AN INTRODUCTION TO PROGRAMMING WITH C++

SEVENTH EDITION

AN INTRODUCTION TO PROGRAMMING WITH C++

DIANE ZAK

Australia • Brazil • Japan • Korea • Mexico • Singapore • Spain • United Kingdom • United States

An Introduction to Programming with C++, Seventh Edition
Diane Zak

Editor-in-Chief: Marie Lee

Senior Product Manager: Alyssa Pratt

Senior Content Project Manager: Matthew Hutchinson

Associate Product Manager: Stephanie Lorenz

Art Director: Cheryl Pearl, GEX

Print Buyer: Julio Esperas

Proofreader: Suzanne Huizenga

Indexer: Liz Cunningham

Compositor: Integra Software Services Pvt. Ltd.

Library of Congress Control Number: 2012945219

ISBN-13: 978-1-285-06147-4
ISBN-10: 1-285-06147-0

Course Technology
20 Channel Center Street
Boston, MA 02210
USA

Printed in the United States of America
1 2 3 4 5 6 7 18 17 16 15 14 13 12

I dedicate this book to the loving memory of Mary Clare Karnick. We all loved you more.

Brief Contents

Contents

Preface

An Introduction to Programming with C++, Seventh Edition uses the C++ programming language to teach programming concepts. This book is designed for a beginning programming course. Although the book provides instructions for using several specific C++ compilers (such as Microsoft® Visual C++®, Dev-C++, and Code::Blocks), it can be used with most C++ compilers, often with little or no modification.

Organization and Coverage

An Introduction to Programming with C++, Seventh Edition contains 15 chapters and several appendices. In the chapters, students with no previous programming experience learn how to plan and create well-structured programs. By the end of the book, students will have learned how to write programs using the sequence, selection, and repetition structures. They also will have learned how to create and manipulate functions, sequential access files, arrays, strings, classes, and objects.

Approach

An Introduction to Programming with C++, Seventh Edition is distinguished from other textbooks because of its unique approach, which motivates students by demonstrating why they need to learn the concepts and skills presented. Each chapter begins with an introduction to one or more programming concepts. The concepts are illustrated with code examples and sample programs. The sample programs allow the student to observe how the current concept can be used before they are introduced to the next concept. The concepts are taught using standard C++ commands. Following the concept portion in each chapter (except Chapter 1) are five labs: Stop and Analyze, Plan and Create, Modify, Desk-Check, and Debug. Each lab teaches students how to apply the chapter concepts; however, each does so in a different way.

Features

An Introduction to Programming with C++, Seventh Edition is an exceptional textbook because it also includes the following features:

READ THIS BEFORE YOU BEGIN This section is consistent with Course Technology's unequaled commitment to helping instructors introduce technology into the classroom. Technical considerations and assumptions about hardware, software, and default settings are listed in one place to help instructors save time and eliminate unnecessary aggravation.

LABS Each chapter (except Chapter 1) contains five labs that teach students how to apply the concepts taught in the chapter to real-world problems. In the first lab, which is the Stop and Analyze lab, students are expected to stop and analyze an existing program. Students plan and create a program in the Plan and Create lab, which is the second lab. The third lab is the Modify lab. This lab requires students to modify an existing program. The fourth lab is the Desk-Check lab, in which students follow the logic of a program by desk-checking it. The fifth lab is the Debug lab. This lab gives students an opportunity to find and correct the errors in an existing program. Answers to the labs are provided in Appendix A.

HOW TO BOXES The How To boxes in each chapter summarize important concepts and provide a quick reference for students. The How To boxes that introduce new statements, operators, stream manipulators, or functions contain the syntax and examples of using the syntax.

STANDARD C++ SYNTAX Like the previous edition of the book, this edition uses the standard C++ syntax in the examples, sample programs, and exercises in each chapter.

TIP These notes provide additional information about the current concept. Examples include alternative ways of writing statements, warnings about common mistakes made when using a particular command, and reminders of related concepts learned in previous chapters.

MINI-QUIZZES Mini-quizzes are strategically placed to test students' knowledge at various points in each chapter. Answers to the quiz questions are provided in Appendix A, allowing students to determine whether they have mastered the material covered thus far before continuing with the chapter.

SUMMARY A Summary section follows the labs in each chapter. The Summary section recaps the programming concepts and commands covered in the chapter.

KEY TERMS Following the Summary section in each chapter is a listing of the key terms introduced throughout the chapter, along with their definitions.

REVIEW QUESTIONS Review Questions follow the Key Terms section in each chapter. The Review Questions test the students' understanding of what they learned in the chapter.

PAPER AND PENCIL EXERCISES The Review Questions are followed by Pencil and Paper Exercises, which are designated as TRY THIS, MODIFY THIS, INTRODUCTORY, INTERMEDIATE, ADVANCED, and SWAT THE BUGS. The answers to the TRY THIS Exercises are provided at the end of the chapter. The ADVANCED Exercises provide practice in applying cumulative programming knowledge or allow students to explore alternative solutions to programming tasks. The SWAT THE BUGS Exercises provide an opportunity for students to detect and correct errors in one or more lines of code.

COMPUTER EXERCISES The Computer Exercises provide students with additional practice of the skills and concepts they learned in the chapter. The Computer Exercises are designated as TRY THIS, MODIFY THIS, INTRODUCTORY, INTERMEDIATE, ADVANCED, and SWAT THE BUGS. The answers to the TRY THIS Exercises are provided at the end of the chapter. The ADVANCED Exercises provide practice in applying cumulative programming knowledge or allow students to explore alternative solutions to programming tasks. The SWAT THE BUGS Exercises provide an opportunity for students to detect and correct errors in an existing program.

New to this Edition!

VIDEOS These notes direct students to videos that accompany each chapter in the book. The videos explain and/or demonstrate one or more of the chapter's concepts. The videos are available online at *www.cengagebrain.com*. Search for the ISBN associated with your book (from the back cover of your book) using the search box at the top of the page. This will take you to the product page where free companion resources can be found.

INSTALLATION VIDEOS These videos show students how to install various C++ compilers (such as Microsoft® Visual C++®, Dev-C++, and Code::Blocks). The videos are named Ch04-Installation *developmentTool*, where *developmentTool* is the name of the C++ development tool covered in the video. The videos are available online at *www.cengagebrain.com*. Search for the ISBN associated with your book (from the back cover of your book) using the search box at the top of the page. This will take you to the product page where free companion resources can be found.

STEP-BY-STEP INSTRUCTIONS This book is accompanied by files that contain step-by-step instructions for completing Labs 4-2, 4-3, 4-5, 5-2, 5-3, and 5-5 using various C++ compilers. The files are named Ch04-Lab4-*X developmentTool*.pdf and Ch05-Lab5-*X developmentTool*.pdf, where *X* represents the lab number, and *developmentTool* is the name of the C++ development tool covered in the file. The files are in PDF format and are available online at *www.cengagebrain.com*. Search for the ISBN associated with your book (from the back cover of your book) using the search box at the top of the page. This will take you to the product page where free companion resources can be found.

PSEUDOCODE AND FLOWCHARTS Both planning tools are now shown for many of the programs within the chapters.

WANT MORE INFO? FILES These notes direct students to files that accompany each chapter in the book. The files contain additional examples and further explanations of the concepts covered in the chapter. The files are in PDF format and are available online at *www.cengagebrain.com*. Search for the ISBN associated with your book (from the back cover of your book) using the search box at the top of the page. This will take you to the product page where free companion resources can be found.

CHAPTER 15 Classes and Objects are now covered in Chapter 15. This topic was covered in Appendix F in the previous edition of the book.

APPENDIX D This appendix contains a listing of common syntax errors that students are likely to encounter.

APPENDIX E This appendix contains a listing of the How To boxes contained in the chapters.

Instructor Resources

The following resources are available on the Instructor Resources CD-ROM or through *www.cengage.com/coursetechnology* to instructors who have adopted this book. Search for this title by ISBN, title, author, or keyword. From the Product Overview page, select the Instructor's Companion Site link to access your complementary resources.

ELECTRONIC INSTRUCTOR'S MANUAL The Instructor's Manual follows the text chapter by chapter to assist you in planning and organizing an effective, engaging course. The manual includes learning objectives, chapter overviews, ideas for classroom activities, and additional resources. A sample course **Syllabus** is also available.

EXAMVIEW® This textbook is accompanied by ExamView, a powerful testing software package that allows instructors to create and administer printed, computer (LAN-based), and Internet exams. ExamView includes hundreds of questions that correspond to the topics covered in this text, enabling students to generate detailed study guides that include page references for further review. The computer-based and Internet testing components allow students to take exams at their computers, and also save the instructor time by grading each exam automatically. Test banks are also available in **Blackboard**, **WebCT**, and **Angel** formats.

POWERPOINT PRESENTATIONS This book comes with Microsoft PowerPoint slides for each chapter. These are included as a teaching aid for classroom presentation, to make available to students on the network for chapter review, or to be printed for classroom distribution. Instructors are encouraged to customize the slides to fit their course needs, and may add slides to cover additional topics using the complete **Figure Files** from the text.

SOLUTION FILES Solutions to the Labs, Review Questions, Pencil and Paper Exercises, and Computer Exercises are password protected. The Solution Files also contain the sample programs that appear in the figures throughout the book.

DATA FILES Data Files are required to complete many Labs and Computer Exercises in this book.

Acknowledgments

Writing a book is a team effort rather than an individual one. I would like to take this opportunity to thank my team, especially Alyssa Pratt (Senior Product Manager), Matt Hutchinson (Senior Content Project Manager), Sreejith Govindan (Full Service Project Manager), and Nicole Ashton (Quality Assurance). Thank you for your support, enthusiasm, patience, and hard work; it made a difficult task much easier. Last, but certainly not least, I want to thank Matthew Alimagham (Spartanburg Community College), Bill Hammerschlag (Brookhaven College), Mark Shellman (Gaston College), and Sharlene Smith (Gaston College) for their invaluable ideas and comments.

Diane Zak

Read This Before You Begin

Technical Information

Data Files

You will need data files to complete the Labs and Computer Exercises in this book. Your instructor may provide the data files to you. You may obtain the files electronically at *www.cengagebrain.com.* Search for the ISBN associated with your book (from the back cover of your book) using the search box at the top of the page. This will take you to the product page where free companion resources can be found.

Each chapter in this book has its own set of data files, which are stored in a separate folder within the Cpp7 folder. The files for Chapter 4 are stored in the Cpp7\Chap04 folder. Similarly, the files for Chapter 5 are stored in the Cpp7\Chap05 folder. Throughout this book, you will be instructed to open files from or save files to these folders.

You can use a computer in your school lab or your own computer to complete the Labs and Computer Exercises in this book.

Using Your Own Computer

To use your own computer to complete the Labs and Computer Exercises in this book, you will need a C++ compiler. This book is accompanied by videos that show students how to install various C++ compilers (such as Microsoft® Visual C++®, Dev-C++, and Code::Blocks). The videos are named Ch04-Installation *developmentTool*, where *developmentTool* is the name of the C++ development tool covered in the video. You may obtain the files electronically at *www.cengagebrain.com.* Search for the ISBN associated with your book (from the back cover of your book) using the search box at the top of the page. This will take you to the product page where free companion resources can be found.

The book was written and Quality Assurance tested using Microsoft Visual C++ 2012. It also was tested using Code::Blocks and Dev-C++. However, the book can be used with most C++ compilers, often with little or no modification. If your book came with a copy of Microsoft Visual C++, then you may install that on your computer and use it to complete the material.

Visit Our Web Site

Additional materials designed for this textbook might be available at *www.cengagebrain.com.* Search this site for more details.

To the Instructor

To complete the Labs and Computer Exercises in this book, your students must use a set of data files. These files are included on the Instructor Resources CD-ROM and Instructor Companion Site. Using the ISBN, title, or author, search *www.cengage.com/coursetechnology* for this title. From the Product Overview page, select the Instructor's Companion Site link to access all complementary resources. Once the files are copied to your server or standalone computer, you should instruct your users how to copy the files to their own computers or workstations.

The material in this book was written and Quality Assurance tested using Microsoft Visual C++ 2012. It also was tested using Code::Blocks and Dev-C++. However, the book can be used with most C++ compilers, often with little or no modification.

Course Technology Data Files

You are granted a license to copy the data files to any computer or computer network used by individuals who have purchased this book.

CHAPTER 1

An Introduction to Programming

After studying Chapter 1, you should be able to:

- Define the terminology used in programming
- Explain the tasks performed by a programmer
- Understand the employment opportunities for programmers and software engineers
- Explain the history of programming languages
- Explain the sequence, selection, and repetition structures
- Write simple algorithms using the sequence, selection, and repetition structures

Programming a Computer

In essence, the word **programming** means *giving a mechanism the directions to accomplish a task.* If you are like most people, you've already programmed several mechanisms, such as your digital video recorder (DVR), cell phone, or coffee maker. Like these devices, a computer also is a mechanism that can be programmed.

The directions given to a computer are called **computer programs** or, more simply, **programs**. The people who write programs are called **programmers**. Programmers use a variety of special languages, called **programming languages**, to communicate with the computer. Some popular programming languages are C++, Visual Basic, C#, Java, and Python. In this book, you will use the C++ programming language.

The Programmer's Job

Ch01-Programmers video

When a company has a problem that requires a computer solution, typically it is a programmer who comes to the rescue. The programmer might be an employee of the company; or he or she might be a freelance programmer, which is a programmer who works on temporary contracts rather than for a long-term employer.

First, the programmer meets with the user, which is the person (or persons) responsible for describing the problem. In many cases, this person or persons also will eventually use the solution. Depending on the complexity of the problem, multiple programmers may be involved, and they may need to meet with the user several times. Programming teams often contain subject matter experts, who may or may not be programmers. For example, an accountant might be part of a team working on a program that requires accounting expertise. The purpose of the initial meetings with the user is to determine the exact problem and to agree on a solution.

After the programmer and user agree on the solution, the programmer begins converting the solution into a computer program. During the conversion phase, the programmer meets periodically with the user to determine whether the program fulfills the user's needs and to refine any details of the solution. When the user is satisfied that the program does what he or she wants it to do, the programmer rigorously tests the program with sample data before releasing it to the user. In many cases, the programmer also provides the user with a manual that explains how to use the program. As this process indicates, the creation of a good computer solution to a problem—in other words, the creation of a good program—requires a great deal of interaction between the programmer and the user.

Employment Opportunities

Ch01-Programmer Qualities video

When searching for a job in computer programming, you will encounter ads for "computer programmers" as well as for "computer software engineers." Although job titles and descriptions vary, computer software engineers typically are responsible for designing an appropriate solution to a user's problem, while computer programmers are responsible for translating the solution into a language that the computer can understand. The process of translating the solution is called **coding**.

Keep in mind that, depending on the employer and the size and complexity of the user's problem, the design and coding tasks may be performed by the same employee, no matter what his or her job title is. In other words, it's not unusual for a software engineer to code her solution, just as it's not unusual for a programmer to have designed the solution he is coding.

Programmers and software engineers need to have strong problem-solving and analytical skills, as well as the ability to communicate effectively with team members, end users, and other nontechnical personnel. Typically, computer software engineers are expected to have at least a bachelor's degree in software engineering, computer science, or mathematics, along with practical work experience, especially in the industry in which they are employed. Computer programmers usually need at least an associate's degree in computer science, mathematics, or information systems, as well as proficiency in one or more programming languages.

Computer programmers and software engineers are employed by companies in almost every industry, such as telecommunications companies, software publishers, financial institutions, insurance carriers, educational institutions, and government agencies. The Bureau of Labor Statistics predicts that employment of computer software engineers will increase by 32% from 2008 to 2018. The employment of computer programmers, on the other hand, will decline slowly, decreasing by 3% over the same period. However, consulting opportunities for freelance programmers and software engineers are expected to increase as companies look for ways to reduce their payroll expenses.

There is a great deal of competition for programming and software engineering jobs, so jobseekers will need to keep up to date with the latest programming languages and technologies. A competitive edge may be gained by obtaining vendor-specific or language-specific certifications. More information about computer programmers and computer software engineers can be found on the Bureau of Labor Statistics Web site at *www.bls.gov*.

A Brief History of Programming Languages

Just as human beings communicate with each other through the use of languages such as English, Spanish, Hindi, and Chinese, programmers use a variety of programming languages to communicate with the computer. In the next sections, you will follow the progression of programming languages from machine languages to assembly languages, and then to high-level languages.

Ch01-History video

Machine Languages

Within a computer, all data is represented by microscopic electronic switches that can be either off or on. The off switch is designated by a 0, and the on switch is designated by a 1. Because computers can understand only these on and off switches, the first programmers had to write the program instructions using nothing but combinations of 0s and 1s; for example, a program might contain the instruction `00101 10001 10000`. Instructions written in 0s and 1s are called **machine language** or **machine code**. The machine languages (each type of machine has its own language) represent the only way to communicate directly with the computer. As you can imagine, programming in machine language is very tedious and error-prone and requires highly trained programmers.

Assembly Languages

Slightly more advanced programming languages are called assembly languages. The **assembly languages** simplify the programmer's job by allowing the programmer to use mnemonics in place of the 0s and 1s in the program. **Mnemonics** are memory aids—in this case, alphabetic abbreviations for instructions. For example, most assembly languages use the mnemonic `ADD` to represent an add operation and the mnemonic `MUL` to represent a multiply operation. An example of an instruction written in an assembly language is `ADD bx, ax`.

Programs written in an assembly language require an **assembler**, which also is a program, to convert the assembly instructions into machine code—the 0s and 1s the computer can understand. Although it is much easier to write programs in assembly language than in machine language, programming in assembly language still is tedious and requires highly trained programmers. Programs written in assembly language are machine specific and usually must be rewritten in a different assembly language to run on a different computer.

High-Level Languages

High-level languages represent the next major development in programming languages. **High-level languages** are a vast improvement over machine and assembly languages because they allow the programmer to use instructions that more closely resemble the English language. An example of an instruction written in a high-level language is `grossPay = hours * rate`. In addition, high-level languages are more machine independent than are machine and assembly languages. As a result, programs written in a high-level language can be used on many different types of computers.

Programs written in a high-level language usually require a compiler, which also is a program, to convert the English-like instructions into the 0s and 1s the computer can understand. Some high-level languages also offer an additional program called an interpreter. Unlike a **compiler**, which translates all of a program's high-level instructions before running the program, an **interpreter** translates the instructions line by line as the program is running.

Like their predecessors, the first high-level languages were used to create procedure-oriented programs. When writing a **procedure-oriented program**, the programmer concentrates on the major tasks that the program needs to perform. A payroll program, for example, typically performs several major tasks, such as inputting the employee data, calculating the gross pay, calculating the taxes, calculating the net pay, and outputting a paycheck. The programmer must instruct the computer every step of the way, from the start of the task to its completion. In a procedure-oriented program, the programmer determines and controls the order in which the computer processes the instructions. In other words, the programmer must determine not only the proper instructions to give the computer, but the correct sequence of those instructions as well. Examples of high-level languages used to create procedure-oriented programs include COBOL (Common Business-Oriented Language), BASIC (Beginner's All-Purpose Symbolic Instruction Code), and C.

More advanced high-level languages can be used to create object-oriented programs in addition to procedure-oriented ones. Different from a procedure-oriented program, which focuses on the individual tasks the program must perform, an **object-oriented program** requires the programmer to focus on the objects that the program can use to accomplish its goal. The objects can take on many different forms. For example, programs written for the Windows environment typically use objects such as check boxes, list boxes, and buttons. A payroll program, on the other hand, might utilize objects found in the real world, such as a time card object, an employee object, or a check object.

Most objects in an object-oriented program are designed to perform multiple tasks. These tasks are programmed using the same techniques used in procedure-oriented programming.

Because each object in an object-oriented program is viewed as an independent unit, an object can be used in more than one program, usually with little or no modification. A check object used in a payroll program, for example, also can be used in a sales revenue program (which receives checks from customers) and an accounts payable program (which issues checks to creditors). The ability to use an object for more than one purpose enables code reuse, which saves programming time and money—an advantage that contributes to the popularity of object-oriented programming. Examples of high-level languages that can be used to create both procedure-oriented and object-oriented programs include C++, Visual Basic, Java, and C#. In this book, you will learn how to use the C++ programming language to create procedure-oriented and object-oriented programs.

The answers to Mini-Quiz questions are located in Appendix A.

Mini-Quiz 1-1

1. Instructions written in 0s and 1s are called ________ language.
2. When writing ________ program, the programmer concentrates on the major tasks needed to accomplish a goal.
   a. a procedure-oriented
   b. an object-oriented
3. When writing ________ program, the programmer breaks up a problem into interacting objects.
   a. a procedure-oriented
   b. an object-oriented
4. Most high-level languages use a(n) ________ to translate the instructions into a language that the computer can understand.

Control Structures

All computer programs, no matter how simple or how complex, are written using one or more of three basic structures: sequence, selection, and repetition. These structures are called **control structures** or **logic structures** because they control the flow of a program's logic. You will use the sequence structure in every program you write. In most programs, you also will use the selection and repetition structures. This chapter gives you an introduction to the three control structures. More detailed information about each structure, as well as how to implement these structures using the C++ language, is provided in subsequent chapters.

The Sequence Structure

You already are familiar with the sequence structure because you use it each time you follow a set of directions, in order, from beginning to end. The directions might be a cookie recipe; or they might be the MapQuest directions to your favorite restaurant. In a computer program, the **sequence structure** directs the computer to process the program instructions, one after another, in the order listed in the program. You will find the sequence structure in every program.

You can observe how the sequence structure works by programming a robotic character named Harold. Like a computer, Harold has a limited instruction set. In other words, he can understand only a specific number of instructions, also called commands. For now, you will use only three of the commands from Harold's instruction set: *walk forward*, *turn left 90 degrees*, and *sit down on the bench*. When told to *walk forward*, Harold takes one complete step forward. In other words, he moves one of his feet forward one step and then moves his other foot to meet it.

For this first example, Harold is standing outside facing a park bench. The bench is two steps away from Harold. Your task is to write the instructions, using only the commands that Harold understands, that direct Harold to sit down on the bench. Figure 1-1 shows the problem specification along with an illustration of the problem. It also shows the five instructions that Harold must follow to get from where he is now to his ultimate destination, which is sitting on the bench. The five instructions are called an **algorithm**, which is a set of step-by-step

Ch01-Harold Sequence video

instructions that accomplish a task. Harold must follow the instructions in order—in other words, in sequence. (You can observe Harold following the algorithm shown in Figure 1-1 by viewing the Ch01-Harold Sequence video.)

Figure 1-1 An example of the sequence structure

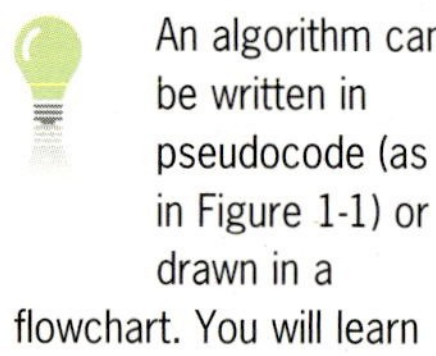

An algorithm can be written in pseudocode (as in Figure 1-1) or drawn in a flowchart. You will learn about pseudocode and flowcharts in Chapter 2.

The Selection Structure

As with the sequence structure, you already are familiar with the **selection structure**, also called the **decision structure**. The selection structure indicates that a decision (based on some condition) needs to be made, followed by an appropriate action derived from that decision. You use the selection structure every time you drive your car and approach a railroad crossing. Your decision, as well as the appropriate action, is based on whether the crossing signals (flashing lights and ringing bells) are on or off. If the crossing signals are on, you stop your car before crossing the railroad tracks; otherwise, you proceed with caution over the railroad tracks. When used in a computer program, the selection structure alerts the computer that a decision needs to be made, and it provides the appropriate action to take based on the result of that decision.

To observe how the selection structure works, we'll make a slight change to the problem specification shown in Figure 1-1. Sometimes Harold's cat Ginger is sitting on the park bench and needs to be gently pushed off before Harold can sit down. What changes will need to be made to the original algorithm from Figure 1-1 as a result of this minor modification? The first two instructions in the original algorithm position Harold directly in front of the bench; Harold will still need to follow those instructions. However, before he follows the third instruction, which is to *turn left 90 degrees* in preparation for sitting down, Harold will need to make a decision about Ginger and then take the appropriate action based on the result. More specifically, he will need to determine whether Ginger is on the bench; if she is on the bench, then he needs to gently shove her off.

To write an algorithm to accomplish the current task, you need to use three additional instructions from Harold's instruction set: *if (Ginger is on the bench)*, *end if*, and *gently shove Ginger off the bench*. The *if (Ginger is on the bench)* instruction allows Harold to make a decision about the status of Ginger, and it represents the beginning of a selection structure. The portion within the parentheses is called the condition and specifies the decision that Harold must make. Notice that the condition results in either a true or a false answer: either Ginger is on the bench (true) or she's not (false). The *end if* instruction denotes the end of a selection structure.

The last three instructions in the original algorithm turn Harold left 180 degrees and then sit him down; Harold will still need to follow those instructions. Figure 1-2 shows the modified problem specification, illustration, and algorithm. Notice that the *gently shove Ginger off the bench* instruction is indented within the selection structure. Indenting in this manner indicates that the instruction should be followed only when Ginger is on the bench—in other words, only when the condition results in an answer of true. The instructions to be followed when a selection structure's condition evaluates to true are referred to as the structure's true path. Although the true path in Figure 1-2 includes only one instruction, it can include many instructions. (You can observe Harold as he follows Figure 1-2's algorithm by viewing the Ch01-Harold Selection video.)

Ch01-Harold Selection video

Harold is standing outside facing a park bench. The bench is two steps away from Harold. Harold's cat Ginger may be on the bench. Write the instructions that direct Harold to gently shove Ginger off the bench (if necessary) and then sit down on the bench.

Ginger might or might not be on the bench

```
1. walk forward
2. walk forward                       [condition]
3. if (Ginger is on the bench)
      gently shove Ginger off the bench —— [indent]
   end if
4. turn left 90 degrees
5. turn left 90 degrees
6. sit down on the bench
```

Figure 1-2 An example of the selection structure

Figure 1-3 shows how the selection structure can be used in a game program. In this game, our superhero gets one shot at the villain. He needs to raise his right arm before taking the shot. If he hits the villain, he should say "Got Him" and then lower his right arm. If he doesn't hit the villain, he should say "Missed Him" before lowering his right arm. Our superhero can understand only these eight instructions: *raise right arm*, *lower right arm*, *shoot at the villain*, *if (the villain was hit)*, *else*, *end if*, *say "Got Him"*, *say "Missed Him"*.

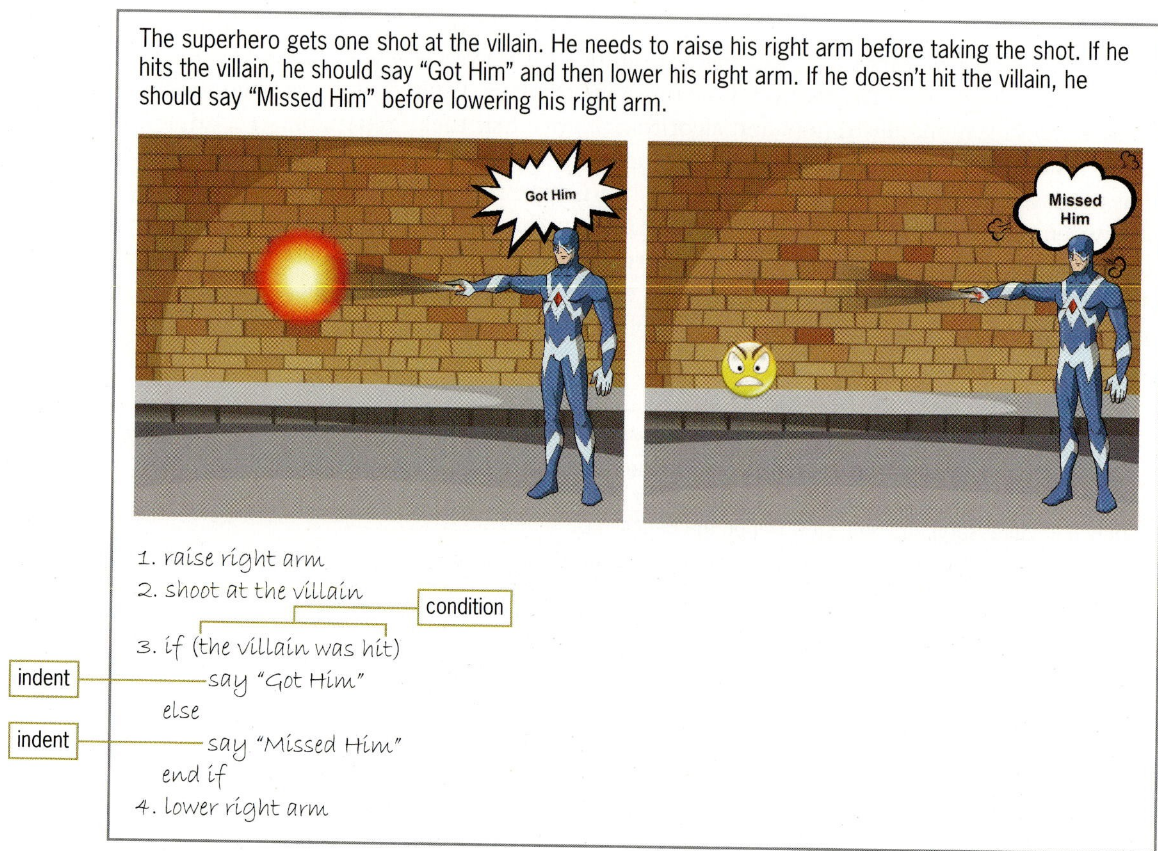

Figure 1-3 Another example of the selection structure

Unlike the selection structure from Figure 1-2, which requires Harold to take a specific action only when the structure's condition evaluates to true, the selection structure in Figure 1-3 requires our superhero to take one action when the condition evaluates to true, but a different action when it evaluates to false. In other words, the selection structure in Figure 1-3 has both a true path and a false path. The *else* instruction marks the beginning of the false path instructions. Notice that the *say "Got Him"* and *say "Missed Him"* instructions are indented within their respective paths. Indenting in this manner clearly indicates the instruction to be followed when the condition evaluates to true (the villain was hit), as well as the one to be followed when the condition evaluates to false (the villain was not hit). Although both paths in Figure 1-3's selection structure contain only one instruction, each can contain many instructions. (You can observe our superhero in action by viewing the Ch01-Superhero Selection video.)

Ch01-Superhero Selection video

The Repetition Structure

The last of the three control structures is the repetition structure. Like the sequence and selection structures, you already are familiar with the repetition structure. For example, shampoo bottles typically include the repetition structure in the directions for washing your hair. Those directions usually tell you to repeat the "apply shampoo to hair," "lather," and "rinse" steps until your hair is clean. When used in a program, the **repetition structure** directs the computer to repeat one or more instructions until some condition is met, at which time the computer should stop repeating the instructions. The repetition structure also is referred to as a **loop** or an **iteration**.

You can use the repetition structure to simplify the algorithm shown in Figure 1-2. To do this, you will need to use two additional instructions from Harold's instruction set: repeat (x times) (where x is the number of times you want Harold to repeat something) and end repeat. The repeat (x times) and end repeat instructions indicate the beginning and end, respectively, of a repetition structure. The modified algorithm, which contains four steps rather than six steps, is shown in Figure 1-4 along with the original algorithm from Figure 1-2. Notice that the two walk forward instructions from the original algorithm, as well as the two turn left 90 degrees instructions, are replaced by repetition structures. The first repetition structure directs Harold to repeat the walk forward instruction two times. The second repetition structure directs him to repeat the turn left 90 degrees instruction two times. The instruction within each repetition structure is indented to indicate that it is part of the repetition structure and, therefore, needs to be repeated the specified number of times. Although each repetition structure in Figure 1-4 includes only one instruction, a repetition structure can include many instructions.

Figure 1-4 Original algorithm and modified algorithm showing the repetition structure

The modified algorithm shown in Figure 1-4 will work only if Harold is two steps away from the park bench. But what if you don't know precisely how many steps separate Harold from the bench? In that case, you need to replace the first repeat (2 times) instruction with another instruction from Harold's instruction set. That instruction is repeat until (you are directly in front of the bench). The new algorithm with the modified condition in the first repetition structure is shown in Figure 1-5. The first repetition structure now tells Harold to keep walking forward until he is directly in front of the bench. Depending on the number of steps between Harold and the bench, Harold may need to walk forward 0 times, 5 times, 10 times, or even 500 times before evaluating the selection structure's condition. (You can observe Harold as he follows the algorithms in Figures 1-4 and 1-5 by viewing the Ch01-Harold Repetition video.)

Ch01-Harold Repetition video

modified condition

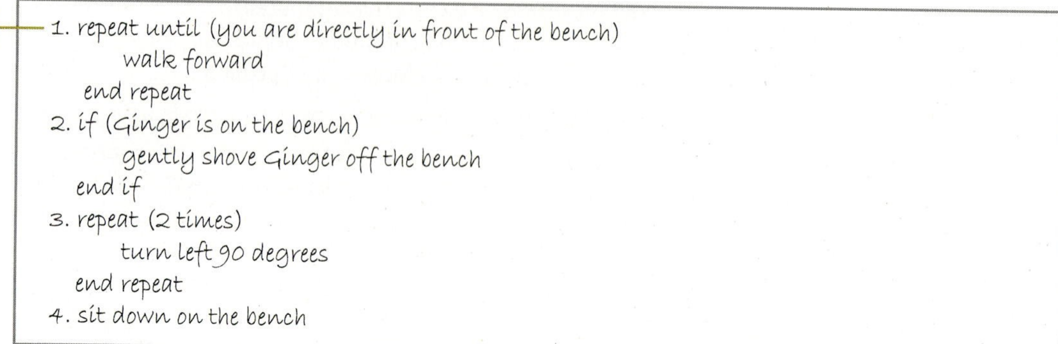

Figure 1-5 Algorithm showing the modified condition in the repetition structure

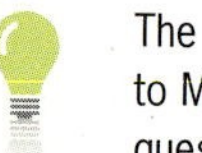

The answers to Mini-Quiz questions are located in Appendix A.

Mini-Quiz 1-2

1. The three basic control structures are ________, ________, and ________.
2. All programs contain the ________ structure.
3. The step-by-step instructions that accomplish a task are called a(n) ________.
4. You use the ________ structure to repeat one or more instructions in a program.
5. The ________ structure ends when its condition has been met.
6. The ________ structure, also called the decision structure, instructs the computer to make a decision and then take some action based on the result of the decision.

The answers to the labs are located in Appendix A.

LAB 1-1 Stop and Analyze

A local business employs five salespeople and pays a 3% bonus on a salesperson's sales. Your task is to create a program that calculates the amount of each salesperson's bonus. The program should display each salesperson's name and bonus amount. Study the algorithm shown in Figure 1-6 and then answer the questions.

```
repeat (5 times)
      enter the salesperson's name and sales amount
      calculate the bonus amount by multiplying the sales amount by 3%
      display the salesperson's name and bonus amount
end repeat
```

Figure 1-6 Algorithm for Lab 1-1

QUESTIONS

1. Which control structures are used in the algorithm shown in Figure 1-6?
2. What will the algorithm shown in Figure 1-6 display when the user enters Mary Smith and 2000 as the salesperson's name and sales amount, respectively?
3. How would you modify the algorithm shown in Figure 1-6 so that it also displays the salesperson's sales amount?

4. How would you modify the algorithm shown in Figure 1-6 so that it can be used for any number of salespeople?
5. How would you modify the algorithm shown in Figure 1-6 so that it allows the user to enter the bonus rate and then uses that rate to calculate the five bonus amounts?

LAB 1-2 Plan and Create

Using only the instructions shown in Figure 1-7, create an algorithm that shows the steps an instructor takes when grading a test that contains 25 questions.

```
end if
end repeat
if (the student's answer is not the same as the correct answer)
mark the student's answer incorrect
read the student's answer and the correct answer
repeat (25 times)
```

Figure 1-7 Instructions for Lab 1-2

LAB 1-3 Modify

Modify the algorithm shown in Figure 1-6 so that it gives a 3.5% bonus to salespeople selling more than $2,000. All other salespeople should receive a 3% bonus.

Summary

- Programs are the step-by-step instructions that tell a computer how to perform a task. Programmers, the people who write computer programs, use various programming languages to communicate with the computer. The first programming languages were machine languages, also called machine code. The assembly languages came next, followed by the high-level languages. The first high-level languages were used to create procedure-oriented programs. More advanced high-level languages are used to create object-oriented programs, as well as procedure-oriented ones.
- An algorithm is the set of step-by-step instructions that accomplish a task. The algorithms for all computer programs contain one or more of the following three control structures: sequence, selection, and repetition. The control structures, also called logic structures, are so named because they control the flow of a program's logic.

- The sequence structure directs the computer to process the program instructions, one after another, in the order listed in the program. The selection structure, also called the decision structure, directs the computer to make a decision and then select an appropriate action based on that decision. The repetition structure directs the computer to repeat one or more program instructions until some condition is met. The sequence structure is used in all programs. Most programs also contain both the selection and repetition structures.

Key Terms

Algorithm—the set of step-by-step instructions that accomplish a task

Assembler—a program that converts assembly instructions into machine code

Assembly languages—programming languages that use mnemonics, such as ADD

Coding—the process of translating a solution into a language that the computer can understand

Compiler—a program that converts high-level instructions into a language that the computer can understand; unlike an interpreter, a compiler converts all of a program's instructions before running the program

Computer programs—the directions given to computers; also called programs

Control structures—the structures that control the flow of a program's logic; also called logic structures; sequence, selection, and repetition

Decision structure—another term for the selection structure

High-level languages—programming languages whose instructions more closely resemble the English language

Interpreter—a program that converts high-level instructions into a language that the computer can understand; unlike a compiler, an interpreter converts a program's instructions, line by line, as the program is running

Iteration—another term for the repetition structure

Logic structures—another term for control structures

Loop—another term for the repetition structure

Machine code—another term for machine language

Machine language—computer instructions written in 0s and 1s; also called machine code

Mnemonics—the alphabetic abbreviations used to represent instructions in assembly languages

Object-oriented program—a program designed by focusing on the objects that the program could use to accomplish its goal

Procedure-oriented program—a program designed by focusing on the individual tasks to be performed

Programmers—the people who write computer programs

Programming—giving a mechanism the directions to accomplish a task

Programming languages—languages used to communicate with a computer

Programs—the directions given to computers; also called computer programs

Repetition structure—the control structure that directs the computer to repeat one or more instructions until some condition is met, at which time the computer should stop repeating the instructions; also called a loop or an iteration

Selection structure—the control structure that directs the computer to make a decision and then take the appropriate action based on that decision; also called the decision structure

Sequence structure—the control structure that directs the computer to process each instruction in the order listed in the program

Review Questions

1. Which of the following is not a programming control structure?
   a. repetition
   b. selection
   c. sequence
   d. sorting

2. Which of the following control structures is used in every program?
   a. repetition
   b. selection
   c. sequence
   d. switching

3. The set of instructions for adding together two numbers is an example of the ________ structure.
   a. control
   b. repetition
   c. selection
   d. sequence

4. The set of step-by-step instructions that solve a problem is called ________.
   a. an algorithm
   b. a list
   c. a plan
   d. a sequential structure

5. The recipe instruction "Beat until smooth" is an example of the ________ structure.
   a. control
   b. repetition
   c. selection
   d. sequence

6. The instruction "If it's raining outside, take an umbrella to work" is an example of the ________ structure.
   a. control
   b. repetition
   c. selection
   d. sequence

7. Which control structure would an algorithm use to determine whether a credit card holder is over his credit limit?
   a. repetition
   b. selection
   c. both repetition and selection

8. Which control structure would an algorithm use to calculate a 5% commission for each of a company's salespeople?
   a. repetition
   b. selection
   c. both repetition and selection

9. A company pays a 3% annual bonus to employees who have been with the company more than 5 years; other employees receive a 1% bonus. Which control structure would an algorithm use to calculate every employee's bonus?
   a. repetition
   b. selection
   c. both repetition and selection

10. Which control structure would an algorithm use to determine whether a customer is entitled to a senior discount?
    a. repetition
    b. selection
    c. both repetition and selection

Exercises

Pencil and Paper

You will use Harold (the robotic character) to complete Pencil and Paper Exercises 1, 3, 4, and 7. Harold's instruction set is shown in Figure 1-8.

```
drop the toy in the toy chest
else
end if
end repeat
if (the flower is red)
jump over Ginger
pick the flower with your left hand
pick the flower with your right hand
repeat (x times)
repeat until (you are directly in front of the chair)
repeat until (you are directly in front of the toy chest)
sit down in the chair
turn left 90 degrees
walk forward
```

Figure 1-8

1. As illustrated in Figure 1-9, Harold is five steps away from his cat Ginger, who is an unknown distance away from a chair. Using only the instructions listed in Figure 1-8, create an algorithm that directs Harold to jump over Ginger and sit in the chair. Be sure to indent the instructions appropriately. (The answers to TRY THIS Exercises are located at the end of the chapter.) TRY THIS

Figure 1-9

2. A store gives a 10% discount to customers who are at least 65 years old. Using only the instructions shown in Figure 1-10, write an algorithm that displays the amount of money a customer owes. Be sure to indent the instructions appropriately. (The answers to TRY THIS Exercises are located at the end of the chapter.) TRY THIS

```
calculate the amount due by multiplying the amount due by 90%
enter the customer's age and the amount due
if (the customer's age is greater than or equal to 65)
end if
display the amount due
```

Figure 1-10

3. Modify the algorithm shown earlier in Figure 1-5 so that Harold gives Ginger a kiss on her head before gently shoving her off the bench. If Ginger is not on the bench, Harold should call her name. You can use the following three additional instructions from Harold's instruction set: *give Ginger a kiss on her head*, *else*, and *call Ginger's name*. MODIFY THIS
4. Harold is facing a toy chest that is zero or more steps away from him. He is carrying a toy in his right hand. Using only the instructions shown earlier in Figure 1-8, create an algorithm that directs Harold to drop the toy in the toy chest. Be sure to indent the instructions appropriately. INTRODUCTORY
5. You have just purchased a new personal computer system. Before putting the system components together, you read the instruction booklet that came with the system. The booklet contains a list of the components that you should have received. The booklet INTRODUCTORY

advises you to verify that you received all of the components by matching those that you received with those on the list. If a component was received, you should cross its name off the list; otherwise, you should draw a circle around the component name in the list. Using only the instructions listed in Figure 1-11, create an algorithm that shows the steps you should take to verify that you received the correct components. Be sure to indent the instructions appropriately.

```
cross the component name off the list
read the component name from the list
circle the component name on the list
search for the component
if (the component was received)
else
repeat for (each component name on the list)
end if
end repeat
```

Figure 1-11

INTERMEDIATE

6. A company pays an annual bonus to its employees. The bonus is calculated by multiplying the employee's annual salary by a bonus rate, which is based on the number of years the employee has been with the company. Employees working at the company for less than 5 years receive a 1% bonus; all others receive a 2% bonus. Using only the instructions shown in Figure 1-12, write two versions of an algorithm that prints each employee's bonus. Be sure to indent the instructions appropriately.

```
calculate the bonus by multiplying the salary by 1%
calculate the bonus by multiplying the salary by 2%
else
end if
end repeat
if (the years employed are greater than or equal to 5)
if (the years employed are less than 5)
print the bonus
enter the salary and years employed
repeat for (each employee)
```

Figure 1-12

INTERMEDIATE

7. Harold is standing in front of a flower bed that contains six flowers, as illustrated in Figure 1-13. Create an algorithm that directs Harold to pick the flowers as he walks to the other side of the flower bed. He should pick all red flowers with his right hand. Flowers that are not red should be picked with his left hand. Use only the instructions shown earlier in Figure 1-8. Be sure to create an algorithm that will work for any combination of colored flowers.

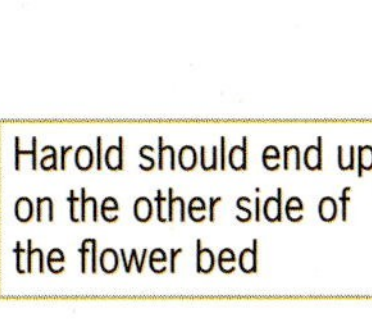

Figure 1-13

8. The algorithm shown in Figure 1-14 should calculate and print the gross pay for five workers; however, some of the instructions are missing from the algorithm. Complete the algorithm. If an employee works more than 40 hours, he or she should receive time and one-half for the hours worked over 40.

ADVANCED

```
_______________________________________________
     enter the employee's name, hours worked, and pay rate
     _____________________________
          calculate gross pay = hours worked times pay rate
     else
          calculate regular pay = pay rate times 40
          calculate overtime hours = hours worked minus 40
          calculate overtime pay = _______________
          calculate gross pay = _______________
     end if
     print the employee's name and gross pay
end repeat
```

Figure 1-14

9. Create an algorithm that tells someone how to evaluate the following expression: 12 / 2 + 3 * 2 – 3. The / operator means division, and the * operator means multiplication. (As you may remember from your math courses, division and multiplication are performed before addition and subtraction.)

ADVANCED

SWAT THE BUGS

10. The algorithm in Figure 1-15 should get Robin seated in the chair, but it does not work correctly. Correct the algorithm.

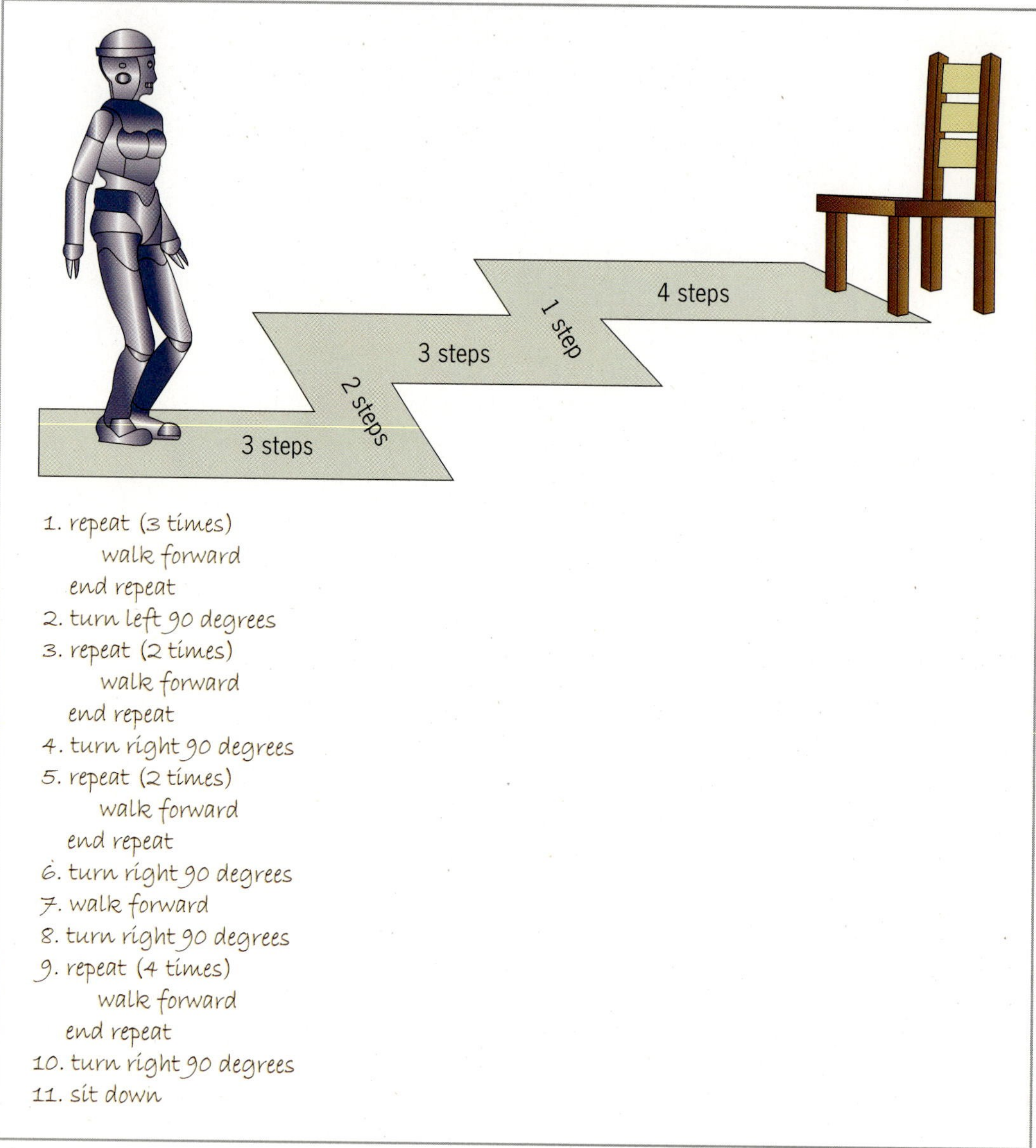

Figure 1-15

SWAT THE BUGS

11. The algorithm in Figure 1-16 does not get Robin through the maze. Correct the algorithm.

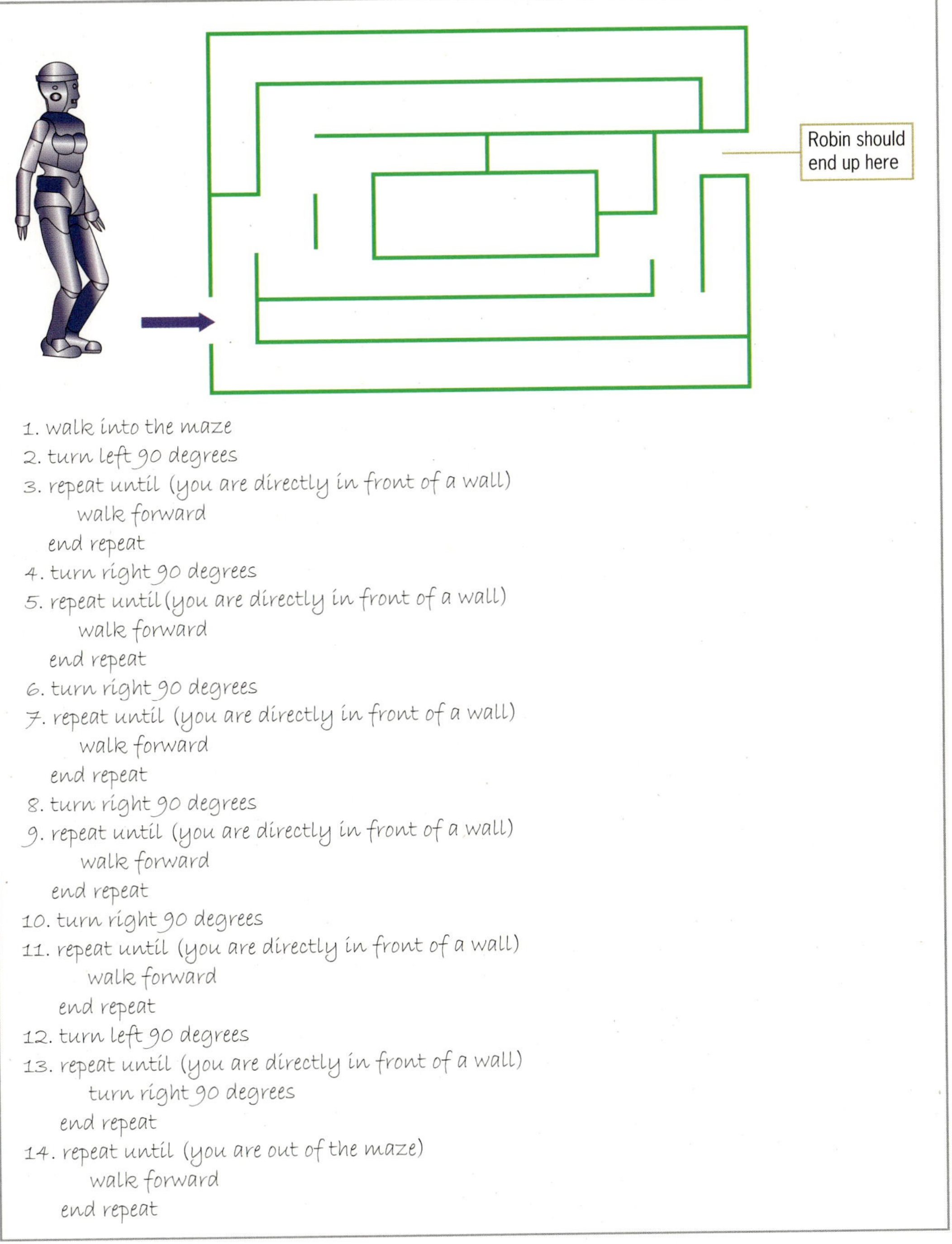

Figure 1-16

Answers to TRY THIS Exercises

1. See Figure 1-17.

```
1. repeat (5 times)
       walk forward
   end repeat
2. jump over Ginger
3. repeat until (you are directly in front of the chair)
       walk forward
   end repeat
4. repeat (2 times)
       turn left 90 degrees
   end repeat
5. sit down in the chair
```

Figure 1-17

2. See Figure 1-18.

```
1. enter the customer's age and the amount due
2. if (the customer's age is greater than or equal to 65)
       calculate the amount due by multiplying the amount due by 90%
   end if
3. display the amount due
```

Figure 1-18

CHAPTER 2

Beginning the Problem-Solving Process

After studying Chapter 2, you should be able to:

- Explain the problem-solving process used to create a computer program
- Analyze a problem
- Complete an IPO chart
- Plan an algorithm using pseudocode and flowcharts
- Desk-check an algorithm

Problem Solving

This chapter introduces you to the process that programmers follow when solving problems that require a computer solution. Although you may not realize it, you use a similar process to solve hundreds of small problems every day. Because most of these problems occur so often, you typically solve them almost automatically, without giving much thought to the process your brain goes through to arrive at the solutions. Unfortunately, problems that are either complex or unfamiliar usually cannot be solved so easily; most require extensive analysis and planning. Understanding the thought process involved in solving simple and familiar problems will make solving complex or unfamiliar ones easier.

In this chapter, you will explore the thought process that you follow when solving common problems. You also will learn how to use a similar process to create a computer solution to a problem—in other words, to create a computer program. The computer solutions you create in this chapter will contain the sequence control structure only, in which each instruction is processed in order from beginning to end. Computer solutions requiring the selection structure are covered in Chapters 5 and 6, and those requiring the repetition structure are covered in Chapters 7 and 8.

Solving Everyday Problems

The first step in solving a familiar problem is to analyze the problem. Next, you plan, review, implement, evaluate, and modify (if necessary) the solution. Consider, for example, how you solve the problem of paying a bill that you received in the mail. First, your mind analyzes the problem to identify its important components. One very important component of any problem is the goal of solving the problem. In this case, the goal is to pay the bill. Other important components of a problem are the things that you can use to accomplish the goal. In this case, you will use the bill itself, as well as the preaddressed envelope that came with the bill. You also will use a bank check, pen, return address label, and postage stamp.

Ch02-Bill Paying video

After analyzing the problem, your mind plans an algorithm. Recall from Chapter 1 that an algorithm is the set of step-by-step instructions that describe how to accomplish a task. In other words, an algorithm is a solution to a problem. The current problem's algorithm, for example, describes how to use the bill, preaddressed envelope, bank check, pen, return address label, and postage stamp to pay the bill. Figure 2-1 shows a summary of the analysis and planning steps for the bill paying problem.

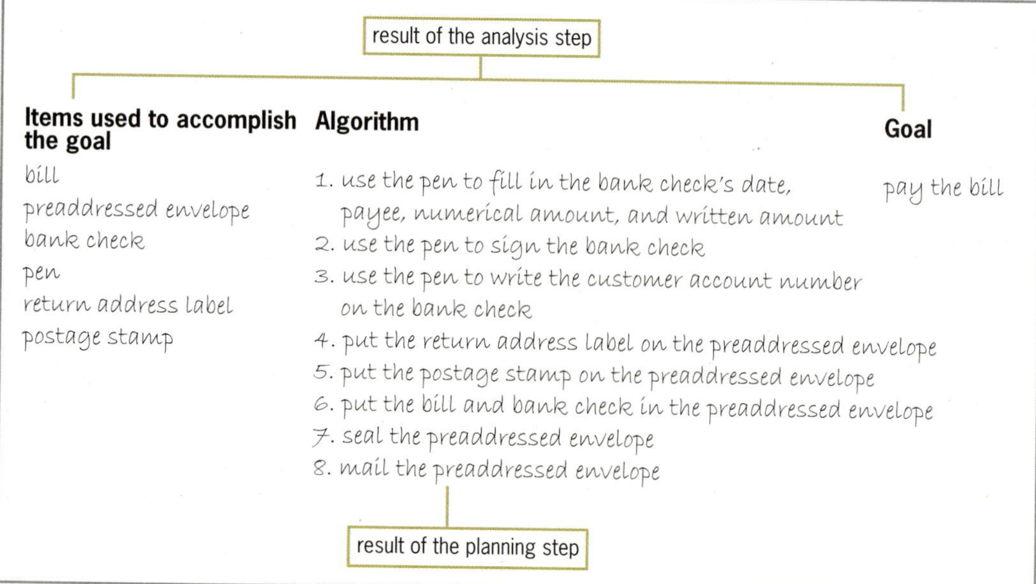

Figure 2-1 Summary of the analysis and planning steps for the bill paying problem

After planning the algorithm, you review it (in your mind) to verify that it will work as intended. When you are satisfied that the algorithm is correct, you implement the algorithm by following each of its instructions in the order indicated. After implementing the algorithm, you evaluate it and, if necessary, you modify it. In this case, for example, you may decide to include the selection structure shown in instruction 6 in Figure 2-2.

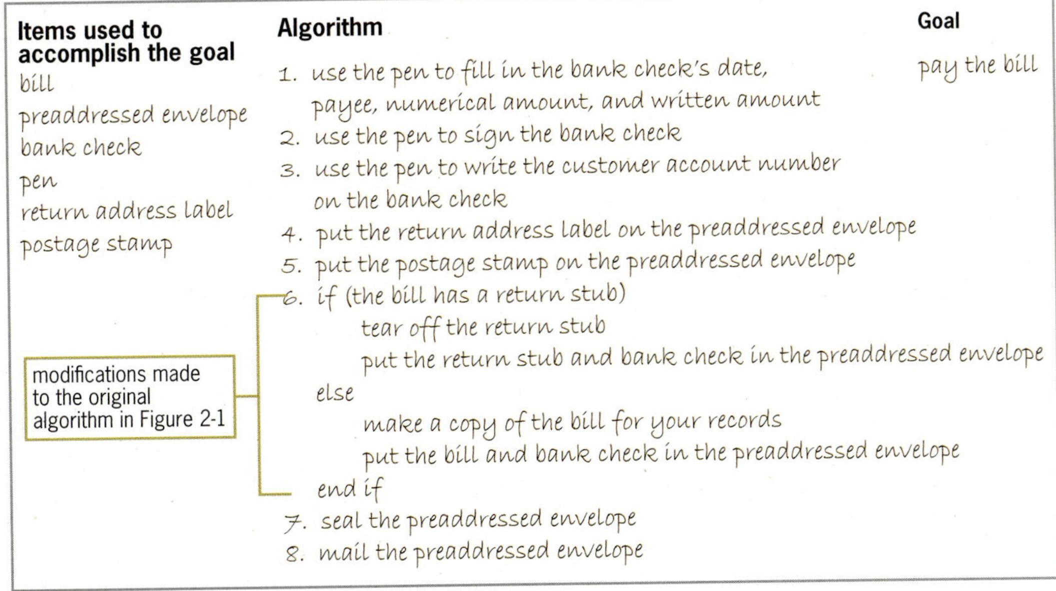

Figure 2-2 Modified algorithm for the bill paying problem

Creating Computer Solutions to Problems

In the previous section, you learned how you create a solution to a familiar problem. A similar problem-solving process is used to create a computer program, which is simply a solution that is implemented with a computer. Figure 2-3 shows the steps that computer programmers follow when solving problems that require a computer solution. This chapter covers the first three steps; the last three steps are covered in Chapters 3 and 4.

HOW TO Create a Computer Solution to a Problem

1. Analyze the problem
2. Plan the algorithm
3. Desk-check the algorithm
4. Code the algorithm into a program
5. Desk-check the program
6. Evaluate and modify (if necessary) the program

Figure 2-3 How to create a computer solution to a problem

Step 1—Analyze the Problem

You cannot solve a problem unless you understand it, and you cannot understand a problem unless you analyze it—in other words, unless you identify its important components. The two most important components of any problem are the problem's output and its input. The **output** is the goal of solving the problem, and the **input** is the item or items needed to achieve the goal. When analyzing a problem, you always search first for the output and then for the input. Let's begin by analyzing the problem specification shown in Figure 2-4.

Problem specification
Treyson Mobley wants a program that calculates and displays the amount he should tip a waiter at a restaurant. The program should subtract any liquor charge from the total bill and then calculate the tip (using a percentage) on the remainder.

Figure 2-4 Problem specification for Treyson Mobley

When searching for the output, ask yourself the following question: *What does the user want to see displayed on the screen, printed on paper, or stored in a file?* The answer to this question typically is stated as nouns and adjectives in the problem specification. The problem specification in Figure 2-4 indicates that Treyson (the program's user) wants to see the amount of the waiter's tip displayed on the screen; therefore, the output is the tip. In this context, the word *tip* is a noun.

After determining the output, you then determine the input, which also is usually stated as nouns and adjectives in the problem specification. Here, look for an answer to the following question: *What information will the computer need to know to display, print, or store the output items?* It helps to think about the information that *you* would need to solve the problem manually because the computer will need to know the same information. In this case, to determine the tip, both you and the computer need to know the total bill, the liquor charge, and the tip percentage; these items, therefore, are the input. In this context, *total, liquor,* and *tip* are adjectives, while *bill, charge,* and *percentage* are nouns. This completes the analysis step for the Treyson Mobley problem. Some programmers use an **IPO chart** to organize and summarize the results of the analysis step, as shown in Figure 2-5. **IPO** is an acronym for Input, Processing, and Output.

Input	Processing	Output
total bill liquor charge tip percentage	Processing items: Algorithm:	tip

Figure 2-5 Partially completed IPO chart showing the input and output items

Hints for Analyzing Problems

Unfortunately, analyzing real-world problems will not be as easy as analyzing the problems found in a textbook. The analysis step is the most difficult of the problem-solving steps, and it requires a lot of time, patience, and effort. If you are having trouble analyzing a problem, try reading the problem specification several times, as it is easy to miss information during the first reading. If the problem still is unclear to you, do not be shy about asking the user for more information. Remember, the more you understand a problem, the easier it will be for you to write a correct and efficient solution.

When reading a problem specification, it helps to use a pencil to lightly cross out the information that you feel is unimportant to the solution, as shown in Figure 2-6. Doing this reduces the amount of information you need to consider in your analysis. If you are not sure whether an item of information is important, ask yourself this question: *If I didn't know this information, could I still solve the problem?* If your answer is *Yes*, then the information is superfluous and you can ignore it. If you later find that the information is important, you can always erase the pencil line.

Problem specification
~~Treyson Mobley wants a program that~~ calculates and displays the amount he should tip ~~a waiter at a restaurant. The program should~~ subtract any liquor charge from the total bill and then calculate the tip (using a percentage) on the remainder.

Figure 2-6 Problem specification with unimportant information crossed out

Some problem specifications, like the one shown in Figure 2-7, are difficult to analyze because they contain incomplete information. In this case, it is clear that the output is the weekly gross pay, and the input is the hourly pay and the number of hours worked during the week. However, most companies pay a premium (such as time and one-half) for the hours worked over 40. You cannot tell whether the premium applies to the additional 10 hours that Jack worked because the problem specification does not contain enough information. Before you can solve this problem, you will need to ask the payroll manager about the company's overtime policy.

Problem specification
Jack Osaki earns $7 per hour. Last week, Jack worked 50 hours. He wants a program that calculates and displays his weekly gross pay.

Figure 2-7 Problem specification that does not contain enough information

As a programmer, it is important to distinguish between information that truly is missing and information that simply is not stated explicitly in the problem specification—that is, information that is implied. For example, consider the problem specification shown in Figure 2-8. To solve the problem, you need to calculate the area of a rectangle; you do this by multiplying the rectangle's length by its width. Therefore, the area is the output, and the length and width are the input. Notice, however, that the words *length* and *width* do not appear in the problem specification. Although both items are not stated explicitly, neither is considered missing information. This is because the formula for calculating the area of a rectangle is common knowledge. (The formula also can be found in any math book or on the Internet.) With practice, you will be able to "fill in the gaps" in a problem specification also.

For more examples of analyzing problems, see the Analyzing Problems section in the Ch02WantMore.pdf file.

Problem specification
Caroline Casey wants a program that calculates and displays the area of any rectangle.

Figure 2-8 Problem specification in which the input is not explicitly stated

The answers to Mini-Quiz questions are located in Appendix A.

Mini-Quiz 2-1

Identify the output and input in each of the following problem specifications. Also identify any information that is missing from the specification.

1. Kendra Chopra lives in a state that charges a 5% sales tax. She wants a program that displays the amount of sales tax due on a purchase.
2. Henry Denton belongs to a CD (compact disc) club. Last year, he bought all of his CDs from the club at $8 per CD. He wants to know how much he saved last year by buying the CDs through the club rather than through a music store.
3. Kelsey Jones saves $1.50 per day. She would like to know the total amount she saved during the month of January.
4. If James Monet saves $2 per day, how much will he save in one year?

Step 2—Plan the Algorithm

The second step in the problem-solving process is to plan the algorithm that will transform the problem's input into its output. You record the algorithm in the Processing column of the IPO chart. Each instruction in the algorithm will describe an action that the computer needs to take. Therefore, each instruction should start with a verb.

Most algorithms begin with an instruction to enter the input items into the computer. Next, you usually record instructions to process the input items to achieve the problem's output. The processing typically involves performing one or more calculations using the input items. Most algorithms end with an instruction to display, print, or store the output items. *Display, print,* and *store* refer to the computer screen, the printer, and a file on a disk, respectively.

Figure 2-9 shows the problem specification and IPO chart for the Treyson Mobley problem. Notice that each instruction in the algorithm starts with a verb: *enter, calculate,* and *display*. The algorithm begins by entering the input items. It then uses the input items to calculate the output item. An algorithm should state both *what* is to be calculated and *how* to calculate it. In this case, the tip is calculated by subtracting the liquor charge from the total bill and then multiplying the remainder by the tip percentage. The last instruction in the algorithm displays the output item. To avoid confusion, it is important that the algorithm is consistent when referring to the input and output items. For example, if the input item is listed as *total bill*, then the algorithm should refer to the item as *total bill* rather than a different name, such as *total* or *total due.*

Problem specification
Treyson Mobley wants a program that calculates and displays the amount he should tip a waiter at a restaurant. The program should subtract any liquor charge from the total bill and then calculate the tip (using a percentage) on the remainder.

Input	Processing	Output
total bill liquor charge tip percentage	Processing items: none Algorithm: 1. enter the total bill, liquor charge, and tip percentage 2. calculate the tip by subtracting the liquor charge from the total bill and then multiplying the remainder by the tip percentage 3. display the tip	tip

each instruction begins with a verb

Figure 2-9 Problem specification and IPO chart for the Treyson Mobley problem

The algorithm in Figure 2-9 is composed of short English statements, referred to as **pseudocode**, which means *false code*. It's called false code because, although it resembles programming language instructions, pseudocode cannot be understood by a computer. Programmers use pseudocode to help them while they are planning an algorithm. It allows them to jot down their ideas using a human-readable language without having to worry about the syntax of the programming language itself. Pseudocode is not standardized; every programmer has his or her own version, but you will find some similarities among the various versions.

Besides using pseudocode, programmers also use flowcharts when planning algorithms. A **flowchart** uses standardized symbols to visually depict an algorithm. You can draw the flowchart symbols by hand; or, you can use the drawing or shapes feature in a word processor. You also can use a flowcharting program, such as SmartDraw or Visio. Figure 2-10 shows the algorithm from Figure 2-9 in flowchart form. The flowchart contains three different symbols: an oval, a parallelogram, and a rectangle. The symbols are connected with lines, called **flowlines**. The oval symbol is called the **start/stop symbol** and is used to indicate the beginning and end of the flowchart. Between the start and stop ovals are two parallelograms, called input/output symbols. You use the **input/output symbol** to represent input tasks (such as getting information from the user) and output tasks (such as displaying, printing, or storing information). The first parallelogram in Figure 2-10 represents an input task, while the last parallelogram represents an output task. The rectangle in a flowchart is called the **process symbol** and is used to represent tasks such as calculations.

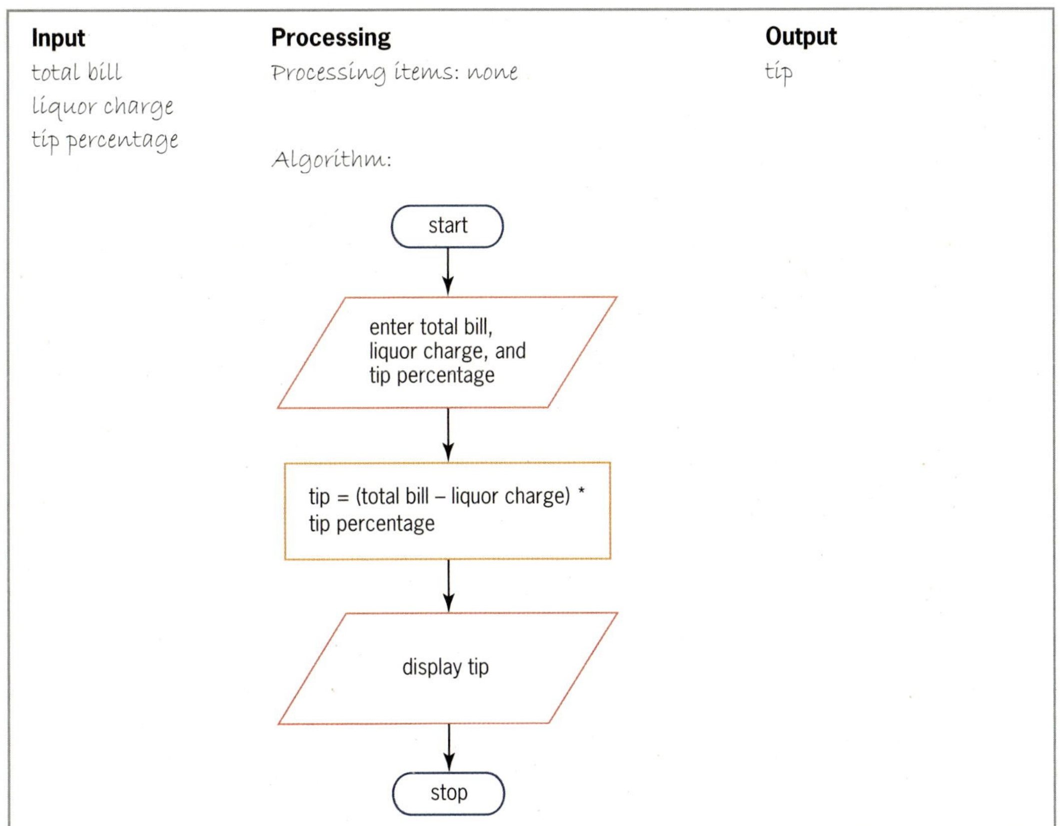

Figure 2-10 Figure 2-9's algorithm in flowchart form

When planning an algorithm, you do not need to create both pseudocode and a flowchart; you need to use only one of these planning tools. The tool you use is really a matter of personal preference. For simple algorithms, pseudocode works just fine. However, when an algorithm becomes more complex, its logic may be easier to see in a flowchart. As the old adage goes, a picture is sometimes worth a thousand words.

Even a very simple problem can have more than one solution. Figure 2-11 shows a different solution to the Treyson Mobley problem. In this solution, the difference between the total bill and liquor charge is calculated in a separate instruction rather than in the instruction that calculates the tip. The total bill without liquor charge item is neither an input item (because it's not provided by the user) nor an output item (because it won't be displayed, printed, or stored in a file). Instead, the total bill without liquor charge is a special item, commonly referred to as a processing item. A **processing item** represents an intermediate value that the algorithm uses when processing the input into the output. In this case, the algorithm uses two of the input items (total bill and liquor charge) to calculate the total bill without liquor charge (an intermediate value). It then uses this intermediate value, along with the tip percentage, to compute the tip.

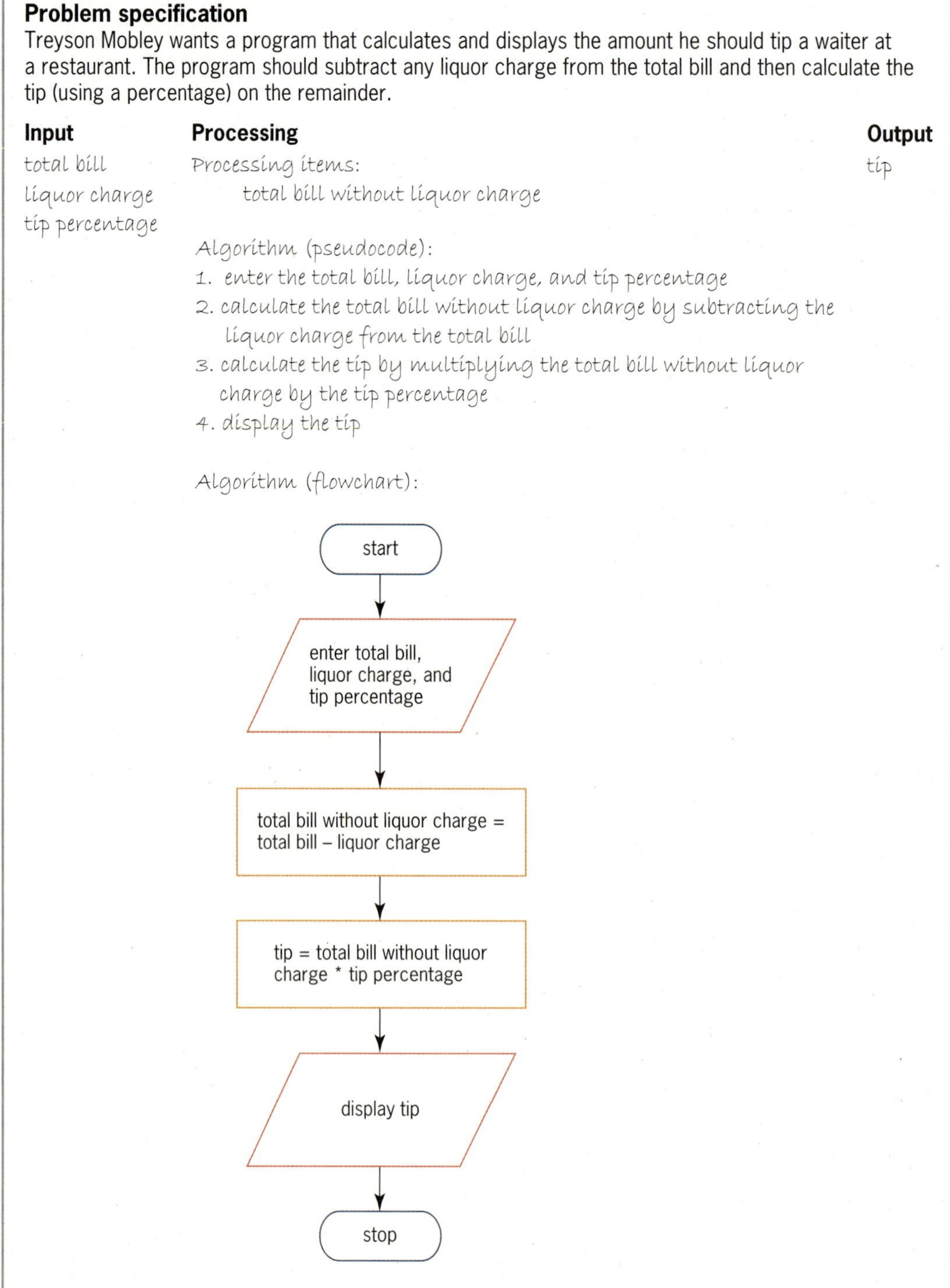

Figure 2-11 A different solution to the Treyson Mobley problem

For more examples of planning algorithms, see the Planning Algorithms section in the Ch02WantMore.pdf file.

The algorithms shown in Figures 2-9 through 2-11 produce the same result and simply represent two different ways of solving the same problem.

Mini-Quiz 2-2

1. The parallelogram in a flowchart is called the ________ symbol.
2. In a flowchart, calculation tasks are placed in a processing symbol, which has a(n) ________ shape.
3. Kendra Chopra lives in a state that charges a 5% sales tax. She wants a program that displays the amount of sales tax due on a purchase. The output is the sales tax. The input is the purchase amount and the sales tax rate. Complete an appropriate IPO chart, using pseudocode in the Algorithm section.
4. Henry Denton belongs to a CD (compact disc) club. Last year, he bought all of his CDs from the club at $8 per CD. He wants to know how much he saved last year by buying the CDs through the club rather than through a music store that charges $12 per CD. The output is the savings. The input is the number of CDs purchased, the club CD price, and the store CD price. Complete an appropriate IPO chart, using a flowchart in the Algorithm section. The algorithm should use two processing items: one for the cost of buying the CDs through the club, and the other for the cost of buying the CDs through the store.

The answers to Mini-Quiz questions are located in Appendix A.

Step 3—Desk-Check the Algorithm

After analyzing a problem and planning its algorithm, you then desk-check the algorithm. The term **desk-checking** refers to the fact that the programmer reviews the algorithm while seated at his or her desk rather than in front of the computer. Desk-checking is also called **hand-tracing** because the programmer uses a pencil and paper to follow each of the algorithm's instructions by hand. You desk-check an algorithm to verify that it is not missing any instructions, and that the existing instructions are correct and in the proper order.

Ch02-Treyson video

Before you begin the desk-check, you first choose a set of sample data for the input values, which you then use to manually compute the expected output value. For the Treyson Mobley solution, you will use input values of $45, $10, and .2 (the decimal equivalent of 20%) as the total bill, liquor charge, and tip percentage, respectively. A manual calculation of the tip results in $7, as shown in Figure 2-12.

```
$ 45  (total bill)
- 10  (liquor charge)
------
  35  (total bill without liquor charge)
*  .2 (tip percentage)
------
$  7  (tip)
```

Figure 2-12 Manual tip calculation for the first desk-check

You now use the sample input values to desk-check the algorithm, which should result in the expected output value of $7. It is helpful to use a desk-check table when desk-checking an algorithm. The table should contain one column for each input item listed in the IPO chart, as well as one column for each output item and one column for each processing item (if any). You can perform the desk-check using either the algorithm's pseudocode or its flowchart.

Figure 2-13 shows one solution for the Treyson Mobley problem along with a partially completed desk-check table. (The flowchart for this solution is shown earlier in Figure 2-11.) Notice that the desk-check table contains five columns: three for the input items, one for the processing item, and one for the output item.

Input
total bill
liquor charge
tip percentage

Processing
Processing items:
total bill without liquor charge

Algorithm:
1. enter the total bill, liquor charge, and tip percentage
2. calculate the total bill without liquor charge by subtracting the liquor charge from the total bill
3. calculate the tip by multiplying the total bill without liquor charge by the tip percentage
4. display the tip

Output
tip

total bill	liquor charge	tip percentage	total bill without liquor charge	tip

Figure 2-13 Treyson Mobley solution and partially completed desk-check table

The first instruction in the algorithm is to enter the input values. You record the results of this instruction by writing 45, 10, and .2 in the total bill, liquor charge, and tip percentage columns, respectively, in the desk-check table. See Figure 2-14.

total bill	liquor charge	tip percentage	total bill without liquor charge	tip
45	10	.2		

Figure 2-14 Input values entered in the desk-check table

The second instruction is to calculate the total bill without liquor charge by subtracting the liquor charge from the total bill. The desk-check table shows that the total bill is 45 and the liquor charge is 10. When making the calculation, always use the table to determine the values of the total bill and liquor charge. Doing this helps to verify the accuracy of the algorithm. If, for example, the table did not show any amount in the total bill column, you would know that your algorithm missed an instruction; in this case, it neglected to enter the total bill amount. When you subtract the liquor charge (10) from the total bill (45), you get 35. You record the number 35 in the total bill without liquor charge column, as shown in Figure 2-15.

total bill	liquor charge	tip percentage	total bill without liquor charge	tip
45	10	.2	35	

Figure 2-15 Processing item's value entered in the desk-check table

The third instruction is to calculate the tip by multiplying the total bill without liquor charge by the tip percentage. The desk-check table shows that the total bill without liquor charge is 35 and the tip percentage is .2. When you multiply 35 by .2, you get 7. You record the number 7 in the tip column, as shown in Figure 2-16.

total bill	liquor charge	tip percentage	total bill without liquor charge	tip
45	10	.2	35	7

Figure 2-16 Output value entered in the desk-check table

The last instruction in the algorithm is to display the tip. In this case, the number 7 will be displayed because that is what appears in the tip column. Notice that this amount agrees with the manual calculation shown in Figure 2-12; therefore, the algorithm appears to be correct. The only way to know for sure, however, is to test the algorithm a few more times with different input values. For the second desk-check, you will test the algorithm using $30, $0, and .15 as the total bill, liquor charge, and tip percentage, respectively. The tip should be $4.50, as shown in Figure 2-17.

```
$  30  (total bill)
-   0  (liquor charge)
-----------------------
   30  (total bill without liquor charge)
*  .15 (tip percentage)
-----------------------
$ 4.50 (tip)
```

Figure 2-17 Manual tip calculation for the second desk-check

Recall that the first instruction in the algorithm is to enter the total bill, liquor charge, and tip percentage. Therefore, you write 30, 0, and .15 in the appropriate columns in the desk-check table, as shown in Figure 2-18. Although it's not required, some programmers find it helpful to lightly cross out the previous value in a column before recording a new value. Doing this helps keep track of the column's current value.

total bill	liquor charge	tip percentage	total bill without liquor charge	tip
~~45~~	~~10~~	~~.2~~	35	7
30	0	.15		

Figure 2-18 Second set of input values entered in the desk-check table

The second instruction is to calculate the total bill without liquor charge. You do this by subtracting the value in the liquor charge column (0) from the value in the total bill column (30). You record the result (30) in the total bill without liquor charge column. See Figure 2-19.

total bill	liquor charge	tip percentage	total bill without liquor charge	tip
~~45~~	~~10~~	~~.2~~	~~35~~	7
30	0	.15	30	

Figure 2-19 Value of the second desk-check's processing item entered in the desk-check table

The third instruction is to calculate the tip by multiplying the value in the total bill without liquor charge column (30) by the value in the tip percentage column (.15). You record the result (4.50) in the tip column, as shown in Figure 2-20. The last instruction in the algorithm is to display the tip. In this case, the number 4.50 will be displayed, which agrees with the manual calculation shown in Figure 2-17.

total bill	liquor charge	tip percentage	total bill without liquor charge	tip
~~45~~	~~10~~	~~.2~~	~~35~~	~~7~~
30	0	.15	30	4.50

Figure 2-20 Value of the second desk-check's output item entered in the desk-check table

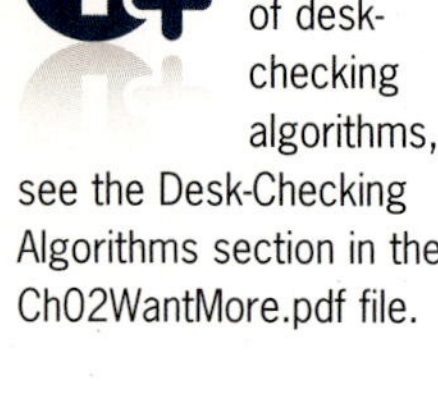

For more examples of desk-checking algorithms, see the Desk-Checking Algorithms section in the Ch02WantMore.pdf file.

To be sure an algorithm works correctly, you should desk-check it several times using both valid and invalid data. **Valid data** is data that the algorithm is expecting the user to enter. For example, the algorithm that you just finished desk-checking expects the user to provide positive numbers for the input values. **Invalid data** is data that the algorithm is not expecting the user to enter, such as a negative number for the total bill. You should test an algorithm with invalid data because users sometimes make mistakes when entering data. In later chapters in this book, you will learn how to write algorithms that correctly handle input errors. For now, however, you can assume that the user will always enter valid data.

The Gas Mileage Problem

The gas mileage problem will help reinforce what you learned in this chapter. Figure 2-21 shows the problem specification.

Ch02-Gas Mileage video

Problem specification
When Cheryl Harrison began her trip from New York to Wyoming, she filled her car's tank with gas and reset its trip meter to zero. After traveling 324 miles, Cheryl stopped at a gas station to refuel; the gas tank required 17 gallons. Cheryl wants a program that calculates and displays her car's gas mileage at any time during the trip. The gas mileage is the number of miles her car can be driven per gallon of gas.

Figure 2-21 Problem specification for the gas mileage problem

First, analyze the problem, looking for nouns and adjectives that represent both the output and the input. The output should answer the question: *What does the user want to see displayed on the screen, printed on paper, or stored in a file?* The input should answer the question: *What information will the computer need to know to display, print, or store the output items?* In the gas mileage problem, the output is the miles per gallon and the input is the miles driven and gallons used.

Next, plan the algorithm. Recall that most algorithms begin with an instruction to enter the input items into the computer, followed by instructions that process the input items and then display, print, or store the output items. Figure 2-22 shows the completed IPO chart for the gas mileage problem.

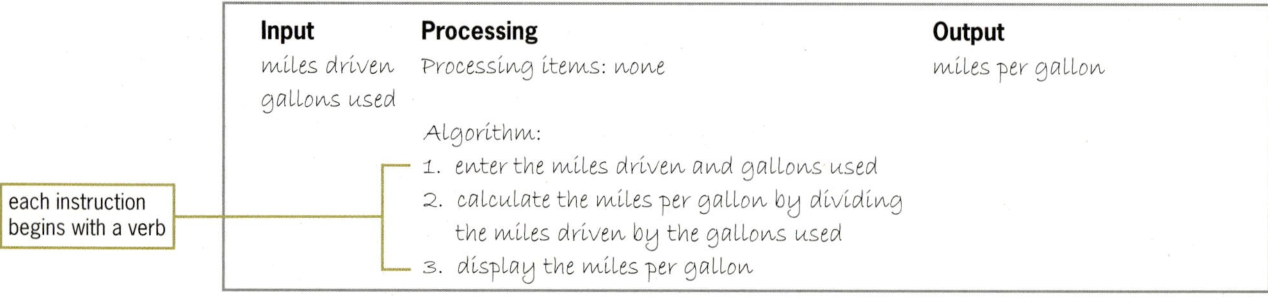

Input	Processing	Output
miles driven gallons used	Processing items: none Algorithm: 1. enter the miles driven and gallons used 2. calculate the miles per gallon by dividing the miles driven by the gallons used 3. display the miles per gallon	miles per gallon

Figure 2-22 IPO chart for the gas mileage problem

After planning the algorithm, you then desk-check it. You will desk-check the algorithm twice, first using 324 and 17 as the miles driven and gallons used, respectively, and then using 200 and 12. Figure 2-23 shows the completed desk-check table for the gas mileage problem. (The miles per gallon are rounded to two decimal places.)

miles driven	gallons used	miles per gallon
~~324~~	~~17~~	~~19.06~~
200	12	16.67

Figure 2-23 Desk-check table for the gas mileage problem

The answers to Mini-Quiz questions are located in Appendix A.

Mini-Quiz 2-3

1. Desk-check the algorithm shown in Figure 2-24 twice. First, use a purchase amount of \$67 and a sales tax rate of .05 (the decimal equivalent of 5%). Then use a purchase amount of \$100 and a sales tax rate of .02 (the decimal equivalent of 2%).
2. Desk-check the algorithm shown in Figure 2-25 twice. Use the numbers 5 and 11 as the first set of input values. Use the numbers 6 and 12 as the second set of input values.

Input	Processing	Output
purchase amount sales tax rate	Processing items: none Algorithm: 1. enter the purchase amount and sales tax rate 2. calculate the sales tax by multiplying the purchase amount by the sales tax rate 3. display the sales tax	sales tax

Figure 2-24 IPO chart for Question 1 in Mini-Quiz 2-3

Input	Processing	Output
first number second number	Processing items: sum Algorithm: 1. enter the first number and second number 2. calculate the sum by adding together the first number and second number 3. calculate the average by dividing the sum by 2 4. display the average	average

Figure 2-25 IPO chart for Question 2 in Mini-Quiz 2-3

The answers to the labs are located in Appendix A.

LAB 2-1 Stop and Analyze

Aiden Nelinski is paid every Friday. He is scheduled to receive either a 2% or 2.5% raise next week. He wants a program that calculates and displays the amount of his new weekly pay. Study the IPO chart and desk-check table shown in Figures 2-26 and 2-27, and then answer the questions.

Input	Processing	Output
current weekly pay raise percentage	Processing items: none Algorithm: 1. enter the current weekly pay and raise percentage 2. calculate the new weekly pay by multiplying the current weekly pay by the raise percentage and then adding the result to the current weekly pay 3. display the new weekly pay	new weekly pay

Figure 2-26 IPO chart for Lab 2-1

current weekly pay	raise percentage	new weekly pay
~~300~~	~~.02~~	~~306~~
500	.025	512.50

Figure 2-27 Desk-check table for Lab 2-1

QUESTIONS

1. What will the algorithm in Figure 2-26 display when the user enters 300 and .02 as the current weekly pay and raise percentage, respectively? What will it display when the user enters 500 and .025?
2. How would you modify Lab 2-1's IPO chart and desk-check table to include the amount of the raise as a processing item?
3. How would you modify Lab 2-1's IPO chart and desk-check table to also display the amount of the raise?

Ch02-Lab 2-2 video

LAB 2-2 Plan and Create

In this lab, you will plan and create an algorithm for the manager of the Lakeview Hotel. The problem specification is shown in Figure 2-28.

Problem specification
The manager of the Lakeview Hotel wants a program that calculates and displays a guest's total bill. Each guest pays a room charge that is based on a per-night rate. For example, if the per-night rate is $100 and the guest stays two nights, the room charge is $200. Customers also may incur a one-time room service charge and a one-time telephone charge.

Figure 2-28 Problem specification for Lab 2-2

First, analyze the problem, looking for the output first and then for the input. Recall that the output and input typically are stated as nouns and adjectives in the problem specification. Asking the question *What does the user want to see displayed on the screen, printed on paper, or stored in a file?* will help you determine the output. In this case, the manager wants to see the guest's total bill displayed on the computer screen. The question *What information will the computer need to know to display, print, or store the output items?* will help you determine the input. In this case, the input is the number of nights, per-night rate, room service charge, and telephone charge. Figure 2-29 shows the input and output items entered in an IPO chart.

Input	Processing	Output
number of nights per-night rate room service charge telephone charge	Processing items: Algorithm:	total bill

Figure 2-29 Partially completed IPO chart for Lab 2-2

After determining a problem's output and input, you then plan its algorithm. Recall that most algorithms begin by entering the input items into the computer. The first instruction in the current problem's algorithm, for example, will be *enter the number of nights, per-night rate, room service charge, and telephone charge.* Notice that the instruction refers to the input items using the same names listed in the Input column of the IPO chart.

After the instruction to enter the input items, you usually record instructions to process those items, typically including the items in one or more calculations. In this case, you first will use the number of nights and per-night rate to calculate an intermediate value: the room charge. You then will calculate the total bill by adding together the room charge, room service charge, and telephone charge.

Recall that most algorithms end with an instruction to display, print, or store the output items. The last instruction in this algorithm will simply display the total bill on the screen. Figure 2-30 shows the completed IPO chart. Notice that each instruction in the algorithm begins with a verb.

Input	Processing	Output
number of nights per-night rate room service charge telephone charge	Processing items: room charge Algorithm: 1. enter the number of nights, per-night rate, room service charge, and telephone charge 2. calculate the room charge by multiplying the number of nights by the per-night rate 3. calculate the total bill by adding together the room charge, room service charge, and telephone charge 4. display the total bill	total bill

each instruction begins with a verb

Figure 2-30 Completed IPO chart for Lab 2-2

You also can write the algorithm in Figure 2-30 without using a processing item, as shown in Figure 2-35.

After completing the IPO chart, you then move on to the third step in the problem-solving process, which is to desk-check the algorithm. You begin by choosing a set of sample data for the input values. You then use the values to manually compute the expected output. You will desk-check the current algorithm twice: first using 4, $100, $12, and $5 as the number of nights, per-night rate, room service charge, and telephone charge, respectively, and then using 2, $55, $20, and $0. For the first desk-check, the total bill should be $417. For the second desk-check, the total bill should be $130. The manual calculations for both desk-checks are shown in Figure 2-31.

First desk-check calculations		Second desk-check calculations	
4	(number of nights)	2	(number of nights)
* 100	(per-night rate)	* 55	(per-night rate)
400	(room charge)	110	(room charge)
+ 12	(room service charge)	+ 20	(room service charge)
+ 5	(telephone charge)	+ 0	(telephone charge)
$ 417	(total bill)	$ 130	(total bill)

Figure 2-31 Manual total bill calculations for the two desk-checks

Next, you create a desk-check table that contains one column for each input, processing, and output item. You then begin desk-checking the algorithm. The first instruction is to enter the input values. Figure 2-32 shows these values entered in the desk-check table.

number of nights	per-night rate	room service charge	telephone charge	room charge	total bill
4	100	12	5		

Figure 2-32 First set of input values entered in the desk-check table

The second and third instructions are to calculate the room charge and total bill. Figure 2-33 shows these values entered in the desk-check table.

number of nights	per-night rate	room service charge	telephone charge	room charge	total bill
4	100	12	5	400	417

Figure 2-33 Room charge and total bill values entered in the desk-check table

The last instruction in the algorithm is to display the total bill. According to the desk-check table in Figure 2-33, the total bill is 417. This amount agrees with the manual calculation shown earlier in Figure 2-31. Now use the second set of input values to desk-check the algorithm. Figure 2-34 shows the result of the second desk-check. Notice that the amount in the total bill column (130) agrees with the manual calculation shown earlier in Figure 2-31.

number of nights	per-night rate	room service charge	telephone charge	room charge	total bill
~~4~~	~~100~~	~~12~~	~~5~~	~~400~~	~~417~~
2	55	20	0	110	130

Figure 2-34 Desk-check table showing the result of the second desk-check

Almost every problem, even simple ones, can be solved in more than one way. Figure 2-35 shows another solution to Lab 2-2's problem. Unlike the solution shown earlier in Figure 2-30, this solution does not use a processing item.

Problem specification
The manager of the Lakeview Hotel wants a program that calculates and displays a guest's total bill. Each guest pays a room charge that is based on a per-night rate. For example, if the per-night rate is $100 and the guest stays two nights, the room charge is $200. Customers also may incur a one-time room service charge and a one-time telephone charge.

Input	**Processing**	**Output**
number of nights per-night rate room service charge telephone charge	Processing items: none	total bill

Algorithm:
1. enter the number of nights, per-night rate, room service charge, and telephone charge
2. calculate the total bill by multiplying the number of nights by the per-night rate and then adding the result to the room service charge and telephone charge
3. display the total bill

Figure 2-35 A different solution for Lab 2-2's problem

LAB 2-3 Modify

Each guest at the Lakeview Hotel pays an entertainment tax, which is a percentage of the room charge only. Make the appropriate modifications to the IPO chart shown earlier in Figure 2-30. Desk-check the algorithm twice. For the first desk-check, use 3, $70, $0, $10, and .05 as the number of nights, per-night rate, room service charge, telephone charge, and entertainment tax rate, respectively. For the second desk-check, use 7, $100, $25, $6, and .03.

LAB 2-4 Desk-Check

The algorithm in Figure 2-36 calculates and displays an annual property tax. Currently, the property tax rate is $1.50 for each $100 of a property's assessed value; however, the tax rate changes each year. Desk-check the algorithm three times. For the first desk-check, use $104,000 and $1.50 as the assessed value and property tax rate, respectively. For the second desk-check, use $239,000 and $1.15. For the third desk-check, use $86,000 and $0.98. Be sure to manually calculate the annual property tax for each set of input values. (The annual property tax using the first set of input values is $1560.)

Input	Processing	Output
assessed value tax rate	Processing items: none Algorithm: 1. enter the assessed value and tax rate 2. calculate the annual property tax by dividing the assessed value by 100 and then multiplying the result by the tax rate 3. display the annual property tax	annual property tax

Figure 2-36 IPO chart for Lab 2-4

LAB 2-5 Debug

The algorithm in Figure 2-37 should calculate and display the average of three numbers, but it is not working correctly. In this lab, you will find and correct the errors in the algorithm.

Input	Processing	Output
first number second number third number	Processing items: sum Algorithm: 1. enter the first number, second number, and third number 2. calculate the average by dividing the sum by 3 3. display the average number	average

Figure 2-37 IPO chart for Lab 2-5

You locate the errors in an algorithm by desk-checking it. First, choose a set of sample data for the input values. In this case, you will use the numbers 25, 63, and 14. Now use the values to manually compute the expected output—in this case, the average. The average of the three numbers is 34. Next, create a desk-check table that contains a column for each input, processing, and output item. This desk-check table will contain five columns. Finally, walk through each of the instructions in the algorithm, recording the appropriate values in the desk-check table. The first instruction in the algorithm in Figure 2-37 is to enter the three input values. Figure 2-38 shows these values entered in the desk-check table.

first number	second number	third number	sum	average
25	63	14		

Figure 2-38 Three input values entered in the desk-check table

The next instruction calculates the average by dividing the sum by 3. Notice that the sum column in the desk-check table does not contain a value. This fact alerts you that the algorithm is missing an instruction. In this case, it is missing the instruction to calculate the sum of the three numbers. The missing instruction is shaded in Figure 2-39.

Input	**Processing**	**Output**
first number second number third number	Processing items: sum Algorithm: 1. enter the first number, second number, and third number 2. calculate the sum by adding together the first number, second number, and third number 3. calculate the average by dividing the sum by 3 4. display the average number	average

Figure 2-39 Missing instruction added to the IPO chart for Lab 2-5

The additional instruction calculates the sum by adding together the first number, second number, and third number. According to the desk-check table shown earlier in Figure 2-38, those values are 25, 63, and 14, respectively. The sum of those values is 102. Figure 2-40 shows the sum entered in the desk-check table.

first number	second number	third number	sum	average
25	63	14	102	

Figure 2-40 Sum entered in the desk-check table

The next instruction calculates the average by dividing the sum by 3. According to the desk-check table, the sum is 102. Dividing 102 by 3 results in 34. Figure 2-41 shows the average entered in the desk-check table.

first number	second number	third number	sum	average
25	63	14	102	34

Figure 2-41 Average entered in the desk-check table

The last instruction in the algorithm displays the average number. Notice that the desk-check table does not contain a column with the heading "average number." Recall that it is important to be consistent when referring to the input, output, and processing items in the IPO chart. In this case, the last instruction in the algorithm should be *display the average* rather than *display the average number.* According to the desk-check table, the average column contains the number 34, which is correct. Figure 2-42 shows the corrected algorithm. The changes made to the original algorithm (shown earlier in Figure 2-37) are shaded in the figure.

Input	Processing	Output
first number second number third number	Processing items: sum Algorithm: 1. enter the first number, second number, and third number 2. calculate the sum by adding together the first number, second number, and third number 3. calculate the average by dividing the sum by 3 4. display the average	average

Figure 2-42 Corrected algorithm for Lab 2-5

On your own, desk-check the corrected algorithm shown in Figure 2-42 using the numbers 33, 56, and 70.

Summary

- The process you follow when creating solutions to everyday problems is similar to the process used to create a computer program, which also is a solution to a problem. This problem-solving process typically involves analyzing the problem and then planning, reviewing, implementing, evaluating, and modifying (if necessary) the solution.
- Programmers use tools such as IPO (Input, Processing, Output) charts, pseudocode, and flowcharts to help them analyze problems and develop algorithms.
- The first step in the problem-solving process is to analyze the problem. During the analysis step, the programmer first determines the output, which is the goal or purpose of solving the problem. The programmer then determines the input, which is the information needed to reach the goal.

- The second step in the problem-solving process is to plan the algorithm. During the planning step, programmers write the instructions that will transform the input into the output. Most algorithms begin by entering some data (the input items), then processing that data (usually by performing some calculations), and then displaying some data (the output items).
- The third step in the problem-solving process is to desk-check the algorithm to determine whether it will work as intended. First, choose a set of sample data for the input values. Then use the values to manually compute the expected output. Next, create a desk-check table that contains a column for each input, processing, and output item. Finally, walk through each of the instructions in the algorithm, recording the appropriate values in the desk-check table.

Key Terms

Desk-checking—the process of manually walking through each of the instructions in an algorithm; also called hand-tracing

Flowchart—a tool that programmers use to help them plan (or depict) an algorithm; consists of standardized symbols connected by flowlines

Flowlines—the lines that connect the symbols in a flowchart

Hand-tracing—another term for desk-checking

Input—the items a program needs in order to achieve the output

Input/output symbol—the parallelogram in a flowchart; used to represent input and output tasks

Invalid data—data that the algorithm is not expecting the user to enter

IPO—an acronym for Input, Processing, and Output

IPO chart—a chart that some programmers use to organize and summarize the results of a problem analysis

Output—the goal of solving a problem; the items the user wants to display, print, or store

Process symbol—the rectangle symbol in a flowchart; used to represent tasks such as calculations

Processing item—an intermediate value (neither input nor output) that an algorithm uses when processing the input into the output

Pseudocode—a tool that programmers use to help them plan an algorithm; consists of short English statements; means *false code*

Start/stop symbol—the oval symbol in a flowchart; used to mark the beginning and end of the flowchart

Valid data—data that the algorithm is expecting the user to enter

Review Questions

1. Which of the following is the first step in the problem-solving process?
   a. Plan the algorithm
   b. Analyze the problem
   c. Desk-check the algorithm
   d. Code the algorithm into a program

2. Programmers refer to the goal of solving a problem as the ________.
   a. input
   b. output
   c. processing
   d. purpose

3. Programmers refer to the items needed to reach a problem's goal as the ________.
   a. input
   b. output
   c. processing
   d. purpose

4. A problem's ________ will answer the question *What does the user want to see displayed on the screen, printed on the printer, or stored in a file?*
   a. input
   b. output
   c. processing
   d. purpose

5. A problem's ________ will answer the question *What information will the computer need to know to display, print, or store the output items?*
   a. input
   b. output
   c. processing
   d. purpose

6. The calculation instructions in an algorithm should state ________.
   a. only *what* is to be calculated
   b. only *how* to calculate something
   c. both *what* is to be calculated and *how* to calculate it
   d. both *what* is to be calculated and *why* it is calculated

7. Most algorithms follow the format of ________.
   a. entering the input items; then displaying, printing, or storing the input items; and then processing the output items
   b. entering the input items; then processing the output items; and then displaying, printing, or storing the output items
   c. entering the input items; then processing the input items; and then displaying, printing, or storing the output items
   d. entering the output items; then processing the output items; and then displaying, printing, or storing the output items

8. The short English statements that represent an algorithm are called ________.
   a. flow diagrams
   b. IPO charts
   c. pseudocharts
   d. pseudocode

9. The oval in a flowchart is called the ________ symbol.
   a. calculation
   b. input/output
   c. process
   d. start/stop

10. A desk-check table should contain ________.
    a. one column for each input item
    b. one column for each output item
    c. one column for each processing item
    d. all of the above

Exercises

Pencil and Paper

TRY THIS

1. The sales manager at Colfax Products wants a program that allows him to enter the sales made in each of two states. The program should calculate and display the commission, which is a percentage of the total sales. Complete an IPO chart for this problem. Plan the algorithm using a flowchart. Also complete a desk-check table for your algorithm. For the first desk-check, use $1000 and $2000 as the two state sales, and use .05 (the decimal equivalent of 5%) as the commission rate. Then use $3000 and $2500 as the two state sales, and use .06 as the commission rate. (The answers to TRY THIS Exercises are located at the end of the chapter.)

TRY THIS

2. Party-On sells individual hot/cold cups and dessert plates for parties. Sue Chen wants a program that allows her to enter the price of a cup, the price of a plate, the number of cups purchased, the number of plates purchased, and the sales tax rate. The program should calculate and display the total cost of the purchase. Complete an IPO chart for this problem. Plan the algorithm using pseudocode. Desk-check the algorithm using $.50 as the cup price, $1 as the plate price, 35 as the number of cups, 35 as the number of plates, and .02 as the sales tax rate. Then desk-check it using $.25, $.75, 20, 10, and .06. (The answers to TRY THIS Exercises are located at the end of the chapter.)

MODIFY THIS

3. Modify the IPO chart shown earlier in Figure 2-9 as follows. Treyson will be charging the total bill, including the tip, to his credit card. Modify the solution so that, in addition to calculating and displaying the appropriate tip, it also calculates and displays the amount charged to Treyson's credit card. Desk-check the algorithm using $50 as the total bill, $5 as the liquor charge, and .2 as the tip percentage. Then desk-check it using $15 as the total bill, $0 as the liquor charge, and .15 as the tip percentage.

INTRODUCTORY

4. Wilma Peterson is paid by the hour. She wants a program that calculates her weekly gross pay. For this exercise, you do not need to worry about overtime pay, as Wilma never works more than 40 hours in a week. Complete an IPO chart for this problem. Desk-check the algorithm using $10 as the hourly pay and 35 as the number of hours worked. Then desk-check it using $15 as the hourly pay and 25 as the number of hours worked.

INTRODUCTORY

5. Jenna Williams is paid based on an annual salary rather than an hourly wage. She wants a program that calculates the amount of her gross pay for each pay period. Complete an IPO chart for this problem. Desk-check the algorithm using $35,000 as the annual salary and 52 as the number of pay periods. Then desk-check it using $50,000 as the annual salary and 24 as the number of pay periods.

INTRODUCTORY

6. Mary wants a program that displays the number of minutes it takes for an airplane to travel a specified distance at a specified speed. The distance will be given in miles, and the speed will be given in miles per hour. Complete an IPO chart for this problem. Desk-check the algorithm using 409 miles as the distance and 340 miles per hour as the speed. Then desk-check it again using 1013 miles as the distance and 494.4 miles per hour as the speed. In each desk-check, round the minutes to the nearest whole number.

INTRODUCTORY

7. An airplane has both first-class and coach seats. The first-class tickets cost more than the coach tickets. The airline wants a program that calculates and displays the total amount of money the passengers paid for a specific flight. Complete an IPO chart for this problem. Desk-check the algorithm using 9, 52, $125, and $90 as the number of first-class tickets sold, the number of coach tickets sold, the price of a first-class ticket, and the price of a coach ticket, respectively. Then desk-check it using your own set of data.

INTERMEDIATE

8. Rent A Van wants a program that calculates the total cost of renting a van. Customers pay a base fee plus a charge per mile driven. Complete an IPO chart for this problem. Desk-check the algorithm using $50, $0.20, and 1000 as the base fee, charge per mile, and number of miles driven, respectively. Then desk-check it using your own set of data.

INTERMEDIATE

9. The accountant at Typing Haven wants a program that will help her prepare a customer's bill. She will enter the number of typed envelopes and the number of typed pages, as well as the charge per typed envelope and the charge per typed page. The program should calculate and display the amount due for the envelopes, the amount due for the pages, and the total amount due. Complete an IPO chart for this problem. Desk-check the algorithm using 50, 100, $0.10, and $0.25 as the number of typed envelopes, the number of typed pages, the charge per typed envelope, and the charge per typed page, respectively. Then desk-check it using your own set of data.

INTERMEDIATE

10. Justin receives 52 weekly paychecks each year. Each week, he contributes a specific percentage of his gross weekly pay to his retirement plan at work. His employer also contributes to his retirement plan, but at a different rate. Justin wants a program that will calculate and display the total annual contribution made to his retirement plan by him and his employer. Complete an IPO chart for this problem. Desk-check the algorithm using $640 as the gross weekly pay, 6% as Justin's contribution rate, and 4% as the employer's contribution rate. Then desk-check it using your own set of data.

ADVANCED

11. The Paper Tree store wants a program that calculates and displays the number of single rolls of wallpaper needed to cover a room. The salesclerk will provide the room's length, width, and ceiling height, in feet. He or she also will provide the number of square feet a single roll will cover. Complete an IPO chart for this problem. Desk-check the algorithm using 10, 12, 8, and 30 as the room's length, width, ceiling height, and number of square feet a single roll will cover, respectively. Then desk-check it using your own set of data.

ADVANCED

12. The payroll clerk at Nosaki Company wants a program that calculates and displays an employee's gross pay, federal withholding tax (FWT), Social Security and Medicare (FICA) tax, state tax, and net pay. The clerk will enter the hours worked (which is never over 40), hourly pay rate, FWT rate, FICA tax rate, and state income tax rate. Complete an IPO chart for this problem. Desk-check the algorithm using 30, $10, .2, .08, and .04 as the hours worked, pay rate, FWT rate, FICA rate, and state tax rate, respectively. Then desk-check it using your own set of data.

SWAT THE BUGS

13. GeeBees Clothiers is having a sale. The store manager wants a program that allows a salesclerk to enter the original price of an item and the discount rate. The program should calculate and display the amount of the discount and the sale price. The algorithm in Figure 2-43 is supposed to solve this problem, but it is not working correctly. Correct the algorithm, and then desk-check it using an original price of $100 and a discount rate of .25 (the decimal equivalent of 25%).

Input	**Processing**	**Output**
original price discount rate	Processing items: none Algorithm: 1. enter the original price and discount rate 2. calculate the sale price by subtracting the discount from the original price 3. display the discount and price	discount sale price

Figure 2-43

SWAT THE BUGS

14. Etola Systems wants a program that displays the ending inventory amount, given the beginning inventory amount, the amount sold, and the amount returned. The algorithm in Figure 2-44 is supposed to solve this problem, but it is not working correctly. First, calculate the expected output using a beginning inventory of 50, an amount sold of 10, and an amount returned of 2. Then use these values to desk-check the algorithm. Correct the algorithm, and then desk-check it again.

Input	**Processing**	**Output**
beginning inventory amount sold amount returned	Processing items: none Algorithm: 1. enter the beginning inventory, amount sold, and amount returned 2. calculate the ending inventory by adding the amount sold to the beginning inventory and then subtracting the amount returned from the result 3. display the ending inventory	ending inventory

Figure 2-44

Answers to TRY THIS Exercises

1. See Figures 2-45 and 2-46.

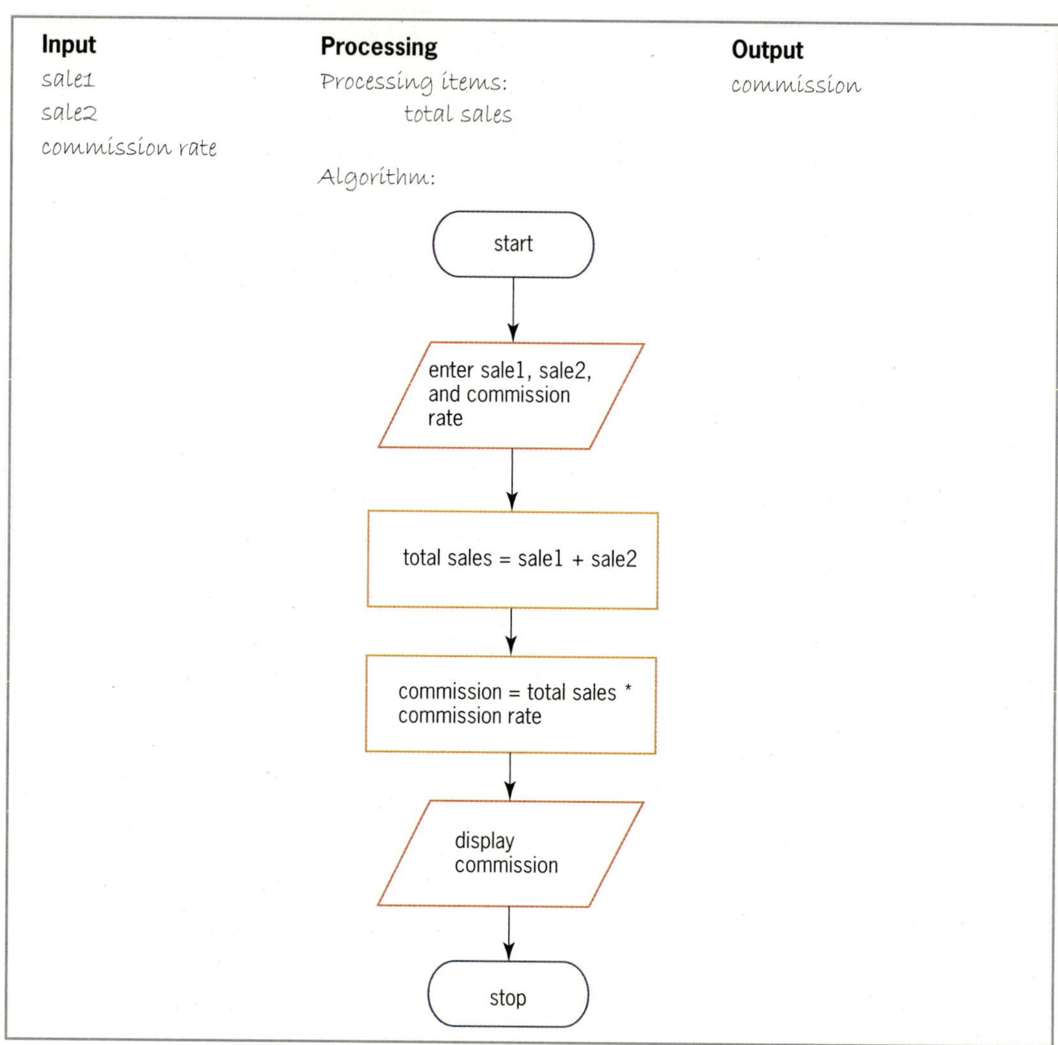

Figure 2-45

sale1	sale2	commission rate	total sales	commission
~~1000~~	~~2000~~	~~.05~~	~~3000~~	~~150~~
3000	2500	.06	5500	330

Figure 2-46

2. See Figures 2-47 and 2-48.

Input

cup price
plate price
cups purchased
plates purchased
sales tax rate

Processing

Processing items:

- total cup cost
- total plate cost
- subtotal

Algorithm:

1. enter the cup price, plate price, cups purchased, plates purchased, and sales tax rate
2. calculate the total cup cost by multiplying the cups purchased by the cup price
3. calculate the total plate cost by multiplying the plates purchased by the plate price
4. calculate the subtotal by adding together the total cup cost and total plate cost
5. calculate the total cost by multiplying the subtotal by the sales tax rate and then adding the result to the subtotal
6. display the total cost

Output

total cost

Figure 2-47

cup price	plate price	cups purchased	plates purchased	sales tax rate
~~.50~~	~~1~~	~~35~~	~~35~~	~~.02~~
.25	.75	20	10	.06

total cup cost	total plate cost	subtotal	total cost
~~17.50~~	~~35~~	~~52.50~~	~~53.55~~
5	7.50	12.50	13.25

Figure 2-48

CHAPTER 3

Variables and Constants

After studying Chapter 3, you should be able to:

- Distinguish among a variable, a named constant, and a literal constant
- Explain how data is stored in memory
- Select an appropriate name, data type, and initial value for a memory location
- Declare a memory location in C++

Beginning Step 4 in the Problem-Solving Process

Ch03-Chapter Preview video

Chapter 2 covered the first three steps in the problem-solving process, which were to analyze the problem, plan the algorithm, and then desk-check the algorithm. When the programmer is satisfied that the algorithm is correct, he or she moves on to the fourth step, which is to code the algorithm into a program. Coding the algorithm refers to the process of translating the algorithm into a language that the computer can understand; in this book, you will use the C++ programming language.

Programmers use the information in the IPO chart, which they created in the analysis and planning steps, as a guide when coding the algorithm. The programmer begins by assigning a descriptive name to each unique input, processing, and output item. The programmer also assigns each item a data type and (optionally) an initial value. The name, data type, and initial value are used to store the input, processing, and output items in the computer's internal memory while the program is running.

Internal Memory

Inside every computer is a component called internal memory. The internal memory of a computer is composed of memory locations, with each memory location having a unique numeric address. It may be helpful to picture memory locations as storage bins, similar to the ones illustrated in Figure 3-1. However, unlike the storage bins shown in the figure, each storage bin (memory location) inside a computer can hold only one item at a time. The item can be a number, such as 5 or 45.89. It also can be **text**, which is a group of characters treated as one unit and not used in a calculation. Examples of text include a name, an address, or a phone number. The item also can be a C++ program instruction.

Figure 3-1 Illustration of storage bins

Some of the memory locations inside the computer are automatically filled with data while you use your computer. For example, when you enter the number 5 at your keyboard, the computer saves the number 5 in a memory location for you. Likewise, when you start an application, each program instruction is placed in a memory location, where it awaits processing. Other memory locations are reserved by programmers for use in a program. Such memory locations are used to store the values of the input, processing, and output items as the program is running. Reserving a memory location is also referred to as declaring the memory location.

A programmer declares a memory location using a C++ instruction that assigns a name, a data type, and (optionally) an initial value to the location. The name allows the programmer to refer to the memory location using one or more descriptive words, rather than a cryptic numeric address, in code. Descriptive words are easier to remember and serve to self-document your code. The data type indicates the type of data—for example, numeric or textual—the memory location will store.

There are two types of memory locations that a programmer can declare: variables and named constants. A **variable** is a memory location whose value can change (vary) during **runtime**, which is when a program is running. Most of the memory locations declared in a program are variables. A **named constant**, on the other hand, is a memory location whose value cannot be changed during runtime. In a program that inputs the radius of any circle and then calculates and outputs the circle's area, a programmer would declare variables to store the values of the radius and area; doing this allows those values to vary while the program is running. However, he or she would declare a named constant to store the value of pi (π), which is used in the formula for calculating the area of a circle. (The formula is πr^2.) A named constant is appropriate in this case because the value of pi (3.141593 when rounded to six decimal places) will always be the same.

Selecting a Name for a Memory Location

Every memory location that a programmer declares must be assigned a name. The name, also called the identifier, should be descriptive in that it should help you remember the memory location's purpose. In other words, it should describe the contents of the memory location. A good name for a memory location is one that is meaningful right after you finish a program and also months or years later when you (or perhaps a coworker) need to modify the program.

Besides being descriptive, a memory location's name must follow several specific rules in C++. It must begin with a letter and contain only letters, numbers, and the underscore character. No punctuation marks, spaces, or other special characters (such as $ or %) are allowed in the name. In addition, the name cannot be a **keyword**, which is a word that has a special meaning in the programming language you are using. Keywords are also referred to as reserved words. Appendix B in this book contains a listing of the C++ keywords, which must be entered using lowercase letters.

Refer to the Tip that appears next to Figure 3-2 for an exception to beginning a memory location's name with a letter.

Finally, memory location names are case sensitive in C++. This means that in addition to using the exact spelling when referring to a specific memory location in a program, you also must use the exact case. For example, if you declare a memory location named `discount` at the beginning of a program, you must use the name `discount`, rather than `Discount` or `DISCOUNT`, to refer to the memory location throughout the program.

Many C++ programmers use uppercase letters when naming named constants and use lowercase letters when naming variables. This practice allows them to easily distinguish between the named constants and variables in a program. If a named constant's name contains more than one word, an underscore character can be used to separate the words, like this: `TAX_RATE`. However, if a variable's name contains two or more words, most C++ programmers enter the name using **camel case**, which means they capitalize the first letter in the second and subsequent words in the name, like this: `grossPay`. Camel case refers to the fact that the uppercase letters appear as "humps" in the name because they are taller than the lowercase letters. The rules for naming memory locations in C++ are shown in Figure 3-2, along with examples of valid and invalid names.

HOW TO Name a Memory Location in C++

1. The name must begin with a letter.
2. The name can contain only letters, numbers, and the underscore character. No punctuation marks, spaces, or other special characters are allowed in the name.
3. The name cannot be a keyword. Appendix B contains a listing of keywords in C++.
4. Names in C++ are case sensitive.

Valid names
`grossPay, interest, TAX_RATE, PI`

Invalid names	Reason
`2011Sales`	the name must begin with a letter
`end Balance`	the name cannot contain a space
`first.name`	the name cannot contain punctuation
`int`	the name cannot be a keyword
`RATE%`	the name cannot contain a special character

Figure 3-2 How to name a memory location in C++

Technically, a memory location's name in C++ can begin with an underscore. However, this usually is done only for the names of memory locations declared within a class. You will learn about classes later in this book.

Revisiting the Treyson Mobley Problem

In Chapter 2, you analyzed a problem specification involving Treyson Mobley and a waiter's tip. You then planned and desk-checked an appropriate algorithm. The problem specification is shown in Figure 3-3, along with one of the IPO charts and desk-check tables you created.

Problem specification
Treyson Mobley wants a program that calculates and displays the amount he should tip a waiter at a restaurant. The program should subtract any liquor charge from the total bill and then calculate the tip (using a percentage) on the remainder.

Input	**Processing**	**Output**
total bill liquor charge tip percentage	Processing items: total bill without liquor charge Algorithm: 1. enter the total bill, liquor charge, and tip percentage 2. calculate the total bill without liquor charge by subtracting the liquor charge from the total bill 3. calculate the tip by multiplying the total bill without liquor charge by the tip percentage 4. display the tip	tip

total bill	liquor charge	tip percentage	total bill without liquor charge	tip
~~45~~	~~10~~	~~.2~~	~~35~~	~~7~~
30	0	.15	30	4.50

Figure 3-3 Problem specification, IPO chart, and desk-check table from Chapter 2

The IPO chart in Figure 3-3 contains a total of five input, processing, and output items. Therefore, five memory locations will be needed to store the values of the items. The memory locations will be variables because each item's value should be allowed to vary during runtime. Figure 3-4 lists possible names (identifiers) for the variables.

IPO chart item	Variable name
total bill	`totalBill`
liquor charge	`liquor`
tip percentage	`tipPercent`
total bill without liquor charge	`totalNoLiquor`
tip	`tip`

Figure 3-4 Names of the variables for the Treyson Mobley problem

Mini-Quiz 3-1

The answers to Mini-Quiz questions are located in Appendix A.

1. How many items can a memory location store at a time?
2. Which of the following should be used in a C++ program to refer to the `quantity` variable?
   a. `quantity`
   b. `QUANTITY`
   c. `Quantity`
   d. Any of the above can be used.
3. Which of the following is a valid name for a memory location?
   a. `jan.Sales`
   b. `2ndQuarterIncome`
   c. `COMMISSION_RATE`
   d. `march$`
4. What are the two types of memory locations that a programmer can declare?

Selecting a Data Type for a Memory Location

Like storage bins, memory locations come in different types and sizes. The type and size you use depends on the item you want the memory location to store. Some memory locations can store a number, while others can hold text, a date, or a Boolean value (true or false). The item that a memory location will accept for storage is determined by the location's data type, which the programmer assigns to the location when he or she declares it in a program. The most commonly used data types in C++ are listed in Figure 3-5, along with the values each type can store and the amount of memory needed to store a value. Except for the `string` data type, the data types listed in the figure belong to a group of data types called fundamental data types. The **fundamental data types** are the basic data types built into the C++ language and often are referred to as primitive data types or built-in data types. The `string` data type, on the other hand, was added to the C++ language through the use of a class and is referred to as a

user-defined data type. A class is simply a group of instructions that the computer uses to create an object. In this case, the `string` class (user-defined data type) creates a `string` variable, which is considered an object. You will learn more about classes and objects in subsequent chapters in this book.

	Data type	Stores	Memory required
fundamental data types	`short`	an integer Range: –32,768 to 32,767	2 bytes
	`int`	an integer Range: –2,147,483,648 to 2,147,483,647	4 bytes
	`float`	a real number with 7 digits of precision Range: -3.4×10^{38} to 3.4×10^{38}	4 bytes
	`double`	a real number with 15 digits of precision Range: -1.7×10^{308} to 1.7×10^{308}	8 bytes
	`bool`	a Boolean value (either `true` or `false`)	1 byte
	`char`	one character	1 byte
user-defined data type	`string`	zero or more characters	1 byte per character

Figure 3-5 Most commonly used data types in C++

The memory requirements and values for the different data types are implementation dependent. However, the ones listed in Figure 3-5 are typical for personal computers.

As Figure 3-5 indicates, `bool` memory locations can store either the Boolean value `true` or the Boolean value `false`. The Boolean values are named in honor of the English mathematician George Boole (1815–1864), who invented Boolean algebra. You could use a `bool` variable in a program to keep track of whether a customer's bill is paid (`true`) or not paid (`false`).

Memory locations assigned the `char` data type can store one character only. A **character** is a letter, a symbol, or a number that will not be used in a calculation. Some programmers pronounce `char` as "care" because it is short for *character*, while others pronounce `char` as in the first syllable of the word *charcoal*. A `string` memory location, on the other hand, can store zero or more characters.

Memory locations assigned either the `short` or `int` data type can store integers only. An **integer** is a whole number, which is a number that does not contain a decimal place. Examples of integers include the numbers 0, 45, and –678. The differences between the `short` and `int` data types are in the range of numbers each type can store and the amount of memory needed to store the number.

Memory locations assigned either the `float` or `double` data type can store **real numbers**, which are numbers that contain a decimal place. Examples of real numbers include the numbers 75.67, –3.45, and 783.5689. The differences between the `float` and `double` data types are in the range of numbers each type can store, the precision with which the number is stored, and the amount of memory needed to store the number.

In most of the programs you create in this book, you will use the `int` data type for memory locations that will store integers, and use the `double` data type for memory locations that will store numbers with a decimal place. The `double` data type was chosen over the `float` data type because it stores real numbers more precisely, using 15 digits of precision rather than only 7 digits. At this point, however, it is important to caution you about real numbers. Even with 15 digits of precision, not all real numbers can be represented exactly within the computer's internal memory. As a result, some calculations may not result in accuracy to the penny.

You will learn more about using real numbers in calculations in Chapter 4. Figure 3-6 shows the data type selected for each variable in the Treyson Mobley problem.

IPO chart item	Variable name	Data type
total bill	totalBill	double
liquor charge	liquor	double
tip percentage	tipPercent	double
total bill without liquor charge	totalNoLiquor	double
tip	tip	double

Figure 3-6 Data type assigned to each variable for the Treyson Mobley problem

How Data Is Stored in Internal Memory

Knowing how data is stored in the computer's internal memory will help you understand the importance of a memory location's data type. Numbers are represented in internal memory using the binary (or *base 2*) number system. The **binary number system** uses only the two digits 0 and 1. Although the binary number system may not be as familiar to you as the **decimal number system**, which uses the 10 digits 0 through 9, it is just as easy to understand. First, we'll review the decimal (or *base 10*) number system that you learned about in elementary school.

Ch03-Number System video

Figure 3-7 illustrates how the decimal number system works. As the figure indicates, the position of each digit in the decimal number system is associated with the system's base number, 10, raised to a power. Starting with the rightmost position, the positions represent the number 10 raised to a power of 0, 1, 2, 3, and so on. In the decimal number 110, the 0 is in the 10^0 position, the middle 1 is in the 10^1 position, and the leftmost 1 is in the 10^2 position. Keep in mind that in all numbering systems, the result of raising the base number to the 0th power is 1, and the result of raising it to the 1st power is the base number itself. A base number raised to the 2nd power indicates that the base number should be squared—in other words, multiplied by itself. As a result, the decimal number 110 means zero 1s (10^0), one 10 (10^1), and one 100 (10^2). The decimal number 3475 means five 1s (10^0), seven 10s (10^1), four 100s (10^2), and three 1000s (10^3); and the decimal number 21509 means nine 1s (10^0), zero 10s (10^1), five 100s (10^2), one 1000 (10^3), and two 10000s (10^4).

HOW TO Use the Decimal (*Base 10*) Number System

Decimal number	10^7	10^6	10^5	10^4	10^3	10^2	10^1	10^0
110						1	1	0
3475					3	4	7	5
21509				2	1	5	0	9

Figure 3-7 How to use the decimal (*base 10*) number system

Compare the decimal number system illustrated in Figure 3-7 with the binary number system illustrated in Figure 3-8. Like the decimal number system, the position of each digit in the binary number system also is associated with the system's base number raised to a power. However, in the binary number system, the base number is 2 rather than 10. Starting with the rightmost position, the positions represent 2 raised to a power of 0, 1, 2, 3, and so on. In the binary number 110, the 0 is in the 2^0 position, the middle 1 is in the 2^1 position, and the leftmost 1 is in the 2^2 position. Therefore, the binary number 110 means zero 1s (2^0), one 2 (2^1), and one 4 (2^2). The decimal equivalent of the binary number 110 is 6, which is calculated by adding together 0 + 2 + 4 (zero 1s + one 2 + one 4). In other words, the decimal number 6 is stored in a memory location using the binary number 110. The binary number 11010 means zero 1s (2^0), one 2 (2^1), zero 4s (2^2), one 8 (2^3), and one 16 (2^4). The decimal equivalent of the binary number 11010 is 26, which is calculated by adding together 0 + 2 + 0 + 8 + 16. The decimal equivalent of the last binary number shown in Figure 3-8 is 9 (one 1 + zero 2s + zero 4s + one 8).

HOW TO Use the Binary (*Base 2*) Number System

Binary number	2^7	2^6	2^5	2^4	2^3	2^2	2^1	2^0	**Decimal equivalent**
110						1	1	0	6
11010				1	1	0	1	0	26
1001					1	0	0	1	9

Figure 3-8 How to use the binary (*base 2*) number system

Unlike numeric data, character data (which is data assigned to memory locations that can store characters) is represented in internal memory using ASCII codes. **ASCII** (pronounced *ASK-ee*) stands for American Standard Code for Information Interchange. The ASCII coding scheme assigns a specific numeric code to each character on your keyboard. Figure 3-9 shows a partial listing of the ASCII codes along with their binary representations. The full ASCII chart is contained in Appendix C in this book.

As Figure 3-9 indicates, the uppercase letter A is assigned the ASCII code 65, which is stored in internal memory using the eight bits ("binary digits") 01000001 (one 64 and one 1). Notice that the lowercase version of each letter is assigned a different ASCII code than the letter's uppercase version. The lowercase letter a, for example, is assigned the ASCII code 97, which is stored in internal memory using the eight bits 01100001. This fact indicates that the computer does not consider both cases of a letter to be equivalent. In other words, the uppercase letter A is not the same as the lowercase letter a. This concept will become important when you compare characters in later chapters.

Character	ASCII	Binary	Character	ASCII	Binary	Character	ASCII	Binary
0	48	00110000	K	75	01001011	g	103	01100111
1	49	00110001	L	76	01001100	h	104	01101000
2	50	00110010	M	77	01001101	i	105	01101001
3	51	00110011	N	78	01001110	j	106	01101010
4	52	00110100	O	79	01001111	k	107	01101011
5	53	00110101	P	80	01010000	l	108	01101100
6	54	00110110	Q	81	01010001	m	109	01101101
7	55	00110111	R	82	01010010	n	110	01101110
8	56	00111000	S	83	01010011	o	111	01101111
9	57	00111001	T	84	01010100	p	112	01110000
:	58	00111010	U	85	01010101	q	113	01110001
;	59	00111011	V	86	01010110	r	114	01110010
A	65	01000001	W	87	01010111	s	115	01110011
B	66	01000010	X	88	01011000	t	116	01110100
C	67	01000011	Y	89	01011001	u	117	01110101
D	68	01000100	Z	90	01011010	v	118	01110110
E	69	01000101	a	97	01100001	w	119	01110111
F	70	01000110	b	98	01100010	x	120	01111000
G	71	01000111	c	99	01100011	y	121	01111001
H	72	01001000	d	100	01100100	z	122	01111010
I	73	01001001	e	101	01100101			
J	74	01001010	f	102	01100110			

Figure 3-9 Partial ASCII chart

At this point, you may be wondering why the numeric characters on your keyboard are assigned ASCII codes. For example, shouldn't a 9 be stored using the binary number system, as you learned earlier? The answer is that the computer uses the binary number system to store the *number* 9, but it uses the ASCII coding scheme to store the *character* 9. But how does the computer know whether the 9 is a number or a character? The answer to this question is simple: by the memory location's data type.

Here is an example of the importance of a memory location's data type: Consider a program that displays the message "Enter your pet's age:" on the computer screen. The program stores your response in a variable named `age`. When you press the 9 key on your keyboard in response to the message, the computer uses the data type of the `age` variable to determine whether to store the 9 as a number (using the binary number system) or as a character (using the ASCII coding scheme). If the variable's data type is `int`, the 9 is stored as the binary number 1001 (one 1 + one 8). If the variable's data type is `char`, on the other hand, the 9 is stored as a character using the ASCII code 57, which is represented in internal memory as 00111001 (one 1 + one 8 + one 16 + one 32).

The memory location's data type also determines how the computer interprets a memory location's existing data. If a program instruction needs to access the value stored in a memory location—perhaps to display the value on the screen—the computer uses the memory location's data type to determine the value's data type. To illustrate this point, assume that a memory location named `inputItem` contains the eight bits 01000001. If the memory location's data type is `char`, the computer displays the uppercase letter A on the screen. This is because the computer interprets the 01000001 as the ASCII code 65, which is equivalent to the uppercase letter A. However, if the memory location's data type is `int`, the computer displays the number 65 on the screen because the 01000001 is interpreted as the binary representation of the decimal number 65. In summary, the data type of a memory location is important because it determines how the data is stored when first entered into the memory location. It also determines how the data is interpreted when the memory location is used in an instruction later in the program.

The answers to Mini-Quiz questions are located in Appendix A.

Mini-Quiz 3-2

1. The `string` data type is one of the fundamental data types in C++.
   a. True
   b. False
2. In the binary number system, the decimal number 32 is represented as ________.
   a. 10000
   b. 10001
   c. 100000
   d. none of the above
3. What is the ASCII code for the lowercase letter b, and how is it represented in the computer's internal memory?
4. Which data type can store a real number?
   a. `double`
   b. `int`
   c. `float`
   d. both a and c

Selecting an Initial Value for a Memory Location

In addition to assigning a name and data type to each variable and named constant used in a program, you also should assign an initial value to each. Assigning an initial (or beginning) value to a memory location is referred to as **initializing**. With the exception of a `bool` memory location, which is initialized using either the C++ keyword `true` or the C++ keyword `false`, you typically initialize a memory location by assigning a literal constant to it. Unlike variables and named constants, literal constants are not memory locations. Rather, a **literal constant** is an item of data that can appear in a program instruction and be stored in a memory location.

Although initializing variables is optional in most programming languages, including C++, it is considered a good programming practice to do so and is highly recommended.

The data type of a literal constant should match the data type of the memory location to which it is assigned. Integers should be assigned to memory locations having the `short` or `int` data type. Memory locations having the `float` or `double` data type should be initialized using real numbers. Integers and real numbers are called **numeric literal constants**; examples include the numbers 146, 0.0, and –2.5. Numeric literal constants can contain numbers, the plus sign, the minus sign, and the decimal point. They also can contain either the letter e or the letter E, both of which are used to represent exponential (or e) notation. Scientific programs use e notation to represent very small and very large numbers. Numeric literal constants cannot contain a space, a comma, or a special character, such as the dollar sign ($) or percent sign (%). A numeric literal constant with no decimal place is considered an `int` data type in C++, whereas a numeric literal constant with a decimal place is considered a `double` data type.

Programmers use character literal constants to initialize `char` memory locations. A **character literal constant** is one character enclosed in single quotation marks, such as the letter 'X', the dollar sign '$', and a space ' ' (two single quotation marks with a space character between). A `string` memory location is initialized using a **string literal constant**, which is zero or more characters enclosed in double quotation marks. The word "Hello", the message "Enter your pet's age:", and the **empty string** "" (two double quotation marks with no space between) are examples of string literal constants.

When a program instructs the computer to assign a value to a memory location, the computer first compares the value's data type with the memory location's data type. The comparison is made to verify that the value is appropriate for the memory location. If the value's data type does not match the memory location's data type, the computer uses a process called **implicit type conversion** to convert the value to fit the memory location. For example, if a program initializes a `double` variable named `price` to the integer 9, the computer converts the integer to a real number before storing the value in the variable. The computer does this by appending a decimal point and the number 0 to the end of the integer, like this: 9.0. The computer then stores the real number 9.0 in the `price` variable. When a value is converted from one data type to another data type that can store larger numbers, the value is said to be **promoted**. In this case, the `int` value 9 is promoted to the `double` value 9.0. (As shown earlier in Figure 3-5, the `double` data type can store larger numbers than can the `int` data type.) In most cases, the implicit promotion of values does not adversely affect a program's output.

Ch03-Type Conversion video

However, now consider a program that declares an `int` named constant called `MIN_WAGE`. If you use a real number (such as 7.25) to initialize the named constant, the computer converts the real number to an integer before storing the value in the memory location. The computer does this by truncating (dropping off) the decimal portion of the number. In this case, the computer converts the real number 7.25 to the integer 7. As a result, the number 7 rather than the number 7.25 is assigned to the `MIN_WAGE` named constant. When a value is converted from one data type to another data type that can store only smaller numbers, the value is said to be **demoted**. In this case, the `double` value 7.25 is demoted to the `int` value 7. The implicit demotion of values can adversely affect a program's output. Therefore, it's important to initialize memory locations using values that have the same data type as the memory location.

Recall that a numeric literal constant with a decimal place is treated as a `double` number.

If a memory location is a named constant, the problem specification and IPO chart will provide the appropriate initial value to use, and that value will remain the same during runtime. (Recall that the contents of a named constant cannot change while the program is running.) The initial value for a variable, on the other hand, is not stated in a problem specification or IPO chart because the user supplies the value while the program is running. As a result, `short` and `int` variables generally are initialized to the integer 0, while `float` and `double` variables are assigned the real number 0.0. Variables declared using the `string` data type usually are initialized to the empty string (""), and `char` variables are initialized to a space (' '). As mentioned earlier, the C++ keywords `true` and `false` are used to initialize `bool` variables. Figure 3-10 shows the initial values for the variables in the Treyson Mobley problem.

IPO chart item	Variable name	Data type	Initial value
total bill	totalBill	double	0.0
liquor charge	liquor	double	0.0
tip percentage	tipPercent	double	0.0
total bill without liquor charge	totalNoLiquor	double	0.0
tip	tip	double	0.0

Figure 3-10 Initial values for the variables in the Treyson Mobley problem

Declaring a Memory Location

Now that you know how to select an appropriate name, data type, and initial value for a memory location, you can learn how to declare variables and named constants in a C++ program. We'll begin with variables.

You declare a variable using a **statement**, which is a C++ instruction that causes the computer to perform some action after being executed (processed) by the computer. A statement that declares a variable, for example, causes the computer to set aside a memory location with the name, data type, and initial value you provide. A variable declaration statement is one of many different types of statements in C++.

The syntax and examples of a variable declaration statement are shown in Figure 3-11. The term **syntax** refers to the rules of a programming language. One rule in C++ is that all statements must end with a semicolon; the syntax and examples in Figure 3-11 follow this rule. Another rule is that the programmer must provide a data type and name for the variable being declared. He or she also can provide an initial value for the variable.

Using the storage bin analogy from the beginning of the chapter, initializing a variable is similar to removing any junk (or garbage) from a bin before using it.

Items that the programmer provides are italicized in a statement's syntax, as shown in Figure 3-11. Items appearing in square brackets in a syntax—in this case, the = symbol and *initialValue*—are optional. In other words, the C++ language does not require variables to be initialized. However, initializing variables is highly recommended. If you do not provide an initial value, the variable may contain a meaningless value. Programmers refer to the meaningless value as *garbage* because it is the remains of what was last stored in the memory location that the variable now occupies. Items in boldface in a syntax are required. In a variable declaration statement, the semicolon is required; the = symbol is required only when the programmer is providing an initial value for the variable.

HOW TO Declare a Variable in C++

Syntax

dataType variableName [= *initialValue*]**;**

Examples

```
int age = 0;
double price = 0.0;
bool paid = false;
char grade = ' ';
string company = "";
```

Figure 3-11 How to declare a variable in C++

After a variable is declared, you then can use its name to refer to it later in the program, such as in a statement that displays the variable's value or uses the value in a calculation. You will learn how to write such statements in Chapter 4. Figure 3-12 shows the declaration statements you would use to declare the five variables in the Treyson Mobley problem.

IPO chart item	Variable name	Data type	Initial value	C++ statement
total bill	`totalBill`	`double`	`0.0`	`double totalBill = 0.0;`
liquor charge	`liquor`	`double`	`0.0`	`double liquor = 0.0;`
tip percentage	`tipPercent`	`double`	`0.0`	`double tipPercent = 0.0;`
total bill without liquor charge	`totalNoLiquor`	`double`	`0.0`	`double totalNoLiquor = 0.0;`
tip	`tip`	`double`	`0.0`	`double tip = 0.0;`

Figure 3-12 C++ declaration statements for the variables in the Treyson Mobley problem

Now we'll look at how you declare a named constant. Figure 3-13 shows the syntax of a declaration statement for a named constant. It also includes examples of using the syntax to declare several named constants. Recall that italicized items in a syntax indicate information that the programmer must supply. In a named constant declaration statement, the programmer must supply the constant's data type, name, and initial value. Items in boldface in a syntax—in this case, the keyword `const`, the = symbol, and the semicolon—are required. The **const** keyword indicates that the memory location being declared is a named constant, which means its value cannot be changed during runtime. If a program statement attempts to change the value stored in a named constant, the C++ compiler will display an error message. As you learned in Chapter 1, a compiler converts the instructions written in a high-level language (such as C++) into the 0s and 1s the computer can understand.

HOW TO Declare a Named Constant in C++

Syntax

const *dataType constantName* **=** *value***;**

Examples

```
const double PI = 3.141593;
const int MIN_AGE = 65;
const bool INSURED = true;
const char YES = 'Y';
const string BANK = "Harrison Trust and Savings";
```

Figure 3-13 How to declare a named constant in C++

As you can with variables, you can use a named constant in another statement that appears after its declaration statement. For example, after entering the `const double PI = 3.141593;`

statement in a program, you can use `PI` in a statement that calculates the area of a circle; the computer will use the value stored in the named constant (3.141593) to calculate the area.

Using named constants in a program has several advantages. First, named constants make a program more self-documenting and easier to modify because they allow the use of meaningful words in place of values that are less clear. The named constant `PI`, for example, is much more meaningful than the number 3.141593, which is the value of pi rounded to six decimal places. Second, unlike the value stored in a variable, the value stored in a named constant cannot be inadvertently changed during runtime. Third, typing `PI` rather than 3.141593 in a statement is easier and less prone to typing errors. If you do mistype `PI` in a statement that calculates a circle's area—for example, if you type `Pi` rather than `PI`—the C++ compiler will display an error message. Mistyping 3.141593 in the area calculation statement, however, will not trigger an error message and will result in an incorrect answer. Finally, if a named constant's value needs to be changed in the future, you will need to modify only the declaration statement, rather than all of the statements that use the value.

For more examples of declaring variables and named constants, see the Declaring Memory Locations section in the Ch03WantMore.pdf file.

The answers to Mini-Quiz questions are located in Appendix A.

Mini-Quiz 3-3

1. Which of the following is a character literal constant?
   a. '56'
   b. '%'
   c. "a"
   d. both a and b
2. Which of the following is a string literal constant?
   a. "$"
   b. "Good Morning!"
   c. ""
   d. all of the above
3. If you assign the number 10.25 to an `int` variable, what will the computer store in the variable?
4. Write a C++ statement that declares and initializes an `int` variable named `population`.
5. Write a C++ statement that declares the `MAX_PAY` named constant. The constant should have the `double` data type and contain the number 25.55.
6. If you earn $10.25 per hour and worked 20 hours, how much less would you be paid if your hourly rate was inadvertently assigned to an `int` variable in a program?

The answers to the labs are located in Appendix A.

LAB 3-1 Stop and Analyze

Study the problem specification, IPO chart, and desk-check table shown in Figure 3-14 and then answer the questions.

Problem specification
Aiden Nelinski is paid every Friday. He is scheduled to receive anywhere from a 2% to 4.5% raise next week. He wants a program that calculates and displays the amount of his new weekly pay.

Input	Processing	Output
current weekly pay raise percentage	Processing items: none Algorithm: 1. enter the current weekly pay and raise percentage 2. calculate the new weekly pay by multiplying the current weekly pay by the raise percentage and then adding the result to the current weekly pay 3. display the new weekly pay	new weekly pay

current weekly pay	raise percentage	new weekly pay
~~300~~	~~.02~~	~~306~~
500	.025	512.50

Figure 3-14 Problem specification, IPO chart, and desk-check table for Lab 3-1

QUESTIONS

1. How many memory locations will the Aiden Nelinski problem require?
2. How many of the memory locations will be variables, and how many will be named constants? Why did you choose one type over the other?
3. If the input and output items are real numbers, which data types could be assigned to the memory locations that store these items?
4. How would you write the appropriate declaration statements? Use the `double` data type and the names `currentPay`, `raiseRate`, and `newPay`.
5. If the raise percentage was always 2%, how would you declare the memory location that will store it? Use the `double` data type and the name `RAISE_RATE`.

LAB 3-2 Plan and Create

In this lab, you will plan and create an algorithm that displays the area of a circle. The problem specification is shown in Figure 3-15.

Ch03-Lab 3-2 video

Problem specification
Professor Chang wants a program that calculates and displays the area of a circle, given the circle's radius. The formula for calculating the area of a circle is πr^2, where π and r represent pi and the radius, respectively. The professor wants to use the value of pi rounded to two decimal places, which is 3.14.

Figure 3-15 Problem specification for Lab 3-2

First, analyze the problem, looking for the output first and then for the input. Recall that the output answers the question *What does the user want to see displayed on the screen, printed on paper, or stored in a file?*, and the input answers the question *What information will the computer need to know to display, print, or store the output items?* In this case, the user wants to see the circle's area displayed on the screen. To do this, the computer will need to know the circle's radius and the value of pi. The radius will be entered by the user, whereas the problem specification indicates that the value to use for pi is 3.14. Figure 3-16 shows the input and output items entered in an IPO chart.

Input	Processing	Output
radius pi (3.14)	Processing items: Algorithm:	area

Figure 3-16 Partially completed IPO chart showing the input and output items

After determining a problem's output and input, you then plan its algorithm. Recall that most algorithms begin with an instruction to enter the input items into the computer, followed by instructions that process the input items, typically including the items in one or more calculations. Most algorithms end with one or more instructions that display, print, or store the output items. Figure 3-17 shows the completed IPO chart for the circle area problem.

Input	Processing	Output
radius pi (3.14)	Processing items: none Algorithm: 1. enter the radius 2. calculate the area by multiplying the radius by itself and then multiplying the result by pi 3. display the area	area

Figure 3-17 Completed IPO chart for Lab 3-2

After completing the IPO chart, you then move on to the third step in the problem-solving process, which is to desk-check the algorithm. You begin by choosing a set of sample data for the input values. You then use the values to manually compute the expected output. You will desk-check the current algorithm twice: first using 4 as the radius and then using 5.5. For the first desk-check, the area should be 50.24. For the second desk-check, the area should be 94.985. The manual calculations for both desk-checks are shown in Figure 3-18.

First desk-check calculation	Second desk-check calculation
4 (radius)	5.5 (radius)
* 4 (radius)	* 5.5 (radius)
* 3.14 (pi)	* 3.14 (pi)
50.24 (area)	94.985 (area)

Figure 3-18 Manual area calculation for the two desk-checks

Next, you create a desk-check table that contains one column for each input, processing, and output item. You then begin desk-checking the algorithm. Figure 3-19 shows the completed desk-check table. Notice that the amounts in the area column agree with the results of the manual calculations shown in Figure 3-18.

radius	pi	area
~~4~~	~~3.14~~	~~50.24~~
5.5	3.14	94.985

Figure 3-19 Completed desk-check table for Lab 3-2

After desk-checking an algorithm to ensure that it works correctly, you can begin coding it. You begin by declaring memory locations that will store the values of the input, processing (if any), and output items. The circle area problem will need three memory locations to store the values of the radius, pi, and area. The radius and area values should be stored in variables because the user should be allowed to change the radius value, which then will change the area value, while the program is running. The value of pi, however, will be stored in a named constant because its value should not change during runtime. The variables and named constant will store real numbers, so you will use the `double` data type for each one. Figure 3-20 shows the input, processing, and output items from the IPO chart, along with the corresponding C++ statements.

IPO chart information	C++ instructions
Input	
radius	`double radius = 0.0;`
pi (3.14)	`const double PI = 3.14;`
Processing	
none	
Output	
area	`double area = 0.0;`

Figure 3-20 IPO chart information and C++ instructions for Lab 3-2

LAB 3-3 Modify

Modify the IPO chart shown earlier in Figure 3-17 so that it includes the radius squared as a processing item. Then make the appropriate modifications to Figure 3-20.

LAB 3-4 Desk-Check

Using the IPO chart modified in Lab 3-3, make the appropriate modifications to the manual calculations and desk-check table shown earlier in Figures 3-18 and 3-19.

LAB 3-5 Debug

Correct the C++ instructions shown in Figure 3-21. The memory locations will store real numbers.

IPO chart information	C++ instructions
Input	
first number	`first = 0.0;`
second number	`second = 0.0;`
third number	`third = 0.0;`
Processing	
sum	`Double sum = 0.0`
Output	
average	`average = 0.0;`

Figure 3-21 IPO chart information and C++ instructions for Lab 3-5

Summary

- The fourth step in the problem-solving process is to code the algorithm, which means to translate it into a language that the computer can understand. You begin by declaring a memory location for each unique input, processing, and output item listed in the IPO chart. The memory locations will store the values of those items while the program is running.
- Numeric data is stored in the computer's internal memory using the binary number system. Character data is stored using the ASCII coding scheme.
- A memory location can store only one value at a time.
- A memory location's data type determines how a value is stored in the location, as well as how the value is interpreted when retrieved.

- Programmers can declare two types of memory locations: variables and named constants. You declare a memory location using a statement that assigns a name, a data type, and an initial value to the memory location. The initial value is required when declaring named constants but is optional when declaring variables. However, it is highly recommended that variables be initialized to ensure they don't contain garbage.
- In most cases, memory locations are initialized using a literal constant. The exception to this is a `bool` memory location, which is initialized using a C++ keyword (`true` or `false`).
- The data type of a literal constant assigned to a memory location should be the same as the memory location's data type. If the data types do not match, the computer uses implicit type conversion to either promote or demote the value to fit the memory location. Promoting a value does not usually affect a program's output; however, demoting a value may cause a program's output to be incorrect.
- The C++ programming language has a set of rules, called syntax, which you must follow when using the language. One rule is that all statements in C++ must end with a semicolon.

Key Terms

ASCII—a coding scheme used to represent character data; stands for American Standard Code for Information Interchange

Binary number system—a system that uses only the two digits 0 and 1; used to represent numeric data in the computer's internal memory

Camel case—a naming convention that capitalizes only the first letter in the second and subsequent words in a memory location's name

Character—a letter, a symbol, or a number that will not be used in a calculation

Character literal constant—one character enclosed in single quotation marks

const—the keyword used to declare a named constant in C++

Decimal number system—a system that represents numbers using the digits 0 through 9

Demoted—refers to the conversion of a number from one data type to another data type that can store only smaller numbers

Empty string—two quotation marks with no space between, like this ""

Fundamental data types—the basic data types built into the C++ language; also called primitive data types or built-in data types

Implicit type conversion—the process the computer follows when converting a numeric value to fit a memory location that has a different data type

Initializing—assigning a beginning value to a memory location

Integer—a whole number, which is a number without a decimal place

Keyword—a word that has a special meaning in the programming language you are using

Literal constant—an item of data that can appear in a program instruction and be stored in a memory location

Named constant—a memory location whose value cannot be changed while a program is running

Numeric literal constants—numbers

Promoted—refers to the conversion of a number from one data type to another data type that can store larger numbers

Real numbers—numbers that contain a decimal place

Runtime—occurs while a program is running

Statement—a C++ instruction that causes the computer to perform some action after being executed (processed) by the computer; all statements in C++ must end with a semicolon

String literal constant—zero or more characters enclosed in double quotation marks

Syntax—the rules you must follow when using a programming language; every programming language has its own syntax

Text—a group of characters treated as one unit and not used in a calculation

User-defined data type—a data type added to the C++ language through the use of a class; an example is the `string` data type

Variable—a memory location whose value can change (vary) while a program is running

Review Questions

1. The rules you must follow when using a programming language are called its ________.
   a. guidelines
   b. procedures
   c. regulations
   d. syntax

2. Which of the following declares a variable that can store a real number?
   a. `commission double = 0.0;`
   b. `double commission = 0.0`
   c. `double commission = 0.0;`
   d. `commission = 0.0;`

3. A C++ statement must end with a ________.
   a. colon
   b. comma
   c. period
   d. semicolon

4. The declaration statement for a named constant requires ________.
   a. a data type
   b. a name
   c. a value
   d. all of the above

5. Which of the following creates a variable that can store whole numbers only?
   a. `int numItems = 0;`
   b. `int numItems = '0';`
   c. `int numItems = "0";`
   d. `integer numItems = 0;`

6. Which of the following is a valid name for a variable?
   a. `amount-sold`
   b. `amountSold`
   c. `1stQtrAmountSold`
   d. both b and c

7. Which of the following declares a `char` named constant called `TOP_GRADE`?
   a. `const char TOP_GRADE = 'A';`
   b. `const char TOP_GRADE = "A";`
   c. `const char TOP_GRADE;`
   d. both a and c

8. A memory location contains the following eight bits: 00110111. If the memory location's data type is `int`, the computer will interpret the eight bits as the number ________.
   a. 7
   b. 55
   c. 56
   d. 110, 111

9. A memory location contains the following eight bits: 00110111. If the memory location's data type is `char`, the computer will interpret the eight bits as the character ________.
   a. 7
   b. 55
   c. 56
   d. none of the above

10. If you use a real number to initialize an `int` variable, the real number will be ________ before it is stored in the variable.
    a. demoted
    b. promoted
    c. reduced
    d. upgraded

Exercises

Pencil and Paper

1. Complete the C++ instructions column in Figure 3-22. Use the `double` data type for the memory locations. (The answers to TRY THIS Exercises are located at the end of the chapter.) TRY THIS

IPO chart information	C++ instructions
Input	
sale1	
sale2	
commission rate	
Processing	
total sales	
Output	
commission	

Figure 3-22

TRY THIS

2. Complete the C++ instructions column in Figure 3-23. The numbers of cups and plates purchased will be integers. All of the remaining items will be real numbers. Use the `int` and `double` data types. (The answers to TRY THIS Exercises are located at the end of the chapter.)

IPO chart information	C++ instructions
Input	
cup price	
plate price	
cups purchased	
plates purchased	
sales tax rate (5.5%)	
Processing	
total cup cost	
total plate cost	
subtotal	
Output	
total cost	

Figure 3-23

MODIFY THIS

3. Complete TRY THIS Exercise 1, and then modify the IPO chart information and C++ instructions to indicate that the commission rate will always be 10%.

INTRODUCTORY

4. Chris Johanson wants a program that calculates and displays a 10%, 15%, and 20% tip on his total restaurant bill. First, create an IPO chart for this problem, and then desk-check the algorithm twice, using $35.80 and $56.78 as the total bill. After desk-checking the algorithm, list the input, processing, and output items in a chart similar to the one shown in Figure 3-23, and then enter the appropriate C++ declaration statements.

INTRODUCTORY

5. Tile Limited wants a program that allows its salesclerks to enter the length and width (both in feet) of a rectangle and the price of a square foot of tile. The program should calculate and display the area of the rectangle and the total price of the tile. First, create an IPO chart for this problem, and then desk-check the algorithm twice. For the first desk-check, use 10 feet, 12 feet, and $2.39 as the length, width, and tile price, respectively. For the second desk-check, use 5.5 feet, 10.5 feet, and $3.50. After desk-checking the algorithm, list the input, processing, and output items in a chart similar to the one shown in Figure 3-23, and then enter the appropriate C++ declaration statements.

6. Builders Inc. wants a program that allows its salesclerks to enter the diameter of a circle and the price of railing material per foot. The program should calculate and display the total price of the railing material. Use 3.1416 as the value of pi. First, create an IPO chart for this problem, and then desk-check the algorithm twice. For the first desk-check, use 35 feet as the diameter and $2 as the price per foot. For the second desk-check, use 15.5 and $3.50. After desk-checking the algorithm, list the input, processing, and output items in a chart similar to the one shown in Figure 3-23, and then enter the appropriate C++ declaration statements. INTERMEDIATE

7. Currency Traders wants a program that converts American dollars to British pounds, Mexican pesos, and Japanese yen, and then displays the results. Use the following conversion rates for one American dollar: .6318 British pounds, 12.8863 Mexican pesos, and 82.34 Japanese yen. First, create an IPO chart for this problem, and then desk-check the algorithm twice, using 1000 and 50 as the number of American dollars. After desk-checking the algorithm, list the input, processing, and output items in a chart similar to the one shown in Figure 3-23, and then enter the appropriate C++ declaration statements. INTERMEDIATE

8. Sharon receives 24 paychecks each year. She always deposits a specific percentage of her gross pay in her savings account. Sharon also receives a bonus check, which is always more than $100, at the end of the year. She always deposits $100 of her bonus in her savings account. Sharon wants a program that will calculate and display the total amount she deposited during the year. Complete an IPO chart for this problem. Desk-check the algorithm twice, using your own sets of data. After desk-checking the algorithm, list the input, processing, and output items in a chart similar to the one shown in Figure 3-23, and then enter the appropriate C++ declaration statements. INTERMEDIATE

9. Crispies Bagels and Bites wants a program that allows its salesclerks to enter the number of bagels, donuts, and cups of coffee a customer orders. Bagels are 99¢, donuts are 75¢, and coffee is $1.20 per cup. The program should calculate and display the total price of the customer's order. First, create an IPO chart for this problem, and then desk-check the algorithm twice. For the first desk-check, use 0, 12, and 2 as the number of bagels, donuts, and cups of coffee, respectively. For the second desk-check, use 2, 6, and 1. After desk-checking the algorithm, list the input, processing, and output items in a chart similar to the one shown in Figure 3-23, and then enter the appropriate C++ declaration statements. ADVANCED

10. The payroll clerk at Cartwright Industries wants a program that displays an employee's weekly net pay. The clerk will enter the employee's weekly gross pay. From the gross pay, the program will need to subtract the appropriate federal and state taxes. Use 20% as the FWT (Federal Withholding Tax) rate, 8% as the FICA (Social Security and Medicare) tax rate, and 4% as the state income tax rate. First, create an IPO chart for this problem, and then desk-check the algorithm twice, using $500 and $235.50 as the weekly gross pay. After desk-checking the algorithm, list the input, processing, and output items in a chart similar to the one shown in Figure 3-23, and then enter the appropriate C++ declaration statements. ADVANCED

SWAT THE BUGS

11. Correct the C++ instructions shown in Figure 3-24.

IPO chart information	C++ instructions
Input	
original price	`double original = 0.0;`
discount rate (10%)	`double DISC_RATE = 10%;`
Processing	
none	
Output	
discount	`int discount = 0;`
new price	`double new price = 0.0;`

Figure 3-24

Answers to TRY THIS Exercises

1. See Figure 3-25.

IPO chart information	C++ instructions
Input	
sale1	`double sale1 = 0.0;`
sale2	`double sale2 = 0.0;`
commission rate	`double commissionRate = 0.0;`
Processing	
total sales	`double totalSales = 0.0;`
Output	
commission	`double commission = 0.0;`

Figure 3-25

2. See Figure 3-26.

IPO chart information	C++ instructions
Input	
cup price	`double cupPrice = 0.0;`
plate price	`double platePrice = 0.0;`
cups purchased	`int cupsPurchased = 0;`
plates purchased	`int platesPurchased = 0;`
sales tax rate (5.5%)	`const double TAX_RATE = .055;`
Processing	
total cup cost	`double totalCupCost = 0.0;`
total plate cost	`double totalPlateCost = 0.0;`
subtotal	`double subtotal = 0.0;`
Output	
total cost	`double totalCost = 0.0;`

Figure 3-26

CHAPTER 4

Completing the Problem-Solving Process

After studying Chapter 4, you should be able to:

- Get numeric and character data from the keyboard
- Display information on the computer screen
- Write arithmetic expressions
- Type cast a value
- Write an assignment statement
- Code the algorithm into a program
- Desk-check a program
- Evaluate and modify a program

Finishing Step 4 in the Problem-Solving Process

Ch04-Chapter Preview video

The fourth step in the problem-solving process is to code the algorithm into a program. As you learned in Chapter 3, the programmer begins the fourth step by declaring a memory location for each unique input, processing, and output item listed in the problem's IPO chart. The memory locations will store the values of those items while the program is running. Recall that each memory location must be assigned a name and data type. If the memory location is a named constant, it also must be assigned a value. Assigning an initial value to a variable is optional but highly recommended to ensure that the variable does not contain garbage.

Figure 4-1 shows the problem specification, IPO chart information, and variable declaration statements for the Treyson Mobley problem from Chapter 3. Recall that the `double` data type was selected for these variables because it allows each to store a real number with the greatest precision.

Problem specification
Treyson Mobley wants a program that calculates and displays the amount he should tip a waiter at a restaurant. The program should subtract any liquor charge from the total bill and then calculate the tip (using a percentage) on the remainder.

IPO chart information	**C++ instructions**
Input	
total bill	`double totalBill = 0.0;`
liquor charge	`double liquor = 0.0;`
tip percentage	`double tipPercent = 0.0;`
Processing	
total bill without liquor charge	`double totalNoLiquor = 0.0;`
Output	
tip	`double tip = 0.0;`

Algorithm
1. enter the total bill, liquor charge, and tip percentage
2. calculate the total bill without liquor charge by subtracting the liquor charge from the total bill
3. calculate the tip by multiplying the total bill without liquor charge by the tip percentage
4. display the tip

Figure 4-1 Problem specification, IPO chart information, and variable declaration statements

After declaring the necessary memory locations, the programmer begins coding the algorithm. The first instruction in the algorithm shown in Figure 4-1 is to enter the three input items. You will have the user enter the items at the keyboard.

Getting Data from the Keyboard

In C++, you use objects to perform standard input and output operations, such as getting a program's input items and displaying its output items. The objects are called **stream objects** because they handle streams. A **stream** is defined in C++ as a sequence of characters.

Ch04-cin video

In this section, you will learn about the standard input stream object, `cin` (pronounced *see in*). The **cin** object tells the computer to pause program execution while the user enters one or more characters at the keyboard; the object temporarily stores the characters as they are typed.

The `cin` object is not a physical object that can be seen or touched. Rather, it is an object created through the use of a class, and it resides in a special area of the computer's internal memory. As you learned in Chapter 3, a class is a group of instructions that the computer uses to create an object. The `cin` object typically is used with the **extraction operator** (>>), which extracts (removes) characters from the object and sends them "in" to the data area of the computer's internal memory. The `cin` object and extraction operator allow the user to communicate with the computer while a program is running.

Figure 4-2 illustrates the relationship among the keyboard, `cin` object, extraction operator, and internal memory. As the figure indicates, the characters you type at the keyboard are sent first to the `cin` object, where they remain until the extraction operator removes them, sending them to the data area of the computer's internal memory.

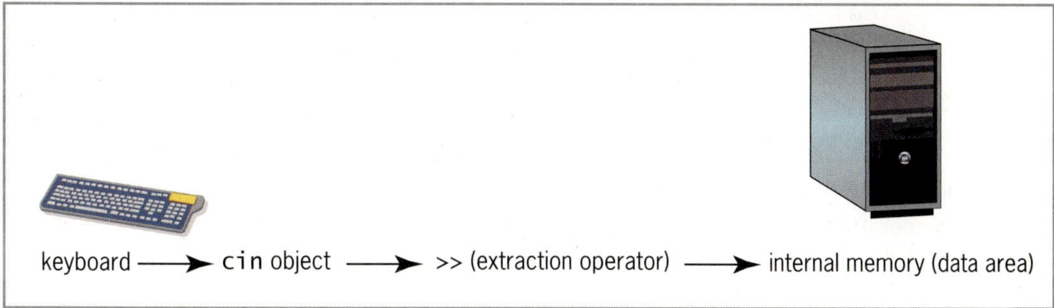

Figure 4-2 Relationship among the keyboard, `cin` object, extraction operator, and internal memory

The extraction operator stops removing characters from the `cin` object when it encounters a **white-space character**, which can be a newline, tab, or blank. You enter a newline character when you press the Enter key on your keyboard. You enter a tab character when you press the Tab key, and you enter a blank character when you press the Spacebar key. Because many strings entered at the keyboard contain one or more blank characters (for example, the string *Raleigh, North Carolina*), the extraction operator is used mainly to get numeric and character data, but not string data. Recall from Chapter 3 that numeric data is a number that will be used in a calculation, while character data is a letter, a symbol, or a number that will not be used in a calculation. String data is zero or more characters treated as one unit. This chapter covers inputting numeric and character data; inputting string data is covered in Chapter 13.

Figure 4-3 shows the syntax and examples of statements that use `cin` and the extraction operator to get numeric and character input from the keyboard. (For clarity, the variable declaration statements are included in the examples.) You can tell that the syntax and examples are statements because a semicolon appears at the end of each. Recall that a statement is a C++ instruction that causes the computer to perform some action after being executed (processed) by the computer. The `cin` portion of the `cin >> price;` statement, for example, tells the computer to pause program execution to allow the user to enter the price at the keyboard. The `cin` object temporarily stores the price as the user types it. When the user presses the Enter key, the extraction operator in the statement removes the price from the `cin` object and sends it to the computer's internal memory, where it is stored in the `price` variable. Similarly, the `cin >> middleInitial;` statement waits for the user to enter a character and ultimately stores the user's response in the `middleInitial` variable.

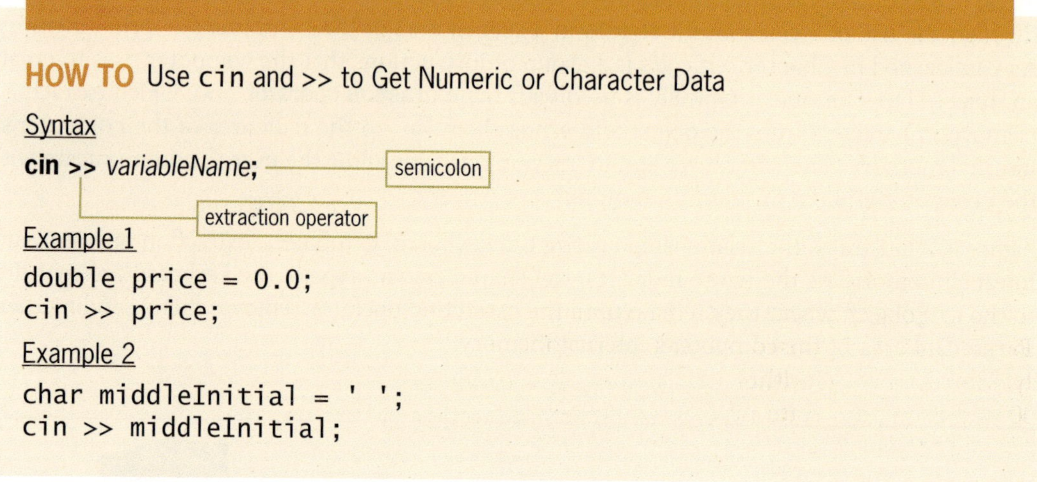

HOW TO Use `cin` and >> to Get Numeric or Character Data

Syntax

cin >> *variableName*; — semicolon; >> — extraction operator

Example 1

```
double price = 0.0;
cin >> price;
```

Example 2

```
char middleInitial = ' ';
cin >> middleInitial;
```

Figure 4-3 How to use `cin` and >> to get numeric or character data

The input items in the Treyson Mobley problem are numeric, so you can use the `cin` object and extraction operator to get the items from the user at the keyboard. The appropriate statements are shaded in Figure 4-4.

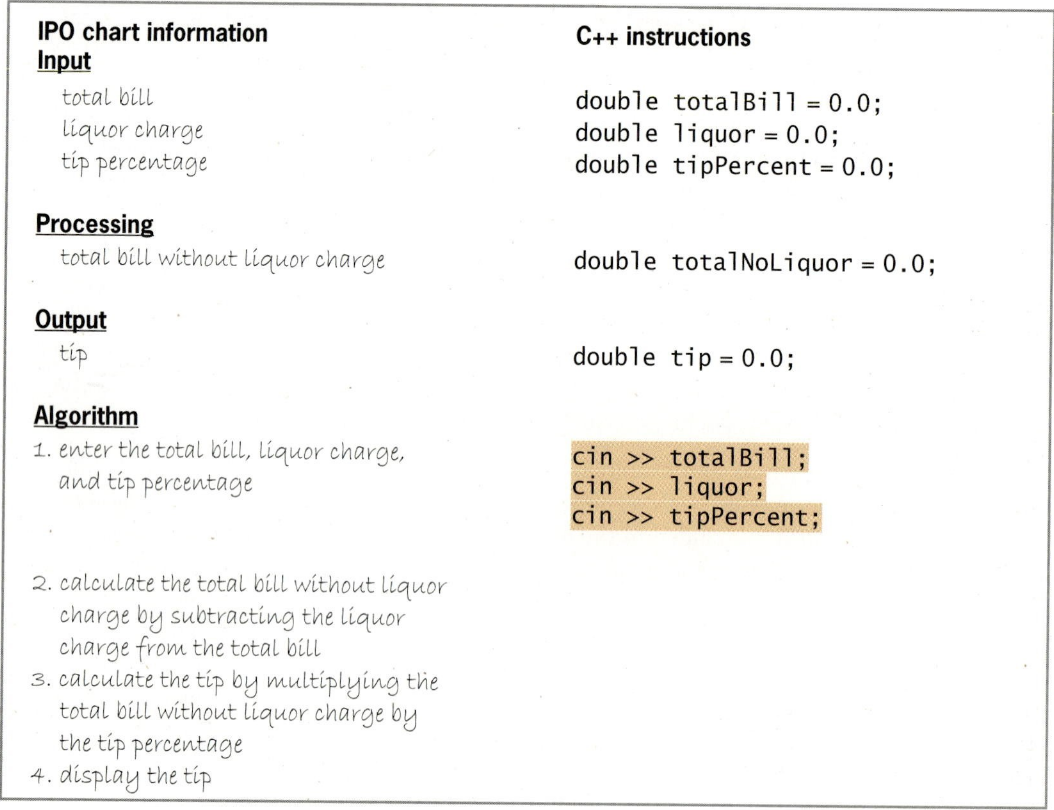

IPO chart information	C++ instructions
Input	
total bill	`double totalBill = 0.0;`
liquor charge	`double liquor = 0.0;`
tip percentage	`double tipPercent = 0.0;`
Processing	
total bill without liquor charge	`double totalNoLiquor = 0.0;`
Output	
tip	`double tip = 0.0;`
Algorithm	
1. enter the total bill, liquor charge, and tip percentage	`cin >> totalBill;` `cin >> liquor;` `cin >> tipPercent;`
2. calculate the total bill without liquor charge by subtracting the liquor charge from the total bill	
3. calculate the tip by multiplying the total bill without liquor charge by the tip percentage	
4. display the tip	

Figure 4-4 Input statements for the Treyson Mobley problem

When the `cin >> totalBill;` statement is processed by the computer while the program is running, a blank window containing a blinking cursor will appear on the computer screen. The blinking cursor indicates that the computer is waiting for the user to enter *something,* but it does not indicate what that *something* is. Should the user enter an age, a price, or a middle initial? You indicate the type of information to enter by displaying a message, called a **prompt**, on the computer screen.

Displaying Messages on the Computer Screen

As you learned earlier, you use objects to perform standard input and output operations in C++. In this section, you will learn about the standard output stream object, `cout` (pronounced *see out*). The **cout** object is used with the **insertion operator** (<<) to display information on the computer screen—in other words, to send information "out" to the user. The information can be any combination of literal constants, named constants, or variables. The `cout` object and insertion operator allow the computer to communicate with the user while a program is running.

Ch04-cout video

Figure 4-5 shows the syntax and examples of statements that use `cout` and the insertion operator. Notice the required semicolon that appears at the end of the syntax and examples. Also notice that you can include more than one insertion operator in a statement. The four `cout` statements in the figure tell the computer to display messages on the computer screen. The first two messages prompt the user to enter specific items of data: an item's price and a middle initial. The third message alerts the user that the program has ended. The message displayed by the last `cout` statement contains the string "Bonus: $" and the contents of the `bonusAmt` variable. If the `bonusAmt` variable contains the number 94.56, the statement will display the message "Bonus: $94.56" on the computer screen. The `endl` in the last `cout` statement is one of the stream manipulators in C++. A **stream manipulator** allows you to manipulate (or manage) the characters in either the input or output stream. When used with the `cout` object, the **endl** stream manipulator advances the cursor to the next line on the computer screen, which is equivalent to pressing the Enter key. When typing `endl` (which stands for *end of line*) in a statement, be sure to type the lowercase letter l rather than the number 1.

Like the `cin` object, the `cout` object is created in the computer's internal memory through the use of a class.

HOW TO Use the `cout` Object

Syntax

cout << *item1* [<< *item2* << *itemN*]; (insertion operator; semicolon)

Examples

```
cout << "Enter the price: ";
cout << "What is your middle initial? ";
cout << "End of program";
cout << "Bonus: $" << bonusAmt << endl;
```

(stream manipulator)

Figure 4-5 How to use the `cout` object

The last `cout` statement is equivalent to the following three lines of code:

```
cout << "Bonus: $";
cout << bonusAmt;
cout << endl;
```

In order for the user to know what to enter when the Treyson Mobley program is run on the computer, you will display a meaningful prompt for each of the three input items. Each prompt should be entered above its corresponding `cin` statement because you want the prompt to appear before the user is expected to enter the information. The three prompts are shaded in Figure 4-6. Keep in mind that the prompts merely display a message on the computer screen. They don't allow the user to actually enter the data being requested; for that, you need the `cin` object and extraction operator.

Also shaded in Figure 4-6 is the statement that displays the tip amount on the computer screen; the statement corresponds to the last instruction in the algorithm. Although it's customary to code an algorithm's instructions in the order they appear in the algorithm, the statement to display the tip amount is included now simply because this section covers displaying messages on the computer screen.

IPO chart information	C++ instructions
Input	
total bill	`double totalBill = 0.0;`
liquor charge	`double liquor = 0.0;`
tip percentage	`double tipPercent = 0.0;`
Processing	
total bill without liquor charge	`double totalNoLiquor = 0.0;`
Output	
tip	`double tip = 0.0;`
Algorithm	

1. enter the total bill, liquor charge, and tip percentage	`cout << "Enter the total bill: ";`
	`cin >> totalBill;`
	`cout << "Enter the liquor charge: ";`
	`cin >> liquor;`
	`cout << "Enter the tip percentage in decimal format: ";`
	`cin >> tipPercent;`

2. calculate the total bill without liquor charge by subtracting the liquor charge from the total bill	
3. calculate the tip by multiplying the total bill without liquor charge by the tip percentage	
4. display the tip	`cout << "Tip: $" << tip << endl;`

Figure 4-6 Prompts and output statement for the Treyson Mobley problem

You also can display the tip amount using the following three lines of code:

```
cout << "Tip: $";
cout << tip;
cout << endl;
```

The answers to Mini-Quiz questions are located in Appendix A.

Mini-Quiz 4-1

1. Which of the following stores the value entered at the keyboard in a variable named `grossPay`?
   a. `cin << grossPay;`
   b. `cin >> grossPay;`
   c. `cout << grossPay;`
   d. `cout >> grossPay;`

2. Which of the following displays the contents of the `grossPay` variable on the computer screen?

   a. `cin << grossPay;`

   b. `cin >> grossPay;`

   c. `cout << grossPay;`

   d. `cout >> grossPay;`

3. Which of the following is considered a white-space character in C++?

   a. a blank

   b. a tab

   c. a newline

   d. all of the above

4. The insertion operator looks like this: ________.

Arithmetic Operators in C++

Instructions 2 and 3 in the algorithm shown in Figure 4-6 involve arithmetic calculations. You direct the computer to perform a calculation by writing an arithmetic expression that contains one or more arithmetic operators. Figure 4-7 lists the standard arithmetic operators available in C++, along with their precedence numbers. The precedence numbers indicate the order in which the computer performs the operation in an expression. Operations with a precedence number of 1 are performed before operations with a precedence number of 2, which are performed before operations with a precedence number of 3, and so on. However, you can use parentheses to override the order of precedence because operations within parentheses are always performed before operations outside of parentheses.

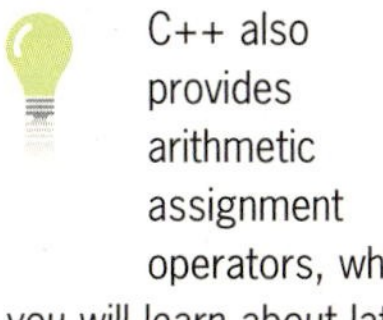

C++ also provides arithmetic assignment operators, which you will learn about later in this chapter.

Operator	Operation	Precedence number
( )	override normal precedence rules	1
–	negation (reverses the sign of a number)	2
*, /, %	multiplication, division, and modulus arithmetic	3
+, –	addition and subtraction	4

Figure 4-7 Standard arithmetic operators and their order of precedence

Ch04-Arithmetic Operators video

Although the negation and subtraction operators use the same symbol (a hyphen), there is a difference between both operators: The negation operator is unary, whereas the subtraction operator is binary. Unary and binary refer to the number of operands required by the operator. Unary operators require one operand, whereas binary operators require two operands. The expression `-7` uses the negation operator to turn the positive number 7 into a negative number. The expression `9 - 4`, on the other hand, uses the subtraction operator to subtract the number 4 from the number 9.

One of the arithmetic operators listed in Figure 4-7, the modulus (or remainder) operator (**%**), might be less familiar to you. The **modulus operator** is used to divide two integers and results in the remainder of the division; the remainder is always an integer. For example, the expression

`211 % 4` (read 211 mod 4) equals 3, which is the remainder after dividing 211 by 4. A common use for the modulus operator is to determine whether a number is even or odd. If you divide a number by 2 and the remainder is 0, the number is even; if the remainder is 1, however, the number is odd.

Some of the operators listed in Figure 4-7, like the addition and subtraction operators, have the same precedence number. When an expression contains more than one operator having the same priority, those operators are evaluated from left to right. In the expression `5 + 12 / 3 - 1`, the division is performed first, then the addition, and then the subtraction. The result of the expression is the number 8, as shown in Figure 4-8. You can use parentheses to change the order in which the operators in an expression are evaluated. For instance, as Figure 4-8 indicates, the expression `5 + 12 / (3 - 1)` evaluates to 11 rather than to 8. This is because the parentheses tell the computer to perform the subtraction operation first.

The modulus operator is used to divide integers only, and the result (remainder) is always an integer.

Original expression	`5 + 12 / 3 - 1`
The division is performed first	`5 + 4 - 1`
The addition is performed next	`9 - 1`
The subtraction is performed last	`8`
Original expression	`5 + 12 / (3 - 1)`
The subtraction is performed first	`5 + 12 / 2`
The division is performed next	`5 + 6`
The addition is performed last	`11`

Figure 4-8 Expressions containing more than one operator having the same precedence

Type Conversions in Arithmetic Expressions

In Chapter 3, you learned about implicit type conversions in statements that declare memory locations. Recall that, if necessary, the computer will either promote or demote the value in a declaration statement to match the memory location's data type. The computer also makes implicit type conversions when processing some arithmetic expressions. More specifically, when performing an arithmetic operation with two values having different data types, the value with the lower-ranking data type is always promoted, temporarily, to the higher-ranking data type. A data type ranks higher than another data type if it can store larger numbers. The value returns to its original data type after the operation is performed.

Ch04-Type Conversions video

Figure 4-9 shows examples of expressions that require implicit type conversions. As you study the examples, keep in mind that a number with a decimal place is considered a `double` number in C++. The figure also explains how each expression is evaluated by the computer. In Examples 2 and 4, `firstNum` is an `int` variable that contains the number 5. When a variable name appears in an expression, the computer uses the value stored in the variable when evaluating the expression.

Example 1 `3 * 1.15`
The integer 3 is implicitly promoted to the **double** number 3.0 before being multiplied by the **double** number 1.15. The result is the **double** number 3.45.

Example 2 `9 * (2.5 + firstNum)`
1. The value stored in the `firstNum` variable (the integer 5) is implicitly promoted to the **double** number 5.0 before it is added to the **double** number 2.5. The result is the **double** number 7.5.
2. The integer 9 is implicitly promoted to the **double** number 9.0 before being multiplied by the **double** number 7.5 (the result of Step 1). The result is the **double** number 67.5.

Example 3 `9.8 / 2`
The integer 2 is implicitly promoted to the **double** number 2.0 before it is divided into the **double** number 9.8. The result is the **double** number 4.9.

Example 4 `firstNum / 2.0`
The value stored in the `firstNum` variable (the integer 5) is implicitly promoted to the **double** number 5.0 before being divided by the **double** number 2.0. The result is the **double** number 2.5.

Figure 4-9 Examples of expressions that require implicit type conversions

When both operands in an expression are integers, the result is an integer. When both are `double` numbers, the result is a `double` number. When one operand is an integer and the other is a `double` number, the result is a `double` number.

At this point, it is important to highlight what happens when you divide one integer by another integer in C++ because the result may not be what you expect. When both the dividend and divisor are integers, the quotient is always an integer in C++. For example, the result of the expression `24 / 5` is the integer 4 rather than the real number 4.8. So how do you get the quotient as a real number? You do so by converting at least one of the integers involved in the division operation to a real number. If the integer is a numeric literal constant, you can convert it to a real number by adding .0 to it. In this case, for example, you can change the expression `24 / 5` to `24.0 / 5`. When the computer evaluates the `24.0 / 5` expression, it will implicitly convert the integer 5 to the `double` number 5.0 before dividing it into the `double` number 24.0; the result will be the `double` number 4.8. You also can use either the expression `24 / 5.0` or the expression `24.0 / 5.0`; both expressions evaluate to 4.8. Similarly, if the `firstNum` variable contains the integer 5, the result of the expression `24.0 / firstNum` also is 4.8. This is because the integer stored in the `firstNum` variable will be implicitly promoted to the `double` data type before the division is performed.

But what if neither of the integers involved in the division operation is a literal constant? For example, what if both the dividend and divisor are `int` variables? Now how do you get the quotient as a real number? In that case, you need to explicitly convert at least one of the `int` variables in the expression to either the `double` or `float` data type. (However, recall that the programs in this book will use the `double` data type for real numbers.) You can use the `static_cast` operator to perform the conversion.

The `static_cast` Operator

C++ provides the **`static_cast` operator** for explicitly converting data from one data type to another. This type of conversion is called an **explicit type conversion** or a **type cast**. Figure 4-10 shows the `static_cast` operator's syntax and includes examples of using the operator. In the syntax, *data* can be a literal constant, named constant, or variable, and *dataType* is the data type to which you want the data converted.

In the examples shown in Figure 4-10, `firstNum` and `secondNum` are `int` variables that contain the numbers 5 and 2, respectively. You can use any of the expressions shown in Examples 1 through 3 to divide the integer stored in the `firstNum` variable by the integer stored in the `secondNum` variable and then return the quotient as a real number having the `double` data type. The expression in Example 4 uses the `static_cast` operator to explicitly promote the integer stored in the `firstNum` variable to the `double` data type before it is multiplied by the `double` number 10.65. Although the same answer would be achieved with implicit type conversion, the type casting makes the programmer's intent clear to anyone reading the program. The statement in Example 5 uses the `static_cast` operator to explicitly convert, or type cast, the `double` number 3.99 to the `float` data type. In this case, the `double` number will be demoted to the `float` data type. (Recall that the `double` data type ranks higher than the `float` data type because it can store larger numbers and also store numbers with greater precision.)

HOW TO Use the `static_cast` Operator

Syntax
static_cast<*dataType*>(*data*)

Example 1 `static_cast<double>(firstNum) / static_cast<double>(secondNum)`
1. The value stored in the `firstNum` variable (the integer 5) is explicitly promoted to the `double` number 5.0.
2. The value stored in the `secondNum` variable (the integer 2) is explicitly promoted to the `double` number 2.0.
3. The `double` number 5.0 (the result of Step 1) is divided by the `double` number 2.0 (the result of Step 2). The result of the division is the `double` number 2.5.

Example 2 `static_cast<double>(firstNum) / secondNum`
1. The value stored in the `firstNum` variable (the integer 5) is explicitly promoted to the `double` number 5.0.
2. The value stored in the `secondNum` variable (the integer 2) is implicitly promoted to the `double` number 2.0.
3. The `double` number 5.0 (the result of Step 1) is divided by the `double` number 2.0 (the result of Step 2). The result of the division is the `double` number 2.5.

Example 3 `firstNum / static_cast<double>(secondNum)`
1. The value stored in the `secondNum` variable (the integer 2) is explicitly promoted to the `double` number 2.0.
2. The value stored in the `firstNum` variable (the integer 5) is implicitly promoted to the `double` number 5.0.
3. The `double` number 5.0 (the result of Step 2) is divided by the `double` number 2.0 (the result of Step 1). The result of the division is the `double` number 2.5.

Example 4 `10.65 * static_cast<double>(firstNum)`
The value stored in the `firstNum` variable (the integer 5) is explicitly promoted to the `double` number 5.0 before being multiplied by the `double` number 10.65. The result is the `double` number 53.25. The `static_cast` operator is not required in this example because the computer will implicitly convert the contents of the `firstNum` variable to the `double` data type before performing the multiplication operation.

Example 5 `const float PRICE = static_cast<float>(3.99);`
The `double` number 3.99 is explicitly converted to the `float` data type before being stored in the `PRICE` named constant.

Figure 4-10 How to use the `static_cast` operator

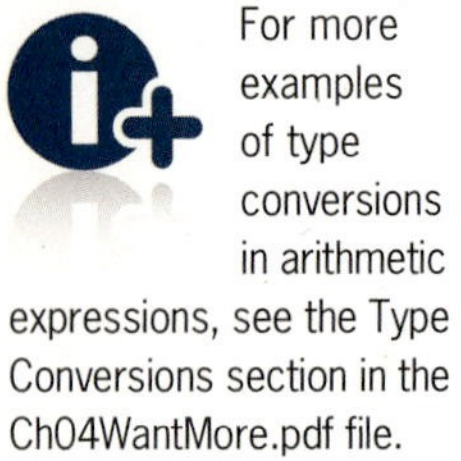
For more examples of type conversions in arithmetic expressions, see the Type Conversions section in the Ch04WantMore.pdf file.

In most cases, the result of an arithmetic expression is assigned to a variable in a program. You do this using an assignment statement.

Assignment Statements

You can use an **assignment statement** to assign a value to a variable while a program is running. When a value is assigned to a variable, it replaces the existing value in the memory location; this is because a variable can store only one value at any time.

Figure 4-11 shows both the syntax and examples of an assignment statement in C++. (For clarity, the variable declaration statements are included in the examples.) The = symbol in an assignment statement is called the **assignment operator**. An assignment statement tells the computer to evaluate the expression that appears on the right side of the assignment operator and then store the result in the variable whose name appears on the left side of the assignment operator. The expression can include one or more items, and the items can be literal constants, named constants, variables, or arithmetic operators.

Ch04-Assignment Statement video

As with declaration statements, the data type of the expression in an assignment statement must match the data type of the variable to which the expression is assigned; otherwise, the computer implicitly converts the value to fit the memory location. However, recall from Chapter 3 that implicit type conversions—more specifically, those that demote the value—do not always give you the expected results. Therefore, it is considered a good programming practice to use a type cast, if necessary, to explicitly convert the value of the expression to fit the memory location. For example, the `static_cast` operator in Example 3 in Figure 4-11 explicitly converts the integer stored in the `firstNum` variable to the `double` data type.

You cannot use an assignment statement to assign a value to a named constant because the contents of a named constant cannot be changed during runtime.

HOW TO Write an Assignment Statement

Syntax
variableName = expression;

Example 1
```
int quantity = 0;
quantity = 1000;
```
The assignment statement assigns the integer 1000 to the `quantity` variable.

Example 2
```
int janOrder = 500;
int febOrder = 225;
int total = 0;
total = janOrder + febOrder;
```
The assignment statement assigns the integer 725 to the `total` variable.

Example 3
```
int firstNum = 5;
int secondNum = 2;
double quotient = 0.0;
quotient = static_cast<double>(firstNum) / secondNum;
```
The assignment statement assigns the `double` number 2.5 to the `quotient` variable.

(continues)

When writing assignment statements that contain a calculation, remember to "compute on the right and assign to the left."

Figure 4-11 How to write an assignment statement

(continued)

Example 4

```
char middleInitial = ' ';
middleInitial = 'C';
```

The assignment statement assigns the letter C to the `middleInitial` variable.

Example 5

```
string customerName = "";
customerName = "Jeff Brown";
```

The assignment statement assigns the string "Jeff Brown" to the `customerName` variable.

Example 6

```
const double DISCOUNT_RATE = .05;
double price = 100.0;
double discount = 0.0;
discount = price * DISCOUNT_RATE;
```

The assignment statement assigns the `double` number 5.0 to the `discount` variable.

Example 7

```
double price = 100.0;
price = price * .95;
```

The assignment statement assigns the `double` number 95.0 to the `price` variable.

For more examples of assignment statements, see the Assignment Statements section in the Ch04WantMore.pdf file.

Figure 4-11 How to write an assignment statement

It is easy to confuse an assignment statement with a variable declaration statement in C++. For example, the assignment statement `hours = 50;` looks very similar to the variable declaration statement `int hours = 50;`. The noticeable difference is the data type that appears at the beginning of the declaration statement. However, keep in mind that a variable declaration statement creates (and optionally initializes) a *new* variable. An assignment statement, on the other hand, assigns a value to an *existing* variable.

Shaded in Figure 4-12 are the appropriate calculation statements for the Treyson Mobley problem. Because all of the items in both calculation statements have the same data type, neither statement requires any implicit or explicit type conversions.

IPO chart information	C++ instructions
Input	
total bill	`double totalBill = 0.0;`
liquor charge	`double liquor = 0.0;`
tip percentage	`double tipPercent = 0.0;`
Processing	
total bill without liquor charge	`double totalNoLiquor = 0.0;`
Output	
tip	`double tip = 0.0;`
Algorithm	

1. enter the total bill, liquor charge, and tip percentage	`cout << "Enter the total bill: ";`
	`cin >> totalBill;`
	`cout << "Enter the liquor charge: ";`
	`cin >> liquor;`
	`cout << "Enter the tip percentage in decimal format: ";`
	`cin >> tipPercent;`

2. calculate the total bill without liquor charge by subtracting the liquor charge from the total bill	`totalNoLiquor = totalBill - liquor;`
3. calculate the tip by multiplying the total bill without liquor charge by the tip percentage	`tip = totalNoLiquor * tipPercent;`
4. display the tip	`cout << "Tip: $" << tip << endl;`

Figure 4-12 Calculation statements for the Treyson Mobley problem

For more examples of coding algorithms, see the Coding Algorithms section in the Ch04WantMore.pdf file.

You now have coded the algorithm into a program, which is Step 4 in the problem-solving process. At this point, it is important to caution you about a problem you might encounter when using real numbers in calculations. As mentioned in Chapter 3, not all real numbers can be represented exactly within the computer's internal memory. As a result, the answer to some calculations may not be accurate to the penny. For example, the expression `7.0 / 3.0` yields a quotient of 2.333333... (with the number 3 repeating indefinitely). The number 2.333333... cannot be stored precisely in the computer's memory; it can be stored only as an approximation. Because many real numbers cannot be stored precisely, some programmers do not use them in monetary calculations where accuracy to the penny is required. Instead, some programmers use integers, while others use special classes designed to perform precise arithmetic using real numbers. These special classes can be purchased from third-party vendors, such as Rogue Wave Software. You can learn more about the problem of using real numbers in monetary calculations by completing Computer Exercise 15 at the end of this chapter. The exercise also allows you to explore the use of integers in calculations. (Your instructor may require you to use integers in monetary calculations; however, for simplicity, this book will use real numbers.)

Arithmetic Assignment Operators

In addition to the standard arithmetic operators listed earlier in Figure 4-7, C++ also provides several arithmetic assignment operators. The **arithmetic assignment operators** allow you to abbreviate an assignment statement that contains an arithmetic operator. However, the assignment statement must have the following format, in which *variableName* is the name of the same variable: *variableName = variableName arithmeticOperator value.* For example, you can use the multiplication assignment operator (*=) to abbreviate the statement `price = price * 1.05;` as follows: `price *= 1.05;`. Both statements tell the computer to multiply the contents of the `price` variable by 1.05 and then store the result in the `price` variable.

In the assignment statement, *value* is usually either a constant (literal or named) or the name of a different variable.

Figure 4-13 shows the syntax of a C++ statement that uses an arithmetic assignment operator. The figure also lists the most commonly used arithmetic assignment operators. Notice that each arithmetic assignment operator consists of an arithmetic operator followed immediately by the assignment operator (=). The arithmetic assignment operators do not contain a space; in other words, the addition assignment operator is +=, not + =. Including a space in an arithmetic assignment operator is a common syntax error.

Figure 4-13 also includes examples of using arithmetic assignment operators to abbreviate assignment statements. To abbreviate an assignment statement, you simply remove the variable name that appears on the left side of the assignment operator (=), and then put the assignment operator immediately after the arithmetic operator.

Ch04-Arithmetic Assignment Operators video

HOW TO Use an Arithmetic Assignment Operator

Syntax
variableName arithmeticAssignmentOperator value;

Operator	Purpose
+=	addition assignment
-=	subtraction assignment
*=	multiplication assignment
/=	division assignment
%=	modulus (remainder) assignment

Example 1
Original statement: `rate = rate + .05;`
Abbreviated statement: `rate += .05;`

Example 2
Original statement: `price = price - discount;`
Abbreviated statement: `price -= discount;`

Figure 4-13 How to use an arithmetic assignment operator

Mini-Quiz 4-2

The answers to Mini-Quiz questions are located in Appendix A.

1. Write a C++ assignment statement that multiplies the number 9.55 by the value stored in an `int` variable named `hours` and then assigns the result to a `double` variable named `grossPay`. Use implicit type conversion.
2. Rewrite the answer to Question 1 using a type cast (explicit type conversion).
3. In C++, the expression `7 / 2 * 4.5` will evaluate to ________, when it should evaluate to ________. Why does the expression evaluate incorrectly?
4. Rewrite the expression from Question 3 so that it will evaluate correctly.
5. Rewrite the `age = age + 1;` statement using an arithmetic assignment operator.

Step 5—Desk-Check the Program

Ch04-Treyson Desk-Check video

The fifth step in the problem-solving process is to desk-check the program to make sure that each instruction in the algorithm was translated correctly. You should desk-check the program using the same sample data used to desk-check the algorithm; the results of both desk-checks should be the same. For your convenience when comparing the results of both desk-checks later in this section, Figure 4-14 shows the desk-check table that you completed for the Treyson Mobley algorithm in Chapter 2.

total bill	liquor charge	tip percentage	total bill without liquor charge	tip
~~45~~	~~10~~	~~.2~~	~~35~~	~~7~~
30	0	.15	30	4.50

Figure 4-14 Algorithm's desk-check table from Chapter 2

When desk-checking a program, you first place the names of the declared memory locations (variables and named constants) in a new desk-check table, along with each memory location's initial value. Figure 4-15 shows the result of desk-checking the variable declaration statements shown earlier in Figure 4-12.

totalBill	liquor	tipPercent	totalNoLiquor	tip
0.0	0.0	0.0	0.0	0.0

Figure 4-15 Variable names and initial values entered in the program's desk-check table

Next, you desk-check the remaining C++ instructions in order, recording in the desk-check table any changes made to the contents of the variables. In the Treyson Mobley program, the first instruction following the declaration statements is the `cout << "Enter the total bill: ";` statement. The statement displays a prompt on the computer screen, but it does not make any changes to the contents of the program's variables; therefore, no entry is necessary in the desk-check table.

The next statement, `cin >> totalBill;`, allows the user to enter the total bill amount, and it stores the user's response in the `totalBill` variable. If the user enters the number 45, the statement stores the number 45.0 in the variable because the variable has the `double` data type.

Therefore, you record 45.0 in the `totalBill` column in the desk-check table. (As you learned in Chapter 2, some programmers find it helpful to lightly cross out the previous value in a column before recording a new value; however, this is not a requirement.)

Next, the `cout << "Enter the liquor charge: ";` statement prompts the user to enter the liquor charge. The `cin >> liquor;` statement waits for the user's response and then stores the response in the `liquor` variable. If the user enters the number 10, you record 10.0 in the desk-check table's `liquor` column.

The next statement, `cout << "Enter the tip percentage in decimal format: ";`, prompts the user to enter the tip percentage. The `cin >> tipPercent;` statement waits for the user's response and then stores the response in the `tipPercent` variable. If the user enters the number .2, you record .2 in the desk-check table. Figure 4-16 shows the input values recorded in the program's desk-check table.

totalBill	liquor	tipPercent	totalNoLiquor	tip
~~0.0~~	~~0.0~~	~~0.0~~	0.0	0.0
45.0	10.0	.2		

Figure 4-16 Input values entered in the program's desk-check table

The `totalNoLiquor = totalBill - liquor;` statement in the program subtracts the contents of the `liquor` variable (10.0) from the contents of the `totalBill` variable (45.0) and then stores the result (35.0) in the `totalNoLiquor` variable. Notice that the expression that appears on the right side of the assignment operator is evaluated first, and then the result is stored in the variable whose name appears on the left side of the assignment operator. As a result of this statement, you record 35.0 in the `totalNoLiquor` column in the desk-check table, as shown in Figure 4-17.

Remember that assignment statements compute on the right and assign to the left.

totalBill	liquor	tipPercent	totalNoLiquor	tip
~~0.0~~	~~0.0~~	~~0.0~~	~~0.0~~	0.0
45.0	10.0	.2	35.0	

Figure 4-17 Desk-check table showing the result of the total bill without liquor charge calculation

The next statement, `tip = totalNoLiquor * tipPercent;`, multiplies the contents of the `totalNoLiquor` variable (35.0) by the contents of the `tipPercent` variable (.2) and then stores the result (7.0) in the `tip` variable. In the desk-check table, you record the number 7.0 in the `tip` column, as shown in Figure 4-18.

totalBill	liquor	tipPercent	totalNoLiquor	tip
~~0.0~~	~~0.0~~	~~0.0~~	~~0.0~~	~~0.0~~
45.0	10.0	.2	35.0	7.0

Figure 4-18 Desk-check table showing the result of the tip calculation

You should perform several desk-checks (using different data) to make sure that a program works correctly.

The last statement in the program displays the `"Tip: $"` message along with the contents of the `tip` variable on the screen. You now have completed desk-checking the program using the first set of test data. If you compare the second row of values in Figure 4-18 with the first row of values shown earlier in Figure 4-14, you will notice that the results obtained when desk-checking the program are the same as the results obtained when desk-checking the algorithm.

For the second desk-check, you will use 30, 0, and .15 as the total bill, liquor charge, and tip percentage, respectively. (This is the same data used in the second desk-check in Figure 4-14.) Each time you desk-check a program, keep in mind that you must complete all of the program's statements, beginning with the first statement and ending with the last statement. In this case, the first statement declares and initializes the `totalBill` variable, and the last statement displays the tip amount on the screen. The completed desk-check table is shown in Figure 4-19. Here again, if you compare the fourth row of values in Figure 4-19 with the second row of values in Figure 4-14, you will notice that the program's results are the same as the algorithm's results.

totalBill	liquor	tipPercent	totalNoLiquor	tip
~~0.0~~	~~0.0~~	~~0.0~~	~~0.0~~	~~0.0~~
~~45.0~~	~~10.0~~	~~.2~~	~~35.0~~	~~7.0~~
~~0.0~~	~~0.0~~	~~0.0~~	~~0.0~~	~~0.0~~
30.0	0.0	.15	30.0	4.50

Figure 4-19 Program's desk-check table showing the results of the second desk-check

Step 6—Evaluate and Modify the Program

The final step in the problem-solving process is to evaluate and modify (if necessary) the program. You evaluate a program by entering your C++ instructions into the computer, along with other instructions that you will learn about later in this section, and then using the computer to run (execute) the program. While the program is running, you enter the same sample data used when desk-checking the program. If the results obtained when running the program differ from those shown in the program's desk-check table, it indicates that the program contains errors, referred to as **bugs**. The bugs must be located and removed from the program before the program is released to the user. The programmer's job is not finished until the program runs without errors and produces the expected results.

The process of locating and correcting the bugs in a program is called **debugging**. Program bugs typically are caused by either syntax errors or logic errors. A **syntax error** occurs when you break one of the programming language's rules. Most syntax errors are a result of typing errors that occur when entering instructions, such as typing `cut` (instead of `cout`) or neglecting to enter a semicolon at the end of a statement. In most cases, syntax errors are easy to both locate and correct because they trigger an error message from the C++ compiler. The error message indicates the general vicinity of the error and includes a brief description of the error. Appendix D contains a listing of common syntax errors.

Another type of error, called a runtime error, can occur while a program is running. Entering a letter when a number is expected will cause a runtime error.

Unlike syntax errors, logic errors are much more difficult to find because they do not trigger an error message from the compiler. A **logic error** can occur for a variety of reasons, such as forgetting to enter an instruction or entering the instructions in the wrong order. Some logic errors occur as a result of calculation statements that are correct syntactically but incorrect mathematically. For example, consider the statement `average = midtermScore + finalScore / 2;`, which is supposed to calculate the average of two numeric test scores. The statement's syntax is correct, but it is incorrect mathematically. This is because it tells the computer to divide the contents of the `finalScore` variable by 2 and then add the quotient to the contents of the `midtermScore` variable. (Recall that division is performed before addition in an arithmetic expression.) The correct instruction for calculating the average is `average = (midtermScore + finalScore) / 2;`. The parentheses tell the computer to add together the contents of the `midtermScore` and `finalScore` variables before dividing the sum by 2.

In order to enter your C++ instructions into the computer, you need to have access to a text editor, more simply referred to as an editor. The instructions you enter are called **source code**.

You save the source code in a file on a disk, giving it the filename extension .cpp (which stands for C plus plus). The .cpp file is called the **source file**. In order to run (execute) the code contained in the source file, you need a C++ compiler. As you learned in Chapter 1, a compiler translates high-level instructions into machine code—the 0s and 1s that the computer can understand. Machine code is usually called **object code**. The compiler generates the object code and saves it in a file whose filename extension is .obj (which stands for object). The file containing the object code is called the **object file**.

After the compiler creates the object file, it then invokes another program called a linker. The **linker** combines the object file with other machine code necessary for your C++ program to run correctly, such as machine code that allows the program to communicate with input and output devices. The linker produces an **executable file**, which is a file that contains all of the machine code necessary to run your C++ program as many times as desired without the need for translating the program again. The executable file has an extension of .exe on its filename. (The exe stands for executable.) Figure 4-20 illustrates the sequence of steps followed when translating your source code into executable code.

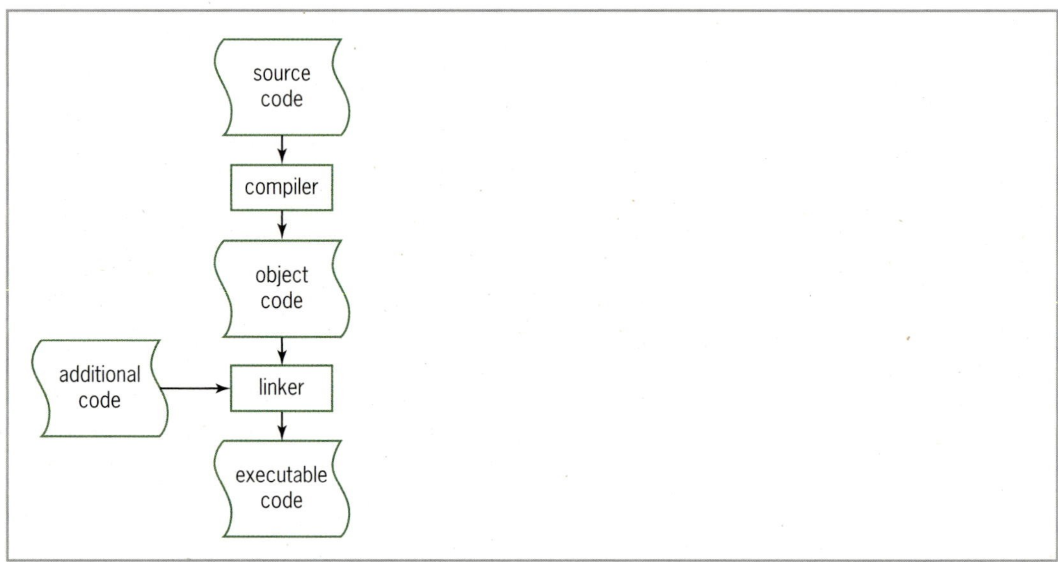

Figure 4-20 Process by which source code is translated into executable code

Many C++ development tools contain both the editor and compiler in one integrated environment, referred to as an **IDE (Integrated Development Environment)**. Examples include Microsoft Visual C++, Dev C++, Code::Blocks, and Xcode. Other C++ development tools, called command-line compilers, contain only the compiler and require you to use a general-purpose editor (such as Notepad, WordPad, or vi) to enter the program instructions into the computer. As noted in this book's *Read This Before You Begin* page, this book is accompanied by video files that show you how to install various development tools on your computer. Also accompanying this book are files, in PDF format, that contain step-by-step directions for using these development tools to enter and run some of the C++ programs in this book. However, keep in mind that you are not limited to the development tools supported by the videos and PDF files. You can enter and run the programs in this book using most C++ development tools, often with little or no modification. Your instructor or technical support person will provide you with the appropriate instructions if you are using a different development tool.

Figure 4-21 shows the source code for the Treyson Mobley program. Each line in the figure is numbered so that it is easier to refer to it in the text; you do not enter the line numbers in the program. The unshaded lines of code are your C++ instructions from Figure 4-12. You do not have to align the initial values in the declaration statements as shown in the figure; however, doing so makes it easier to verify that each memory location has been initialized.

Besides entering your C++ instructions, you also need to enter other instructions in the source file. Some of the additional instructions are required by the C++ compiler, while others are optional but highly recommended. The additional instructions are shaded in Figure 4-21.

```
1 //Fig4-21.cpp - displays the amount of a tip
2 //Created/revised by <your name> on <current date>
3
4 #include <iostream>
5 using namespace std;
6
7 int main()
8 {
9     //declare variables
10    double totalBill      = 0.0;
11    double liquor         = 0.0;
12    double tipPercent     = 0.0;
13    double totalNoLiquor  = 0.0;
14    double tip            = 0.0;
15
16    //enter input items
17    cout << "Enter the total bill: ";
18    cin >> totalBill;
19    cout << "Enter the liquor charge: ";
20    cin >> liquor;
21    cout << "Enter the tip percentage in decimal format: ";
22    cin >> tipPercent;
23
24    //calculate the total without liquor and the tip
25    totalNoLiquor = totalBill - liquor;
26    tip = totalNoLiquor * tipPercent;
27
28    //display the output item
29    cout << "Tip: $" << tip << endl;
30
31    system("pause");
32    return 0;
33 }  //end of main function
```

function header (line 7)

depending on your C++ development tool, this statement may not be necessary (line 31)

Figure 4-21 Treyson Mobley program

Everything after the two forward slashes (//) to the end of the line is treated as a comment.

Lines 1, 2, 9, 16, 24, and 28 in the program are comments; there also is a comment on line 33. You create a comment by typing two forward slashes (//) before the text you want treated as a comment. A **comment** is simply a message to the person reading the program and is referred to as internal documentation. The comments on lines 1 and 2 indicate the program's name and purpose, as well as the programmer's name and the date the program was either created or revised. The remaining comments explain various sections of the code. The comment on line 9, for example, indicates that the instructions that follow it are variable declaration statements. The C++ compiler does not require you to include comments in a program. However, it is a good programming practice to do so because they make your code more readable and easier to understand by anyone viewing it. The C++ compiler does not process (execute) the comments in a program. Instead, the compiler ignores the comments when it translates the source code into object code. Comments do not end with a semicolon because they are not statements in C++.

Lines 4 and 5 in Figure 4-21 are directives. C++ programs typically contain at least one directive, and most contain many directives. Line 4 is a #include directive and line 5 is a using directive. A **#include directive** provides a convenient way to merge the source code from one file with the source code in another file, without having to retype the code. The `#include <iostream>` directive, for example, tells the C++ compiler to include the contents of the iostream file in the current program. The iostream file must be included in any program that uses the `cin` or `cout` objects. A #include directive is not a C++ statement; therefore, it does not end with a semicolon.

A using directive, on the other hand, *is* a statement; therefore, it must end with a semicolon. A **using directive** tells the compiler where (in the computer's internal memory) it can find the definitions of keywords and classes, such as `double` or `string`. The `using namespace std;` directive indicates that the definitions of the standard C++ keywords and classes are located in the `std` (which stands for *standard*) namespace. A namespace is a special area in the computer's internal memory.

In line 7 of the program, `main` is the name of a function and must be typed using lowercase letters. A **function** is a block of code that performs a task. Functions have parentheses following their names, like this: `main()`. Some functions require you to enter information between the parentheses; other functions, like `main`, do not. Every C++ program must have a `main` function because that is where the execution of a C++ program always begins.

A C++ program can contain many functions; however, only one can be the `main` function. Some functions, like `main`, return a value after completing their assigned task. If a function returns a value, the data type of the value it returns appears to the left of the function name; otherwise, the keyword `void` appears to the left of the name. The `int` in line 7 indicates that the `main` function returns an integer. The entire line of code, `int main()`, is referred to as a **function header** because it marks the beginning of the function.

After the function header, you enter the code that directs the function on how to perform its assigned task. Examples of such code include statements that declare variables, as well as statements that input, calculate, and output data. In C++, you enclose a function's code within a set of braces (`{}`). The braces mark the beginning and end of the code block that constitutes the function. You enter the opening brace (`{`) immediately below the function's header in the program, and you enter the closing brace (`}`) at the end of the function. In Figure 4-21, the opening brace appears on line 8, immediately below the `int main()` function header; the closing brace appears on line 33.

Everything between the opening and closing braces in Figure 4-21 is included in the `main` function and is referred to as the **function body**. Notice that you can include a comment (in this case, `//end of main function`) on the same line with a C++ instruction. However, you must be sure to enter the comment *after* the instruction because only the text appearing after the two forward slashes (`//`) on a line is interpreted as a comment.

Line 31 contains the `system("pause");` statement, which pauses program execution and displays the *Press any key to continue* message in a Command Prompt window on the computer screen, as shown in Figure 4-22. Depending on the C++ development tool you are using, your programs may not need the `system("pause");` statement. This is because many C++ development tools automatically pause program execution and display the *Press any key to continue* message when a program ends. Although you may need to include the statement in the files submitted to your instructor, the statement is never included in the final executable file given to the user.

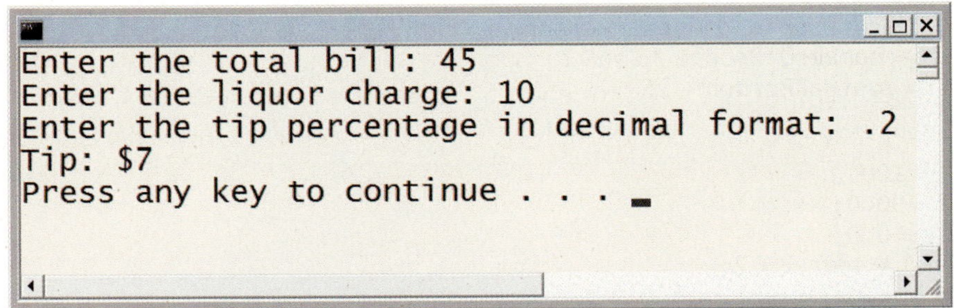

Figure 4-22 Command Prompt window

The `return 0;` statement, which appears on Line 32 in Figure 4-21, returns the number 0 to the operating system to indicate that the program ended normally. (As mentioned earlier, the `main` function returns an integer.)

Mini-Quiz 4-3

The answers to Mini-Quiz questions are located in Appendix A.

1. Typing `cin > age;` rather than `cin >> age;` is an example of a(n) ________ error.
2. The .cpp file that contains your C++ instructions is called the ________ file.
   a. executable
   b. object
   c. source
   d. statement
3. In a C++ program, the body of a function is enclosed in ________.
   a. braces
   b. parentheses
   c. square brackets
   d. none of the above

The answers to the labs are located in Appendix A.

LAB 4-1 Stop and Analyze

Study the three examples shown in Figure 4-23, and then answer the questions.

Example 1
```
int numberOfPeople = 10;
double costPerPerson = 7.45;
double totalCost = 0.0;
totalCost = numberOfPeople * costPerPerson;
numberOfPeople = numberOfPeople / 2;
costPerPerson = costPerPerson + 3;
```

Example 2
```
double score1 = 100.0;
double score2 = 90.0;
double average = 0.0;
average = score1 + score2 / 2;
```

Example 3
```
int juneSales = 933;
int julySales = 1216;
double avgSales = 0.0;
avgSales = (juneSales + julySales) / 2;
```

Figure 4-23 Examples for Lab 4-1

QUESTIONS

1. Explain how the computer evaluates the total cost calculation statement in Example 1. What value will be assigned to the `totalCost` variable? Is the value correct? If not, how can you fix the statement so it evaluates correctly?
2. Explain how the computer evaluates the number of people calculation statement in Example 1. The statement should divide the number of people by 2 and then assign the result to the `numberOfPeople` variable. What value will be assigned to the variable? Is the value correct? If not, how can you fix the statement so it evaluates correctly?
3. Explain how the computer evaluates the cost per person calculation statement in Example 1. What value will be assigned to the `costPerPerson` variable? Is the value correct? If not, how can you fix the statement so it evaluates correctly?
4. Explain how the computer evaluates the average calculation statement in Example 2. What value will be assigned to the `average` variable? Is the value correct? If not, how can you fix the statement so it evaluates correctly?
5. Explain how the computer evaluates the average sales calculation statement in Example 3. What value will be assigned to the `avgSales` variable? Is the value correct? If not, how can you fix the statement so it evaluates correctly?

LAB 4-2 Plan and Create

In this lab, you will plan and create an algorithm that displays the total amount a student owes for a semester. After doing this, you will code the algorithm into a program and then enter and run the program using the computer. The problem specification is shown in Figure 4-24.

Ch04-Lab4-2 video

> **Problem specification**
> The cashier at Hoover College wants a program that calculates and displays the total amount a student owes for the semester, including tuition and room and board. The fee per semester hour is \$100, and the room and board fee is \$2,000 per semester. Courses at the college can be 1, 2, or 3 semester hours.

Figure 4-24 Problem specification for Lab 4-2

First, analyze the problem, looking for the output first and then for the input. In this case, the user wants the program to display the total amount the student owes. To calculate the total amount, the computer will need to know the number of semester hours for which the student is enrolled, as well as the fee per semester hour and the room and board fee. The number of semester hours will be entered by the user, whereas the problem specification indicates that the fee per semester hour is \$100, and the room and board fee is \$2,000. Figure 4-25 shows the input and output items entered in an IPO chart.

Input	Processing	Output
hours enrolled fee per hour (100) room & board fee (2000)	Processing items: Algorithm:	total owed

Figure 4-25 Partially completed IPO chart showing the input and output items

As you know, most algorithms begin with an instruction to enter the input items into the computer, followed by instructions that process the input items, typically including the items in one or more calculations. Most algorithms end with one or more instructions that display, print, or store the output items. Figure 4-26 shows the completed IPO chart for the Hoover College problem.

Input	Processing	Output
hours enrolled fee per hour (100) room & board fee (2000)	Processing items: none Algorithm: 1. enter the hours enrolled 2. calculate the total owed by multiplying the hours enrolled by the fee per hour and then adding the room & board fee to the result 3. display the total owed	total owed

Figure 4-26 Completed IPO chart for the Hoover College problem

After completing the IPO chart, you then move on to the third step in the problem-solving process, which is to desk-check the algorithm. You will desk-check the Hoover College algorithm twice, using 9 and 11 as the number of hours enrolled. Manually calculating the total owed results in $2,900 for the first desk-check and $3,100 for the second desk-check. Figure 4-27 shows the completed desk-check table. Notice that the amounts in the total owed column agree with the results of the manual calculations.

hours enrolled	fee per hour	room & board fee	total owed
~~9~~	~~100~~	~~2000~~	~~2900~~
11	100	2000	3100

Figure 4-27 Completed desk-check table for the Hoover College algorithm

The fourth step in the problem-solving process is to code the algorithm into a program. You begin by declaring memory locations that will store the values of the input, processing (if any), and output items. The Hoover College problem will need four memory locations to store the values of the hours enrolled, fee per hour, room & board fee, and total owed. The hours enrolled and total owed values should be stored in variables because the user should be allowed to change the hours enrolled value, which then will change the total owed value, while the program is running. The fee per hour and room & board fee, however, will be stored in named constants because those values should not change during runtime. The variables and named constants will store integers, so you will use the `int` data type for each one. Figure 4-28 shows the input, processing, and output items from the IPO chart, along with the corresponding C++ statements.

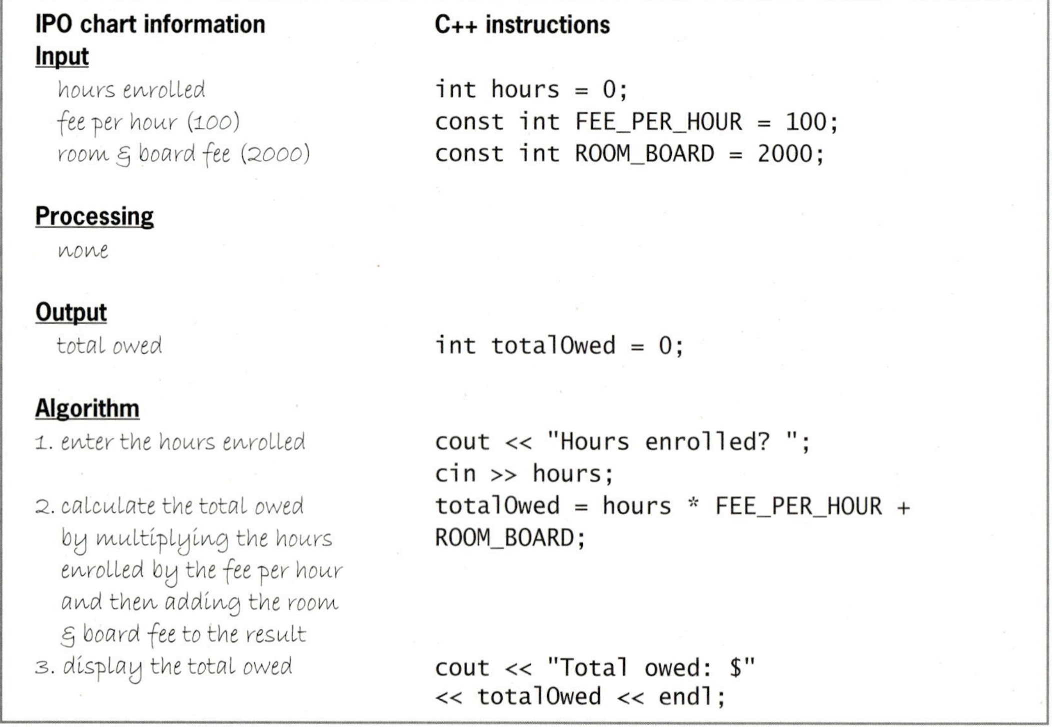

IPO chart information	C++ instructions
Input	
hours enrolled	`int hours = 0;`
fee per hour (100)	`const int FEE_PER_HOUR = 100;`
room & board fee (2000)	`const int ROOM_BOARD = 2000;`
Processing	
none	
Output	
total owed	`int totalOwed = 0;`
Algorithm	
1. enter the hours enrolled	`cout << "Hours enrolled? ";` `cin >> hours;`
2. calculate the total owed by multiplying the hours enrolled by the fee per hour and then adding the room & board fee to the result	`totalOwed = hours * FEE_PER_HOUR +` `ROOM_BOARD;`
3. display the total owed	`cout << "Total owed: $"` `<< totalOwed << endl;`

Figure 4-28 IPO chart information and C++ instructions for the Hoover College problem

The fifth step in the problem-solving process is to desk-check the program. You begin by placing the names of the declared variables and named constants in a new desk-check table, along with their values. You then desk-check the remaining C++ instructions in order, recording in the desk-check table any changes made to the variables. Figure 4-29 shows the completed desk-check table for the program. The results agree with those shown in the algorithm's desk-check table in Figure 4-27.

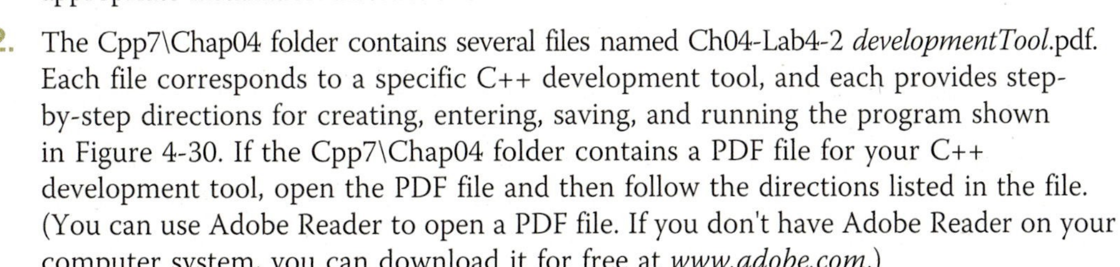

Figure 4-29 Completed desk-check table for the Hoover College program

The final step in the problem-solving process is to evaluate and modify (if necessary) the program. Recall that you evaluate a program by entering its instructions into the computer and then using the computer to run (execute) it. While the program is running, you enter the same sample data used when desk-checking the program.

DIRECTIONS

Ch04-Installation *developmentTool* video

1. Determine whether your C++ development tool has been installed on your computer. If it hasn't, then you will need to install it before you can enter and run the program shown in Figure 4-30. If you need help with the installation, watch the video that corresponds to your development tool. The videos are named Ch04-Installation *developmentTool*, where *developmentTool* is the name of the C++ development tool covered in the video. If your development tool is not covered in any of these videos, you will need to contact your instructor or technical support person for the appropriate installation instructions.
2. The Cpp7\Chap04 folder contains several files named Ch04-Lab4-2 *developmentTool*.pdf. Each file corresponds to a specific C++ development tool, and each provides step-by-step directions for creating, entering, saving, and running the program shown in Figure 4-30. If the Cpp7\Chap04 folder contains a PDF file for your C++ development tool, open the PDF file and then follow the directions listed in the file. (You can use Adobe Reader to open a PDF file. If you don't have Adobe Reader on your computer system, you can download it for free at *www.adobe.com*.)

   If the Cpp7\Chap04 folder does *not* contain a PDF file for your C++ development tool, contact your instructor or technical support person for the appropriate instructions. Follow the instructions you are given for starting your C++ development tool. Depending on the development tool you are using, you may need to create a new project; if so, name the project Lab4-2 Project and save it in the Cpp7\Chap04 folder. Enter the instructions shown in Figure 4-30 in a source file named Lab4-2.cpp. (Do not enter the line numbers.) Save the file in either the project folder or the Cpp7\Chap04 folder. Now follow the appropriate instructions for running the Lab4-2.cpp file. Run the program twice, using the sample data values of 9 and 11 for the hours enrolled. If necessary, correct any bugs (errors) in the program.

```
//Lab4-2.cpp - displays the total owed
//Created/revised by <your name> on <current date>

#include <iostream>
using namespace std;

int main()
{
    //declare variables and named constants
    int hours                = 0;
    int totalOwed            = 0;
    const int FEE_PER_HOUR = 100;
    const int ROOM_BOARD   = 2000;

    //enter hours enrolled
    cout << "Hours enrolled? ";
    cin >> hours;

    //calculate total owed
    totalOwed = hours * FEE_PER_HOUR + ROOM_BOARD;

    //display total owed
    cout << "Total owed: $" << totalOwed << endl;

    //system("pause");
    return 0;
}   //end of main function
```

if your C++ development tool requires this statement, delete the two forward slashes

Figure 4-30 Hoover College program

LAB 4-3 Modify

In this lab, you will modify the program created in Lab 4-2. Hoover College now has courses that can be .5, 1, 2, or 3 semester hours. In addition, the fee per hour has been raised to $105.

The Cpp7\Chap04 folder contains several files named Ch04-Lab4-3 *developmentTool*.pdf. Each file corresponds to a specific C++ development tool, and each provides step-by-step directions for completing Lab 4-3. If the Cpp7\Chap04 folder contains a PDF file for your C++ development tool, open the PDF file and then follow the directions listed in the file. (You can use Adobe Reader to open a PDF file.)

If the Cpp7\Chap04 folder does *not* contain a PDF file for your C++ development tool, create a new project (if necessary) named Lab4-3 Project and save it in the Cpp7\Chap04 folder. Copy the program instructions from Lab 4-2 into a new source file named Lab4-3.cpp. Modify the program instructions appropriately. Be sure to change Lab4-2.cpp in the first comment to Lab4-3.cpp. Test the program twice, using 9.5 and 11 as the number of hours enrolled. The total owed should be $2997.5 and $3155. (Don't be concerned that the $2997.5 has only one decimal place. You will learn how to format numbers in Chapter 5.)

LAB 4-4 Desk-Check

Desk-check the three lines of code shown in Figure 4-31.

```
int num 75;
int answer = 0;
answer = num % 2;
```

Figure 4-31 Code for Lab 4-4

LAB 4-5 Debug

The Cpp7\Chap04 folder contains several files named Ch04-Lab4-5 *developmentTool*.pdf. Each file corresponds to a specific C++ development tool, and each provides step-by-step directions for completing Lab 4-5. If the Cpp7\Chap04 folder contains a PDF file for your C++ development tool, open the PDF file and then follow the directions listed in the file. (You can use Adobe Reader to open a PDF file.)

If the Cpp7\Chap04 folder does *not* contain a PDF file for your C++ development tool, start your C++ development tool and open the Lab4-5.cpp file. If necessary, delete the two forward slashes that appear before the `system("pause");` statement, and then save the program. The program should calculate and display a 3% raise, but it is not working correctly. Run and then debug the program.

Summary

- The fourth step in the problem-solving process is to code the algorithm. You begin by declaring a memory location for each unique input, processing, and output item listed in the IPO chart. You then translate each instruction in the algorithm into one or more C++ statements.
- In C++, you perform standard input and output operations using stream objects. The standard input stream object is called `cin`. The standard output stream object is called `cout`.
- You use `cin` along with the extraction operator (>>) to get either numeric or character input from the computer keyboard. You use `cout` along with the insertion operator (<<) to display information on the computer screen.
- The extraction operator stops removing characters from the `cin` object when it encounters a white-space character.
- The `endl` stream manipulator advances the cursor to the next line on the computer screen.
- A program should display (on the computer screen) a separate and meaningful prompt for each item of data the user should enter.

- You direct the computer to perform a calculation by writing an arithmetic expression that contains one or more arithmetic operators.
- Each arithmetic operator is associated with a precedence number, which controls the order in which the operation is performed in an expression. When an arithmetic expression contains more than one operator having the same priority, those operators are evaluated from left to right. You can use parentheses to override the normal order of precedence.
- When an arithmetic operation involves two values having different data types, the computer implicitly promotes the value with the lower-ranking data type to the higher-ranking data type. The value returns to its original data type upon completion of the arithmetic operation.
- The quotient obtained by dividing one integer by another integer is always an integer in C++.
- You can use the `static_cast` operator to explicitly convert data from one data type to another.
- You can use an assignment statement to assign a value to a variable during runtime. An assignment statement tells the computer to evaluate the expression that appears on the right side of the assignment operator (=) and then store the result in the variable whose name appears on the left side of the assignment operator.
- The fifth step in the problem-solving process is to desk-check the program. You should use the same sample data used to desk-check the algorithm.
- The sixth (and final) step in the problem-solving process is to evaluate and modify (if necessary) the program.
- The errors in a program are called bugs and typically fall into one of two categories: syntax errors or logic errors.
- In order for you to enter your C++ instructions into the computer and then run the program, you need to have access to a text editor and a C++ compiler.
- The C++ instructions entered in a program are called source code and are saved in a source file, which has a .cpp filename extension.
- The compiler translates source code into machine code, also called object code.
- The linker produces an executable file that contains all the machine code necessary to run a C++ program. The executable file has an .exe filename extension.
- Programmers use comments to document a program internally. Doing this makes the program easier to understand by anyone viewing it. Comments are not statements and are ignored by the compiler.
- The `#include <iostream>` directive tells the computer to include the contents of the iostream file in the current program.
- The `using namespace std;` directive tells the computer that the definitions of standard C++ keywords and classes are located in the `std` namespace. A namespace is a special area in the computer's internal memory.
- The execution of a C++ program begins with the `main` function. Therefore, every C++ program must have one (and only one) `main` function.
- The first line in a function is called the function header. Following the function header is the function body, which must be enclosed in braces.
- C++ provides arithmetic assignment operators that allow you to abbreviate an assignment statement as follows: *variableName arithmeticAssignmentOperator value*;. However, the original assignment statement must have the following format, in which *variableName* is the name of the same variable: *variableName* = *variableName arithmeticOperator value*.

Key Terms

#include directive—an instruction that tells the computer to merge the source code from one file with the source code from another file

%—modulus (remainder) operator; divides two integers and returns the remainder as an integer

<<—the insertion operator in C++

>>—the extraction operator in C++

Arithmetic assignment operators—operators composed of an arithmetic operator and the assignment operator; used to abbreviate an assignment statement that follows a specific format

Assignment operator—the = symbol in an assignment statement

Assignment statement—used to assign a value to a variable during runtime

Bugs—the errors in a program

cin—the standard input stream object in C++; tells the computer to pause program execution while the user enters one or more characters at the keyboard; temporarily stores the characters entered at the keyboard

Comment—a message used to document a program internally; begins with two forward slashes (//) in C++

cout—the standard output stream object in C++; used with the insertion operator to display information on the computer screen

Debugging—the process of locating and correcting any errors in a program

endl—a stream manipulator that can be used to advance the cursor to the next line on the computer screen

Executable file—a file that contains all of the machine code necessary to run a program; executable files have an .exe filename extension

Explicit type conversion—the explicit conversion of data from one data type to another; usually performed with the `static_cast` operator; also called a type cast

Extraction operator—two greater-than signs (>>); extracts (removes) characters from the `cin` object and sends them "in" to the computer's internal memory

Function—a block of code that performs a task

Function body—the code contained between a function's opening and closing braces

Function header—the first line in a function; marks the beginning of the function

IDE—an acronym for Integrated Development Environment

Insertion operator—two less-than signs (<<); used with the `cout` object to display information on the computer screen

Integrated Development Environment—a system that includes both an editor and a compiler

Linker—a program that combines the code contained in a C++ program's object file with other machine code necessary to run the C++ program

Logic error—an error (bug) that occurs when you neglect to enter a program instruction or enter the instructions in the wrong order; also occurs as a result of calculation statements that are correct syntactically but incorrect mathematically

Modulus operator—the percent sign (%); divides two integers and returns the remainder as an integer

Object code—another name for machine code

Object file—a file that contains the object code associated with a program; automatically generated by the compiler

Prompt—a message (displayed on the computer screen) indicating the type of data the user should enter at the keyboard

Source code—the program instructions you enter using an editor; the instructions are saved in a source file

Source file—a file that contains a program's source code; source files have a .cpp filename extension

`static_cast` operator—explicitly converts (or type casts) data from one data type to another

Stream—a sequence of characters

Stream manipulator—allows a C++ program to manipulate (or manage) the characters in either the input or output stream

Stream objects—objects used to perform standard input and output operations in C++

Syntax error—an error (bug) that occurs when a program instruction violates a programming language's syntax

Type cast—another term for an explicit type conversion

using directive—an instruction that tells the computer where it can find the definitions of keywords and classes

White-space character—a newline character, a tab character, or a blank (space) character

Review Questions

1. Which of the following prompts the user to enter a price?
   a. `cin >> "What is the price? ";`
   b. `cin << "What is the price? ";`
   c. `cout << "What is the price? ";`
   d. `cout >> "What is the price? ";`

2. Which of the following sends keyboard input to a variable named `price`?
   a. `cin >> price;`
   b. `cin << price;`
   c. `cin <> price;`
   d. `cin > price;`

3. If the `price` variable has the `double` data type, which of the following statements will require an explicit type conversion to evaluate correctly?
   a. `price = 25;`
   b. `price = price * 1.05;`
   c. `price = price / 2;`
   d. none of the above

4. The num1 and num2 variables have the int data type and contain the numbers 13 and 5, respectively. The answer variable has the double data type. Which of the following statements will require an explicit type conversion to evaluate correctly?

   a. answer = num1 / 4.0;

   b. answer = num1 + num1 / num2;

   c. answer = num1 - num2;

   d. none of the above

5. Which of the following assigns the letter T to a char variable named insured?

   a. insured = 'T';

   b. insured = "T";

   c. insured = T;

   d. none of the above

6. Which of the following explicitly converts the contents of an int variable named quantity to the double data type?

   a. castToDouble(quantity)

   b. explicit_cast<double>(quantity)

   c. static_cast<double>(quantity)

   d. type_cast<double>(quantity)

7. Which of the following statements advances the cursor to the next line on the computer screen?

   a. cout << endl;

   b. cout << endline;

   c. cout << newline;

   d. none of the above

8. Which of the following tells the compiler to merge the code contained in the iostream file with the current file's code?

   a. #include iostream;

   b. #include <iostream>

   c. #include <iostream>;

   d. #include (iostream)

9. Which of the following is equivalent to the rate = rate / 100; statement?

   a. rate = rate =/ 100;

   b. rate /= 100;

   c. rate =/ 100;

   d. none of the above

10. Which of the following is a valid comment in C++?

    a. **This is a comment

    b. @/This is a comment

    c. /This is a comment

    d. none of the above

Exercises

Pencil and Paper

TRY THIS

1. Complete the C++ instructions column in Figure 4-32. (The answers to TRY THIS Exercises are located at the end of the chapter.)

IPO chart information	C++ instructions
Input	
sale1	`double sale1 = 0.0;`
sale2	`double sale2 = 0.0;`
commission rate	`double commissionRate = 0.0;`
Processing	
total sales	`double totalSales = 0.0;`
Output	
commission	`double commission = 0.0;`
Algorithm	
1. enter sale1, sale2, and the commission rate	
2. calculate the total sales by adding sale1 to sale2	
3. calculate the commission by multiplying the total sales by the commission rate	
4. display the commission	

Figure 4-32

TRY THIS

2. Complete the C++ instructions column in Figure 4-33. (The answers to TRY THIS Exercises are located at the end of the chapter.)

IPO chart information	**C++ instructions**
Input	
cup price	`double cupPrice = 0.0;`
plate price	`double platePrice = 0.0;`
cups purchased	`int cupsPurchased = 0;`
plates purchased	`int platesPurchased = 0;`
sales tax rate (5.5%)	`const double TAX_RATE = .055;`
Processing	
total cup cost	`double totalCupCost = 0.0;`
total plate cost	`double totalPlateCost = 0.0;`
subtotal	`double subtotal = 0.0;`
Output	
total cost	`double totalCost = 0.0;`
Algorithm 1. enter cup price, plate price, cups purchased, and plates purchased 2. calculate the total cup cost by multiplying the cups purchased by the cup price 3. calculate the total plate cost by multiplying the plates purchased by the plate price 4. calculate the subtotal by adding the total cup cost to the total plate cost 5. calculate the total cost by multiplying the subtotal by the sales tax rate and then adding the result to the subtotal 6. display the total cost	

Figure 4-33

MODIFY THIS

3. Complete TRY THIS Exercise 1, and then modify the IPO chart information and C++ instructions so that the commission rate will always be 10%.

INTRODUCTORY

4. Complete the C++ instructions column in Figure 4-34.

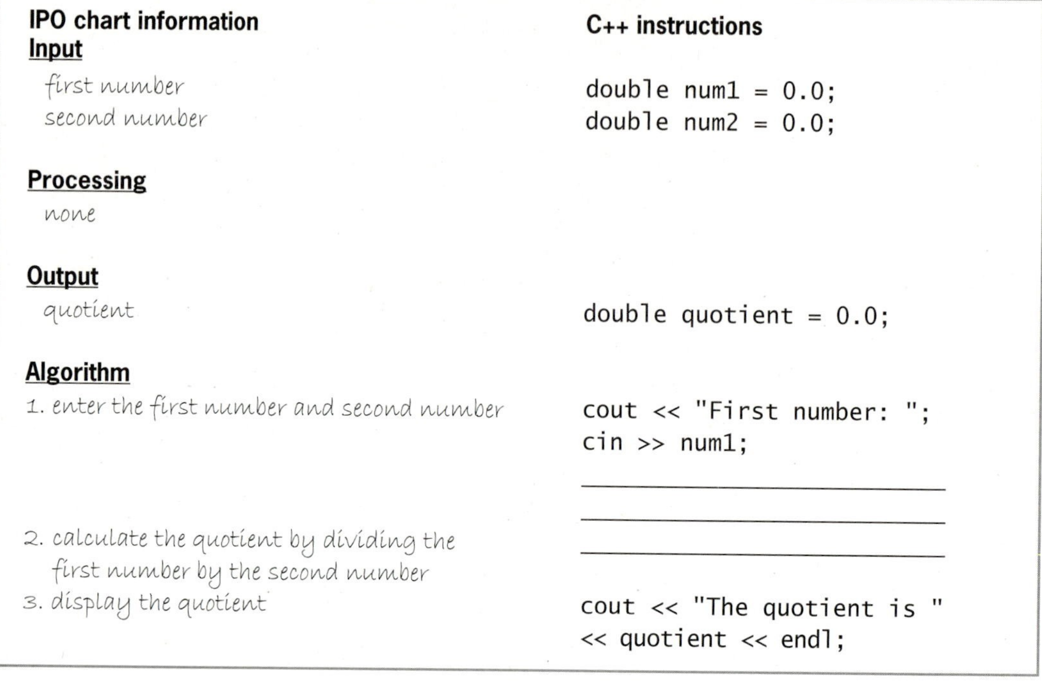

Figure 4-34

INTERMEDIATE

5. Complete the C++ instructions column in Figure 4-35.

IPO chart information	C++ instructions
Input	
miles driven	`int milesDriven = 0;`
gallons used	`int gallonsUsed = 0;`
Processing	
none	
Output	
miles per gallon	`double milesPerGal = 0.0;`
Algorithm	
1. enter the miles driven and gallons used	____________________ ____________________ ____________________ ____________________ ____________________
2. calculate the miles per gallon by dividing the miles driven by the gallons used	
3. display the miles per gallon	`cout << "MPG: " << milesPerGal << endl;`

Figure 4-35

ADVANCED

6. Complete the C++ instructions column in Figure 4-36.

IPO chart information	C++ instructions
Input	
assessed value	`int assessedValue = 0;`
tax rate ($1.02)	________________
Processing	
none	
Output	
annual property tax	`double tax = 0.0;`
Algorithm	
1. enter the assessed value	________________ ________________
2. calculate the annual property tax by dividing the assessed value by 100 and then multiplying the result by the tax rate	________________
3. display the annual property tax	________________

Figure 4-36

SWAT THE BUGS

7. Correct the errors in the lines of code shown in Figure 4-37. (The code contains nine errors.)

```
#include <iostreem>
using std namespace;

int main
{
    /declare variables
    Int quantity = 0;

    //enter the input item
    cout "Enter the quantity ordered: ";
    cin << quantity;

    //display a message
    cout << "You entered " << quantity << endl

    //system("pause");        your C++ development tool may require this statement
    return 0;
{   //end of main function
```

Figure 4-37

Computer

TRY THIS

8. The answer to TRY THIS Exercise 1 is shown in Figure 4-38 at the end of the chapter. If necessary, create a new project named TryThis8 Project and save it in the Cpp7\Chap04 folder. Enter the C++ instructions from the figure into a source file named TryThis8.cpp. Also enter appropriate comments and any additional instructions required by the compiler. Save and run the program. Test the program using 345.55 and 576.34 as the two sale amounts and .05 as the commission rate. The answer should be $46.0945. (Don't be concerned if your answer has more decimal places.) Now test it using 3000, 2500, and .06. (The answers to TRY THIS Exercises are located at the end of the chapter.)

TRY THIS

9. The answer to TRY THIS Exercise 2 is shown in Figure 4-39 at the end of the chapter. If necessary, create a new project named TryThis9 Project and save it in the Cpp7\Chap04 folder. Enter the C++ instructions from the figure into a source file named TryThis9.cpp. Also enter appropriate comments and any additional instructions required by the compiler. Save and run the program. Test the program using .50 as the cup price, 1.05 as the plate price, 35 as the number of cups purchased, and 35 as the number of plates purchased. The answer should be $57.2338. (Don't be concerned if your answer has more decimal places.) Then test it using .25, .75, 20, and 10. (The answers to TRY THIS Exercises are located at the end of the chapter.)

MODIFY THIS

10. Complete TRY THIS Exercise 8. If necessary, create a new project named ModifyThis10 Project and save it in the Cpp7\Chap04 folder. Enter (or copy) the instructions from the TryThis8.cpp file into a new source file named ModifyThis10.cpp. Modify the code in the ModifyThis10.cpp file so that the commission rate will always be 10%. Save and run the program. Test the program using 345.55 and 576.34 as the two sale amounts. Then test it using 3000 and 2500.

INTRODUCTORY

11. A-1 Appliances needs a program that allows the store clerks to enter the number of dishwashers in stock at the beginning of the month, the number purchased by the store during the month, and the number sold to customers during the month. The program should calculate and display the number of dishwashers in stock at the end of the month.

    a. Create an IPO chart for the problem, and then desk-check the algorithm twice. For the first desk-check, use 5000 as the number of dishwashers at the beginning of the month, 1000 as the number purchased, and 3500 as the number sold. For the second desk-check, use 450, 20, and 125.

    b. List the input, processing, and output items, as well as the algorithm, in a chart similar to the one shown in Figure 4-12 in the chapter. Then code the algorithm into a program.

    c. Desk-check the program using the same data used to desk-check the algorithm.

    d. If necessary, create a new project named Introductory11 Project and save it in the Cpp7\Chap04 folder. Enter your C++ instructions into a source file named Introductory11.cpp. Also enter appropriate comments and any additional instructions required by the compiler.

    e. Save and run the program. Test the program using the same data used to desk-check the program.

INTRODUCTORY

12. A concert hall has three seating categories: Orchestra, Main floor, and Balcony. Orchestra seats are $25. Main floor seats are $30, and Balcony seats are $15. The manager wants a program that allows him to enter the number of tickets sold in each seating category. The program should calculate and display the amount of revenue generated by each seating category, as well as the total revenue.

    a. Create an IPO chart for the problem, and then desk-check the algorithm twice. For the first desk-check, use 50, 100, and 75 as the number of Orchestra, Main floor, and Balcony seats, respectively. For the second desk-check, use 30, 25, and 99.

b. List the input, processing, and output items, as well as the algorithm, in a chart similar to the one shown in Figure 4-12 in the chapter. Then code the algorithm into a program.

c. Desk-check the program using the same data used to desk-check the algorithm.

d. If necessary, create a new project named Introductory12 Project and save it in the Cpp7\Chap04 folder. Enter your C++ instructions into a source file named Introductory12.cpp. Also enter appropriate comments and any additional instructions required by the compiler.

e. Save and run the program. Test the program using the same data used to desk-check the program.

INTERMEDIATE

13. The manager of Mama Calari's Pizza Palace wants a program that calculates and displays the number of slices of pizza into which a circular pizza can be divided. The manager will enter the radius of the entire pizza. For this exercise, use the number 14.13 as the area of a pizza slice, and use 3.14 as the value of pi.

a. Create an IPO chart for the problem, and then desk-check the algorithm twice. For the first desk-check, use 10 as the radius of the pizza. For the second desk-check, use 6. Hint: For the first desk-check, the number of slices should be a little over 22.

b. List the input, processing, and output items, as well as the algorithm, in a chart similar to the one shown in Figure 4-12 in the chapter. Then code the algorithm into a program.

c. Desk-check the program using the same data used to desk-check the algorithm.

d. If necessary, create a new project named Intermediate13 Project and save it in the Cpp7\Chap04 folder. Enter your C++ instructions into a source file named Intermediate13.cpp. Also enter appropriate comments and any additional instructions required by the compiler.

e. Save and run the program. Test the program using the same data used to desk-check the program.

ADVANCED

14. Complete INTRODUCTORY Exercise 12. If necessary, create a new project named Advanced14 Project and save it in the Cpp7\Chap04 folder. Enter (or copy) the instructions from the Introductory12.cpp file into a new source file named Advanced14.cpp. Modify the code in the Advanced14.cpp file so that it also calculates and displays the percentage of the total revenue contributed by each seating category. Save and run the program. Test the program using 50, 100, and 75 as the number of Orchestra, Main floor, and Balcony seats, respectively. Then test it using 30, 25, and 99. (Don't be concerned about the extra decimal places in the answers.)

ADVANCED

15. In this exercise, you explore the use of integers in monetary calculations.

a. Follow the instructions for starting C++ and opening the Advanced15.cpp file. If necessary, delete the two forward slashes that appear before the `system("pause");` statement, and then save the program. Run the program. When you are prompted to enter the gross pay, type 45.13 and press Enter. The net pay that appears on the computer screen is incorrect because it is not the result of subtracting the taxes from the gross pay. Press any key to stop the program.

b. Review the code contained in the Advanced15.cpp file. The `#include <iomanip>` directive tells the C++ compiler to include the contents of the iomanip file in the current program. The iomanip file contains the definition of the `setprecision` stream manipulator, which appears in the `cout << fixed << setprecision(2) << endl;` statement. The `fixed` stream manipulator is defined in the iostream file, and it forces a real number to display a specific number of decimal places, as specified by the `setprecision` stream manipulator. In this program, the output values will display with two decimal places. You will learn about the directive and both stream manipulators in Chapter 5.

c. Why does the net pay appear as $33.85 rather than $33.84? Hint: Change the `cout << fixed << setprecision(2) << endl;` statement to a comment, and then save and run the program. Type 45.13 as the gross pay and press Enter. Study the output, and then stop the program and change the comment back to a statement.

d. Use the comments that appear in the Advanced15.cpp file to modify the program's code. (Start with the comment on Line 14 in the program.) Why do you need to add .5 to the expressions that calculate the federal and state taxes?

e. Save, run, and test the program to verify that it is working correctly, and then stop the program.

SWAT THE BUGS

16. Follow the instructions for starting C++ and opening the SwatTheBugs16.cpp file. The program declares and initializes a `double` variable. It then adds 1.5 to the variable before displaying the variable's value. If necessary, delete the two forward slashes that appear before the `system("pause");` statement, and then save the program. Run the program. (If you are asked whether you want to run the last successful build, click the No button.) Debug the program.

Answers to TRY THIS Exercises

Pencil and Paper

1. See Figure 4-38.

IPO chart information	C++ instructions
Input	
sale1	`double sale1 = 0.0;`
sale2	`double sale2 = 0.0;`
commission rate	`double commissionRate = 0.0;`
Processing	
total sales	`double totalSales = 0.0;`
Output	
commission	`double commission = 0.0;`
Algorithm	

1. enter sale1, sale2, and the commission rate	`cout << "First sale? ";`
	`cin >> sale1;`
	`cout << "Second sale? ";`
	`cin >> sale2;`
	`cout << "Commission rate in decimal format? ";`
	`cin >> commissionRate;`

2. calculate the total sales by adding sale1 to sale2	`totalSales = sale1 + sale2;`
3. calculate the commission by multiplying the total sales by the commission rate	`commission = totalSales * commissionRate;`
4. display the commission	`cout << "Commission: $" << commission << endl;`

Figure 4-38

2. See Figure 4-39.

IPO chart information	C++ instructions
Input	
cup price	`double cupPrice = 0.0;`
plate price	`double platePrice = 0.0;`
cups purchased	`int cupsPurchased = 0;`
plates purchased	`int platesPurchased = 0;`
sales tax rate (5.5%)	`const double TAX_RATE = .055;`
Processing	
total cup cost	`double totalCupCost = 0.0;`
total plate cost	`double totalPlateCost = 0.0;`
subtotal	`double subtotal = 0.0;`
Output	
total cost	`double totalCost = 0.0;`
Algorithm	

1. enter cup price, plate price, cups purchased, and plates purchased	`cout << "Cup price: ";`
	`cin >> cupPrice;`
	`cout << "Plate price: ";`
	`cin >> platePrice;`
	`cout << "Cups purchased: ";`
	`cin >> cupsPurchased;`
	`cout << "Plates purchased: ";`
	`cin >> platesPurchased;`

2. calculate the total cup cost by multiplying the cups purchased by the cup price	`totalCupCost = cupsPurchased * cupPrice;`
3. calculate the total plate cost by multiplying the plates purchased by the plate price	`totalPlateCost = platesPurchased * platePrice;`
4. calculate the subtotal by adding the total cup cost to the total plate cost	`subtotal = totalCupCost + totalPlateCost;`
5. calculate the total cost by multiplying the subtotal by the sales tax rate and then adding the result to the subtotal	`totalCost = subtotal * TAX_RATE + subtotal;`
6. display the total cost	`cout << "Total cost: $" << totalCost << endl;`

Figure 4-39

Computer

8. See Figure 4-40.

```
//TryThis8.cpp - calculates and displays the commission
//Created/revised by <your name> on <current date>

#include <iostream>
using namespace std;

int main()
{
    //declare variables
    double sale1          = 0.0;
    double sale2          = 0.0;
    double commissionRate = 0.0;
    double totalSales     = 0.0;
    double commission     = 0.0;

    //enter input items
    cout << "First sale? ";
    cin >> sale1;
    cout << "Second sale? ";
    cin >> sale2;
    cout << "Commission rate in decimal format? ";
    cin >> commissionRate;

    //calculate total sales and commission
    totalSales = sale1 + sale2;
    commission = totalSales * commissionRate;

    //display the commission
    cout << "Commission: $" << commission << endl;

    //system("pause");
    return 0;
}   //end of main function
```

if your C++ development tool requires this statement, delete the two forward slashes

Figure 4-40

9. See Figure 4-41.

```
//TryThis9.cpp - calculates and displays the total owed
//Created/revised by <your name> on <current date>

#include <iostream>
using namespace std;

int main()
{
    //declare variables and named constant
    int cupsPurchased      = 0;
    int platesPurchased    = 0;
    double cupPrice        = 0.0;
    double platePrice      = 0.0;
    double totalCupCost    = 0.0;
    double totalPlateCost  = 0.0;
    double subtotal        = 0.0;
    double totalCost       = 0.0;
    const double TAX_RATE  = .055;

    //enter input items
    cout << "Cup price: ";
    cin >> cupPrice;
    cout << "Plate price: ";
    cin >> platePrice;
    cout << "Cups purchased: ";
    cin >> cupsPurchased;
    cout << "Plates purchased: ";
    cin >> platesPurchased;

    //calculate total cup cost, total plate
    //cost, the subtotal, and the total cost
    totalCupCost = cupsPurchased * cupPrice;
    totalPlateCost = platesPurchased * platePrice;
    subtotal = totalCupCost + totalPlateCost;
    totalCost = subtotal * TAX_RATE + subtotal;

    //display total cost
    cout << "Total cost: $" << totalCost << endl;

    //system("pause");
    return 0;
}   //end of main function
```

if your C++ development tool requires this statement, delete the two forward slashes

Figure 4-41

CHAPTER 5

The Selection Structure

After studying Chapter 5, you should be able to:

- Include the selection structure in pseudocode and in a flowchart
- Code a selection structure using the `if` statement
- Include comparison operators in a selection structure's condition
- Include logical operators in a selection structure's condition
- Format numeric output

Making Decisions

As you learned in Chapter 1, all computer programs are written using one or more of three basic control structures: sequence, selection, and repetition. You used the sequence structure in the programs you coded in Chapter 4. Recall that during runtime, the computer processed the instructions in those programs sequentially—in other words, in the order the instructions appeared in the program. Many times, however, a program will need the computer to make a decision before selecting the next instruction to process. A payroll program, for example, typically has the computer determine whether the number of hours an employee worked is greater than 40. The computer then would select either an instruction that computes regular pay only or an instruction that computes regular pay plus overtime pay. Programs that need the computer to make a decision require the use of the selection structure (also called the decision structure).

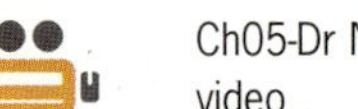

Ch05-Dr N video

The **selection structure** indicates that a decision (based on some condition) needs to be made, followed by an appropriate action derived from that decision. But how does a programmer determine whether a problem's solution requires a selection structure? The answer to this question is by studying the problem specification. The first problem specification you will examine in this chapter involves an evil scientist named Dr. N. The problem specification and an illustration of the problem are shown in Figure 5-1 along with a solution to the problem. The solution, which is written in pseudocode, requires only the sequence structure.

Problem specification
Dr. N is sitting in a chair in his lair, facing a control deck and an electronic screen. At times, visitors come to the door located at the rear of the lair. Before opening the door, which is accomplished by pressing the blue button on the control deck, Dr. N likes to view the visitor on the screen; he can do this by pressing the orange button on the control deck. Write the instructions that direct Dr. N to view the visitor first, and then open the door and say "Welcome".

1. press the orange button on the control deck to view the visitor on the screen
2. press the blue button on the control deck to open the door
3. say "Welcome"

Figure 5-1 A problem that requires the sequence structure only

Now we'll make a slight change to the problem specification shown in Figure 5-1. In this case, Dr. N should open the door only if the visitor knows the secret password. The modified problem specification and solution are shown in Figure 5-2. The solution contains both the sequence and selection structures. The selection structure's condition, which is enclosed in parentheses in the pseudocode, directs Dr. N to make a decision about the visitor's password. More specifically, he needs to determine whether the visitor's password matches the secret password. As you may remember from Chapter 1, the condition in a selection structure must be phrased so that it evaluates to either a true or a false answer. In this case, either the visitor's password matches the secret password (true) or it doesn't match the secret password (false). Only if both passwords are the same does Dr. N need to follow the two indented instructions, which are to press the blue button on the control deck to open the door and say "Welcome". The selection structure in Figure 5-2 is referred to as a **single-alternative selection structure** because it requires one or more actions to be taken *only* when its condition evaluates to true.

Other examples of single-alternative selection structures include if (it's raining), take an umbrella and if (it's night), turn your headlights on.

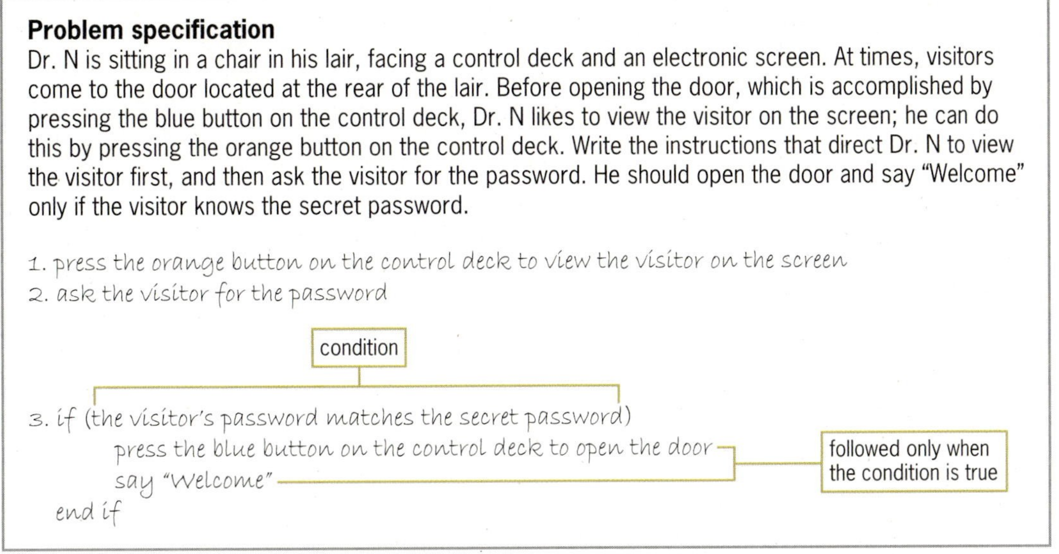

Problem specification
Dr. N is sitting in a chair in his lair, facing a control deck and an electronic screen. At times, visitors come to the door located at the rear of the lair. Before opening the door, which is accomplished by pressing the blue button on the control deck, Dr. N likes to view the visitor on the screen; he can do this by pressing the orange button on the control deck. Write the instructions that direct Dr. N to view the visitor first, and then ask the visitor for the password. He should open the door and say "Welcome" only if the visitor knows the secret password.

```
1. press the orange button on the control deck to view the visitor on the screen
2. ask the visitor for the password
3. if (the visitor's password matches the secret password)
       press the blue button on the control deck to open the door
       say "Welcome"
   end if
```


Figure 5-2 A problem that requires the sequence structure and a single-alternative selection structure

In pseudocode, programmers use the words if and end if to denote the beginning and end, respectively, of a selection structure. They also indent the instructions within the selection structure.

Figure 5-3 shows a modified version of the previous problem specification. In this version, Dr. N will say "Sorry, you are wrong" and then destroy the visitor if the passwords do not match. Also shown in Figure 5-3 are two possible solutions to the problem; both solutions produce the same result. The condition in Solution 1's selection structure determines whether the visitor's password is *correct*. If it is correct, Dr. N will open the door and welcome the visitor to his lair; otherwise, he will tell the visitor that the password is wrong and then destroy the visitor. The condition in Solution 2's selection structure, on the other hand, determines whether the visitor's password is *incorrect*. If it is incorrect, Dr. N will tell the visitor that the password is wrong and then destroy the visitor; otherwise, he will open the door and welcome the visitor to his lair.

Unlike the selection structure in Figure 5-2, which provides instructions for Dr. N to follow only when the selection structure's condition is true, the selection structures in Figure 5-3 require Dr. N to perform one set of instructions when the condition is true but a different set of instructions when the condition is false. The instructions to follow when the condition evaluates to true are called the **true path**. The true path begins with the if and ends with either the else (if there is one) or the end if. The instructions to follow when the condition evaluates to false are called the **false path**. The false path begins with the else and ends with the end if. For clarity, the instructions in each path should be indented as shown in Figure 5-3. Selection structures that contain instructions in both paths, like the ones in Figure 5-3, are referred to as **dual-alternative selection structures**.

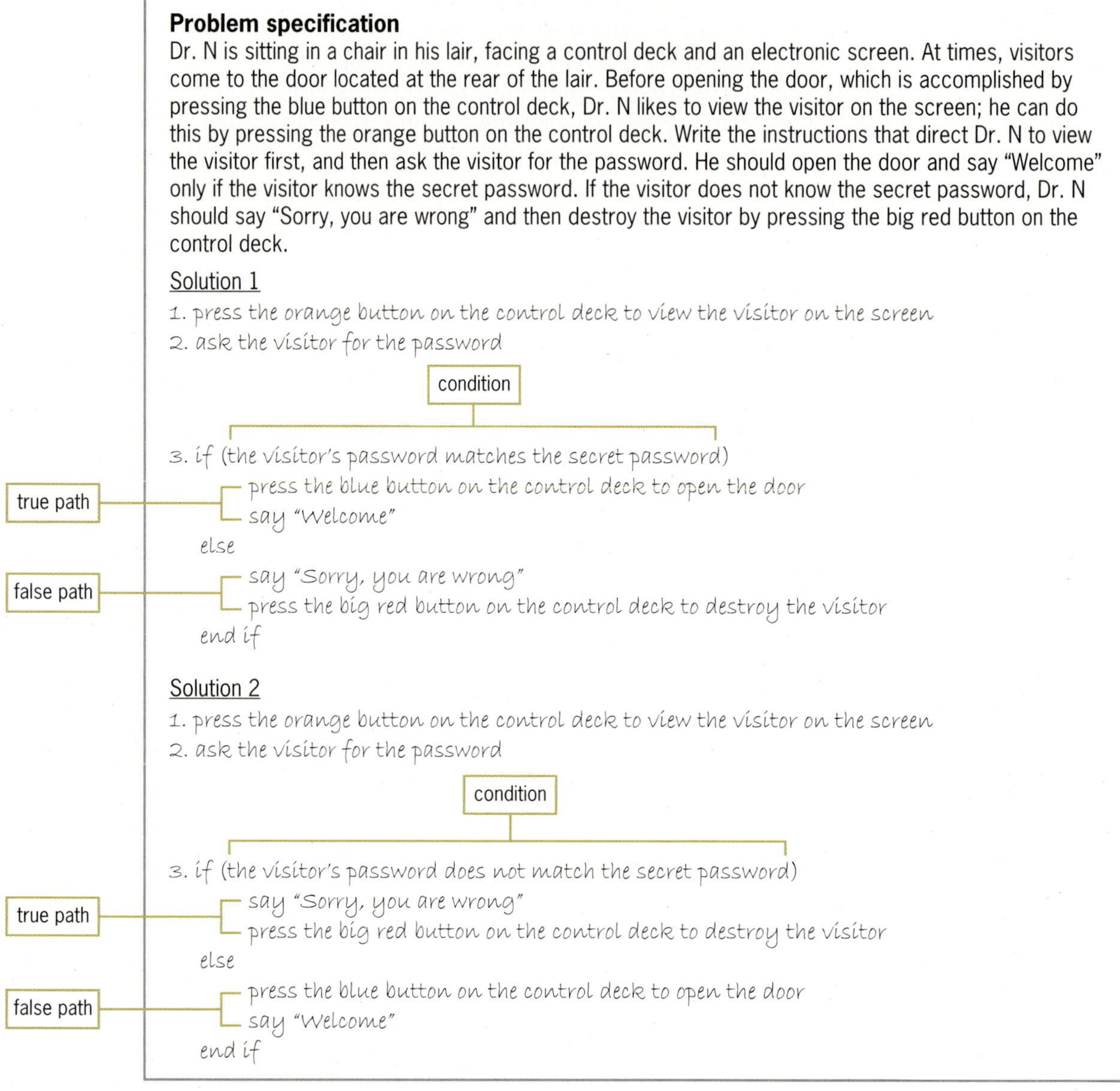

Problem specification

Dr. N is sitting in a chair in his lair, facing a control deck and an electronic screen. At times, visitors come to the door located at the rear of the lair. Before opening the door, which is accomplished by pressing the blue button on the control deck, Dr. N likes to view the visitor on the screen; he can do this by pressing the orange button on the control deck. Write the instructions that direct Dr. N to view the visitor first, and then ask the visitor for the password. He should open the door and say "Welcome" only if the visitor knows the secret password. If the visitor does not know the secret password, Dr. N should say "Sorry, you are wrong" and then destroy the visitor by pressing the big red button on the control deck.

Solution 1

```
1. press the orange button on the control deck to view the visitor on the screen
2. ask the visitor for the password
3. if (the visitor's password matches the secret password)
        press the blue button on the control deck to open the door
        say "Welcome"
   else
        say "Sorry, you are wrong"
        press the big red button on the control deck to destroy the visitor
   end if
```


Solution 2

```
1. press the orange button on the control deck to view the visitor on the screen
2. ask the visitor for the password
3. if (the visitor's password does not match the secret password)
        say "Sorry, you are wrong"
        press the big red button on the control deck to destroy the visitor
   else
        press the blue button on the control deck to open the door
        say "Welcome"
   end if
```


Figure 5-3 A problem that requires the sequence structure and a dual-alternative selection structure

Flowcharting a Selection Structure

As you learned in Chapter 2, many programmers use flowcharts (rather than pseudocode) when planning solutions to problems. Unlike pseudocode, which consists of short phrases, a flowchart uses standardized symbols to show the steps needed to accomplish a task. Figures 5-4 and 5-5 show two problem specifications along with the correct solutions in flowchart form. Recall that the oval in a flowchart is the start/stop symbol, the rectangle is the process symbol, and the parallelogram is the input/output symbol. The diamond in a flowchart is called the **decision symbol** because it is used to represent the condition (decision) in both the selection and repetition structures. The diamonds in Figures 5-4 and 5-5 represent the condition in a selection structure. (You will learn how to use the diamond to represent a repetition structure's condition in Chapter 7.)

The flowchart in Figure 5-4 contains a single-alternative selection structure. You can tell that it's a single-alternative selection structure because it requires a special set of actions to be taken only when its condition evaluates to true. Figure 5-5's flowchart contains a dual-alternative selection structure. You can tell that it's a dual-alternative selection structure because it requires two different sets of actions: one to be taken only when its condition evaluates to true, and the other to be taken only when its condition evaluates to false.

The condition in Figure 5-4's diamond checks whether the customer purchased more than five items. It's necessary to do this because the customer receives a 10% discount when more than five items are purchased. The condition in Figure 5-5's diamond, on the other hand, determines whether Mary's sales are at least $15,000. In this case, the result (either true or false) determines whether Mary receives a 2% or 1.5% bonus. Notice that the conditions in both diamonds evaluate to either true or false only. Also notice that both diamonds have one flowline entering the symbol and two flowlines leaving the symbol. One of the flowlines leading out of a diamond in a flowchart should be marked with a "T" (for true) and the other should be marked with an "F" (for false). The "T" flowline points to the next instruction to be processed when the condition evaluates to true. In Figure 5-4, the next instruction calculates the 10% discount; in Figure 5-5, it calculates the 2% bonus. The "F" flowline points to the next instruction to be processed when the condition evaluates to false. In Figure 5-4, that instruction displays the total owed; in Figure 5-5, it calculates the 1.5% bonus. You also can mark the flowlines leading out of a diamond with a "Y" and an "N" (for yes and no).

Problem specification
Jerrili's Trading Store wants a program that allows a salesclerk to enter an item's price and the quantity purchased by a customer. The store gives the customer a 10% discount when the quantity purchased is over 5. The program should calculate and display the total amount the customer owes.

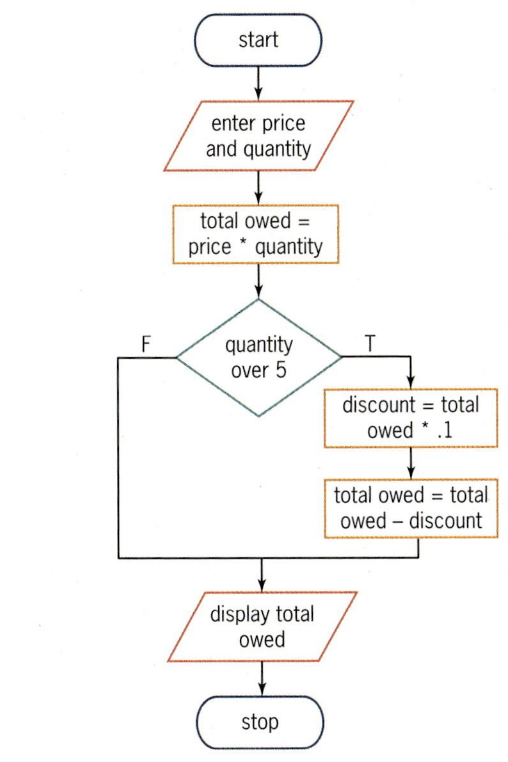

Figure 5-4 Flowchart showing a single-alternative selection structure

For more experience in examining problem specifications, see the Problem Specifications section in the Ch05WantMore.pdf file.

Problem specification
Mary Kettleson wants a program that calculates and displays her annual bonus, given her annual sales amount. Mary receives a 2% bonus when her annual sales are at least $15,000; otherwise, she receives a 1.5% bonus.

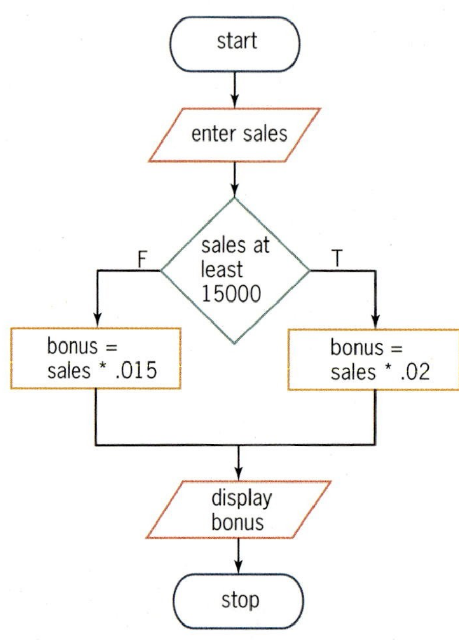

Figure 5-5 Flowchart showing a dual-alternative selection structure

The answers to Mini-Quiz questions are located in Appendix A.

Mini-Quiz 5-1

1. Most programmers use the words ______ to denote the end of a selection structure in pseudocode.
2. The true path in a selection structure can contain only one instruction.
   a. True
   b. False
3. Which of the following is the decision symbol in a flowchart?
   a. diamond
   b. oval
   c. parallelogram
   d. rectangle
4. A problem specification states that only customers who live in California are charged sales tax. Which type of selection structure would the solution to this problem require?
   a. dual-alternative
   b. single-alternative
5. A problem specification states that salespeople who sell more than $10,000 in product receive a 10% commission. All other salespeople receive a 5% commission. Which type of selection structure would the solution to this problem require?
   a. dual-alternative
   b. single-alternative

Coding a Selection Structure in C++

In most C++ programs, you will use the `if` statement to code single-alternative and dual-alternative selection structures. The statement's syntax is shown in Figure 5-6. The square brackets in the syntax indicate that the `else` portion, referred to as the `else` clause, is optional. Recall, however, that boldfaced items in a statement's syntax are required. In this case, the keyword `if` and the parentheses that surround the condition are required. The keyword `else` is necessary only in a dual-alternative selection structure.

Italicized items in the syntax indicate where the programmer must supply information. In the `if` statement, the programmer must supply the condition that the computer needs to evaluate before further processing can occur. The condition must be a Boolean expression, which is an expression that results in a Boolean value (true or false). Besides providing the condition, the programmer must provide the statements to be processed in the true path and (optionally) in the false path. If a path contains more than one statement, the statements must be entered as a **statement block**, which means they must be enclosed in a set of braces ({}).

Ch05-if Statement video

Although not a requirement, it is a good programming practice to use a comment (such as `//end if`) to mark the end of the `if` statement in a program. The comment will make your program easier to read and understand. It also will help you keep track of the required `if` and `else` clauses when you nest `if` statements—in other words, when you include one `if` statement inside another `if` statement. You will learn how to nest `if` statements in Chapter 6.

The six examples in Figure 5-6 show various ways of using the `if` statement to code selection structures. Examples 1 and 2 are single-alternative selection structures. The remaining four examples are dual-alternative selection structures. Notice that when a path contains multiple statements, the statements are entered as a statement block by enclosing them in braces. Although not shown in Figure 5-6, you also can include the braces even when a path contains only one statement. By doing this, you won't need to remember to enter the braces when statements are added subsequently to the path. Forgetting to enter the braces is a common error made when typing the `if` statement in a C++ program.

HOW TO Use the `if` Statement

Syntax

if (*condition***)**
    one or more statements to be processed when the condition is true
[**else**
    one or more statements to be processed when the condition is false]
`//end if`

Example 1—one statement in only the true path

```
if (condition)
      one statement
//end if
```

Example 2—multiple statements in only the true path

```
if (condition)
{
      multiple statements enclosed in braces
}     //end if
```

(continues)

Figure 5-6 How to use the `if` statement

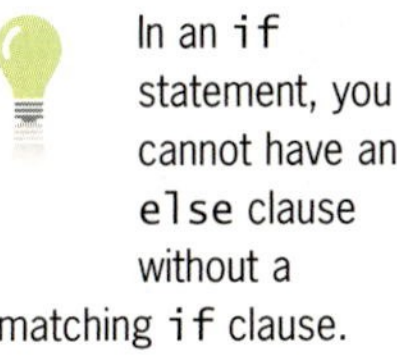

In an `if` statement, you cannot have an `else` clause without a matching `if` clause.

(continued)

Example 3—one statement in each path

```
if (condition)
      one statement
else
      one statement
//end if
```

Example 4—multiple statements in the true path and one statement in the false path

```
if (condition)
{
      multiple statements enclosed in braces
}
else
      one statement
//end if
```

Example 5—one statement in the true path and multiple statements in the false path

```
if (condition)
      one statement
else
{
      multiple statements enclosed in braces
} //end if
```

Example 6—multiple statements in both paths

```
if (condition)
{
      multiple statements enclosed in braces
}
else
{
      multiple statements enclosed in braces
} //end if
```

Figure 5-6 How to use the `if` statement

As mentioned earlier, an `if` statement's condition must be a Boolean expression, which is an expression that evaluates to either true or false. The expression can contain variables, constants, arithmetic operators, comparison operators, and logical operators. You already know about variables, constants, and arithmetic operators. You will learn about comparison operators and logical operators in this chapter. We'll begin with comparison operators.

Comparison Operators

The C++ operators listed in Figure 5-7 are called **comparison operators** (also referred to as relational operators). Comparison operators are used in expressions to compare two values having the same data type. Expressions containing a comparison operator always evaluate to a Boolean value: either true or false. The precedence numbers in the figure indicate the order in which the computer performs comparisons in an expression. Comparisons with a precedence number of 1 are performed before comparisons with a precedence number of 2; however, you can use parentheses to override the order of precedence.

Notice that four of the C++ comparison operators contain two symbols. When entering these operators, be sure you do not enter a space between the symbols and be sure to enter both symbols in the exact order shown in Figure 5-7. Also included in Figure 5-7 are examples of using comparison operators in an `if` statement's condition.

HOW TO Use Comparison Operators in an `if` Statement's Condition

Operator	Operation	Precedence number
<	less than	1
<=	less than or equal to	1
>	greater than	1
>=	greater than or equal to	1
==	equal to	2
!=	not equal to	2

<u>Examples</u> (All of the variables have the `int` data type.)

```
if (quantity < 50)
if (age >= 25)
if (onhand == target)
if (quantity != 7500)
```

Figure 5-7 How to use comparison operators in an `if` statement's condition

Keep in mind that == (equal to) is the opposite of != (not equal to), > (greater than) is the opposite of <= (less than or equal to), and < (less than) is the opposite of >= (greater than or equal to).

As Figure 5-7 indicates, you use two equal signs (==) to test for equality in C++. To test for inequality, you use an exclamation point (which stands for *not*) followed by an equal sign, like this: !=. Keep in mind that you should never use either the equality operator (==) or the inequality operator (!=) to compare two real numbers. Because some real numbers cannot be stored precisely in memory, the numbers should never be compared for equality or inequality. Instead, you should test that the difference between the real numbers you are comparing is less than some acceptable small value, such as .00001. You will learn how to determine whether two real numbers are equal in Computer Exercise 15 at the end of this chapter.

Numbers are compared using their binary equivalents.

When an expression contains more than one comparison operator with the same precedence number, the computer evaluates the comparison operators from left to right in the expression, similar to what is done with arithmetic operators. Comparison operators are evaluated after any arithmetic operators in an expression. For example, when processing the expression 5 - 2 > 1 + 2, the computer will evaluate the two arithmetic operators before it evaluates the comparison operator. The result of the expression is the Boolean value false, as shown in Figure 5-8.

Original expression	5 - 2 > 1 + 2
The subtraction is performed first	3 > 1 + 2
The addition is performed next	3 > 3
The > comparison is performed last	`false`

Figure 5-8 Evaluation steps for an expression containing arithmetic and comparison operators

It is easy to confuse the equality operator (==) with the assignment operator (=). You use the equality operator to compare two values to determine whether they are equal, as in the condition in the following `if` clause: `if (num == 1)`. You use the assignment operator, on the other hand, to assign a value to a memory location. An example of this is the statement `num = 1;`. In the next two sections, you will view programs that contain a comparison operator in an `if` statement's condition.

Swapping Numeric Values

Figure 5-9 shows the IPO chart information and C++ code for a program that displays the lowest and highest of two integers entered by the user. The program contains a single-alternative selection structure. The `firstNum > secondNum` condition in the `if` clause compares the contents of the `firstNum` variable with the contents of the `secondNum` variable. If the value in the `firstNum` variable is greater than the value in the `secondNum` variable, the condition evaluates to true and the four instructions in the `if` statement's true path swap both values. Swapping the values places the smaller number in the `firstNum` variable and places the larger number in the `secondNum` variable.

Ch05-Swapping video

Notice that the four instructions in the `if` statement's true path are enclosed in braces. As you learned earlier, when more than one instruction needs to be processed when the `if` statement's condition is true, the C++ syntax requires those instructions to be entered as a statement block. If the condition in the `if` clause in Figure 5-9 evaluates to false, the instructions in the true path are skipped over because the `firstNum` variable already contains a number that is smaller than (or possibly equal to) the number stored in the `secondNum` variable.

IPO chart information	C++ instructions
Input	
first number	`int firstNum = 0;`
second number	`int secondNum = 0;`
Processing	
none	
Output	
first number (lowest)	
second number (highest)	
Algorithm	

1. enter the first number and the second number	`cout << "Enter an integer: ";`
	`cin >> firstNum;`
	`cout << "Enter another integer: ";`
	`cin >> secondNum;`

2. if (the first number is greater than the second number)
swap the numbers so that the first number is the lowest number
end if
	`if (firstNum > secondNum)`
	`{`
	`int temp = 0;`
	`temp = firstNum;`
	`firstNum = secondNum;`
	`secondNum = temp;`
	`}  //end if`

3. display the first number and the second number	`cout << "Lowest: " <<`
	`firstNum << endl;`
	`cout << "Highest: " <<`
	`secondNum << endl;`

Figure 5-9 IPO chart information and C++ instructions for the swapping program

The shaded instructions in Figure 5-9 swap the values stored in the `firstNum` and `secondNum` variables. The first instruction, `int temp = 0;`, declares and initializes a variable named `temp`. Because the `temp` variable is declared in the `if` statement's true path, it can be used only by the instructions within that path. More specifically, it can be used only by the instructions that follow its declaration statement within the true path. A variable that can be used only within the statement block in which it is defined is referred to as a **local variable**. In this case, the `temp` variable is local to the `if` statement's true path.

You may be wondering why the `temp` variable was not declared at the beginning of the `main` function, along with the `firstNum` and `secondNum` variables. Although there is nothing wrong with declaring the `temp` variable in that location, there is no reason to create the variable until it is needed, which (in this case) is only when a swap is necessary. (You will learn more about local variables in Chapter 9.)

The second instruction in the `if` statement's true path, `temp = firstNum;`, assigns the value in the `firstNum` variable to the `temp` variable. If you do not store the `firstNum` variable's value in the `temp` variable, the value will be lost when the computer processes the next statement, `firstNum = secondNum;`, which replaces the contents of the `firstNum` variable with the contents of the `secondNum` variable. Finally, the `secondNum = temp;` instruction assigns the `temp` variable's value to the `secondNum` variable; this completes the swap.

Figure 5-10 illustrates the concept of swapping, assuming the user enters the numbers 10 and 3. Figures 5-11 and 5-12 show the corresponding flowchart and a sample run of the number swapping program.

	firstNum	secondNum	temp
values stored in the variables after the `cin` and `int temp = 0;` statements are processed	10	3	0
result of the `temp = firstNum;` statement	10	3	10
result of the `firstNum = secondNum;` statement	3	3	10
result of the `secondNum = temp;` statement	3	10	10

the values were swapped

Figure 5-10 Illustration of the swapping concept

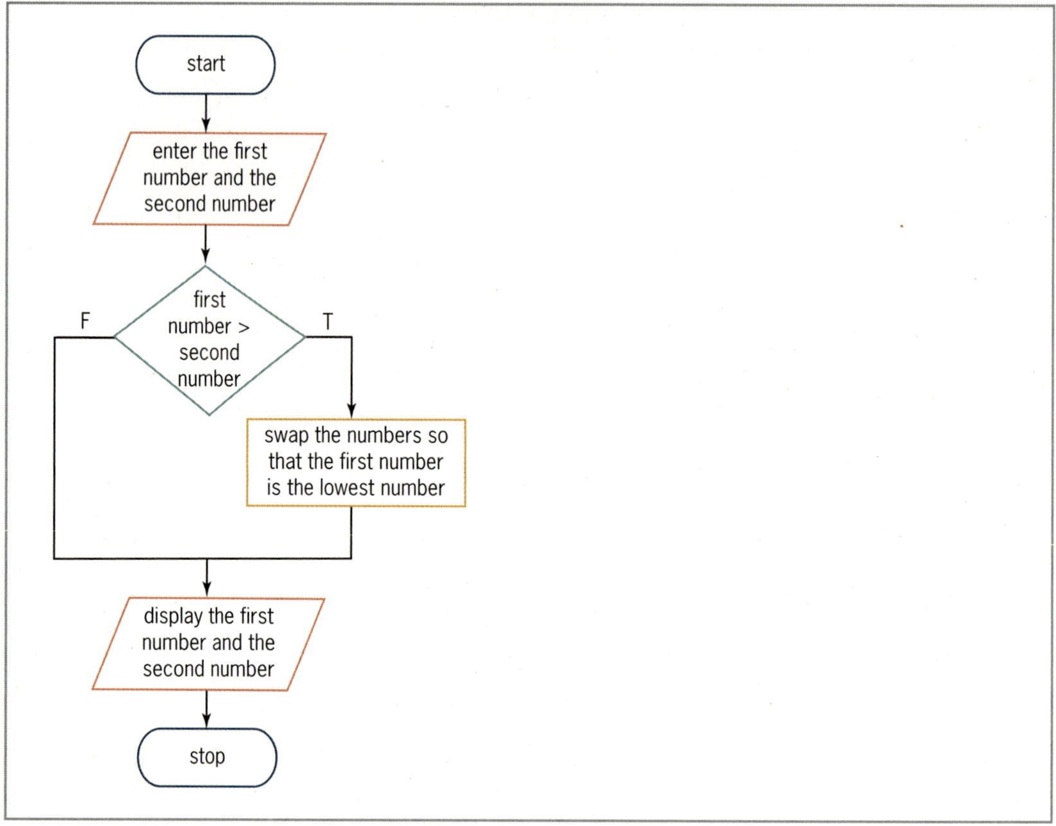

Figure 5-11 Flowchart for the swapping program

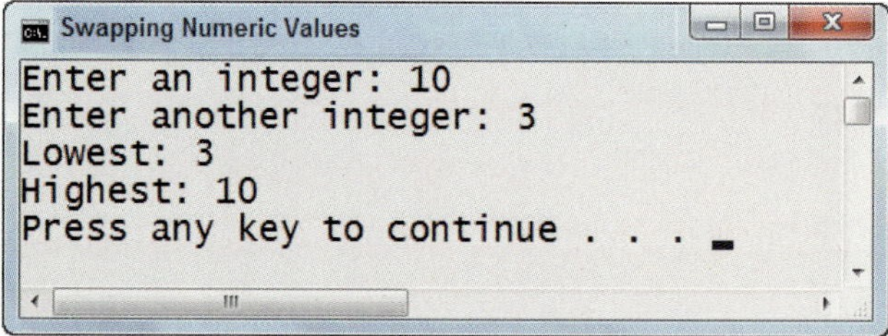

Figure 5-12 Sample run of the swapping program

Displaying the Sum or Difference

Figure 5-13 shows the IPO chart information and C++ code for a program that displays either the sum of or difference between two numbers entered by the user. The program contains a dual-alternative selection structure. The program uses an `int` variable named `operation` and three `double` variables named `janSales`, `febSales`, and `answer`. The program prompts the user to enter either the number 1 (for addition) or the number 2 (for subtraction); it stores the user's response in the `operation` variable. The program then prompts the user to enter two sales amounts, which it stores in the `janSales` and `febSales` variables.

After the program in Figure 5-13 gets the input items from the user, the `operation == 1` condition in the `if` clause compares the contents of the `operation` variable with the number 1. The condition will evaluate to true only when the user enters the number 1. It will evaluate to false when the user enters anything other than the number 1. If the condition evaluates to true, the instructions in the selection structure's true path calculate and display the sum of the sales amounts stored in the `janSales` and `febSales` variables. If the condition evaluates to false, the instructions in the selection structure's false path calculate and display the difference between the two sales amounts. Notice that the instructions in each path are entered as a statement block. Figures 5-14 and 5-15 show the corresponding flowchart and a sample run of the sum or difference program.

IPO chart information	C++ instructions
Input	
operation	`int operation = 0;`
January sales	`double janSales = 0.0;`
February sales	`double febSales = 0.0;`
Processing	
none	
Output	
either the sum of or the difference between the January sales and February sales	`double answer = 0.0;`
Algorithm	

1. enter the operation, January sales, and February sales	`cout << "Enter 1 (add) or 2 (subtract): ";`
	`cin >> operation;`
	`cout << "January sales: ";`
	`cin >> janSales;`
	`cout << "February sales: ";`
	`cin >> febSales;`

2. if (the operation is 1)	`if (operation == 1)` `{`
calculate the answer by adding the January sales to the February sales	`answer = janSales + febSales;`
display "Sum:" and the answer	`cout << "Sum: " << answer << endl;` `}`
else	`else` `{`
calculate the answer by subtracting the February sales from the January sales	`answer = janSales - febSales;`
display "Difference:" and the answer	`cout << "Difference: " << answer << endl;`
end if	`} //end if`

Figure 5-13 IPO chart information and C++ instructions for the sum or difference program

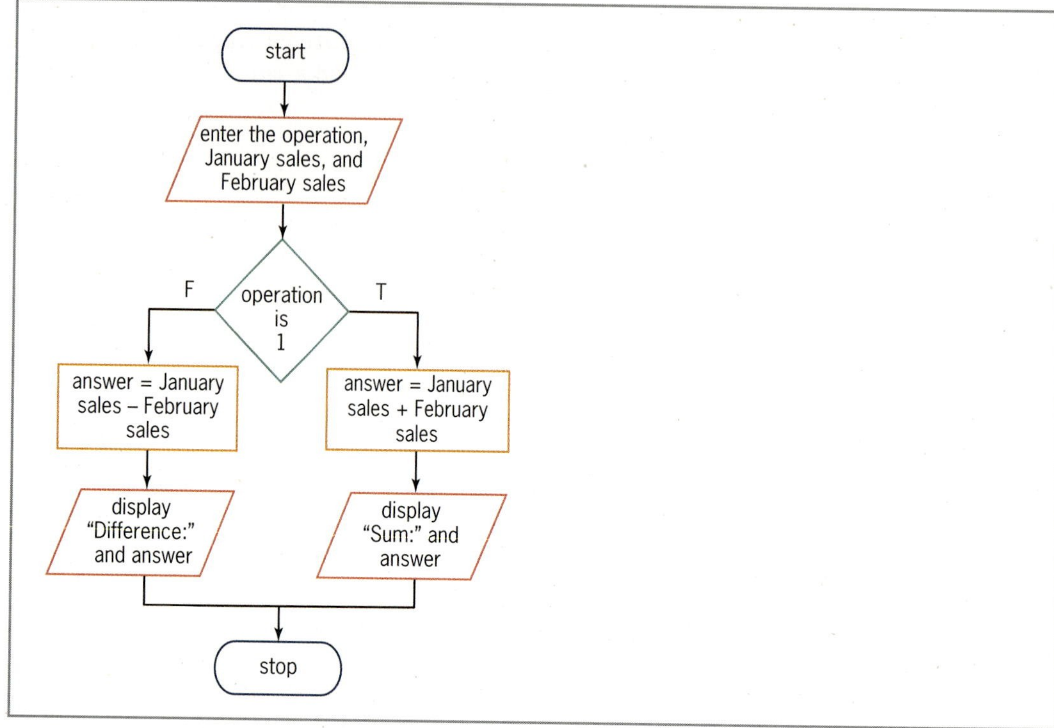

Figure 5-14 Flowchart for the sum or difference program

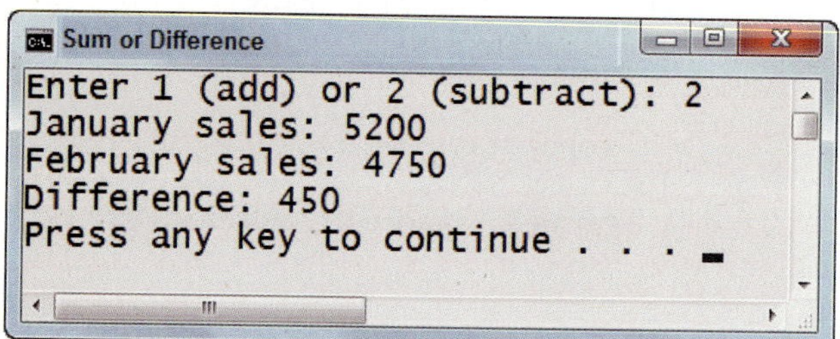

Figure 5-15 Sample run of the sum or difference program

The answers to Mini-Quiz questions are located in Appendix A.

Mini-Quiz 5-2

1. You create a statement block by enclosing one or more statements in ________.
   a. parentheses
   b. square brackets
   c. quotation marks
   d. none of the above
2. Which of the following determines whether an `int` variable named `quantity` contains the number 100?
   a. `if (quantity = 100)`
   b. `if quantity = 100`
   c. `if (quantity == 100)`
   d. none of the above

3. Which of the following determines whether the value contained in the `sales` variable is at least $300.99?

   a. `if (sales >= 300.99)`
   b. `if (sales => 300.99)`
   c. `if (sales > = 300.99)`
   d. both a and c

4. Which of the following is the inequality operator in C++?

   a. &=
   b. =/
   c. !=
   d. none of the above

5. Which of the following is the opposite of the < operator?

   a. <=
   b. >=
   c. =>
   d. >

Logical Operators

You also can use logical operators in an `if` statement's condition. **Logical operators** allow you to combine two or more conditions, referred to as sub-conditions, into one compound condition. Logical operators sometimes are referred to as **Boolean operators** because the compound condition in which they are contained always evaluates to either true or false only.

Figure 5-16 lists the two most commonly used logical operators: And and Or. When the And logical operator is used to create a compound condition, *all* of the sub-conditions must be true for the compound condition to be true. However, when the Or logical operator is used, only *one* of the sub-conditions must be true for the compound condition to be true. C++ uses special symbols to represent the And and Or logical operators in a program. The And operator in C++ is two ampersands (&&); the Or operator is two pipe symbols (||). On most computer keyboards, the pipe symbol (|) is located on the same key as the backslash (\).

Figure 5-16 also shows the order of precedence for the And and Or operators, as well as examples of using the operators in an `if` statement's condition. Notice that the compound condition in each example evaluates to either true or false only. Logical operators are evaluated after any arithmetic or comparison operators in an expression.

HOW TO Use Logical Operators in an `if` Statement's Condition

Operator	Operation	Precedence number
And (&&)	*all* sub-conditions must be true for the compound condition to evaluate to true	1
Or (||)	only *one* of the sub-conditions needs to be true for the compound condition to evaluate to true	2

(continues)

Figure 5-16 How to use logical operators in an `if` statement's condition

(continued)

Example 1
```
int quantity = 0;
cin >> quantity;
if (quantity > 0 && quantity < 50)
```
The compound condition evaluates to true when the number stored in the `quantity` variable is greater than 0 and, at the same time, less than 50; otherwise, it evaluates to false.

Example 2
```
int age = 0;
cin >> age;
if (age == 21 || age > 55)
```
The compound condition evaluates to true when the number stored in the `age` variable is either equal to 21 or greater than 55; otherwise, it evaluates to false.

Example 3
```
int quantity = 0;
double price = 0.0;
cin >> quantity;
cin >> price;
if (quantity < 100 && price < 10.35)
```
The compound condition evaluates to true when the number stored in the `quantity` variable is less than 100 and, at the same time, the number stored in the `price` variable is less than 10.35; otherwise, it evaluates to false.

Example 4
```
int quantity = 0;
double price = 0.0;
cin >> quantity;
cin >> price;
if (quantity > 0 && quantity < 100 || price > 34.55)
```
The compound condition evaluates to true when either (or both) of the following is true: the number stored in the `quantity` variable is between 0 and 100 or the number stored in the `price` variable is greater than 34.55; otherwise, it evaluates to false. (The && operator is evaluated before the || operator because it has a higher precedence.)

Figure 5-16 How to use logical operators in an `if` statement's condition

You already are familiar with logical operators because you use them on a daily basis. Examples of this include the following: *if (you finished your homework and you studied for tomorrow's exam), watch a movie*; *if (your cell phone rings and (it's your spouse calling or it's your child calling)), answer the phone*; and *if (it's raining or it's foggy or there is bug splatter on your windshield), turn your wipers on.*

As mentioned earlier, all expressions containing a logical operator result in an answer of either true or false only. The tables shown in Figure 5-17, called **truth tables**, summarize how the computer evaluates the logical operators in an expression. As the figure indicates, when you use the And operator to combine two sub-conditions (sub-condition1 && sub-condition2), the resulting compound condition is true only when both sub-conditions are true. If either sub-condition is false or if both sub-conditions are false, then the compound condition is false. However, when you use the Or operator to combine two sub-conditions (sub-condition1 || sub-condition2), the compound condition is false only when both sub-conditions are false. If either sub-condition is true or if both sub-conditions are true, then the compound condition is true.

Truth table for the And (&&) operator

sub-condition1	sub-condition2	sub-condition1 && sub-condition2
true	true	true
true	false	false
false	true (not evaluated)	false
false	false (not evaluated)	false

Truth table for the Or (||) operator

sub-condition1	sub-condition2	sub-condition1 || sub-condition2
true	true (not evaluated)	true
true	false (not evaluated)	true
false	true	true
false	false	false

Figure 5-17 Truth tables for the logical operators

As indicated in Figure 5-17, when the computer evaluates the "sub-condition1 && sub-condition2" expression, it will not evaluate sub-condition2 when sub-condition1 is false. Because both sub-conditions combined with the And operator need to be true for the compound condition to be true, there is no need to evaluate sub-condition2 when sub-condition1 is false. When the computer evaluates the "sub-condition1 || sub-condition2" expression, on the other hand, it will not evaluate sub-condition2 when sub-condition1 is true. Because only one of the sub-conditions combined with the Or operator needs to be true for the compound condition to be true, there is no need to evaluate sub-condition2 when sub-condition1 is true. The concept of evaluating sub-condition2 based on the result of sub-condition1 is referred to as **short-circuit evaluation**.

Using the Truth Tables

A program needs to calculate a bonus for each A-rated salesperson whose monthly sales are more than $5,000. The program uses a `char` variable named `rating` and an `int` variable named `sales` to store the salesperson's rating and sales amount, respectively. Therefore, you can phrase sub-condition1 as `rating == 'A'` and phrase sub-condition2 as `sales > 5000`. (Notice that the values being compared in each sub-condition have the same data type.) Which logical operator should you use to combine both sub-conditions into one compound condition? Let's use the truth tables from Figure 5-17 to answer this question.

For a salesperson to receive a bonus, both sub-condition1 and sub-condition2 must be true at the same time. If either sub-condition is false or if both sub-conditions are false, then the compound condition should be false and the salesperson should not receive a bonus. According to the truth tables, both logical operators evaluate a compound condition as true when both sub-conditions are true. However, only the And operator evaluates a compound condition as false when either one or both of the sub-conditions are false. Therefore, the correct compound condition to use here is `rating == 'A' && sales > 5000`.

Now assume you want to send a letter to all A-rated salespeople and all B-rated salespeople. If the rating is stored in the `rating` variable, you can phrase sub-condition1 as `rating == 'A'` and phrase sub-condition2 as `rating == 'B'`. Now which logical operator should you use to combine both sub-conditions? At first it might appear that the And operator is the correct one to use because the example says to send the letter to "all A-rated salespeople and all B-rated salespeople." In everyday conversations, people sometimes use the word *and* when what they really mean is *or*. Although both words do not mean the same thing, using *and* instead of *or* generally does not cause a problem because we are able to infer what another person means. Computers, however, cannot infer anything; they simply process the directions you give them, word for word. In this case, you actually want to send a letter to all salespeople with either an A or a B rating (a salesperson can have only one rating), so you will need to use the Or operator. As the truth tables indicate, the Or operator is the only operator that evaluates the compound condition as true when at least one of the sub-conditions is true. Therefore, the correct compound condition to use in this case is `rating == 'A' || rating == 'B'`. In the next two sections, you will view programs that contain a logical operator in an `if` statement's condition.

Calculating Gross Pay

A program needs to calculate and display an employee's gross pay. To keep this example simple, no one at the company works more than 40 hours per week and everyone earns the same hourly rate, $10. Before making the gross pay calculation, the program should verify that the number of hours entered by the user is greater than or equal to 0 but less than or equal to 40. Programmers refer to the process of verifying that the input data is within the expected range as **data validation**. If the number of hours is valid, the program should calculate and display the gross pay. Otherwise, it should display an error message alerting the user that the number of hours is incorrect.

You can use either of the examples in Figure 5-18 to code the gross pay program. Both examples contain a dual-alternative selection structure whose compound condition includes a logical operator. The compound condition in Example 1 uses the And operator to determine whether the value stored in the `hoursWorked` variable is greater than or equal to 0 and, at the same time, less than or equal to 40. If the compound condition evaluates to true, the selection structure's true path calculates and displays the gross pay; otherwise, its false path displays the "Incorrect number of hours" message. The compound condition in Example 2, on the other hand, uses the Or operator to determine whether the value stored in the `hoursWorked` variable is either less than 0 or greater than 40. If the compound condition evaluates to true, the selection structure's true path displays the "Incorrect number of hours" message; otherwise, its false path calculates and displays the gross pay.

Both examples in Figure 5-18 produce the same result and simply represent two different ways of performing the same task. Figures 5-19 and 5-20 show sample runs of a program that contains the code shown in either of the examples in Figure 5-18.

Example 1

```
//declare constant and variables
const int PAY_RATE = 10;
int hoursWorked    = 0;
int grossPay       = 0;

//enter input items
cout << "Hours worked (0 through 40): ";
cin >> hoursWorked;

//calculate and display output
if (hoursWorked >= 0 && hoursWorked <= 40)
{
    grossPay = hoursWorked * PAY_RATE;
    cout << "Gross pay: $" << grossPay << endl;
}
else
    cout << "Incorrect number of hours" << endl;
//end if
```

And operator

Example 2

```
//declare constant and variables
const int PAY_RATE =  10;
int hoursWorked    =  0;
int grossPay       =  0;

//enter input items
cout << "Hours worked (0 through 40): ";
cin >> hoursWorked;

//calculate and display output

if (hoursWorked < 0 || hoursWorked > 40)
    cout << "Incorrect number of hours" << endl;
else
{
    grossPay = hoursWorked * PAY_RATE;
    cout << "Gross pay: $" << grossPay << endl;
}   //end if
```

Or operator

Figure 5-18 Examples of C++ instructions for the gross pay program

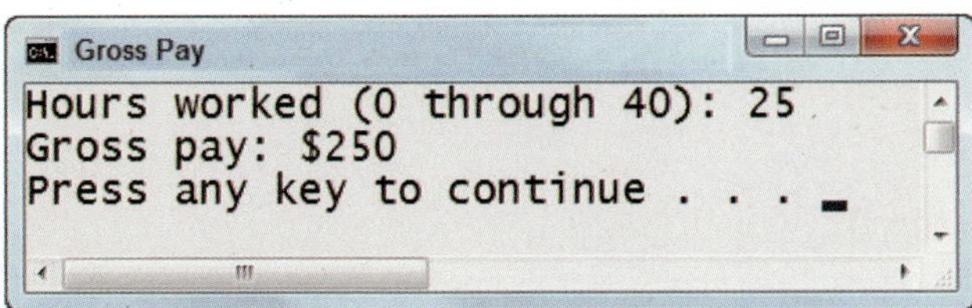

Figure 5-19 First sample run of the gross pay program's code

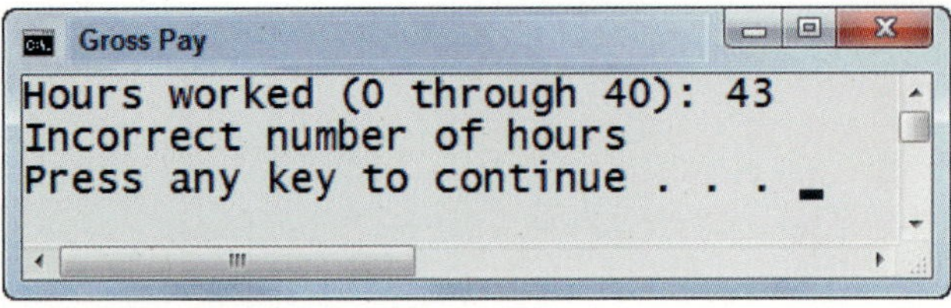

Figure 5-20 Second sample run of the gross pay program's code

Pass/Fail Program

A program needs to display the word "Pass" when the user enters the letter P (in either uppercase or lowercase) and display the word "Fail" when the user enters anything else. You can use either of the examples in Figure 5-21 to code the program. Both examples contain a dual-alternative selection structure. The compound condition in Example 1 uses the Or operator to determine whether the character stored in the `letter` variable is either the uppercase letter P or the lowercase letter p. When the variable contains one of those two letters, the compound condition evaluates to true and the selection structure's true path displays the word "Pass" on the screen; otherwise, its false path displays the word "Fail". The compound condition in Example 2, on the other hand, uses the And operator to determine whether the value in the `letter` variable is not equal to the uppercase letter P and also not equal to the lowercase letter p. When the variable does not contain either of those two letters, the compound condition evaluates to true and the selection structure's true path displays the word "Fail" on the screen; otherwise, its false path displays the word "Pass".

Example 1

```
//declare variable
char letter = ' ';

//enter input item, then display message
cout << "Enter a letter: ";
cin >> letter;

if (letter == 'P' || letter == 'p')
    cout << "Pass" << endl;
else
    cout << "Fail" << endl;
//end if
```

Or operator

character literal constants are enclosed in single quotation marks

string literal constants are enclosed in double quotation marks

Example 2

```
//declare variable
char letter = ' ';

//enter input item, then display message
cout << "Enter a letter: ";
cin >> letter;

if (letter != 'P' && letter != 'p')
    cout << "Fail" << endl;
else
    cout << "Pass" << endl;
//end if
```

And operator

Figure 5-21 Examples of C++ instructions for the Pass/Fail program

You may be wondering why you need to compare the contents of the `letter` variable with both the uppercase and lowercase forms of the letter P. As is true in many programming languages, character comparisons in C++ are case sensitive, which means that the uppercase version of a letter is not the same as its lowercase counterpart. So, although a human being recognizes P and p as being the same letter, a computer does not; to a computer, a P is different from a p. You learned the reason for this differentiation in Chapter 3. Recall that each character on a computer keyboard is assigned a unique ASCII code, which is stored in the computer's internal memory using a group of 0s and 1s. The ASCII code for the uppercase letter P is 80 and is stored using the eight bits 01010000. The ASCII code for the lowercase letter p, on the other hand, is 112 and is stored using the eight bits 01110000. (The full ASCII chart is contained in Appendix C in this book.) Figures 5-22 and 5-23 show sample runs of a program that contains the code shown in either of the examples in Figure 5-21.

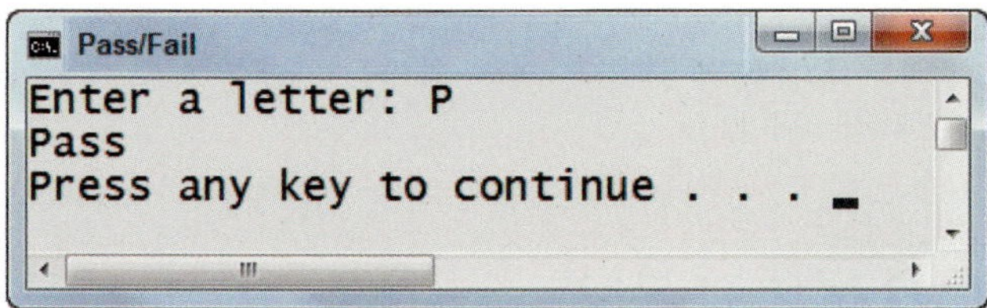

Figure 5-22 First sample run of the Pass/Fail program's code

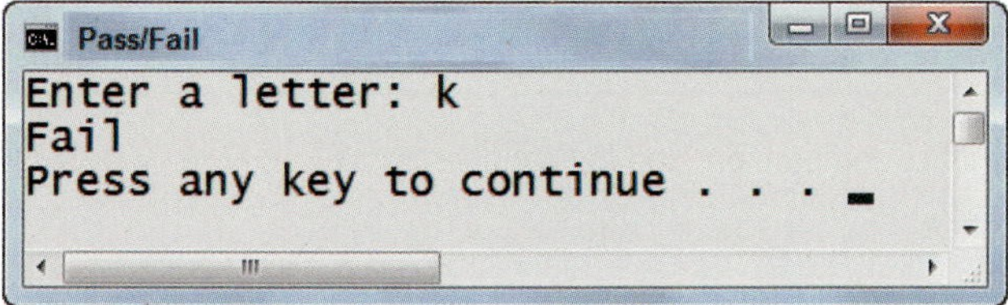

Figure 5-23 Second sample run of the Pass/Fail program's code

Summary of Operators

Figure 5-24 shows the order of precedence for the arithmetic, comparison, and logical operators you have learned so far. Recall that operators with the same precedence number are evaluated from left to right in an expression. Notice that logical operators are evaluated after any arithmetic operators or comparison operators in an expression. As a result, when the computer processes the expression 30 > 75 / 3 && 5 < 10 * 2, it evaluates the arithmetic operators first, followed by the comparison operators, and then the logical operator. The expression evaluates to true, as shown in the example included in the figure.

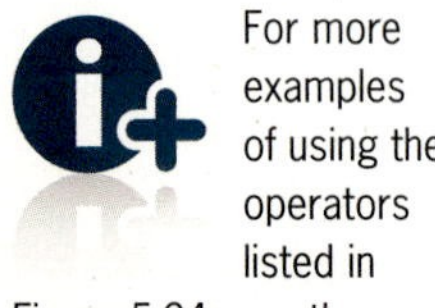

Ch05-Fig5-24 video

Operator	Operation	Precedence number
( )	override normal precedence rules	1
–	negation (reverses the sign of a number)	2
*, /, %	multiplication, division, and modulus arithmetic	3
+, –	addition and subtraction	4
<, <=, >, >=	less than, less than or equal to, greater than, greater than or equal to	5
==, !=	equal to, not equal to	6
And (&&)	*all* sub-conditions must be true for the compound condition to evaluate to true	7
Or (||)	only *one* of the sub-conditions needs to be true for the compound condition to evaluate to true	8

Example

Original expression	30 > 75 / 3 && 5 < 10 * 2
75 / 3 is evaluated first	30 > 25 && 5 < 10 * 2
10 * 2 is evaluated second	30 > 25 && 5 < 20
30 > 25 is evaluated third	`true && 5 < 20`
5 < 20 is evaluated fourth	`true && true`
`true && true` is evaluated last	`true`

For more examples of using the operators listed in Figure 5-24, see the Operators section in the Ch05WantMore.pdf file.

Figure 5-24 Listing and an example of arithmetic, comparison, and logical operators

The answers to Mini-Quiz questions are located in Appendix A.

Mini-Quiz 5-3

1. The compound condition `true || false` will evaluate to ________.
2. The compound condition `7 > 3 && 5 < 2` will evaluate to ________.
3. The compound condition `5 * 4 < 20 || true` will evaluate to ________.
4. Which of the following `if` clauses determines whether the value in an `int` variable named `age` is between 30 and 40, including 30 and 40?
   a. `if (age <= 30 || age >= 40)`
   b. `if (age >= 30 && age <= 40)`
   c. `if (age >=30 && <= 40)`
   d. `if (age <=30 || >= 40)`
5. Which of the following `if` clauses determines whether a `char` variable named `code` contains the letter R (in any case)?
   a. `if (code == 'R' || code == 'r')`
   b. `if (code = 'R' || code = 'r')`
   c. `if (code == "R" || code == "r")`
   d. none of the above

Converting a Character to Uppercase or Lowercase

Earlier, in Figure 5-21, you viewed two examples of C++ code for the Pass/Fail program. In both examples, the `if` clause contains a compound condition that compares the character stored in the `letter` variable with both the uppercase and lowercase forms of the letter P. However, that is not the only way of comparing a variable's contents to both versions of a letter. You also can use either of the following C++ built-in functions: `toupper` or `tolower`. The **`toupper` function** temporarily converts a character to uppercase, while the **`tolower` function** converts it to lowercase.

Figure 5-25 shows the syntax of the `toupper` and `tolower` functions. An item that appears between parentheses in a function's syntax is called an **argument**, and it represents information that the function needs to perform its task. In this case, the `toupper` and `tolower` functions need the name of a variable whose data type is `char`. Both functions copy the character stored in the *charVariable* to a temporary location in the computer's internal memory. The functions convert the temporary character to the appropriate case (if necessary) and then return the temporary character. Keep in mind that the `toupper` and `tolower` functions do not change the contents of the *charVariable*; they change the contents of the temporary location only. In addition, the `toupper` and `tolower` functions affect only characters that represent letters of the alphabet, as these are the only characters that have uppercase and lowercase forms.

Also included in Figure 5-25 are examples of using the `toupper` and `tolower` functions. When using the `toupper` function in a comparison, be sure that everything you are comparing is uppercase; otherwise, the comparison will not evaluate correctly. For instance, the clause `if (toupper(letter) == 'p')` is not correct: The condition will always evaluate to false because the uppercase version of a letter will never be equal to its lowercase counterpart. Likewise, when using the `tolower` function in a comparison, be sure that everything you are comparing is lowercase.

HOW TO Use the `toupper` and `tolower` Functions

Syntax

toupper(*charVariable***)**
tolower(*charVariable***)**

Example 1

```
if (toupper(letter) == 'P')
```

The condition compares the uppercase character returned by the `toupper` function with the uppercase letter P. The condition evaluates to true when the character stored in the `letter` variable is either P or p.

Example 2

```
if (tolower(letter) == 'p')
```

The condition compares the lowercase character returned by the `tolower` function with the lowercase letter p. The condition evaluates to true when the character stored in the `letter` variable is either P or p.

Example 3

```
initial = toupper(initial);
```

The assignment statement changes the contents of the `initial` variable to uppercase.

Figure 5-25 How to use the `toupper` and `tolower` functions

Formatting Numeric Output

In a C++ program, numbers with a decimal place are displayed by the compiler in either fixed-point or e (exponential) notation, depending on the size of the number. Recall that a number with a decimal place is called a real number. Smaller real numbers—those containing six or fewer digits to the left of the decimal point—usually are displayed in fixed-point notation. For example, the number 1234.56 would be displayed in fixed-point notation as 1234.560000. Larger real numbers—those containing more than six digits to the left of the decimal point—typically are displayed in e notation. The number 1,225,000.00, for example, would be displayed in e notation as 1.225e+006. The type of program you are creating determines the appropriate format to use when displaying numbers with a decimal place. Business programs usually display real numbers in fixed-point notation, while many scientific programs use e notation.

C++ provides stream manipulators that allow you to control the format used to display real numbers. You use the **`fixed` stream manipulator** to display real numbers in fixed-point notation. To display real numbers in e notation, you use the **`scientific` stream manipulator**. The appropriate manipulator must appear in a `cout` statement, and it must be processed before the real numbers you want formatted are displayed. After being processed, the manipulator remains in effect either until the end of the program or until the computer encounters another manipulator that changes the format, whichever occurs first. Figure 5-26 shows examples of using both manipulators. As the examples indicate, a stream manipulator can appear by itself in a `cout` statement; or, it can be included with other information in a `cout` statement.

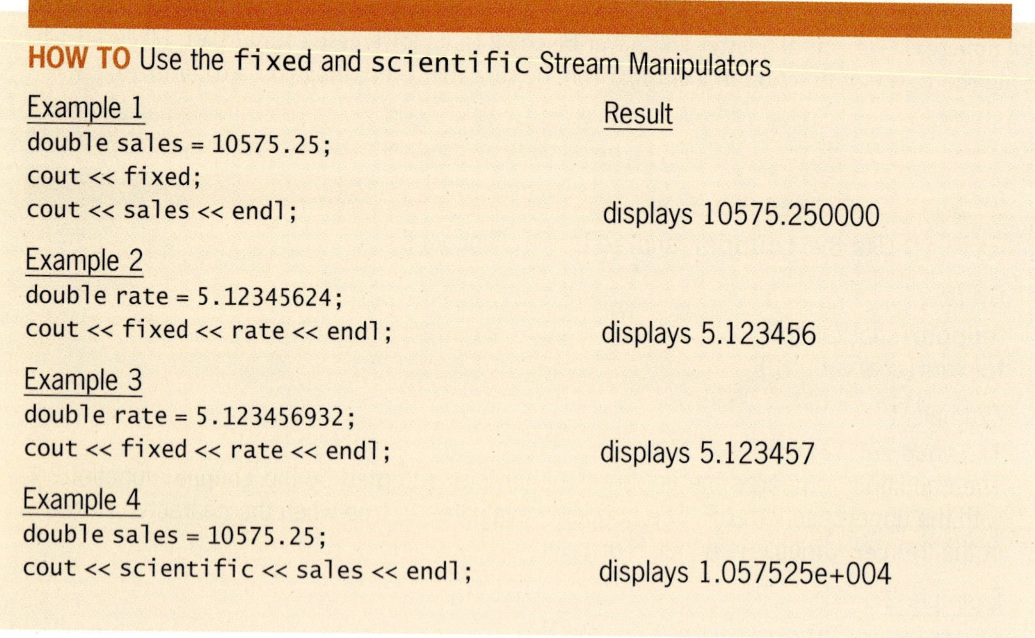

HOW TO Use the `fixed` and `scientific` Stream Manipulators

Example 1	Result
`double sales = 10575.25;`	
`cout << fixed;`	
`cout << sales << endl;`	displays 10575.250000
Example 2	
`double rate = 5.12345624;`	
`cout << fixed << rate << endl;`	displays 5.123456
Example 3	
`double rate = 5.123456932;`	
`cout << fixed << rate << endl;`	displays 5.123457
Example 4	
`double sales = 10575.25;`	
`cout << scientific << sales << endl;`	displays 1.057525e+004

Figure 5-26 How to use the `fixed` and `scientific` stream manipulators

Study closely the examples in Figure 5-26. Notice that the code in Example 1 displays 10575.250000 rather than 10575.25. This is because all real numbers formatted by the `fixed` stream manipulator will have six digits to the right of the decimal point. If the unformatted number contains fewer than six decimal places, the `fixed` stream manipulator pads the number with zeros until it has six decimal places. The number 10575.25, for instance, is padded with four zeros to make 10575.250000.

If the unformatted number contains more than six decimal places, on the other hand, the additional decimal places are truncated (dropped off). Before the truncation occurs, however, the number in the sixth decimal place is either rounded up one number or left as is, depending on the value of the numbers being truncated. For example, when the `rate` variable contains the number 5.12345624, as it does in Example 2 in Figure 5-26, the `cout` statement displays the number 5.123456. Notice that the digits 2 and 4, which occupy the seventh and eighth decimal places in the number 5.12345624, are truncated. Also notice that the number in the sixth decimal place (6) remains the same; no rounding occurs because the value of the truncated numbers (24) is less than 50. On the other hand, when the `rate` variable contains the number 5.123456932, as it does in Example 3, the `cout` statement displays 5.123457. In this case, the digits in the seventh, eighth, and ninth decimal places (9, 3, and 2) are truncated. However, because the value of the truncated numbers (932) is greater than 500, the number in the sixth decimal place (6) is rounded up to 7. The `cout << scientific << sales << endl;` statement in Example 4 in Figure 5-26 displays the contents of the `sales` variable in e notation; the result is 1.057525e+004.

In most programs, especially business programs, numeric output is displayed with either zero or two decimal places. Rarely does a program require numbers to be displayed with the six decimal places you get from the `fixed` stream manipulator. You can use the C++ **`setprecision` stream manipulator** to control the number of decimal places that appear when a real number is displayed. The definition of the `setprecision` manipulator is contained in the iomanip file, which comes with your C++ compiler. (The "io" stands for "input/output".) For a program to use the `setprecision` manipulator, it must contain the `#include <iomanip>` directive.

Figure 5-27 shows the `setprecision` manipulator's syntax. The *numberOfDecimalPlaces* argument in the syntax is an integer that specifies the number of decimal places to include when displaying a real number. The `setprecision` manipulator remains in effect either until the end of the program or until the computer encounters another `setprecision` manipulator. Also included in Figure 5-27 are examples of using the `setprecision` manipulator in a C++ statement. As Example 2 shows, you can include the `setprecision` and `fixed` manipulators in the same statement.

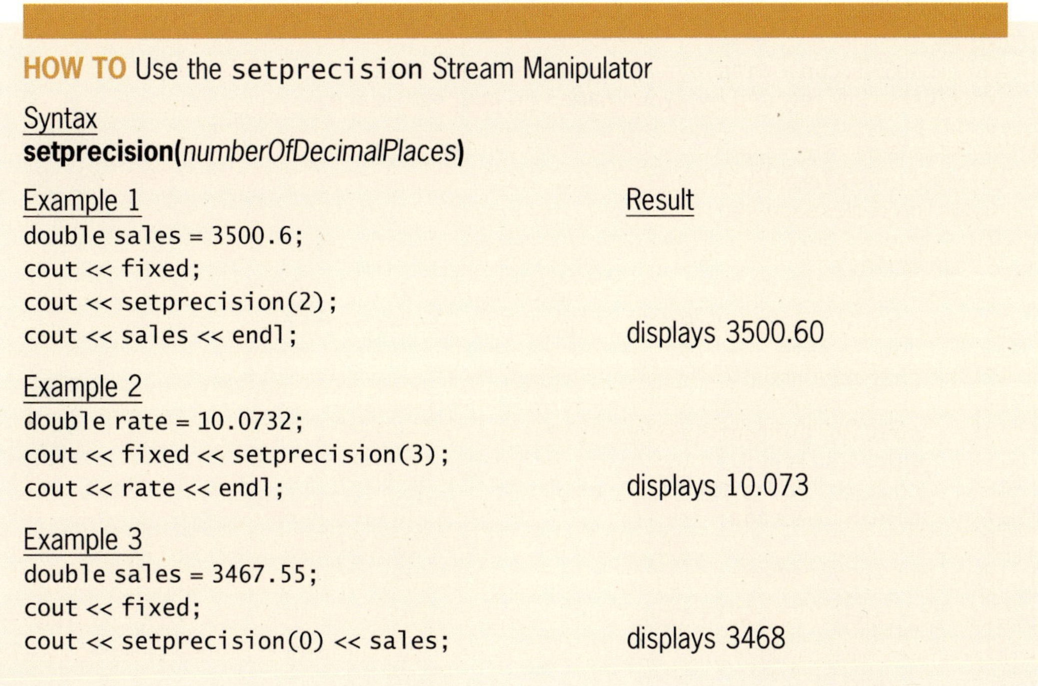

HOW TO Use the `setprecision` Stream Manipulator

Syntax
setprecision(*numberOfDecimalPlaces***)**

Example 1	Result
`double sales = 3500.6;`	
`cout << fixed;`	
`cout << setprecision(2);`	
`cout << sales << endl;`	displays 3500.60

Example 2	
`double rate = 10.0732;`	
`cout << fixed << setprecision(3);`	
`cout << rate << endl;`	displays 10.073

Example 3	
`double sales = 3467.55;`	
`cout << fixed;`	
`cout << setprecision(0) << sales;`	displays 3468

Figure 5-27 How to use the `setprecision` stream manipulator

Stream manipulators with arguments (such as `setprecision`) are defined in the iomanip file. Stream manipulators that do not have arguments (such as `fixed` and `scientific`) are defined in the iostream file.

The answers to Mini-Quiz questions are located in Appendix A.

Mini-Quiz 5-4

1. Which of the following tells the computer to display real numbers in fixed-point notation with two decimal places?
   a. `cout << fixed << decimal(2);`
   b. `cout << fixedPoint << precision(2);`
   c. `cout << fixedPoint << setdecimal(2);`
   d. `cout << fixed << setprecision(2);`
2. Which of the following changes the contents of a `char` variable named `letter` to lowercase?
   a. `tolower(letter) = letter;`
   b. `letter == tolower(letter);`
   c. `letter = tolower(letter);`
   d. `tolower('letter');`
3. If the `num` variable contains the number 34.65, the `cout << fixed << num;` statement will display the number as ________.
   a. 34.65
   b. 34.650
   c. 34.6500
   d. 34.650000

The answers to the labs are located in Appendix A.

LAB 5-1 Stop and Analyze

Study the program shown in Figure 5-28, and then answer the questions.

```
//Lab5-1.cpp - displays an employee's new salary
//Created/revised by <your name> on <current date>

#include <iostream>
#include <iomanip>
using namespace std;

int main()
{
    double salary = 0.0;
    double rate   = 0.0;
    char payGrade = ' ';

    cout << "Current salary: ";
    cin >> salary;
    cout << "Pay grade (1, 2, or 3): ";
    cin >> payGrade;

    if (payGrade == '1')
        rate = .03;
    else
        rate = .02;
     //end if
```

Figure 5-28 Program for Lab 5-1 *(continues)*

(continued)

```
24
25     salary = salary + salary * rate;
26     cout << fixed << setprecision(2);
27     cout << "New salary: " << salary << endl;
28
29     //system("pause");
30     return 0;
31 }  //end of main function
```

Figure 5-28 Program for Lab 5-1

QUESTIONS

1. What rate will be assigned to the `rate` variable when the user enters the following pay grades: 1, 3, and 5?
2. Why is the directive on Line 5 necessary?
3. Why is the 1 in the `if` statement's condition on Line 19 enclosed in single quotation marks?
4. How would you rewrite the `if` statement on Lines 19 through 23 to use the `!=` operator in the condition?
5. In addition to using `salary = salary * rate + salary`, how else could you write the `salary = salary + salary * rate;` statement on Line 25?
6. What changes would you need to make to the program so that it doesn't use the `rate` variable?

LAB 5-2 Plan and Create

In this lab, you will plan and create an algorithm for the manager of Willow Springs Health Club. The problem specification is shown in Figure 5-29.

Problem specification
The manager of Willow Springs Health Club wants a program that allows her to enter the number of calories and grams of fat contained in a specific food. The program should calculate and display two values: the food's fat calories and its fat percentage. The fat calories are the number of calories attributed to fat and are calculated by multiplying the food's fat grams by the number 9; this is because each gram of fat contains nine calories. The fat percentage is the ratio of the food's fat calories to its total calories. You calculate the fat percentage by dividing the food's fat calories by its total calories and then multiplying the result by 100. The fat percentage should be displayed with zero decimal places. The program should display an appropriate error message if either or both input values are less than 0.

Figure 5-29 Problem specification for Lab 5-2

First, analyze the problem, looking for the output first and then for the input. In this case, the user wants the program to display a food's fat calories and its fat percentage. To calculate these values, the computer will need to know the food's total calories and its grams of fat; both of these items will be entered by the user. Next, plan the algorithm. As you know, most algorithms begin with an instruction to enter the input items into the computer, followed by instructions that process the input items, typically including the items in one or more calculations. Most algorithms end with one or more instructions that display, print, or store the output items. Figure 5-30 shows the completed IPO chart for the health club problem. Notice that the solution requires a dual-alternative selection structure. First, the selection structure's condition determines whether the input data is valid. Then the selection structure's true and false paths take the appropriate action(s).

Input	Processing	Output

total calories
grams of fat
	Processing items: none
	
	Algorithm:
	1. enter the total calories and grams of fat
	2. if (both the total calories and grams of fat are greater than or equal to 0)
	    calculate fat calories by multiplying grams of fat by 9
	    calculate fat percentage by dividing fat calories by total calories and then multiplying the result by 100
	    display the fat calories and fat percentage
	else
	    display an error message
	end if
		fat calories
		fat percentage (zero decimal places)

Figure 5-30 Completed IPO chart for the health club problem

After completing the IPO chart, you then move on to the third step in the problem-solving process, which is to desk-check the algorithm. You will desk-check the health club algorithm three times. For the first desk-check, you will use 150 as the total calories and 6 as the grams of fat; the fat calories and fat percentage should be 54 and 36%, respectively. For the second desk-check, you will use 105 as the total calories and 2 as the grams of fat. Using this data, the fat calories and fat percentage should be 18 and 17%, respectively. For the third desk-check, you will use 100 as the total calories and –3 as the grams of fat. Using this data, the program should display an error message. Figure 5-31 shows the completed desk-check table. Notice that the amounts in the fat calories and fat percentage columns agree with the results of the manual calculations.

total calories	grams of fat	fat calories	fat percentage
~~150~~	~~6~~	~~54~~	~~36~~
~~105~~	~~2~~	18	17
100	-3		

Figure 5-31 Completed desk-check table for the health club algorithm

The fourth step in the problem-solving process is to code the algorithm into a program. You begin by declaring memory locations that will store the values of the input, processing (if any), and output items. The health club problem will need four memory locations to store the input and output items. The input items (total calories and grams of fat) will be stored in variables because the user should be allowed to change the value of those items during runtime. The output items (fat calories and fat percentage) also will be stored in variables because their values are based on the current values of the input items. The total calories, grams of fat, and fat calories will be integers; therefore, you will store those values in `int` variables. You will store the fat percentage in a `double` variable because its value will be a real number.

Figure 5-32 shows the input, processing, and output items from the IPO chart, along with the corresponding C++ instructions. Pay particular attention to the shaded statement, which calculates the fat percentage. The statement uses the `static_cast` operator to convert the integers stored in the `fatCals` and `totalCals` variables to `double` numbers before performing the division operation. As you learned in Chapter 4, the `static_cast` operator ensures that the quotient obtained when dividing one `int` variable by another `int` variable is a real number rather than an integer. Although the statement converts the contents of both `int` variables to `double`, recall that only one of the two integers involved in a division operation needs to be converted. As a result, you also can write the division part of the statement as either `static_cast<double>(fatCals) / totalCals` or `fatCals / static_cast<double>(totalCals)`.

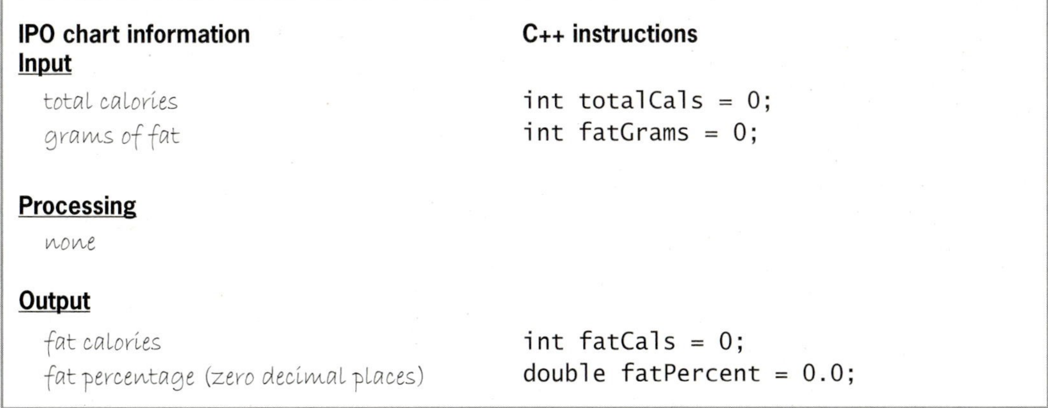

IPO chart information	**C++ instructions**
Input	
total calories	`int totalCals = 0;`
grams of fat	`int fatGrams = 0;`
Processing	
none	
Output	
fat calories	`int fatCals = 0;`
fat percentage (zero decimal places)	`double fatPercent = 0.0;`

Figure 5-32 IPO chart information and C++ instructions for the health club problem *(continues)*

(continued)

Algorithm

1. enter the total calories and grams of fat

```
cout << "Total calories: ";
cin >> totalCals;
cout << "Grams of fat: ";
cin >> fatGrams;
```

2. if (both the total calories and grams of fat are greater than or equal to 0)

```
if (totalCals >= 0 && fatGrams >= 0)
{
```

calculate fat calories by multiplying grams of fat by 9

```
    fatCals = fatGrams * 9;
```

calculate fat percentage by dividing fat calories by total calories and then multiplying the result by 100

```
    fatPercent =
    static_cast<double>(fatCals) /
    static_cast<double>(totalCals)
    * 100;
```

display fat calories and fat percentage

```
    cout << "Fat calories: " <<
    fatCals << endl;
    cout << fixed << setprecision(0);
    cout << "Fat percentage: " <<
    fatPercent << "%" << endl;
}
```

else
display an error message
end if

```
else
    cout << "Input error" << endl;
//end if
```

Figure 5-32 IPO chart information and C++ instructions for the health club problem

The fifth step in the problem-solving process is to desk-check the program. You begin by placing the names of the declared variables and named constants (if any) in a new desk-check table, along with their initial values. You then desk-check the remaining C++ instructions in order, recording in the desk-check table any changes made to the variables. Figure 5-33 shows the completed desk-check table for the program. The results agree with those shown in the algorithm's desk-check table in Figure 5-31.

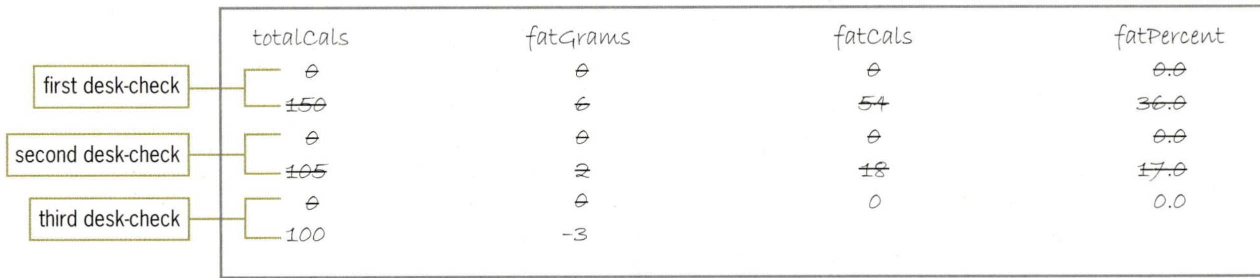

	totalCals	fatGrams	fatCals	fatPercent
first desk-check	~~0~~	~~0~~	~~0~~	~~0.0~~
	~~150~~	~~6~~	~~54~~	~~36.0~~
second desk-check	~~0~~	~~0~~	~~0~~	~~0.0~~
	~~105~~	~~2~~	~~18~~	~~17.0~~
third desk-check	~~0~~	~~0~~	0	0.0
	100	-3		

Figure 5-33 Completed desk-check table for the health club program

The final step in the problem-solving process is to evaluate and modify (if necessary) the program. Recall that you evaluate a program by entering its instructions into the computer and then using the computer to run (execute) it. While the program is running, you enter the same sample data used when desk-checking the program.

DIRECTIONS

The Cpp7\Chap05 folder contains several files named Ch05-Lab5-2 *developmentTool*.pdf. Each file corresponds to a specific C++ development tool, and each provides step-by-step directions for creating, entering, saving, and running the program shown in Figure 5-34. If the Cpp7\Chap05 folder contains a PDF file for your C++ development tool, open the PDF file and then follow the directions listed in the file. (You can use Adobe Reader to open a PDF file.)

If the Cpp7\Chap05 folder does *not* contain a PDF file for your C++ development tool, contact your instructor or technical support person for the appropriate instructions. Follow the instructions you are given for starting your C++ development tool. Depending on the development tool you are using, you may need to create a new project; if so, name the project Lab5-2 Project and save it in the Cpp7\Chap05 folder. Enter the instructions shown in Figure 5-34 in a source file named Lab5-2.cpp. (Do not enter the line numbers.) Save the file in either the project folder or the Cpp7\Chap05 folder. Now follow the appropriate instructions for running the Lab5-2.cpp file. Use the sample data from Figure 5-33 to test the program. If necessary, correct any bugs (errors) in the program.

```
//Lab5-2.cpp - displays a food's fat
//calories and fat percentage
//Created/revised by <your name> on <current date>

#include <iostream>
#include <iomanip>
using namespace std;

int main()
{
    //declare variables
    int totalCals     = 0;
    int fatGrams      = 0;
    int fatCals       = 0;
    double fatPercent = 0.0;

    //enter input items
    cout << "Total calories: ";
    cin >> totalCals;
    cout << "Grams of fat: ";
    cin >> fatGrams;

```

Figure 5-34 Health club program *(continues)*

(continued)

```
    //determine whether the data is valid
    if (totalCals >= 0 && fatGrams >= 0)
    {
          //calculate and display the output
          fatCals = fatGrams * 9;
          fatPercent = static_cast<double>(fatCals)
                / static_cast<double>(totalCals) * 100;

          cout << "Fat calories: " << fatCals << endl;
          cout << fixed << setprecision(0);
          cout << "Fat percentage: " << fatPercent
                << "%" << endl;
    }
    else
          cout << "Input error" << endl;
    //end if

    //system("pause");
    return 0;
 } //end of main function
```

if your C++ development tool requires this statement, delete the two forward slashes

Figure 5-34 Health club program

LAB 5-3 Modify

In the program created in Lab 5-2, the `if` statement's true path handles valid data, while its false path handles invalid data. In this lab, you will modify the `if` statement so that invalid data is handled in the true path and valid data is handled in the false path.

The Cpp7\Chap05 folder contains several files named Ch05-Lab5-3 *developmentTool*.pdf. Each file corresponds to a specific C++ development tool, and each provides step-by-step directions for completing Lab 5-3. If the Cpp7\Chap05 folder contains a PDF file for your C++ development tool, open the PDF file and then follow the directions listed in the file. (You can use Adobe Reader to open a PDF file.)

If the Cpp7\Chap05 folder does *not* contain a PDF file for your C++ development tool, create a new project (if necessary) named Lab5-3 Project and save it in the Cpp7\Chap05 folder. Copy the program instructions from Lab 5-2 into a new source file named Lab5-3.cpp file. Modify the program instructions appropriately. Be sure to change Lab5-2.cpp in the first comment to Lab5-3.cpp. Use the sample data from Figure 5-33 to test the program.

LAB 5-4 Desk-Check

Desk-check the code shown in Figure 5-35 using the letter P. Although the code displays the appropriate message, it is considered inefficient. Why? How can you fix the code to make it more efficient?

```
//declare variable
char letter = ' ';

//enter input item, then display message
cout << "Enter a letter: ";
cin >> letter;

if (letter == 'P' || letter == 'p')
    cout << "Pass" << endl;
//end if
if (letter != 'P' || letter != 'p')
    cout << "Fail" << endl;
//end if
```

Figure 5-35 Code for Lab 5-4

LAB 5-5 Debug

The Cpp7\Chap05 folder contains several files named Ch05-Lab5-5 *developmentTool*.pdf. Each file corresponds to a specific C++ development tool, and each provides step-by-step directions for completing Lab 5-5. If the Cpp7\Chap05 folder contains a PDF file for your C++ development tool, open the PDF file and then follow the directions listed in the file. (You can use Adobe Reader to open a PDF file.)

If the Cpp7\Chap05 folder does *not* contain a PDF file for your C++ development tool, start your C++ development tool and open the Lab5-5.cpp file. Read the comments entered at the beginning of the program. If necessary, delete the two forward slashes that appear before the `system("pause");` statement. Test the program using codes of 1, 2, and 3. Use 100 as the purchase price. Debug the program.

Summary

- You use the selection structure when you want a program to make a decision before selecting the next instruction to process.
- Studying the problem specification will help you determine whether a solution requires a selection structure.
- A selection structure's condition must evaluate to either true or false. In single-alternative and dual-alternative selection structures, the instructions to follow when the structure's condition is true are placed in the structure's true path. In a dual-alternative selection structure, the instructions to follow when the structure's condition is false are placed in the structure's false path. You should indent the instructions in both paths.
- A diamond, called the decision symbol, is used to represent a selection structure's condition in a flowchart. Each selection structure diamond has one flowline entering the symbol and two flowlines leaving the symbol. One of the flowlines leading out of a diamond should be marked with a "T" (for true) and the other should be marked with an "F" (for false).

- In most C++ programs, you will use the `if` statement to code single-alternative and dual-alternative selection structures. The statement's condition must evaluate to either true or false.
- If either an `if` statement's true path or its false path contains more than one statement, the statements in the path must be entered as a statement block, which means the statements must be enclosed in a set of braces ({}).
- It is a good programming practice to include a comment (such as `//end if`) to identify the end of an `if` statement in a program.
- You use comparison operators to compare values in expressions; the values should have the same data type. Expressions containing comparison operators always evaluate to either true or false. If more than one comparison operator with the same precedence number appears in a C++ expression, the computer evaluates those operators from left to right in the expression.
- You shouldn't use either the equality operator (==) or the inequality operator (!=) to compare two real numbers because not all real numbers can be stored precisely in memory.
- A memory location declared in an `if` statement's true path can be used only by the instructions following its declaration statement within the true path. Likewise, a memory location declared in an `if` statement's false path can be used only by the instructions following its declaration statement within the false path.
- The And and Or logical operators are represented in C++ by the symbols && and ||, respectively. All expressions containing a logical operator evaluate to either true or false.
- In an expression, arithmetic operators are evaluated first, followed by comparison operators and then logical operators.
- Character comparisons in C++ are case sensitive.
- C++ provides the `toupper` and `tolower` functions for temporarily converting a character to uppercase and lowercase, respectively.
- C++ provides the `fixed` and `scientific` stream manipulators for formatting the display of real numbers. It provides the `setprecision` stream manipulator for controlling the number of decimal places that appear when a real number is displayed. The `fixed` and `scientific` stream manipulators are defined in the iostream file. The `setprecision` stream manipulator is defined in the iomanip file.

Key Terms

Argument—an item that appears between the parentheses that follow a function's name; represents information that the function needs to perform its task

Boolean operators—another term for logical operators

Comparison operators—operators used to compare values having the same data type in an expression; also called relational operators; <, <=, >, >=, ==, !=

Data validation—the process of verifying that a program's input data is within the expected range

Decision symbol—the diamond in a flowchart; used to represent the condition in either a selection or repetition structure

Dual-alternative selection structures—selection structures that require two sets of actions: one to be taken only when the structure's condition is true, and the other only when the condition is false

False path—contains the instructions to be processed when a dual-alternative selection structure's condition evaluates to false

`fixed` stream manipulator—the manipulator used to display real numbers in fixed-point notation

Local variable—a variable declared within a statement block; can be used only by the instructions within the statement block in which it is declared, and the instructions must appear after its declaration statement

Logical operators—operators used to combine two or more sub-conditions into one compound condition; also called Boolean operators

`scientific` stream manipulator—the manipulator used to display real numbers in scientific (e) notation

Selection structure—one of the three control structures; tells the computer to make a decision before selecting the next instruction to process; also called the decision structure

`setprecision` stream manipulator—the manipulator used to control the number of decimal places that appear when a real number is displayed

Short-circuit evaluation—refers to the way the computer evaluates two sub-conditions connected by a logical operator; when the logical operator is And, the computer does not evaluate sub-condition2 when sub-condition1 is false; when the logical operator is Or, the computer does not evaluate sub-condition2 when sub-condition1 is true

Single-alternative selection structure—a selection structure that requires a special set of actions to be taken only when the structure's condition is true

Statement block—one or more instructions enclosed in a set of braces ({})

`tolower` function—temporarily converts a character to lowercase

`toupper` function—temporarily converts a character to uppercase

True path—contains the instructions to be processed when a selection structure's condition evaluates to true

Truth tables—tables that summarize how the computer evaluates the logical operators in an expression

Review Questions

1. If an `if` statement's false path contains the statement `int sum = 0;`, where can the `sum` variable be used?
    a. in any instruction after the declaration statement in the entire program
    b. in any instruction after the declaration statement in the `if` statement
    c. in any instruction after the declaration statement in the `if` statement's false path
    d. none of the above, because you can't declare a variable in an `if` statement's false path

2. Which of the following is a valid `if` clause? (The `sales` variable has the `double` data type.)
    a. `if (sales > 500.0 && < 800.0)`
    b. `if (sales > 500.0 || < 800.0)`
    c. `if (sales > 500.0 And sales < 800.0)`
    d. `if (sales > 500.0 && sales < 800.0)`

3. Which of the following conditions evaluates to true when the initial variable contains the letter A in either uppercase or lowercase?
   a. if (initial = 'A' || initial = 'a')
   b. if (initial == 'A' || initial == 'a')
   c. if (initial = 'A' || initial = 'a')
   d. if (initial == 'A' && initial = 'a')

4. The expression 3 < 6 && 7 < 4 evaluates to ________.
   a. true
   b. false

5. The computer will perform short-circuit evaluation when processing which of the following if clauses?
   a. if (3 * 2 < 4 && 5 > 3)
   b. if (6 < 9 || 5 > 3)
   c. if (12 > 4 * 4 && 6 > 2)
   d. all of the above

6. If an expression does not contain any parentheses, which of the following operators is performed first in the expression?
   a. arithmetic
   b. comparison
   c. logical
   d. you can't tell without seeing the expression

7. The expression 4 * 3 < 6 + 7 && 7 < 6 + 9 evaluates to ________.
   a. true
   b. false

8. Which of the following compares the contents of an int variable named quantity with the number 5?
   a. if (quantity = 5)
   b. if (quantity == 5)
   c. if (quantity 5)
   d. if (quantity =! 5)

9. Which of the following is required in a program that uses the setprecision stream manipulator?
   a. #include <iostream>
   b. #include <setprecision>
   c. #include <iomanip>
   d. #include <manipulators>

10. Which of the following tells the computer to display real numbers in fixed-point notation with no decimal places?

    a. `cout << fixed << decimal(0);`

    b. `cout << fixed << precision(0);`

    c. `cout << fixed << setprecision(0);`

    d. `cout << fixed << setdecimal(0);`

Exercises

Pencil and Paper

TRY THIS

1. Write the C++ code to compare the contents of an `int` variable named `quantity` with the number 10. If the variable's value is equal to 10, display the "Equal" message; otherwise, display the "Not equal" message. (The answers to TRY THIS Exercises are located at the end of the chapter.)

TRY THIS

2. Write the C++ code that corresponds to the partial flowchart shown in Figure 5-36. Use `int` variables named `sold` and `bonus`. (The answers to TRY THIS Exercises are located at the end of the chapter.)

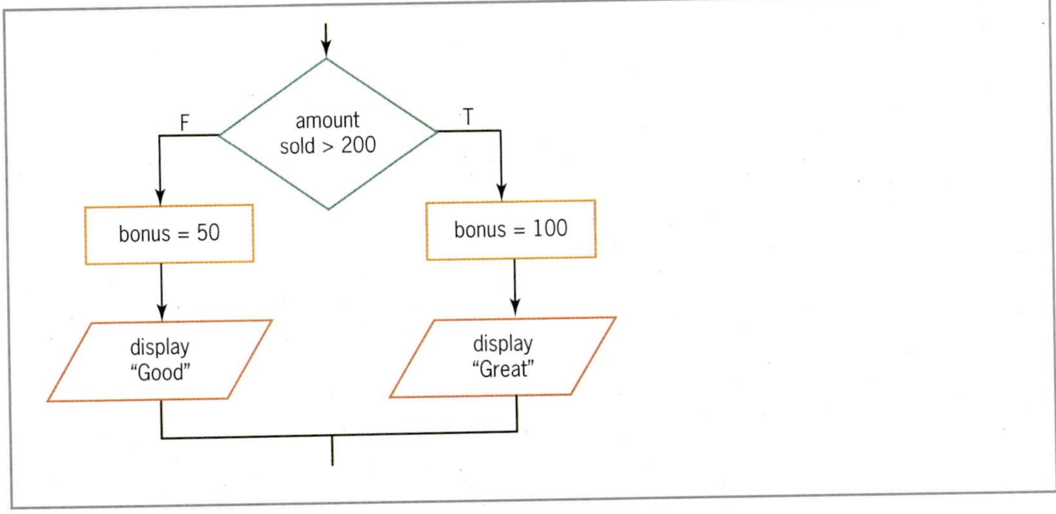

Figure 5-36

MODIFY THIS

3. Complete TRY THIS Exercise 1, and then modify the code so that the true path displays "Not equal" and the false path displays "Equal".

INTRODUCTORY

4. Write the C++ code to display the message "Entry error" when the value in the `units` variable is less than or equal to 0. Otherwise, calculate the total owed by multiplying the `units` variable's value by 5. Store the total owed in the `total` variable, and then display the total owed.

INTERMEDIATE

5. A program stores sales amounts in two `double` variables named `marySales` and `jimSales`. Write the C++ code to assign the highest and lowest sales amounts to the `highSales` and `lowSales` variables, respectively, and then display the contents of those variables. (You can assume that both sales amounts are different.)

ADVANCED

6. A program uses a `char` variable named `department` and two `double` variables named `salary` and `raise`. The `department` variable contains one of the following letters (entered in either uppercase or lowercase): A, B, or C. Employees in departments A and B are receiving a 2% raise. Employees in department C are receiving a 1.5% raise. Write the C++ code to calculate and display the appropriate raise amount. Display the raise amount in fixed-point notation with two decimal places.

SWAT THE BUGS

7. Correct the errors in the lines of code shown in Figure 5-37. The `code` variable has the `char` data type.

```
if (toupper(code) = 'x')
      cout << "Discontinued" << endl;
else
      cout << "Available" << endl;
      cout << "The item will be shipped ASAP" << endl;
//end if
```

Figure 5-37

Computer

TRY THIS

8. Code the flowchart shown earlier in Figure 5-4. If necessary, create a new project named TryThis8 Project and save it in the Cpp7\Chap05 folder. Enter the C++ instructions into a source file named TryThis8.cpp. Also enter appropriate comments and any additional instructions required by the compiler. Display the total owed in fixed-point notation with two decimal places. Save and run the program. Test the program using 2.25 and 6 as the price and quantity, respectively. The answer should be $12.15. Now test it using 2.25 and 5. (The answers to TRY THIS Exercises are located at the end of the chapter.)

TRY THIS

9. Complete Figure 5-38 by writing the algorithm and corresponding C++ instructions. Employees with a pay code of either 4 or 9 receive a 5% raise; all other employees receive a 3% raise. If necessary, create a new project named TryThis9 Project and save it in the Cpp7\Chap05 folder. Enter the C++ instructions into a source file named TryThis9.cpp. Also enter appropriate comments and any additional instructions required by the compiler. Display the new pay in fixed-point notation with two decimal places. Save and run the program. Test the program using 1 and 500 as the pay code and current pay, respectively. The new pay should be $515.00. Now test the program using the following three sets of input values: 4 and 450, 9 and 500, 2 and 625. (The answers to TRY THIS Exercises are located at the end of the chapter.)

IPO chart information	C++ instructions
Input	
pay code	`char code = ' ';`
current pay	`double currentPay = 0.0;`
raise rate 1 (3%)	`const double RATE1 = .03;`
raise rate 2 (5%)	`const double RATE2 = .05;`
Processing	
raise	`double raise = 0.0;`
Output	
new pay	`double newPay = 0.0;`
Algorithm	

Figure 5-38

MODIFY THIS

10. Complete TRY THIS Exercise 9. If necessary, create a new project named ModifyThis10 Project and save it in the Cpp7\Chap05 folder. Enter (or copy) the instructions from the TryThis9.cpp file into a new source file named ModifyThis10.cpp. Modify the code in the ModifyThis10.cpp file so that a 5% raise is also given to employees with pay codes of 2 and 6. Save and run the program. Test the program using 1 and 500 as the pay code and current pay, respectively. Now test it using the following four sets of input values: 4 and 450, 9 and 500, 2 and 625, 6 and 150.

INTRODUCTORY

11. Tea Time Company wants a program that allows a clerk to enter the number of pounds of tea ordered, the price per pound, and whether the customer should be charged a $15 shipping fee. The program should calculate and display the total amount the customer owes. Use an `int` variable for the number of pounds, a `double` variable for the price per pound, and a `char` variable for the shipping information.

    a. Create an IPO chart for the problem, and then desk-check the algorithm twice. For the first desk-check, use 10 as the number of pounds and 12.54 as the price per pound; the customer should be charged the shipping fee. For the second desk-check, use 5 as the number of pounds and 11.59 as the price; the customer should not be charged the shipping fee.

    b. List the input, processing, and output items, as well as the algorithm, in a chart similar to the one shown earlier in Figure 5-32. Then code the algorithm into a program.

    c. Desk-check the program using the same data used to desk-check the algorithm.

    d. If necessary, create a new project named Introductory11 Project and save it in the Cpp7\Chap05 folder. Enter your C++ instructions into a source file named Introductory11.cpp. Also enter appropriate comments and any additional instructions required by the compiler. Display the total amount owed in fixed-point notation with two decimal places.

    e. Save and run the program. Test the program using the same data used to desk-check the program.

INTRODUCTORY

12. Marcy's Department store is having a BoGoHo (Buy One, Get One Half Off) sale. The store manager wants a program that allows the salesclerk to enter the prices of two items. The program should calculate and display the total amount the customer owes. The half-off should always be taken on the item having the lowest price. For example, if the items cost $24.99 and $10, the half-off would be taken on the $10 item.

    a. Create an IPO chart for the problem, and then desk-check the algorithm twice. For the first desk-check, use 24.99 and 10 as the prices. For the second desk-check, use 11.50 and 30.99.

    b. List the input, processing, and output items, as well as the algorithm, in a chart similar to the one shown earlier in Figure 5-32. Then code the algorithm into a program.

    c. Desk-check the program using the same data used to desk-check the algorithm.

    d. If necessary, create a new project named Introductory12 Project and save it in the Cpp7\Chap05 folder. Enter your C++ instructions into a source file named Introductory12.cpp. Also enter appropriate comments and any additional instructions required by the compiler. Display the total amount owed in fixed-point notation with two decimal places.

    e. Save and run the program. Test the program using the same data used to desk-check the program.

INTERMEDIATE

13. Allenton Water Department wants a program that calculates a customer's monthly water bill. The clerk will enter the current and previous meter readings. The program should calculate and display the number of gallons of water used and the total charge for the water. The charge for water is $7 per 1,000 gallons. However, there is a minimum charge of $16.67. (In other words, every customer must pay at least $16.67.)

    a. Create an IPO chart for the problem, and then desk-check the algorithm twice. For the first desk-check, use 16000 and 13000 as the current and previous meter readings, respectively. For the second desk-check, use 3675 and 1650.

    b. List the input, processing, and output items, as well as the algorithm, in a chart similar to the one shown earlier in Figure 5-32. Then code the algorithm into a program.

    c. Desk-check the program using the same data used to desk-check the algorithm.

    d. If necessary, create a new project named Intermediate13 Project and save it in the Cpp7\Chap05 folder. Enter your C++ instructions into a source file named Intermediate13.cpp. Also enter appropriate comments and any additional instructions required by the compiler. Display the total charge in fixed-point notation with two decimal places.

    e. Save and run the program. Test the program using the same data used to desk-check the program.

ADVANCED

14. A third-grade teacher at Plano Elementary School wants a program that allows a student to enter the amount of money a customer owes and the amount of money the customer paid. The program should calculate and display the amount of change, as well as how many dollars, quarters, dimes, nickels, and pennies to return to the customer. Display an appropriate message when the amount paid is less than the amount owed.

    a. Create an IPO chart for the problem, and then desk-check the algorithm three times. For the first desk-check, use 75.34 and 80 as the amount owed and paid, respectively. For the second desk-check, use 39.67 and 50. For the third desk-check, use 10.55 and 9.75.

b. List the input, processing, and output items, as well as the algorithm, in a chart similar to the one shown earlier in Figure 5-32. Then code the algorithm into a program.

c. Desk-check the program using the same data used to desk-check the algorithm.

d. If necessary, create a new project named Advanced14 Project and save it in the Cpp7\Chap05 folder. Enter your C++ instructions into a source file named Advanced14.cpp. Also enter appropriate comments and any additional instructions required by the compiler. Display the change in fixed-point notation with two decimal places. Display the remaining output in fixed-point notation with no decimal places.

e. Save and run the program. Test the program using the same data used to desk-check the program.

ADVANCED

15. As you learned in the chapter, you must be careful when comparing two real numbers for either equality or inequality because some real numbers cannot be stored precisely in memory. To determine whether two real numbers are either equal or unequal, you should test that the difference between both numbers is less than some acceptable small value, such as .00001.

a. Start your C++ development tool and view the Advanced15.cpp file. The file is contained in either the Cpp7\Chap05\Advanced15 Project folder or the Cpp7\Chap05 folder. (Depending on your C++ development tool, you may need to open this exercise's solution/project file first.) Notice that the code divides the contents of the `num1` variable (10.0) by the contents of the `num2` variable (3.0), storing the result (approximately 3.33333) in the `quotient` variable. An `if` statement is used to compare the contents of the `quotient` variable with the number 3.33333. The `if` statement displays a message that indicates whether the numbers are equal.

b. If necessary, delete the two forward slashes that appear before the `system("pause");` statement and then save the program. Run the program. Even though the message on the screen states that the quotient is 3.33333, the message indicates that this value is not equal to 3.33333. Stop the program.

c. If you need to compare two real numbers for equality or inequality, first find the difference between both numbers and then compare the absolute value of that difference to a small number, such as .00001. You can use the C++ `fabs` function to find the absolute value of a real number. The absolute value of a number is a positive number that represents the distance the number is from 0 on the number line. For example, the absolute value of the number 5 is 5. The absolute value of the number –5 also is 5. To use the `fabs` function, the program must contain the `#include <cmath>` directive. Modify the program appropriately. Save and then run the program. This time, the message "Yes, the quotient 3.33333 is equal to 3.33333." appears. Stop the program.

SWAT THE BUGS

16. Start your C++ development tool and view the SwatTheBugs16.cpp file. The file is contained in either the Cpp7\Chap05\SwatTheBugs16 Project folder or the Cpp7\Chap05 folder. (Depending on your C++ development tool, you may need to open this exercise's solution/project file first.) If necessary, delete the two forward slashes that appear before the `system("pause");` statement. The program should display a 10% bonus for sales over $10,000. Correct the syntax errors and then save, run, and test the program.

Answers to TRY THIS Exercises

Pencil and Paper

1. See Figure 5-39.

```
if (quantity == 10)
      cout << "Equal" << endl;
else
      cout << "Not equal" << endl;
//end if
```

Figure 5-39

2. See Figure 5-40.

```
if (sold > 200)
{
      bonus = 100;
      cout << "Great" << endl;
}
else
{
      bonus = 50;
      cout << "Good" << endl;
}     //end if
```

Figure 5-40

Computer

8. See Figure 5-41.

```
//TryThis8.cpp - displays the total owed
//Created/revised by <your name> on <current date>

#include <iostream>
#include <iomanip>
using namespace std;

int main()
{
    //declare variables
    int quantity    = 0;
    double price    = 0.0;
    double discount = 0.0;
    double total    = 0.0;

    cout << "Price: ";
    cin >> price;
    cout << "Quantity: ";
    cin >> quantity;

    //calculate total owed
    total = price * quantity;

    //calculate discount, if necessary
    if (quantity > 5)
    {
        discount = total * .1;
        total = total - discount;
    }

    //display total owed
    cout << fixed << setprecision(2);
    cout << "Total owed: $" << total << endl;

    //system("pause");
    return 0;
}   //end of main function
```

if your C++ development tool requires this statement, delete the two forward slashes

Figure 5-41

9. See Figures 5-42 and 5-43.

IPO chart information	C++ instructions
Input	
pay code	`char code = ' ';`
current pay	`double currentPay = 0.0;`
raise rate 1 (3%)	`const double RATE1 = .03;`
raise rate 2 (5%)	`const double RATE2 = .05;`
Processing	
raise	`double raise = 0.0;`
Output	
new pay	`double newPay = 0.0;`
Algorithm	

1. enter the pay code and current pay	`cout << "Pay code: ";`
	`cin >> code;`
	`cout << "Current pay: ";`
	`cin >> currentPay;`

2. if (the pay code is 4 or 9) calculate the raise by multiplying the current pay by raise rate 2	`if (code == '4' || code == '9')` `raise = currentPay * RATE2;`
else calculate the raise by multiplying the current pay by raise rate 1	`else` `raise = currentPay * RATE1;`
end if	`//end if`
3. calculate the new pay by adding the raise to the current pay	`newPay = currentPay + raise;`
4. display the new pay	`cout << "New pay: $" <<` `newPay << endl;`

Figure 5-42

```
//TryThis9.cpp - displays the new pay
//Created/revised by <your name> on <current date>

#include <iostream>
#include <iomanip>
using namespace std;

int main()
{
    //declare named constants and variables
    const double RATE1 = .03;
    const double RATE2 = .05;
    char code          = ' ';
    double currentPay  = 0.0;
    double raise       = 0.0;
    double newPay      = 0.0;

    //enter input items
    cout << "Pay code: ";
    cin >> code;
    cout << "Current pay: ";
    cin >> currentPay;

    //calculate raise and new pay
    if (code == '4' || code == '9')
        raise = currentPay * RATE2;
    else
        raise = currentPay * RATE1;
    //end if
    newPay = currentPay + raise;

    //display new pay
    cout << fixed << setprecision(2);
    cout << "New pay: $" << newPay << endl;

    //system("pause");
    return 0;
}   //end of main function
```

if your C++ development tool requires this statement, delete the two forward slashes

Figure 5-43

CHAPTER 6

More on the Selection Structure

After studying Chapter 6, you should be able to:

- Include a nested selection structure in pseudocode and in a flowchart
- Code a nested selection structure
- Recognize common logic errors in selection structures
- Include a multiple-alternative selection structure in pseudocode and in a flowchart
- Code a multiple-alternative selection structure in C++

Making Decisions

In Chapter 5, you learned that you use the selection structure when you want the computer to make a decision and then select the appropriate path—either the true path or the false path—based on the result. Both paths in a selection structure can include instructions that declare variables, perform calculations, and so on. In this chapter, you will learn that both paths also can include other selection structures. When either a selection structure's true path or its false path contains another selection structure, the inner selection structure is referred to as a **nested selection structure** because it is contained (nested) entirely within the outer selection structure.

Ch06-Maleek video

A programmer determines whether a problem's solution requires a nested selection structure by studying the problem specification. The first problem specification you will examine in this chapter involves a basketball player named Maleek. The problem specification and an illustration of the problem are shown in Figure 6-1, along with an appropriate solution. The solution requires a selection structure, but not a nested one. This is because only one decision—whether the basketball went through the hoop—is necessary.

Problem specification

Maleek is practicing for an upcoming basketball game. Write the instructions that direct Maleek to shoot the basketball and then say one of two phrases, depending on whether or not the basketball went through the hoop.

Result of shot	Phrase
Basketball went through the hoop	I did it!
Basketball did not go through the hoop	Missed it!

```
1. shoot the basketball
2. if (the basketball went through the hoop)      ← condition
       say "I did it!"                            ← true path
   else
       say "Missed it!"                           ← false path
   end if
```

Figure 6-1 A problem that requires the selection structure

Now we'll make a slight change to the problem specification shown in Figure 6-1. This time, Maleek should say either one or two phrases, depending not only on whether or not the ball went through the hoop, but also on where he was standing when he made the basket. Figure 6-2 shows the modified problem specification and solution. The modified solution contains an outer dual-alternative selection structure and a nested dual-alternative selection structure. The outer selection structure begins with *if (the basketball went through the hoop)*, and it ends with the last *end if*. The last *else* belongs to the outer selection structure and separates the structure's true path from its false path. Notice that the instructions in both paths are indented within the outer selection structure. Indenting in this manner clearly indicates the instructions to be followed when the basketball went through the hoop, as well as the ones to be followed when the basketball did not go through the hoop.

The nested selection structure in Figure 6-2 appears in the outer selection structure's true path. The nested selection structure begins with *if (Maleek was either inside or on the 3-point line)*, and it ends with the first *end if*. The indented *else* belongs to the nested selection structure and separates the nested structure's true path from its false path. For clarity, the instructions in the nested selection structure's true and false paths are indented within the structure. For a nested selection structure to work correctly, it must be contained entirely within either the outer selection structure's true path or its false path. The nested selection structure in Figure 6-2, for example, appears entirely within the outer selection structure's true path.

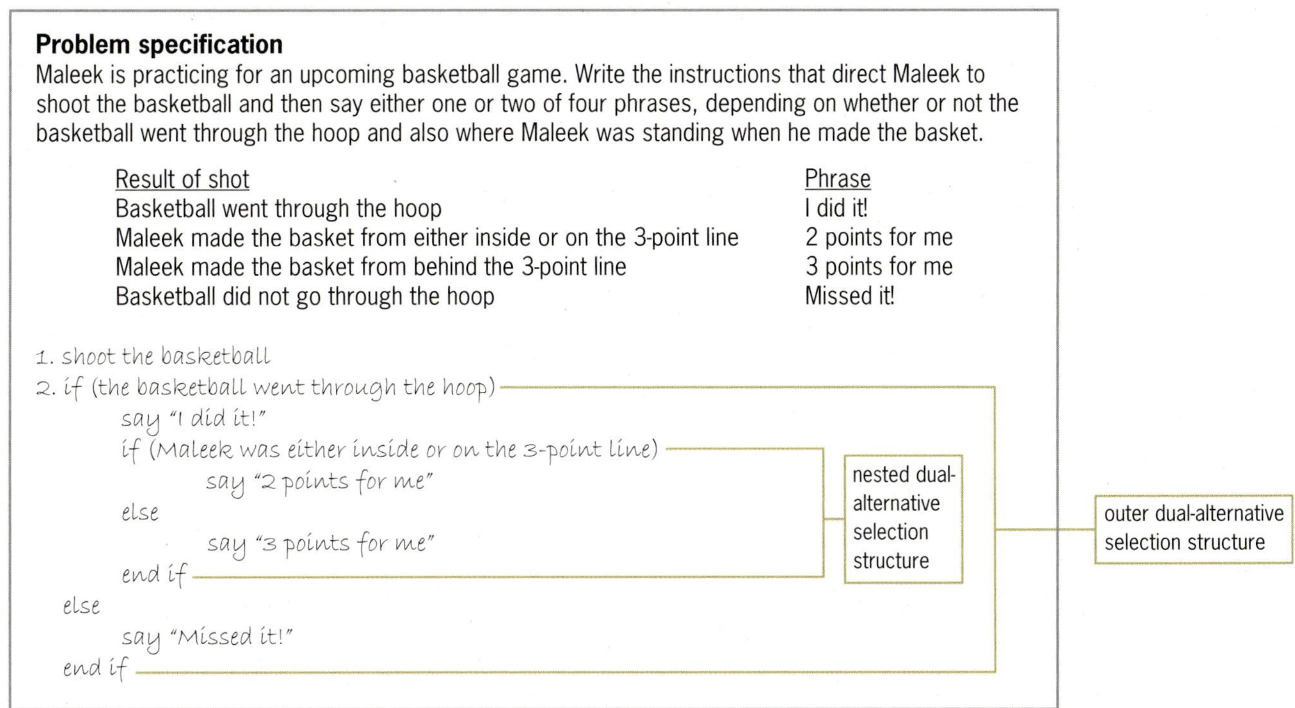

Figure 6-2 A problem that requires a nested selection structure

Figure 6-3 shows a modified version of the previous problem specification, along with the modified solution. In this version of the problem, Maleek should still say "Missed it!" when the basketball misses its target. However, if the basketball hits the rim, he also should say "So close". In addition to the nested dual-alternative selection structure from the previous solution, the modified solution also contains a nested single-alternative selection structure, which appears in the outer selection structure's false path. The nested single-alternative selection structure begins with *if (the basketball hit the rim)*, and it ends with the second *end if*. Notice that the nested single-alternative selection structure is contained entirely within the outer selection structure's false path.

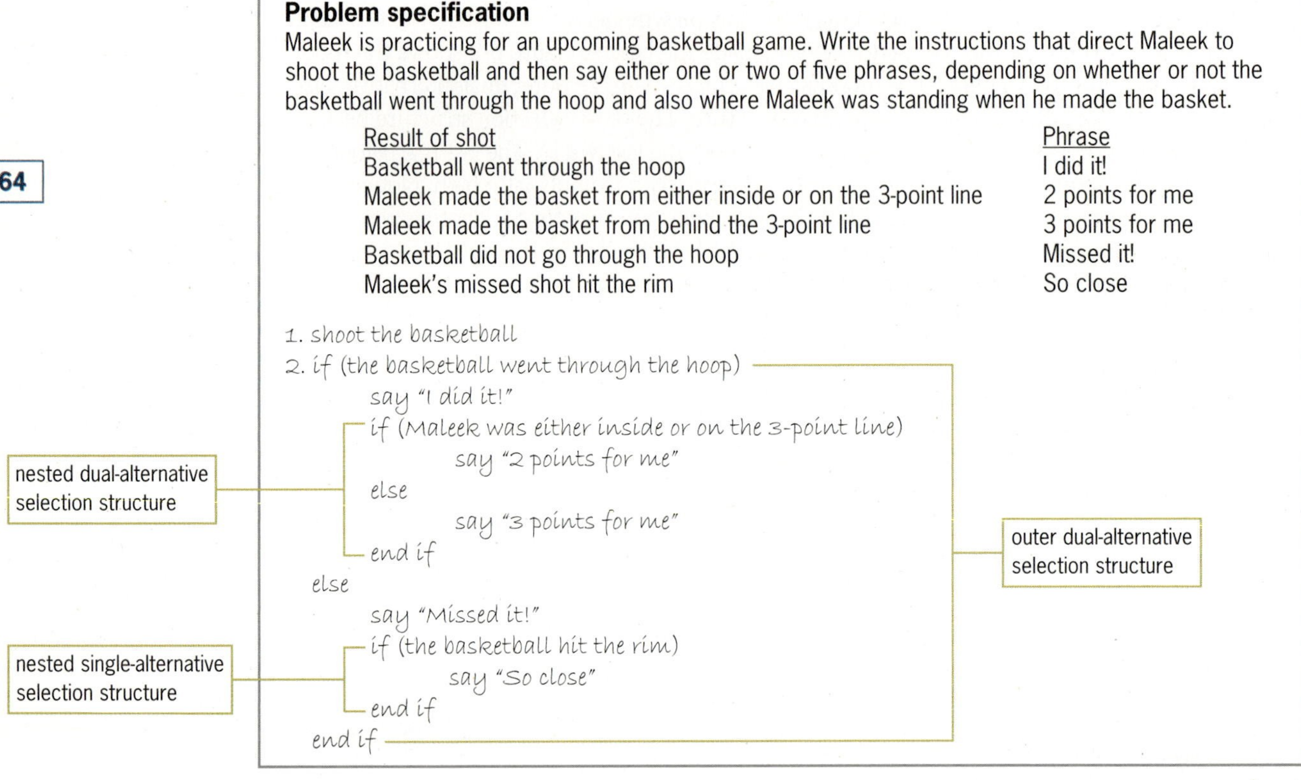

Figure 6-3 A problem that requires two nested selection structures

The answers to Mini-Quiz questions are located in Appendix A.

Mini-Quiz 6-1

1. A nested selection structure can appear ________.
   a. only in an outer selection structure's false path
   b. only in an outer selection structure's true path
   c. in either an outer selection structure's false path or its true path
2. Travis is standing in front of two containers: one marked Trash and the other marked Recycle. He is holding a bag, which contains either trash or recyclables, in his right hand. Travis needs to lift the lid from the appropriate container (if necessary), then drop the bag in the container, and then put the lid back on the container. Write an appropriate algorithm, using only the instructions listed in Figure 6-4.
3. Caroline is at a store's checkout counter. She'd like to use one of her credit cards—either her Discovery card or her Vita card, but preferably her Discovery card—to pay for the items she is purchasing. However, she is not sure whether the store accepts either card. If the store doesn't accept either card, she will need to pay cash for the items. Write an appropriate algorithm, using only the instructions listed in Figure 6-5.

```
else
end if
drop the bag of recyclables in the Recycle container
drop the bag of trash in the Trash container
if (the bag contains trash)
if (the lid is on the Recycle container)
if (the lid is on the Trash container)
lift the Recycle container's lid using your left hand
lift the Trash container's lid using your left hand
put the lid back on the Recycle container using your left hand
put the lid back on the Trash container using your left hand
```

Figure 6-4 Instructions for Question 2 in Mini-Quiz 6-1

```
else
end if
pay for your items using your Vita card
pay for your items using your Discovery card
pay for your items using cash
if (the store accepts the Vita card)
if (the store accepts the Discovery card)
ask the store clerk whether the store accepts the Vita card
ask the store clerk whether the store accepts the Discovery card
```

Figure 6-5 Instructions for Question 3 in Mini-Quiz 6-1

Flowcharting a Nested Selection Structure

Figure 6-6 shows a problem specification for a voter eligibility program. The program determines whether a person can vote and then displays one of three different messages. The appropriate message depends on the person's age and voter registration status. For example, if the person is younger than 18 years old, the program should display the message "You are too young to vote." However, if the person is at least 18 years old, the program should display one of two messages. The correct message to display is determined by the person's voter registration status. If the person is registered, then the appropriate message is "You can vote."; otherwise, it is "You must register before you can vote." Notice that determining the person's voter registration status is important only *after* his or her age is determined. Because of this, the decision regarding the age is considered the primary decision, while the decision regarding the registration status is considered the secondary decision because whether it needs to be made depends on the result of the primary decision. A primary decision is always made by an outer selection structure, while a secondary decision is always made by a nested selection structure.

Also included in Figure 6-6 is a correct solution to the voter eligibility problem in flowchart form. The first diamond in the flowchart represents the outer selection structure's condition, which checks whether the age entered by the user is greater than or equal to 18. If the condition evaluates to false, it means that the person is not old enough to vote. In that case, the outer selection structure's false path will display the "You are too young to vote." message before the outer selection structure ends. However, if the outer selection structure's condition evaluates to true, it means that the person *is* old enough to vote. Before displaying the appropriate message, the outer selection structure's true path gets the registration status from the user. It then uses a nested selection structure to determine whether the person is registered and then take the appropriate action. The nested selection structure's condition is represented by the second diamond in Figure 6-6. If the person is registered, the nested selection structure's true path displays the "You can vote." message; otherwise, its false path displays the "You must register before you can vote." message. After the appropriate message is displayed, the nested and outer selection structures end. Notice that the nested selection structure is processed only when the outer selection structure's condition evaluates to true.

Problem specification

The Danville city manager wants a program that determines voter eligibility and displays one of three messages. The messages and the criteria for displaying each message are as follows:

Message	Criteria
You are too young to vote.	person is younger than 18 years old
You can vote.	person is at least 18 years old and is registered to vote
You must register before you can vote.	person is at least 18 years old but is not registered to vote

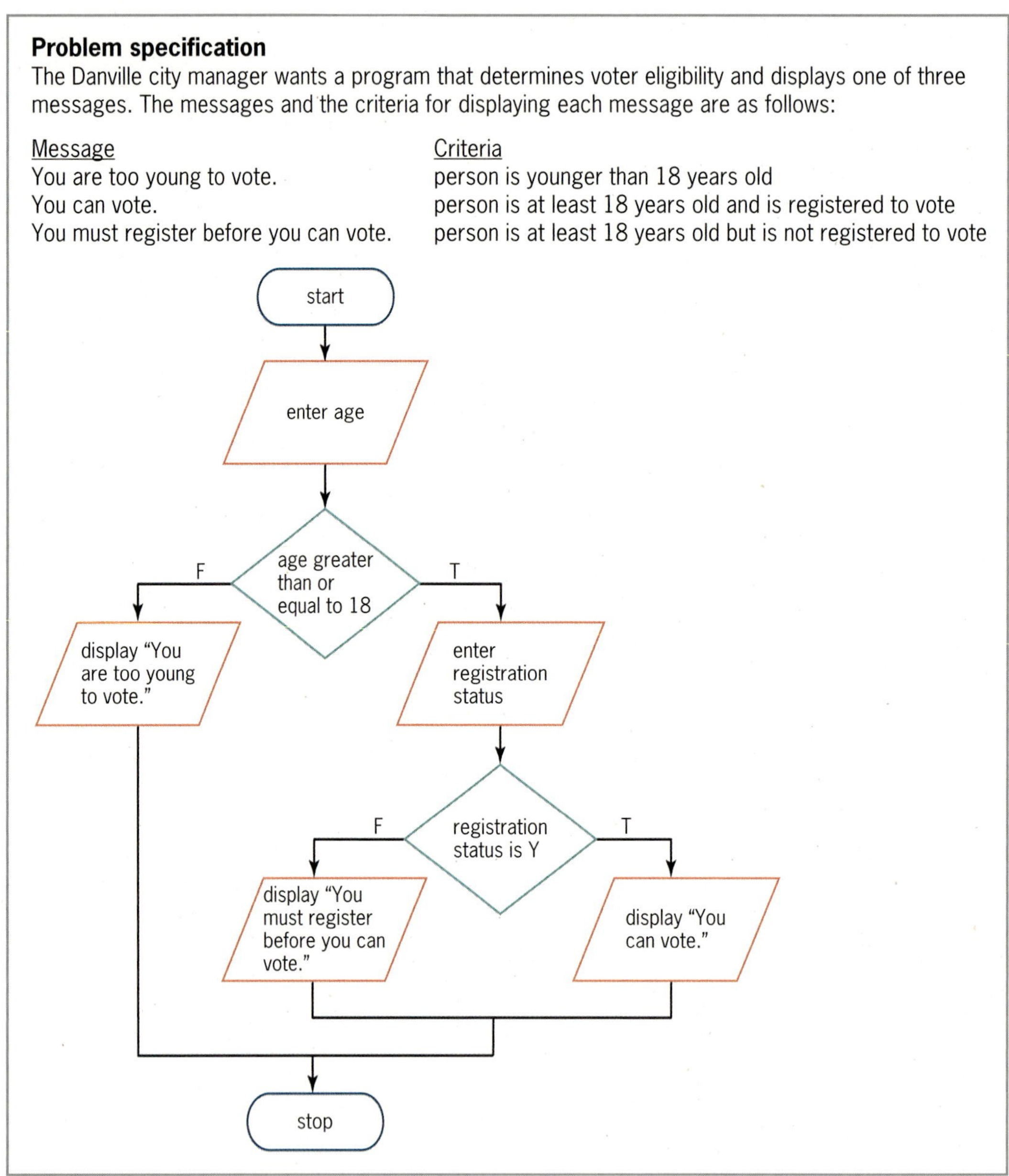

Figure 6-6 Problem specification and a correct solution for the voter eligibility problem

Figure 6-7 shows another correct solution, also in flowchart form, for the voter eligibility problem. As in the previous solution, the outer selection structure in this solution determines the age (the primary decision), and the nested selection structure determines the voter registration status (the secondary decision). In this solution, however, the outer selection structure's condition is the opposite of the one in Figure 6-6: It checks whether the age is less than 18, rather than checking if it is greater than or equal to 18. (Recall that *less than* is the opposite of *greater than or equal to.*) In addition, the nested selection structure appears in the outer selection structure's false path in this solution, which means it will be processed only when the outer selection structure's condition evaluates to false. The solutions in Figures 6-6 and 6-7 produce the same results. Neither solution is better than the other. Each simply represents a different way of solving the same problem.

Problem specification
The Danville city manager wants a program that determines voter eligibility and displays one of three messages. The messages and the criteria for displaying each message are as follows:

Message	Criteria
You are too young to vote.	person is younger than 18 years old
You can vote.	person is at least 18 years old and is registered to vote
You must register before you can vote.	person is at least 18 years old but is not registered to vote

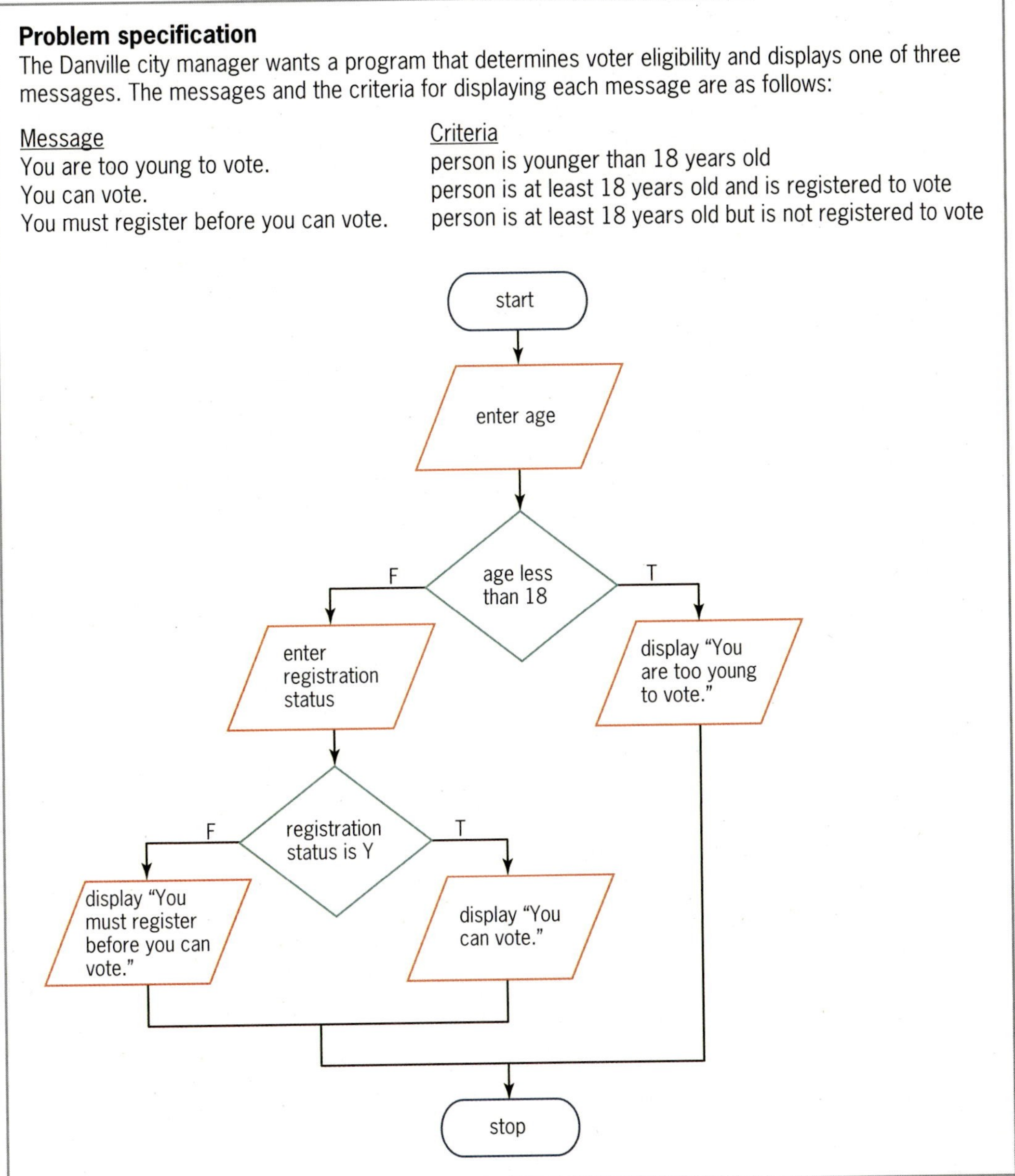

Figure 6-7 Another correct solution for the voter eligibility problem

Coding a Nested Selection Structure

In Lab 5-2 in Chapter 5, you created a program for the manager of Willow Springs Health Club. The program allows the manager to enter the number of calories and grams of fat contained in a specific food. The program then calculates and displays two values: the food's fat calories and its fat percentage. The health club's manager now wants the program to display the message "High in fat" when the food's fat percentage is greater than 30%; otherwise, the program should display the message "Not high in fat". To accomplish this task, you will need to add a nested dual-alternative selection structure to the program. You will code the nested selection structure using the dual-alternative form of the `if` statement. Recall that the dual-alternative form is simply an `if` statement that contains an `else` clause. The modified problem specification and program are shown in Figure 6-8. The modifications made to the original specification and program are shaded in the figure.

Problem specification

The manager of Willow Springs Health Club wants a program that allows her to enter the number of calories and grams of fat contained in a specific food. The program should calculate and display two values: the food's fat calories and its fat percentage. The fat calories are the number of calories attributed to fat and are calculated by multiplying the food's fat grams by the number 9; this is because each gram of fat contains nine calories. The fat percentage is the ratio of the food's fat calories to its total calories. You calculate the fat percentage by dividing the food's fat calories by its total calories and then multiplying the result by 100. The fat percentage should be displayed with zero decimal places. If the fat percentage is greater than 30%, the program should display the message "High in fat"; otherwise, it should display the message "Not high in fat". The program should display an appropriate error message if either or both input values are less than 0.

```
//Fig6-8.cpp - displays a food's fat
//calories and fat percentage
//Created/revised by <your name> on <current date>

#include <iostream>
#include <iomanip>
using namespace std;

int main()
{
    //declare variables
    int totalCals     = 0;
    int fatGrams      = 0;
    int fatCals       = 0;
    double fatPercent = 0.0;

    //enter input items
    cout << "Total calories: ";
    cin >> totalCals;
    cout << "Grams of fat: ";
    cin >> fatGrams;

    //determine whether the data is valid
    if (totalCals >= 0 && fatGrams >= 0)
    {
         //calculate and display the output
         fatCals = fatGrams * 9;
         fatPercent = static_cast<double>(fatCals)
               / static_cast<double>(totalCals) * 100;

         cout << "Fat calories: " << fatCals << endl;
         cout << fixed << setprecision(0);
         cout << "Fat percentage: " << fatPercent
              << "%" << endl;
```

Figure 6-8 Modified problem specification and program for the health club problem from Chapter 5 's Lab 5-2 *(continues)*

(continued)

```
35            if (fatPercent > 30.0)
36                cout << "High in fat" << endl;
37            else
38                cout << "Not high in fat" << endl;
39            //end if
40        }
41        else
42            cout << "Input error" << endl;
43        //end if
44
45        //system("pause");
46        return 0;
47    }   //end of main function
```

nested selection structure

your C++ development tool may require this statement

Figure 6-8 Modified problem specification and program for the health club problem from Chapter 5 's Lab 5-2

The outer selection structure's condition appears on Line 24 in the program, and it determines whether the user's input is valid. If the input is *not* valid, the outer selection structure's false path (which begins on Line 41) displays the "Input error" message. If the input *is* valid, on the other hand, the instructions in the outer selection structure's true path are processed. The true path begins on Line 25 and ends on Line 40. First, the true path calculates and then displays the food's fat calories and fat percentage. It then uses the nested selection structure shaded in Figure 6-8 to determine whether the fat percentage is greater than the `double` number 30.0. If the fat percentage is greater than 30.0, the nested selection structure's true path displays the message "High in fat"; otherwise, its false path displays the message "Not high in fat". Figure 6-9 shows a sample run of the modified health club program, and Figure 6-10 shows the modified program's flowchart.

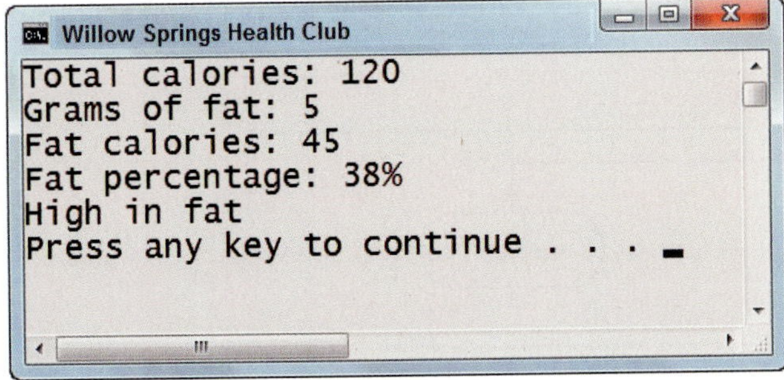

Figure 6-9 Sample run of the modified health club program

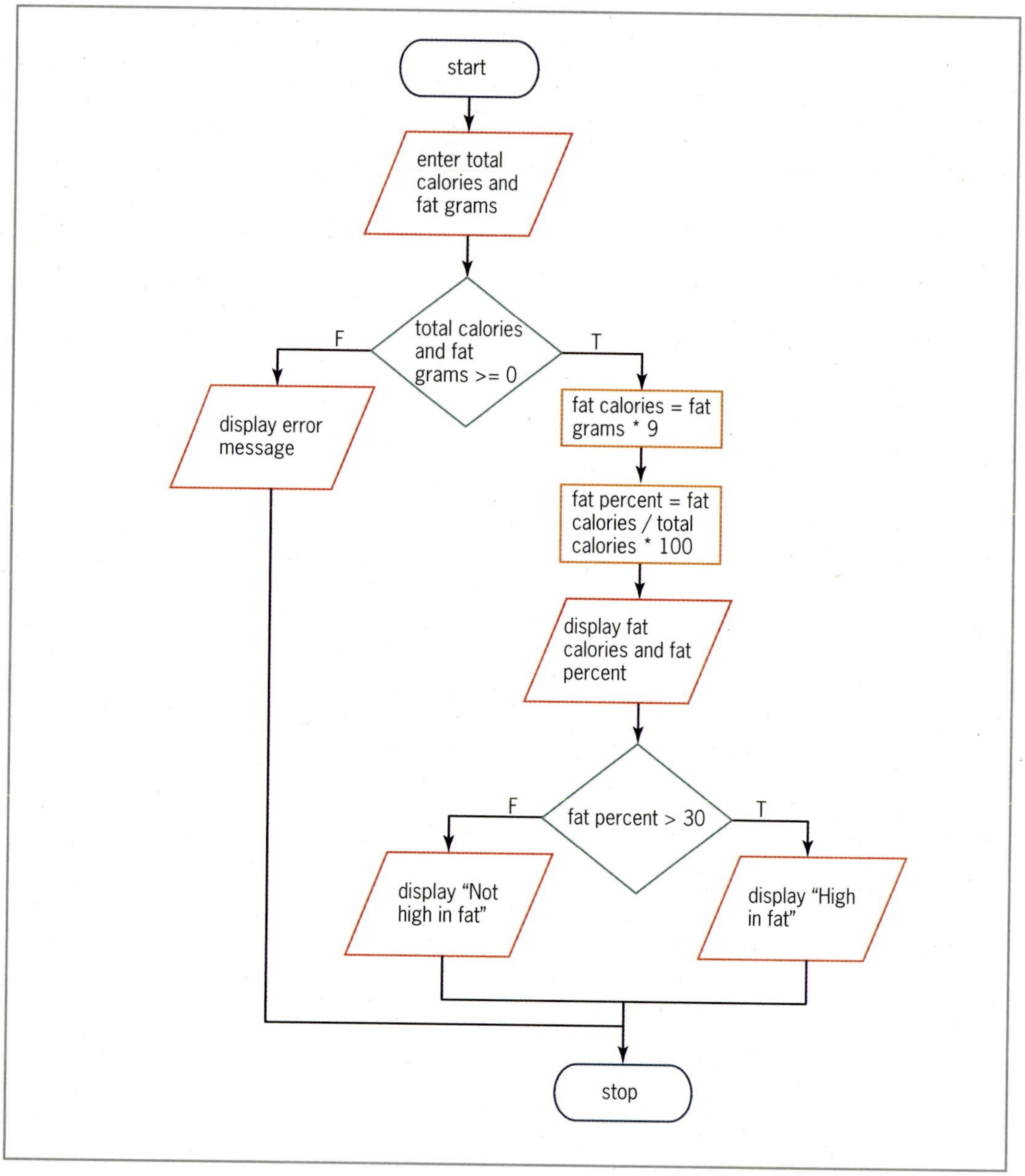

Figure 6-10 Flowchart for the modified health club program

The answers to Mini-Quiz questions are located in Appendix A.

Mini-Quiz 6-2

1. A selection structure should display one of the following messages, depending on a student's test score. Write the pseudocode for the selection structure.

Message	Test score
Great score!	at least 90
Good score	70 through 89
Retake the test	below 70

2. Draw a flowchart of the selection structure from Question 1.

3. Write the C++ code for the selection structure from either Question 1 or Question 2. The test score is stored in an `int` variable named `score`.

4. The manager of a golf course wants a program that displays the appropriate fee to charge a golfer. Club members pay a $5 fee. Non-members golfing on Monday through Thursday pay $15. Non-members golfing on Friday through Sunday pay $25. The condition in the program's outer selection structure should check the ______, while the condition in its nested selection structure should check the ______.
   a. membership status, day of the week
   b. day of the week, membership status
   c. membership status, fee
   d. fee, day of the week

Logic Errors in Selection Structures

In the next few sections, you will observe some of the common logic errors made when writing selection structures. Being aware of these errors will help prevent you from making them. In most cases, logic errors in selection structures are a result of one of the following three mistakes:

1. using a compound condition rather than a nested selection structure
2. reversing the decisions in the outer and nested selection structures
3. using an unnecessary nested selection structure

The ABC Company's bonus program will be used to demonstrate the logic errors listed above. The company pays each salesperson an 8% bonus on his or her sales. However, salespeople having a sales code of X receive an additional $150 bonus when their sales are greater than or equal to $10,000; otherwise, they receive an additional $125 bonus. Notice that the salesperson's code determines whether he or she receives an additional bonus. If the salesperson is entitled to the additional bonus, then the amount of his or her sales determines the appropriate additional amount. In this case, the decision regarding the salesperson's code is the primary decision, while the decision regarding the sales amount is the secondary decision. The pseudocode shown in Figure 6-11 represents a correct algorithm for the bonus program.

Ch06-ABC Correct Desk-Check video

```
1. enter the code and sales
2. calculate the bonus by multiplying the sales by .08
3. if (the code is X)
        if (the sales are greater than or equal to 10000)
                add 150 to the bonus
        else
                add 125 to the bonus
        end if
   end if
4. display the bonus
```

Figure 6-11 A correct algorithm for the bonus problem

You also can write the nested selection structure's condition as follows: *if (the sales are less than 10000)*. You then would reverse the instructions in the true and false paths.

To verify its accuracy, you will desk-check the algorithm from Figure 6-11 three times. Figure 6-12 shows the values you will use for the desk-checks and also includes the manually calculated results.

Code	Sales ($)	Bonus ($)
X	15000	1350
X	9000	845
A	13000	1040

Figure 6-12 Test data and manually calculated results

The first instruction in Figure 6-11's algorithm is to enter the code and sales. For the first desk-check, the code and sales are X and 15000, respectively. The second instruction calculates the bonus by multiplying the sales by .08; the answer is 1200. Figure 6-13 shows the current status of the desk-check table.

code	sales	bonus
X	15000	1200

Figure 6-13 Current status of the desk-check table

Next, the outer selection structure in the algorithm determines whether the salesperson's code is X. It is, so the nested selection structure checks whether the sales are greater than or equal to 10000. The sales are greater than 10000, so the nested selection structure's true path adds 150 to the bonus; the answer is 1350. After the bonus is calculated, both selection structures end. The last instruction in the algorithm displays the bonus on the screen. Figure 6-14 shows the desk-check table after completing the first desk-check. The 1350 in the bonus column agrees with the manual calculation shown earlier in Figure 6-12.

code	sales	bonus
X	15000	~~1200~~
		1350

Figure 6-14 Desk-check table after completing the first desk-check

Using the second set of test data, the user enters X as the code and 9000 as the sales. The second instruction in the algorithm calculates the bonus (720). Next, the outer selection structure determines whether the salesperson's code is X. It is, so the nested selection structure checks whether the sales are greater than or equal to 10000. The sales are not greater than or equal to 10000, so the nested selection structure's false path adds 125 to the bonus amount; the answer is 845. After the bonus is calculated, both selection structures end. The last instruction in the algorithm displays the bonus on the screen. Figure 6-15 shows the desk-check table after completing the second desk-check. The 845 in the bonus column agrees with the manual calculation shown earlier in Figure 6-12.

code	sales	bonus
~~X~~	~~15000~~	~~1200~~
		~~1350~~
X	9000	~~720~~
		845

Figure 6-15 Desk-check table after completing the second desk-check

Using the third set of test data, the user enters A as the code and 13000 as the sales. The second instruction in the algorithm calculates the bonus (1040). Next, the outer selection structure determines whether the salesperson's code is X. The code is not X, so the outer selection structure ends. Notice that the nested selection structure is not processed when the outer selection structure's condition is false. The last instruction in the algorithm displays the bonus on the screen. Figure 6-16 shows the desk-check table after completing the third desk-check. The final entry in the bonus column (1040) agrees with the manual calculation shown earlier in Figure 6-12.

code	sales	bonus
~~X~~	~~15000~~	~~1200~~
		~~1350~~
~~X~~	~~9000~~	~~720~~
		~~845~~
A	13000	1040

Figure 6-16 Desk-check table after completing the third desk-check

First Logic Error: Using a Compound Condition Rather Than a Nested Selection Structure

A common error made when writing selection structures is to use a compound condition in the outer selection structure when a nested selection structure is needed. Figure 6-17 shows an example of this error in the bonus algorithm. The correct algorithm is included in the figure for comparison. Notice that the incorrect algorithm uses one selection structure rather than two selection structures and that the selection structure contains a compound condition. Consider why the selection structure in the incorrect algorithm cannot be used in place of the selection structures in the correct one. In the correct algorithm, the outer and nested selection structures indicate that a hierarchy exists between the code and sales decisions: The code decision is always made first, followed by the sales decision (if necessary). In the incorrect algorithm, however, the compound condition indicates that no hierarchy exists between the code and sales decisions. Consider how this difference changes the algorithm.

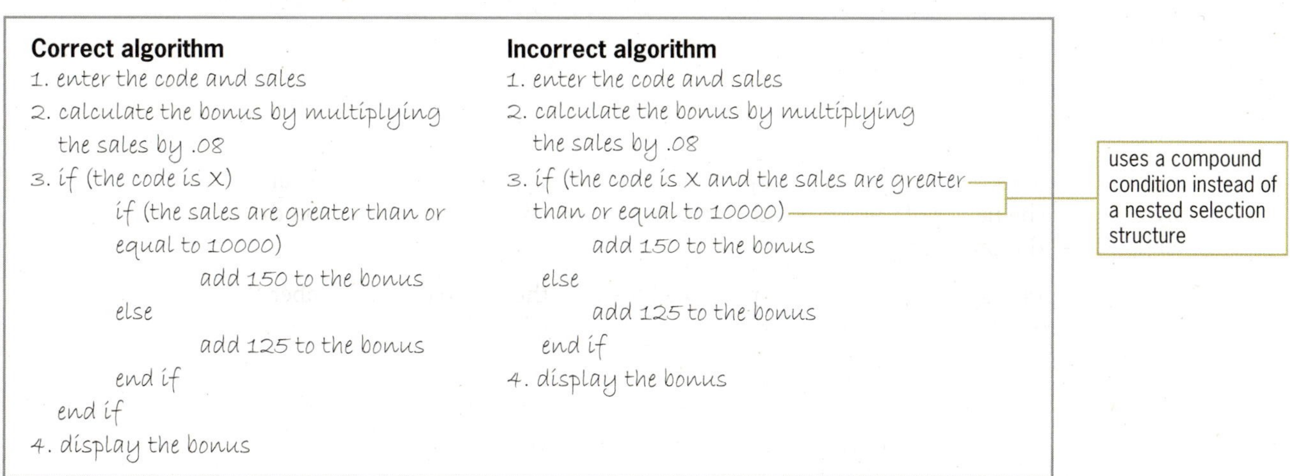

Correct algorithm

```
1. enter the code and sales
2. calculate the bonus by multiplying
   the sales by .08
3. if (the code is X)
        if (the sales are greater than or
        equal to 10000)
              add 150 to the bonus
        else
              add 125 to the bonus
        end if
   end if
4. display the bonus
```

Incorrect algorithm

```
1. enter the code and sales
2. calculate the bonus by multiplying
   the sales by .08
3. if (the code is X and the sales are greater
   than or equal to 10000)
        add 150 to the bonus
   else
        add 125 to the bonus
   end if
4. display the bonus
```


Figure 6-17 Correct algorithm and an incorrect algorithm containing the first logic error

To understand why the incorrect algorithm in Figure 6-17 will not work correctly, you will desk-check it using the same test data used to desk-check the correct algorithm. The first instruction in the incorrect algorithm is to enter the code and sales. For the first desk-check, the code and sales are X and 15000, respectively. The second instruction calculates the bonus by multiplying the sales by .08; the answer is 1200. The compound condition in the third instruction determines whether the salesperson's code is X and, at the same time, the sales are greater than or equal to 10000. In this case, the compound condition evaluates to true. Therefore, the selection structure's true path adds 150 to the bonus, giving 1350, and then the selection structure ends. The last instruction in the incorrect algorithm displays the bonus (1350) on the screen. Even though its selection structure is phrased incorrectly, the incorrect algorithm produces the same result as the correct algorithm using the first set of test data.

Ch06-First Logic Error Desk-Check video

Using the second set of test data, the user enters X as the code and 9000 as the sales. The second instruction in the incorrect algorithm calculates the bonus (720). The compound condition in the third instruction determines whether the salesperson's code is X and, at the same time, the sales are greater than or equal to 10000. In this case, the compound condition evaluates to false because the sales do not meet the specified criteria. As a result, the selection structure's false path adds 125 to the bonus, giving 845, and then the selection structure ends. The last instruction in the incorrect algorithm displays the bonus (845) on the screen. Here again, using the second set of test data, the incorrect algorithm produces the same result as the correct algorithm.

Using the third set of test data, the user enters A as the code and 13000 as the sales. The second instruction in the incorrect algorithm calculates the bonus (1040). The compound condition in the third instruction determines whether the salesperson's code is X and, at the same time, the sales are greater than or equal to 10000. In this case, the compound condition evaluates to false because the salesperson's code is not X. As a result, the selection structure's false path adds 125 to the bonus, giving 1165, and then the selection structure ends. The last instruction in the incorrect algorithm displays the bonus (1165) on the screen. Notice that the incorrect algorithm produces erroneous results using the third set of test data: According to Figure 6-12, the correct bonus is 1040.

Figure 6-18 shows the desk-check table for the incorrect algorithm. As indicated in the figure, the results of the first and second desk-checks are correct, but the result of the third desk-check is not correct.

code	sales	bonus	
~~X~~	~~15000~~	~~1200~~	
		~~1350~~	(correct result for the first desk-check)
~~X~~	~~9000~~	~~720~~	
		~~845~~	(correct result for the second desk-check)
A	13000	~~1040~~	
		1165	(incorrect result for the third desk-check)

Figure 6-18 Desk-check table for the incorrect algorithm in Figure 6-17

The importance of desk-checking an algorithm several times using different data cannot be emphasized enough. In this case, if you had used only the first two sets of data to desk-check the incorrect algorithm, you would not have discovered the error.

Second Logic Error: Reversing the Outer and Nested Decisions

Another common error made when writing selection structures is to reverse the decisions made by the outer and nested structures. Figure 6-19 shows an example of this error in the bonus algorithm. The correct algorithm is included in the figure for comparison. Unlike the selection structures in the correct algorithm, which determine the salesperson's code before determining his or her sales, the selection structures in the incorrect algorithm determine the sales before determining the code. Consider how this difference changes the algorithm. In the correct algorithm, the selection structures indicate that only salespeople who have a code of X receive an additional bonus. The selection structures in the incorrect algorithm, on the other hand, indicate that the additional bonus is given to all salespeople who have sales greater than or equal to 10000.

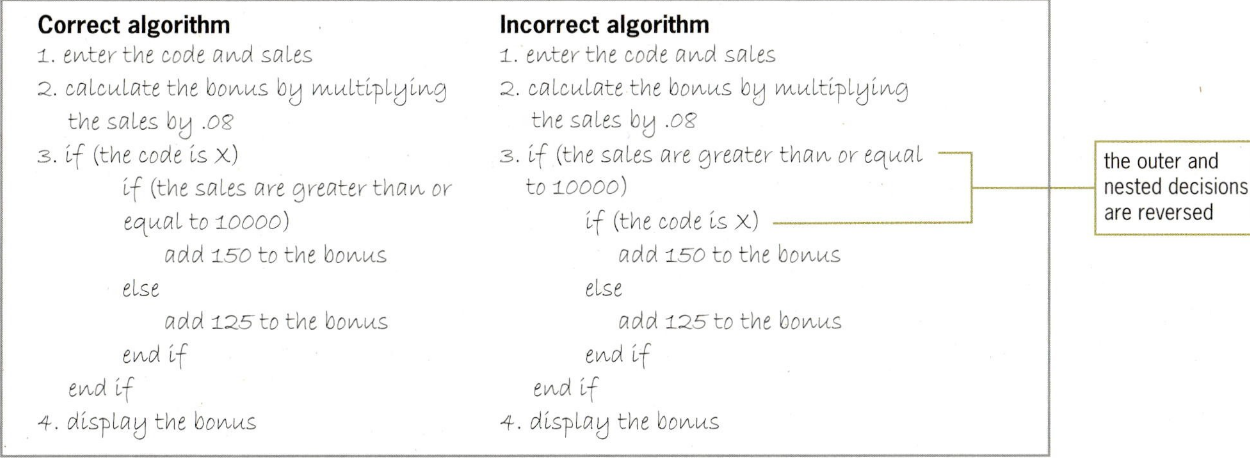

Figure 6-19 Correct algorithm and an incorrect algorithm containing the second logic error

Desk-checking the incorrect algorithm in Figure 6-19 will show you why the algorithm will not work correctly. The first instruction in the incorrect algorithm is to enter the code and sales—in this case, X and 15000. The second instruction multiplies the sales by .08; doing this results in a bonus of 1200. The condition in the outer selection structure in the third instruction determines whether the sales are greater than or equal to 10000. They are, so the nested selection structure's condition determines whether the salesperson's code is X. It is, so the nested selection structure's true path adds 150 to the bonus amount, giving 1350. After the bonus is calculated, both selection structures end. The last instruction in the incorrect algorithm displays the bonus (1350) on the screen. Even though its selection structures are phrased incorrectly, the incorrect algorithm produces the same result as the correct algorithm using the first set of test data.

Ch06-Second Logic Error Desk-Check video

Using the second set of test data, the user enters X as the code and 9000 as the sales. The second instruction in the incorrect algorithm calculates the bonus (720). The condition in the outer selection structure in the third instruction determines whether the sales are greater than or equal to 10000. They aren't, so the outer selection structure ends. Notice that the nested selection structure is not processed when the outer selection structure's condition evaluates to false. The last instruction in the incorrect algorithm displays 720 as the bonus, which is not correct.

Using the third set of test data, the user enters A as the code and 13000 as the sales. The second instruction in the incorrect algorithm calculates the bonus (1040). The condition in the outer selection structure in the third instruction determines whether the sales are greater than or equal to 10000. They are, so the nested selection structure's condition determines whether the salesperson's code is X. It isn't, so the nested selection structure's false path adds 125 to the bonus; this results in 1165. After the bonus is calculated, both selection structures end. The last instruction in the incorrect algorithm displays 1165 as the bonus, which is not correct. Figure 6-20 shows the desk-check table for the incorrect algorithm. As indicated in the figure, only the result of the first desk-check is correct.

code	sales	bonus	
~~X~~	~~15000~~	~~1200~~	
		~~1350~~	(correct result for the first desk-check)
~~X~~	~~9000~~	~~720~~	(incorrect result for the second desk-check)
A	13000	~~1040~~	
		1165	(incorrect result for the third desk-check)

Figure 6-20 Desk-check table for the incorrect algorithm in Figure 6-19

Third Logic Error: Using an Unnecessary Nested Selection Structure

Another error often made when writing selection structures is to include an unnecessary nested selection structure. In most cases, a selection structure containing this error will still produce the correct results. However, it will do so less efficiently than selection structures that are properly structured. Figure 6-21 shows an example of this error in the bonus algorithm. The correct algorithm is included in the figure for comparison. Unlike the correct algorithm, which contains two selection structures, the inefficient algorithm contains three selection structures. Notice that the condition in the third selection structure determines whether the sales are less than 10000; that condition is processed only when the second selection structure's condition evaluates to false. In other words, it is processed only when the sales are not greater than or equal to 10000. However, if the sales are not greater than or equal to 10000, then they would have to be less than 10000, so the third selection structure is unnecessary.

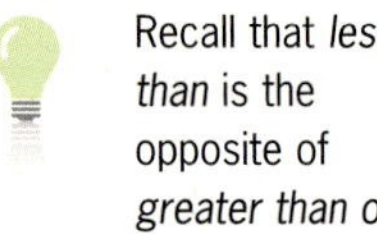

Recall that *less than* is the opposite of *greater than or equal to*.

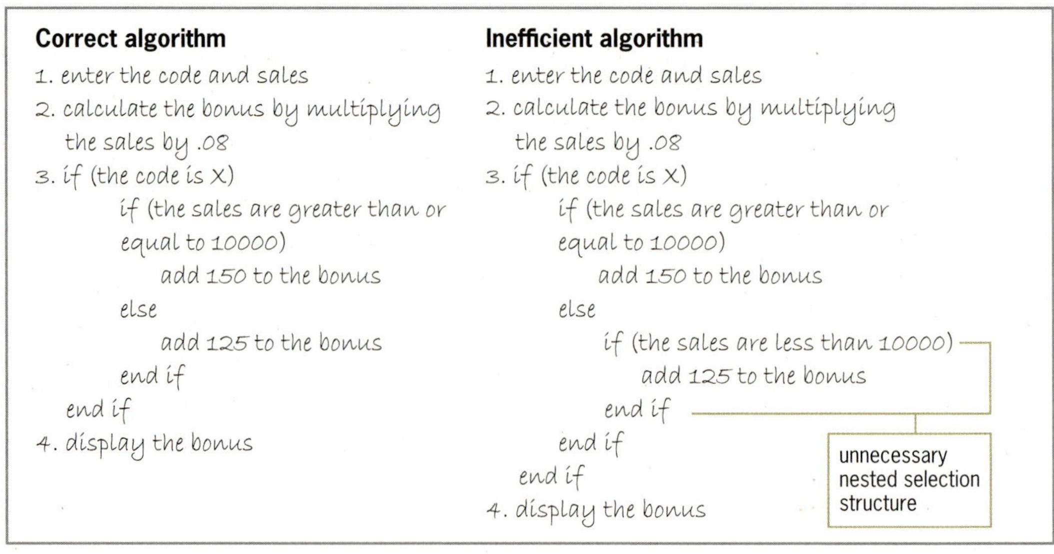

Correct algorithm

```
1. enter the code and sales
2. calculate the bonus by multiplying
   the sales by .08
3. if (the code is X)
        if (the sales are greater than or
        equal to 10000)
            add 150 to the bonus
        else
            add 125 to the bonus
        end if
   end if
4. display the bonus
```

Inefficient algorithm

```
1. enter the code and sales
2. calculate the bonus by multiplying
   the sales by .08
3. if (the code is X)
        if (the sales are greater than or
        equal to 10000)
            add 150 to the bonus
        else
            if (the sales are less than 10000)
                add 125 to the bonus
            end if
        end if
   end if
4. display the bonus
```


Figure 6-21 Correct algorithm and an inefficient algorithm containing the third logic error

We'll desk-check the inefficient algorithm in Figure 6-21 so you can observe why the last selection structure is unnecessary. The first instruction in the inefficient algorithm is to enter the code and sales—in this case, X and 15000. The second instruction calculates the bonus by multiplying the sales by .08; the answer is 1200. The condition in the first selection structure determines whether the salesperson's code is X. It is, so the condition in the second selection structure checks whether the sales are greater than or equal to 10000. They are, so the second selection structure's true path adds 150 to the bonus amount, giving 1350. The last instruction in the inefficient algorithm displays 1350 as the bonus, which is correct.

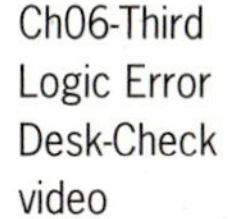

Ch06-Third Logic Error Desk-Check video

Using the second set of test data, the user enters X as the code and 9000 as the sales. The second instruction in the inefficient algorithm calculates the bonus (720). The condition in the first selection structure determines whether the salesperson's code is X. It is, so the condition in the second selection structure checks whether the sales are greater than or equal to 10000. They aren't, so the condition in the third selection structure determines whether the sales are less than 10000—an unnecessary decision. In this case, the sales are less than 10000, so the third selection structure's true path adds 125 to the bonus, giving 845. The last instruction in the inefficient algorithm displays 845 as the bonus, which is correct.

Using the third set of test data, the user enters A as the code and 13000 as the sales. The second instruction in the inefficient algorithm calculates the bonus (1040). The condition in the first selection structure determines whether the salesperson's code is X. It's not, so the first selection structure ends. Notice that the two nested selection structures are not processed when the first selection structure's condition evaluates to false. The last instruction in the inefficient algorithm displays 1040 as the bonus, which is correct.

For more experience with problems containing nested selection structures, see the Nested Selection Structures section in the Ch06WantMore.pdf file.

Figure 6-22 shows the desk-check table for the inefficient algorithm. Although the results of the three desk-checks are correct, the result of the second desk-check is obtained in a less efficient manner.

code	sales	bonus	
~~X~~	~~15000~~	~~1200~~	
		~~1350~~	(correct result for the first desk-check)
~~X~~	~~9000~~	~~720~~	
		~~845~~	(correct but inefficient result for the second desk-check)
A	13000	1040	(correct result for the third desk-check)

Figure 6-22 Desk-check table for the inefficient algorithm in Figure 6-21

Mini-Quiz 6-3

1. List the three errors commonly made when writing selection structures.
2. Which of the errors from Question 1 makes the selection structure inefficient but still produces the correct results?
3. What is wrong with the algorithm shown in Figure 6-23?
4. Does Algorithm A in Figure 6-24 give you the same results as the solution shown earlier in Figure 6-2? If not, why not?
5. Does Algorithm B in Figure 6-24 give you the same results as the solution shown earlier in Figure 6-2? If not, why not?

The answers to Mini-Quiz questions are located in Appendix A.

```
1. shoot the basketball
2. if (the basketball went through the hoop)
        say "I did it!"
   else
        if (the basketball did not go through the hoop)
              say "Missed it!"
        end if
   end if
```

Figure 6-23 Algorithm for Question 3 in Mini-Quiz 6-3

```
Algorithm A
1. shoot the basketball
2. if (the basketball went through the hoop and Maleek was either inside or on the 3-point line)
        say "I did it!"
        say "2 points for me"
   else
        if (Maleek was behind the 3-point line)
              say "I did it!"
              say "3 points for me"
        else
              say "Missed it!"
        end if
   end if

Algorithm B
1. shoot the basketball
2. if (the basketball did not go through the hoop)
        say "Missed it!"
   else
        say "I did it!"
        if (Maleek was either inside or on the 3-point line)
              say "2 points for me"
        else
              say "3 points for me"
        end if
   end if
```

Figure 6-24 Algorithms for Questions 4 and 5 in Mini-Quiz 6-3

Multiple-Alternative Selection Structures

Figure 6-25 shows the problem specification and IPO chart for the Kindlon High School problem. The problem's solution requires a selection structure that can choose from several alternatives. In this case, it can choose from several different letter grades. As the figure indicates, when the letter grade is A, the selection structure should display the message "Excellent". When the letter grade is B, the selection structure should display the message "Above Average", and so on. Selection structures containing several alternatives are referred to as **multiple-alternative selection structures** or **extended selection structures**.

Problem specification

Mr. Jacoby teaches math at Kindlon High School. He wants a program that displays a message based on a letter grade he enters. The valid letter grades and their corresponding messages are shown below. If the letter grade is not valid, the program should display the "Invalid grade" message.

Letter grade	Message
A	Excellent
B	Above Average
C	Average
D	Below Average
F	Below Average

Input	**Processing**	**Output**
grade	Processing items: none	message

```
Algorithm:
1. enter the grade
2. if (the grade is one of the following:)
        A          display "Excellent" message
        B          display "Above Average" message
        C          display "Average" message
        D or F     display "Below Average" message
   else
        display "Invalid grade"
   end if
```

Figure 6-25 Problem specification and IPO chart for the Kindlon High School problem

Figure 6-26 shows the Kindlon High School algorithm in flowchart form. The diamond in the flowchart represents the multiple-alternative selection structure's condition. Recall that the diamond is also used to represent the condition in both single-alternative and dual-alternative selection structures. However, unlike the diamond in both of those selection structures, the diamond in a multiple-alternative selection structure has several flowlines (rather than only two flowlines) leading out of the symbol. Each flowline represents a possible path and must be marked appropriately, indicating the value or values necessary for the path to be chosen.

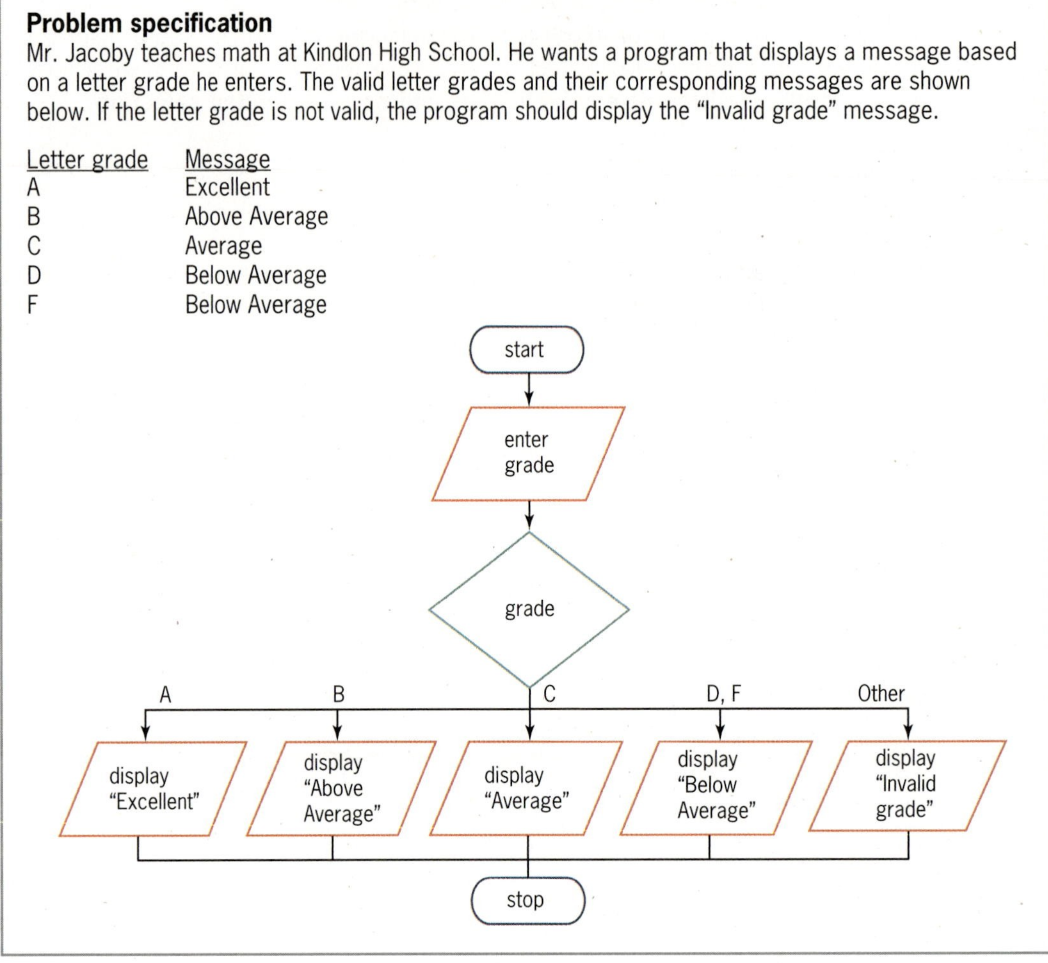

Figure 6-26 Flowchart for the Kindlon High School problem

Figure 6-27 shows two ways of coding the multiple-alternative selection structure from Figures 6-25 and 6-26. In both examples, `grade` is a `char` variable that gets its value from the user at the keyboard. Both examples use the multiple-alternative form of the `if` statement to code the selection structure. The multiple-alternative form contains several `if` and `else` clauses. Although both examples produce the same result, Example 2 provides a more convenient way of using the `if` statement to code a multiple-alternative selection structure.

Example 1

```
grade = toupper(grade);
if (grade == 'A')
        cout << "Excellent";
else
        if (grade == 'B')
                cout << "Above Average";
        else
                if (grade == 'C')
                        cout << "Average";
                else
                        if (grade == 'D' || grade == 'F')
                                cout << "Below Average";
                        else    //default
                                cout << "Invalid grade";
                        //end if
                //end if
        //end if
//end if
```

you get here when the grade is not A

you get here when the grade is not A and not B

you get here when the grade is not A, B, or C

you get here when the grade is not A, B, C, D, or F

Example 2

```
grade = toupper(grade);
if (grade == 'A')
     cout << "Excellent";
else if (grade == 'B')
     cout << "Above Average";
else if (grade == 'C')
     cout << "Average";
else if (grade == 'D' || grade == 'F')
     cout << "Below Average";
else //default
     cout << "Invalid grade";
//end if
```

you can use one comment to mark the end of the entire structure

Figure 6-27 Two ways of coding the multiple-alternative selection structure from Figures 6-25 and 6-26

The `switch` Statement

Instead of using the `if` statement to code a multiple-alternative selection structure in C++, you sometimes (but not always) can use the **`switch` statement**. Figure 6-28 shows the `switch` statement's syntax and includes an example of using the statement in place of the `if` statements shown in Figure 6-27. The `switch` statement begins with the `switch` clause, which contains a *selectorExpression* enclosed in parentheses. The *selectorExpression* can contain any combination of variables, constants, functions, and operators; however, the combination must result in a value whose data type is `bool`, `char`, `short`, `int`, or `long`. In the example in Figure 6-28, the *selectorExpression* is a `char` variable named `grade`.

Following the `switch` clause is a statement block. Recall from Chapter 5 that a statement block is one or more statements enclosed in a set of braces. Between the `switch` statement's opening and closing braces are one or more `case` clauses; you can include as many `case` clauses as necessary. Each `case` clause in a `switch` statement represents a different alternative.

Notice that each `case` clause contains a value followed by a colon. The value can be a literal constant, a named constant, or an expression composed of literal and named constants. The data type of the value should be compatible with the data type of the *selectorExpression*. When the *selectorExpression* is numeric, the values in the `case` clauses should be numeric. Likewise, when the *selectorExpression* is a character, the values should be characters. In the example in Figure 6-28, the data type of the *selectorExpression* is `char`, and so is the data type of the values in the `case` clauses (`'A'`, `'B'`, `'C'`, `'D'`, and `'F'`). (Recall that `char` literal constants are enclosed in single quotation marks.) Following the colon in each `case` clause are one or more statements that are processed when the *selectorExpression* matches that `case`'s value.

The `switch` statement is often used in programs that display a menu of choices for the user.

HOW TO Use the `switch` Statement

Syntax

switch (*selectorExpression***)**
{
case *value1***:**
  one or more statements
  [**break;**]
[**case** *value2***:**
  one or more statements
  [**break;**]]
[**case** *valueN***:**
  one or more statements
  [**break;**]]
[**default:**
  one or more statements to be processed when the selectorExpression does not match any of the values in the `case` *clauses*
  [**break;**]]
} `//end switch`

Example

```
grade = toupper(grade);
switch (grade)
{
case 'A':
      cout << "Excellent";
      break;
case 'B':
      cout << "Above Average";
      break;
case 'C':
      cout << "Average";
      break;
case 'D':
case 'F':
      cout << "Below Average";
      break;
default:
      cout << "Invalid grade";
}     //end switch
```


Figure 6-28 How to use the `switch` statement

After the computer processes the instructions in a `case` clause, you typically want the computer to leave the `switch` statement without processing the remaining instructions in the statement. You do this by including the `break` statement as the last statement in the `case` clause. The **`break` statement** tells the computer to leave ("break out of") the `switch` statement at that point. If you do not use the `break` statement in a `case` clause, the computer continues processing the remaining instructions in the `switch` statement; this may or may not be what you intended. After processing the `break` statement, the computer processes the instruction that follows the `switch` statement's closing brace. For clarity, it is a good programming practice to document the end of the `switch` statement with a comment, such as `//end switch`.

In addition to the `case` clauses, you also can include one `default` clause in a `switch` statement. Although the `default` clause can appear anywhere within the `switch` statement, it usually is entered as the last clause in the statement, as shown in Figure 6-28. When it is in that position, it does not need a `break` statement; however, some programmers include the `break` statement for clarity. If the `default` clause is not the last clause, a `break` statement is required in order to stop the computer from processing the instructions in the next `case` clause. In Computer Exercises 19 and 20, you will observe the result of not using the `break` statement to break out of the `switch` statement.

The `switch` statement sounds more difficult than it really is. When processing the statement, the computer simply compares the value of the *selectorExpression* with the value listed in each of the `case` clauses, one `case` clause at a time beginning with the first. If a match is found, the computer processes the instructions contained in that `case` clause, stopping only when it encounters either a `break` statement or the `switch` statement's closing brace; the computer then skips to the instruction following the closing brace. If a match is *not* found and there is a `default` clause, the computer processes the instructions in the `default` clause, stopping only when it encounters either a `break` statement or the `switch` statement's closing brace; the computer then skips to the instruction following the closing brace. If a match is *not* found and there isn't a `default` clause, the computer just skips to the instruction following the closing brace.

Desk-checking the code in Figure 6-28 will help you understand how the `switch` statement is processed by the computer. You will desk-check the code using the following three letter grades: B, D, and X. The `switch (grade)` clause tells the computer to compare the value in the `grade` variable (the letter B) with the value listed in the first `case` clause (the letter A). Both letters do not match, so the computer compares the letter stored in the `grade` variable (B) with the letter listed in the second `case` clause (B). In this case, both letters match, so the computer processes the instructions contained in the second `case` clause. The first statement in the second `case` clause displays the message "Above Average" on the screen. The next statement, `break;`, tells the computer to skip the remaining instructions in the `switch` statement and continue processing with the instruction that follows the `switch` statement's closing brace.

Ch06-Switch Statement Desk-Checks video

Now use the letter D to desk-check the code. The switch (grade) clause tells the computer to compare the value in the grade variable (the letter D) with the value listed in the first case clause (the letter A). Both letters do not match, so the computer compares the letter stored in the grade variable (D) with the letter listed in the second case clause (B). Here again, both letters do not match, so the computer compares the letter stored in the grade variable (D) with the letter listed in the third case clause (C). Here too, both letters do not match, so the computer compares the letter stored in the grade variable (D) with the letter listed in the fourth case clause (D); this time, the computer finds a match. However, notice that there is no statement immediately below the case 'D': clause. So, what (if anything) will appear when the grade is D?

Recall that when the value of the *selectorExpression* matches the value in a case clause, the computer processes the instructions contained in that clause until it encounters either a break statement or the switch statement's closing brace. In this case, not finding any instructions in the case 'D': clause, the computer continues processing with the instructions in the next clause, which is the case 'F': clause. The first instruction in the case 'F': clause displays the message "Below Average", which is the correct message to display. The second instruction tells the computer to break out of the switch statement. In other words, the cout << "Below Average"; and break; statements are processed when the grade is either D or F. The computer then skips to the instruction following the switch statement's closing brace. As this example shows, you can process the same instructions for more than one value by listing each value in a separate case clause, as long as the clauses appear together in the switch statement. The last case clause in the group of related clauses should contain the instructions you want the computer to process when one of the values in the group matches the *selectorExpression*. Only the last case clause in the group of related clauses should contain the break statement.

Finally, you will use the letter X to desk-check the code. When processing the switch statement, the computer compares the value stored in the grade variable (the letter X) with the value listed in each of the case clauses, one case clause at a time beginning with the first. Notice that the letter X does not appear as a value in any of the case clauses. When the *selectorExpression* does not match any of the values listed in the case clauses, the computer processes the instructions contained in the default clause. If there is no default clause, the computer skips to the instruction following the switch statement's closing brace. In the example shown earlier in Figure 6-28, the instruction in the default clause displays the message "Invalid grade" on the screen. If the default clause is the last clause in the switch statement, as it is in Figure 6-28, the computer then skips to the instruction following the switch statement's closing brace.

Figure 6-29 shows another example of a multiple-alternative selection structure. In this example, a product's ID determines its price. The ID is stored in an int variable named productId. The switch statement used to code the multiple-alternative selection structure is shaded in the figure. The statement assigns 50.55 to the price variable when the product ID is 1. When the product ID is either 2 or 9, the switch statement assigns 12.35 to the price variable. It assigns 11.46 to the price variable when the product ID is one of the following: 5, 7, or 11. Finally, it assigns –1 to the price variable when the product ID is anything other than 1, 2, 5, 7, 9, or 11. The if statement in the example compares the value stored in the price variable with the number –1 and then displays either the "Invalid product ID" message or the product's price. The flowchart for the program is shown in Figure 6-30.

Problem specification
The sales manager at Warren Company wants a program that displays a price based on a product ID she enters. The valid product IDs and their corresponding prices are shown here. If the product ID is not valid, the program should display the "Invalid product ID" message.

Product ID	Price
1	50.55
2	12.35
5	11.46
7	11.46
9	12.35
11	11.46

IPO chart information	C++ instructions
Input	
product ID	`int productId = 0;`
Processing	
none	
Output	
price	`double price = 0.0;`

Algorithm

1. enter the product ID

```
cout << "Product ID (1, 2, 5,
7, 9, or 11): ";
cin >> productId;
```

2. if (the product ID is one of the following:)
       1   assign 50.55 as the price
       2 or 9   assign 12.35 as the price
       5, 7, or 11 assign 11.46 as the price
   else
       assign -1 as the price
   end if

```
switch (productId)
{
    case 1:
        price = 50.55;
        break;
    case 2:
    case 9:
        price = 12.35;
        break;
    case 5:
    case 7:
    case 11:
        price = 11.46;
        break;
    default:
        price = -1;
} //end switch
```

3. if (the price is -1)
       display "Invalid product ID" message
   else
       display the price
   end if

```
if (price == -1)
    cout << "Invalid product ID"
    << endl;
else
    cout << "Price: $" << price
    << endl;
//end if
```

Figure 6-29 Problem specification, IPO chart information, and C++ instructions for the Warren Company problem

For more experience with problems containing multiple-alternative selection structures, see the Multiple Alternative Selection Structures section in the Ch06WantMore.pdf file.

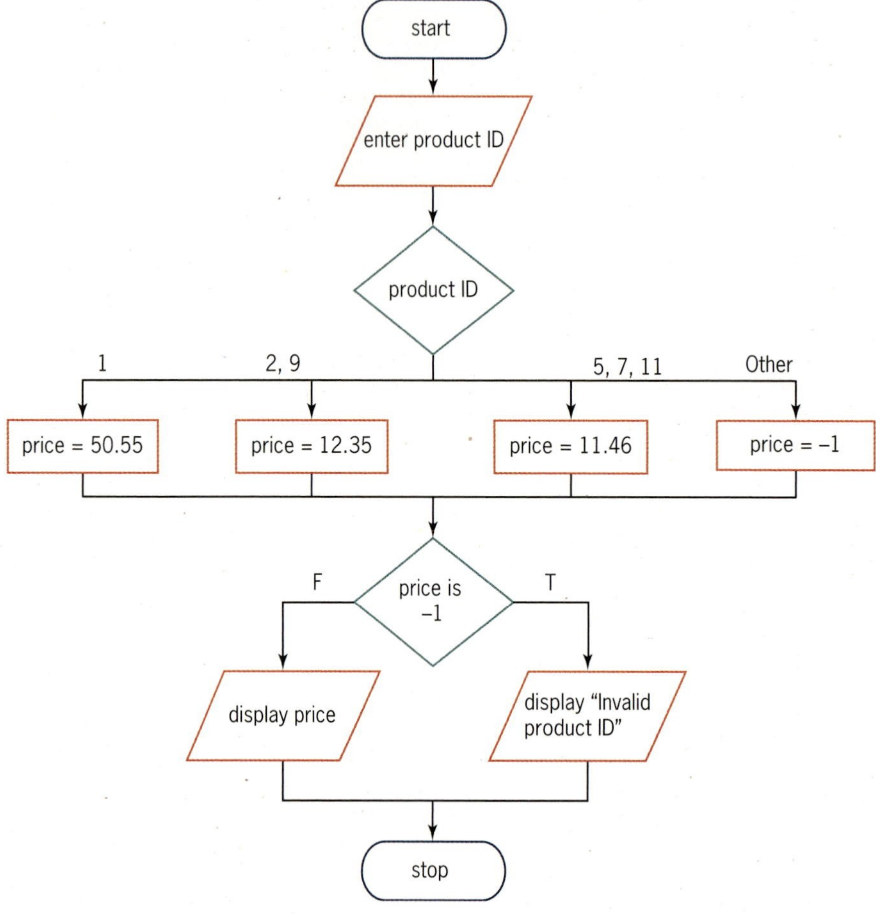

Figure 6-30 Flowchart for the Warren Company problem

The answers to Mini-Quiz questions are located in Appendix A.

Mini-Quiz 6-4

1. A selection structure should display one of the following messages, depending on a student's test score. Write the C++ code using the more convenient form of the `if` statement.

Message	Test score
Great score!	at least 90
Good score	70 through 89
Retake the test	0 through 69
Invalid test score	less than 0

2. If a `switch` statement's *selectorExpression* is an `int` variable named `stateCode`, which of the following `case` clauses will be processed when the `stateCode` variable contains the number 2?

   a. `case "2":`
   b. `case 2:`
   c. `case = 2;`
   d. `case == 2;`

3. The ________ statement tells the computer to leave the `switch` statement at that point.

LAB 6-1 Stop and Analyze

Study the flowchart shown in Figure 6-31, and then answer the questions.

The answers to the labs are located in Appendix A.

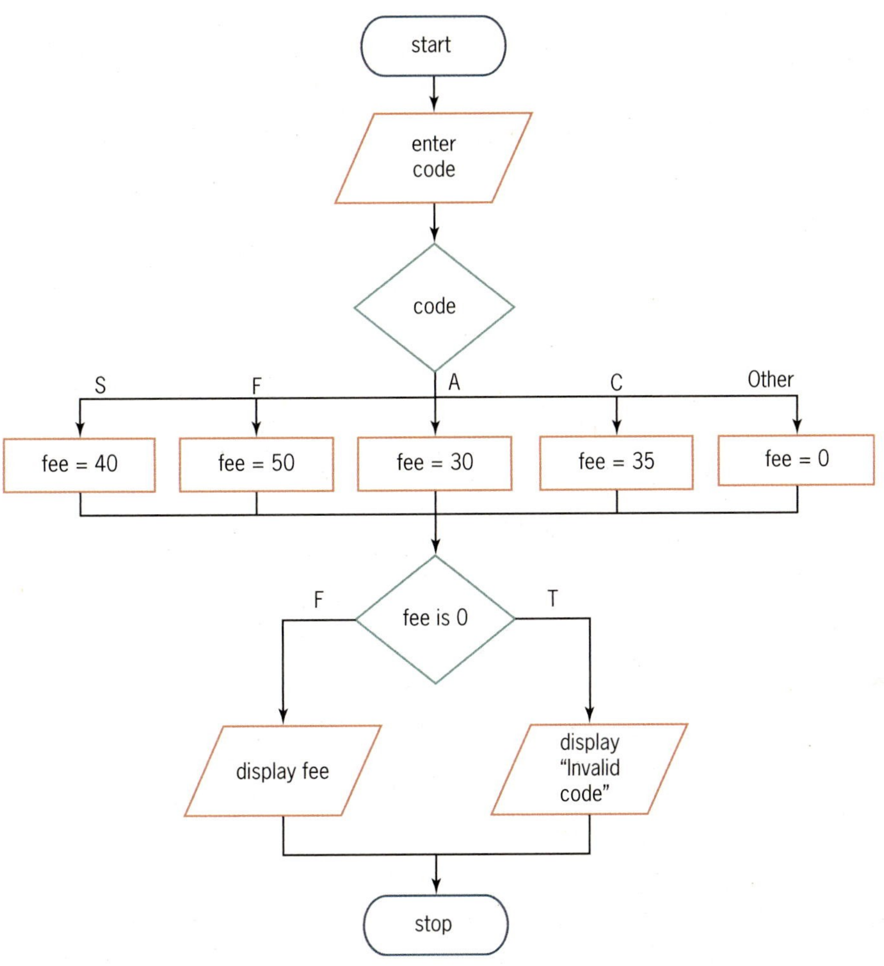

Figure 6-31 Flowchart for Lab 6-1

QUESTIONS

1. What will the program display when the code is the letter C?
2. How can you write the multiple-alternative selection structure in Figure 6-31 using the longer form of the `if` statement?
3. How can you write the multiple-alternative selection structure in Figure 6-31 using the shorter form of the `if` statement?
4. How can you write the multiple-alternative selection structure in Figure 6-31 using the `switch` statement?
5. What changes would you need to make to the code from Question 4 so that each `case` clause displays the appropriate fee, and the `default` clause displays the "Invalid code" message?

LAB 6-2 Plan and Create

In this lab, you will plan and create an algorithm for Golf Pro. The problem specification and examples of calculations are shown in Figure 6-32.

Problem specification

Jennifer Yardley is the owner of Golf Pro, a U.S. company that sells golf equipment both domestically and abroad. She wants a program that displays the amount of a salesperson's commission. A commission is a percentage of the sales made by the salesperson. Some companies use a fixed rate to calculate the commission, while others (like Golf Pro) use a rate that varies with the amount of sales.

Golf Pro's commission schedule is shown below, along with examples of using the schedule to calculate the commission on three different sales amounts. Notice that the commission for each range in the schedule is calculated differently. The commission for sales in the first range is calculated by multiplying the sales by 2%. As Example 1 shows, if the sales are $15,000, the commission is $300. The commission for sales in the second range is calculated by multiplying the sales over $100,000 by 5% and then adding $2,000 to the result. As Example 2 shows, if the sales are $250,000, the commission is $9,500. The commission for sales starting at $400,001 is calculated by multiplying the sales over $400,000 by 10%, and then adding $17,000 to the result. Example 3 indicates that the commission for sales of $500,000 is $27,000.

If the sales do not fall in any of the sales ranges (in other words, they are less than 0), the program should display the message "The sales cannot be less than 0."

Sales range	Commission
$0 – 100,000	multiply the sales by 2%
$100,001 – 400,000	multiply the sales over 100,000 by 5% and then add 2,000 to the result
$400,001 and over	multiply the sales over 400,000 by 10% and then add 17,000 to the result

Example 1

Sales: $15,000
Commission: 15,000 * .02 = 300

Example 2

Sales: $250,000
Commission: (250,000 – 100,000) * .05 + 2,000 = 9,500

Example 3

Sales: $500,000
Commission: (500,000 – 400,000) * .1 + 17,000 = 27,000

Figure 6-32 Problem specification and calculation examples for Lab 6-2

First, analyze the problem, looking for the output first and then for the input. In this case, the user wants the program to display a salesperson's commission. To calculate the commission, the computer will need to know the salesperson's sales and how to calculate the commission. The sales amount will be entered by the user. The calculation instructions, on the other hand, are specified in the problem specification.

Next, plan the algorithm. Recall that most algorithms begin with an instruction to enter the input items into the computer, followed by instructions that process the input items, typically including the items in one or more calculations. Most algorithms end with one or more instructions that display, print, or store the output items. Figure 6-33 shows the completed IPO chart for the Golf Pro problem.

Input	Processing	Output
sales	Processing items: none	commission

```
Algorithm:
1. enter the sales
2. if (the sales are less than 0)
      commission = -1
   else if (the sales are one of the following:)
      0 through 100,000
             commission = sales * .02
      100,001 through 400,000
             commission = (sales - 100,000) * .05 + 2000
      400,001 and over
             commission = (sales - 400,000) * .1 + 17000
   end if
3. if (the commission is not -1)
      display the commission
   else
      display an error message
   end if
```

Figure 6-33 Completed IPO chart for the Golf Pro problem

After completing the IPO chart, you then move on to the third step in the problem-solving process, which is to desk-check the algorithm. You will desk-check the Golf Pro algorithm four times, using sales of 15,000; 250,000; 500,000; and –500. Figure 6-34 shows the completed desk-check table. Notice that the amounts in the commission column for the first three desk-checks agree with the results of the manual calculations from Figure 6-32.

sales	commission
~~15000~~	~~300~~
~~250000~~	~~9500~~
~~500000~~	~~27000~~
-500	-1

Figure 6-34 Completed desk-check table for the Golf Pro algorithm

The fourth step in the problem-solving process is to code the algorithm into a program. You begin by declaring memory locations that will store the values of the input, processing (if any), and output items. The Golf Pro problem will need two memory locations to store the input and output items. The input item (sales) will be stored in a variable because the user should be allowed to change its value during runtime. The output item (commission) also will be stored in a variable; this is because its value is based on the current value of the input item. The sales amount will always be an integer, so you will store it in an `int` variable. You will store the commission in a `double` variable because its value will be a real number. Figure 6-35 shows the IPO chart information and corresponding C++ instructions.

IPO chart information	C++ instructions
Input	
sales	`int sales = 0;`
Processing	
none	
Output	
commission	`double commission = 0.0;`
Algorithm	
1. enter the sales	`cout << "Sales: ";` `cin >> sales;`
2. if (the sales are less than 0)	`if (sales < 0)`
commission = -1	`commission = -1;`
else if (the sales are one of the following:)	`else if (sales <= 100000)`
0 through 100,000	`commission = sales * .02;`
commission = sales * .02	`else if (sales <= 400000)`
100,001 through 400,000	`commission = (sales - 100000)`
commission = (sales - 100,000)	`* .05 + 2000;`
* .05 + 2000	`else`
400,001 and over	`commission = (sales - 400000)`
commission = (sales - 400,000)	`* .1 + 17000;`
* .1 + 17000	`//end if`
end if	
3. if (the commission is not -1)	`if (commission != -1)`
display the commission	`cout << "Commission: $" <<`
else	`commission << endl;`
display an error message	`else`
end if	`cout << "The sales cannot`
	`be less than 0." << endl;`
	`//end if`

Figure 6-35 IPO chart information and C++ instructions for the Golf Pro problem

The fifth step in the problem-solving process is to desk-check the program. You begin by placing the names of the declared variables and named constants (if any) in a new desk-check table, along with their initial values. You then desk-check the remaining C++ instructions in order, recording in the desk-check table any changes made to the variables. Figure 6-36 shows the completed desk-check table for the Golf Pro program. The results agree with those shown in the algorithm's desk-check table in Figure 6-34.

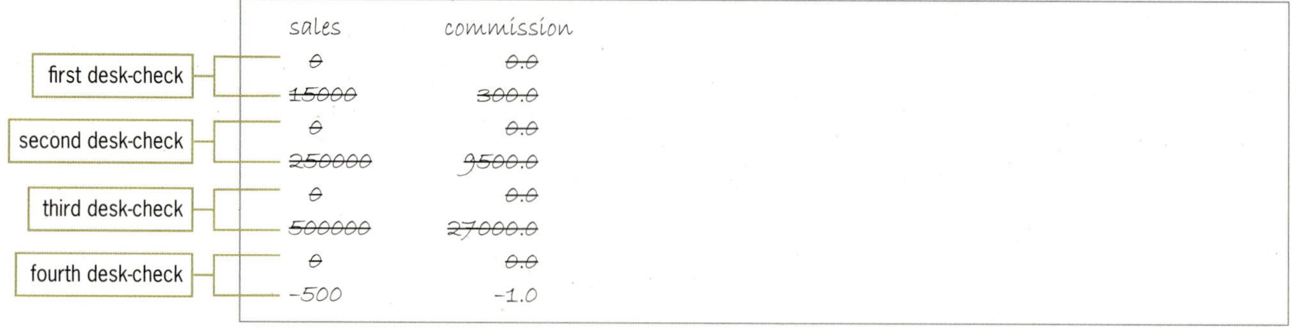

	sales	commission
first desk-check	~~0~~	~~0.0~~
	~~15000~~	~~300.0~~
second desk-check	~~0~~	~~0.0~~
	~~250000~~	~~9500.0~~
third desk-check	~~0~~	~~0.0~~
	~~500000~~	~~27000.0~~
fourth desk-check	~~0~~	~~0.0~~
	-500	-1.0

Figure 6-36 Completed desk-check table for the Golf Pro program

The final step in the problem-solving process is to evaluate and modify (if necessary) the program. Recall that you evaluate a program by entering its instructions into the computer, and then using the computer to run (execute) it. While the program is running, you enter the same sample data used when desk-checking the program.

DIRECTIONS

Follow the instructions for starting your C++ development tool. Depending on the development tool you are using, you may need to create a new project; if so, name the project Lab6-2 Project and save it in the Cpp7\Chap06 folder. Enter the instructions shown in Figure 6-37 in a source file named Lab6-2.cpp. (Do not enter the line numbers.) Save the file in either the project folder or the Cpp7\Chap06 folder. Now follow the appropriate instructions for running the Lab6-2.cpp file. Use the sample data from Figure 6-36 to test the program. If necessary, correct any bugs (errors) in the program.

```
//Lab6-2.cpp - displays a salesperson's commission
//Created/revised by <your name> on <current date>

#include <iostream>
#include <iomanip>
using namespace std;

int main()
{
      //declare variables
      int sales         = 0;
      double commission = 0.0;

      //enter input
      cout << "Sales: ";
      cin >> sales;

      //determine commission
      if (sales < 0)
          commission = -1;
      else if (sales <= 100000)
          commission = sales * .02;
      else if (sales <= 400000)
          commission = (sales - 100000) * .05 + 2000;
      else
          commission = (sales - 400000) * .1 + 17000;
      //end if

      //display commission or error message
      if (commission != -1)
      {
          cout << fixed << setprecision(2);
          cout << "Commission: $" << commission << endl;
      }
      else
          cout << "The sales cannot be less than 0." << endl;
      //end if

      //system("pause");
      return 0;
  } //end of main function
```

if your C++ development tool requires this statement, delete the two forward slashes

Figure 6-37 Golf Pro program

LAB 6-3 Modify

If necessary, create a new project named Lab6-3 Project and save it in the Cpp7\Chap06 folder. Enter (or copy) the Lab6-2.cpp instructions into a new source file named Lab6-3.cpp. Change Lab6-2.cpp in the first comment to Lab6-3.cpp.

Golf Pro now uses the commission chart shown in Figure 6-38 to determine a salesperson's commission. Modify the program appropriately. Use the `switch` statement to determine the commission. If the sales are less than 0, display the message "The sales cannot be less than 0." If the code is not 1, 2, or 3, display the message "Invalid code" and don't ask the user for a sales amount.

Test the program three times using the following valid test data: 1 and 1000; 2 and 110000; and 3 and 500000. Now test it a fourth time using an invalid code. Finally, test it a fifth time using a valid code but an invalid sales amount.

Code	Commission
1	multiply the sales by 2%
2	multiply the sales over 100,000 by 5% and then add 2,000 to the result
3	multiply the sales over 400,000 by 10% and then add 17,000 to the result

Example 1
Code: 1
Sales: $1,000
Commission: 1,000 * .02 = 20

Example 2
Code: 2
Sales: $110,000
Commission: (110,000 – 100,000) * .05 + 2,000 = 2,500

Example 3
Code: 3
Sales: $500,000
Commission: (500,000 – 400,000) * .1 + 17,000 = 27,000

Figure 6-38 Commission chart and calculation examples for Lab 6-3

LAB 6-4 Desk-Check

Desk-check the code shown in Figure 6-39 three times, using the numbers 2, 5, and 100.

```
int number = 0;

cout << "Enter a number: ";
cin >> number;

switch (number)
{
      case 1:
      case 2:
      case 3:
            number = number * 2;
            break;
      case 4:
      case 5:
            number = number + 5;
            break;
      default:
            number = number - 50;
}     //end switch

cout << "Final number: " << number << endl;
```

Figure 6-39 Code for Lab 6-4

LAB 6-5 Debug

Follow the instructions for starting C++ and viewing the Lab6-5.cpp file, which is contained in either the Cpp7\Chap06\Lab6-5 Project folder or the Cpp7\Chap06 folder. (Depending on your C++ development tool, you may need to open Lab6-5's solution/project file first.) If necessary, delete the two forward slashes that appear before the `system("pause");` statement, and then save the program. Run the program. Test the program using the following codes: 1, 2, 3, 4, 5, 9, and –3. Debug the program.

Summary

- You can nest a selection structure within either the true or false path of another selection structure.
- Logic errors commonly made when writing selection structures usually are a result of one of the following three mistakes: using a compound condition rather than a nested selection structure, reversing the decisions in the outer and nested selection structures, or using an unnecessary nested selection structure.

- Some solutions require selection structures that can choose from several alternatives. The selection structures are commonly referred to as multiple-alternative selection structures or extended selection structures. You can code these selection structures using either the multiple-alternative form of the `if` statement or the `switch` statement.
- In a flowchart, a diamond is used to represent the condition in a multiple-alternative selection structure. The diamond has one flowline leading into the symbol and several flowlines leading out of the symbol. Each flowline leading out of the diamond represents a possible path and must be marked to indicate the value or values necessary for the path to be chosen.
- In a `switch` statement, the data type of the value in each `case` clause should be compatible with the data type of the statement's *selectorExpression*. The *selectorExpression* must evaluate to a value whose data type is `bool`, `char`, `short`, `int`, or `long`.
- Most `case` clauses in a `switch` statement contain a `break` statement, which tells the computer to leave the `switch` statement at that point.
- It is a good programming practice to include a comment (such as `//end switch`) to identify the end of a `switch` statement in a program.

Key Terms

`break` statement—a C++ statement used to tell the computer to leave a `switch` statement

Extended selection structures—another name for multiple-alternative selection structures

Multiple-alternative selection structures—selection structures that contain several alternatives; also called extended selection structures; can be coded using either the multiple-alternative form of the `if` statement or the `switch` statement

Nested selection structure—a selection structure that is wholly contained (nested) within either the true or false path of another selection structure

`switch` statement—a C++ statement that can be used to code a multiple-alternative selection structure

Review Questions

Use the code shown in Figure 6-40 to answer Review Questions 1 through 3.

```
int number = 0;
cout << "Number: ";
cin >> number;

if (number <= 100)
     number = number * 2;
else
     if (number > 500)
          number = number * 3;
     //end if
//end if
```

Figure 6-40

1. If the `number` variable contains the integer 90, what value will be in the `number` variable after the code shown in Figure 6-40 is processed?

   a. 0
   b. 90
   c. 180
   d. 270

2. If the `number` variable contains the integer 1000, what value will be in the `number` variable after the code shown in Figure 6-40 is processed?

   a. 0
   b. 1000
   c. 2000
   d. 3000

3. If the `number` variable contains the integer 200, what value will be in the `number` variable after the code shown in Figure 6-40 is processed?

   a. 0
   b. 200
   c. 400
   d. 600

Use the code shown in Figure 6-41 to answer Review Questions 4 through 7.

```
int id = 0;
cout << "ID: ";
cin >> id;

if (id == 1)
    cout << "Janet";
else if (id == 2 || id == 3)
    cout << "Mark";
else if (id == 4)
    cout << "Jerry";
else
    cout << "Sue";
//end if
```

Figure 6-41

4. What will the code in Figure 6-41 display when the `id` variable contains the number 2?

   a. Janet
   b. Jerry
   c. Mark
   d. Sue

5. What will the code in Figure 6-41 display when the `id` variable contains the number 4?
   a. Janet
   b. Jerry
   c. Mark
   d. Sue

6. What will the code in Figure 6-41 display when the `id` variable contains the number 3?
   a. Janet
   b. Jerry
   c. Mark
   d. Sue

7. What will the code in Figure 6-41 display when the `id` variable contains the number 8?
   a. Janet
   b. Jerry
   c. Mark
   d. Sue

Use the code shown in Figure 6-42 to answer Review Questions 8 through 10.

```
int id = 0;
cout << "ID: ";
cin >> id;

switch (id)
{
      case 1:
            cout << "Janet";
            break;
      case 2:
            cout << "Mark";
            break;
      case 3:
      case 5:
            cout << "Jerry";
            break;
      default:
            cout << "Sue";
}     //end switch
```

Figure 6-42

8. What will the code in Figure 6-42 display when the `id` variable contains the number 2?
   a. Janet
   b. Jerry
   c. Mark
   d. Sue

9. What will the code in Figure 6-42 display when the `id` variable contains the number 4?
    a. Janet
    b. Jerry
    c. Mark
    d. Sue

10. What will the code in Figure 6-42 display when the `id` variable contains the number 3?
    a. Janet
    b. Jerry
    c. Mark
    d. Sue

Exercises

Pencil and Paper

TRY THIS

1. Using the multiple-alternative form of the `if` statement, write the C++ code for a multiple-alternative selection structure that displays the month corresponding to the number entered by the user. The number is stored in an `int` variable named `monthNum`. For example, if the `monthNum` variable contains the number 1, the selection structure should display the string "January". If the month number is not 1 through 12, display the "Incorrect month number" message. (The answers to TRY THIS Exercises are located at the end of the chapter.)

TRY THIS

2. Using the `switch` statement, write the C++ code that corresponds to the partial flowchart shown in Figure 6-43. Use a `char` variable named `code` and a `double` variable named `rate`. (The answers to TRY THIS Exercises are located at the end of the chapter.)

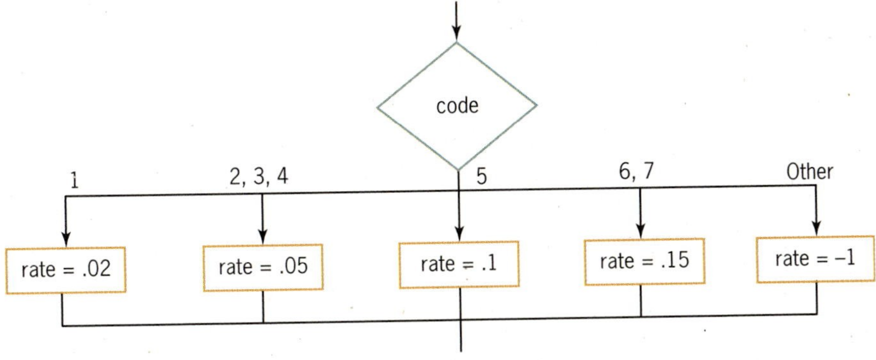

Figure 6-43

MODIFY THIS

3. Complete TRY THIS Exercise 1, and then rewrite the code using the `switch` statement.

MODIFY THIS

4. Complete TRY THIS Exercise 2, and then change the `switch` statement to the multiple-alternative form of the `if` statement.

INTRODUCTORY

5. Write the C++ code to display the message "Entry error" when the value in the `units` variable is less than or equal to 0. Otherwise, calculate the total owed as follows: If the `units` variable's value is less than 10, multiply the value by $5; otherwise, multiply it by $10. Store the total owed in the `total` variable.

INTRODUCTORY

6. A program stores sales amounts in two `int` variables named `marySales` and `jimSales`. Write the C++ code to compare the two sales amounts and then display one of the following messages: "Mary and Jim sold the same amount", "Mary sold more than Jim", or "Jim sold more than Mary".

INTERMEDIATE

7. A program uses a `char` variable named `department` and two `double` variables named `salary` and `raise`. The `department` variable contains one of the following letters (entered in either uppercase or lowercase): A, B, C, or D. Employees in departments A and B are receiving a 2% raise. Employees in department C are receiving a 1.5% raise, and employees in department D are receiving a 3% raise. Using the `switch` statement, write the C++ code to calculate the appropriate raise amount.

ADVANCED

8. A program uses a `char` variable named `membership` and an `int` variable named `age`. The `membership` variable contains one of the following letters (entered in either uppercase or lowercase): M or N. The letter M stands for *member*, and the letter N stands for *non-member*. The program should display the appropriate seminar fee, which is based on a person's membership status and age. The fee schedule is shown in Figure 6-44. Write the C++ code to display the fee.

Seminar fee	Criteria
$10	Club member less than 65 years old
$5	Club member at least 65 years old
$20	Non-member

Figure 6-44

SWAT THE BUGS

9. The C++ code shown in Figure 6-45 should display "Illinois" when the state code is 1, "Kentucky" when it's 2, "New Hampshire" when it's 3, "Vermont" when it's 4, and "Massachusetts" when it's 5. If the state code is not 1 through 5, the code should display the "Unknown state" message. Correct the errors in the code.

```
char stateCode = ' ';
cout << "State code (1, 2, 3, 4, or 5): ";
cin >> stateCode;
switch (stateCode)
{
     case "1":
               cout << "Illinois";
               break;
     case '2':
               break;
               cout << "Kentucky";
     case 3:
               cout << "New Hampshire";
     case 4:
               cout << "Vermont";
     case 5:
               cout << "Massachusetts";
               break;
     default:
               cout << "Unknown state";
}    //end switch
```

Figure 6-45

Computer

TRY THIS

10. Complete Figure 6-46 by writing the algorithm and corresponding C++ instructions. Employees with a pay code of either 4 or 9 receive a 5% raise. Employees with a pay code of either 2 or 10 receive a 4% raise. All other employees receive a 3% raise. Use the multiple-alternative form of the `if` statement to code the multiple-alternative selection structure.

    If necessary, create a new project named TryThis10 Project and save it in the Cpp7\Chap06 folder. Enter the C++ instructions into a source file named TryThis10.cpp. Also enter appropriate comments and any additional instructions required by the compiler. Display the new pay in fixed-point notation with two decimal places. Save and run the program. Test the program using 1 and 500 as the pay code and current pay, respectively. The new pay should be $515.00. Now test the program using the following four sets of input values: 4 and 450, 9 and 500, 2 and 625, 10 and 500. (The answers to TRY THIS Exercises are located at the end of the chapter.)

IPO chart information	C++ instructions
Input	
pay code	`int code = 0;`
current pay	`double currentPay = 0.0;`
raise rate 1 (3%)	`const double RATE1 = .03;`
raise rate 2 (4%)	`const double RATE2 = .04;`
raise rate 3 (5%)	`const double RATE3 = .05;`
Processing	
raise	`double raise = 0.0;`
Output	
new pay	`double newPay = 0.0;`
Algorithm	

Figure 6-46

TRY THIS

11. Code the algorithm shown in Figure 6-47. Use the `switch` statement to code the multiple-alternative selection structure. If necessary, create a new project named TryThis11 Project and save it in the Cpp7\Chap06 folder. Enter the C++ instructions into a source file named TryThis11.cpp. Also enter appropriate comments and any additional instructions required by the compiler. Save and run the program. Test the program using the following codes: 1, 2, 3, and 7. (The answers to TRY THIS Exercises are located at the end of the chapter.)

IPO chart information	C++ instructions
Input	
department code (1, 2, or 3)	`int deptCode = 0;`
Processing	
none	
Output	
salary	`int salary = 0;`

Algorithm

1. enter the department code
2. if (the department code is one of the following:)
   - 1 salary = 25000
   - 2 salary = 30000
   - 3 salary = 32000
   - other display "Invalid code" salary = 0

   end if
3. display salary

Figure 6-47

MODIFY THIS

12. Complete TRY THIS Exercise 10. If necessary, create a new project named ModifyThis12 Project and save it in the Cpp7\Chap06 folder. Enter (or copy) the instructions from the TryThis10.cpp file into a new source file named ModifyThis12.cpp. Be sure to change the filename in the first comment. Modify the code in the ModifyThis12.cpp file so that it verifies that the pay code is 1 through 10. If the pay code is not 1 through 10, don't prompt the user for the current pay. Instead, display the "Invalid pay code" message. Save and run the program. Test the program using 1 and 500 as the pay code and current pay, respectively. Now test it using the following six sets of input values: 4 and 450, 9 and 500, 2 and 625, 10 and 500, 6 and 150, and 11.

INTRODUCTORY

13. Karlton Learning wants a program that displays the amount of money a company owes for a seminar. The fee per person is based on the number of people the company registers, as shown in Figure 6-48. For example, if the company registers seven people, then the total amount owed is $560. If the user enters a number that is less than or equal to 0, the program should display an appropriate error message.

Number of registrants	Fee per person
1 through 4	$100
5 through 10	$ 80
11 or more	$ 60

Figure 6-48

a. Create an IPO chart for the problem, and then desk-check the algorithm five times, using the numbers 4, 8, 12, 0, and –2 as the number of people registered.

b. List the input, processing, and output items, as well as the algorithm, in a chart similar to the one shown earlier in Figure 6-47. Then code the algorithm into a program.

c. Desk-check the program using the same data used to desk-check the algorithm.

d. If necessary, create a new project named Introductory13 Project and save it in the Cpp7\Chap06 folder. Enter your C++ instructions into a source file named Introductory13.cpp. Also enter appropriate comments and any additional instructions required by the compiler.

e. Save and run the program. Test the program using the same data used to desk-check the program.

INTRODUCTORY

14. The owner of Harry's Car Sales pays each salesperson a commission based on his or her monthly sales. The sales ranges and corresponding commission rates are shown in Figure 6-49.

Monthly sales ($)	Commission rate
0 – 19,999.99	4%
20,000 – 29,999.99	5%
30,000 – 39,999.99	6%
40,000 – 49,999.99	7%
50,000 or more	9%
Less than 0	0%

Figure 6-49

a. Create an IPO chart for the problem, and then desk-check the algorithm six times, using sales of 2500, 28500.35, 35678.99, 42300, 50000, and –3.

b. List the input, processing, and output items, as well as the algorithm, in a chart similar to the one shown earlier in Figure 6-47. Then code the algorithm into a program.

c. Desk-check the program using the same data used to desk-check the algorithm.

d. If necessary, create a new project named Introductory14 Project and save it in the Cpp7\Chap06 folder. Enter your C++ instructions into a source file named Introductory14.cpp. Also enter appropriate comments and any additional instructions required by the compiler. Display the commission in fixed-point notation with two decimal places.

e. Save and run the program. Test the program using the same data used to desk-check the program.

INTERMEDIATE

15. In this exercise, you will create a program that displays the number of daily calories needed to maintain your current weight. The number of calories is based on your gender, activity level, and weight. The formulas for calculating the daily calories are shown in Figure 6-50.

Moderately active female: total daily calories = weight multiplied by 12 calories per pound
Relatively inactive female: total daily calories = weight multiplied by 10 calories per pound
Moderately active male: total daily calories = weight multiplied by 15 calories per pound
Relatively inactive male: total daily calories = weight multiplied by 13 calories per pound

Gender	Activity	Weight
F	I	150
F	A	120
M	I	180
M	A	200

Figure 6-50

a. Create an IPO chart for the problem, and then desk-check the algorithm using the test data included in Figure 6-50. Also desk-check it using X as the gender code, and then desk-check it again using F as the gender code and K as the activity code.

b. List the input, processing, and output items, as well as the algorithm, in a chart similar to the one shown earlier in Figure 6-47. Then code the algorithm into a program.

c. Desk-check the program using the same data used to desk-check the algorithm.

d. If necessary, create a new project named Intermediate15 Project and save it in the Cpp7\Chap06 folder. Enter your C++ instructions into a source file named Intermediate15.cpp. Also enter appropriate comments and any additional instructions required by the compiler.

e. Save and run the program. Test the program using the same data used to desk-check the program.

INTERMEDIATE

16. In this exercise, you will create a program that adds, subtracts, multiplies, or divides two integers. The program will need to get a letter (A for addition, S for subtraction, M for multiplication, or D for division) and two integers from the user. If the user enters an invalid letter, the program should not ask the user for the two integers. Instead, it should display an appropriate error message before the program ends. If the letter is A (or a), the program should calculate and display the sum of both integers. If the letter is S (or s), the program should display the difference between both integers. When calculating the difference, always subtract the smaller number from the larger one. If the letter is M (or m), the program should display the product of both integers. If the letter is D (or d), the program should divide both integers, always dividing the larger number by the smaller one. Figure 6-51 shows the test data you will use for this exercise.

Operation	First integer	Second integer
A	10	20
a	45	15
S	65	50
s	7	13
G		
M	10	20
d	45	15
d	50	100

Figure 6-51

a. Create an IPO chart for the problem, and then desk-check the algorithm using the test data shown in Figure 6-51.

b. List the input, processing, and output items, as well as the algorithm, in a chart similar to the one shown earlier in Figure 6-47. Then code the algorithm into a program.

c. Desk-check the program using the same data used to desk-check the algorithm.

d. If necessary, create a new project named Intermediate16 Project and save it in the Cpp7\Chap06 folder. Enter your C++ instructions into a source file named Intermediate16.cpp. Also enter appropriate comments and any additional instructions required by the compiler.

e. Save and run the program. Test the program using the same data used to desk-check the program.

17. In this exercise, you will create a program that converts U.S. dollars to a different currency. The number of American dollars should always be an integer that is greater than or equal to zero. The currencies and exchange rates are listed in Figure 6-52. The user should be allowed to choose the currency. Hint: Designate a code for each currency and use `cout` statements to display a menu that lists each code and its corresponding currency. ADVANCED

Currency	Exchange rate
Canadian Dollar	.9813
Euro	.757
Indian Rupee	52.53
Japanese Yen	80.92
Mexican Peso	13.1544
South African Rand	7.7522
British Pound	.6178

Figure 6-52

a. Create an IPO chart for the problem, and then desk-check the algorithm nine times. For the first seven desk-checks, convert 10 American dollars to each of the seven different currencies. For the eighth desk-check, test the algorithm using –3 as the number of American dollars. For the last desk-check, test the algorithm using an invalid currency code.

b. List the input, processing, and output items, as well as the algorithm, in a chart similar to the one shown earlier in Figure 6-47. Then code the algorithm into a program.

c. Desk-check the program using the same data used to desk-check the algorithm.

d. If necessary, create a new project named Advanced17 Project and save it in the Cpp7\Chap06 folder. Enter your C++ instructions into a source file named Advanced17.cpp. Also enter appropriate comments and any additional instructions required by the compiler. Display the results in fixed-point notation with two decimal places.

e. Save and run the program. Test the program using the same data used to desk-check the program.

18. Shopper Haven wants a program that displays the number of reward points a customer earns each month. The reward points are based on the customer's membership type and total monthly purchase amount, as shown in Figure 6-53. ADVANCED

Membership type	Total monthly purchase ($)	Reward points
Standard	Less than 75 75 – 149.99 150 and over	5% of the total monthly purchase 7.5% of the total monthly purchase 10% of the total monthly purchase
Plus	Less than 150 150 and over	6% of the total monthly purchase 13% of the total monthly purchase
Premium	Less than 200 200 and over	4% of the total monthly purchase 15% of the total monthly purchase

Figure 6-53

a. Create an IPO chart for the problem, and then desk-check the algorithm appropriately.

b. List the input, processing, and output items, as well as the algorithm, in a chart similar to the one shown earlier in Figure 6-47. Then code the algorithm into a program.

c. Desk-check the program using the same data used to desk-check the algorithm.

d. If necessary, create a new project named Advanced18 Project and save it in the Cpp7\Chap06 folder. Enter your C++ instructions into a source file named Advanced18.cpp. Also enter appropriate comments and any additional instructions required by the compiler. Display the reward points in fixed-point notation with no decimal places.

e. Save and run the program. Test the program using the same data used to desk-check the program.

ADVANCED

19. In this exercise, you will experiment with the `switch` statement.

a. Follow the instructions for starting C++ and viewing the Advanced19.cpp file, which is contained in either the Cpp7\Chap06\Advanced19 Project folder or the Cpp7\Chap06 folder. (Depending on your C++ development tool, you may need to open this exercise's project/solution file first.) If necessary, delete the two forward slashes that appear before the `system("pause");` statement, and then save the program. Run the program. When you are prompted to enter a grade, type d and press Enter. What, if anything, did the `switch` statement display on the screen? Stop the program.

b. Enter a `break;` statement in the `case 'd':` clause. Save and then run the program. When you are prompted to enter a grade, type d and press Enter. What, if anything, did the `switch` statement display on the screen? Stop the program.

c. Remove the `break;` statement from the `case 'd':` clause. Also remove the `break;` statement from the `case 'f':` clause. Save and then run the program. When you are prompted to enter a grade, type d and press Enter. What, if anything, did the `switch` statement display on the screen? Stop the program.

d. Put the `break;` statement back in the `case 'f':` clause, and then save and run the program. When you are prompted to enter a grade, type d and press Enter. Stop the program.

ADVANCED

20. In this exercise, you will experiment with the `switch` statement.

a. Follow the instructions for starting C++ and viewing the Advanced20.cpp file, which is contained in either the Cpp7\Chap06\Advanced20 Project folder or the Cpp7\Chap06 folder. (Depending on your C++ development tool, you may need to open this exercise's project/solution file first.) If necessary, delete the two forward slashes that appear before the `system("pause");` statement, and then save the program. The program uses the `switch` statement to display the names of the gifts mentioned in the song "The Twelve Days of Christmas."

b. Run the program. When you are prompted to enter the day, type the number 1 and press Enter. The names of the gifts for the first through the twelfth days appear on the screen. Stop the program.

c. Run the program again. When you are prompted to enter the day, type the number 9 and press Enter. The names of the gifts for the ninth through the twelfth days appear on the screen. Stop the program.

d. Modify the program so that it displays only the name of the gift corresponding to the day entered by the user. For example, when the user enters the number 4, the program should display the "4 calling birds" message only.

e. Save and then run the program. When you are prompted to enter the day, type the number 4 and press Enter. The "4 calling birds" message should appear on the screen. Stop the program, and then test it using the numbers 1 and 9.

ADVANCED

21. In this exercise, you will include a Boolean value in a `switch` statement. Follow the instructions for starting C++ and viewing the Advanced21.cpp file, which is contained in either the Cpp7\Chap06\Advanced21 Project folder or the Cpp7\Chap06 folder. (Depending on your C++ development tool, you may need to open this exercise's project/solution file first.) If necessary, delete the two forward slashes that appear before the `system("pause");` statement, and then save the program. Replace the dual-alternative `if` statement with a `switch` statement. Save and then run the program. Test the program appropriately.

SWAT THE BUGS

22. Follow the instructions for starting C++ and viewing the SwatTheBugs22.cpp file, which is contained in either the Cpp7\Chap06\SwatTheBugs22 Project folder or the Cpp7\Chap06 folder. (Depending on your C++ development tool, you may need to open this exercise's project/solution file first.) If necessary, delete the two forward slashes that appear before the `system("pause");` statement, and then save the program. The program should calculate and display an item's new price, but it is not working correctly. Test the program using 1 as the code and 10 as the old price. Then test it using the following data: 2 and 10, 3 and 20, and 4. Debug the program.

Answers to TRY THIS Exercises

Pencil and Paper

1. See Figure 6-54.

```
if (monthNum == 1)
      cout << "January";
else if (monthNum == 2)
      cout << "February";
else if (monthNum == 3)
      cout << "March";
else if (monthNum == 4)
      cout << "April";
else if (monthNum == 5)
      cout << "May";
else if (monthNum == 6)
      cout << "June";
else if (monthNum == 7)
      cout << "July";
else if (monthNum == 8)
      cout << "August";
else if (monthNum == 9)
      cout << "September";
else if (monthNum == 10)
      cout << "October";
else if (monthNum == 11)
      cout << "November";
else if (monthNum == 12)
      cout << "December";
else
      cout << "Incorrect month number";
//end if
```

Figure 6-54

2. See Figure 6-55.

```
switch (code)
{
      case '1':
                  rate = .02;
                  break;
      case '2':
      case '3':
      case '4':
                  rate = .05;
                  break;
      case '5':
                  rate = .1;
                  break;
      case '6':
      case '7':
                  rate = .15;
                  break;
      default:
                  rate = -1;
}     //end switch
```

Figure 6-55

Computer

10. See Figures 6-56 and 6-57.

IPO chart information	C++ instructions
Input	
pay code	`int code = 0;`
current pay	`double currentPay = 0.0;`
raise rate 1 (3%)	`const double RATE1 = .03;`
raise rate 2 (4%)	`const double RATE2 = .04;`
raise rate 3 (5%)	`const double RATE3 = .05;`
Processing	
raise	`double raise = 0.0;`
Output	
new pay	`double newPay = 0.0;`
Algorithm	

1. enter the pay code and current pay	`cout << "Pay code: ";`
	`cin >> code;`
	`cout << "Current pay: ";`
	`cin >> currentPay;`

2. if (the pay code is 4 or 9) calculate the raise by multiplying the current pay by raise rate 3	`if (code == 4 || code == 9)` `raise = currentPay * RATE3;`
else if (the pay code is 2 or 10) calculate the raise by multiplying the current pay by raise rate 2	`else if (code == 2 || code == 10)` `raise = currentPay * RATE2;`

else
calculate the raise by multiplying the current pay by raise rate 1
end if
	`else`
	`raise = currentPay * RATE1;`
	`//end if`

3. calculate the new pay by adding the raise to the current pay	`newPay = currentPay + raise;`
4. display the new pay	`cout << "New pay: $" <<` `newPay << endl;`

Figure 6-56

```
//TryThis10.cpp - displays the new pay
//Created/revised by <your name> on <current date>

#include <iostream>
#include <iomanip>
using namespace std;

int main()
{
     //declare named constants and variables
     const double RATE1 = .03;
     const double RATE2 = .04;
     const double RATE3 = .05;
     int code             = 0;
     double currentPay    = 0.0;
     double raise         = 0.0;
     double newPay        = 0.0;

     //enter input items
     cout << "Pay code: ";
     cin >> code;
     cout << "Current pay: ";
     cin >> currentPay;

     //calculate raise and new pay
     if (code == 4 || code == 9)
          raise = currentPay * RATE3;
     else if (code == 2 || code == 10)
          raise = currentPay * RATE2;
     else
          raise = currentPay * RATE1;
     //end if
     newPay = currentPay + raise;

     //display new pay
     cout << fixed << setprecision(2);
     cout << "New pay: $" << newPay << endl;

     //system("pause");
     return 0;
}    //end of main function
```

if your C++ development tool requires this statement, delete the two forward slashes

Figure 6-57

11. See Figures 6-58 and 6-59.

IPO chart information	**C++ instructions**
Input	
department code (1, 2, or 3)	`int deptCode = 0;`
Processing	
none	
Output	
salary	`int salary = 0;`
Algorithm	
1. enter the department code	`cout << "Department code (1, 2, or 3): ";` `cin >> deptCode;`
2. if (the department code is one of the following:)	`switch (deptCode)` `{`

1 salary = 25000	`case 1:`
	`salary = 25000;`
	`break;`

2 salary = 30000	`case 2:`
	`salary = 30000;`
	`break;`

3 salary = 32000	`case 3:`
	`salary = 32000;`
	`break;`

other display "Invalid code"
salary = 0
	`default:`
	`cout << "Invalid code" << endl;`
	`salary = 0;`

end if	`}     //end switch`
3. display salary	`cout << "Salary: $" << salary << endl;`

Figure 6-58

```
//TryThis11.cpp
//displays the salary associated with a department code
//Created/revised by <your name> on <current date>

#include <iostream>
using namespace std;

int main()
{
     //declare variables
     int deptCode = 0;
     int salary   = 0;

     //get the department code
     cout << "Department code (1, 2, or 3): ";
     cin >> deptCode;

     //determine the salary
     switch (deptCode)
     {
     case 1:
          salary = 25000;
          break;
     case 2:
          salary = 30000;
          break;
     case 3:
          salary = 32000;
          break;
     default:
          cout << "Invalid code" << endl;
          salary = 0;
     }    //end switch

     //display the salary
     cout << "Salary: $" << salary << endl;

     //system("pause");
     return 0;
}    //end of main function
```

if your C++ development tool requires this statement, delete the two forward slashes

Figure 6-59

CHAPTER 7

The Repetition Structure

After studying Chapter 7, you should be able to:

- Differentiate between a pretest loop and a posttest loop
- Include a pretest loop in pseudocode
- Include a pretest loop in a flowchart
- Code a pretest loop using the C++ `while` statement
- Utilize counter and accumulator variables
- Code a pretest loop using the C++ `for` statement

Repeating Program Instructions

Recall that all computer programs are written using one or more of three control structures: sequence, selection, and repetition. You learned about the sequence and selection structures in previous chapters. This chapter provides an introduction to the repetition structure.

Programmers use the **repetition structure**, referred to more simply as a **loop**, when they need the computer to repeatedly process one or more program instructions. The loop contains a condition that controls whether the instructions are repeated. In many programming languages, the condition can be phrased in one of two ways. It can either specify the requirement for repeating the instructions or specify the requirement for *not* repeating them. The requirement for repeating the instructions is referred to as the **looping condition** because it indicates when the computer should continue "looping" through the instructions. The requirement for *not* repeating the instructions is referred to as the **loop exit condition** because it tells the computer when to exit (or stop) the loop. Every looping condition has an opposing loop exit condition; one is the opposite of the other.

Some examples may help illustrate the difference between the looping condition and the loop exit condition. You've probably heard the old adage "Make hay while the sun shines." The "while the sun shines" is the looping condition because it tells you when to *continue* making hay. The adage also could be phrased as "Make hay until the sun is no longer shining." In this case, the "until the sun is no longer shining" is the loop exit condition because it indicates when you should *stop* making hay. In the phrase "Keep your car's windshield wipers on while it is raining," the "while it is raining" is the looping condition. To use the loop exit condition, you would change the phrase to "Keep your car's windshield wipers on until it stops raining." Similarly, the idiom "While the cat's away, the mice will play" uses the looping condition "While the cat's away" to indicate when the mice will continue playing. You also could phrase the idiom using a loop exit condition, as follows: "Until the cat returns, the mice will play." The loop exit condition indicates when the mice will stop playing. In the C++ programming language, the repetition structure's condition is always phrased as a looping condition, which means it always contains the requirement for repeating the instructions within the loop.

The programmer determines whether a problem's solution requires a repetition structure by studying the problem specification. The first problem specification you will examine in this chapter involves a superheroine named Isis. The problem specification and an illustration of the problem are shown in Figure 7-1, along with a correct solution written in pseudocode. The solution uses only the sequence and selection structures because no instructions need to be repeated.

Ch07-Isis video

Problem specification
A superheroine named Isis must prevent a poisonous yellow spider from attacking King Khafra and Queen Rashida. Isis has one weapon at her disposal: a laser beam that shoots out from her right hand. Unfortunately, Isis gets only one shot at the spider, which is flying around the palace looking for the king and queen. Before taking the shot, she needs to position both her right arm and her right hand toward the spider. After taking the shot, she should return her right arm and right hand to their original positions. In addition, she should say "You are safe now. The spider is dead." if the laser beam hit the spider; otherwise, she should say "Run for your lives, my king and queen!"

```
1. position both your right arm and your right hand toward the spider
2. shoot a laser beam at the spider
3. return your right arm and right hand to their original positions
4. if (the laser beam hit the spider)
        say "You are safe now. The spider is dead."
   else
        say "Run for your lives, my king and queen!"
   end if
```

Figure 7-1 A problem that requires the sequence and selection structures

Now let's change the problem specification slightly. This time, rather than taking only one shot, Isis can take as many shots as needed to destroy the poisonous yellow spider. Because of this, she will never need to tell the king and queen to run for their lives again. Figure 7-2 shows the modified problem specification along with the modified solution, which contains the sequence and repetition structures. The repetition structure begins with the repeat while (the laser beam did not hit the spider) clause and ends with the end repeat clause. The instructions between both clauses are indented to indicate that they are part of the repetition structure. The instructions between both clauses are called the **loop body**.

The portion within parentheses in the repeat while (the laser beam did not hit the spider) clause specifies the repetition structure's condition. The condition is phrased as a looping condition because it tells Isis when to repeat the instructions. In this case, she should repeat the instructions as long as (or while) "the laser beam did not hit the spider." Similar to the condition in a selection structure, the condition in a repetition structure must evaluate to a Boolean value: either true or false. The condition in Figure 7-2 evaluates to true when the laser beam did *not* hit the spider and evaluates to false when the laser beam *did* hit the spider. If the condition evaluates to true, Isis should follow the loop body instructions. She should skip over those instructions when the condition evaluates to false.

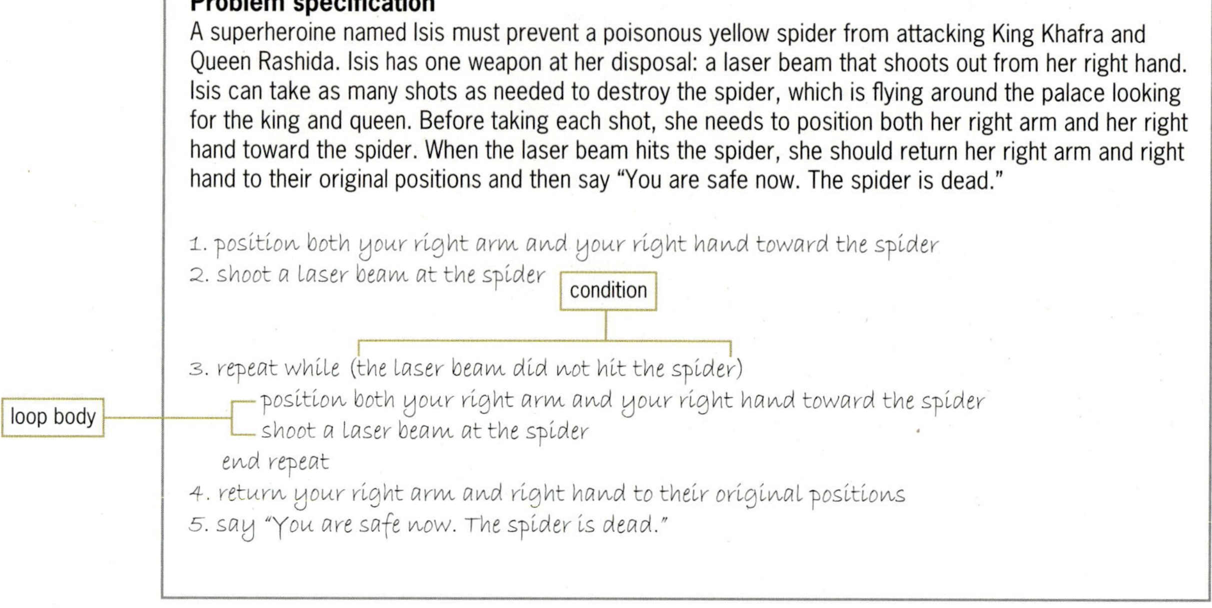
Problem specification
A superheroine named Isis must prevent a poisonous yellow spider from attacking King Khafra and Queen Rashida. Isis has one weapon at her disposal: a laser beam that shoots out from her right hand. Isis can take as many shots as needed to destroy the spider, which is flying around the palace looking for the king and queen. Before taking each shot, she needs to position both her right arm and her right hand toward the spider. When the laser beam hits the spider, she should return her right arm and right hand to their original positions and then say "You are safe now. The spider is dead."

1. position both your right arm and your right hand toward the spider
2. shoot a laser beam at the spider
3. repeat while (the laser beam did not hit the spider)
   position both your right arm and your right hand toward the spider
   shoot a laser beam at the spider
   end repeat
4. return your right arm and right hand to their original positions
5. say "You are safe now. The spider is dead."

Figure 7-2 A problem that requires the sequence and repetition structures

Pretest and posttest loops are also called top-driven and bottom-driven loops, respectively.

A repetition structure can be either a pretest loop or a posttest loop. In both types of loops, the condition is evaluated with each repetition (or iteration) of the loop. In a **pretest loop**, the condition is evaluated *before* the instructions within the loop are processed. In a **posttest loop**, the evaluation occurs *after* the instructions within the loop are processed. The loop shown in Figure 7-2 is a pretest loop.

Depending on the result of the evaluation, the instructions in a pretest loop may never be processed. The solution in Figure 7-2 can be used to illustrate this point. If the laser beam shot in Step 2 hit the spider, the instructions in the loop body would never be processed because the loop's condition in Step 3 would evaluate to false. The instructions in a posttest loop, on the other hand, will always be processed at least once. Of the two types of loops, the pretest loop is the most commonly used. You will learn about pretest loops in this chapter; posttest loops are covered in Chapter 8 along with nested loops.

The answers to Mini-Quiz questions are located in Appendix A.

Mini-Quiz 7-1

1. Using only the following five instructions, write an algorithm for printing the pages in a document: end repeat, print the next page, print the first page, repeat while (there is another page to print), say "Done printing".
2. Modify the algorithm from Question 1 so that it prints all of the pages except page 3. (You will need to add your own instructions to the algorithm.)
3. Jane wants to pick all of the roses in her garden and place them in one of two baskets, depending on the rose's color. Pink roses should be placed in the pink basket. All of the other roses should be placed in the brown basket. Write an appropriate algorithm using only the instructions shown in Figure 7-3.

```
else
end if
end repeat
if (the rose is pink)
try to pick a rose
put the rose in the brown basket
put the rose in the pink basket
repeat while (a rose was picked)
```

Figure 7-3 Instructions for Question 3 in Mini-Quiz 7-1

Using a Pretest Loop to Solve a Real-World Problem

As you already know, not every solution to a problem requires a loop. Consider, for example, the problem specification and IPO chart shown in Figure 7-4. The problem specification indicates that the gross pay for only one employee needs to be calculated and displayed. Therefore, the three instructions in the algorithm will need to be processed only once. Because no instructions need to be repeated, the algorithm does not require a loop.

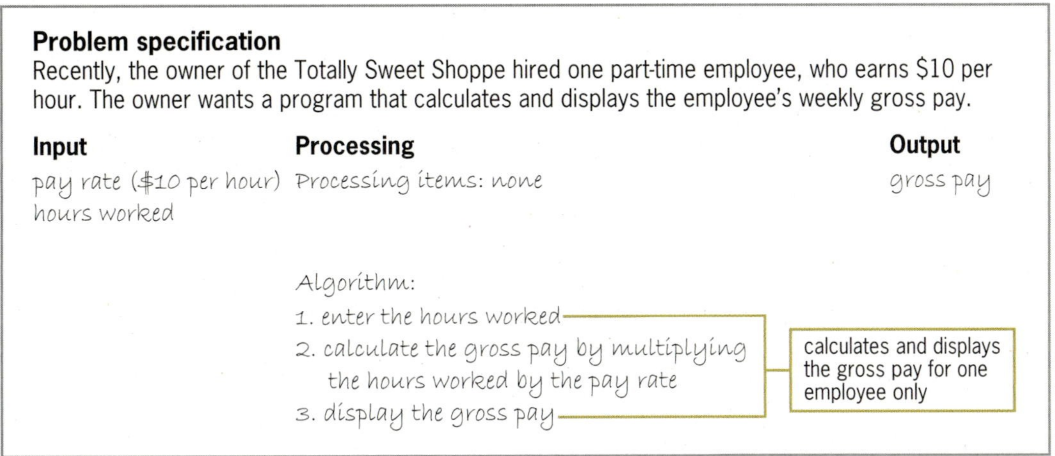

Figure 7-4 Problem specification and IPO chart for the Totally Sweet Shoppe program

Now consider the Wheels & More problem specification and IPO chart shown in Figure 7-5. The problem specification is similar to the previous one, except it indicates that the program will need to calculate and display the gross pay for more than one employee. You could use the algorithm from Figure 7-4 to solve the problem. However, that algorithm is inefficient for the current problem because it calculates and displays only one gross pay amount. A program based on the algorithm in Figure 7-4 would need to be executed once for each employee receiving a paycheck. In other words, if the company had 100 employees, the store manager would need to run the program 100 times.

To calculate and display each employee's gross pay amount without having to run the program more than once, the Wheels & More algorithm will need a repetition structure, as shown in Figure 7-5. After running a program based on this algorithm, the store manager can calculate and display the gross pay amount for any number of employees. The program will end when the store manager enters –1 (a negative number one) as the number of hours worked.

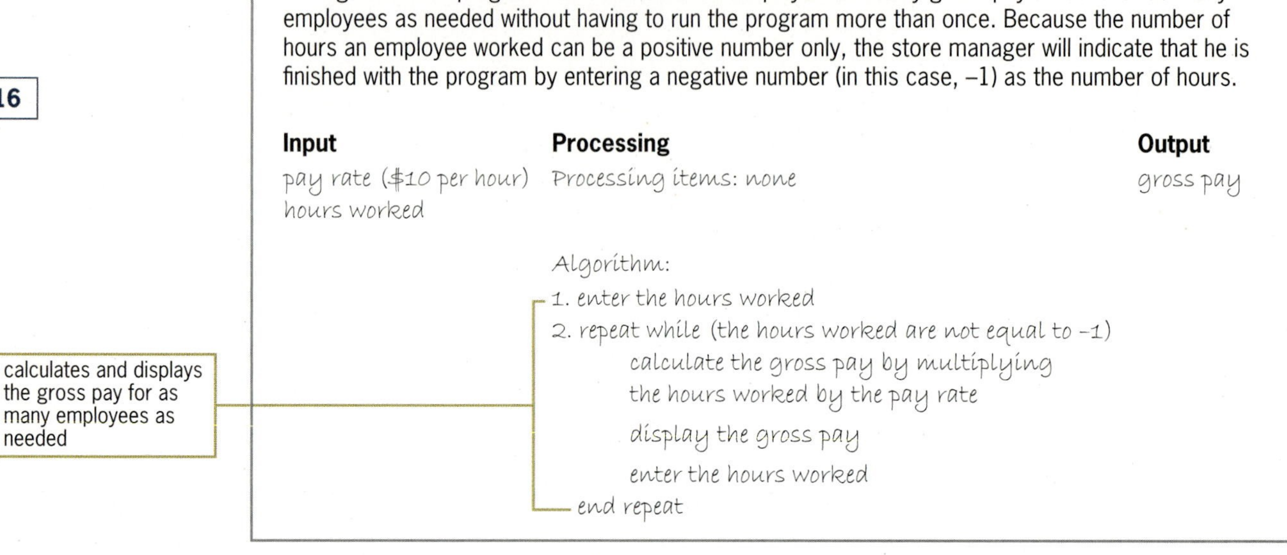

Figure 7-5 Problem specification and IPO chart for the Wheels & More program

Figure 7-6 identifies the important components of the algorithm from Figure 7-5. With very rare exceptions, every loop has a condition and a loop body. In a pretest loop, the condition appears at the beginning of the loop. As mentioned earlier, the condition must result in a Boolean value: either true or false. The condition in Figure 7-6 evaluates to true when the hours worked entry is *not* equal to –1, and evaluates to false when it *is* equal to –1.

Sentinel values are often referred to as trip values because they release the loop from its task. And, because they are the last values entered before the loop ends, they are also called trailer values.

Some loops, such as the one in Figure 7-6, require the user to enter a special value to end the loop. Values that are used to end loops are referred to as **sentinel values**. The sentinel value should be one that is easily distinguishable from the valid data recognized by the program. In the loop in Figure 7-6, the sentinel value is –1. The number 15 would not be a good sentinel value for the loop because it is possible for an employee to work 15 hours. The number –1, on the other hand, is a good sentinel value for the loop because the problem specification states that the number of hours worked is always a positive number.

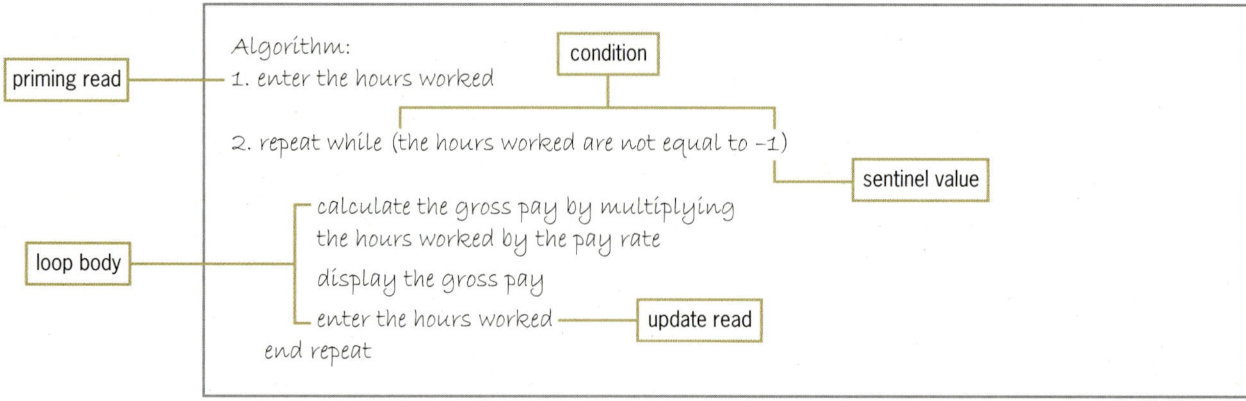

Figure 7-6 Components of the Wheels & More algorithm

When a loop's condition evaluates to true, the one or more instructions listed in the loop body are processed; otherwise, the loop body instructions are skipped over. After each processing of the loop body instructions, the loop's condition is reevaluated to determine whether the instructions should be processed again. The loop body instructions are processed and the loop's condition is evaluated until the condition evaluates to false, at which time the loop ends and processing continues with the instruction immediately following the end of the loop. Keep in mind that, because the condition in a pretest loop is evaluated *before* any of the instructions within the loop body are processed, it is possible that the loop body instructions may not be processed at all. For example, if the store manager enters the number –1 as the first number of hours worked, the condition in Figure 7-6's loop will evaluate to false and the instructions in the loop body will not be processed during that run of the program.

Notice that the algorithm in Figure 7-6 contains two *enter the hours worked* instructions. One of the instructions appears above the loop, and the other appears as the last instruction in the loop body. The *enter the hours worked* instruction above the loop is referred to as the **priming read** because it is used to prime (prepare or set up) the loop. The priming read initializes the loop condition by providing its first value. In this case, the priming read gets only the first hours worked entry from the store manager. This first entry is compared to the sentinel value (–1) and determines whether the loop body instructions are processed at all. If the loop body instructions are processed, the *enter the hours worked* instruction in the loop body gets the remaining hours worked entries (if any) from the store manager. This instruction is referred to as the **update read** because it allows the store manager to update the value of the input item (in this case, the number of hours worked) that controls the looping condition. The update read is often an exact copy of the priming read.

The importance of the update read cannot be stressed enough. If you don't include the update read in the loop body, there will be no way to enter the sentinel value after the loop body instructions are processed the first time. This is because the priming read is processed only once and gets only the first input entry from the user. Without the update read, the loop will have no way of stopping on its own. You will learn more about this in the section titled "The `while` Statement" later in the chapter. (You can observe the effect of not including the update read by completing Lab 7-5.)

Flowcharting a Pretest Loop

Figure 7-7 shows the Wheels & More algorithm in flowchart form. The diamond in the figure indicates the beginning of a repetition structure (loop). Like the diamond in a selection structure, the diamond in a repetition structure contains a condition that evaluates to either true or false only. The condition determines whether the instructions within the loop body are processed. Also like the diamond in a selection structure, the diamond in a repetition structure has one flowline entering the symbol and two flowlines leaving the symbol. The two flowlines leading out of the diamond are marked with a "T" (for true) and an "F" (for false). The flowline marked with a "T" leads to the loop body, which contains the instructions to be processed when the loop's condition evaluates to true. The flowline marked with an "F", on the other hand, leads to the instructions to be processed when the loop's condition evaluates to false. Notice that a circle or loop is formed by the flowline entering the diamond combined with the diamond and the symbols and flowlines within the true path. It is this loop (circle) that distinguishes the repetition structure from the selection structure in a flowchart.

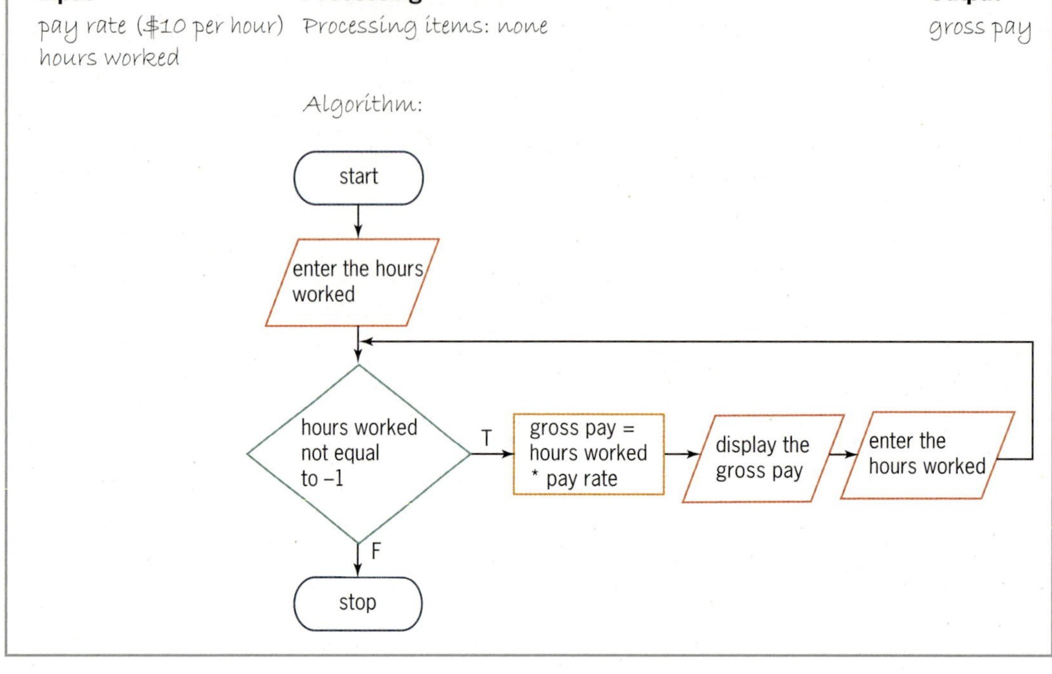

Figure 7-7 Wheels & More algorithm shown in flowchart form

The first and last parallelograms in Figure 7-7 represent the priming and update reads, respectively.

To illustrate how a loop operates in a program, you will desk-check the algorithm in Figure 7-7 using the following numbers of hours worked: 15, 8, and –1 (the sentinel value). The gross pay amounts should be $150 and $80. First, you record the input and output items in a desk-check table, as shown in Figure 7-8.

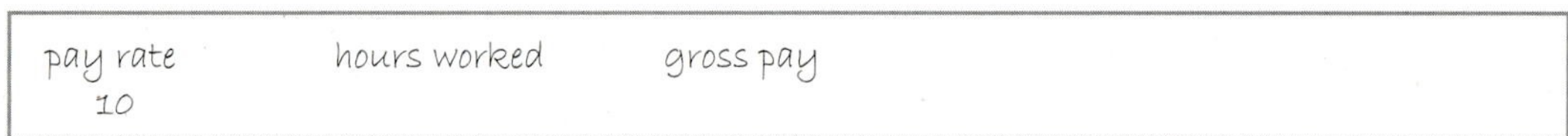

Figure 7-8 Input and output items entered in the desk-check table

Ch07-Wheels Desk-Check video

Next, you follow each of the symbols in the flowchart, from top to bottom, recording in the desk-check table any changes made to the values of the input and output items. The first symbol is the start oval, which merely marks the beginning of the flowchart. The next symbol is a parallelogram that gets the first hours worked entry from the store manager. This symbol represents the priming read. Figure 7-9 shows this first entry recorded in the desk-check table.

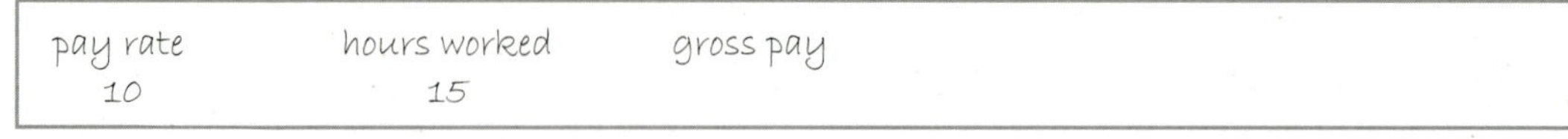

Figure 7-9 First hours worked entry recorded in the desk-check table

The next symbol in the flowchart is a diamond that represents the condition in a pretest loop. You can tell that the loop is a pretest loop (rather than a posttest loop) because the diamond appears *before* the symbols in both the true and false paths. The loop's condition tells the computer to compare the number entered by the user with the sentinel value (–1). In this case, the condition evaluates to true because 15 is not equal to –1. When the condition evaluates to true, the computer processes the instructions in the loop body. The first two instructions in the loop body calculate and display the gross pay. Figure 7-10 shows the first employee's information recorded in the desk-check table. The gross pay amount agrees with the manually calculated results.

pay rate	hours worked	gross pay
10	15	150

Figure 7-10 First employee's information recorded in the desk-check table

The last instruction in the loop body in Figure 7-7 is contained in a parallelogram. The instruction allows the store manager to enter the number of hours the next employee worked—in this case, 8. Recall that this instruction is the update read. After the store manager enters the number of hours worked, the loop's condition is reevaluated to determine whether the loop should be processed again (a true condition) or end (a false condition). Recall that the condition is contained in the diamond located at the top of the loop. In this case, the condition evaluates to true because 8 is not equal to –1. As a result, the gross pay amount is calculated and then displayed on the screen. Figure 7-11 shows the second employee's information recorded in the desk-check table.

pay rate	hours worked	gross pay
10	~~15~~	~~150~~
	8	80

Figure 7-11 Second employee's information recorded in the desk-check table

The last parallelogram in the loop body gets the number of hours worked by the next employee. In this case, the store manager enters the sentinel value (–1). Next, the loop's condition is reevaluated to determine whether the loop should be processed again (a true condition) or end (a false condition). In this case, the condition evaluates to false because the store manager's entry is equal to –1. When the loop's condition evaluates to false, the computer skips over the loop body instructions and processes the instruction immediately following the end of the loop. In Figure 7-7's flowchart, the stop oval follows the loop and marks the end of the flowchart. The completed desk-check table is shown in Figure 7-12.

pay rate	hours worked	gross pay
10	~~15~~	~~150~~
	~~8~~	80
	-1	

Figure 7-12 Completed desk-check table

You can code a pretest loop in C++ using either the `while` statement or the `for` statement. We'll begin with the `while` statement.

The `while` Statement

Figure 7-13 shows the syntax of the **`while` statement**, which can be used to code a pretest loop in a C++ program. As the boldfaced text in the syntax indicates, the keyword `while` and the parentheses that surround the *condition* are essential components of the statement. The italicized items in the syntax indicate where the programmer must supply information. In this case, the programmer needs to supply the *condition*, which must be phrased as a looping condition. The condition must be a Boolean expression, which is an expression that evaluates to either true or false. The expression can contain variables, constants, functions, arithmetic operators, comparison operators, and logical operators.

Besides providing the condition, the programmer also must provide the loop body statements, which are the statements to be processed when the condition evaluates to true. If more than one statement needs to be processed, the statements must be entered as a statement block by enclosing them in a set of braces ({}). You also can include the braces when a loop body contains only one statement. By doing this, you won't need to remember to enter the braces when statements are added subsequently to the loop body. Forgetting to enter the braces is a common error made when typing the `while` statement in a program. Although not a requirement, it is a good programming practice to use a comment (such as `//end while`) to mark the end of the `while` statement, as shown in Figure 7-13. The comment will make your program easier to read and understand.

Also included in Figure 7-13 are examples of using the `while` statement. In Example 1, the `while (age > 0)` clause tells the computer to repeat the loop body instructions as long as (or while) the value in the `age` variable is greater than 0. The loop will stop when the user enters either the number 0 or a negative number. In Example 2, the `while (anotherSale == 'Y' || anotherSale == 'y')` clause indicates that the loop body instructions should be repeated as long as the value in the `anotherSale` variable is either the uppercase letter Y or the lowercase letter y. In this case, the loop will stop when the user enters anything other than the letter Y or the letter y. You also could write the `while` clause as either `while (toupper(anotherSale) == 'Y')` or `while (tolower(anotherSale) == 'y')`.

HOW TO Use the `while` Statement

Syntax

while (*condition***)**
    either one statement or a statement block to be processed as long as the condition is true
//end while

Example 1

```
int age = 0;

cout << "Enter age: ";
cin >> age;
while (age > 0)
{
      cout << "You entered " << age << endl;
      cout << "Enter age: ";
      cin >> age;
}     //end while
```

Example 2

```
char anotherSale = ' ';
double sales = 0.0;

cout << "Enter a sales amount? (Y/N) ";
cin >> anotherSale;
while (anotherSale == 'Y' || anotherSale == 'y')
{
      cout << "Enter the sales: ";
      cin >> sales;
      cout << "You entered " << sales << endl;
      cout << "Enter a sales amount? (Y/N) ";
      cin >> anotherSale;
}     //end while
```

Figure 7-13 How to use the `while` statement

Figure 7-14 shows the IPO chart information and corresponding C++ instructions for the Wheels & More program. The first three statements in the figure declare and initialize the `RATE` named constant and the `hours` and `gross` variables. The first `cout` statement prompts the user to enter the first number of hours worked, and the `cin >> hours;` statement (the priming read) stores the user's response in the `hours` variable. The looping condition in the `while (hours != -1)` clause compares the value stored in the `hours` variable with the sentinel value. If the `hours` variable does not contain the sentinel value, the looping condition evaluates to true and the loop body instructions are processed. Those instructions calculate and display the gross pay. They then use a `cout` statement to prompt the user to enter the next number of hours worked, and use a `cin` statement (the update read) to store the user's response in the `hours` variable. Each time the user enters a number of hours worked, the looping condition in the `while` clause compares the entry to the sentinel value. When the user enters the sentinel value (−1) as the hours worked, the looping condition evaluates to false. As a result, the loop body instructions are skipped over and processing continues with the instruction located immediately below the end of the loop.

IPO chart information	C++ instructions
Input	
pay rate ($10 per hour)	`const double RATE = 10.0;`
hours worked	`double hours = 0.0;`
Processing	
none	
Output	
gross pay	`double gross = 0.0;`
Algorithm	
1. enter the hours worked	`cout << "First hours worked (-1 to stop): ";` `cin >> hours;`
2. repeat while (the hours worked are not equal to -1)	`while (hours != -1)` `{`
calculate the gross pay by multiplying the hours worked by the pay rate	`gross = hours * RATE;`
display the gross pay	`cout << "Gross pay: $" << gross;` `cout << endl << endl;`
enter the hours worked	`cout << "Next hours worked (-1 to stop): ";` `cin >> hours;`
end repeat	`}     //end while`

Figure 7-14 IPO chart information and C++ instructions for the Wheels & More program

The loop in Figure 7-14 will stop when the number of hours worked is equal to −1 because "equal to" is the opposite of "not equal to."

The importance of the update read was mentioned earlier. In this case, if you forget to enter the `cin >> hours;` statement in the loop body, the computer will process the loop body instructions indefinitely. This is because without that `cin` statement, there will be no way to change the value stored in the `hours` variable once the loop body instructions are processed. A loop whose instructions are processed indefinitely is referred to as either an **endless loop** or an **infinite loop**. Usually, you can stop a program that contains an endless loop by pressing Ctrl+c (press and hold down the Ctrl key as you tap the letter c, and then release both keys); you also can use the Command Prompt window's Close button. (You can practice stopping an endless loop by completing either Lab 7-5 or Computer Exercise 19.)

A sample run of the Wheels & More program is shown in Figure 7-15. (The program uses the `fixed` and `setprecision` stream manipulators to display the gross pay amounts in fixed-point notation with two decimal places.)

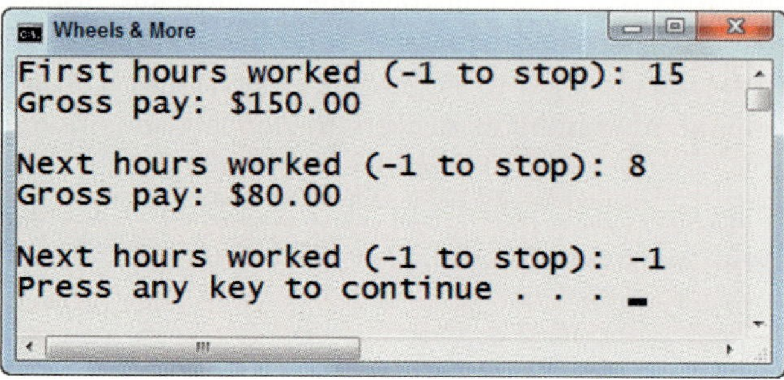

Figure 7-15 A sample run of the Wheels & More program

The answers to Mini-Quiz questions are located in Appendix A.

Mini-Quiz 7-2

1. Write a C++ `while` clause that processes the loop body instructions as long as the value in the `quantity` variable is greater than the number 0.
2. Write a C++ `while` clause that stops the loop when the value in the `quantity` variable is less than the number 0. Hint: Change the loop exit condition to a looping condition.
3. Write a C++ `while` clause that processes the loop body instructions as long as the value in the `inStock` variable is greater than the value in the `reorder` variable.
4. Write a C++ `while` clause that processes the loop body instructions as long as the value in a `char` variable named `letter` is either Y or y.
5. Which of the following is a good sentinel value for a program that inputs a test score?
   a. –9
   b. 32
   c. 45.5
   d. 7

Using Counters and Accumulators

Some algorithms require you to calculate a subtotal, a total, or an average. You make these calculations using a repetition structure that includes a counter, an accumulator, or both. A **counter** is a numeric variable used for counting something, such as the number of employees paid in a week. An **accumulator** is a numeric variable used for accumulating (adding together) something, such as the total dollar amount of a week's payroll.

Two tasks are associated with counters and accumulators: initializing and updating. **Initializing** means to assign a beginning value to the counter or accumulator. Typically, counters and accumulators are initialized to the number 0. However, they can be initialized to any number, depending on the value required by the algorithm. The initialization task is performed before the loop is processed because it needs to be performed only once. **Updating**, often referred to as **incrementing**, means adding a number to the value stored in the counter or accumulator. The number can be either positive or negative, integer or non-integer. A counter is always updated by a constant value—typically the number 1—whereas an accumulator is updated by a value that varies. The assignment statement that updates a counter or an accumulator is placed in the body of a loop. This is because the update task must be performed each time the loop body instructions are processed.

Game programs make extensive use of counters and accumulators. The partial game program shown in Figure 7-16, for example, uses a counter to keep track of the number of smiley faces that Eddie (the character in the figure) destroys. After he destroys three smiley faces and then jumps through the manhole, he advances to the next level in the game, as shown in the figure.

Ch07-Eddie Game video

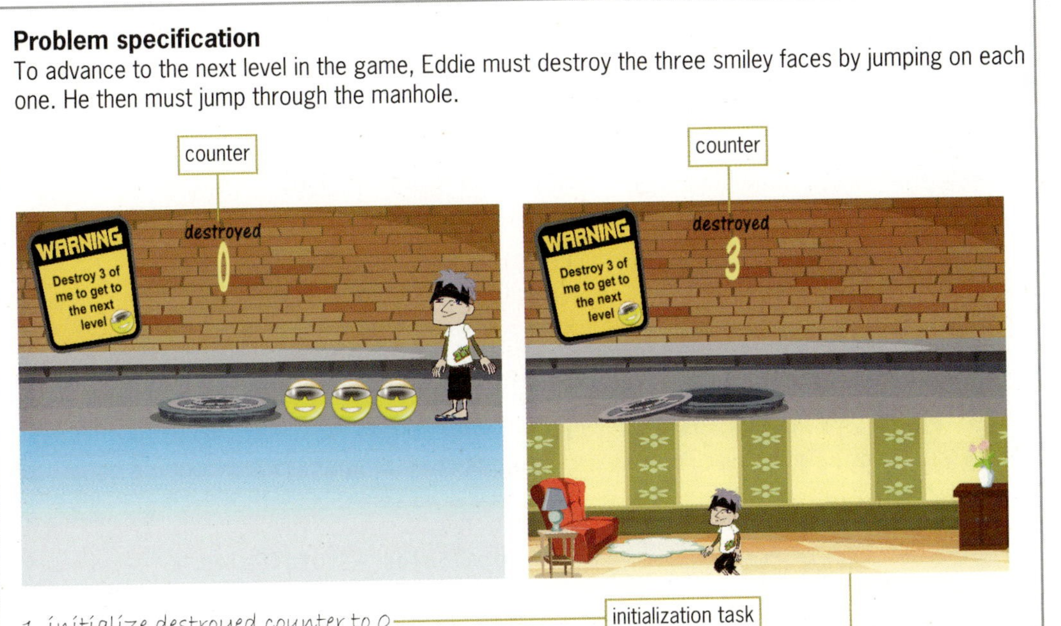

1. initialize destroyed counter to 0 — initialization task
2. repeat while (destroyed counter is less than 3)
   jump on smiley face to destroy it
   add 1 to destroyed counter — update task
   end repeat
3. jump into manhole to get to the next level

next level

Figure 7-16 Example of a partial game program that uses a counter

The Sales Express program, which you view next, includes a counter, an accumulator, and a repetition structure.

The Sales Express Program

Figure 7-17 shows the problem specification, IPO chart information, and C++ instructions for the Sales Express program, and Figure 7-18 shows the corresponding flowchart. The program's input is each salesperson's sales amount, and its output is the average sales amount. The program uses two processing items: a counter and an accumulator. The counter (an `int` variable named `numSales`) keeps track of the number of sales amounts entered and is initialized to the number 0. The accumulator (a `double` variable named `totalSales`) keeps track of the total sales and is initialized to 0.0.

Problem specification

Sales Express wants a program that displays the average amount the company sold during the prior year. The sales manager will enter each salesperson's sales. The program will use a counter to keep track of the number of sales amounts entered and an accumulator to total the sales amounts. When the sales manager has finished entering the sales amounts, the program will calculate the average sales amount by dividing the value stored in the accumulator by the value stored in the counter. It then will display the average sales amount on the screen. The sales manager will indicate that she is finished with the program by entering a negative number as the sales amount. If the sales manager does not enter any sales amounts, the program should display the "No sales entered" message.

IPO chart information	**C++ instructions**
Input	
sales	`double sales = 0.0;`
Processing	
number of sales entered (counter)	`int numSales = 0;`
total sales (accumulator)	`double totalSales = 0.0;`
Output	
average sales	`double average = 0.0;`
Algorithm	
1. enter the sales	`cout << "First sales amount (negative number to stop): ";` `cin >> sales;`
2. repeat while (the sales are at least 0)	`while (sales >= 0.0)` `{`
add 1 to the number of sales entered	`numSales = numSales + 1;`
add the sales to the total sales	`totalSales = totalSales + sales;`
enter the sales	`cout << "Next sales amount (negative number to stop): ";` `cin >> sales;`
end repeat	`}  //end while`
3. if (the number of sales entered is greater than 0)	`if (numSales > 0)` `{`
calculate the average sales by dividing the total sales by the number of sales entered	`average = totalSales / numSales;`
display the average sales	`cout << "Average sales: $" << average << endl;` `}`
else	`else`
display "No sales entered" message	`cout << "No sales entered" << endl;`
end if	`// end if`

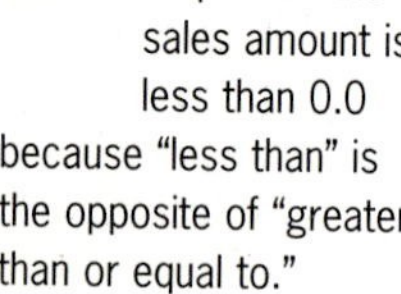

The loop in Figure 7-17 will stop when the sales amount is less than 0.0 because "less than" is the opposite of "greater than or equal to."

Figure 7-17 Problem specification, IPO chart information, and C++ instructions for the Sales Express program

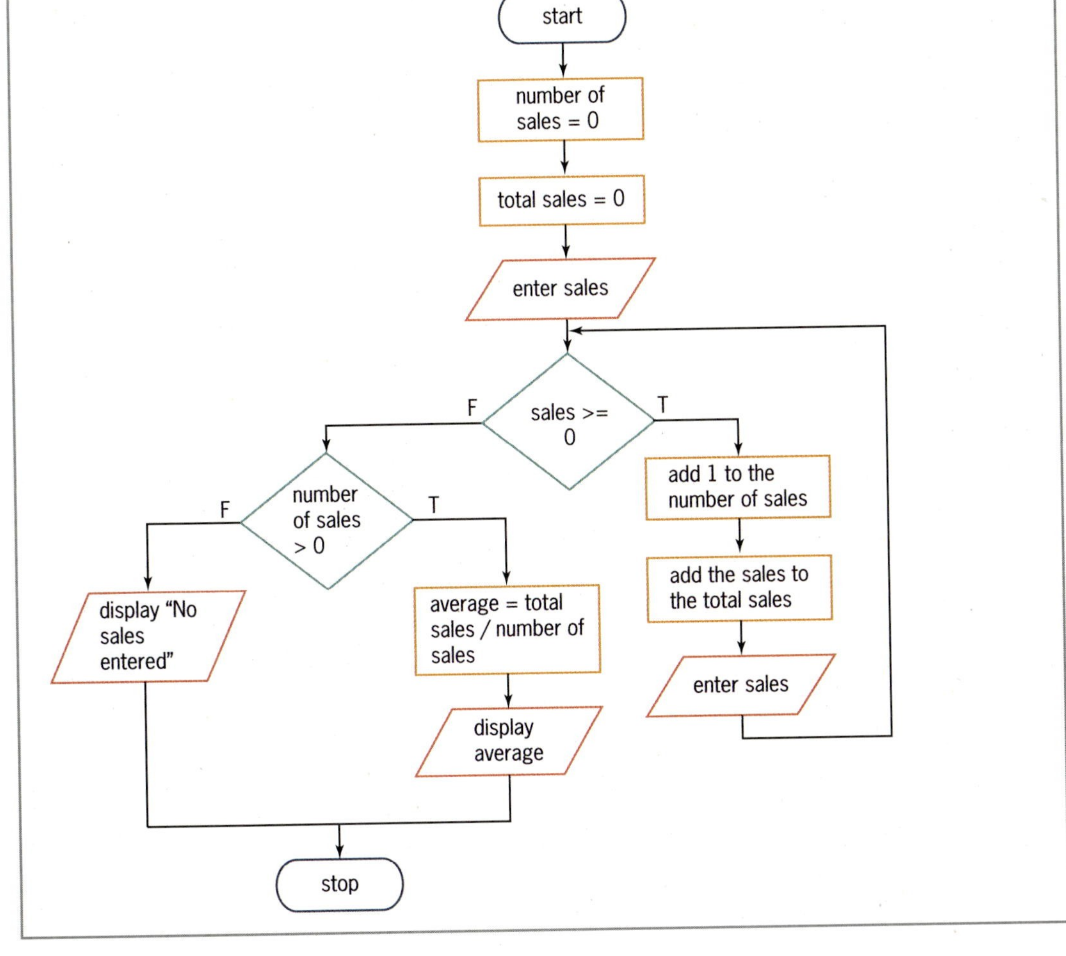

Figure 7-18 Flowchart for the Sales Express program

The "enter sales" parallelogram above the loop represents the priming read, and the one within the loop represents the update read.

You can observe the way counters and accumulators are used in a program by desk-checking the code shown earlier in Figure 7-17. You will do this using the following sales amounts: 30000, 40000, and –3. The average sales amount should be $35,000. After declaring and initializing the appropriate variables, the code prompts the user to enter the first sales amount and then stores the user's response in the `sales` variable. See Figure 7-19.

Ch07-Sales Express Desk-Check video

sales	numSales	totalSales	average
~~0.0~~	0	0.0	0.0
30000.0			

Figure 7-19 Desk-check table after the first sales amount is entered

The `while (sales >= 0.0)` clause begins a pretest loop that repeats the loop body instructions as long as (or while) the `sales` variable contains a value that is greater than or equal to 0.0. Notice that the condition compares the variable's value with 0.0 rather than with 0. This is because the values being compared should have the same data type—in this case, `double`. The loop stops when the `sales` variable contains a sentinel value. For this loop, a sentinel value is any value that is less than 0.0. The current value in the `sales` variable is greater than or equal to 0.0; therefore, the computer will process the instructions in the loop body.

Unlike the loop in the Wheels & More program (shown earlier in Figure 7-14), the loop in the Sales Express program has more than one sentinel value.

The first instruction in the loop body updates the counter variable's value; it does this by adding the number 1 to the value. The second instruction updates the accumulator variable's value by adding the current contents of the `sales` variable to it. You also can write the first two instructions in the loop body as `numSales += 1;` and `totalSales += sales;`. The desk-check table in Figure 7-20 shows the updated values assigned to the counter and accumulator variables.

sales	numSales	totalSales	average
~~0.0~~	~~0~~	~~0.0~~	0.0
30000.0	1	30000.0	

Figure 7-20 Desk-check table showing the first update to the counter and accumulator variables

The last two instructions in the loop body prompt the user to enter the next sales amount and then store the user's response—in this case, 40000—in the `sales` variable. Next, the condition in the `while (sales >= 0.0)` clause is reevaluated to determine whether the loop body instructions should be processed again (a true condition) or skipped over (a false condition). Here again, the loop's condition evaluates to true. As a result, the first two instructions in the loop body update the counter and accumulator variables. See Figure 7-21.

sales	numSales	totalSales	average
~~0.0~~	~~0~~	~~0.0~~	0.0
~~30000.0~~	~~1~~	~~30000.0~~	
40000.0	2	70000.0	

Figure 7-21 Desk-check table after the second update to the counter and accumulator variables

The last two instructions in the loop body prompt the user to enter the next sales amount and then store the user's response in the `sales` variable. In this case, the user enters the number –3, which is a sentinel value. Next, the condition in the `while (sales >= 0.0)` clause is reevaluated to determine whether the loop body instructions should be processed again or skipped over. In this case, the loop's condition evaluates to false because the value in the `sales` variable is not greater than or equal to 0.0. When the condition evaluates to false, the loop body instructions are skipped over and the loop ends; processing continues with the statement immediately following the loop.

In the Sales Express program, an `if` statement follows the loop. The `if` statement's condition verifies that the value stored in the counter variable (`numSales`) is greater than the number 0, which is the variable's initial value. This verification is necessary because the first instruction in the `if` statement's true path uses the `numSales` variable as the divisor when calculating the average sales amount. Before using a variable as the divisor in an expression, you always should verify that the variable contains a value other than 0. This is because division by 0 is not mathematically possible and will cause the program to end abruptly with an error.

Currently, the `numSales` variable contains the number 2. Therefore, the instructions in the `if` statement's true path first calculate the average sales amount (35000) and then display the amount on the screen before the program ends. Figure 7-22 shows the completed desk-check table for the Sales Express program, and Figures 7-23 and 7-24 show sample runs of the program. (The program uses the `fixed` and `setprecision` stream manipulators to display the average sales amount in fixed-point notation with no decimal places.)

sales	numSales	totalSales	average
~~0.0~~	~~0~~	~~0.0~~	~~0.0~~
~~30000.0~~	~~1~~	~~30000.0~~	35000.0
~~40000.0~~	2	70000.0	
-3.0			

Figure 7-22 Completed desk-check table for the Sales Express program

```
Sales Express
First sales amount (negative number to stop): 30000
Next sales amount (negative number to stop): 40000
Next sales amount (negative number to stop): -3
Average sales: $35000
Press any key to continue . . .
```

Figure 7-23 First sample run of the Sales Express program

```
Sales Express
First sales amount (negative number to stop): -1
No sales entered
Press any key to continue . . . _
```

Figure 7-24 Second sample run of the Sales Express program

The answers to Mini-Quiz questions are located in Appendix A.

Mini-Quiz 7-3

1. Usually, a(n) ________ is updated by an amount that varies.
   a. accumulator
   b. counter
2. Write a C++ assignment statement that updates the `quantity` counter variable by 2.
3. Write a C++ assignment statement that updates the `total` counter variable by –3.
4. Write a C++ assignment statement that updates the `totalPurchases` accumulator variable by the value stored in the `purchases` variable.

Counter-Controlled Pretest Loops

In both the Wheels & More and Sales Express programs, the termination of the loop is determined by a sentinel value that is entered by the user at the keyboard. Other loops, like the one used earlier in the partial game program (shown in Figure 7-16), are controlled using a counter rather than a sentinel value; such loops are referred to as **counter-controlled loops**.

Figure 7-25 shows the problem specification, IPO chart information, and C++ instructions for the Jasper Music Company program, which uses a counter-controlled loop. The program's corresponding flowchart is shown in Figure 7-26. The input is the quarterly sales for each of the three regions, and the output is the total quarterly sales. The program uses one processing item: a counter that will keep track of the number of times the loop instructions are repeated. In this case, the loop instructions need to be repeated three times: once for each sales region. Notice in the C++ instructions that the `numRegions` counter variable is initialized to the number 1, which corresponds to the first sales region. It's also updated by 1 each time the loop instructions are processed. The initialization and update of the counter variable in counter-controlled loops are comparable to the priming and update reads in loops controlled by a sentinel value.

Problem specification
The sales manager at Jasper Music Company wants a program that allows him to enter the quarterly sales amount made in each of three regions: Region 1, Region 2, and Region 3. The program should calculate the total quarterly sales and then display the result on the screen. The program will use a counter to ensure that the sales manager enters exactly three sales amounts. It will use an accumulator to total the sales amounts.

IPO chart information	**C++ instructions**
Input	
region's quarterly sales	`int regionSales = 0;`
Processing	
number of regions (counter: 1 to 3)	`int numRegions = 1;`
Output	
total quarterly sales (accumulator)	`int totalSales = 0;`
Algorithm	
1. repeat while (the number of regions is less than 4)	`while (numRegions < 4)` `{`

enter the region's quarterly sales	`cout << "Enter region "`
	`<< numRegions <<`
	`"'s quarterly sales: ";`
	`cin >> regionSales;`

add the region's quarterly sales to the total quarterly sales	`totalSales += regionSales;`
add 1 to the number of regions	`numRegions += 1;`
end repeat	`}   //end while`
2. display the total quarterly sales	`cout << "Total quarterly sales: $"` `<< totalSales << endl;`

Figure 7-25 Problem specification, IPO chart information, and C++ instructions for the Jasper Music Company program

The loop in Figure 7-25 will stop when the number of regions is equal to 4 because "greater than or equal to" is the opposite of "less than."

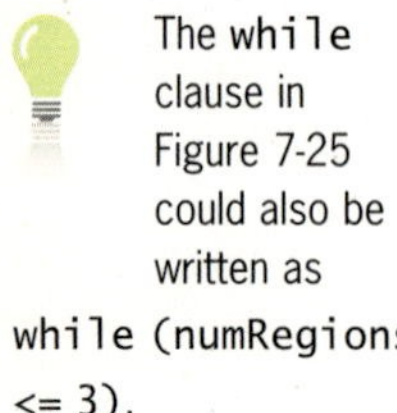

The `while` clause in Figure 7-25 could also be written as `while (numRegions <= 3)`.

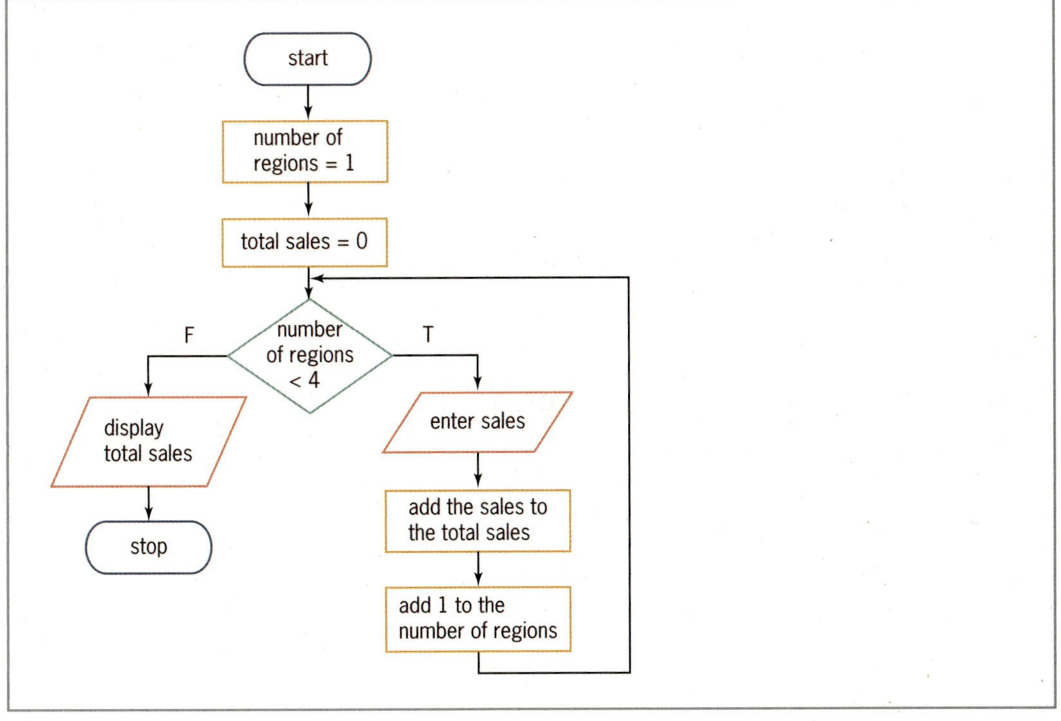

Figure 7-26 Flowchart for the Jasper Music Company

You can observe the way a counter is used to stop a loop by desk-checking the code shown earlier in Figure 7-25. You will do this using the following three sales amounts: 2500, 6000, and 2000. The first three statements in the code create and initialize three variables. Figure 7-27 shows the desk-check table after these statements are processed.

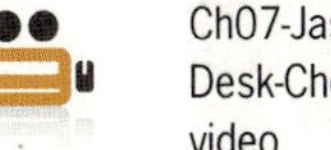

Ch07-Jasper Desk-Check video

regionSales	numRegions	totalSales
0	1	0

Figure 7-27 Desk-check table after the variable declaration statements are processed

The `while (numRegions < 4)` clause begins a pretest loop that repeats its instructions as long as (or while) the value in the `numRegions` counter variable is less than 4. The loop stops when the variable's value is 4 because that is the first integer that is not less than 4. The desk-check table in Figure 7-27 indicates that the value stored in the `numRegions` variable is less than 4. As a result, the loop's condition evaluates to true and the statements in the loop body are processed.

The first statement in the loop body prompts the user to enter Region 1's quarterly sales. The second statement stores the user's response (in this case, 2500) in the `regionSales` variable. The third statement adds the value stored in the `regionSales` variable to the value stored in the `totalSales` accumulator variable; the sum of both values is 2500. The last statement in the loop body adds the number 1 to the value stored in the `numRegions` counter variable; the result is 2. You also can write the last two instructions in the loop body as `totalSales = totalSales + regionSales;` and `numRegions = numRegions + 1;`. Figure 7-28 shows the desk-check table after the loop body instructions are processed the first time.

regionSales	numRegions	totalSales
~~0~~	~~1~~	~~0~~
2500	2	2500

Figure 7-28 Results of processing the loop body instructions the first time

Next, the condition in the `while (numRegions < 4)` clause is reevaluated to determine whether the loop body instructions should be processed again (a true condition) or skipped over (a false condition). Currently, the value stored in the `numRegions` variable is less than 4. As a result, the condition evaluates to true and the statements in the loop body are processed. The first two statements prompt the user to enter Region 2's quarterly sales and then store the user's response (in this case, 6000) in the `regionSales` variable. The next two statements update the accumulator and counter variables. Figure 7-29 shows the desk-check table after the loop body instructions are processed the second time.

regionSales	numRegions	totalSales
~~0~~	~~1~~	~~0~~
~~2500~~	~~2~~	~~2500~~
6000	3	8500

Figure 7-29 Results of processing the loop body instructions the second time

Next, the condition in the `while (numRegions < 4)` clause is reevaluated to determine whether the loop body instructions should be processed again or skipped over. Here again, the condition evaluates to true because the value stored in the `numRegions` variable is still less than 4. Therefore, the statements in the loop body are processed. The first two statements prompt the user to enter Region 3's quarterly sales and then store the user's response (in this case, 2000) in the `regionSales` variable. The next two statements update the accumulator and counter variables. Figure 7-30 shows the desk-check table after the loop body instructions are processed the third (and last) time.

regionSales	numRegions	totalSales
0	~~1~~	~~0~~
~~2500~~	~~2~~	~~2500~~
~~6000~~	~~3~~	~~8500~~
2000	4	10500

Figure 7-30 Results of processing the loop body instructions the third time

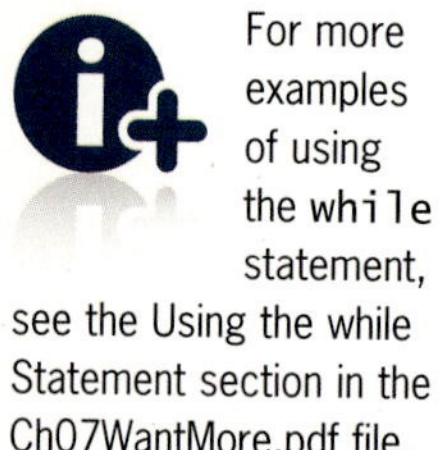

For more examples of using the `while` statement, see the Using the while Statement section in the Ch07WantMore.pdf file.

Next, the condition in the `while (numRegions < 4)` clause is reevaluated to determine whether the loop body instructions should be processed again or skipped over. At this point, the loop's condition evaluates to false because the value stored in the `numRegions` variable is not less than 4. When the condition evaluates to false, the instructions in the loop body are skipped over and the loop ends; processing continues with the statement located immediately below the loop. In the code shown earlier in Figure 7-25, the statement immediately below the loop displays the contents of the `totalSales` variable on the screen. Notice that the termination of the loop is controlled by the loop itself, rather than by the user at the keyboard. Figure 7-31 shows a sample run of the Jasper Music Company program.

```
Enter region 1's quarterly sales: 2500
Enter region 2's quarterly sales: 6000
Enter region 3's quarterly sales: 2000
Total quarterly sales: $10500
Press any key to continue . . .
```


Figure 7-31 A sample run of the Jasper Music Company program

The for Statement

Besides using the `while` statement to code pretest loops, you also can use the **for statement** in C++. However, the most common use of the `for` statement is to code counter-controlled pretest loops. This is because the `for` statement provides a more compact and clearer way of writing that type of loop. The `for` statement's syntax is shown in Figure 7-32. The statement begins with the `for` clause, which contains three arguments separated by two semicolons. As the brackets indicate, the first and third arguments are optional.

In most `for` clauses, the *initialization* argument creates and initializes a counter variable that the computer uses to keep track of the number of times the loop body instructions are processed. The variable is local to the `for` statement, which means it can be used only within the statement's loop body. The variable will be removed from the computer's internal memory when the loop ends.

The *condition* argument in the `for` clause is a looping condition because it specifies the requirement for repeating the loop instructions.

The *condition* argument in the `for` clause specifies the condition that must be true for the loop body instructions to be processed. The condition must be a Boolean expression, which is an expression that evaluates to either true or false. The expression can contain variables, constants, functions, arithmetic operators, comparison operators, and logical operators. The loop stops when its condition evaluates to false. The `for` clause's *update* argument usually contains an expression that updates the counter variable specified in the *initialization* argument.

Following the `for` clause is the body of the loop. The loop body contains the one or more statements that you want the computer to repeat. If the loop body contains more than one statement, the statements must be entered as a statement block by enclosing them in a set of braces ({}). However, you also can include the braces even when the loop body contains only one statement, as shown in Example 2 in Figure 7-32.

Although it is not required by the C++ syntax, it is helpful to use a comment (such as `//end for`) to document the end of the `for` statement, as shown in Figure 7-32. The comment will make your program easier to read and understand.

Also included in Figure 7-32 are examples of using the `for` statement. Example 1 displays the numbers 1, 2, and 3 on separate lines on the screen, and Example 2 displays the numbers 3, 2, and 1. You also could write the *condition* arguments in Examples 1 and 2 as `x <= 3` and `x >= 1`, respectively. In addition, you could write the *update* arguments in Examples 1 and 2 as `x = x + 1` and `x -= 1`, respectively.

HOW TO Use the `for` Statement

Syntax

semicolons

for ([*initialization*]; *condition*; [*update*]**)**
    either one statement or a statement block to be processed as long as the condition is true
```
//end for
```

Example 1: displays the numbers 1, 2, and 3 on separate lines on the screen
```
for (int x = 1; x < 4; x += 1)
     cout << x << endl;
//end for
```

Example 2: displays the numbers 3, 2, and 1 on separate lines on the screen
```
for (int x = 3; x > 0; x = x - 1)
{
     cout << x << endl;
}    //end for
```

A common error made when typing the `for` clause is to use commas rather than semicolons.

Figure 7-32 How to use the `for` statement

Ch07-for Statement video

Figure 7-33 describes the way the computer processes the code shown in Example 1 in Figure 7-32. Notice that the `for` statement in the example ends when the `x` variable contains the number 4. This is because that is the first integer that is not less than 4.

Processing steps for Example 1

1. The *initialization* argument (`int x = 1`) creates a variable named x and initializes it to 1.
2. The *condition* argument (x < 4) checks whether the x variable's value is less than 4. It is, so the statement in the loop body displays the x variable's value (1) on the screen.
3. The *update* argument (x += 1) adds 1 to the contents of the x variable, giving 2.
4. The *condition* argument checks whether the x variable's value is less than 4. It is, so the statement in the loop body displays the x variable's value (2) on the screen.
5. The *update* argument adds 1 to the contents of the x variable, giving 3.
6. The *condition* argument checks whether the x variable's value is less than 4. It is, so the statement in the loop body displays the x variable's value (3) on the screen.
7. The *update* argument adds 1 to the contents of the x variable, giving 4.
8. The *condition* argument checks whether the x variable's value is less than 4. It's not, so the `for` loop ends. Processing continues with the statement following the end of the loop.

Figure 7-33 Processing steps for the code shown in Example 1 in Figure 7-32

In the remaining sections in this chapter, you will view three programs that use the `for` statement.

The Holmes Supply Program

Figure 7-34 shows the problem specification, IPO chart information, and C++ instructions for the Holmes Supply program, which uses the `for` statement to code the pretest loop.

Problem specification
The payroll manager at Holmes Supply wants a program that allows her to enter the payroll amount for each of three stores: Store 1, Store 2, and Store 3. The program should calculate the total payroll and then display the result on the screen. The program will use a counter to ensure that the payroll manager enters exactly three payroll amounts. It will use an accumulator to total the amounts.

IPO chart information	**C++ instructions**
Input	
store's payroll	`int storePayroll = 0;`
Processing	
number of stores (counter: 1 to 3)	this variable is created and initialized in the for clause
Output	
total payroll (accumulator)	`int totalPayroll = 0;`
Algorithm	

1. repeat for (number of stores from 1 to 3)	`for (int numStores = 1;`
	`numStores <= 3; numStores += 1)`
	`{`

enter the store's payroll	`cout << "Store " << numStores`
	`<< " payroll: ";`
	`cin >> storePayroll;`

add the store's payroll to the total payroll	`totalPayroll += storePayroll;`
end repeat	`}  //end for`
2. display the total payroll	`cout << "Total payroll: $"` `<< totalPayroll << endl;`

Figure 7-34 Problem specification, IPO chart information, and C++ instructions for the Holmes Supply program

The loop in Figure 7-34 will stop when the value in the `numStores` variable is greater than 3 because "greater than" is the opposite of "less than or equal to."

The condition argument in Figure 7-34 also could be written as `numStores < 4`.

Desk-checking the code shown in Figure 7-34 will help you understand how the `for` statement works. You will desk-check the code using the following three payroll amounts: 15000, 25000, and 60000. First, the code declares and initializes two `int` variables named `storePayroll` and `totalPayroll`. The `for` clause in the `for` statement is processed next. The clause's *initialization* argument creates an `int` variable named `numStores` and initializes the variable to the number 1. The *initialization* argument is processed only once, at the beginning of the loop. Figure 7-35 shows the desk-check table after the declaration statements and *initialization* argument have been processed.

Ch07-Holmes Desk-Check video

storePayroll	totalPayroll	numStores
0	0	1

Figure 7-35 Results of processing the declaration statements and *initialization* argument

Next, the `for` clause's *condition* argument is evaluated to determine whether the loop body instructions should be processed (a true condition) or skipped over (a false condition). Notice that, like the condition in a `while` statement, the condition in a `for` statement is evaluated *before* the loop body instructions are processed. In this case, the loop body instructions will be processed only when the value in the `numStores` variable is less than or equal to the number 3. The desk-check table in Figure 7-35 indicates that the `numStores` variable contains the number 1. Therefore, the loop's condition evaluates to true and the statements in the loop body are processed.

The first statement in the loop body prompts the user to enter the amount of Store 1's payroll, and the second statement stores the user's response (in this case, 15000) in the `storePayroll` variable. The last statement in the loop body adds the value stored in the `storePayroll` variable to the value stored in the `totalPayroll` accumulator variable; the sum of both values is 15000. The `for` clause's *update* argument is processed next. The *update* argument adds the number 1 to the value stored in the `numStores` variable, giving 2. Figure 7-36 shows the desk-check table after the *update* argument is processed the first time.

storePayroll	totalPayroll	numStores
~~0~~	~~0~~	~~1~~
15000	15000	2

Figure 7-36 Desk-check table after the *update* argument is processed the first time

Next, the `for` clause's *condition* argument is reevaluated to determine whether the loop body instructions should be processed again or skipped over. Unlike the *initialization* argument, which is processed only once, the *condition* argument is processed with each repetition (or iteration) of the loop. Currently, the `numStores` variable contains the number 2. Therefore, the `numStores` <= 3 condition evaluates to true, and the statements in the loop body are processed again.

The first statement in the loop body prompts the user to enter Store 2's payroll, and the second statement stores the user's response (in this case, 25000) in the `storePayroll` variable. The last statement in the loop body adds the store's payroll to the total payroll; the sum of both values is 40000. The `for` clause's *update* argument is processed next. Like the *condition* argument, the *update* argument is processed with each repetition of the loop. The *update* argument adds the number 1 to the value stored in the `numStores` variable, giving 3. Figure 7-37 shows the desk-check table after the *update* argument is processed the second time.

storePayroll	totalPayroll	numStores
~~0~~	~~0~~	~~1~~
~~15000~~	~~15000~~	~~2~~
25000	40000	3

Figure 7-37 Desk-check table after the *update* argument is processed the second time

Next, the `for` clause's *condition* argument is reevaluated to determine whether the loop body instructions should be processed again or skipped over. Currently, the `numStores` variable contains the number 3. Therefore, the `numStores` <= 3 condition evaluates to true, and the statements in the loop body are processed again. The first statement prompts the user to enter Store 3's payroll, and the second statement stores the user's response (in this case, 60000) in the `storePayroll` variable. The last statement in the loop body adds the store's payroll to the total payroll; the sum of both values is 100,000. The `for` clause's *update* argument is processed next. The *update* argument adds the number 1 to the value stored in the `numStores` variable, giving 4. Figure 7-38 shows the desk-check table after the *update* argument is processed the third (and last) time.

storePayroll	totalPayroll	numStores
~~0~~	~~0~~	~~1~~
~~15000~~	~~15000~~	~~2~~
~~25000~~	~~40000~~	~~3~~
60000	100000	4

Figure 7-38 Desk-check table after the *update* argument is processed the third time

Next, the `for` clause's *condition* argument is reevaluated to determine whether the loop body instructions should be processed again or skipped over. At this point, the `numStores <= 3` condition evaluates to false because the `numStores` variable contains the number 4. When the *condition* argument evaluates to false, the instructions in the loop body are skipped over and the loop ends. As a result, the computer removes the `for` statement's local variable, `numStores`, from internal memory. Processing continues with the instruction located immediately below the end of the loop. Notice that the loop stops when the `numStores` variable contains the number 4, which is the first integer that is not less than or equal to 3. Figure 7-39 shows a sample run of the Holmes Supply program.

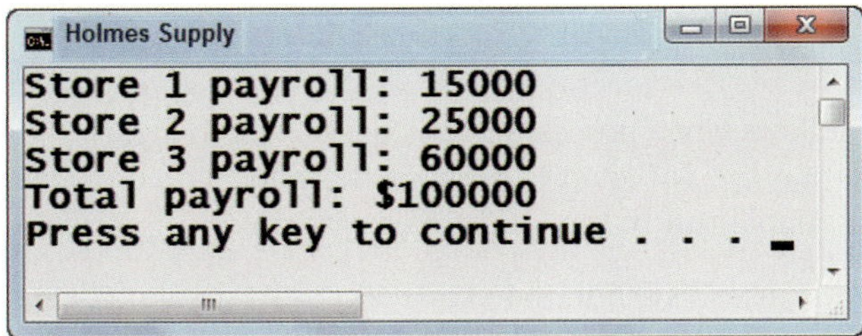

Figure 7-39 A sample run of the Holmes Supply program

The Colfax Sales Program

Figure 7-40 shows the problem specification, IPO chart information, and C++ instructions for the Colfax Sales program, which uses the `for` statement.

Problem specification
The sales manager at Colfax Sales wants a program that allows him to enter a sales amount. The program should calculate and display the appropriate commission using rates of 10%, 15%, 20%, and 25%. The program will use a counter to keep track of the four rates.

IPO chart information	C++ instructions
Input	
sales amount	`double sales = 0.0;`
Processing	
rate (counter: 10% to 25% in increments of 5%)	this variable is created and initialized in the for clause
Output	
commission	`double commission = 0.0;`

Figure 7-40 Problem specification, IPO chart information, and C++ instructions for the Colfax Sales program *(continues)*

(continued)

Algorithm

1. enter the sales amount	`cout << "Enter the sales: ";` `cin >> sales;`

2. repeat for (rate from 10% to 25% in increments of 5%)	`for (double rate = .1;`
	`rate <= .25; rate = rate + .05)`
	`{`

calculate the commission by multiplying the sales amount by the rate	`commission = sales * rate;`

display the commission	`cout << rate * 100 <<`
	`"% commission: $" <<`
	`commission << endl;`

end repeat	`}    //end for`

Figure 7-40 Problem specification, IPO chart information, and C++ instructions for the Colfax Sales program

Figure 7-41 lists the steps the computer follows when processing the code shown in Figure 7-40, using a sales amount of $25,000. Notice that the `for` loop ends when the value stored in the `rate` variable is .3. Figure 7-42 shows a sample run of the Colfax Sales program.

Processing steps

1. The declaration statements create the `sales` and `commission` variables and initialize them to 0.0.
2. The first `cout` statement prompts the user to enter a sales amount, and the `cin` statement stores the user's response (in this case, 25000) in the `sales` variable.
3. The `for` clause's *initialization* argument (`double rate = .1`) creates the `rate` variable and initializes it to .1.
4. The `for` clause's *condition* argument (`rate <= .25`) checks whether the `rate` variable's value is less than or equal to .25. It is, so the statements in the loop body calculate a 10% commission and display the result (2500) on the screen.
5. The `for` clause's *update* argument (`rate = rate + .05`) adds .05 to the value stored in the `rate` variable, giving .15.
6. The `for` clause's *condition* argument checks whether the `rate` variable's value is less than or equal to .25. It is, so the statements in the loop body calculate a 15% commission and display the result (3750) on the screen.
7. The `for` clause's *update* argument adds .05 to the value stored in the `rate` variable, giving .2.
8. The `for` clause's *condition* argument checks whether the `rate` variable's value is less than or equal to .25. It is, so the statements in the loop body calculate a 20% commission and display the result (5000) on the screen.
9. The `for` clause's *update* argument adds .05 to the value stored in the `rate` variable, giving .25.
10. The `for` clause's *condition* argument checks whether the `rate` variable's value is less than or equal to .25. It is, so the statements in the loop body calculate a 25% commission and display the result (6250) on the screen.
11. The `for` clause's *update* argument adds .05 to the value stored in the `rate` variable, giving .3.
12. The `for` clause's *condition* argument checks whether the `rate` variable's value is less than or equal to .25. It's not, so the `for` loop ends. Processing continues with the statement following the end of the loop.

Figure 7-41 Processing steps for the code shown in Figure 7-40

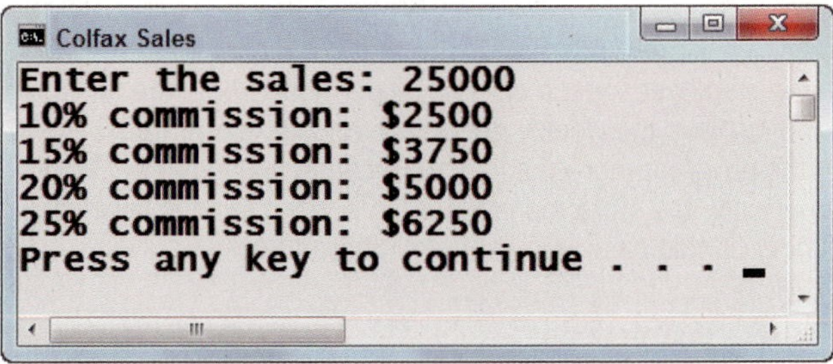

Figure 7-42 A sample run of the Colfax Sales program

Many programmers use a hexagon, which is a six-sided figure, to represent the `for` clause in a flowchart. The hexagon contains four items, as shown in Figure 7-43. Going counterclockwise from the top of the hexagon, the four items are the name of the counter variable (`rate`), the variable's initial value (.1), the value used to update the variable (.05), and the last value for which the condition will evaluate to true (.25). Notice that a less than or equal to sign (<=) precedes the .25 in the hexagon in Figure 7-43. The <= sign indicates that the loop body instructions will be processed as long as the `rate` variable's value is less than or equal to .25.

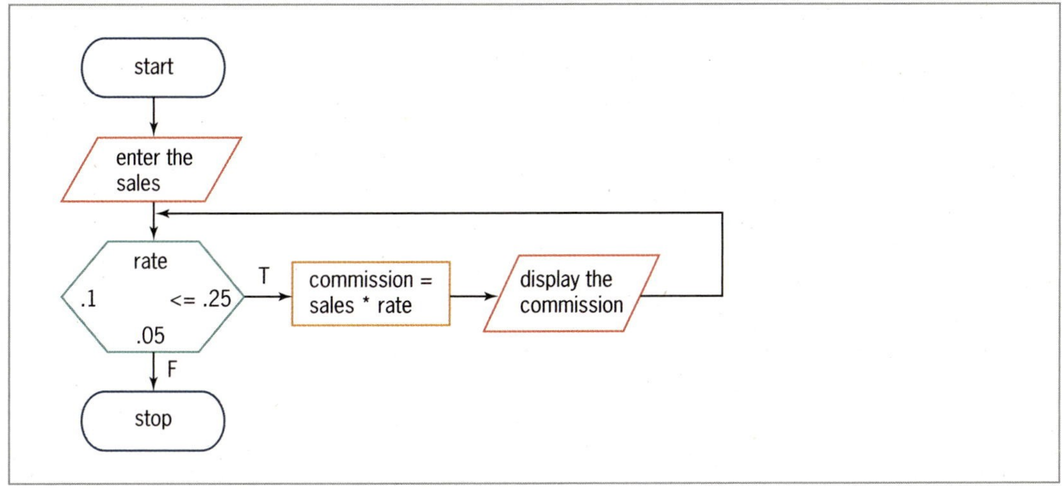

Figure 7-43 Colfax Sales algorithm shown in flowchart form

Some programmers use the hexagon to represent any counter-controlled loop, even those coded with the `while` statement.

Another Version of the Wheels & More Program

Although the `for` statement is more commonly used to code counter-controlled loops, it can be used to code any pretest loop in C++. For example, you can use it to code the pretest loop in the Wheels & More program, shown earlier in Figure 7-14. As you may remember, that program's loop allows the user to calculate and display the gross pay amount for as many employees as needed without having to run the program again. The loop stops when the user enters the sentinel value (–1). Figure 7-44 shows how you would code the loop using the `for` statement rather than the `while` statement used in Figure 7-14. The modifications made to the original code are shaded in the figure.

Unlike the `for` statements in the previous two programs (shown in Figures 7-34 and 7-40), the `for` statement in Figure 7-44 is controlled by the user at the keyboard instead of by a counter. Notice that the `for` clause in Figure 7-44 contains only the *condition* argument. Although the *initialization* and *update* arguments are omitted from the `for` clause, the semicolons after the *initialization* and *condition* arguments must be included.

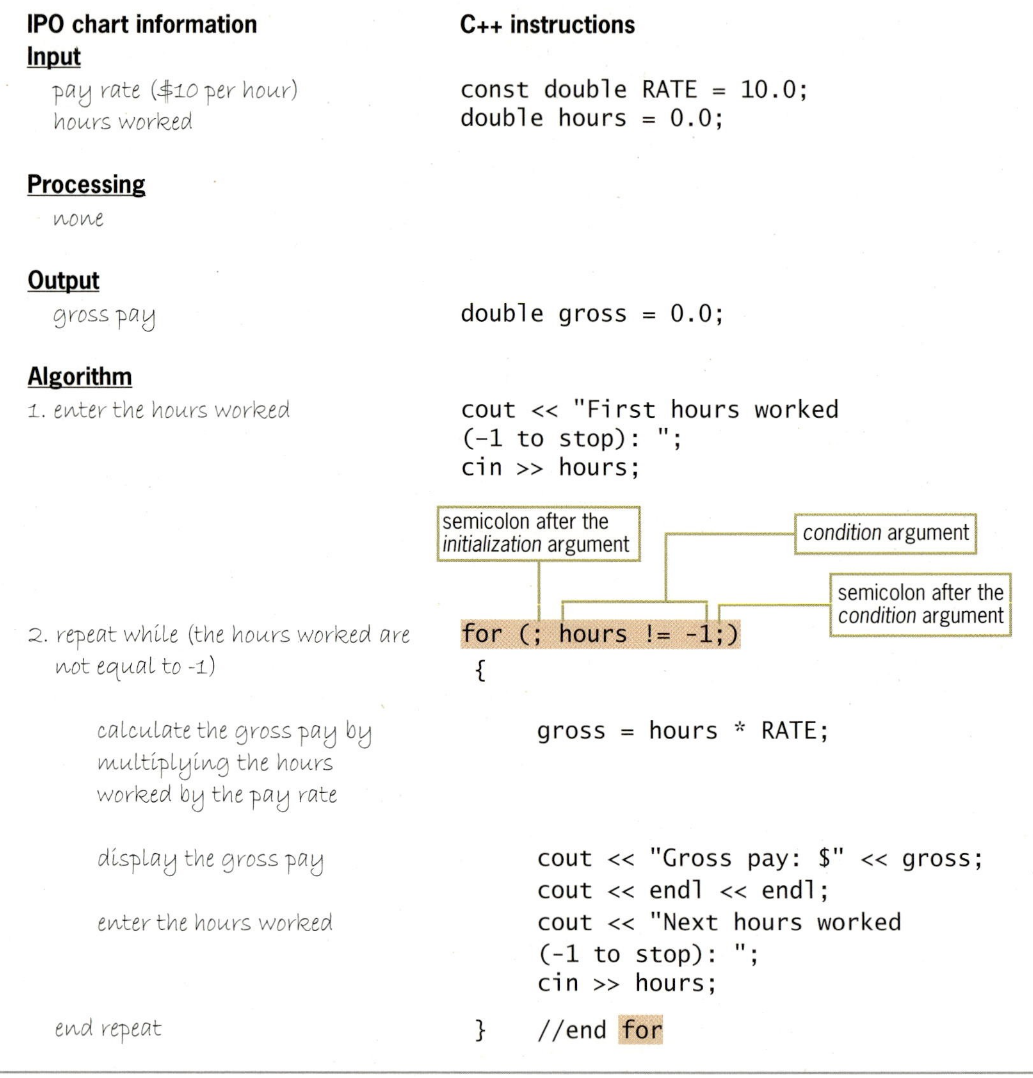

Problem specification
The Wheels & More store has several part-time employees; each earns $10 per hour. The store manager wants a program that calculates and displays the weekly gross pay amount for as many employees as needed without having to run the program more than once. Because the number of hours an employee worked can be a positive number only, the store manager will indicate that he is finished with the program by entering a negative number (in this case, –1) as the number of hours.

IPO chart information	C++ instructions
Input	
pay rate ($10 per hour)	`const double RATE = 10.0;`
hours worked	`double hours = 0.0;`
Processing	
none	
Output	
gross pay	`double gross = 0.0;`
Algorithm	
1. enter the hours worked	`cout << "First hours worked (-1 to stop): ";` `cin >> hours;`
2. repeat while (the hours worked are not equal to -1)	`for (; hours != -1;)` `{`
calculate the gross pay by multiplying the hours worked by the pay rate	`gross = hours * RATE;`
display the gross pay	`cout << "Gross pay: $" << gross;` `cout << endl << endl;`
enter the hours worked	`cout << "Next hours worked (-1 to stop): ";` `cin >> hours;`
end repeat	`}   //end for`

Figure 7-44 IPO chart information and modified C++ instructions for the Wheels & More program

Figure 7-45 lists the steps the computer follows when processing the code shown in Figure 7-44, using the following hours worked entries: 15, 8, and –1 (the sentinel value). A sample run of the Wheels & More program is shown earlier in Figure 7-15.

Processing steps

1. The `const` statement creates the `RATE` named constant and initializes it to 10.0.
2. The declaration statements create the `hours` and `gross` variables and initialize them to 0.0.
3. The first `cout` statement prompts the user to enter the first number of hours worked, and the `cin` statement stores the user's response (in this case, 15) in the `hours` variable.

Figure 7-45 Processing steps for the code shown in Figure 7-44 *(continues)*

(continued)

4. The `for` clause's *condition* argument (`hours != -1`) checks whether the `hours` variable's value is not equal to –1. The condition evaluates to true, so the statements in the loop body calculate and display the gross pay (150). They also prompt the user for the next hours worked entry and store the user's response (in this case, 8) in the `hours` variable.
5. The `for` clause's *condition* argument checks whether the `hours` variable's value is not equal to –1. The condition evaluates to true, so the statements in the loop body calculate and display the gross pay (80). They also prompt the user for the next hours worked entry and store the user's response (in this case, –1) in the `hours` variable.
6. The `for` clause's *condition* argument checks whether the `hours` variable's value is not equal to –1. In this case, the condition evaluates to false, so the `for` loop ends. Processing continues with the statement following the end of the loop.

Figure 7-45 Processing steps for the code shown in Figure 7-44

For more examples of using the `for` statement, see the Using the for Statement section in the Ch07WantMore.pdf file.

Whether you use the `for` statement or the `while` statement to code the loop shown earlier in Figure 7-44 is a matter of personal preference. However, most programmers use the `for` statement only when they know the exact number of times they want the loop instructions repeated. For all other pretest loops, they typically use the `while` statement.

Mini-Quiz 7-4

The answers to Mini-Quiz questions are located in Appendix A.

1. A program declares an `int` variable named `evenNum` and initializes it to 2. Write a C++ `while` loop that uses the `evenNum` variable to display the even integers between 1 and 9.
2. Which of the following `for` clauses processes the loop instructions as long as the `x` variable's value is less than or equal to the number 100?
   a. `for (int x = 10; x <= 100; x = x + 10)`
   b. `for (int x = 10, x <= 100, x = x + 10)`
   c. `for (int x == 10; x <= 100; x = x + 10)`
   d. `for (int x = x + 10; x <= 100; x = 10)`
3. The computer will stop processing the loop associated with the `for` clause from Question 2 when the `x` variable contains the number ________.
   a. 100
   b. 111
   c. 101
   d. 110
4. Write a `for` clause that processes the loop instructions as long as the value stored in the `x` variable is greater than the number 0. The `x` variable should be an `int` variable. Initialize the variable to the number 25 and update it by –5 with each repetition of the loop.
5. The computer will stop processing the loop associated with the `for` clause from Question 4 when the `x` variable contains the number ________.
6. Write a `for` statement that displays the even integers between 2 and 9 (inclusive) on the screen. Use `num` as the name of the counter variable.

The answers to the labs are located in Appendix A.

LAB 7-1 Stop and Analyze

Study the program shown in Figure 7-46, and then answer the questions. The program calculates the average outside temperature.

```
1  //Lab7-1.cpp - calculates the average temperature
2  //Created/revised by <your name> on <current date>
3
4  #include <iostream>
5  #include <iomanip>
6  using namespace std;
7
8  int main()
9  {
10      //declare variables
11      int numberOfTemps = 0;  //counter
12      int totalTemp     = 0;  //accumulator
13      int temp          = 0;
14      double average    = 0.0;
15
16      //get first temperature
17      cout << "First temperature (999 to stop): ";
18      cin >> temp;
19
20      while (temp != 999)
21      {
22          //update counter and accumulator
23          numberOfTemps += 1;
24          totalTemp += temp;
25
26          //get remaining temperatures
27          cout << "Next temperature (999 to stop): ";
28          cin >> temp;
29      }   //end while
30
31      //verify that at least one temperature was entered
32      if (numberOfTemps > 0)
33      {
34           //calculate and display average temperature
35           average = static_cast<double>(totalTemp) /
36                 static_cast<double>(numberOfTemps);
37           cout << fixed << setprecision(1);
38           cout << endl << "Average temperature: "
39                << average << endl;
40      }
41      else
42           cout << "No temperatures were entered." << endl;
43      //end if
44
45      //system("pause");
46      return 0;
47 }    //end of main function
```

Figure 7-46 Code for Lab 7-1

QUESTIONS

1. What are the program's input, processing, and output items?
2. Why do you think the number 999 was chosen as the sentinel value in the `while` clause on Line 20? Would a negative number be a good sentinel value for this program? Why or why not?

3. Why is the selection structure on Lines 32 through 43 necessary?
4. Are the type casts in the statement on Lines 35 and 36 necessary? Why or why not?
5. What is the purpose of the statement on Line 37?
6. Why was the `numberOfTemps` counter variable initialized to 0 rather than to 1?
7. Desk-check the program using the following temperatures and sentinel value: 78, 85, 67, and 999. What is the average temperature?
8. Follow the instructions for starting C++ and viewing the Lab7-1.cpp file, which is contained in either the Cpp7\Chap07\Lab7-1 Project folder or the Cpp7\Chap07 folder. (Depending on your C++ development tool, you may need to open Lab 7-1's project/solution file first.) If necessary, delete the two forward slashes that appear before the `system("pause");` statement, and then save the program. Run the program and then enter the temperatures and sentinel value from Question 7. What does the program display as the average temperature? (The program's output should agree with the results of your desk-check from Question 7.)
9. Run the program again. Enter the sentinel value. What does the program display?
10. Change the `while` statement to a `for` statement. Save and then run the program. Enter the sentinel value. What does the program display?
11. Run the program again. Enter the following temperatures and sentinel value: –3, 32, –10, 40, and 999. What is the average temperature?

LAB 7-2 Plan and Create

In this lab, you will plan and create an algorithm for Professor Chang. The problem specification and example calculations are shown in Figure 7-47.

Problem specification

Professor Chang wants a program that allows him to enter a student's project and test scores, which will always be integers. The professor assigns three projects and two tests. Each project is worth 50 points, and each test is worth 100 points. The program should calculate and display the total points the student earned on the projects and tests. It also should display the student's grade, which is based on the total points earned. Shown below is the grading scale that Professor Chang uses when assigning grades.

Total points earned	Grade
315 – 350	A
280 – 314	B
245 – 279	C
210 – 244	D
below 210	F

Example 1
Project and test scores: 45, 40, 41, 96, 89
Total points earned and grade: 311, B

Example 2
Project and test scores: 40, 35, 37, 73, 68
Total points earned and grade: 253, C

Figure 7-47 Problem specification and calculation examples for Lab 7-2

First, analyze the problem, looking for the output first and then for the input. In this case, Professor Chang wants the program to display the total points a student earned and his or her grade. To calculate the total points earned, the computer will need to know the student's project and test scores. The scores are the problem's input items and will be entered by Professor Chang. To determine the grade, the computer will need to know the professor's grading scale. The grading scale is provided in the problem specification.

Next, plan the algorithm. Recall that most algorithms begin with an instruction to enter the input items into the computer, followed by instructions that process the input items, typically including the items in one or more calculations. Most algorithms end with one or more instructions that display, print, or store the output items. Figure 7-48 shows the completed IPO chart for the Professor Chang problem.

Input	Processing	Output

score (5 of them)	Processing items: none
	
	Algorithm:
	1. enter the first score
	2. repeat while (the score is not -1)
	        add the score to the total points earned
	        enter the next score
	    end repeat
	3. if (the total points earned >= 315)
	        assign A as the grade
	    else if (the total points earned >= 280)
	        assign B as the grade
	    else if (the total points earned >= 245)
	        assign C as the grade
	    else if (the total points earned >= 210)
	        assign D as the grade
	    else
	        assign F as the grade
	    end if
	4. display the total points earned and the grade
		total points earned
		grade

Figure 7-48 Completed IPO chart for the Professor Chang problem

After completing the IPO chart, you then move on to the third step in the problem-solving process, which is to desk-check the algorithm. You will desk-check the algorithm in Figure 7-48 two times. For the first desk-check, you will use the following five scores and sentinel value: 45, 40, 41, 96, 89, and –1. You will use the following five scores and sentinel value for the second desk-check: 40, 35, 37, 73, 68, and –1. Figure 7-49 shows the completed desk-check table. Notice that the values in the total points earned and grade columns agree with the results of the manual calculations shown in Figure 7-47.

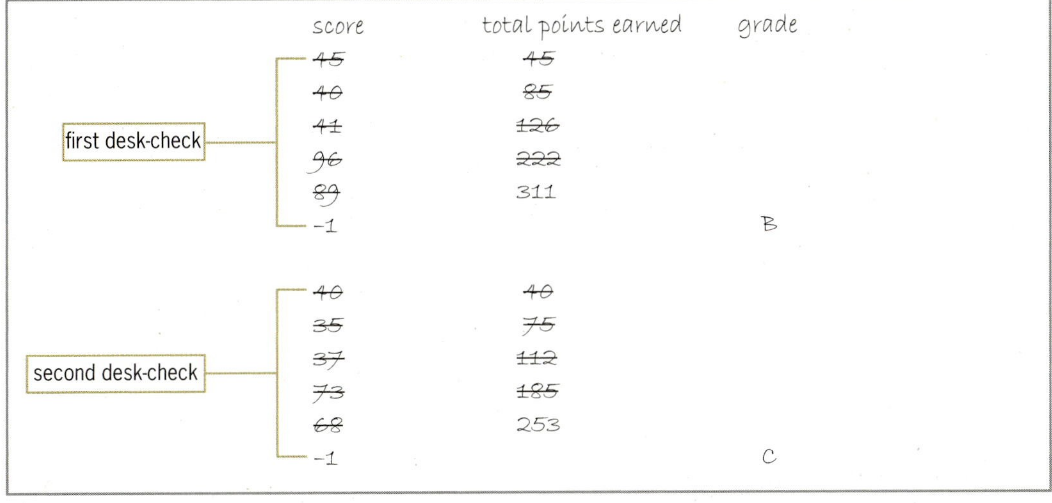

Figure 7-49 Completed desk-check table for the Professor Chang algorithm

The fourth step in the problem-solving process is to code the algorithm into a program. You begin by declaring memory locations that will store the values of the input, processing (if any), and output items. The Professor Chang problem will need three memory locations to store the input and output items. The input item (score) will be stored in a variable because the user should be allowed to change its value during runtime. The output items (total points earned and grade) also will be stored in variables because their values will change based on the current value of the input item. The score and total points earned will always be integers, so you will store both in `int` variables. You will store the grade in a `char` variable. Figure 7-50 shows the IPO chart information and corresponding C++ instructions.

IPO chart information	C++ instructions
Input	
score (5 of them)	`int score = 0;`
Processing	
none	
Output	
total points earned	`int totalPoints = 0;`
grade	`char grade = ' ';`
Algorithm	
1. enter the first score	`cout << "First score (-1 to stop): ";` `cin >> score;`
2. repeat while (the score is not -1)	`while (score != -1)` `{`
add the score to the total points earned	`totalPoints += score;`
enter the next score	`cout << "Next score (-1 to stop): ";` `cin >> score;`
end repeat	`}   //end while`

Figure 7-50 IPO chart information and C++ instructions for the Professor Chang program (*continues*)

(continued)

```
3. if (the total points earned >= 315)
       assign A as the grade
   else if (the total points earned >= 280)
       assign B as the grade
   else if (the total points earned >= 245)
       assign C as the grade
   else if (the total points earned >= 210)
       assign D as the grade
   else
       assign F as the grade
   end if

4. display the total points earned
   and the grade
```

```
if (totalPoints >= 315)
     grade = 'A';
else if (totalPoints >= 280)
     grade = 'B';
else if (totalPoints >= 245)
     grade = 'C';
else if (totalPoints >= 210)
     grade = 'D';
else
     grade = 'F';
//end if

cout << "Total points earned: "
<< totalPoints << endl;
cout << "Grade: "
<< grade << endl;
```

Figure 7-50 IPO chart information and C++ instructions for the Professor Chang program

The fifth step in the problem-solving process is to desk-check the program. You begin by placing the names of the declared variables and named constants (if any) in a new desk-check table, along with their initial values. You then desk-check the remaining C++ instructions in order, recording in the desk-check table any changes made to the variables. Figure 7-51 shows the completed desk-check table for the Professor Chang program. The results agree with those shown in the algorithm's desk-check table in Figure 7-49.

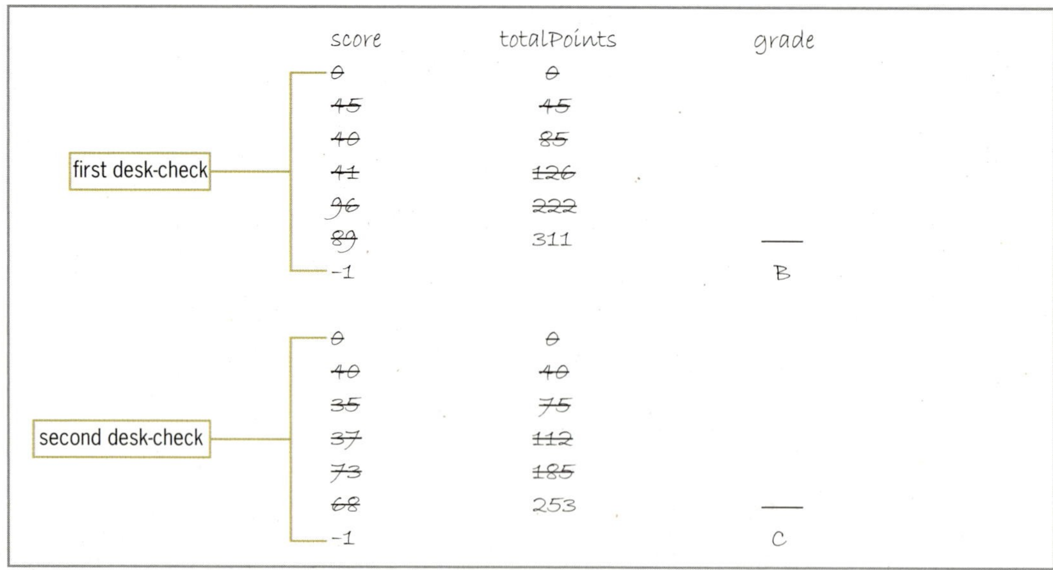

Figure 7-51 Completed desk-check table for the Professor Chang program

The final step in the problem-solving process is to evaluate and modify (if necessary) the program. Recall that you evaluate a program by entering its instructions into the computer and then using the computer to run (execute) it. While the program is running, you enter the same sample data used when desk-checking the program.

DIRECTIONS

Follow the instructions for starting your C++ development tool. Depending on the development tool you are using, you may need to create a new project; if so, name the project Lab7-2 Project and save it in the Cpp7\Chap07 folder. Enter the instructions shown in Figure 7-52 in a source file named Lab7-2.cpp. (Do not enter the line numbers.) Save the file in either the project folder or the Cpp7\Chap07 folder. Now follow the appropriate instructions for running the Lab7-2.cpp file. Use the sample data from Figure 7-51 to test the program. If necessary, correct any bugs (errors) in the program.


```
//Lab7-2.cpp
//displays the total points earned and grade
//Created/revised by <your name> on <current date>

#include <iostream>

using namespace std;

int main()
{
    //declare variables
    int score       = 0;
    int totalPoints = 0;  //accumulator
    char grade      = ' ';

    //get first score
    cout << "First score (-1 to stop): ";
    cin >> score;

    while (score != -1)
    {
        //update accumulator
        //then get another score
        totalPoints += score;
        cout << "Next score (-1 to stop): ";
        cin >> score;
    }   //end while

    //determine grade
    if (totalPoints >= 315)
        grade = 'A';
    else if (totalPoints >= 280)
        grade = 'B';
    else if (totalPoints >= 245)
        grade = 'C';
    else if (totalPoints >= 210)
        grade = 'D';
    else
        grade = 'F';
    //end if
```

you also can use `totalPoints = totalPoints + score;`

Figure 7-52 Professor Chang program (*continues*)

(continued)

```

    //display the total points and grade
    cout << "Total points earned: "
         << totalPoints << endl;
    cout << "Grade: " << grade << endl;

    //system("pause");
    return 0;
}   //end of main function
```

if your C++ development tool requires this statement, delete the two forward slashes

Figure 7-52 Professor Chang program

LAB 7-3 Modify

If necessary, create a new project named Lab7-3 Project and save it in the Cpp7\Chap07 folder. Enter (or copy) the Lab7-2.cpp instructions into a new source file named Lab7-3.cpp. Change Lab7-2.cpp in the first comment to Lab7-3.cpp. Professor Chang now wants the program to display the total number of scores he enters. Modify the program appropriately, and then save and run the program. Test the program using the following five scores and sentinel value: 45, 40, 41, 96, 89, and –1. The total points earned and grade should be 311 and B, respectively. In addition, the program should indicate that Professor Chang entered 5 scores.

Now test the program a second time using the following scores and sentinel value: 25, 500 (Professor Chang inadvertently enters 500 rather than 50), 38, –500 (Professor Chang corrects his mistake by entering a negative number 500), 50, 64, 78, and –1. Does the program display the correct total points earned and grade? How many scores does the program indicate that Professor Chang entered?

LAB 7-4 Desk-Check

The code shown in Figure 7-53 should display the squares of the numbers from 1 through 5. In other words, it should display the numbers 1, 4, 9, 16, and 25. Desk-check the code. Did your desk-check reveal any errors in the code? If so, correct the code and then desk-check it again.

```
int squaredNumber = 0;
for (int number = 1; number < 5; number += 1)
{
      squaredNumber = number * number;
      cout << squaredNumber << endl;
}     //end for
```

Figure 7-53 Code for Lab 7-4

LAB 7-5 Debug

Follow the instructions for starting C++ and viewing the Lab7-5.cpp file, which is contained in either the Cpp7\Chap07\Lab7-5 Project folder or the Cpp7\Chap07 folder. (Depending on your C++ development tool, you may need to open Lab 7-5's project/solution file first.) If necessary, delete the two forward slashes that appear before the `system("pause");` statement, and then save the program. Run the program. When you are prompted to enter a price, type 15.45 and press Enter. The "Next price:" prompt appears over and over again in the Command Prompt window, as shown in Figure 7-54. This is a result of the computer repeatedly processing the `cout << "Next price: ";` statement contained in the body of the `while` loop, and it indicates that the program contains an endless (or infinite) loop. You can stop an endless loop by pressing Ctrl+c (press and hold down the Ctrl key as you tap the letter c, and then release both keys). Or, you can use the Close button on the Command Prompt window's title bar. Use either method to stop the endless loop, and then debug the program.

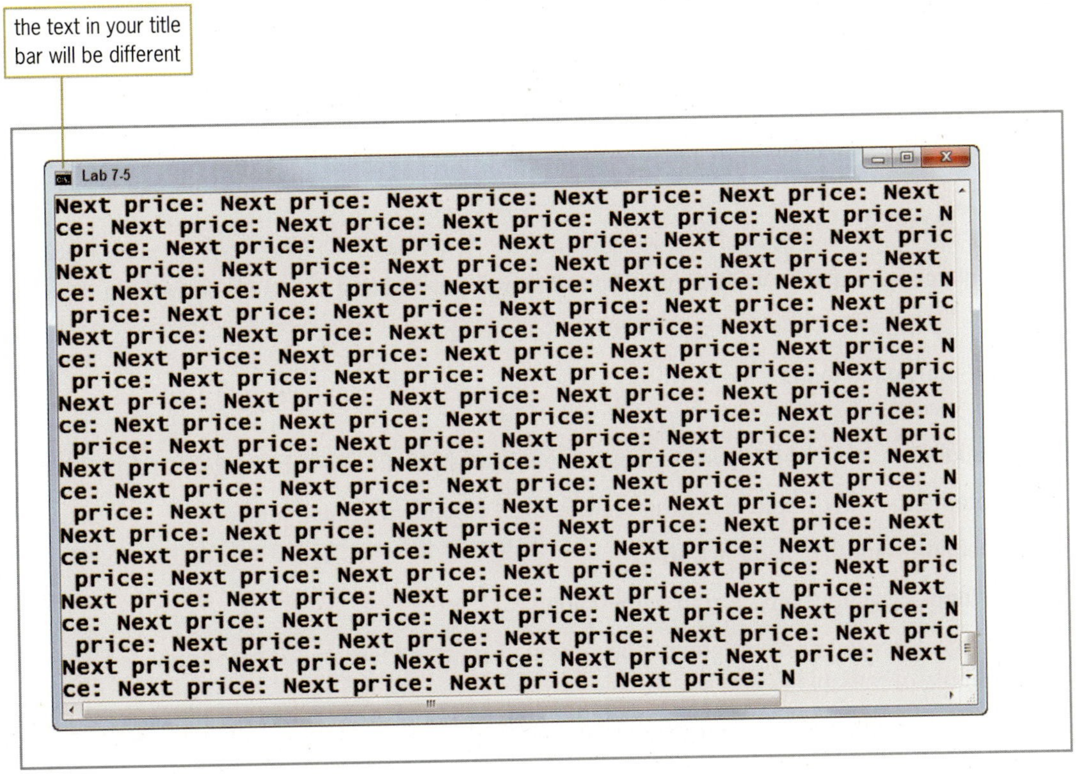

the text in your title bar will be different

```
Lab 7-5
Next price: Next price: Next price: Next price: Next price: Next
ce: Next price: Next price: Next price: Next price: Next price: N
 price: Next price: Next price: Next price: Next price: Next pric
Next price: Next price: Next price: Next price: Next price: Next
ce: Next price: Next price: Next price: Next price: Next price: N
 price: Next price: Next price: Next price: Next price: Next pric
Next price: Next price: Next price: Next price: Next price: Next
ce: Next price: Next price: Next price: Next price: Next price: N
 price: Next price: Next price: Next price: Next price: Next pric
Next price: Next price: Next price: Next price: Next price: Next
ce: Next price: Next price: Next price: Next price: Next price: N
 price: Next price: Next price: Next price: Next price: Next pric
Next price: Next price: Next price: Next price: Next price: Next
ce: Next price: Next price: Next price: Next price: Next price: N
 price: Next price: Next price: Next price: Next price: Next pric
Next price: Next price: Next price: Next price: Next price: Next
ce: Next price: Next price: Next price: Next price: Next price: N
 price: Next price: Next price: Next price: Next price: Next pric
Next price: Next price: Next price: Next price: Next price: Next
ce: Next price: Next price: Next price: Next price: Next price: N
 price: Next price: Next price: Next price: Next price: Next pric
Next price: Next price: Next price: Next price: Next price: Next
ce: Next price: Next price: Next price: Next price: N
```

Figure 7-54 Command Prompt window showing that the program is in an endless loop

Summary

- You use the repetition structure, also called a loop, when you need the computer to repeatedly process one or more program instructions while the looping condition is true (or until the loop exit condition has been met).
- A repetition structure can be either a pretest loop or a posttest loop. In a pretest loop, the loop condition is evaluated *before* the instructions within the loop are processed. In a posttest loop, which is covered in Chapter 8, the evaluation occurs *after* the instructions within the loop are processed. Of the two types of loops, the pretest loop is the most commonly used.
- The condition appears at the beginning of a pretest loop and determines whether the instructions within the loop, referred to as the loop body, are processed. The loop's

condition must result in either a true or false answer only. When the condition evaluates to true, the instructions listed in the loop body are processed; otherwise, the loop body instructions are skipped over.

- Some loops require the user to enter a special value, called a sentinel value, to end the loop. You should use a sentinel value that is easily distinguishable from the valid data recognized by the program. Other loops are terminated through the use of a counter.
- The input instruction that appears above the pretest loop's condition is referred to as the priming read because it is used to prime (prepare or set up) the loop. The priming read gets only the first value from the user. The input instruction that appears within the loop gets the remaining values (if any) and is referred to as the update read.
- In most flowcharts, a diamond is used to represent a repetition structure's condition. The diamond is called the decision symbol.
- Counters and accumulators are used within a repetition structure to calculate subtotals, totals, and averages. All counters and accumulators must be initialized and updated. Counters are updated by a constant value, whereas accumulators are updated by an amount that varies.
- Many programmers use a hexagon to represent the `for` clause in a `for` statement.
- You can use either the `while` statement or the `for` statement to code a pretest loop in C++.

Key Terms

Accumulator—a numeric variable used for accumulating (adding together) something

Counter—a numeric variable used for counting something

Counter-controlled loops—loops whose processing and termination are controlled by a counter variable

Endless loop—a loop whose instructions are processed indefinitely; also called an infinite loop

`for` statement—a C++ statement that can be used to code a pretest loop

Incrementing—another name for updating

Infinite loop—another name for an endless loop

Initializing—the process of assigning a beginning value to a memory location, such as a counter or accumulator variable

Loop—another name for the repetition structure

Loop body—the instructions within a loop

Loop exit condition—the requirement that must be met for the computer to *stop* processing the loop body instructions

Looping condition—the requirement that must be met for the computer to *continue* processing the loop body instructions

Posttest loop—a loop whose condition is evaluated *after* the instructions in its loop body are processed

Pretest loop—a loop whose condition is evaluated *before* the instructions in its loop body are processed

Priming read—the input instruction that appears above the loop that it controls; used to get the first input item from the user

Repetition structure—the control structure used to repeatedly process one or more program instructions; also called a loop

Sentinel values—values that are used to end loops; also called trip values or trailer values

Update read—the input instruction that appears within a loop and is associated with the priming read

Updating—the process of adding a number to the value stored in a counter or accumulator variable; also called incrementing

`while` statement—a C++ statement that can be used to code a pretest loop

Review Questions

Refer to Figure 7-55 to answer Review Questions 1 through 4.

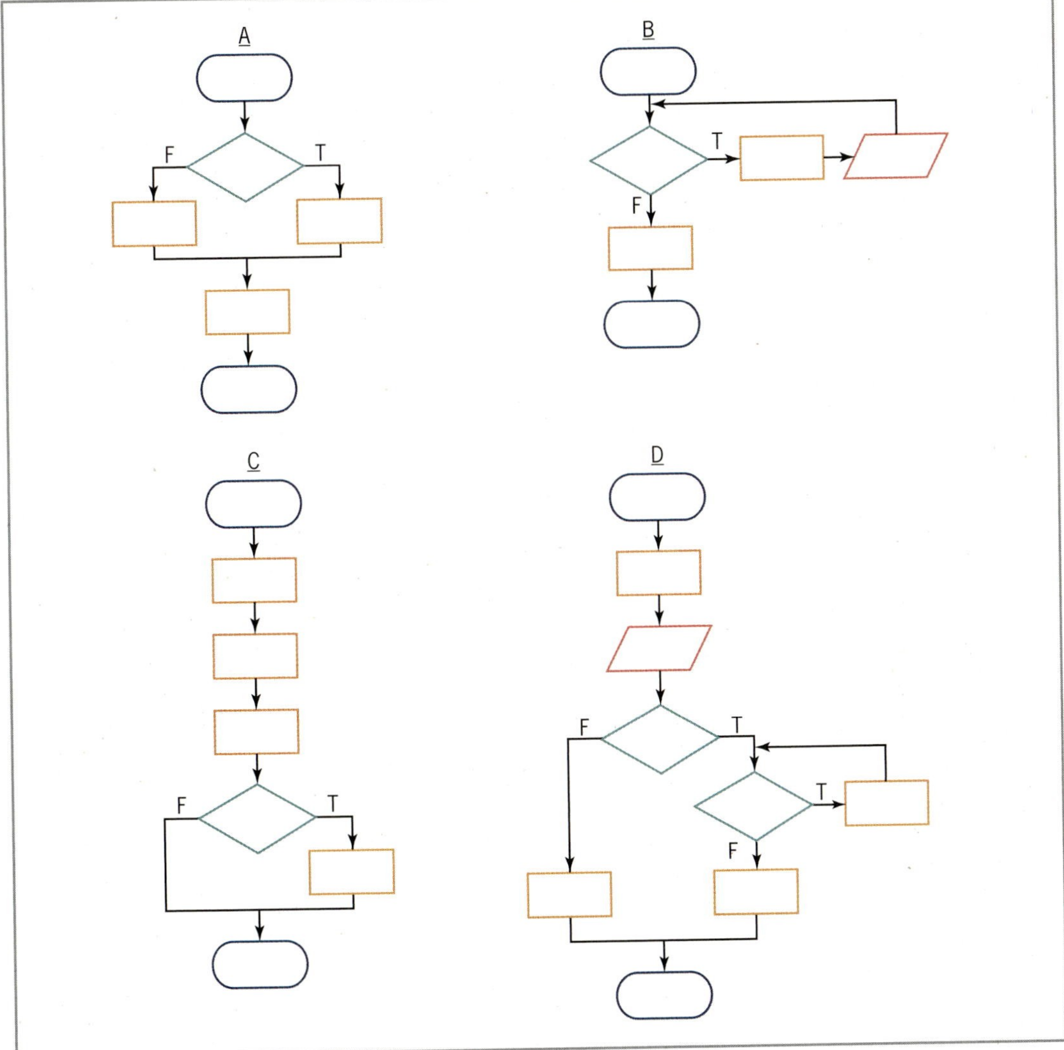

Figure 7-55

1. Which of the following control structures are used in flowchart A in Figure 7-55? (Select all that apply.)
   a. sequence
   b. selection
   c. repetition

2. Which of the following control structures are used in flowchart B in Figure 7-55? (Select all that apply.)
   a. sequence
   b. selection
   c. repetition
3. Which of the following control structures are used in flowchart C in Figure 7-55? (Select all that apply.)
   a. sequence
   b. selection
   c. repetition
4. Which of the following control structures are used in flowchart D in Figure 7-55? (Select all that apply.)
   a. sequence
   b. selection
   c. repetition
5. Which of the following `while` clauses tells the computer to exit the loop when the value in the `age` variable is less than the number 0?
   a. `while (age < 0)`
   b. `while age >= 0;`
   c. `while (age !> 0)`
   d. `while (age >= 0)`
6. Which of the following is a good sentinel value for a program that allows the user to enter a person's age?
   a. –4
   b. 350
   c. 999
   d. all of the above
7. Values that are used to end loops are referred to as ________ values.
   a. closing
   b. ending
   c. sentinel
   d. stop
8. A program allows the user to enter one or more numbers. The first input instruction will get the first number only and is referred to as the ________ read.
   a. entering
   b. initializer
   c. initializing
   d. priming

9. How many times will the computer process the `cout << numTimes << endl;` statement in the following code?

```
int numTimes = 0;
while (numTimes > 3)
{
        cout << numTimes << endl;
        numTimes += 1;
}      //end while
```

   a. 0
   b. 1
   c. 3
   d. 4

10. How many times will the computer process the `cout << numTimes << endl;` statement in the following code?

```
for (int numTimes = 1; numTimes < 6; numTimes += 1)
     cout << numTimes << endl;
//end for
```

   a. 0
   b. 1
   c. 5
   d. 6

11. What value in the `numTimes` variable stops the loop in Review Question 10?

   a. 1
   b. 5
   c. 6
   d. 7

12. How many times will the computer process the `cout << numTimes << endl;` statement in the following code?

```
for (int numTimes = 4; numTimes <= 10; numTimes += 2)
     cout << numTimes << endl;
//end for
```

   a. 0
   b. 3
   c. 4
   d. 12

13. What value in the `numTimes` variable stops the loop in Review Question 12?

   a. 4
   b. 6
   c. 10
   d. 12

14. Which of the following updates the `total` accumulator variable by the value in the `sales` variable?
    a. `total = total + sales;`
    b. `total = sales + total;`
    c. `total += sales;`
    d. all of the above

15. Which of the following statements can be used to code a loop whose instructions you want processed 10 times?
    a. `for`
    b. `repeat`
    c. `while`
    d. either a or c

Exercises

Pencil and Paper

TRY THIS

1. Complete a desk-check table for the code shown in Figure 7-56. What will the code display on the computer screen? What `temp` variable value stops the loop? (The answers to TRY THIS Exercises are located at the end of the chapter.)

```
int temp = 0;
while (temp < 5)
{
        cout << temp << endl;
        temp = temp + 1;
}       //end while
```

Figure 7-56

TRY THIS

2. Complete a desk-check table for the code shown in Figure 7-57. What will the code display on the computer screen? What `num` variable value stops the loop? (The answers to TRY THIS Exercises are located at the end of the chapter.)

```
for (int num = 0; num <= 5; num += 2)
{
        cout << "Number: ";
        cout << num << endl;
}       //end for
```

Figure 7-57

MODIFY THIS

3. Rewrite the code shown in Figure 7-56 to use the `for` statement.

MODIFY THIS

4. Rewrite the code shown in Figure 7-57 to use the `while` statement.

INTRODUCTORY

5. Complete a desk-check table for the code shown in Figure 7-58. What will the code display on the computer screen? What `totalEmployee` variable value stops the loop?

```
int totalEmployee = 0;
while (totalEmployee <= 5)
{
      cout << totalEmployee << endl;
      totalEmployee = totalEmployee + 2;
}     //end while
```

Figure 7-58

INTRODUCTORY

6. Write an assignment statement that updates a counter variable named `numStudents` by 1.

INTRODUCTORY

7. Write an assignment statement that updates an accumulator variable named `totalPay` by the value in the `grossPay` variable.

INTRODUCTORY

8. Write a C++ `while` clause that processes the loop instructions as long as the value in the `quantity` variable is greater than the number 100.

INTRODUCTORY

9. Write a C++ `for` clause that processes the loop instructions 10 times. Use `numTimes` as the counter variable's name.

INTRODUCTORY

10. Figure 7-32 in the chapter showed two examples of the `for` statement. List the processing steps for the code shown in Example 2. (Use Figure 7-33 as a guide.)

INTRODUCTORY

11. Using only the instructions listed in Figure 7-59, write an algorithm that directs an author to sign each customer's book.

```
accept the book from the customer
close the book
end repeat
open the front cover of the book
place the book on the table
repeat for (each customer in line)
return the book to the customer
sign your name on the first page
thank the customer
```

Figure 7-59

INTERMEDIATE

12. Write a C++ `while` clause that stops the loop when the value in the `inStock` variable is less than or equal to the value in the `reorder` variable.

INTERMEDIATE

13. Write an assignment statement that updates a counter variable named `quantity` by –5.

INTERMEDIATE

14. Write an assignment statement that subtracts the contents of the `salesReturns` variable from the `sales` accumulator variable.

INTERMEDIATE

15. Modify the solution shown earlier in Figure 7-2. The solution should now keep track of the number of times Isis's laser beam missed the spider. After saying "You are safe now. The spider is dead.", Isis should say one of the following: "I got him immediately.", "I missed him one time.", or "I missed him *x* times." (where *x* is the value in the counter).

ADVANCED

16. Write two versions of the code to display the numbers 10 through 1 on the computer screen. In the first version, use the `for` statement. In the second version, use the `while` statement.

SWAT THE BUGS

17. The code shown in Figure 7-60 should display the numbers 1, 2, 3, and 4 on the computer screen. However, the code is not working correctly. Correct the errors in the code.

```
int num = 1;
while (num < 5)
      cout << num << endl;
//end while
```

Figure 7-60

SWAT THE BUGS

18. The code shown in Figure 7-61 should display each salesperson's commission. The commission is calculated by multiplying the salesperson's sales by 10%. The code is not working correctly. Correct the errors in the code.

```
double sales = 0.0;
double commission = 0.0;
cout << "Enter a sales amount: ";
cin >> sales;
while (sales > 0.0)
{
      commission = sales * .1;
      cout << commission << endl;
}     //end while
```

Figure 7-61

Computer

TRY THIS

19. In this exercise, you learn two ways to stop a program that is in an endless (infinite) loop.
    a. Follow the instructions for starting C++ and viewing the TryThis19.cpp file, which is contained in either the Cpp7\Chap07\TryThis19 Project folder or the Cpp7\Chap07 folder. (You may need to open the project/solution file first.) If necessary, delete the two forward slashes that appear before the `system("pause");` statement, and then save the program.
    b. Run the program. You can tell that the program is in an endless loop because it displays the number 0 over and over again in the Command Prompt window. In most cases, you can stop an endless loop by pressing Ctrl+c (press and hold down the Ctrl key as you tap the letter c, and then release both keys). Use the Ctrl+c key combination to stop the program. If necessary, close the Command Prompt window.
    c. Run the program again. You also can use the Command Prompt window's Close button to stop an endless loop. Click the Command Prompt window's Close button.

TRY THIS

20. Follow the instructions for starting C++ and viewing the TryThis20.cpp file, which is contained in either the Cpp7\Chap07\TryThis20 Project folder or the Cpp7\Chap07 folder. (You may need to open the project/solution file first.) If necessary, delete the two forward slashes that appear before the `system("pause");` statement. Complete the program by entering a `while`

clause that processes the loop instructions when the user enters a number that is at least 0. Save and then run the program. Test the program using the following numbers: 4, 10, 0, and –3. (The answers to TRY THIS Exercises are located at the end of the chapter.)

TRY THIS

21. Follow the instructions for starting C++ and viewing the TryThis21.cpp file, which is contained in either the Cpp7\Chap07\TryThis21 Project folder or the Cpp7\Chap07 folder. (You may need to open the project/solution file first.) If necessary, delete the two forward slashes that appear before the `system("pause");` statement. Complete the program by entering a `while` clause that stops the loop when the user enters the letter N in either uppercase or lowercase. Save and then run the program. Test the program using the following characters: a, 4, $, and n. (The answers to TRY THIS Exercises are located at the end of the chapter.)

MODIFY THIS

22. Follow the instructions for starting C++ and viewing the ModifyThis22.cpp file, which is contained in either the Cpp7\Chap07\ModifyThis22 Project folder or the Cpp7\Chap07 folder. (You may need to open the project/solution file first.) If necessary, delete the two forward slashes that appear before the `system("pause");` statement. Change the `while` statement to a `for` statement. Save and then run the program. The word "Hello" should appear on the screen 10 times.

MODIFY THIS

23. In this exercise, you modify the program from Lab7-2.

    a. If necessary, create a new project named ModifyThis23 Project and save it in the Cpp7\Chap07 folder. Enter (or copy) the Lab7-2.cpp instructions into a new source file named ModifyThis23.cpp. Change Lab7-2.cpp in the first comment to ModifyThis23.cpp.

    b. If Professor Chang enters a score that is greater than 100 points, the program should ask him whether the score is correct. The program should not add a score that is more than 100 points to the accumulator without the professor's permission. Modify the program appropriately.

    c. Save and then run the program. Enter 35, 45, and 50 as the first three scores, and then enter 105. When you are asked whether the 105 score is correct, respond that it is not correct. Now enter 100, 90, and –1. The program should display 320 as the total points earned and A as the grade.

    d. Run the program again. Enter 27, 15, and 30 as the first three scores, and then enter 105. When you are asked whether the 105 score is correct, respond that it is correct. Now enter 70 and –1. The program should display 247 as the total points earned and C as the grade.

INTRODUCTORY

24. Follow the instructions for starting C++ and viewing the Introductory24.cpp file, which is contained in either the Cpp7\Chap07\Introductory24 Project folder or the Cpp7\Chap07 folder. (You may need to open the project/solution file first.) If necessary, delete the two forward slashes that appear before the `system("pause");` statement. Complete the program by entering a `while` clause that processes the loop instructions as long as the user enters the letter Y in either uppercase or lowercase. Save and then run the program. Test the program using the following three sets of data: y and 100, Y and 200, and n. The total sales amount should be $300. Run the program again. When you are asked whether you want to enter a sales amount, type N and press Enter. Notice that you were not asked to enter the sales amount. Explain why.

INTRODUCTORY

25. Figure 7-62 shows the flowchart for an algorithm that displays the numbers 20, 40, 60, 80, 100, 120, 140, 160, and 180 on the screen. Code the algorithm into a program; use the `while` statement. The counter variable should be an `int` variable named `number`. If necessary, create a new project named Introductory25 Project and save it in the Cpp7\Chap07 folder. Enter your C++ instructions into a source file named Introductory25.cpp. Also enter appropriate comments and any additional instructions required by the compiler. Save and then run the program.

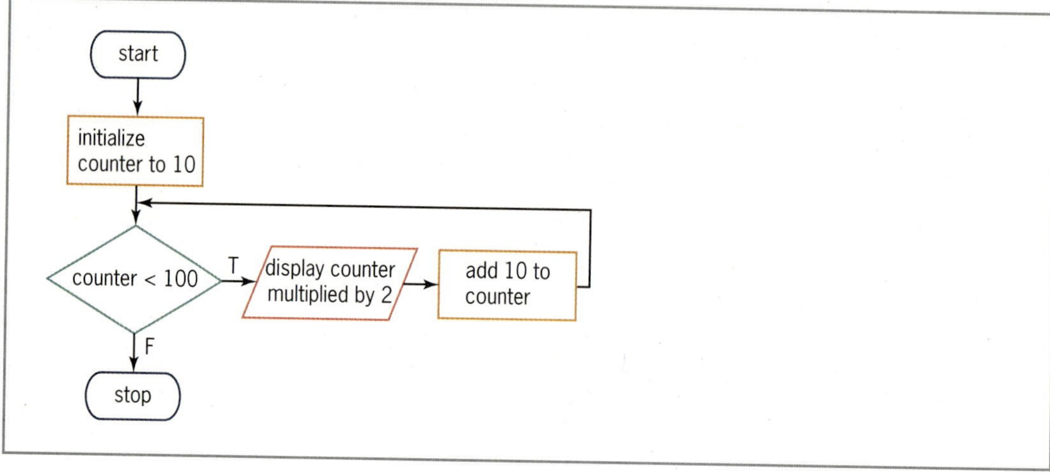

Figure 7-62

INTRODUCTORY

26. Figure 7-63 shows the flowchart for an algorithm that displays the numbers 10, 30, 50, 70, and 90 on the screen. Code the algorithm into a program; use the `for` statement. The counter variable should be an `int` variable named `number`. If necessary, create a new project named Introductory26 Project and save it in the Cpp7\Chap07 folder. Enter your C++ instructions into a source file named Introductory26.cpp. Also enter appropriate comments and any additional instructions required by the compiler. Save and then run the program.

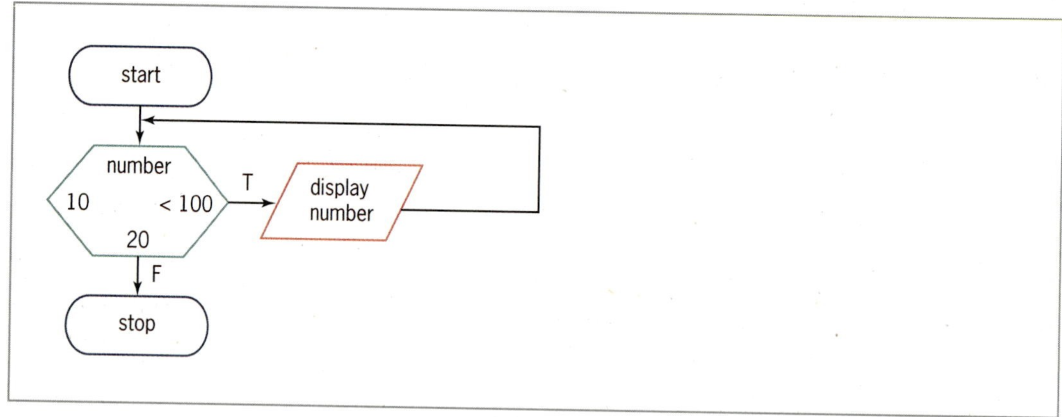

Figure 7-63

INTRODUCTORY

27. In this exercise, you create a program that displays the numbers 0 through 117, in increments of 9. Write two versions of the appropriate code: one using the `for` statement and the other using the `while` statement. If necessary, create a new project named Introductory27 Project and save it in the Cpp7\Chap07 folder. Enter the C++ instructions into a source file named Introductory27.cpp. Also enter appropriate comments and any additional instructions required by the compiler. Save and then run the program. The numbers 0, 9, 18 and so on should appear twice on the screen.

INTERMEDIATE

28. The problem specification, IPO chart information, and C++ instructions for the Jasper Music Company program are shown in Figure 7-25 in the chapter.

    a. If necessary, create a new project named Intermediate28 Project and save it in the Cpp7\Chap07 folder. Enter the C++ instructions into a source file named Intermediate28.cpp. Also enter appropriate comments and any additional instructions required by the compiler.

b. Save and then run the program. Test the program using the following sales amounts: 2500, 6000, and 2000.

c. Modify the program so it uses the `for` statement rather than the `while` statement.

d. Save and then run the program. Test the program using the following sales amounts: 2500, 6000, and 2000.

INTERMEDIATE

29. The problem specification, IPO chart information, and C++ instructions for the Holmes Supply program are shown in Figure 7-34 in the chapter.

a. If necessary, create a new project named Intermediate29 Project and save it in the Cpp7\Chap07 folder. Enter the C++ instructions into a source file named Intermediate29.cpp. Also enter appropriate comments and any additional instructions required by the compiler.

b. Save and then run the program. Test the program using the following payroll amounts: 15000, 25000, and 60000.

c. Modify the program so it uses the `while` statement rather than the `for` statement.

d. Save and then run the program. Test the program using the following payroll amounts: 15000, 25000, and 60000.

INTERMEDIATE

30. The problem specification, IPO chart information, and C++ instructions for the Colfax Sales program are shown in Figure 7-40 in the chapter.

a. If necessary, create a new project named Intermediate30 Project and save it in the Cpp7\Chap07 folder. Enter the C++ instructions into a source file named Intermediate30.cpp. Also enter appropriate comments and any additional instructions required by the compiler.

b. Save and then run the program. Test the program using the number 25000 as the sales amount.

c. Modify the program so it uses the `while` statement rather than the `for` statement.

d. Save and then run the program. Test the program using the number 25000 as the sales amount.

INTERMEDIATE

31. Effective January 1st of each year, Gabriela receives a 5% raise on her previous year's salary. She wants a program that calculates and displays the amount of her annual raises for the next three years. The program also should calculate and display her total salary for the next three years.

a. Create an IPO chart for the problem, and then desk-check the algorithm using an annual salary of $10,000. (The raise amounts are $500.00, $525.00, and $551.25. The total salary is $33101.25.)

b. List the input, processing, and output items, as well as the algorithm, in a chart similar to the one shown earlier in Figure 7-14. Then code the algorithm into a program.

c. Desk-check the program using the same data used to desk-check the algorithm.

d. If necessary, create a new project named Intermediate31 Project and save it in the Cpp7\Chap07 folder. Enter your C++ instructions into a source file named Intermediate31.cpp. Also enter appropriate comments and any additional instructions required by the compiler.

e. Save and then run the program. Test the program using the same data used to desk-check the program.

ADVANCED

32. In this exercise, you create a program that displays the sum of the even integers between and including two numbers entered by the user. In other words, if the user enters an even number, that number should be included in the sum. For example, if the user enters the integers 2 and 7, the sum is 12 (2 + 4 + 6). If the user enters the integers 2 and 8, the sum is 20 (2 + 4 + 6 + 8). Display an error message if the first integer entered by the user is greater than the second integer.

    a. Create an IPO chart for the problem, and then desk-check the algorithm three times. For the first desk-check, use the integers 1 and 5. For the second desk-check, use the integers 12 and 21. For the third desk-check, use the integers 50 and 3.

    b. List the input, processing, and output items, as well as the algorithm, in a chart similar to the one shown earlier in Figure 7-14. Then code the algorithm into a program.

    c. Desk-check the program using the same data used to desk-check the algorithm.

    d. If necessary, create a new project named Advanced32 Project and save it in the Cpp7\Chap07 folder. Enter your C++ instructions into a source file named Advanced32.cpp. Also enter appropriate comments and any additional instructions required by the compiler.

    e. Save and then run the program. Test the program using the same data used to desk-check the program.

ADVANCED

33. The sales manager at Premium Paper wants a program that allows her to enter the company's income and expense amounts, which will always be integers. The number of income and expense amounts may vary each time the program is run. For example, the sales manager may need to enter five income amounts and three expense amounts. Or, she may need to enter 20 income amounts and 30 expense amounts. The program should calculate and display the company's total income, total expenses, and profit (or loss).

    a. Create an IPO chart for the problem, and then desk-check the algorithm three times. For the first desk-check, use the following income amounts: 5000, 7500, and 3350. Also use the following expense amounts: 125 and 999. For the second desk-check, use the following income amounts: 2450, 6700, 9000, and 5600. Also use the following expense amount: 4000. For the third desk-check, use an income amount of 8000 and an expense amount of 10000.

    b. List the input, processing, and output items, as well as the algorithm, in a chart similar to the one shown earlier in Figure 7-14. Then code the algorithm into a program.

    c. Desk-check the program using the same data used to desk-check the algorithm.

    d. If necessary, create a new project named Advanced33 Project and save it in the Cpp7\Chap07 folder. Enter your C++ instructions into a source file named Advanced33.cpp. Also enter appropriate comments and any additional instructions required by the compiler.

    e. Save and then run the program. Test the program using the same data used to desk-check the program.

ADVANCED

34. In this exercise, you create a program for the sales manager at Computer Haven, a small business that offers motivational seminars to local companies. Figure 7-64 shows the charge for attending a seminar. Notice that the charge per person depends on the number of people the company registers. For example, the cost for four registrants is $400; the cost for two registrants is $300. The program should allow the sales manager to enter the number of registrants for as many companies as needed. When the sales manager has finished entering the data, the program should calculate and display the

total number of people registered, the total charge for those registrants, and the average charge per registrant. For example, if one company registers four people and another company registers two people, the total number of people registered is six, the total charge is $700, and the average charge per registrant is $116.67.

Number of people a company registers	Charge per person ($)
1 – 3	150
4 – 9	100
10 or more	90

Figure 7-64

a. Create an IPO chart for the problem, and then desk-check the algorithm appropriately.

b. List the input, processing, and output items, as well as the algorithm, in a chart similar to the one shown earlier in Figure 7-14. Then code the algorithm into a program.

c. Desk-check the program using the same data used to desk-check the algorithm.

d. If necessary, create a new project named Advanced34 Project and save it in the Cpp7\Chap07 folder. Enter your C++ instructions into a source file named Advanced34.cpp. Also enter appropriate comments and any additional instructions required by the compiler. Display the average charge in fixed-point notation with two decimal places.

e. Save and then run the program. Test the program using the same data used to desk-check the program.

ADVANCED

35. In this exercise, you create a program that displays the first 10 Fibonacci numbers (1, 1, 2, 3, 5, 8, 13, 21, 34, and 55). Notice that beginning with the third number in the series, each Fibonacci number is the sum of the prior two numbers. In other words, 2 is the sum of 1 plus 1, 3 is the sum of 1 plus 2, 5 is the sum of 2 plus 3, and so on. Write two versions of the code: one using the `while` statement and the other using the `for` statement. If necessary, create a new project named Advanced35 Project and save it in the Cpp7\Chap07 folder. Enter the C++ instructions into a source file named Advanced35.cpp. Also enter appropriate comments and any additional instructions required by the compiler. Save and then run the program. The Fibonacci numbers should appear twice on the screen.

SWAT THE BUGS

36. Follow the instructions for starting C++ and viewing the SwatTheBugs36.cpp file, which is contained in either the Cpp7\Chap07\SwatTheBugs36 Project folder or the Cpp7\Chap07 folder. (You may need to open the project/solution file first.) If necessary, delete the two forward slashes that appear before the `system("pause");` statement, and then save the program. The program should display the number of positive integers and the number of negative integers entered by the user, but it is not working correctly. Debug the program.

Answers to TRY THIS Exercises

Pencil and Paper

1. See Figure 7-65. The code will display the numbers 0, 1, 2, 3, and 4 on separate lines on the computer screen. The loop stops when the `temp` variable's value is 5.

```
temp
0 (crossed out)
1 (crossed out)
2 (crossed out)
3 (crossed out)
4 (crossed out)
5
```

Figure 7-65

2. See Figure 7-66. The code will display Number: 0, Number: 2, and Number: 4 on separate lines on the computer screen. The loop stops when the `num` variable's value is 6.

```
num
0 (crossed out)
2 (crossed out)
4 (crossed out)
6
```

Figure 7-66

Computer

19. No answer required.
20. To complete the program, enter the following `while` clause: `while (number >= 0)`.
21. To complete the program, enter one of the following `while` clauses: `while (toupper(more) != 'N')`, `while (tolower(more) != 'n')`, or `while (more != 'N' && more != 'n')`.

CHAPTER 8

More on the Repetition Structure

After studying Chapter 8, you should be able to:

- Include a posttest loop in pseudocode
- Include a posttest loop in a flowchart
- Code a posttest loop using the C++ do while statement
- Nest repetition structures
- Raise a number to a power using the pow function

Posttest Loops

Recall that a repetition structure can be either a pretest loop or a posttest loop. The difference between both types of loops pertains to when the loop's condition is evaluated. Unlike a pretest loop's condition, which is evaluated *before* the instructions within the loop are processed, a posttest loop's condition is evaluated *after* the instructions within the loop are processed. As a result, the instructions in a posttest loop will always be processed at least once, whereas the instructions in a pretest loop may never be processed.

Pretest and posttest loops are also called top-driven and bottom-driven loops, respectively.

You learned about pretest loops in Chapter 7. You will learn about posttest loops in this chapter. Although pretest loops are the most commonly used, it is essential to understand the way posttest loops work. You may encounter a situation where a posttest loop is the better choice. Or, you may encounter a posttest loop in another programmer's code that you are either modifying or debugging.

The problem specification, illustrations, and solutions shown in Figure 8-1 will help clarify the difference between pretest and posttest loops. Both solutions contain the instructions for getting Sherri from her current location to one that is directly in front of the fountain. Solution 1 contains a pretest loop, and Solution 2 contains a posttest loop. Compare the first and last lines in the pretest loop with the first and last lines in the posttest loop. More specifically, notice the location of the loop's condition. In the pretest loop, the condition appears in the first line, which indicates that Sherri should evaluate it *before* she follows the walk forward instruction in the loop body. In the posttest loop, the condition appears in the last line, indicating that Sherri should evaluate it only *after* following the walk forward instruction in the loop body. The pretest loop in Solution 1 will work when Sherri is zero or more steps away from the fountain. The posttest loop in Solution 2, however, will work only when Sherri is at least one step away from the fountain.

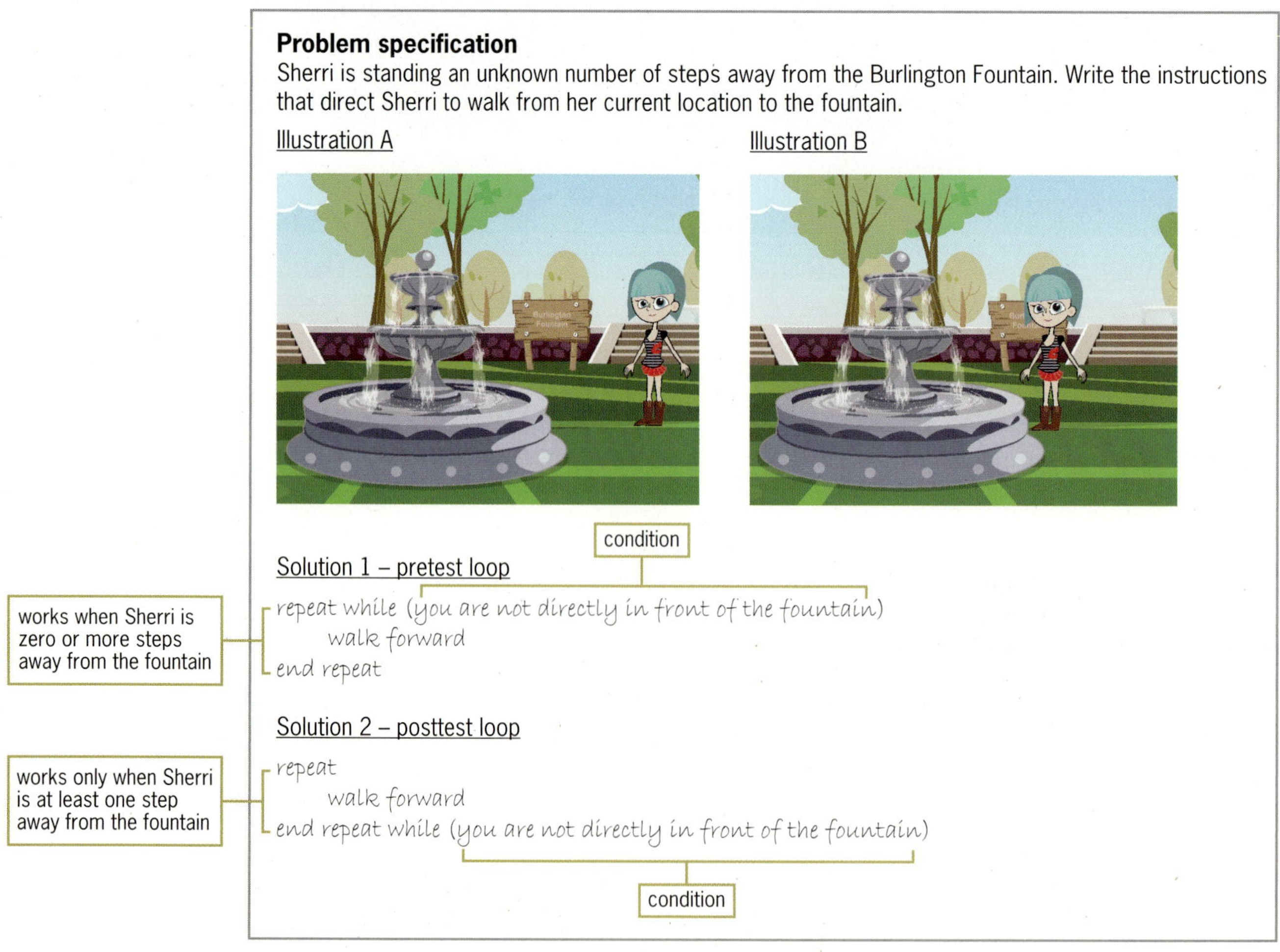

Figure 8-1 Problem specification, illustrations, and solutions containing pretest and posttest loops

To understand why the loops in Figure 8-1 are not interchangeable, you will desk-check them using the two illustrations shown in the figure. For the first desk-check, we'll use Illustration A, which shows Sherri at least one step away from the fountain. For the purposes of this desk-check, we'll assume that Sherri is three steps away from her final destination. In the pretest loop, the loop's condition checks Sherri's current location. Sherri is not directly in front of the fountain, so she is told to walk forward (her first step) and then the loop's condition is evaluated again. The condition evaluates to true, so Sherri is told to walk forward (her second step) and then the loop's condition is evaluated again. The condition evaluates to true, so Sherri is told to walk forward (her third step) and then the loop's condition is evaluated again. At this point, Sherri is directly in front of the fountain, so the condition evaluates to false and the pretest loop ends.

The posttest loop, on the other hand, instructs Sherri to walk forward (her first step) before evaluating the loop's condition. Sherri still is not directly in front of the fountain, so she is told to walk forward (her second step) and then the loop's condition is evaluated again. The condition evaluates to true, so Sherri is told to walk forward (her third step) and then the loop's condition is evaluated again. At this point, Sherri is directly in front of the fountain, so the condition evaluates to false and the posttest loop ends. Notice that when Sherri is three steps away from the fountain, the pretest and posttest loops produce the same result: Both place her right in front of the fountain. If you desk-check both loops using other values for the number of steps, you will find that both loops are interchangeable when Sherri is at least one step away from her final destination.

For the second desk-check, we'll use Illustration B, which shows Sherri already standing in front of the fountain. The condition in the pretest loop checks Sherri's current location. Sherri is already positioned correctly, so the walk forward instruction is bypassed and the loop ends. The posttest loop, on the other hand, instructs Sherri to walk forward before the loop's condition is evaluated. But if Sherri walks forward, she will bump into the fountain. Obviously, the posttest loop in Solution 2 does not work correctly when Sherri starts out directly in front of the fountain. You can fix this problem by adding a selection structure to the solution. The modified solution is shown in Figure 8-2.

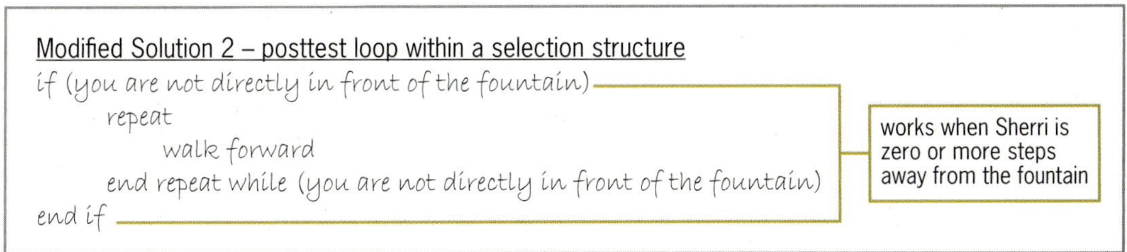

Figure 8-2 Selection structure added to Solution 2 from Figure 8-1

The posttest loop in Figure 8-2 is identical to the posttest loop in Figure 8-1 except it is processed only when the selection structure's condition evaluates to true, which is when Sherri is not directly in front of the fountain. To understand how the selection and repetition structures in Figure 8-2 work, you will desk-check the solution twice. For the first desk-check, Sherri is one step away from the fountain. The solution in Figure 8-2 begins with a single-alternative selection structure whose condition checks Sherri's initial location. The condition evaluates to true because Sherri is not directly in front of the fountain. Therefore, the instructions in the selection structure's true path are processed. The first instruction in the true path (repeat) marks the beginning of a posttest loop. Next, the instruction in the loop body directs Sherri to walk forward (her first step). The loop's condition is evaluated next. At this point, Sherri is positioned correctly; so the loop ends and so does the selection structure.

For the second desk-check, Sherri is directly in front of the fountain. Here again, the condition in the selection structure checks Sherri's initial location. In this case, Sherri is already in front of the fountain, so the selection structure's condition evaluates to false. As a result, the selection structure ends without processing the posttest loop contained in its true path.

Although the modified solution works correctly, most programmers prefer to use a pretest loop, rather than a posttest loop within a selection structure, because it is easier to write and understand. Posttest loops should be used only when their instructions must be processed at least once. You often will find a posttest loop in programs that allow the user to select from a menu, such as a game program. This type of program uses the posttest loop to control the display of the menu, which must appear on the screen at least once.

Flowcharting a Posttest Loop

For many people, it's easier to understand the difference between a pretest loop and a posttest loop by viewing both loops in flowchart form. Figure 8-3 shows the problem specification for the Wheels & More program from Chapter 7. It also shows two correct algorithms written in pseudocode and drawn in a flowchart. Algorithm 1, which you viewed in Figures 7-5 and 7-7 in Chapter 7, uses a pretest loop to get the hours worked entry from the user; Algorithm 2 uses a posttest loop. Notice that the decision diamond, which contains the loop's condition, appears at the top of a pretest loop in a flowchart; however, it appears at the bottom of a posttest loop.

Problem specification
The Wheels & More store has several part-time employees; each earns $10 per hour. The store manager wants a program that calculates and displays the weekly gross pay amount for as many employees as needed without having to run the program more than once. Because the number of hours an employee worked can be a positive number only, the store manager will indicate that he is finished with the program by entering a negative number (in this case, –1) as the number of hours.

Input	**Processing**	**Output**
pay rate ($10 per hour) hours worked	Processing items: none	gross pay

```
Algorithm 1 (pretest loop):
1. enter the hours worked
2. repeat while (the hours worked are not equal to -1)
       calculate the gross pay by multiplying
       the hours worked by the pay rate
       display the gross pay
       enter the hours worked
   end repeat
```

Figure 8-3 Wheels & More problem specification and algorithms *(continues)*

(continued)

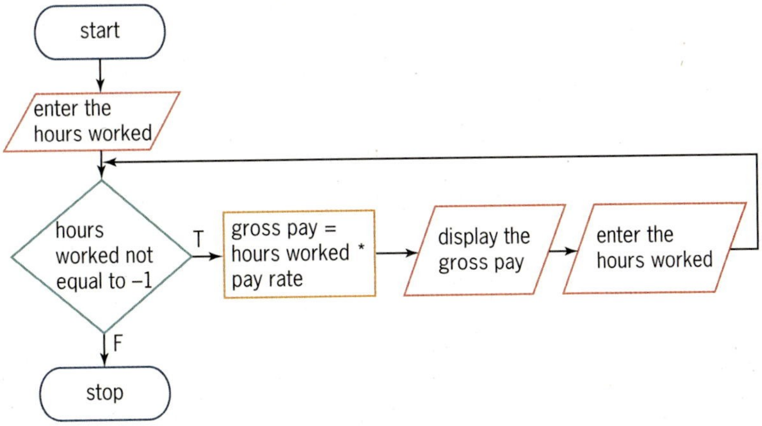

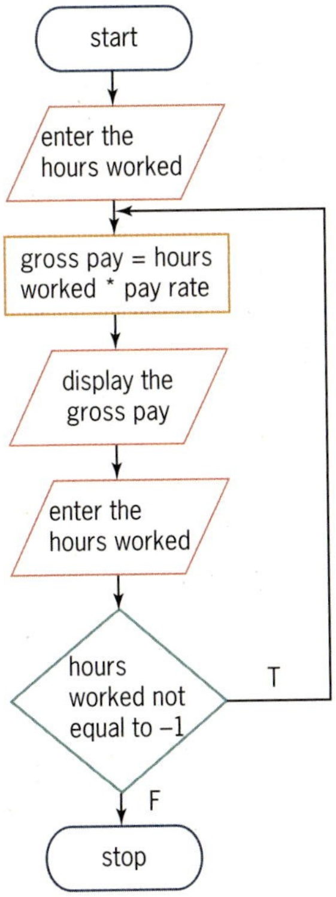

Figure 8-3 Wheels & More problem specification and algorithms

You can observe how a posttest loop operates in a program by desk-checking Algorithm 2's flowchart. You will desk-check the algorithm using the following numbers of hours worked: 15, 8, and −1 (the sentinel value). First, you record the input and output items in a desk-check table, as shown in Figure 8-4.

Ch08-Wheels Desk-Check video

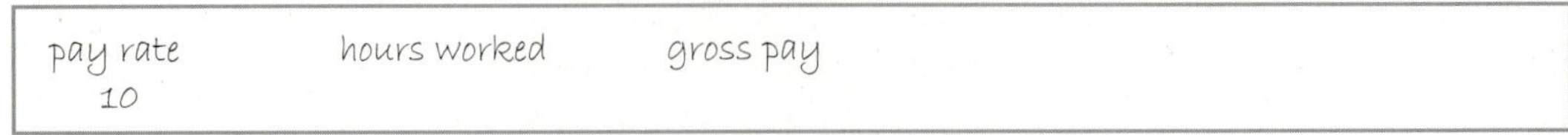

Figure 8-4 Input and output items entered in the desk-check table

Next, you follow each symbol in the flowchart, from top to bottom, recording in the desk-check table any changes made to the values of the input and output items. The first symbol in Algorithm 2's flowchart is the start oval, which merely marks the beginning of the flowchart. The next symbol is an input parallelogram that represents the priming read. In this case, the priming read gets the first hours worked entry (15) from the user. The instruction in the processing rectangle is handled next and is the first instruction in the loop body. The instruction calculates the gross pay by multiplying the hours worked by the pay rate. Notice that the first hours worked entry is not compared to the sentinel value in a posttest loop. Figure 8-5 shows the first hours worked and gross pay amounts recorded in the desk-check table.

pay rate	hours worked	gross pay
10	15	150

Figure 8-5 First hours worked and gross pay amounts recorded in the desk-check table

An output parallelogram follows the processing rectangle in Algorithm 2's flowchart. The output parallelogram, which is part of the loop body, contains the instruction to display the gross pay on the screen. In this case, the number 150 will be displayed. Following the output parallelogram is an input parallelogram, which also is part of the loop body. This input parallelogram gets the next hours worked entry (8) from the user, and it represents the update read. Figure 8-6 shows the second hours worked entry recorded in the desk-check table.

pay rate	hours worked	gross pay
10	~~15~~	150
	8	

Figure 8-6 Second hours worked entry recorded in the desk-check table

The next symbol in the flowchart is the decision diamond. The diamond contains the posttest loop's condition, which always marks the end of a posttest loop. The condition, which is phrased as a looping condition, compares the current hours worked entry with the sentinel value to determine whether the loop should be processed again (a true condition) or end (a false condition). Notice that this is the first time the loop's condition is evaluated. In this case, the condition evaluates to true because 8 is not equal to –1. When the condition evaluates to true, the computer processes the instructions in the loop body. Those instructions calculate and display the gross pay for the second employee and then get another hours worked entry (in this case, the sentinel value) from the user. Figure 8-7 shows the current status of the desk-check table.

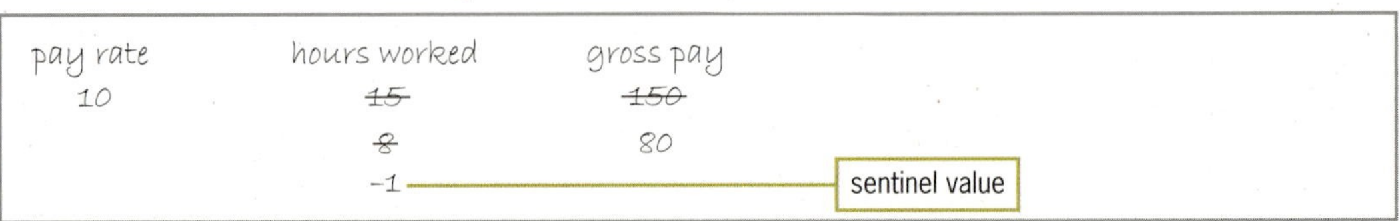

Figure 8-7 Current status of the desk-check table

Next, the loop's condition is reevaluated to determine whether the loop should be processed again (a true condition) or end (a false condition). In this case, the condition evaluates to false because the current hours worked entry is equal to the sentinel value. When the condition evaluates to false, the loop ends and processing continues with the instruction immediately following the loop. In Algorithm 2's flowchart in Figure 8-3, the loop is followed by the stop oval, which marks the end of the flowchart.

Mini-Quiz 8-1

The answers to Mini-Quiz questions are located in Appendix A.

1. If the user enters the numbers 5, 8, 9, and –1, how many times will the condition in the following algorithm be evaluated?

```
1.  enter number
2.  repeat while (number is greater than or equal to 0)
        display number
        enter number
    end repeat
```

2. If the user enters the number –4, how many times will the condition in Question 1's algorithm be evaluated?
3. If the user enters the numbers 5, 8, 9, and –1, how many times will the condition in the following algorithm be evaluated?

```
1.  enter number
2.  repeat
        display number
        enter number
    end repeat while (number is greater than or equal to 0)
```

4. If the user enters the numbers 0 and –4, how many times will the condition in Question 3's algorithm be evaluated?
5. Robin is standing in her hallway facing her bedroom door. The door is an unknown number of steps away from her, and it may or may not be closed. Robin wants to go inside her bedroom. Write two appropriate algorithms using only the instructions shown in Figure 8-8. One of the algorithms should contain a pretest loop; the other should contain a posttest loop.

```
end if
end repeat
end repeat while (you are not directly in front of your bedroom door)
if (the bedroom door is closed)
if (you are not directly in front of your bedroom door)
open the bedroom door
repeat
repeat while (you are not directly in front of your bedroom door)
walk forward
```

Figure 8-8 Instructions for Question 5 in Mini-Quiz 8-1

The do while Statement

C++ provides the **do while statement** for coding a posttest loop. The statement's syntax is shown in Figure 8-9. As the boldfaced text in the syntax indicates, essential components of the statement include the do and while keywords, the parentheses that surround the condition, the braces, and the semicolon. The italicized items indicate where the programmer must supply information. In this case, the programmer must supply the loop's *condition*, which must be phrased as a looping condition. Recall that a looping condition indicates the requirement for repeating the loop body instructions.

As in the while statement, the condition in the do while statement must evaluate to either true or false. The condition can contain variables, constants, functions, arithmetic operators, comparison operators, and logical operators. Besides providing the condition, the programmer also must provide the statements to be processed when the condition evaluates to true. Although not a requirement, some programmers use a comment (such as //begin loop) to mark the beginning of the do while statement because it makes the program easier to read and understand.

Also included in Figure 8-9 are examples of using the do while statement. The while clause in Example 1 indicates that the loop body instructions should be repeated as long as (or while) the value in the age variable is greater than 0. The loop will stop when the second number entered by the user is either less than or equal to 0. The while clause in Example 2 indicates that the loop body instructions should be repeated as long as the value in the makeEntry variable is either the uppercase letter Y or the lowercase letter y. In this case, the loop will stop when the user's second entry is anything other than the letter Y entered in either uppercase or lowercase. You also could write the last line in the loop more simply as either `} while (toupper(makeEntry) == 'Y');` or `} while (tolower(makeEntry) == 'y');`.

HOW TO Use the do while Statement

Syntax

do //begin loop
{
    one or more statements to be processed one time, and thereafter as long as the condition is true
}   **while (***condition***);** — the statement ends with a semicolon

Example 1

```
int age = 0;

cout << "Enter an age greater than 0: ";
cin >> age;                                    // priming read
do   //begin loop
{
     cout << "You entered " << age << endl << endl;
     cout << "Enter an age greater than 0: ";
     cin >> age;                               // update read
}    while (age > 0);                          // semicolon
```

Figure 8-9 How to use the do while statement *(continues)*

(continued)

Example 2

```
char makeEntry = ' ';
double sales = 0.0;

cout << "Enter a sales amount? (Y/N) ";
cin >> makeEntry;                              priming read
do    //begin loop
{
      cout << "Enter the sales: ";                      update read
      cin >> sales;
      cout << "You entered " << sales << endl << endl;
      cout << "Enter a sales amount? (Y/N) ";
      cin >> makeEntry;
}     while (makeEntry == 'Y' || makeEntry == 'y');     semicolon
```

Figure 8-9 How to use the do while statement

The braces in a do while statement are not required when the loop body contains only one statement. However, a one-statement loop body is rare.

Earlier, in Figure 8-3, you viewed the problem specification and algorithms for the Wheels & More program, which calculates and displays the gross pay amount for any number of employees. Figure 8-10 shows the pseudocode and C++ instructions corresponding to Algorithm 2 in that figure. The first three statements in the figure declare and initialize the `RATE` named constant and the `hours` and `gross` variables. Next, the `cout` statement prompts the user to enter the first number of hours worked, and the `cin` statement stores the user's response in the `hours` variable. (This `cin` statement represents the priming read.) The `do` clause appears next in the code and marks the beginning of a posttest loop. The first three instructions in the loop body calculate the gross pay and then display the result, followed by two blank lines, on the computer screen. The last two instructions in the loop body prompt the user to enter the next number of hours worked and then store the user's response in the `hours` variable. (The `cin` statement within the loop represents the update read.) Notice that the loop body instructions are processed *before* the condition in the `while` clause is evaluated.

After the loop body instructions are processed, the looping condition in the `while` clause in Figure 8-10 compares the value stored in the `hours` variable with the sentinel value (–1). If the `hours` variable does not contain the sentinel value, the condition evaluates to true and the loop body instructions are processed again. Those instructions calculate the gross pay and then display the gross pay and two blank lines on the computer screen. They then prompt the user to enter the next number of hours worked and store the user's response in the `hours` variable. From now on, each time the user enters the hours worked, the condition in the `while` clause compares the entry with the sentinel value. When the user enters the sentinel value (in this case, –1) as the number of hours worked, the loop body instructions are not processed again. Instead, the loop is exited and processing continues with the instruction located immediately below the loop. A sample run of the Wheels & More program is shown in Figure 8-11. (The program uses the `fixed` and `setprecision` stream manipulators to display the gross pay amounts in fixed-point notation with two decimal places.)

IPO chart information	C++ instructions
Input	
pay rate ($10 per hour)	`const double RATE = 10.0;`
hours worked	`double hours = 0.0;`
Processing	
none	
Output	
gross pay	`double gross = 0.0;`
Algorithm	
1. enter the hours worked	`cout << "First hours worked (-1 to stop): ";` `cin >> hours;`
2. repeat	`do //begin loop` `{`
calculate the gross pay by multiplying the hours worked by the pay rate	`gross = hours * RATE;`
display the gross pay	`cout << "Gross pay: $" << gross;` `cout << endl << endl;`
enter the hours worked	`cout << "Next hours worked (-1 to stop): ";` `cin >> hours;`
end repeat while (the hours worked are not equal to -1)	`} while (hours != -1);`

Figure 8-10 IPO chart information and C++ instructions for the Wheels & More program

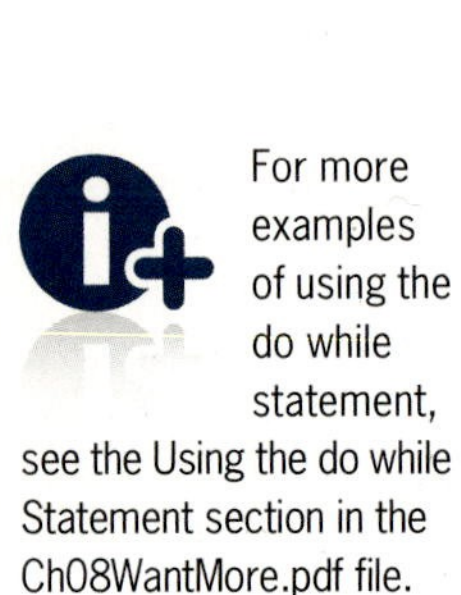

For more examples of using the do while statement, see the Using the do while Statement section in the Ch08WantMore.pdf file.

```
Wheels & More
First hours worked (-1 to stop): 12
Gross pay: $120.00

Next hours worked (-1 to stop): 22.5
Gross pay: $225.00

Next hours worked (-1 to stop): -1
Press any key to continue . . .
```

Figure 8-11 A sample run of the Wheels & More program

The answers to Mini-Quiz questions are located in Appendix A.

Mini-Quiz 8-2

1. The `do while` clause marks the beginning of the C++ `do while` statement.
   a. True
   b. False

2. The `while` clause in the C++ `do while` statement ends with a ________.
   a. brace
   b. colon
   c. comma
   d. semicolon
3. Write a C++ `while` clause that processes the body of a posttest loop as long as the value in the `inStock` variable is greater than the value in the `reorder` variable.
4. Write a C++ `while` clause that processes the body of a posttest loop as long as the value in a `char` variable named `letter` is either Y or y. Use the built-in `toupper` function.

Nested Repetition Structures

Like selection structures, repetition structures can be nested, which means you can place one loop (called the nested or inner loop) within another loop (called the outer loop). Both loops can be pretest loops, or both can be posttest loops. Or, one can be a pretest loop and the other a posttest loop.

A clock uses nested repetition structures to keep track of the time. For simplicity, consider a clock's minute and second hands only. The second hand on a clock moves one position, clockwise, for every second that has elapsed. After the second hand moves 60 positions, the minute hand moves one position, also clockwise. The second hand then begins its journey around the clock again. Figure 8-12 shows the logic used by a clock's minute and second hands. As the figure indicates, an outer loop controls the minute hand, while an inner (nested) loop controls the second hand. Notice that the entire nested loop is contained within the outer loop. This must be true for the loop to be nested and work correctly.

Ch08-Nested Loop video

```
1. start minutes at 0
2. repeat while (minutes are less than 60)
        start seconds at 0
        repeat while (seconds are less than 60)
            move second hand 1 position, clockwise
            add 1 to seconds
        end repeat
        move minute hand 1 position, clockwise
        add 1 to minutes
   end repeat
```

Figure 8-12 Logic used by a clock's minute and second hands

The next iteration of the outer loop (which controls the minute hand) occurs only after the nested loop (which controls the second hand) has finished processing.

A programmer determines whether a problem's solution requires a **nested loop** by studying the problem specification. The first problem specification you will examine in this chapter involves a waitress named Trixie. The problem specification and an illustration of the problem are shown in Figure 8-13, along with an appropriate solution. The solution requires a loop because the instructions for telling each table about the daily specials must be repeated for every table that needs to be waited on. However, the solution does not require a nested loop. This is because the instructions within the loop should be followed only once per table.

Problem specification

A waitress named Trixie works at a local diner. The diner just opened for the day and there are customers already sitting at several of the tables. Write the instructions that direct Trixie to go over to each table that needs to be waited on and tell the customers about the daily specials.

```
repeat for (each table that needs to be waited on)
    go to a table that needs to be waited on
    tell the customers at the table about the daily specials
end repeat
```

follow these instructions for each table

Figure 8-13 Problem specification and solution that requires a loop

Now let's add some additional tasks for Trixie to perform. This time, after telling the customers at a table about the daily specials, Trixie should take each customer's order and then submit the order for the entire table to the cook. Figure 8-14 shows the modified problem specification along with the modified solution, which requires a nested selection structure. The outer loop begins with *repeat for (each table that needs to be waited on)*, and it ends with the last *end repeat*. The nested loop begins with *repeat for (each customer at the table)*, and it ends with the first *end repeat*. Here again, notice that the entire nested loop is contained within the outer loop. Recall that this is a requirement for the loop to be nested and work correctly.

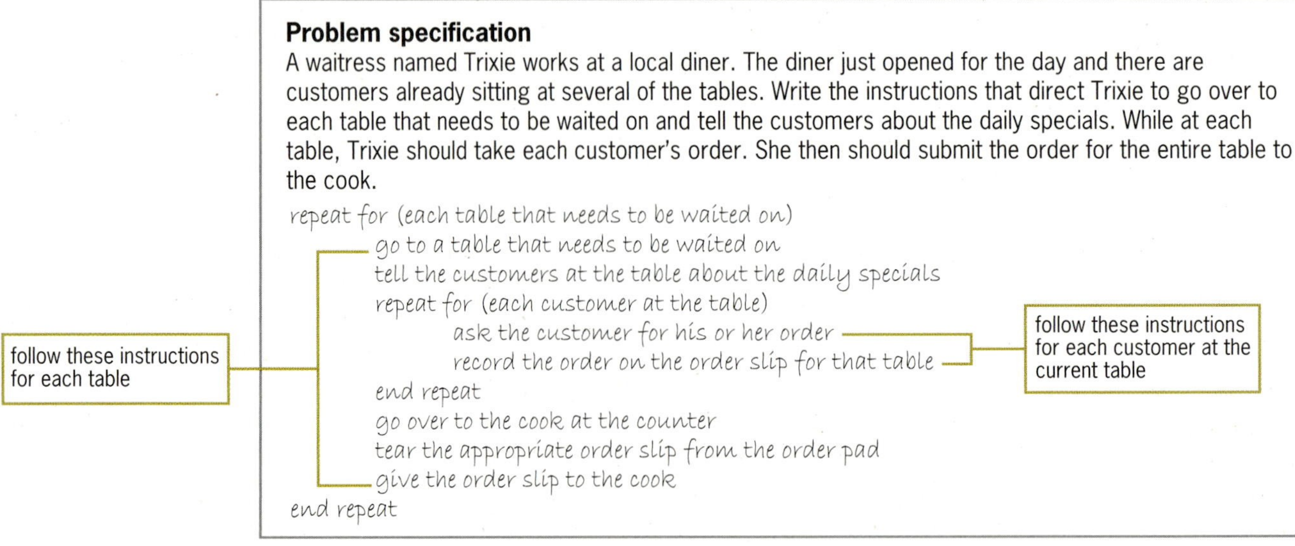

Problem specification

A waitress named Trixie works at a local diner. The diner just opened for the day and there are customers already sitting at several of the tables. Write the instructions that direct Trixie to go over to each table that needs to be waited on and tell the customers about the daily specials. While at each table, Trixie should take each customer's order. She then should submit the order for the entire table to the cook.

```
repeat for (each table that needs to be waited on)
    go to a table that needs to be waited on
    tell the customers at the table about the daily specials
    repeat for (each customer at the table)
        ask the customer for his or her order
        record the order on the order slip for that table
    end repeat
    go over to the cook at the counter
    tear the appropriate order slip from the order pad
    give the order slip to the cook
end repeat
```


Figure 8-14 Modified problem specification and solution that requires a nested loop

The Asterisks Program

Figure 8-15 shows the problem specification, IPO chart information, and C++ instructions for a program that displays an asterisk on three separate lines on the computer screen. The algorithm, which is shown in both pseudocode and a flowchart, does not require a nested loop. This is because all of the instructions within the loop need to be repeated the same number of times: three. Figure 8-16 shows the completed desk-check table, and Figure 8-17 shows a sample run of the program.

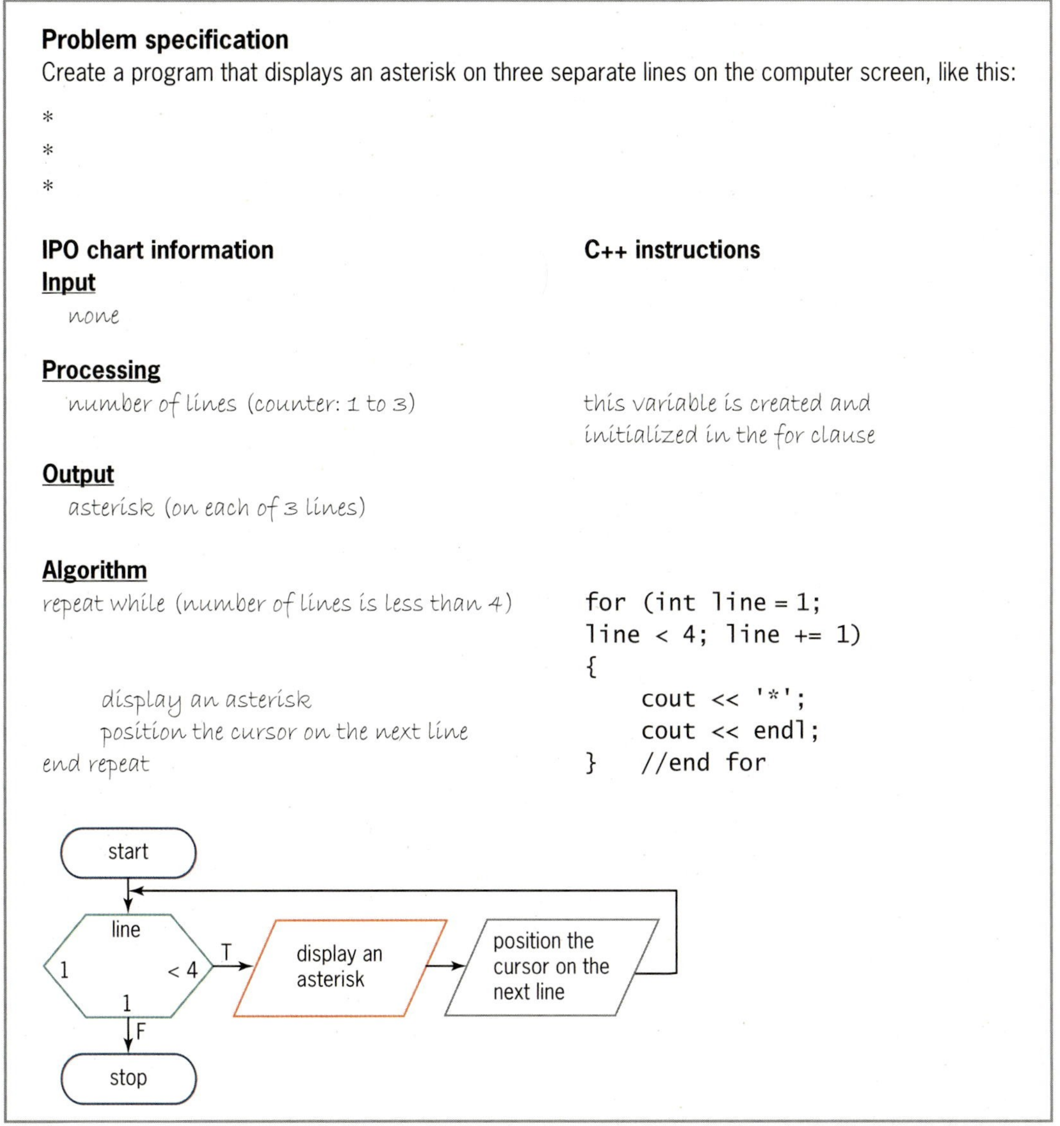

Problem specification
Create a program that displays an asterisk on three separate lines on the computer screen, like this:

```
*
*
*
```

IPO chart information	**C++ instructions**
Input	
none	
Processing	
number of lines (counter: 1 to 3)	*this variable is created and initialized in the for clause*
Output	
asterisk (on each of 3 lines)	

Algorithm

```
repeat while (number of lines is less than 4)      for (int line = 1;
                                                   line < 4; line += 1)
                                                   {
     display an asterisk                               cout << '*';
     position the cursor on the next line              cout << endl;
end repeat                                         }   //end for
```


Figure 8-15 Problem specification, IPO chart information, and C++ instructions for the asterisks program

line
~~1~~
~~2~~
~~3~~
4

Figure 8-16 Completed desk-check table for the asterisks program

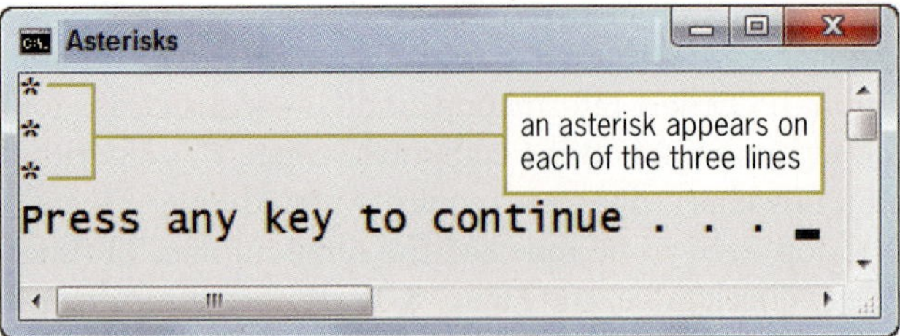

Figure 8-17 Sample run of the asterisks program

Figure 8-18 shows a modified version of the previous problem specification, along with the corresponding IPO chart information and C++ instructions. In the modified version, the program needs to display two asterisks on each of three separate lines on the computer screen. The modified algorithm will use two loops to accomplish this task: an outer pretest loop to keep track of the number of lines, and a nested pretest loop to keep track of the number of asterisks. The changes made to the IPO chart information and C++ instructions are shaded in Figure 8-18.

In the code in Figure 8-18, the outer loop begins with the first `for` clause, which directs the computer to repeat the loop body instructions three times. The outer loop ends with the closing brace (}). Braces are required in the outer loop because its loop body contains more than one statement. The nested loop begins with the second `for` clause, which directs the computer to repeat the `cout << '*';` statement two times. The nested loop ends with the `//end for` comment. Braces are not needed in the nested loop because its loop body contains only one statement. Here again, notice that the entire nested loop is contained within the outer loop. Although both loops in Figure 8-18 are coded using the `for` statement, one or both could be coded using the `while` statement. In addition, the algorithm could have been written using one or more posttest loops. Recall that you use the `do while` statement to code a posttest loop in C++.

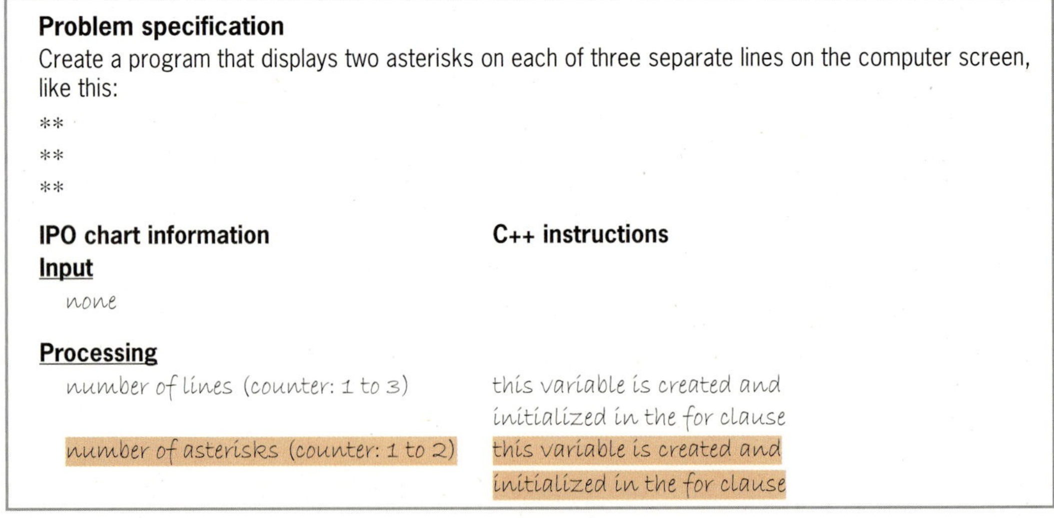

Problem specification

Create a program that displays two asterisks on each of three separate lines on the computer screen, like this:

```
**
**
**
```

IPO chart information	C++ instructions
Input	
none	
Processing	
number of lines (counter: 1 to 3)	*this variable is created and initialized in the for clause*
number of asterisks (counter: 1 to 2)	*this variable is created and initialized in the for clause*

Figure 8-18 Problem specification, IPO chart information, and C++ instructions for the modified asterisks program *(continues)*

(continued)

Output

asterisk (2 on each of 3 lines)

Algorithm

repeat while (number of lines is less than 4)	`for (int line = 1;` `line < 4; line += 1)` `{`
repeat while (number of asterisks is less than 3)	`for (int numAsterisks = 1;` `numAsterisks < 3;` `numAsterisks += 1)`
display an asterisk	`cout << '*';`
end repeat	`//end for`
position the cursor on the next line	`cout << endl;`
end repeat	`} //end for`

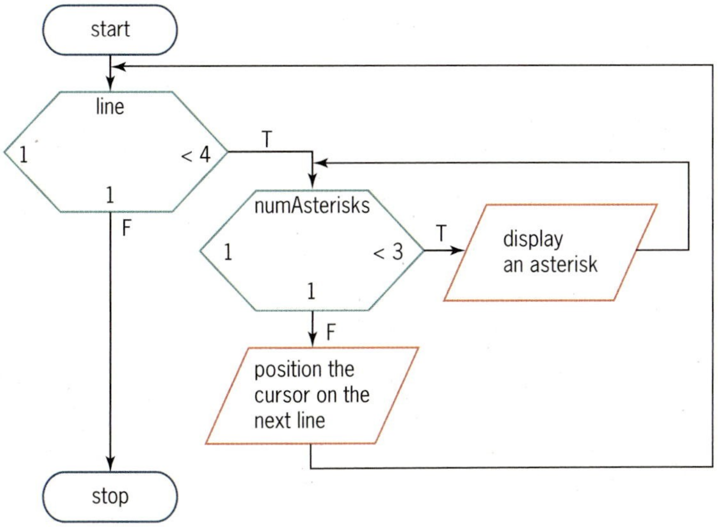

```
for (int line = 1;
line < 4; line += 1)
{
    for (int numAsterisks = 1;
    numAsterisks < 3;
    numAsterisks += 1)
        cout << '*';
    //end for
    cout << endl;
}   //end for
```

start
line
1
< 4
1
T
F
numAsterisks
1
< 3
1
T
display an asterisk
F
position the cursor on the next line
stop

Figure 8-18 Problem specification, IPO chart information, and C++ instructions for the modified asterisks program

You can observe the way the computer processes a nested loop by desk-checking the code shown in Figure 8-18. First, the *initialization* argument in the outer loop's `for` clause tells the computer to create the `line` variable and initialize it to 1. The *condition* argument then directs the computer to check whether the `line` variable's value is less than the number 4. It is, so the instructions in the body of the outer loop are processed. The first instruction is the nested loop's `for` clause. The clause's *initialization* argument tells the computer to create the `numAsterisks` variable and initialize it to the number 1. Its *condition* argument then directs the computer to check whether the value in the `numAsterisks` variable is less than 3. It is, so the `cout << '*';` statement in the body of the nested loop is processed. That statement displays an asterisk on the current line on the computer screen. Figure 8-19 shows the desk-check table and output after the nested loop's `cout` statement is processed the first time.

Ch08-Modified Asterisks Desk-Check video

Recall that the `for` clause's *condition* argument must be phrased as a looping condition, which means it must specify the requirement for processing the loop body instructions.

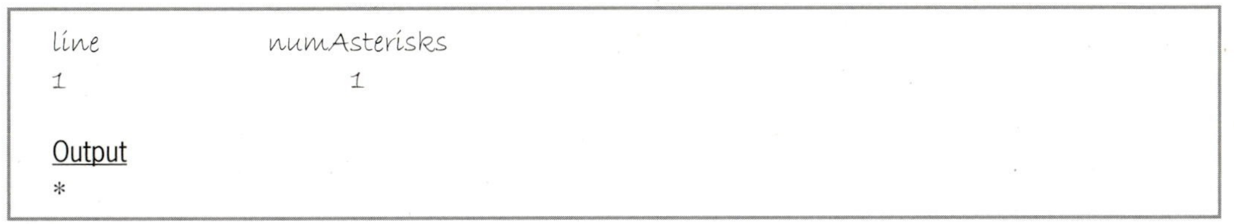

line	numAsterisks
1	1

Output

*

Figure 8-19 Desk-check table and output after the nested loop's `cout` statement is processed the first time

Next, the *update* argument in the nested loop's `for` clause tells the computer to add the number 1 to the value stored in the `numAsterisks` variable; the result is 2. Once again, the *condition* argument in the nested loop's `for` clause directs the computer to check whether the variable's value is less than 3. It is, so the nested loop's `cout << '*';` statement displays another asterisk on the current line on the computer screen. Figure 8-20 shows the desk-check table and output after the `cout` statement is processed the second time.

Figure 8-20 Desk-check table and output after the nested loop's `cout` statement is processed the second time

> Recall that the variable created in the `for` clause is local to the `for` statement and is removed from memory when the `for` loop ends.

The computer again adds the number 1 to the value stored in the `numAsterisks` variable, giving 3. It then checks whether the variable's value is less than 3. It's not, so the nested loop ends and the `numAsterisks` variable is removed from the computer's internal memory. Processing continues with the first statement following the end of the nested loop. That statement is the `cout << endl;` statement, which positions the cursor on the next line on the computer screen.

> Notice that the nested loop is completely processed prior to the next iteration of the outer loop.

After processing the `cout << endl;` statement, which is the last statement in the body of the outer loop, the computer returns to the outer loop's `for` clause to process its *update* and *condition* arguments. The *update* argument tells the computer to add the number 1 to the value stored in the `line` variable; the result is 2. The *condition* argument directs the computer to check whether the variable's value is less than 4. It is, so the instructions in the body of the outer loop are processed again. The first instruction is the nested loop's `for` clause, whose *initialization* and *condition* arguments tell the computer to create the `numAsterisks` variable and initialize it to the number 1, and then check whether its value is less than 3. At this point, the variable's value is less than 3, so the `cout << '*';` statement in the nested loop is processed. That statement displays an asterisk on the second line on the computer screen. Figure 8-21 shows the current status of the desk-check table and output.

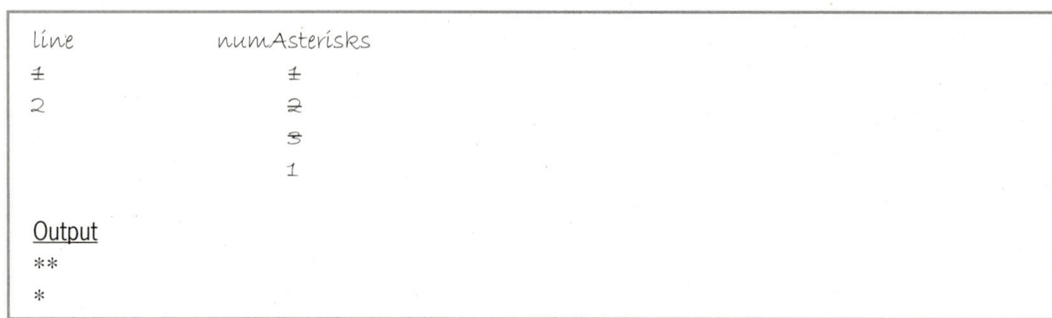

Figure 8-21 Current status of the desk-check table and output

Next, the computer updates the value in the `numAsterisks` variable by adding the number 1 to it; the result is 2. The computer then checks whether the variable's value is less than 3. It is, so the nested loop's `cout << '*';` statement displays another asterisk on the current line on the computer screen. The computer again adds the number 1 to the value stored in the `numAsterisks` variable, giving 3. It then checks whether the variable's value is less than 3. It's not, so the nested loop ends and the `numAsterisks` variable is removed from the computer's internal memory. Figure 8-22 shows the desk-check table and output after the nested loop ends the second time.

line	numAsterisks
~~1~~	~~1~~
2	~~2~~
	~~3~~
	~~1~~
	~~2~~
	3

Output
**
**

Figure 8-22 Desk-check table and output after the nested loop ends the second time

Processing continues with the first statement located below the nested loop. That statement is the `cout << endl;` statement, which positions the cursor on the next line on the computer screen. After processing the statement, the computer returns to the outer loop's `for` clause to process its *update* and *condition* arguments. The *update* argument tells the computer to add the number 1 to the value stored in the `line` variable; the result is 3. The *condition* argument directs the computer to check whether the variable's value is less than 4. It is, so the instructions in the body of the outer loop are processed again. The first instruction is the nested loop's `for` clause, whose *initialization* and *condition* arguments tell the computer to create the `numAsterisks` variable and initialize it to the number 1, and then check whether its value is less than 3. At this point, the variable's value is less than 3, so the `cout << '*';` statement in the nested loop is processed. That statement displays the first asterisk on the third line on the computer screen. The computer will continue processing the nested loop until the value stored in the `numAsterisks` variable is the number 3. Figure 8-23 shows the desk-check table and output after the nested loop ends the third time.

Figure 8-23 Desk-check table and output after the nested loop ends the third time

Processing continues with the `cout << endl;` statement, which follows the nested loop and is the last statement in the body of the outer loop. The statement positions the cursor on the next line on the computer screen. After processing the statement, the computer returns to the outer loop's `for` clause to process its *update* and *condition* arguments. The *update* argument tells the computer to add the number 1 to the value stored in the `line` variable; the result is 4. The *condition* argument directs the computer to check whether the variable's value is less than 4. It's not, so the outer loop ends and the `line` variable is removed from the computer's internal memory. Processing will continue with the first statement located below the end of the outer loop. Figure 8-24 shows a sample run of the modified asterisks program.

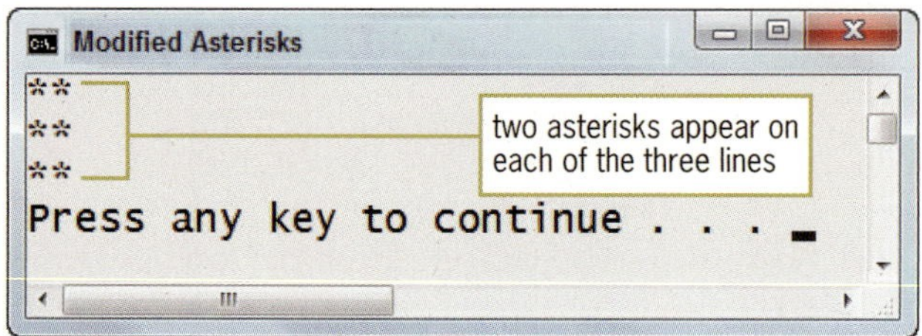

Figure 8-24 Sample run of the modified asterisks program

The Savings Calculator Program

Figure 8-25 shows the problem specification for the savings calculator program, which calculates the value of a one-time deposit of $1,000 into a savings account that earns a specific amount of interest for a certain amount of time. The figure also includes sample calculations. The formula in Example 1 calculates the savings account balance at the end of the first year. It does this by adding the number 1 to the interest rate of .02 and then raising the sum (1.02) to the first power. Recall that the result of raising a number to a power of 1 is the number itself; in this case, the result is 1.02. The formula then multiplies the number 1.02 by the number 1000, giving 1020.

The formula in Example 2 calculates the account balance at the end of the third year. Here again, the formula begins by adding the number 1 to the interest rate of .02. However, this time it raises the sum (1.02) to the third power. Raising a number to a power of 3 means multiplying it by itself three times; in this case, the expression 1.02 * 1.02 * 1.02 yields 1.061208. The formula then multiplies the number 1.061208 by the number 1000, giving 1061.21 when rounded to two decimal places.

Figure 8-25 also contains the problem's IPO chart and a desk-check table. Notice that the algorithm uses a counter to keep track of the years, which are from 1 to 5. In addition, it uses a posttest loop to calculate and display the account balance at the end of each year. (You also can use a pretest loop to calculate and display the savings account balances.) The problem's flowchart is shown in Figure 8-26.

Problem specification
For your 21st birthday, your grandmother opens a savings account for you and deposits $1,000 into the account. The savings account pays a 2% interest on the account balance. If you don't deposit any more money into the account, and you don't withdraw any money from the account, how much will your savings account be worth at the end of 1 through 5 years? Create a program that gives you the answers. You can calculate the answers using the following formula: $b = p * (1 + r)^n$. In the formula, p is the principal (the amount of the deposit), r is the annual interest rate, n is the number of years, and b is the balance in the savings account at the end of the nth year.

Example 1
$b = 1000 * (1 + .02)^1$
$b = \$1020$

Example 2
$b = 1000 * (1 + .02)^3$
$b = \$1061.21$ (rounded to two decimal places)

Input	Processing	Output
principal (1000) annual interest rate (2%) number of years (counter: 1 to 5)	Processing items: none	account balance (at end of each of the 5 years)

Algorithm:
repeat
    calculate the account
    balance = principal
    * (1 + annual interest rate)$^{\text{number of years}}$

    display the current number
    of years and account balance

    add 1 to the number of years
end repeat while (number of years
is less than 6)

principal	annual interest rate	years	account balance
1000	.02	~~1~~	~~1020.00~~
		~~2~~	~~1040.40~~
		~~3~~	~~1061.21~~
		~~4~~	~~1082.43~~
		~~5~~	1104.08
		6	

Figure 8-25 Problem specification, sample calculations, IPO chart, and desk-check table for the savings calculator program

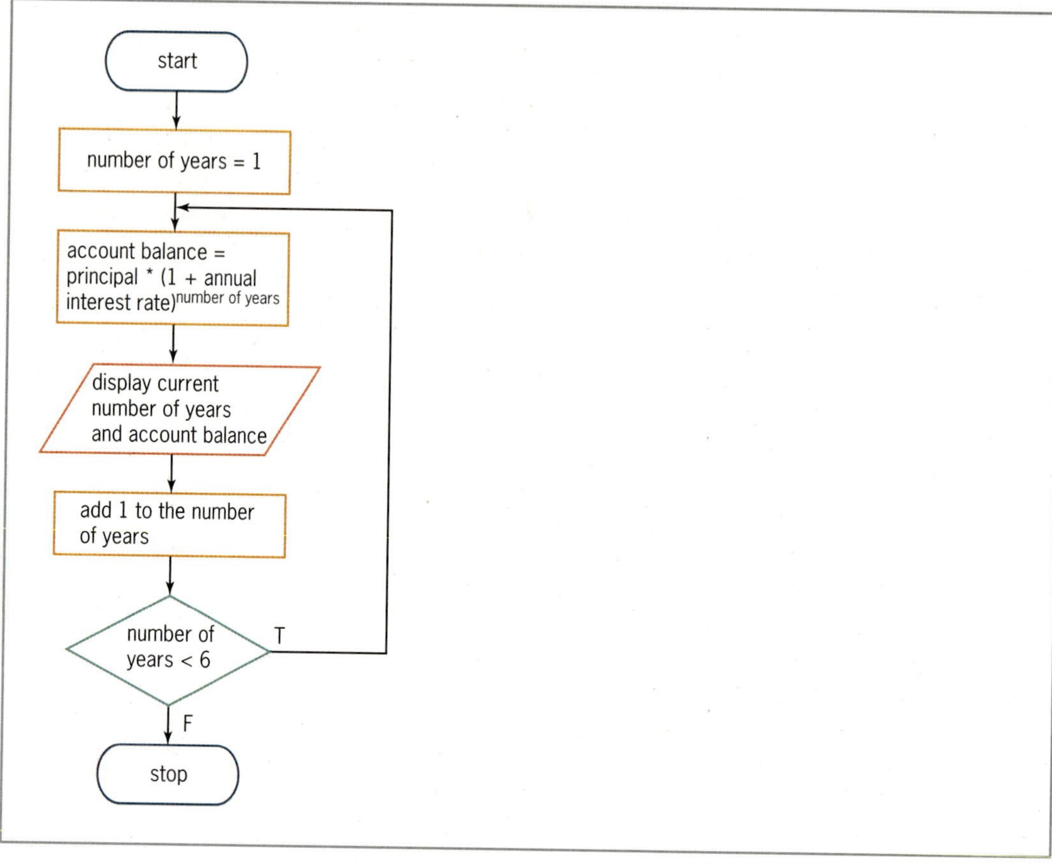

Figure 8-26 Flowchart for the savings calculator program

Before coding the savings calculator algorithm, you will learn about the built-in C++ pow function. The function provides a convenient way to code a formula that raises a number to a power.

The pow Function

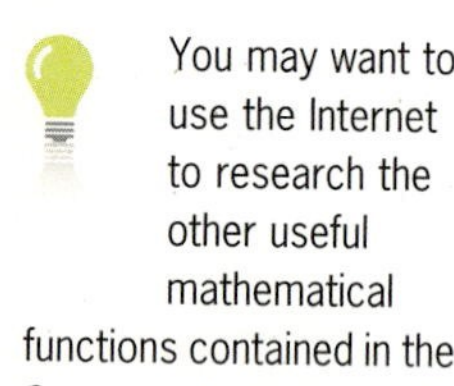

You may want to use the Internet to research the other useful mathematical functions contained in the C++ cmath library.

Some mathematical expressions require a number to be raised to a power. Raising a number to a power is referred to as **exponentiation**. An example of exponentiation is found in the πr^2 expression, where r is the radius of a circle. The expression calculates the circle's area by raising its radius to the second power and then multiplying the result by pi.

C++ provides the built-in pow function for performing exponentiation. To use the pow function in a program, the program must contain the `#include <cmath>` directive. The **pow function** raises a number to a power and then returns the result as a `double` number. Figure 8-27 shows the function's syntax, which contains two arguments: *x* and *y*. The *x* argument represents the number you want raised to power *y*. At least one of the two arguments must be a `double` number.

Also included in Figure 8-27 are examples of C++ statements that contain the pow function. For clarity, the variable declaration statements are included in the examples. The `cube = pow(4.0, 3);` statement in Example 1 raises the `double` number 4.0 to the third power. In other words, it multiplies the `double` number 4.0 by itself three times (4.0 * 4.0 * 4.0). The statement then assigns the result, which is the `double` number 64.0, to the `cube` variable. The `cout << pow(100, .5);` statement in Example 2 raises the number 100 to the .5 power and is equivalent to finding the square root of the number. The statement displays the number 10 on the screen. The `area = 3.14 * pow(radius, 2.0);` statement in Example 3 raises the number contained in the `radius` variable (5.0) to the second power; in other words, it squares the number. It then multiplies the result by 3.14 and assigns the product (78.5) to the `area` variable.

HOW TO Use the pow Function

Syntax
pow(*x*, *y***)**

Example 1
```
double cube = 0.0;
cube = pow(4.0, 3);
```
The assignment statement assigns the number 64.0, which is 4.0 raised to the third power, to the cube variable.

Example 2
```
cout << pow(100, .5);
```
The statement displays the number 10, which is 100 raised to the .5 power. The pow(100, .5) expression is equivalent to finding the square root of the number 100.

Example 3
```
double area = 0.0;
double radius = 5.0;
area = 3.14 * pow(radius, 2.0);
```
The assignment statement raises the value stored in the radius variable to the second power; in other words, it squares the value. The result is 25.0. The assignment statement then multiplies the 25.0 by 3.14 and assigns the product (78.5) to the area variable.

Figure 8-27 How to use the pow function

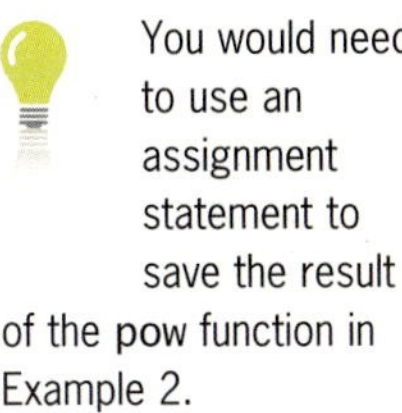

You would need to use an assignment statement to save the result of the pow function in Example 2.

Now that you know how to use the pow function, you can code the savings calculator program.

Coding the Savings Calculator Program

Figure 8-28 contains the information from the IPO chart shown earlier in Figure 8-25. It also contains the corresponding C++ instructions. The pow function is shaded in the figure.

IPO chart information	C++ instructions
Input	
principal (1000)	`int principal = 1000;`
annual interest rate (2%)	`double rate = .02;`
number of years (counter: 1 to 5)	`int years = 1;`
Processing	
none	
Output	
account balance (at end of each of the 5 years)	`double balance = 0.0;`

Figure 8-28 IPO chart information and C++ instructions for the savings calculator program *(continues)*

(continued)

Algorithm	
repeat	`do //begin loop` `{`
calculate the account balance = principal * (1 + annual interest rate)$^{\text{number of years}}$	`balance = principal *` `pow(1 + rate, years);`

display the current number of years and account balance	`cout << "Year " << years`
	 `<< ":" << endl;`
	 `cout << "     $" << balance`
	 `<< endl;`

add 1 to the number of years	`years += 1;`
end repeat while (number of years is less than 6)	`} while (years < 6);`

Figure 8-28 IPO chart information and C++ instructions for the savings calculator program

Figure 8-29 shows the complete savings calculator program, and Figure 8-30 shows a sample run of the program. Notice that the account balances in Figure 8-30 agree with the amounts in the desk-check table shown earlier in Figure 8-25.

```
//Savings Calculator.cpp - displays the balance
//in a savings account at the end of 1 through 5 years
//Created/revised by <your name> on <current date>

#include <iostream>
#include <iomanip>
#include <cmath>
using namespace std;

int main()
{
    int principal  = 1000;
    double rate    = .02;
    int years      = 1;          //counter
    double balance = 0.0;

    //display output with two decimal places
    cout << fixed << setprecision(2);

    do  //begin loop
    {
        balance = principal * pow(1 + rate, years);
        cout << "Year " << years << ":" << endl;
        cout << "     $" << balance << endl;
        //update years counter
        years += 1;
    }   while (years < 6);

    //system("pause");
    return 0;
}   //end of main function
```

required for the pow function (#include <cmath>)

if your C++ development tool requires this statement, delete the two forward slashes (//system("pause");)

Figure 8-29 Savings calculator program

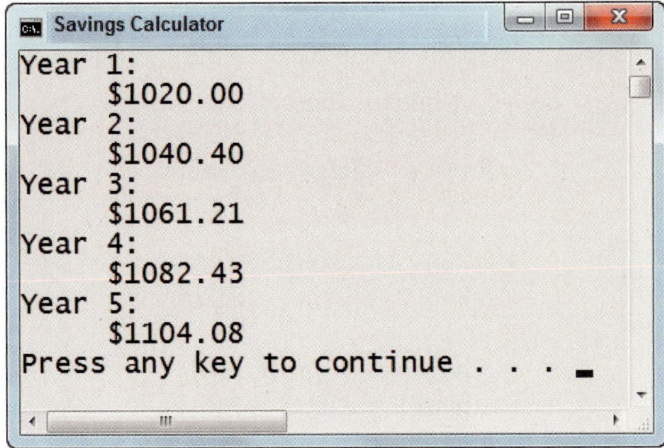

Figure 8-30 Sample run of the savings calculator program

Modifying the Savings Calculator Program

Currently, the savings calculator program calculates each account balance using an annual interest rate of 2%. In this section, you'll modify the program to use annual interest rates of 2%, 3%, and 4%. Figure 8-31 shows the modified IPO chart information and C++ instructions. The modifications made to the original information and instructions (shown earlier in Figure 8-28) are shaded in Figure 8-31. Notice that the algorithm and C++ instructions now contain two loops: an outer posttest loop to keep track of the years, and a nested pretest loop to keep track of the rates. (You also can use a pretest loop for the years and a posttest loop for the rates.) The flowchart for the modified algorithm is shown in Figure 8-32.

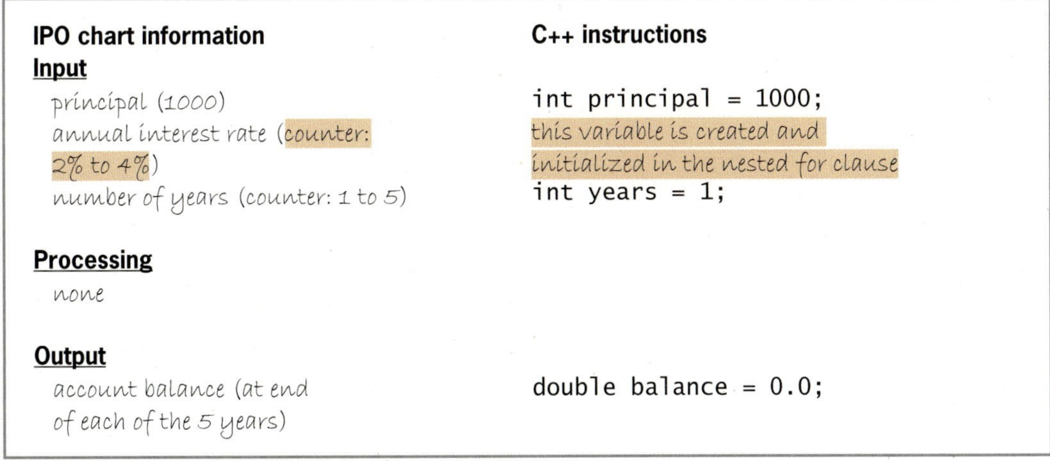

IPO chart information	C++ instructions
Input	
principal (1000)	`int principal = 1000;`
annual interest rate (counter: 2% to 4%)	this variable is created and initialized in the nested for clause
number of years (counter: 1 to 5)	`int years = 1;`
Processing	
none	
Output	
account balance (at end of each of the 5 years)	`double balance = 0.0;`

Figure 8-31 IPO chart information and C++ instructions for the modified savings calculator program *(continues)*

(continued)

Algorithm

repeat
 display the current number of years
 repeat for (annual interest rate from 2% to 4%)
  calculate the account balance = principal * (1 + annual interest rate)$^{\text{number of years}}$
  display the current rate with no decimal places
  display the current account balance with two decimal places
 end repeat
 add 1 to the number of years
end repeat while (number of years is less than 6)

```
do     //begin loop
{
    cout << "Year " << years <<
    ":" << endl;

    for (double rate = .02;
    rate < .05; rate += .01)
    {
        balance = principal *
        pow(1 + rate, years);

        cout << fixed <<
        setprecision(0);
        cout << "    Rate " << rate
        * 100 << "%: $";
        cout << setprecision(2) <<
        balance << endl;
    } //end for
    years += 1;
} while (years < 6);
```

Figure 8-31 IPO chart information and C++ instructions for the modified savings calculator program

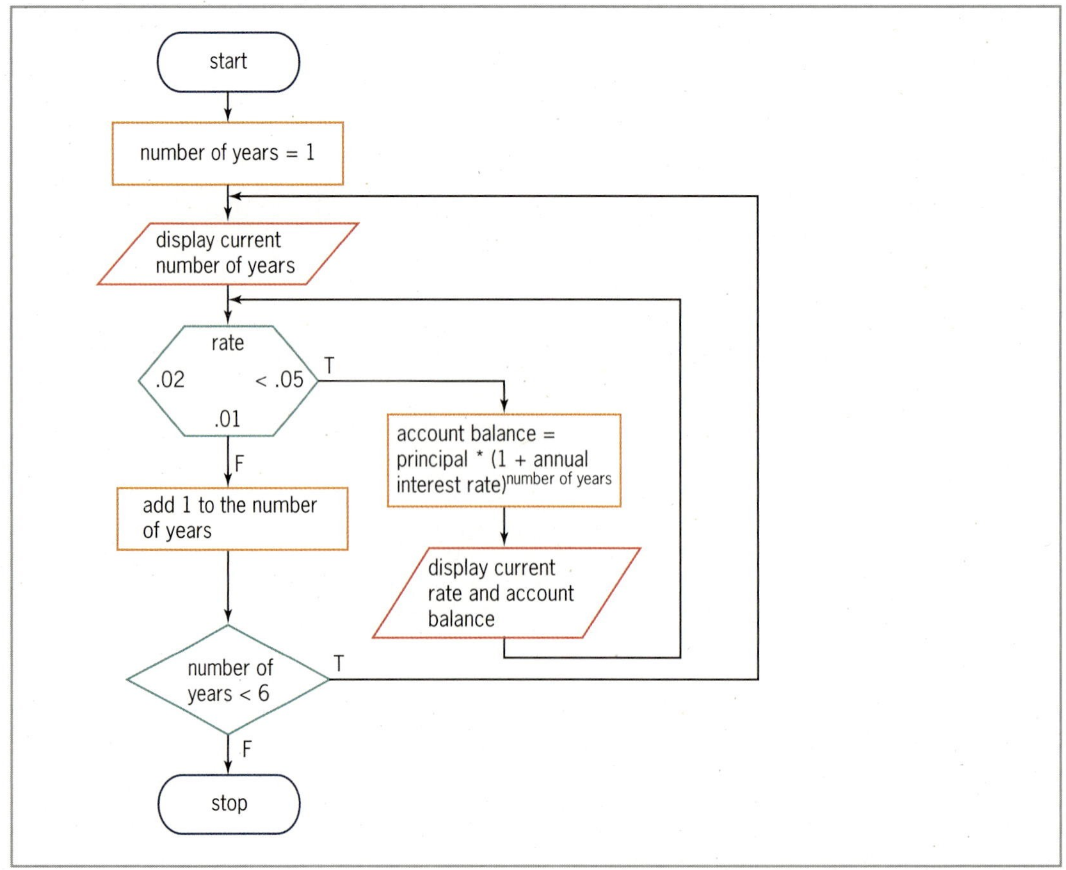

Figure 8-32 Flowchart for the modified savings calculator program

Figure 8-33 shows the modified savings calculator program with the nested loop shaded, and Figure 8-34 shows a sample run of the modified program.

```
//Modified Savings Calculator.cpp - displays the balance
//in a savings account at the end of 1 through 5 years
//using interest rates of 2%, 3%, and 4%
//Created/revised by <your name> on <current date>

#include <iostream>
#include <iomanip>
#include <cmath>
using namespace std;

int main()
{
    int principal  = 1000;
    int years      = 1;            //counter
    double balance = 0.0;

    do  //begin loop
    {
        cout << "Year " << years << ":" << endl;

        for (double rate = .02; rate < .05; rate += .01)
        {
            balance = principal * pow(1 + rate, years);
            //display rate with zero decimal places
            cout << fixed << setprecision(0);
            cout << "    Rate " << rate * 100 << "%: $";
            //display balance with two decimal places
            cout << setprecision(2) << balance << endl;
        }   //end for

        //update years counter
        years += 1;
    }   while (years < 6);

    //system("pause");
    return 0;
}   //end of main function
```

if your C++ development tool requires this statement, delete the two forward slashes

Figure 8-33 Modified savings calculator program

For more examples of nested loops, see the Nested Loops section in the Ch08WantMore.pdf file.

```
Modified Savings Calculator
Year 1:
   Rate 2%: $1020.00
   Rate 3%: $1030.00
   Rate 4%: $1040.00
Year 2:
   Rate 2%: $1040.40
   Rate 3%: $1060.90
   Rate 4%: $1081.60
Year 3:
   Rate 2%: $1061.21
   Rate 3%: $1092.73
   Rate 4%: $1124.86
Year 4:
   Rate 2%: $1082.43
   Rate 3%: $1125.51
   Rate 4%: $1169.86
Year 5:
   Rate 2%: $1104.08
   Rate 3%: $1159.27
   Rate 4%: $1216.65
Press any key to continue . . .
```

Figure 8-34 Sample run of the modified savings calculator program

The answers to Mini-Quiz questions are located in Appendix A.

Mini-Quiz 8-3

1. A nested loop can be a pretest loop only.
   a. True
   b. False
2. For a nested loop to work correctly, it must be contained entirely within an outer loop.
   a. True
   b. False
3. Consider a clock's hour and minute hands only. The hour hand is controlled by a(n) ______ loop, while the minute hand is controlled by a(n) ______ loop.
   a. outer, nested
   b. nested, outer
4. Which of the following can be used to code the mathematical expression 10^2?
   a. `pow(10.0, 2.0)`
   b. `pow(10.0, 2)`
   c. `pow(10, 2.0)`
   d. all of the above
5. Chakura is sitting at a table in a bookstore, attending her book signing. Customers are standing in line waiting for her to sign their copy of her book. She needs to sign each customer's book. It's possible that some customers in line may not have a book; they are in line simply to meet her. It's also possible that some customers may have more than one book for her to sign. Write an appropriate algorithm using only the instructions listed in Figure 8-35.

```
accept the book from the customer
close the book
end repeat
open the front cover of the book
place the book on the table
repeat while (the customer has a book that needs signing)
repeat while (there are customers in line)
return the book to the customer
sign your name on the first page
thank the customer
```

Figure 8-35 Instructions for Question 5 in Mini-Quiz 8-3

LAB 8-1 Stop and Analyze

The program shown in Figure 8-36 displays the total sales made in Region 1 and the total sales made in Region 2. Study the program and then answer the questions.

The answers to the labs are located in Appendix A.

```
//Lab8-1.cpp - displays each region's total sales
//Created/revised by <your name> on <current date>

#include <iostream>
using namespace std;

int main()
{
      //declare variables
      int sales            = 0;
      int region           = 1;  //counter
      int totalRegionSales = 0;  //accumulator

      while (region < 3)
      {
          //get current region's first sales amount
          cout << "First sales amount for Region "
               << region << " (negative number to end): ";
          cin >> sales;

          while (sales >= 0)
          {
              //add sales amount to region total
              totalRegionSales += sales;
              //get next sales amount for
              //current region
              cout << "Next sales amount for Region "
                   << region << " (negative number to end): ";
              cin >> sales;
          }   //end while

          //display current region's total sales
          cout << "****************Region " << region
               << " sales: $" << totalRegionSales
               << endl << endl;

```

Figure 8-36 Code for Lab 8-1 *(continues)*

(continued)

```
37            //update counter
38            region += 1;
39            ____________
40        }   //end while
41
42        //system("pause");
43        return 0;
44    } //end of main function
```

missing statement

Figure 8-36 Code for Lab 8-1

QUESTIONS

1. How many pretest loops does the program contain? How many posttest loops does the program contain?
2. Which of the two loops is controlled by a counter? For what counter values will the loop's condition evaluate to true? What counter value will make the loop condition evaluate to false?
3. Which of the two loops is controlled by a sentinel value? What are the valid sentinel values for this loop?
4. The statement on Line 39 is missing from the program. To determine the missing statement, desk-check the program using sales amounts of 1000, 2000, and –1 for Region 1, and sales amounts of 400, 500, and –3 for Region 2. What is the missing statement and why is it necessary? How would you modify the comment on Line 37 so it documents the purpose of the additional statement?
5. After entering the missing statement on Line 39, desk-check the program using the data from Question 4. What are the total sales for Region 1? What are the total sales for Region 2?
6. Follow the instructions for starting C++ and viewing the Lab8-1.cpp file, which is contained in either the Cpp7\Chap08\Lab8-1 Project folder or the Cpp7\Chap08 folder. (Depending on your C++ development tool, you may need to open Lab8-1's project/solution file first.) If necessary, delete the two forward slashes that appear before the `system("pause");` statement. Enter the missing statement on Line 39. Also modify the comment on Line 37. Run the program and then enter the data from Question 4. What does the program display as the total sales for each region? (The program's output should agree with the results of your desk-check from Question 5.)
7. Modify the program to use a `for` statement for the region loop and a `do while` statement for the sales loop. Save and then run the program. Enter the data from Question 4. What does the program display as the total sales for each region? (The program's output should agree with the results from Question 6.)

LAB 8-2 Plan and Create

In this lab, you will plan and create an algorithm for Mrs. Johansen. The problem specification is shown in Figure 8-37.

Problem specification

Last month, Mrs. Johansen began teaching multiplication to the students in her second grade class. She wants a program that displays one or more multiplication tables. A sample multiplication table is shown below. The x entries represent the number entered by the user and are called the multiplicand. The numbers 1 through 9 are called the multiplier. The y entries represent the product, which is the result of multiplying the multiplicand (x) by the multiplier (the numbers 1 through 9).

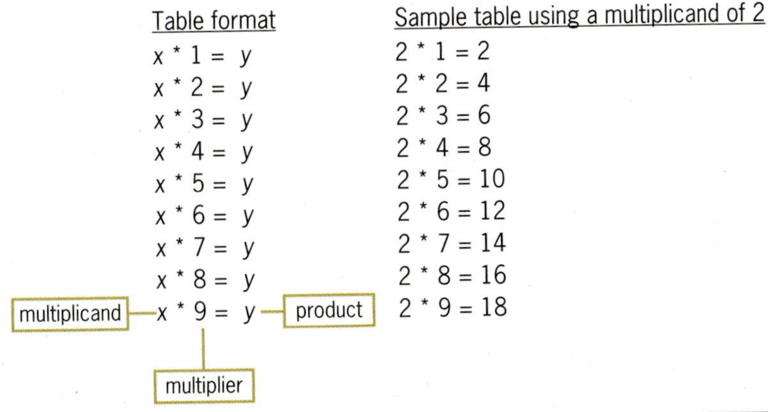

Figure 8-37 Problem specification for Lab 8-2

First, analyze the problem, looking for the output first and then for the input. In this case, Mrs. Johansen wants the program to display a multiplication table. The table will show the multiplicand entered by the user, the multipliers provided in the problem specification, and the products calculated by the program.

Next, plan the algorithm. Recall that most algorithms begin with an instruction to enter the input items into the computer, followed by instructions that process the input items, typically including the items in one or more calculations. Most algorithms end with one or more instructions that display, print, or store the output items. Figure 8-38 shows the completed IPO chart for the multiplication table problem.

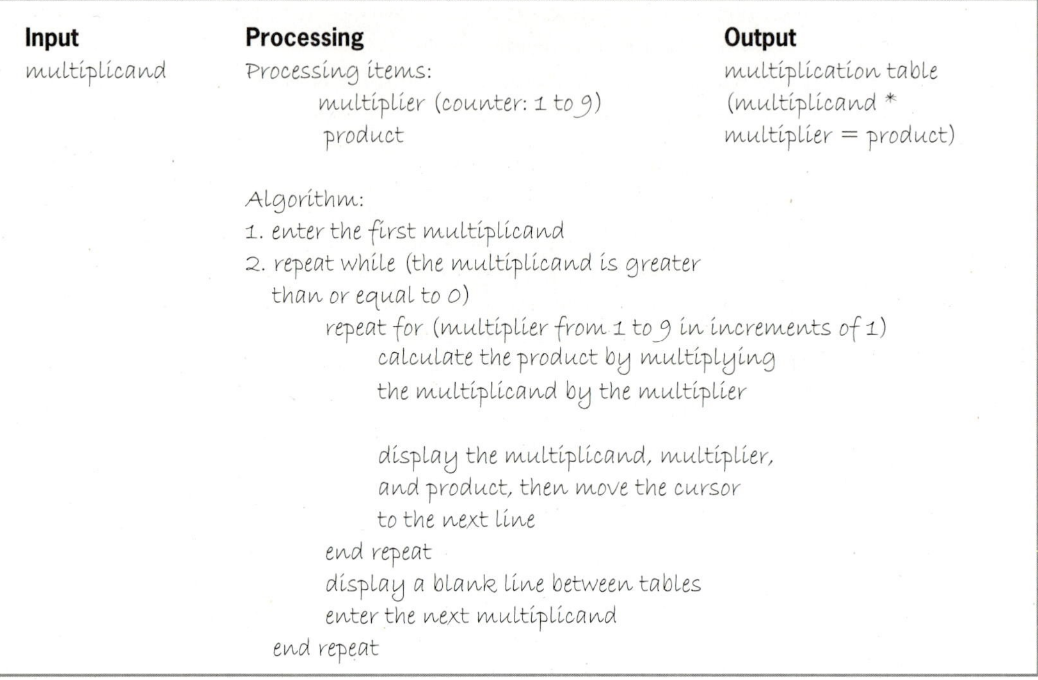

Input
multiplicand

Processing
Processing items:
multiplier (counter: 1 to 9)
product

Algorithm:
1. enter the first multiplicand
2. repeat while (the multiplicand is greater than or equal to 0)
   repeat for (multiplier from 1 to 9 in increments of 1)
      calculate the product by multiplying the multiplicand by the multiplier

      display the multiplicand, multiplier, and product, then move the cursor to the next line
   end repeat
   display a blank line between tables
   enter the next multiplicand
end repeat

Output
multiplication table
(multiplicand * multiplier = product)

Figure 8-38 Completed IPO chart for the multiplication table problem

After completing the IPO chart, you then move on to the third step in the problem-solving process, which is to desk-check the algorithm. You will desk-check the algorithm in Figure 8-38 using multiplicands of 2 and 4, followed by a sentinel value of –1. Figure 8-39 shows the completed desk-check table. Notice that the products corresponding to a multiplicand of 2 agree with the amounts shown in the sample table in Figure 8-37.

multiplicand	multiplier	product
2	1	2
	2	4
	3	6
	4	8
	5	10
	6	12
	7	14
	8	16
	9	18
	10	
4	1	4
	2	8
	3	12
	4	16
	5	20
	6	24
	7	28
	8	32
	9	36
	10	
-1		

Figure 8-39 Completed desk-check table for the multiplication table algorithm

The fourth step in the problem-solving process is to code the algorithm into a program. You begin by declaring memory locations that will store the values of the input, processing, and output items. The multiplication table program will need three memory locations to store the multiplicand, multiplier, and product. You will store the multiplicand in a variable because the user should be allowed to change its value during runtime. The multiplier also will be stored in a variable to allow its value to change from 1 to 9 in increments of 1. Finally, you will store the product in a variable because its value will change based on the current values of the multiplicand and multiplier. The multiplicand, multiplier, and product will always be integers, so you will store them in `int` variables. Figure 8-40 shows the IPO chart information and corresponding C++ instructions.

IPO chart information	**C++ instructions**
Input	
multiplicand	`int multiplicand = 0;`
Processing	
multiplier (counter: 1 to 9)	this variable is created and initialized in the for clause
product	`int product = 0;`
Output	
multiplication table (multiplicand * multiplier = product)	contains the multiplicand, multiplier, and product
Algorithm	
1. enter the first multiplicand	`cout << "Multiplicand (negative number to end): ";` `cin >> multiplicand;`
2. repeat while (the multiplicand is greater than or equal to 0)	`while (multiplicand >= 0)` `{`
repeat for (multiplier from 1 to 9 in increments of 1)	`for (int multiplier = 1; multiplier < 10; multiplier += 1)` `{`
calculate the product by multiplying the multiplicand by the multiplier	`product = multiplicand * multiplier;`
display the multiplicand, multiplier, and product, then move the cursor to the next line	`cout << multiplicand << " * " << multiplier << " = " << product << endl;`
end repeat	`} //end for`
display a blank line between tables	`cout << endl;`
enter the next multiplicand	`cout << "Multiplicand (negative number to end): ";` `cin >> multiplicand;`
end repeat	`} //end while`

Figure 8-40 IPO chart information and C++ instructions for the multiplication table program

The fifth step in the problem-solving process is to desk-check the program. You begin by placing the names of the declared variables and named constants (if any) in a new desk-check table, along with their initial values. You then desk-check the remaining C++ instructions in order, recording in the desk-check table any changes made to the variables. Figure 8-41 shows the completed desk-check table for the multiplication table program. The results agree with those shown in the algorithm's desk-check table in Figure 8-39.

multiplicand	multiplier	product
~~0~~	~~0~~	
2	~~1~~	~~2~~
	~~2~~	~~4~~
	~~3~~	~~6~~
	~~4~~	~~8~~
	~~5~~	~~10~~
	~~6~~	~~12~~
	~~7~~	~~14~~
	~~8~~	~~16~~
	~~9~~	~~18~~
	~~10~~	
~~4~~	~~1~~	~~4~~
	~~2~~	~~8~~
	~~3~~	~~12~~
	~~4~~	~~16~~
	~~5~~	~~20~~
	~~6~~	~~24~~
	~~7~~	~~28~~
	~~8~~	~~32~~
	~~9~~	36
	10	
-1		

Figure 8-41 Completed desk-check table for the multiplication table program

The final step in the problem-solving process is to evaluate and modify (if necessary) the program. Recall that you evaluate a program by entering its instructions into the computer and then using the computer to run (execute) it. While the program is running, you enter the same sample data used when desk-checking the program.

DIRECTIONS

Follow the instructions for starting your C++ development tool. Depending on the development tool you are using, you may need to create a new project; if so, name the project Lab8-2 Project and save it in the Cpp7\Chap08 folder. Enter the instructions shown in Figure 8-42 in a source file named Lab8-2.cpp. (Do not enter the line numbers.) Save the file in either the project folder or the Cpp7\Chap08 folder. Now follow the appropriate instructions for running the Lab8-2.cpp file. Test the program using multiplicands of 2 and 4, followed by a sentinel value. If necessary, correct any bugs (errors) in the program.

```
//Lab8-2.cpp - displays a multiplication table
//Created/revised by <your name> on <current date>

#include <iostream>
using namespace std;

int main()
{
     //declare variables
     int multiplicand = 0;
     int product      = 0;

     cout << "Multiplicand (negative number to end): ";
     cin >> multiplicand;

```

Figure 8-42 Multiplication table program *(continues)*

(continued)

```
    while (multiplicand >= 0)
    {
        for (int multiplier = 1; multiplier < 10;
            multiplier += 1)
        {
            product = multiplicand * multiplier;
            cout << multiplicand << " * "
                 << multiplier << " = "
                 << product << endl;
        }   //end for

        cout << endl;
        cout << "Multiplicand (negative number to end): ";
        cin >> multiplicand;
    }   //end while

    //system("pause");
    return 0;
}   //end of main function
```

if your C++ development tool requires this statement, delete the two forward slashes

Figure 8-42 Multiplication table program

LAB 8-3 Modify

If necessary, create a new project named Lab8-3 Project and save it in the Cpp7\Chap08 folder. Enter (or copy) the Lab8-2.cpp instructions into a new source file named Lab8-3.cpp. Change Lab8-2.cpp in the first comment to Lab8-3.cpp. Change both loops to posttest loops. Save and then run the program. Use the program to display the multiplication tables for the following multiplicands: 6, 9, and 2.

LAB 8-4 Desk-Check

Desk-check the code shown in Figure 8-43. What will the code display on the computer screen?

```
int number = 1;

while (number < 3)
{
      cout << number << ' ';
      for (int x = 1; x <= 4; x += 1)
           cout << number + x << ' ';
      //end for
      number += 1;
      cout << endl;
}     //end while
```

Figure 8-43 Code for Lab 8-4

LAB 8-5 Debug

Follow the instructions for starting C++ and viewing the Lab8-5.cpp file, which is contained in either the Cpp7\Chap08\Lab8-5 Project folder or the Cpp7\Chap08 folder. (Depending on your C++ development tool, you may need to open Lab8-5's project/solution file first.) If necessary, delete the two forward slashes that appear before the `system("pause");` statement. The program should display a store's quarterly sales, but it is not working correctly. Debug the program.

Summary

- A repetition structure can be either a pretest loop or a posttest loop. In a pretest loop, the loop condition is evaluated *before* the instructions within the loop are processed. In a posttest loop, the evaluation occurs *after* the instructions within the loop are processed.
- The condition appears at the end of a posttest loop and determines whether the instructions within the loop body will be processed more than once. The loop's condition must result in either a true or false answer only. When the condition evaluates to true, the instructions listed in the loop body are processed again; otherwise, the loop is exited.
- You use the `do while` statement to code a posttest loop in C++. To code a pretest loop in C++, you can use either the `while` statement or the `for` statement.
- Repetition structures can be nested, which means one loop can be placed inside another loop. For nested repetition structures to work correctly, the entire inner (nested) loop must be contained entirely within the outer loop.
- You can use the built-in C++ `pow` function to raise a number to a power. The function returns the result as a `double` number.

Key Terms

`do while` statement—the statement used to code a posttest loop in C++

Exponentiation—the process of raising a number to a power

Nested loop—a loop (repetition structure) contained entirely within another loop (repetition structure)

`pow` function—a built-in C++ function that raises a number to a power and then returns the result as a `double` number

Review Questions

1. The condition in the `do while` statement is evaluated ________ the instructions in the loop body are processed.
   a. after
   b. before

2. The instructions in the body of the ______ statement are always processed at least once during runtime.

   a. `do while`

   b. `for`

   c. `while`

   d. both a and b

3. It's possible that the instructions in the body of the ______ statement will not be processed during runtime.

   a. `do while`

   b. `for`

   c. `while`

   d. both b and c

4. What numbers will the following code display on the computer screen?

```
int x = 1;
do
{
    cout << x << endl;
    x = x + 1;
} while (x < 5);
```

   a. 0, 1, 2, 3, 4

   b. 0, 1, 2, 3, 4, 5

   c. 1, 2, 3, 4

   d. 1, 2, 3, 4, 5

5. What numbers will the following code display on the computer screen?

```
int x = 20;
do
{
    cout << x << endl;
    x -= 4;
} while (x > 10);
```

   a. 16, 12, 8

   b. 16, 12

   c. 20, 16, 12, 8

   d. 20, 16, 12

6. What value of `x` causes the loop in Review Question 5 to end?

   a. 0

   b. 8

   c. 10

   d. 12

7. What numbers will the following code display on the computer screen?

```
int total = 1;
do
{
    cout << total << endl;
    total += 2;
} while (total <= 3);
```

a. 1, 2

b. 1, 3

c. 1, 3, 5

d. 0, 1, 3

8. What will the following code display on the computer screen?

```
for (int x = 1; x < 3; x += 1)
{
    for (int y = 1; y < 4; y += 1)
        cout << "*";
    //end for
    cout << endl;
} //end for
```

a.
```
***
***
```

b.
```
***
***
***
```

c.
```
**
**
**
```

d.
```
***
***
***
***
```

9. What number will the following code display on the computer screen?

```
int sum = 0;
int y = 0;
do
{
    for (int x = 1; x < 5; x += 1)
        sum = sum + x;
    //end for
    y += 1;
} while (y < 3);
cout << sum << endl;
```

a. 5

b. 8

c. 15

d. 30

10. Which of the following raises the number 6 to the third power?
    a. `cube(6)`
    b. `pow(3.0, 6)`
    c. `pow(6.0, 3)`
    d. none of the above

Exercises

Pencil and Paper

1. Complete a desk-check table for the code shown in Figure 8-44. What will the code display on the computer screen? What value causes the nested loop to end? What value causes the outer loop to end? (The answers to TRY THIS Exercises are located at the end of the chapter.) TRY THIS

```
int nested = 0;
for (int outer = 1; outer <= 2; outer += 1)
{
     nested = 1;
     do    //begin loop
     {
          cout << nested;
          cout << "   ";
          nested += 1;
     } while (nested < 4);
     cout << endl;
} //end for
```

Figure 8-44

2. Write a C++ `while` clause that stops a posttest loop when the value in the `quantity` variable is less than the number 0. (The answers to TRY THIS Exercises are located at the end of the chapter.) TRY THIS
3. Rewrite the code shown in Figure 8-44 so it uses the `while` statement for the outer loop and the `for` statement for the nested loop. MODIFY THIS
4. Rewrite the code shown in Figure 8-44 so it uses the `do while` statement for the outer loop. MODIFY THIS
5. Write a C++ `while` clause that processes a posttest loop's instructions as long as the value in the `inStock` variable is greater than the value in the `reorder` variable. INTRODUCTORY
6. Write a C++ `while` clause that stops a posttest loop when the value in a `char` variable named `letter` is anything other than the letter Y (in either uppercase or lowercase). INTRODUCTORY
7. Write an assignment statement that raises the number 2 to the 25th power and then assigns the result to a `double` variable named `answer`. INTRODUCTORY
8. A program declares an `int` variable named `oddNum` and initializes it to 1. Write the C++ code to display the odd integers 1, 3, 5, 7, and 9 on separate lines on the computer screen. Use the `do while` statement. INTERMEDIATE

INTERMEDIATE

9. Write the code to display a table consisting of four rows and six columns. The first column should contain the numbers 1 through 4 raised to the first power. The second column should contain the result of raising the number in the first column to the second power. The third column should contain the result of raising the number in the first column to the third power, and so on. The table will look similar to the one shown in Figure 8-45. Use two `for` statements: one to keep track of the numbers 1 through 4, and the other to keep track of the powers (1 through 6).

1	1	1	1	1	1
2	4	8	16	32	64
3	9	27	81	243	729
4	16	64	256	1024	4096

Figure 8-45

INTERMEDIATE

10. Rewrite the code from Pencil and Paper Exercise 9 to use two `while` statements.

INTERMEDIATE

11. Rewrite the code from Pencil and Paper Exercise 9 to use two `do while` statements.

INTERMEDIATE

12. Rewrite the code from Pencil and Paper Exercise 9 to use a `while` statement in the outer loop.

INTERMEDIATE

13. Rewrite the code from Pencil and Paper Exercise 9 to use the `do while` statement in the nested loop.

SWAT THE BUGS

14. The code shown in Figure 8-46 should display three rows of asterisks on the computer screen. The first row should contain one asterisk, the second row should contain two asterisks, and the third row should contain three asterisks. The code is not working correctly because it displays three asterisks on each of the three rows. Debug the code.

```
for (int row = 1; row < 4; row += 1)
{
     for (int asterisks = 1; asterisks <= 3; asterisks += 1)
          cout << '*';
     //end for
     cout << endl;
}    //end for
```

Figure 8-46

Computer

TRY THIS

15. In this exercise, you create a program that uses two `for` statements to display the pattern of asterisks shown in Figure 8-47. If necessary, create a new project named TryThis15 Project and save it in the Cpp7\Chap08 folder. Enter the C++ instructions into a source file named TryThis15.cpp. Also enter appropriate comments and any additional instructions required by the compiler. Save and then run the program. (The answers to TRY THIS Exercises are located at the end of the chapter.)

```
**
****
******
********
**********
```


Figure 8-47

TRY THIS

16. In this exercise, you create a program that uses two `while` statements to display the pattern of asterisks shown in Figure 8-48. If necessary, create a new project named TryThis16 Project and save it in the Cpp7\Chap08 folder. Enter the C++ instructions into a source file named TryThis16.cpp. Also enter appropriate comments and any additional instructions required by the compiler. Save and then run the program. (The answers to TRY THIS Exercises are located at the end of the chapter.)

```
*********
********
*******
******
*****
****
***
**
*
```

Figure 8-48

MODIFY THIS

17. In this exercise, you modify the code from Computer Exercise 16. If necessary, create a new project named ModifyThis17 Project and save it in the Cpp7\Chap08 folder. Enter (or copy) the TryThis16.cpp instructions into a new source file named ModifyThis17.cpp. Change TryThis16.cpp in the first comment to ModifyThis17.cpp. Replace the two `while` statements with `do while` statements. Save and then run the program.

INTRODUCTORY

18. The savings calculator program is shown in Figure 8-29 in the chapter. If necessary, create a new project named Introductory18 Project and save it in the Cpp7\Chap08 folder. Enter the C++ instructions from the figure into a source file named Introductory18.cpp. Change the filename in the first comment. Save and then run the program. The output is shown in Figure 8-30 in the chapter. Replace the `do while` statement with a `for` statement, and then save and run the program again.

INTRODUCTORY

19. The modified savings calculator program is shown in Figure 8-33 in the chapter. If necessary, create a new project named Introductory19 Project and save it in the Cpp7\Chap08 folder. Enter the C++ instructions from the figure into a source file named Introductory19.cpp. Change the filename in the first comment. Save and then run the program. The output is shown in Figure 8-34 in the chapter. Replace the `for` statement with a `while` statement, and then save and run the program again.

INTERMEDIATE

20. In this exercise, you modify the code from Lab 8-2. If necessary, create a new project named Intermediate20 Project and save it in the Cpp7\Chap08 folder. Enter (or copy) the C++ instructions from the Lab8-2.cpp file into a source file named Intermediate20.cpp. Change the filename in the first comment. Replace both pretest loops with posttest loops. Save and then run the program.

INTERMEDIATE

21. The modified savings calculator program is shown in Figure 8-33 in the chapter. If necessary, create a new project named Intermediate21 Project and save it in the Cpp7\Chap08 folder. Enter the C++ instructions from the figure into a source file named Intermediate21.cpp. Modify the program to allow the user to enter the principal. Use a sentinel value to end the program. Save and then run the program. Test the program using the following principals, followed by your sentinel value: 1000, 3000, and 10000.

INTERMEDIATE

22. Write the code to display a table consisting of four rows and 11 columns. The first column should contain the numbers 1 through 4. The second and subsequent columns should contain the result of multiplying the number in the first column by the numbers 0 through 9. The table will look similar to the one shown in Figure 8-49. (Don't be concerned about the alignment of the numbers in each column.) Use two `for` statements. If necessary, create a new project named Intermediate22 Project and save it in the Cpp7\Chap08 folder. Enter your C++ instructions into a source file named Intermediate22.cpp. Also enter appropriate comments and any additional instructions required by the compiler. Save and then run the program.

```
1    0    1    2    3    4    5    6    7    8    9
2    0    2    4    6    8    10   12   14   16   18
3    0    3    6    9    12   15   18   21   24   27
4    0    4    8    12   16   20   24   28   32   36
```

Figure 8-49

INTERMEDIATE

23. The payroll manager at Kenton Incorporated wants a program that allows him to enter an unknown number of payroll amounts for each of three stores: Store 1, Store 2, and Store 3. The program should calculate the total payroll and then display the result on the screen.

    a. Create an IPO chart for the problem, and then desk-check the algorithm using 23000 and 15000 as the payroll amounts for Store 1; 12000, 16000, 34000, and 10000 for Store 2; and 64000, 12000, and 70000 for Store 3.

    b. List the input, processing, and output items, as well as the algorithm, in a chart similar to the one shown earlier in Figure 8-40. Then code the algorithm into a program.

    c. Desk-check the program using the same data used to desk-check the algorithm.

    d. If necessary, create a new project named Intermediate23 Project and save it in the Cpp7\Chap08 folder. Enter your C++ instructions into a source file named Intermediate23.cpp. Also enter appropriate comments and any additional instructions required by the compiler.

    e. Save and then run the program. Test the program using the same data used to desk-check the program.

INTERMEDIATE

24. In this exercise, you modify the program from Lab 7-2 in Chapter 7. If necessary, create a new project named Intermediate24 Project and save it in the Cpp7\Chap08 folder. Copy the instructions from the Lab7-2.cpp file into a source file named Intermediate24.cpp. The Lab7-2.cpp file is contained in either the Cpp7\Chap07\Lab7-2 Project folder or the Cpp7\Chap07 folder. (Alternatively, you can enter the instructions from

Figure 7-52 into the Intermediate24.cpp file.) Change the filename in the first comment. Modify the program to allow Professor Chang to display more than one student's total points and grade. Save and then run the program. Test the program appropriately.

ADVANCED

25. At the beginning of every year, Khalid receives a raise on his previous year's salary. He wants a program that calculates and displays the amount of his annual raises for the next three years, using rates of 3%, 4%, 5%, and 6%. The program should end when Khalid enters a sentinel value as the salary.

    a. Create an IPO chart for the problem, and then desk-check the algorithm using annual salaries of 30000 and 50000, followed by your sentinel value.

    b. List the input, processing, and output items, as well as the algorithm, in a chart similar to the one shown earlier in Figure 8-40. Then code the algorithm into a program.

    c. Desk-check the program using the same data used to desk-check the algorithm.

    d. If necessary, create a new project named Advanced25 Project and save it in the Cpp7\Chap08 folder. Enter your C++ instructions into a source file named Advanced25.cpp. Also enter appropriate comments and any additional instructions required by the compiler.

    e. Save and then run the program. Test the program using the same data used to desk-check the program.

ADVANCED

26. In this exercise, you modify the program from Computer Exercise 15. The modified program will allow the user to specify the outer loop's ending value and its increment value. The ending value determines the maximum number of asterisks to display. The increment value determines the number of asterisks to repeat.

    a. If necessary, create a new project named Advanced26 Project and save it in the Cpp7\Chap08 folder. Enter (or copy) the TryThis15.cpp instructions into a new source file named Advanced26.cpp. Change TryThis15.cpp in the first comment to Advanced26.cpp. Make the appropriate modifications to the program.

    b. Save and then run the program. Test the program by entering the numbers 4 and 1 as the maximum number of asterisks and increment value, respectively. The program should display four rows of asterisks as follows: one asterisk, two asterisks, three asterisks, and four asterisks.

    c. Run the program again. This time, enter the numbers 9 and 3 as the maximum number of asterisks and the increment value, respectively. The program should display three rows of asterisks as follows: three asterisks, six asterisks, and nine asterisks.

ADVANCED

27. In this exercise, you modify the program from Computer Exercise 16. The modified program will allow the user to display the asterisks using one of two different patterns. Pattern 1 contains nine rows of asterisks as follows: nine asterisks, eight asterisks, seven asterisks, six asterisks, five asterisks, four asterisks, three asterisks, two asterisks, and one asterisk. Pattern 2 contains nine rows of asterisks as follows: one asterisk, two asterisks, three asterisks, four asterisks, five asterisks, six asterisks, seven asterisks, eight asterisks, and nine asterisks.

    a. If necessary, create a new project named Advanced27 Project and save it in the Cpp7\Chap08 folder. Enter (or copy) the TryThis16.cpp instructions into a new source file named Advanced27.cpp. Change TryThis16.cpp in the first comment to Advanced27.cpp. Make the appropriate modifications to the program.

    b. Save and then run the program. Display the asterisks using the first pattern, and then display them using the second pattern.

ADVANCED

28. The modified savings calculator program is shown in Figure 8-33 in the chapter. If necessary, create a new project named Advanced28 Project and save it in the Cpp7\Chap08 folder. Enter the C++ instructions from the figure into a source file named Advanced28.cpp. Modify the program to allow the user to enter the principal, the minimum and maximum interest rates, and the number of years. Save and then run the program. Test the program appropriately. Include the following values in your test data: 1000, .02, .04, and 5. Your answers should agree with those shown earlier in Figure 8-34..

SWAT THE BUGS

29. Follow the instructions for starting C++ and viewing the SwatTheBugs29.cpp file, which is contained in either the Cpp7\Chap08\SwatTheBugs29 Project folder or the Cpp7\Chap08 folder. (Depending on your C++ development tool, you may need to open this exercise's project/solution file first.) If necessary, delete the two forward slashes that appear before the `system("pause");` statement. Read the program's comments and then debug the program.

Answers to TRY THIS Exercises

Pencil and Paper

1. See Figure 8-50. The number 4 causes the nested loop to end. The number 3 causes the outer loop to end.

outer	nested
	~~0~~
~~1~~	~~1~~
~~2~~	~~2~~
3	~~3~~
	~~4~~
	~~1~~
	~~2~~
	~~3~~
	4

The program will display the following output:

```
1  2  3
1  2  3
```

Figure 8-50

2. `} while (quantity >= 0);`

Computer

15. See Figure 8-51.

```
//TryThis15.cpp - displays a pattern of asterisks
//Created/revised by <your name> on <current date>

#include <iostream>
using namespace std;

int main()
{
    for (int outer = 2; outer < 11; outer += 2)
    {
        for (int nested = 1; nested <= outer; nested += 1)
             cout << '*';
        //end for
        cout << endl;
    }   //end for

    //system("pause");
    return 0;
}  //end of main function
```


Figure 8-51

16. See Figure 8-52.

```
//TryThis16.cpp - displays a pattern of asterisks
//Created/revised by <your name> on <current date>

#include <iostream>
using namespace std;

int main()
{
    int outer  = 9;
    int nested = 1;

    while (outer > 0)
    {
        while (nested <= outer)
        {
            cout << '*';
            nested += 1;  //update nested counter
        }   //end while
        outer -= 1;    //update outer counter
        nested = 1;    //reset nested counter
        cout << endl;
    }   //end while

    //system("pause");
    return 0;
}   //end of main function
```

if your C++ development tool requires this statement, delete the two forward slashes

Figure 8-52

CHAPTER 9

Value-Returning Functions

After studying Chapter 9, you should be able to:

- Use the `sqrt` function to return the square root of a number
- Generate random numbers
- Create and invoke a function that returns a value
- Pass information *by value* to a function
- Write a function prototype
- Understand a variable's scope and lifetime

Functions

As you learned in Chapter 4, a function is a block of code that performs a task. Every C++ program contains at least one function, which is named `main`. However, most C++ programs contain many functions. Some of the functions used in a program are built into the C++ language. The code for these **built-in functions** resides in C++ libraries, which are special files that come with the C++ language. Examples of built-in functions with which you are already familiar include `pow` and `toupper`.

In some programming languages, functions are called methods, subroutines, or procedures.

Other program functions, like `main`, are created by the programmer. These functions are often referred to as **program-defined functions** because the function definitions are contained in the program itself rather than in a different file. But why would a programmer need more than the `main` function? One reason is to avoid the duplication of code. If the same task needs to be performed in more than one section of a program, it is more efficient for the programmer to enter the code once, in a function. Any section in the program can then call (or invoke) the function to perform the required task. Program-defined functions also allow large and complex programs, which typically are written by a team of programmers, to be broken into small and manageable tasks. Each member of the team is assigned one or more tasks to code as a function. Doing this allows more than one programmer to work on a program at the same time, decreasing the time it takes to write the program. When each programmer completes his or her function, all of the functions are gathered together into one program. Typically, a program's `main` function is responsible for calling (or invoking) each of the other program-defined functions. However, any program-defined function can call any other program-defined or built-in function.

All program-defined and built-in functions are categorized as either value-returning functions or void functions. The difference between both categories is that value-returning functions return a value after performing their assigned task, whereas void functions do not return a value after completing their task. Although the concept of something being either value-returning or void may sound confusing at first, it is a concept with which you are already familiar. We'll use the two illustrations shown in Figure 9-1 to demonstrate this fact.

In Illustration A, Helen is at the ticket counter in her local movie theater, requesting a ticket for the current movie. Helen gives the ticket agent a $5 bill and expects a ticket in return. The ticket agent is similar to a value-returning function. He performs his task (fulfilling her request for a ticket) and then returns a value (a ticket) to Helen. Compare that with Illustration B, where Helen and her granddaughter, Penelope, are at the Blast Off Games arcade. Helen wants Penelope to have fun, so she gives Penelope a $5 bill to play some games. But, unlike with the ticket agent, Helen expects nothing from Penelope in return. This is similar to the way a void function works. Penelope performs her task (having fun by playing games), but doesn't need to return any value to her grandmother.

Illustration A

Helen:

1. ask ticket agent for a senior ticket
2. give ticket agent $5
3. receive senior ticket from ticket agent

Ticket agent (value-returning function):

1. take $5 from Helen
2. give Helen a senior ticket

Illustration B

Helen:

1. tell Penelope to have fun playing games
2. give Penelope $5

Penelope (void function):

1. take $5 from Helen
2. buy game tickets with the $5
3. play games and have fun

Figure 9-1 Illustrations of value-returning and void functions

You will learn about value-returning functions in this chapter. Void functions are covered in Chapter 10.

Value-Returning Functions

All **value-returning functions**, whether built-in or program-defined, perform a task and then return precisely one value after the task is completed. The built-in value-returning `toupper` function, for example, temporarily converts a character to uppercase and then returns the result. The built-in value-returning `pow` function, on the other hand, returns the result of raising a number to a specified power. In almost all cases, a value-returning function returns its one value to the statement from which it was called (invoked). One exception is the `main` function, which returns its one value to the operating system. Typically, the statement that invokes a function assigns the return value to a variable. However, it also may use the return value in a calculation or comparison; or it simply may display the return value.

The value that the `main` function returns to the operating system indicates whether the program ended normally.

In the first part of this chapter, you will learn how to use several built-in value-returning functions. Later in the chapter, you will learn how to create program-defined value-returning functions. At this point, it's important to point out that functions are one of the more challenging topics for beginning programmers. Therefore, don't be concerned if you don't understand everything right away. If you still feel overwhelmed by the end of the chapter, try reading the chapter again, paying particular attention to the examples and programs shown in the figures.

The Hypotenuse Program

Figure 9-2 shows the problem specification and IPO chart for the hypotenuse program, and Figure 9-3 shows the program's flowchart. The program calculates and displays the length of a right triangle's hypotenuse, which is the longest side of the triangle. The figure also includes an example of using the Pythagorean Theorem to calculate the length. The theorem requires raising a number to the second power (in other words, squaring the number) and also taking the square root of a number. You already know how to square a number using the C++ built-in pow function. In the next section, you will learn how to use the built-in sqrt function to find the square root of a number. Both functions are value-returning functions because they return a value after performing their assigned task.

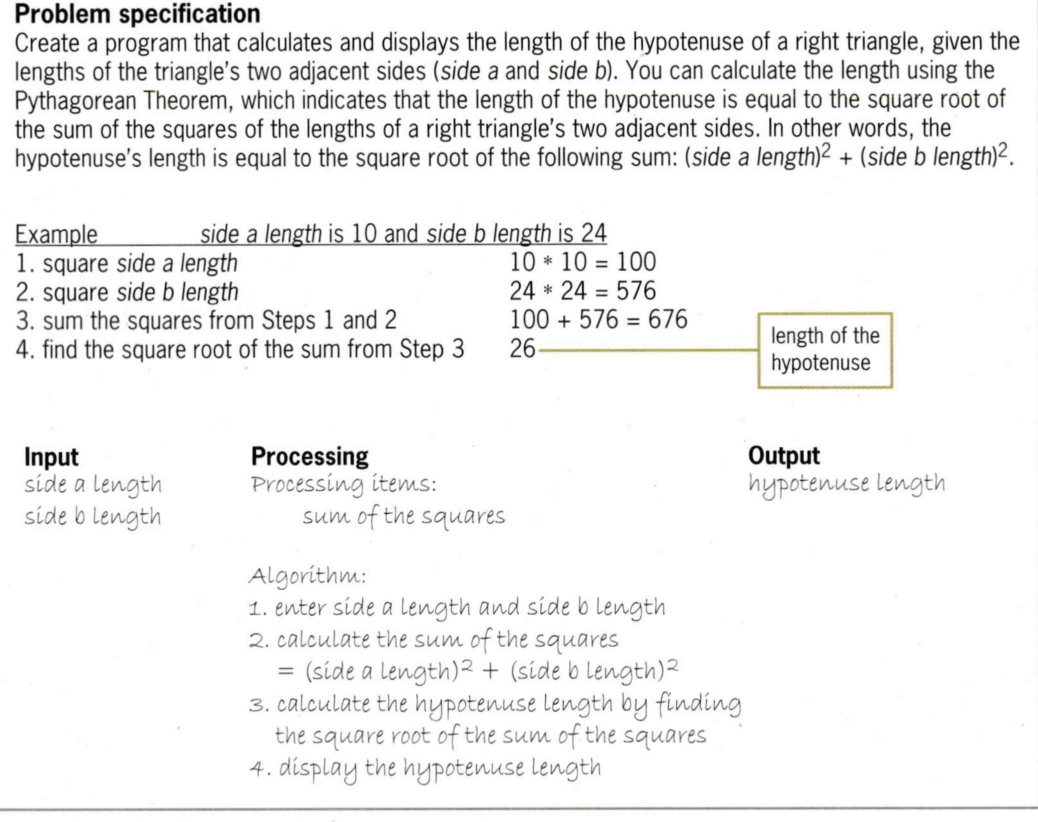

Figure 9-2 Problem specification, calculation example, and IPO chart for the hypotenuse program

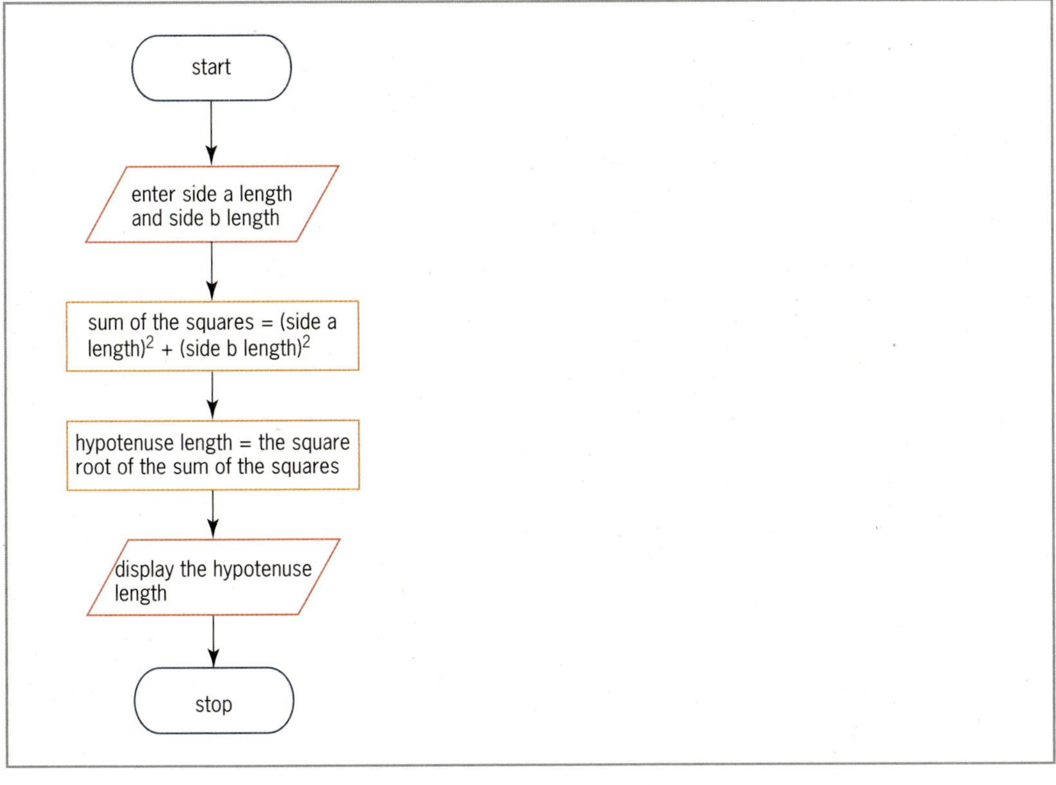

Figure 9-3 Flowchart for the hypotenuse program

Finding the Square Root of a Number

In Chapter 8, you learned that you can find the square root of a number by raising the number to the .5 power, like this: `pow(100, .5)`. Although you can use the `pow` function to determine a square root, C++ provides the `sqrt` function specifically for that purpose. The **`sqrt` function** is a built-in value-returning function that calculates a number's square root and then returns the result as a `double` number. The `sqrt` function's code is contained in the cmath library file. Therefore, a program must contain the `#include <cmath>` directive in order to use the function. The directive tells the C++ compiler the location of the function's code.

Recall from Chapter 4 that a `#include` directive provides a convenient way to merge the source code from one file with the source code in another file, without having to retype the code.

The `sqrt` function's syntax is shown in Figure 9-4. Recall from Chapter 5 that an item within parentheses in a function's syntax—in this case, *x*—is called an argument; more specifically, it is called an actual argument. An **actual argument** represents information that the function needs to perform its task. The `sqrt` function contains one actual argument (*x*) because it requires only one item of information: the number whose square root you want to find. The *x* actual argument must have either the `double` or `float` data type. The actual argument is passed to the function when the function is invoked. Invoking a function is also referred to as calling a function. You call a function simply by including its name and actual arguments (if any) in a program statement.

Also included in Figure 9-4 are examples of using the `sqrt` function. (For clarity, the variable declaration statements are included in the examples.) The assignment statement in Example 1 calls (invokes) the `sqrt` function, passing it the `double` number 100.0. The function calculates the number's square root and then returns the answer (10.0) to the assignment statement, which assigns the answer to the `squareRoot` variable. Similarly, the second `cout` statement in Example 2 calls the `sqrt` function, passing it the `double` number stored in the `num` variable. The function calculates the number's square root and then returns the answer to the `cout` statement, which displays the answer on the computer screen.

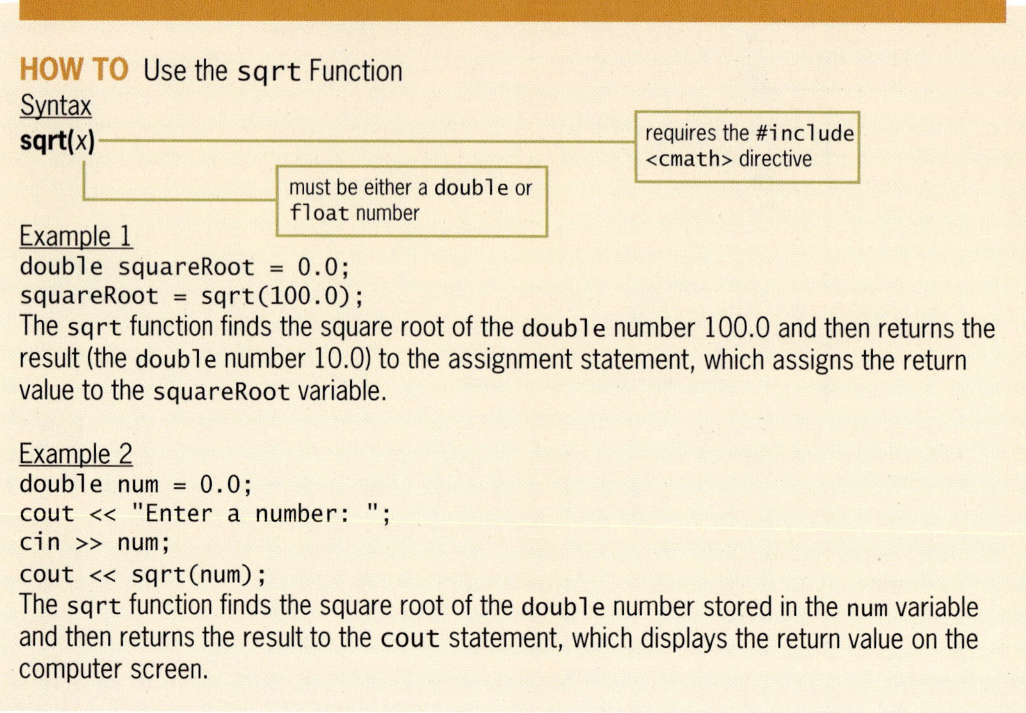

HOW TO Use the `sqrt` Function

Syntax

sqrt(*x*)

Example 1

```
double squareRoot = 0.0;
squareRoot = sqrt(100.0);
```

The `sqrt` function finds the square root of the `double` number 100.0 and then returns the result (the `double` number 10.0) to the assignment statement, which assigns the return value to the `squareRoot` variable.

Example 2

```
double num = 0.0;
cout << "Enter a number: ";
cin >> num;
cout << sqrt(num);
```

The `sqrt` function finds the square root of the `double` number stored in the `num` variable and then returns the result to the `cout` statement, which displays the return value on the computer screen.

Figure 9-4 How to use the `sqrt` function

Figure 9-5 shows the IPO chart information and corresponding C++ instructions for the hypotenuse program.

IPO chart information	**C++ instructions**
Input	
side a length	`double sideA = 0.0;`
side b length	`double sideB = 0.0;`
Processing	
sum of the squares	`double sumSqrs = 0.0;`
Output	
hypotenuse length	`double hypotenuse = 0.0;`
Algorithm	

1. enter side a length and side b length	`cout << "Side a length: ";`
	`cin >> sideA;`
	`cout << "Side b length: ";`
	`cin >> sideB;`

2. calculate the sum of the squares = (side a length)^2 + (side b length)^2	`sumSqrs = pow(sideA, 2) +` `pow(sideB, 2);`
3. calculate the hypotenuse length by finding the square root of the sum of the squares	`hypotenuse = sqrt(sumSqrs);`
4. display the hypotenuse length	`cout << "Hypotenuse length: "` `<< hypotenuse << endl;`

Figure 9-5 IPO chart information and C++ instructions for the hypotenuse program

Figure 9-6 shows the hypotenuse program's code. The #include <cmath> directive on Line 6 is required because the program uses the sqrt function. The directive tells the C++ compiler to include the contents of the cmath file, which contains the sqrt function's code, in the current program. The sqrt function appears in the assignment statement on Line 25. The assignment statement calls the function, passing it the value stored in the sumSqrs variable. When the computer encounters the assignment statement in the code, it temporarily leaves the main function to process the sqrt function's code. The sqrt function calculates the square root of the value passed to it and then returns the value to the statement that called it. In this case, it returns the value to the assignment statement on Line 25. The assignment statement assigns the return value to the double hypotenuse variable. A sample run of the hypotenuse program is shown in Figure 9-7.

```
1  //Hypotenuse.cpp - displays the length of the
2  //hypotenuse of a right triangle
3  //Created/revised by <your name> on <current date>
4
5  #include <iostream>
6  #include <cmath>
7  using namespace std;
8
9  int main()
10 {
11     //declare variables
12     double sideA      = 0.0;
13     double sideB      = 0.0;
14     double sumSqrs    = 0.0;
15     double hypotenuse = 0.0;
16
17     //get lengths of two sides
18     cout << "Side a length: ";
19     cin >> sideA;
20     cout << "Side b length: ";
21     cin >> sideB;
22
23     //calculate the length of the hypotenuse
24     sumSqrs = pow(sideA, 2) + pow(sideB, 2);
25     hypotenuse = sqrt(sumSqrs);
26
27     //display the length of the hypotenuse
28     cout << "Hypotenuse length: "
29          << hypotenuse << endl;
30
31     //system("pause");
32     return 0;
33 }  //end of main function
```

required for the sqrt function (Line 6)

uses the sqrt function (Line 25)

your C++ development tool may require this statement (Line 31)

Figure 9-6 Hypotenuse program

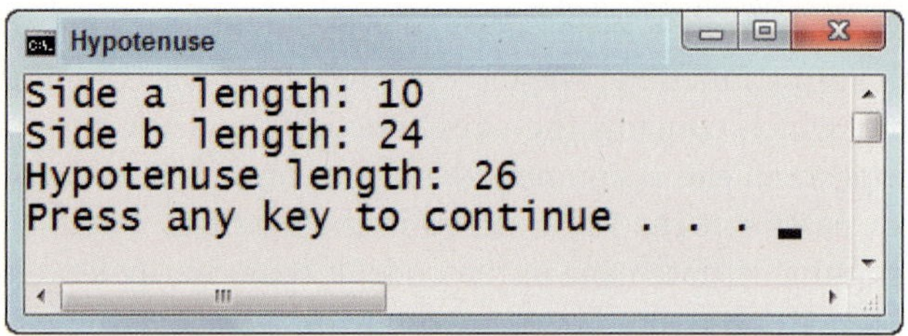

Figure 9-7 Sample run of the hypotenuse program

The Random Addition Problems Program

Figure 9-8 shows the problem specification and IPO chart for the random addition problems program, and Figure 9-9 shows the program's flowchart. The algorithm requires the computer to generate two random integers from 1 to 10, inclusive. You will learn how to generate random integers in the next section.

Problem specification
Create a program that displays five random addition problems, one at a time, on the computer screen. Each problem should be displayed as a question, like this: *What is the sum of* x + *y?*. The x and y in the question represent numbers from 1 to 10, inclusive. After displaying the question, the program should allow the user to enter the answer. It then should compare the user's answer with the correct answer. If the user's answer matches the correct answer, the program should display the "Correct!" message. Otherwise, it should display the "Sorry, the correct answer is" message followed by the correct answer and a period.

Input	Processing	Output
user's answer	Processing items: first random number (1 to 10) second random number (1 to 10) counter (1 to 5) correct answer	addition problem message

```
Algorithm:
1. initialize the random number generator
2. repeat for (counter from 1 to 5)
      generate the first random number

      generate the second random number

      calculate the correct answer by adding
      together the first random number and
      the second random number

      display the addition problem

      enter the user's answer

      if (user's answer matches correct answer)
         display "Correct!" message
      else
         display "Sorry, the correct answer is" message
         followed by the correct answer and a period
      end if
      display two blank lines
   end repeat
```

Figure 9-8 Problem specification and IPO chart for the random addition problems program

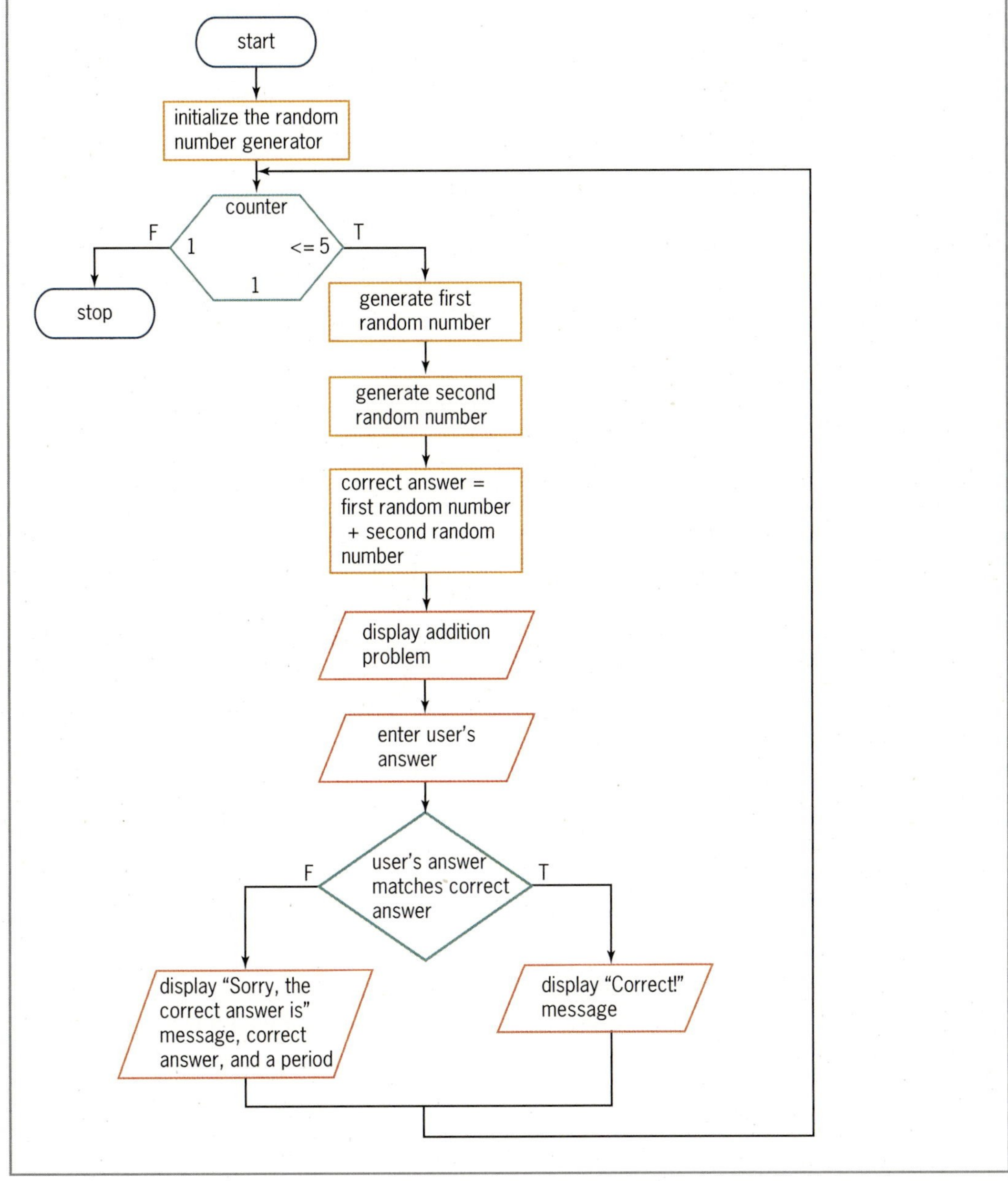

Figure 9-9 Flowchart for the random addition problems program

Generating Random Integers

Many programs require the use of random numbers. Examples of such programs include game programs, lottery programs, and programs used to practice elementary math skills. Most programming languages provide a **pseudo-random number generator**, which is a device that produces a sequence of numbers that meet certain statistical requirements for randomness. Pseudo-random numbers are chosen with equal probability from a finite set of numbers. The chosen numbers are not completely random because a definite mathematical algorithm is used to select them. However, they are sufficiently random for practical purposes.

The random number generator in C++ is a built-in value-returning function named `rand`. The **rand function** returns an integer that is greater than or equal to 0 but less than or equal to the value stored in the RAND_MAX constant, which is one of many constants built into the C++ language. Although the value of **RAND_MAX** varies with different systems, its value is always at least 32,767. (You can display your computer system's RAND_MAX value using the statement `cout << RAND_MAX;`.) Figure 9-10 shows the `rand` function's syntax and includes examples of using the function to generate random integers. The `rand` function's syntax does not contain any actual arguments because the function does not require any information to perform its task. However, the parentheses after the function's name are required. Depending on your C++ development tool, you may need to include the `#include <cstdlib>` directive in your program in order to use `rand` and `RAND_MAX`.

In C++, every function's name is followed by a set of parentheses, which may or may not contain actual arguments.

HOW TO Use the rand Function

Syntax

rand()

Example 1

```
int randomNum = 0;
randomNum = rand();
```

The `rand` function generates a random integer that is greater than or equal to 0 but less than or equal to `RAND_MAX`. It then returns the random integer to the assignment statement, which assigns the random integer to the `randomNum` variable.

Example 2

```
cout << rand();
```

The `rand` function generates a random integer that is greater than or equal to 0 but less than or equal to `RAND_MAX`. It then returns the random integer to the `cout` statement, which displays the random integer on the computer screen.

Example 3

```
int tripleNum = 0;
tripleNum = rand() * 3;
```

The `rand` function generates a random integer that is greater than or equal to 0 but less than or equal to `RAND_MAX`. It then returns the random integer to the assignment statement, which multiplies the random integer by 3 and assigns the result to the `tripleNum` variable.

Figure 9-10 How to use the rand function

As you learned in Chapter 4, the modulus operator divides two integers and then returns the remainder as an integer.

Ch09-Random Range video

Most programs that use random numbers require the numbers to be within a range that is more specific than 0 through RAND_MAX. For example, a program that simulates rolling dice will require integers from 1 through 6 only. A program that displays arithmetic problems for elementary school students, on the other hand, may require integers from 10 through 100. Figure 9-11 shows the syntax of an expression that you can use to specify the desired range of integers. In the syntax, *lowerBound* and *upperBound* are the lowest integer and highest integer, respectively, in the range. Also included in Figure 9-11 are examples of using the expression in a C++ statement. The expression in Example 1 will produce integers in the range of 1 through 6, whereas the expression in Example 2 will produce integers from 10 through 100. You also can write the expressions in Figure 9-1 as `1 + rand() % 6` and `10 + rand() % 91`. However, including the *lowerBound* and *upperBound* values within the parentheses makes the expression clearer and more self-documenting.

Figure 9-11 also shows how the computer evaluates the expressions in both examples using sample values generated by the `rand` function. The first sample value for Example 1 is 27. When processing the `1 + 27 % (6 - 1 + 1)` expression, the computer first evaluates the part of the expression within parentheses; in this case, `6 - 1 + 1` evaluates to 6. The expression now becomes `1 + 27 % 6`. The modulus (remainder) operation in the expression is evaluated next. The modulus operator (%) tells the computer to divide the number 27 by the number 6 and then find the remainder; in this case, the remainder is 3. The expression now becomes `1 + 3`. Finally, the computer adds the number 1 to the number 3, giving 4. In other words, the expression in Example 1 evaluates to the integer 4 when the `rand` value is 27. As Figure 9-11 indicates, the expression will evaluate to the integers 3 and 1 when the `rand` value is 8 and 324, respectively. Notice that the three random integers (4, 3, and 1) are within the range of 1 through 6.

Now look closely at the sample `rand` values used in Example 2 in Figure 9-11; the first sample value is 352. When processing the `10 + 352 % (100 - 10 + 1)` expression, the computer first evaluates the part of the expression within parentheses; in this case, `100 - 10 + 1` evaluates to 91. The expression now becomes `10 + 352 % 91`. The modulus operator (%) in the expression tells the computer to divide the number 352 by the number 91 and then find the remainder; in this case, the remainder is 79. The expression now becomes `10 + 79`. Finally, the computer adds the number 10 to the number 79, giving 89. Therefore, the expression in Example 2 evaluates to the integer 89 when the `rand` value is 352. The expression will evaluate to the integers 14 and 53 when the `rand` value is 4 and 2500, respectively. Notice that in this case, the three random integers (89, 14, and 53) are within the required range of 10 through 100.

HOW TO Generate Random Integers within a Specific Range

Syntax

lowerBound **+ rand() % (***upperBound* **–** *lowerBound* **+ 1)**

Example 1

```
cout << 1 + rand() % (6 - 1 + 1);
```

displays a random integer from 1 through 6 on the computer screen

`rand` value: 27	`1 + 27 % (6 - 1 + 1)`
`6 - 1 + 1` is evaluated first and results in 6	`1 + 27 % 6`
`27 % 6` is evaluated next and results in 3	`1 + 3`
`1 + 3` is evaluated last and results in 4	`4`

`rand` value: 8	`1 + 8 % (6 - 1 + 1)`
`6 - 1 + 1` is evaluated first and results in 6	`1 + 8 % 6`
`8 % 6` is evaluated next and results in 2	`1 + 2`
`1 + 2` is evaluated last and results in 3	`3`

`rand` value: 324	`1 + 324 % (6 - 1 + 1)`
`6 - 1 + 1` is evaluated first and results in 6	`1 + 324 % 6`
`324 % 6` is evaluated next and results in 0	`1 + 0`
`1 + 0` is evaluated last and results in 1	`1`

(continues)

Figure 9-11 How to generate random integers within a specific range

(continued)

Example 2
```
int num = 0;
num = 10 + rand() % (100 - 10 + 1);
```
assigns a random integer from 10 through 100 to the `num` variable

`rand` value: 352	`10 + 352 % (100 - 10 + 1)`
`100 - 10 + 1` is evaluated first and results in 91	`10 + 352 % 91`
`352 % 91` is evaluated next and results in 79	`10 + 79`
`10 + 79` is evaluated last and results in 89	`89`
`rand` value: 4	`10 + 4 % (100 - 10 + 1)`
`100 - 10 + 1` is evaluated first and results in 91	`10 + 4 % 91`
`4 % 91` is evaluated next and results in 4	`10 + 4`
`10 + 4` is evaluated last and results in 14	`14`
`rand` value: 2500	`10 + 2500 % (100 - 10 + 1)`
`100 - 10 + 1` is evaluated first and results in 91	`10 + 2500 % 91`
`2500 % 91` is evaluated next and results in 43	`10 + 43`
`10 + 43` is evaluated last and results in 53	`53`

Figure 9-11 How to generate random integers within a specific range

You should initialize the random number generator in each program in which it is used. Otherwise, it will generate the same series of numbers each time the program is executed. Typically, the initialization task is performed at the beginning of the program. You initialize the random number generator using the **`srand` function**. Like the `rand` function, the `srand` function is a built-in C++ function. However, unlike the `rand` function, the `srand` function is a void function, which means it does not return a value. (You will learn more about void functions in Chapter 10.) Depending on your C++ development tool, you may need to include the `#include <cstdlib>` directive in your program in order to use `srand`.

Figure 9-12 shows the syntax of the `srand` function and includes examples of using the function. The *seed* actual argument in the syntax is an integer that represents the starting point for the random number generator. The computer uses the starting point (or seed) in the mathematical algorithm it employs when selecting the random numbers. You can have the user enter the seed, as shown in Example 1 in Figure 9-12. However, a more common way to initialize the random number generator is to use the C++ `time` function as the seed; this is shown in Examples 2 and 3.

The **`time` function** is a built-in value-returning function that returns the current time (according to your computer system's clock) as seconds elapsed since midnight on January 1, 1970. However, because the `time` function returns a `time_t` object, you will need to use a type cast to convert the function's return value to an integer, as shown in Examples 2 and 3 in Figure 9-12. In both examples, the `time` function is passed one actual argument: the number 0. Using the `time` function as the `srand` function's seed ensures that the random number generator is initialized with a unique integer each time the program is executed. The unique integer will produce a unique series of random numbers. To use the `time` function in a program, the program must contain the `#include <ctime>` directive.

HOW TO Use the srand Function

Syntax

srand(*seed*)

Example 1

```
int x = 0;
cout << "Enter an integer: ";
cin >> x;
srand(x);
cout << rand() << endl;
cout << rand() << endl;
```

The srand function initializes the random number generator using the intege entered by the user. The cout statements display two random integers on ther computer screen. The random integers will be greater than or equal to 0 but less than or equal to RAND_MAX.

Example 2

the time function requires the #include <ctime> directive

```
srand(static_cast<int>(time(0)));
cout << rand() << endl;
cout << rand() << endl;
```

The srand function initializes the random number generator using the value returned by the time function after it has been converted to the int data type. The cout statements display two random integers on the computer screen. The random integers will be greater than or equal to 0 but less than or equal to RAND_MAX.

Example 3

the time function requires the #include <ctime> directive

```
int randNum = 0;
srand(static_cast<int>(time(0)));
randNum = 1 + rand() % (10 - 1 + 1);
```

The srand function initializes the random number generator using the value returned by the time function after it has been converted to the int data type. The assignment statement assigns a random integer to the randNum variable. The random integer will be greater than or equal to 1 but less than or equal to 10.

Figure 9-12 How to use the srand function

Figure 9-13 shows the IPO chart information and corresponding C++ instructions for the random addition problems program.

IPO chart information	C++ instructions
Input	
user's answer	`int userAnswer = 0;`
Processing	
first random number (1 to 10)	`int num1 = 0;`
second random number (1 to 10)	`int num2 = 0;`
counter (1 to 5)	this variable is created and initialized in the for clause
correct answer	`int correctAnswer = 0;`
Output	
addition problem	this contains string literal constants and the num1 and num2 variables
message	this is one of two messages composed of either a string literal constant or string literal constants and the correctAnswer variable
Algorithm	
1. initialize the random number generator	`srand(static_cast<int>(time(0)));`
2. repeat for (counter from 1 to 5)	`for (int x = 1; x < 6; x += 1)` `{`
generate the first random number	`num1 = 1 + rand() % (10 - 1 + 1);`
generate the second random number	`num2 = 1 + rand() % (10 - 1 + 1);`
calculate the correct answer by adding together the first random number and the second random number	`correctAnswer = num1 + num2;`
display the addition problem	`cout << "What is the sum of "` `<< num1 << " + " << num2 << "? ";`
enter the user's answer	`cin >> userAnswer;`
if (user's answer matches correct answer)	`if (userAnswer == correctAnswer)`
display "Correct!" message	`cout << "Correct!";`
else	`else`
display "Sorry, the correct answer is" message followed by the correct answer and a period	`cout << "Sorry, the correct answer is " << correctAnswer << ".";`
end if	`//end if`
display two blank lines	`cout << endl << endl;`
end repeat	`} //end for`

Figure 9-13 IPO chart information and C++ instructions for the random addition problems program

Figure 9-14 shows the code for the random addition problems program. The `#include <ctime>` directive on Line 9 is required when using the `time` function. The statement on Line 22 uses the `time` and `srand` functions to initialize the random number generator. The `rand` function appears in the assignment statements on Lines 29 and 30; each assigns a random integer from 1 through 10 to a variable. A sample run of the program is shown in Figure 9-15.

```
1  //Random Addition.cpp
2  //Displays random addition problems
3  //Allows the user to enter the answer and then
4  //displays a message that indicates whether the
5  //user's answer is correct or incorrect
6  //Created/revised by <your name> on <current date>
7
8  #include <iostream>
9  #include <ctime>
10 //#include <cstdlib>
11 using namespace std;
12
13 int main()
14 {
15     //declare variables
16     int num1          = 0;
17     int num2          = 0;
18     int correctAnswer = 0;
19     int userAnswer    = 0;
20
21     //initialize rand function
22     srand(static_cast<int>(time(0)));
23
24     for (int x = 1; x < 6; x += 1)
25     {
26         //generate two random integers
27         //from 1 through 10, then
28         //calculate the sum
29         num1 = 1 + rand() % (10 - 1 + 1);
30         num2 = 1 + rand() % (10 - 1 + 1);
31         correctAnswer = num1 + num2;
32
33         //display addition problem and get user's answer
34         cout << "What is the sum of " << num1
35              << " + " << num2 << "? ";
36         cin >> userAnswer;
37
38         //determine whether user's answer is correct
39         if (userAnswer == correctAnswer)
40             cout << "Correct!";
```

required for the `time` function

your C++ development tool may require this directive

uses the `srand` and `time` functions

uses the `rand` function

Figure 9-14 Random addition problems program *(continues)*

(continued)

```
            else
                cout << "Sorry, the correct answer is "
                    << correctAnswer << ".";
            //end if
            cout << endl << endl;
        }   //end for

        //system("pause");
        return 0;
    }   //end of main function
```

your C++ development tool may require this statement (refers to `//system("pause");`)

Figure 9-14 Random addition problems program

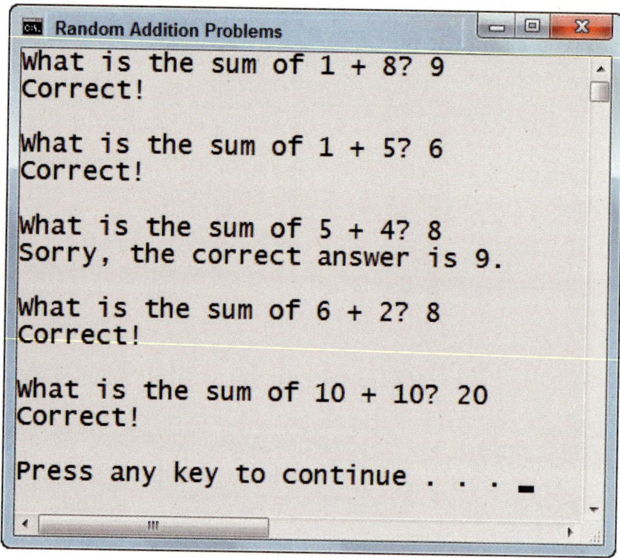

Figure 9-15 Sample run of the random addition problems program

The answers to Mini-Quiz questions are located in Appendix A.

Mini-Quiz 9-1

1. Which of the following will return the square root of the number 16?
   a. `pow(16.0, 2)`
   b. `sqrt(16.0)`
   c. `sqrt(16.0, .5)`
   d. both a and b

2. Which of the following expressions will generate a random integer from 25 through 50, inclusive?
   a. `1 + rand() % (50 - 25 + 1)`
   b. `50 + rand() % (50 - 25 + 1)`
   c. `25 + rand() % (50 - 25 + 1)`
   d. `25 + rand() % (50 - 25 - 1)`

3. Which of the following functions initializes the random number generator in C++?
   a. `initialize()`
   b. `startRand()`
   c. `rand(time(0))`
   d. none of the above

4. Which of the following directives is necessary for a program to use the C++ `time` function?
   a. `#include <ctime>`
   b. `#include <stime>`
   c. `#include <time>`
   d. none of the above

Creating Program-Defined Value-Returning Functions

In addition to using the value-returning functions built into the C++ language, you also can create your own value-returning functions. As mentioned earlier, such functions are referred to as program-defined value-returning functions because the function definitions are contained in the program itself rather than in a different file. You already know how to create one program-defined value-returning function: `main`. In this section, you will learn how to create other program-defined value-returning functions.

The first program-defined value-returning function you will create is for the random addition problems program from the previous section. Because that program is short and simple, it's perfectly acceptable to have the `main` function perform all of the program's tasks, as it does now. However, when coding large and complex programs, programmers typically divide the program into small and manageable tasks and then assign some of the tasks to program-defined functions. Doing this makes the program easier to code because it allows the programmer to concentrate on coding one small piece of the program at a time. It also allows more than one programmer to work on a program at the same time. In this case, you will remove the task of generating the random numbers from the `main` function and assign that responsibility to a program-defined value-returning function instead.

Figure 9-16 shows the modified IPO chart for the `main` function. The changes made to the function's original IPO chart, shown earlier in Figure 9-8, are shaded in Figure 9-16. The figure also shows the IPO chart for a program-defined value-returning function named `getRandomNumber`. When invoked by a statement in the `main` function, the `getRandomNumber` function will generate a random number from 1 through 10 and then return the random number to the statement that called it. The `main` function will need to call the `getRandomNumber` function twice. This is because the program needs two random numbers, and the `getRandomNumber` function can return only one random number at a time.

Recall that a value-returning function can return only one value at a time.

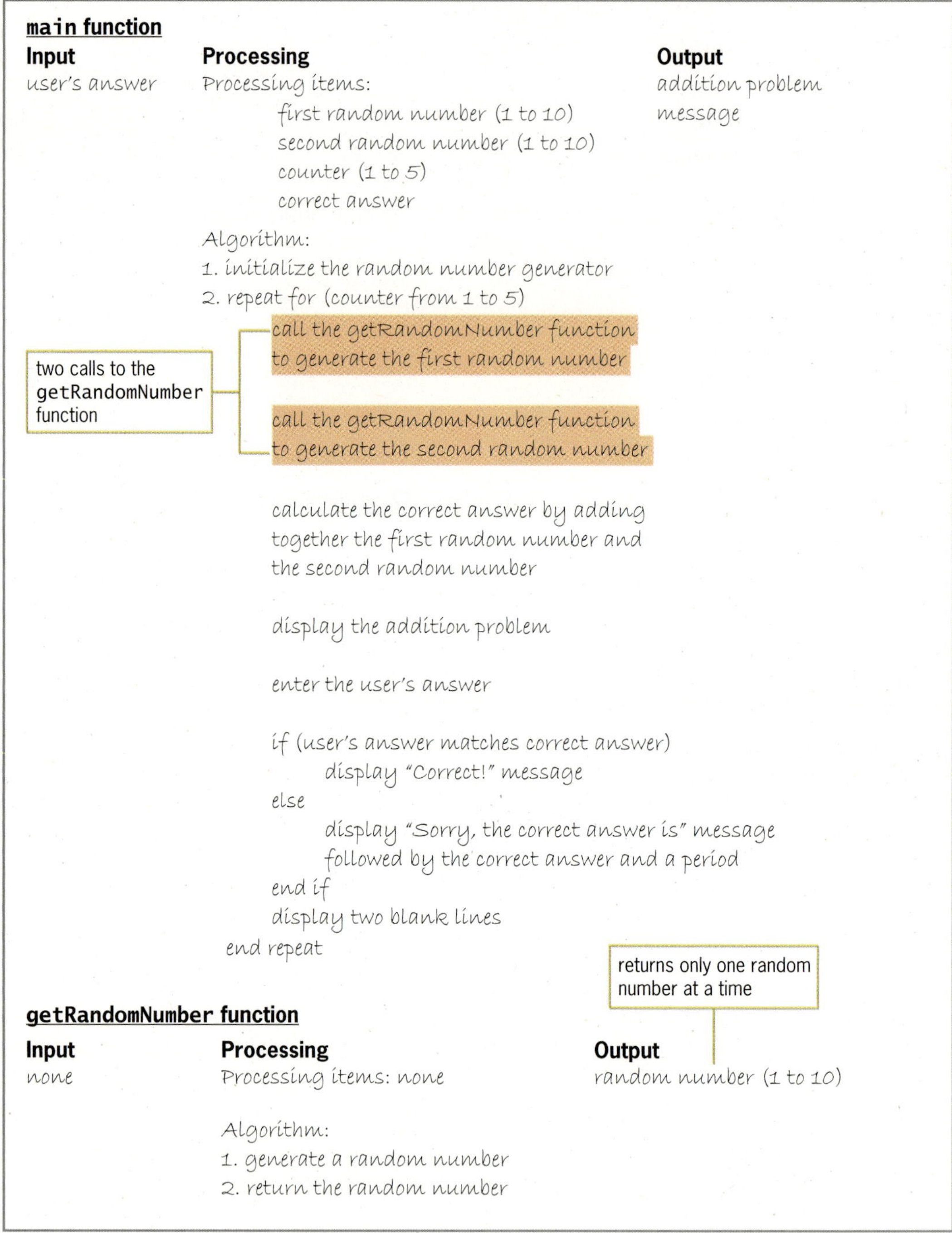

Figure 9-16 IPO charts for the modified random addition problems program

Figure 9-17 shows the syntax used to create (or define) a value-returning function in a C++ program. The figure also shows examples of program-defined value-returning functions. The `getRandomNumber` function in Example 1 returns a random integer from 1 through 10. The `getRectangleArea` function in Example 2 calculates and returns the area of a rectangle, using the values stored in the `len` and `wid` variables. The values for the `len` and `wid` variables will be passed to the function by the statement from which it is called. The function returns the area as a `double` number. The `getBonus` function in Example 3 uses the values passed to it to calculate the amount of a salesperson's bonus, which the function returns as a `double` number. For now, don't be concerned if you don't fully understand the examples. They will become clearer to you as you progress through the chapter.

HOW TO Create a Program-Defined Value-Returning Function

Syntax

returnDataType functionName(**[***parameterList***]**) — function header

```
{
        one or more statements
        return expression;
}       //end of functionName function
```

function body

Example 1

```
int getRandomNumber()
{
        int randInteger = 0;
        randInteger = 1 + rand() % (10 - 1 + 1);
        return randInteger;
}       //end of getRandomNumber function
```

function definition

The function generates a random integer from 1 through 10 and then returns the random integer.

Example 2

```
double getRectangleArea(double len, double wid)
{
        return len * wid;
}       //end of getRectangleArea function
```

The function calculates the area of a rectangle and then returns the result as a `double` number.

Example 3

```
double getBonus(int sold, double bonusRate)
{
        double bonus = 0.0;

        bonus = sold * bonusRate;
        return bonus;
}       //end of getBonus function
```

The function calculates the amount of a salesperson's bonus and then returns the result as a `double` number.

Figure 9-17 How to create a program-defined value-returning function

Rather than using an empty set of parentheses when a function is not passed any information, some programmers enter the keyword `void` within the parentheses.

As Figure 9-17 indicates, a function definition is composed of a function header and a function body. The function header is the first line in a function definition. The function header for a value-returning function begins with *returnDataType*, which indicates the data type of the value the function returns. The `getRandomNumber` function in Figure 9-17 returns an integer; therefore, its *returnDataType* is `int`. The `getRectangleArea` and `getBonus` functions, on the other hand, return a `double` number and have a *returnDataType* of `double`.

The function header also specifies the name of the function. The rules for naming functions are the same as for naming variables. However, it is a common practice to begin a function's name with a verb. To make your programs more self-documenting and easier to understand, you should use meaningful names that describe the task the function performs. The names of the functions in Figure 9-17 indicate that the functions return a random number, the area of a rectangle, and a bonus amount.

The function header also contains an optional *parameterList* enclosed in parentheses. Keep in mind that only the *parameterList* is optional; the parentheses are a required part of the syntax. The *parameterList* contains the data type and name of one or more memory locations. The memory locations in a function's *parameterList* are called **formal parameters**. Each formal parameter will store an item of information that is passed to the function when the function is called. In Example 1 in Figure 9-17, the empty set of parentheses in the function header indicates that the `getRandomNumber` function will not be passed any information by the statement that calls it. The function header in Example 2, however, contains two formal parameters and indicates that the `getRectangleArea` function will be passed two items of information when it is invoked. Both items will have the `double` data type. The `getBonus` function in Example 3 will receive an `int` item followed by a `double` item from the statement that invokes it. You will learn more about the *parameterList* later in the chapter and also in Chapter 10.

You can provide a default value for one or more of a function's formal parameters. This topic is covered in Computer Exercise 25.

In addition to the function header, a function definition also contains a function body. The function body contains the instructions for performing the function's assigned task. The function body begins with the opening brace ({) and ends with the closing brace (}). In most cases, the last statement in the function body of a value-returning function is `return` *expression*`;`, in which *expression* represents the function's one and only return value. The data type of the *expression* must agree with the *returnDataType* specified in the function header. The **`return` statement** returns the *expression*'s value to the statement that called the function.

After the `return` statement is processed, the function ends and program execution continues in the calling function. Although not a requirement, it is a good programming practice to use a comment (such as `//end of getRandomNumber function`) to mark the end of a program-defined function. The comment will make your program easier to read and understand.

The answers to Mini-Quiz questions are located in Appendix A.

Mini-Quiz 9-2

1. A value-returning function's header contains ______________.
   a. the data type of the function's return value
   b. the function's name
   c. an optional *parameterList*
   d. all of the above
2. Which of the following is a valid function header for the `getArea` function? The function returns a `double` number and does not have any formal parameters.
   a. `double getArea()`
   b. `double getArea`
   c. `double getArea();`
   d. `double getArea;`
3. Write the function header for the `getGrossPay` function. The function returns a `double` number and has two formal parameters: an `int` variable named `hours` and a `double` variable named `rate`.
4. The `getGrossPay` function from Question 3 calculates and returns an employee's gross pay. Write a C++ statement that returns the gross pay to the statement that called the function. The gross pay is stored in a `double` variable named `gross`.

Calling a Function

For a function to perform its task, it must be called (or invoked). The `main` function in a C++ program is invoked automatically when the program is executed. Functions other than `main`, however, must be called by a statement within the program. You do this by including the function's name and actual arguments (if any) in the statement, as indicated in the syntax in Figure 9-18. The actual arguments are listed in the optional *argumentList*, which appears within parentheses after the function's name.

Value-returning functions typically are called from statements that do one of the following: assign the return value to a variable, use the return value in a calculation or comparison, or display the return value. The `cout` statement in Example 1 in Figure 9-18 calls the built-in value-returning `rand` function and then displays the function's return value on the computer screen. The assignment statement in Example 2 invokes the built-in value-returning `sqrt` function, passing it one actual argument: the `double` number 100.0. The `sqrt` function calculates the square root of the number 100.0 and then returns the answer (10.0) to the assignment statement, which assigns the answer to the `squareRoot` variable.

Unlike a call to a value-returning function, a call to a void function is an independent statement. In other words, it's not part of a statement that either assigns or displays the return value; this is because a void function does not return a value. Example 3 in Figure 9-18 shows a statement that calls a built-in void function: `srand`. Recall that you learned about the `srand` function earlier in the chapter. The `srand(5);` statement passes the integer 5 to the function, which uses the integer to initialize the random number generator. As mentioned earlier, you will learn more about void functions in Chapter 10.

Although the examples just cited call built-in functions, the same method is used to call program-defined functions. The assignment statement in Example 4, for instance, calls the program-defined value-returning `getRandomNumber` function shown earlier in Figure 9-17. The function generates a random integer from 1 through 10 and then returns the integer to the assignment statement, which assigns it to the `num1` variable. The function calls in the remaining two examples in Figure 9-18 pass actual arguments to program-defined functions.

HOW TO Call a Function

Syntax

functionName(**[***argumentList***]**)

Example 1

```
cout << rand();
```

The `cout` statement calls the built-in value-returning `rand` function and then displays the function's return value on the computer screen.

Example 2

```
double squareRoot = 0.0;
squareRoot = sqrt(100.0);
```

The assignment statement calls the built-in value-returning `sqrt` function, passing it the `double` number 100.0. It then assigns the function's return value to the `squareRoot` variable.

(continues)

Figure 9-18 How to call a function

(continued)

Example 3

```
srand(5);
```

a void function call is a self-contained statement

The statement calls the built-in void `srand` function, passing it the integer 5. The function uses the integer to initialize the random number generator.

Example 4

```
int num1 = 0;
num1 = getRandomNumber();
```

The assignment statement calls the `getRandomNumber` function and then assigns the function's return value to the `num1` variable.

Example 5

```
cout << getRectangleArea(7.25, 21.0);
```

The `cout` statement calls the `getRectangleArea` function, passing it the `double` numbers 7.25 and 21.0. It then displays the function's return value on the computer screen.

Example 6

```
int sales = 0;
double rate = 0.0;
cin >> sales;
cin >> rate;
if (getBonus(sales, rate) > 999.99)
```

The `if` clause calls the `getBonus` function, passing it the integer stored in the `sales` variable and the `double` number stored in the `rate` variable. It then compares the function's return value to the `double` number 999.99.

Figure 9-18 How to call a function

An actual argument can be a variable, named constant, literal constant, or keyword; however, in most cases it will be a variable. Each variable you declare in a program has both a value and a unique address that represents the location of the variable in the computer's internal memory. C++ allows you to pass either a copy of the variable's value or its address to a function. Passing a copy of a variable's value is referred to as **passing *by value***. Passing a variable's address is referred to as **passing *by reference***. Unless you specify otherwise, variables in C++ are automatically passed *by value*. For now, you do not need to concern yourself with passing *by reference* because all variables passed to functions in this chapter are passed *by value*. You will learn how to pass variables *by reference* in Chapter 10.

The number of actual arguments passed to a function should match the number of formal parameters in its function header. In addition, the data type and order (or position) of each actual argument must agree with the data type and order (position) of its corresponding formal parameter. This is because when the function is called, the computer stores the value of the first actual argument in the function's first formal parameter, the value of the second actual argument in its second formal parameter, and so on. To illustrate this point, let's compare the last two function calls shown in Figure 9-18 with their corresponding function definitions. The function calls and function definitions are shown together in Figure 9-19, with the function calls shaded. The call to the `getRectangleArea` function passes two `double` numbers (7.25 and 21.0) to the function. This is because the function's header contains two formal parameters, both of which have the `double` data type. The function uses the values stored in its formal parameters to calculate the area. It then returns the area to the `cout` statement that called it. That statement displays the area on the computer screen.

Ch09-Pass By Value video

The call to the `getBonus` function appears in an `if` clause in Figure 9-19. The function's header indicates that the function is expecting to receive two values, in this order: an integer that represents the amount sold and a `double` number that represents the bonus rate. Because of this, the function call passes two actual arguments in the required data type and order: the `int sales` variable first and the `double rate` variable second. The computer stores the values of the actual arguments in the `getBonus` function's formal parameters, which are named `sold` and `bonusRate`. Notice that the names of the actual arguments do not have to be identical to the names of their corresponding formal parameters. In fact, to avoid confusion, you should use different names for the actual arguments and formal parameters. The `getBonus` function uses the values in its formal parameters to calculate the salesperson's bonus. It then returns the bonus as a `double` number to the `if` clause, whose condition compares the return value to the `double` number 999.99. The condition will evaluate to true when the return value is greater than 999.99. It will evaluate to false when the return value is either less than or equal to 999.99.

<u>`getRectangleArea` function call (Figure 9-18) and function definition (Figure 9-17)</u>

```
cout << getRectangleArea(7.25, 21.0);

double getRectangleArea(double len, double wid)
{
      return len * wid;
}     //end of getRectangleArea function
```

<u>`getBonus` function call (Figure 9-18) and function definition (Figure 9-17)</u>

```
if (getBonus(sales, rate) > 999.99)

double getBonus(int sold, double bonusRate)
{
      double bonus = 0.0;

      bonus = sold * bonusRate;
      return bonus;
}     //end of getBonus function
```

Figure 9-19 Function calls and function definitions

Keep in mind that when the computer encounters a statement that calls a function, it temporarily leaves the calling function to process the code contained in the called function. It returns to the calling function only after the called function ends.

Now that you know how to both create and call a program-defined value-returning function, you can code the `main` and `getRandomNumber` functions. Figure 9-20 shows the IPO chart information and C++ instructions for both functions. The statements that call the `getRandomNumber` function are shaded in the figure. (The IPO charts for both functions are shown earlier in Figure 9-16.)

`main` function **IPO chart information**	**C++ instructions**
Input	
user's answer	`int userAnswer = 0;`
Processing	
first random number (1 to 10)	`int num1 = 0;`
second random number (1 to 10)	`int num2 = 0;`
counter (1 to 5)	*this variable is created and initialized in the for clause*
correct answer	`int correctAnswer = 0;`
Output	
addition problem	*this contains string literal constants and the num1 and num2 variables*
message	*this is one of two messages composed of either a string literal constant or string literal constants and the correctAnswer variable*
Algorithm	
1. initialize the random number generator	`srand(static_cast<int>(time(0)));`
2. repeat for (counter from 1 to 5)	`for (int x = 1; x < 6; x += 1)` `{`
call the getRandomNumber function to generate the first random number	`num1 = getRandomNumber();`
call the getRandomNumber function to generate the second random number	`num2 = getRandomNumber();`
calculate the correct answer by adding together the first random number and the second random number	`correctAnswer = num1 + num2;`
display the addition problem	`cout << "What is the sum of "` `<< num1 << " + " << num2 << "? ";`
enter the user's answer	`cin >> userAnswer;`
if (user's answer matches correct answer)	`if (userAnswer == correctAnswer)`
display "Correct!" message	`cout << "Correct!";`
else	`else`
display "Sorry, the correct answer is" message followed by the correct answer and a period	`cout << "Sorry, the correct answer is " << correctAnswer << ".";`
end if	`//end if`
display two blank lines	`cout << endl << endl;`
end repeat	`} //end for`

Figure 9-20 IPO chart information and C++ instructions for the modified random addition problems program *(continues)*

(continued)

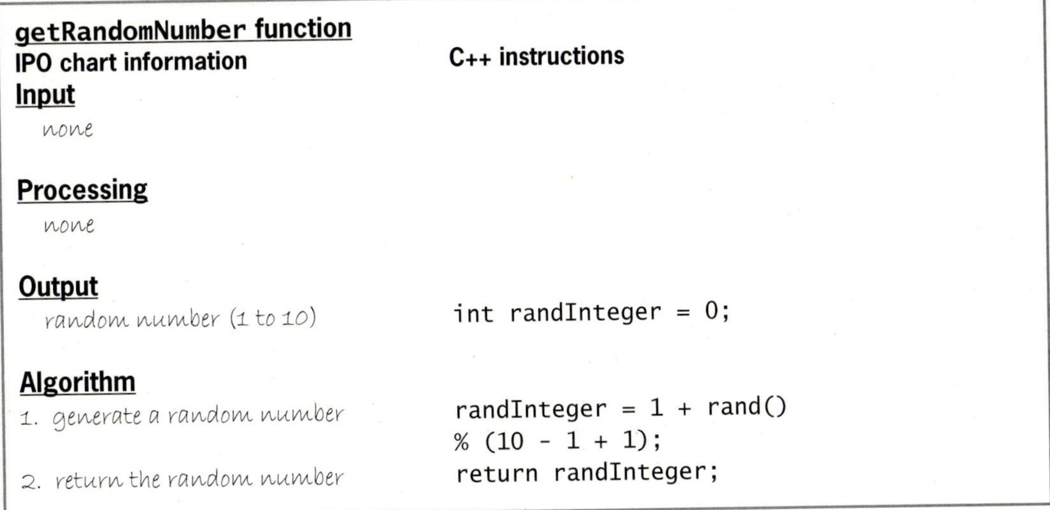

getRandomNumber function IPO chart information	C++ instructions
Input none	
Processing none	
Output random number (1 to 10)	`int randInteger = 0;`
Algorithm 1. generate a random number	`randInteger = 1 + rand() % (10 - 1 + 1);`
2. return the random number	`return randInteger;`

Figure 9-20 IPO chart information and C++ instructions for the modified random addition problems program

Function Prototypes

Most C++ programmers enter the function definitions below the `main` function in a program. When a function definition appears below the `main` function, you must enter a function prototype *above* the `main` function; otherwise, the compiler won't recognize the function's name when it is used in the `main` function. A **function prototype** is a statement that specifies the function's name, the data type of its return value, and the data type of each of its formal parameters (if any). You also can include the name of each of the formal parameters; however, that is not a requirement.

A program will have one function prototype for each function defined below the `main` function. You usually place the function prototypes at the beginning of the program, after the `#include` directives and `using namespace std;` statement. A function prototype alerts the C++ compiler that the function will be defined later in the program. The function prototypes in a program are similar to the table of contents in a book. As does each entry in a table of contents, each prototype is simply a preview of what will be expanded on later in the program (or in the book).

Keep in mind that a function prototype is necessary only when the function is defined *below* the `main` function in the program. It is not needed for a function whose definition appears *above* the `main` function. In this book, the function definitions will be entered below the `main` function because that is the format used by most C++ programmers. This means that each program-defined function will need a corresponding function prototype above the `main` function.

Figure 9-21 shows a function prototype's syntax, which is almost identical to a function header's syntax. However, unlike a function header, a function prototype ends with a semicolon. Also included in Figure 9-21 are function prototypes for the functions defined earlier in Figure 9-17. As Examples 2 and 3 indicate, it is not necessary to include the names of the formal parameters in a function prototype. However, many programmers include the names to make the program easier to read and understand. Some also include the names for convenience because it makes entering the function prototype an easy task: All you need to do is copy the function's header, then paste it in the function prototype section of the program, and then type a semicolon at the end of it.

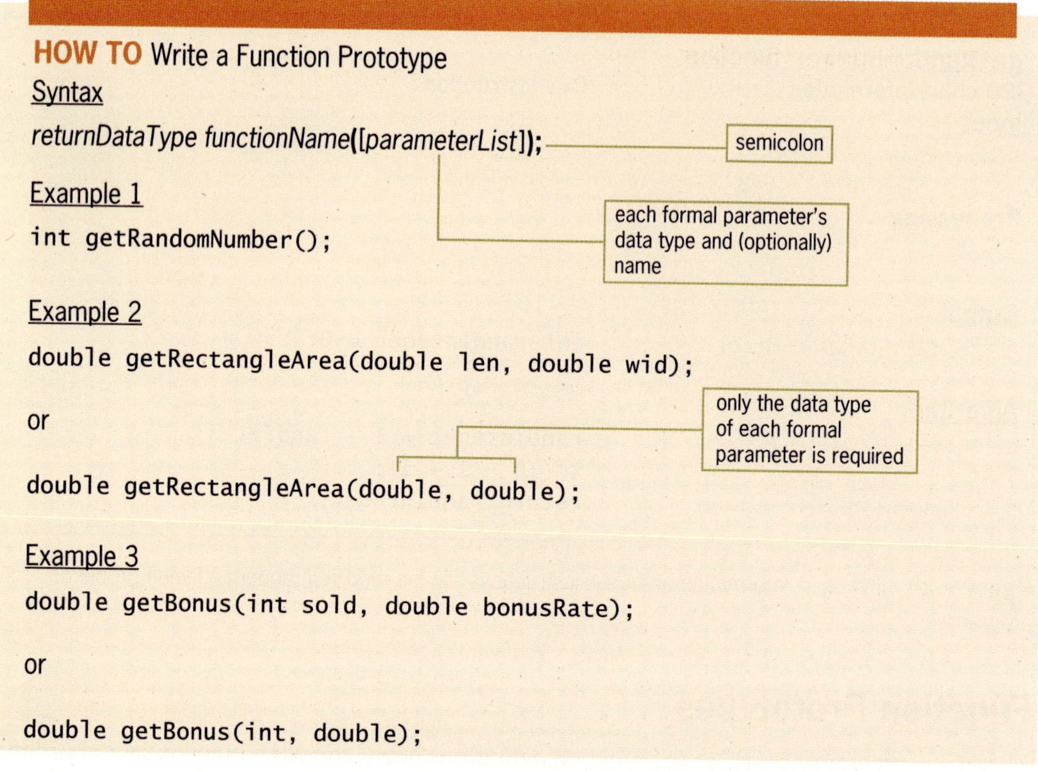

Figure 9-21 How to write a function prototype

Ch09-Modified Random video

Figure 9-22 shows the complete code for the modified random numbers addition program. Changes made to the original program's code (shown earlier in Figure 9-14) are shaded in the figure. The program contains a function prototype on Line 14. The prototype alerts the computer that the `getRandomNumber` function is defined somewhere below the `main` function in the program. In this case, the function definition appears on Lines 56 through 62. Some programmers use a comment to separate the function definitions from the `main` function, as shown on Line 55; however, this is not a requirement.

The statements that call the `getRandomNumber` function are on Lines 32 and 33 in Figure 9-22. When the computer processes the `num1 = getRandomNumber();` statement, it temporarily leaves the `main` function to process the `getRandomNumber` function's code. The function header is processed first and simply marks the beginning of the function. The statements in the function body are processed next. The first statement creates and initializes the `randInteger` variable. The second statement generates a random integer from 1 through 10 and then assigns the random integer to the variable. The third (and last) statement returns the value stored in the `randInteger` variable to the statement that called the function. In this case, it returns the value to the `num1 = getRandomNumber();` statement, which assigns the value to the `num1` variable. After the `return` statement is processed, the `getRandomNumber` function ends and the computer removes the `randInteger` variable from its internal memory. Processing continues with the statement that called the `getRandomNumber` function. The same procedure is followed when the computer processes the `num2 = getRandomNumber();` statement, except the `getRandomNumber` function's return value is assigned to the `num2` variable.

```
//Modified Random Addition.cpp
//Displays random addition problems
//Allows the user to enter the answer and then
//displays a message that indicates whether the
//user's answer is correct or incorrect
//Created/revised by <your name> on <current date>

#include <iostream>
#include <ctime>
//#include <cstdlib>
using namespace std;

//function prototype
int getRandomNumber();

int main()
{
    //declare variables
    int num1          = 0;
    int num2          = 0;
    int correctAnswer = 0;
    int userAnswer    = 0;

    //initialize rand function
    srand(static_cast<int>(time(0)));

    for (int x = 1; x < 6; x += 1)
    {
        //generate two random integers
        //from 1 through 10, then
        //calculate the sum
        num1 = getRandomNumber();
        num2 = getRandomNumber();
        correctAnswer = num1 + num2;

        //display addition problem and get user's answer
        cout << "What is the sum of " << num1
            << " + " << num2 << "? ";
        cin >> userAnswer;

        //determine whether user's answer is correct
        if (userAnswer == correctAnswer)
            cout << "Correct!";
        else
            cout << "Sorry, the correct answer is "
                << correctAnswer << ".";
        //end if
        cout << endl << endl;
    }   //end for

    //system("pause");
    return 0;
}   //end of main function
```

your C++ development tool may require this directive

function prototype

function calls

your C++ development tool may require this statement

Figure 9-22 Modified random addition problems program *(continues)*

(continued)

```
//*****function definitions*****
int getRandomNumber()
{
    int randInteger = 0;
    //generate random integer from 1 through 10
    randInteger = 1 + rand() % (10 - 1 + 1);
    return randInteger;
} //end of getRandomNumber function
```

function definition

Figure 9-22 Modified random addition problems program

The Western Elementary School Program

The principal of Western Elementary School would like to use the random addition problems program that you completed in the previous section. However, she wants the ability to specify the range of random numbers that appear each time the program is run. To accomplish this, the program will need to allow the user to enter the smallest and largest integer in the desired range. The two function calls in the program will send that information to the `getRandomNumber` function. Figure 9-23 shows the Western Elementary School program. The changes made to the code shown in Figure 9-22 are shaded in Figure 9-23.

```
//Western Elementary.cpp
//Displays random addition problems
//Allows the user to enter the answer and then
//displays a message that indicates whether the
//user's answer is correct or incorrect
//Created/revised by <your name> on <current date>

#include <iostream>
#include <ctime>
//#include <cstdlib>
using namespace std;

//function prototype
int getRandomNumber(int lower, int upper);

int main()
{
    //declare variables
    int smallest      = 0;
    int largest       = 0;
    int num1          = 0;
    int num2          = 0;
    int correctAnswer = 0;
    int userAnswer    = 0;

    //initialize rand function
    srand(static_cast<int>(time(0)));

```

your C++ development tool may require this directive

the names are not required

Figure 9-23 Western Elementary School program *(continues)*

(continued)

```
29        cout << "Smallest integer: ";
30        cin >> smallest;
31        cout << "Largest integer: ";
32        cin >> largest;
33        cout << endl;
34
35        for (int x = 1; x < 6; x += 1)
36        {
37            //generate two random integers
38            //from smallest through largest, then
39            //calculate the sum
40            num1 = getRandomNumber(smallest, largest);
41            num2 = getRandomNumber(smallest, largest);
42            correctAnswer = num1 + num2;
43
44            //display addition problem and get user's answer
45            cout << "What is the sum of " << num1
46                 << " + " << num2 << "? ";
47            cin >> userAnswer;
48
49            //determine whether user's answer is correct
50            if (userAnswer == correctAnswer)
51                 cout << "Correct!";
52            else
53                 cout << "Sorry, the correct answer is "
54                        << correctAnswer << ".";
55            //end if
56            cout << endl << endl;
57       }    //end for
58
59       //system("pause");
60       return 0;
61   } //end of main function
62
63   //*****function definitions*****
64   int getRandomNumber(int lower, int upper)
65   {
66       int randInteger = 0;
67       //generate random integer from lower through upper
68       randInteger = lower + rand() % (upper - lower + 1);
69       return randInteger;
70   } //end of getRandomNumber function
```

gets the smallest and largest integers in the range

passes the smallest and largest integers to the `getRandomNumber` function

your C++ development tool may require this statement

receives the smallest and largest integers from each function call on Lines 39 and 40

Figure 9-23 Western Elementary School program

The Western Elementary School program provides an example of code reuse. It also demonstrates how you can use functions to improve programming productivity by splitting larger problems into a series of smaller problems. Each small problem can be assigned to a member of the programming team. In this case, for example, you can code the `main` function while your friend Sam codes the `getRandomNumber` function. By splitting the work in this manner, you won't need to worry about the code for generating the random numbers. Whenever the `main` function needs a random number, you can simply call Sam's function to get one. Actually, you can use Sam's function in any program that requires a random integer within a specific range; you just need to enter the function definition in the program. (Depending on where you enter the function definition, you also may need the function prototype.) Sam will also be using another programmer's code in his `getRandomNumber` function. More specifically, he'll be using the C++ built-in `rand` function. Figure 9-24 shows a sample run of the Western Elementary School program.

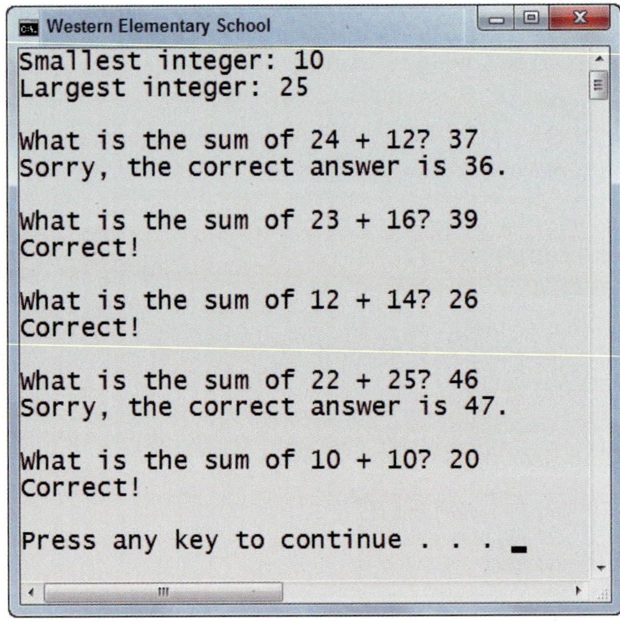

Figure 9-24 Sample run of the Western Elementary School program

The answers to Mini-Quiz questions are located in Appendix A.

Mini-Quiz 9-3

1. The `getArea` function returns a `double` number and has no formal parameters. Which of the following calls the `getArea` function and assigns its return value to a `double` variable named `area`?

   a. `area = getArea`

   b. `area = getArea();`

   c. `area = getArea(double);`

   d. `getArea(area);`

2. Which of the following is a valid function prototype for the `getArea` function from Question 1?
   a. `double getArea()`
   b. `double getArea`
   c. `double getArea();`
   d. `double getArea;`
3. Write a C++ statement that will display the value returned by the `getArea` function from Question 1.
4. Write a function prototype for the `getGrossPay` function. The function returns a `double` number and has two formal parameters: an `int` variable named `hours` and a `double` variable named `rate`.
5. Write a statement that invokes the `getGrossPay` function from Question 4. The statement should pass the function the integer 40 and a copy of the value stored in a `double` variable named `payRate`. The statement should assign the function's return value to a `double` variable named `weekGross`.

The Area Calculator Program

Figure 9-25 shows the problem specification and IPO charts for the area calculator program. The program uses a program-defined value-returning function to calculate the area of a rectangle, given the rectangle's length and width measurements. The program displays the area on the computer screen.

Problem specification
Create a program that allows the user to enter a rectangle's length and width (in feet). The program should calculate and display the rectangle's area in square feet.

`main` function

Input	Processing	Output
length (feet) width (feet)	Processing items: none Algorithm: 1. enter the length and width 2. call the getRectangleArea function to calculate the area; pass the length and width 3. display the area	area (square feet)

Figure 9-25 Problem specification and IPO charts for the area calculator program *(continues)*

(continued)

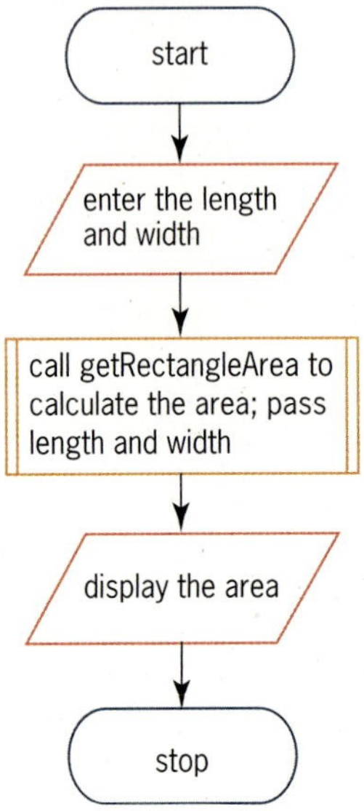

start

enter the length and width

call getRectangleArea to calculate the area; pass length and width

display the area

stop

getRectangleArea function

Input	**Processing**	**Output**
length (feet) width (feet)	Processing items: none Algorithm: 1. return the area, which is the result of multiplying the length by the width	area (square feet)

start

return the area, which is the result of multiplying the length by the width

stop

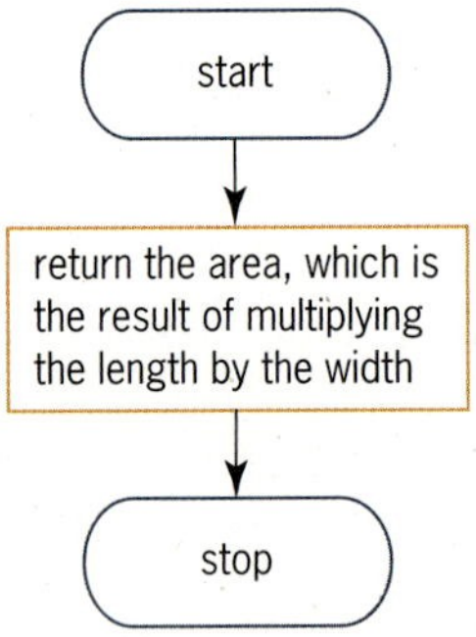

Figure 9-25 Problem specification and IPO charts for the area calculator program

Figure 9-26 shows a sample run of the program, and Figure 9-27 shows the program's code.

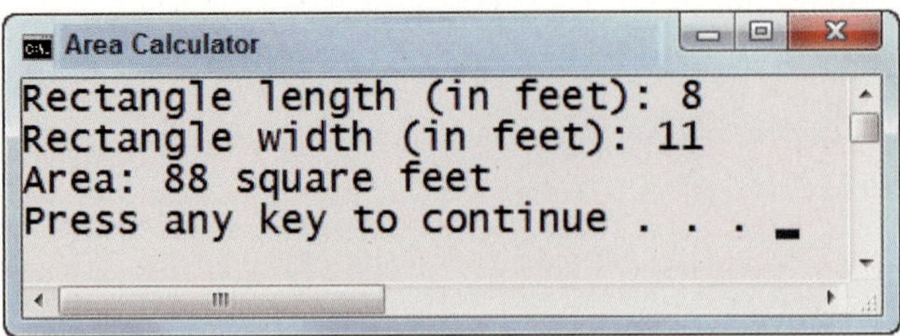

Figure 9-26 Sample run of the area calculator program

```
1   //Area Calculator.cpp - displays the area of a rectangle
2   //Created/revised by <your name> on <current date>
3
4   #include <iostream>
5   using namespace std;
6
7   //function prototype
8   double getRectangleArea(double len, double wid);
9
10  int main()
11  {
12      double length = 0.0;
13      double width  = 0.0;
14      double area   = 0.0;
15
16      cout << "Rectangle length (in feet): ";
17      cin >> length;
18      cout << "Rectangle width (in feet): ";
19      cin >> width;
20
21      area = getRectangleArea(length, width);
22      cout << "Area: " << area << " square feet" << endl;
23
24      //system("pause");
25      return 0;
26  }   //end of main function
27
28  //*****function definitions*****
29  double getRectangleArea(double len, double wid)
30  {
31      return len * wid;
32  }   //end of getRectangleArea function
```

the names are not required

function call

your C++ development tool may require this statement

function header

Figure 9-27 Area calculator program

You will desk-check the area calculator program shown in Figure 9-27 using the `double` numbers 8.0 and 11.0 as the rectangle's length and width, respectively. Desk-checking the program will help you understand how the computer processes a program-defined value-returning function when it is invoked. The statements on Lines 12 through 14 in the program create and initialize three `double` variables named `length`, `width`, and `area`. The statements on Lines 16 through 19 prompt the user to enter the length and width of the rectangle and then store the user's responses in the `length` and `width` variables, respectively. Figure 9-28 shows the desk-check table after the statements are processed.

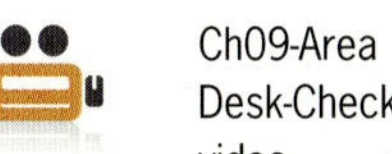

Ch09-Area Desk-Check video

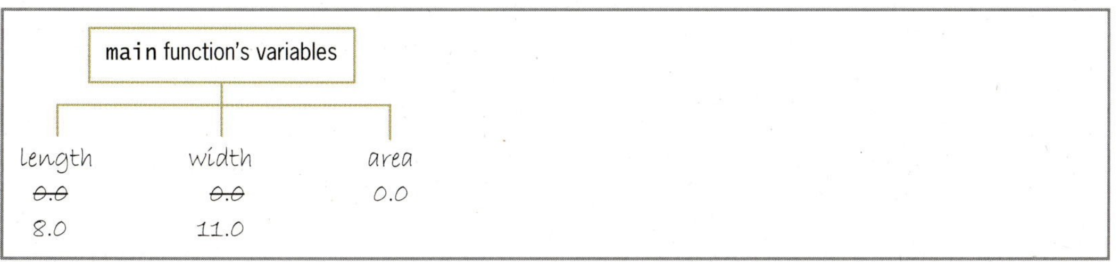

Figure 9-28 Desk-check table after the statements on Lines 12 through 19 are processed

The assignment statement on Line 21 calls the `getRectangleArea` function, passing it two actual arguments: the `double length` variable and the `double width` variable. Recall that unless specified otherwise, variables in C++ are passed *by value*, which means that only a copy of the variable's contents is passed to the function. In this case, the computer passes the numbers 8.0 and 11.0 to the `getRectangleArea` function. At this point, the computer temporarily leaves the `main` function to process the `getRectangleArea` function's code, beginning with the function header on Line 29 in the program.

The `getRectangleArea` function's header contains two formal parameters. The formal parameters tell the computer to reserve two memory locations: a `double` variable named `len` and a `double` variable named `wid`. After reserving the `len` and `wid` variables, the computer stores the values passed to the function—in this case, the numbers 8.0 and 11.0—in the variables. Figure 9-29 shows the desk-check table after the `getRectangleArea` function header is processed.

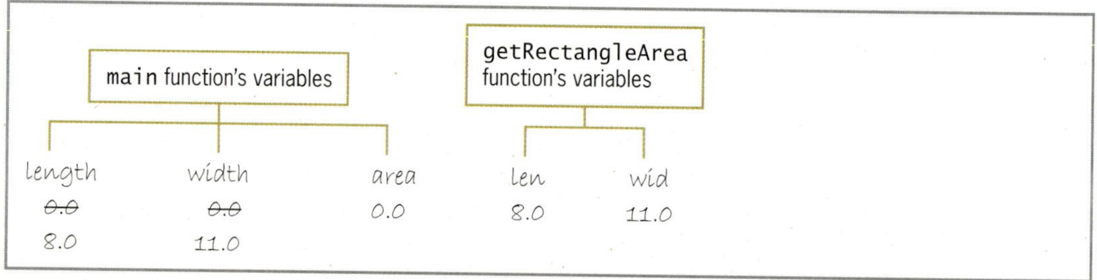

Figure 9-29 Desk-check table after the `getRectangleArea` function header is processed

Next, the computer processes the `return len * wid;` statement on Line 31 in the `getRectangleArea` function. The statement multiplies the `len` variable's value by the `wid` variable's value and then returns the result to the statement that called the `getRectangleArea` function. In this case, it returns the `double` number 88.0 to the assignment statement on Line 21 in the `main` function. The statement assigns the `double` number to the `area` variable.

After the `getRectangleArea` function's `return` statement is processed, the function ends and the computer removes the `len` and `wid` variables from its internal memory. Figure 9-30 shows the desk-check table at this point in the program. Notice that only the `main` function's variables are still in the computer's internal memory.

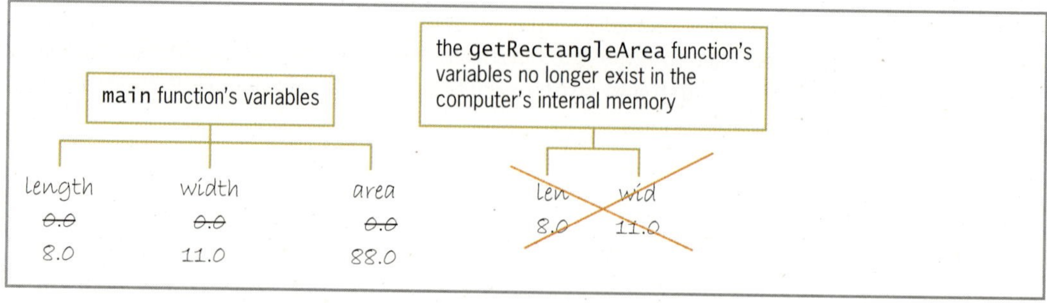

Figure 9-30 Desk-check table after the `getRectangleArea` function ends

Next, the computer processes the `cout` statement on Line 22. The statement displays the contents of the `area` variable on the screen. The `return 0;` statement is processed next. The statement returns the number 0 to the operating system to indicate that the program ended normally. After the statement is processed, the `main` function ends and the computer removes the `length`, `width`, and `area` variables from its internal memory.

At this point, you may be wondering why the program needs to pass the contents of the `length` and `width` variables to the `getRectangleArea` function. Why can't the function just use both variables in its `return` statement, like this: `return length * width;`? You also may be wondering why the computer removes the `len` and `wid` variables from memory after the `getRectangleArea` function ends, but waits until the `main` function ends before it removes the `length`, `width`, and `area` variables. Why are the variables removed from memory at different times? To answer these questions, you will need to learn about the scope and lifetime of a variable. The scope and lifetime of a variable are the last topics covered in this chapter.

The Scope and Lifetime of a Variable

A variable's **scope** indicates where in the program the variable can be used, and its **lifetime** indicates how long the variable remains in the computer's internal memory. Although variables can have either local or global scope, most of the variables used in a program will have local scope. This is because fewer unintentional errors occur in programs when the variables are declared using the minimum scope needed, which usually is local scope.

You can experiment with the concepts of scope and lifetime by completing Computer Exercise 19 at the end of the chapter.

A variable's scope and lifetime are determined by where you declare the variable in the program. Variables declared within a function, and those that appear in a function's *parameterList*, have a local scope and are referred to as local variables. **Local variables** can be used only by the function in which they are declared or in whose *parameterList* they appear. Local variables remain in the computer's internal memory until the function ends.

Unlike local variables, **global variables** are declared outside of any function in the program, and they remain in memory until the program ends. Also unlike a local variable, any statement in the program can use a global variable. Declaring a variable as global rather than local allows unintentional errors to occur when a function that should not have access to the variable inadvertently changes the variable's contents. Because of this, you should avoid using global variables in your programs. If more than one function needs access to the same variable, it is better to create a local variable in one of the functions and then pass that variable to the other functions that need it.

In the area calculator program shown earlier in Figure 9-27, the `length`, `width`, and `area` variables are declared on Lines 12 through 14 in the `main` function. As a result, the variables are local to the `main` function and can be used only by statements below Line 14 within the `main` function. The `getRectangleArea` function is not even aware of the existence of these variables in memory. If you want the `getRectangleArea` function to use the values stored in the `length` and `width` variables, you will need to pass each variable's value to the function.

The `len` and `wid` variables, on the other hand, are local to the `getRectangleArea` function because they appear in the function's *parameterList*. Therefore, only the statements within the `getRectangleArea` function can use the `len` and `wid` variables. As mentioned earlier, local variables remain in the computer's internal memory until the function in which they are created ends. This explains why the `len` and `wid` variables are removed from memory after the `getRectangleArea` function ends. It also explains why the computer waits until the `main` function ends before it removes the `length`, `width`, and `area` variables from memory.

Now that you understand the concepts of scope and lifetime, you will view and desk-check a program that uses two program-defined value-returning functions.

The Bonus Calculator Program

Figure 9-31 shows the problem specification for the bonus calculator program. The program calculates and displays a salesperson's bonus, which is 5% of his or her sales. The figure also shows the IPO chart information and C++ instructions for the `main` function, which calls two program-defined value-returning functions named `getSales` and `getBonus`. The IPO charts and C++ instructions for the `getSales` and `getBonus` functions are shown in Figures 9-32 and 9-33, respectively.

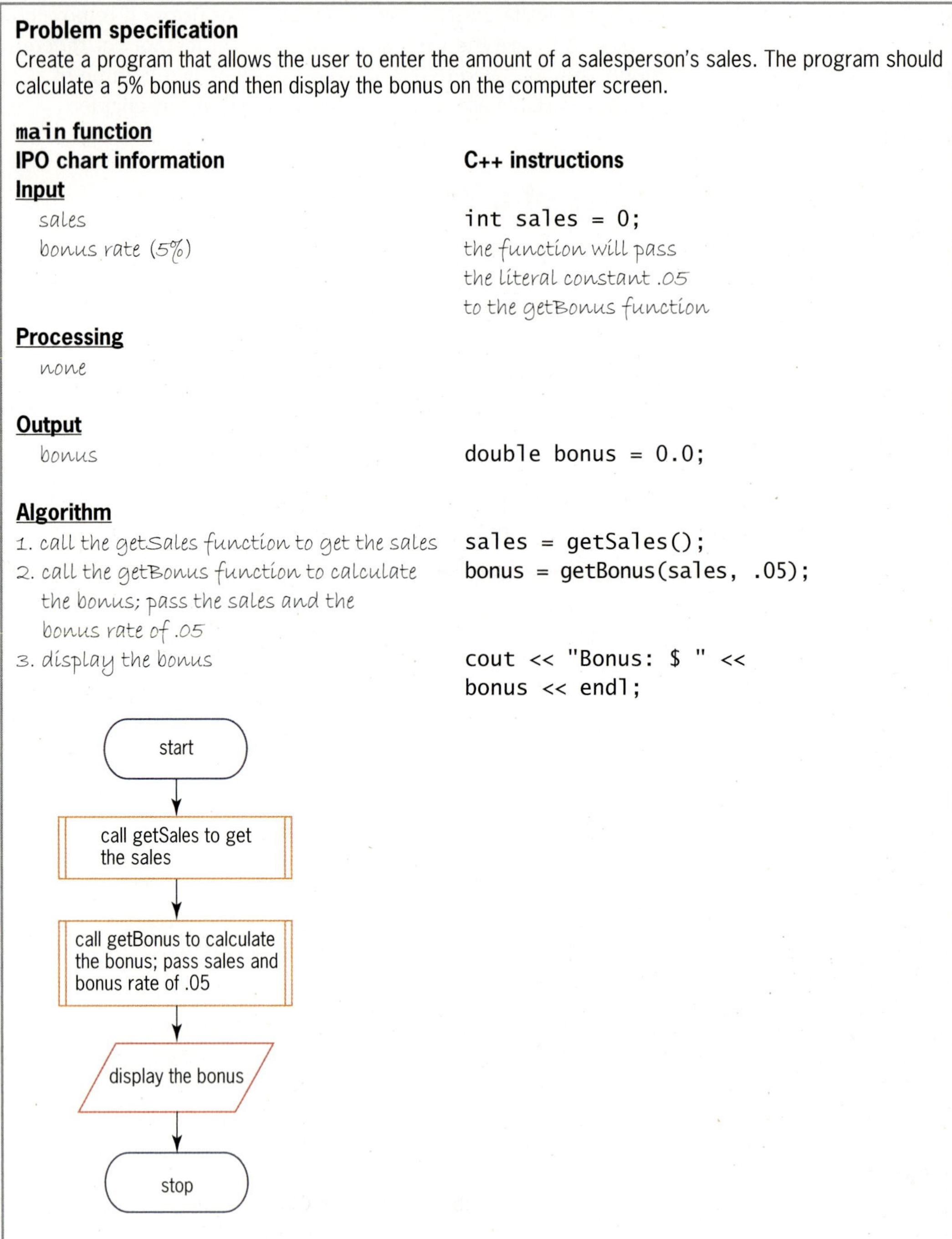

Problem specification

Create a program that allows the user to enter the amount of a salesperson's sales. The program should calculate a 5% bonus and then display the bonus on the computer screen.

`main` function

IPO chart information	C++ instructions
Input	
sales	`int sales = 0;`
bonus rate (5%)	the function will pass the literal constant .05 to the getBonus function
Processing	
none	
Output	
bonus	`double bonus = 0.0;`
Algorithm	
1. call the getSales function to get the sales	`sales = getSales();`
2. call the getBonus function to calculate the bonus; pass the sales and the bonus rate of .05	`bonus = getBonus(sales, .05);`
3. display the bonus	`cout << "Bonus: $ " << bonus << endl;`

Figure 9-31 Problem specification, IPO chart information, and C++ code for the `main` function

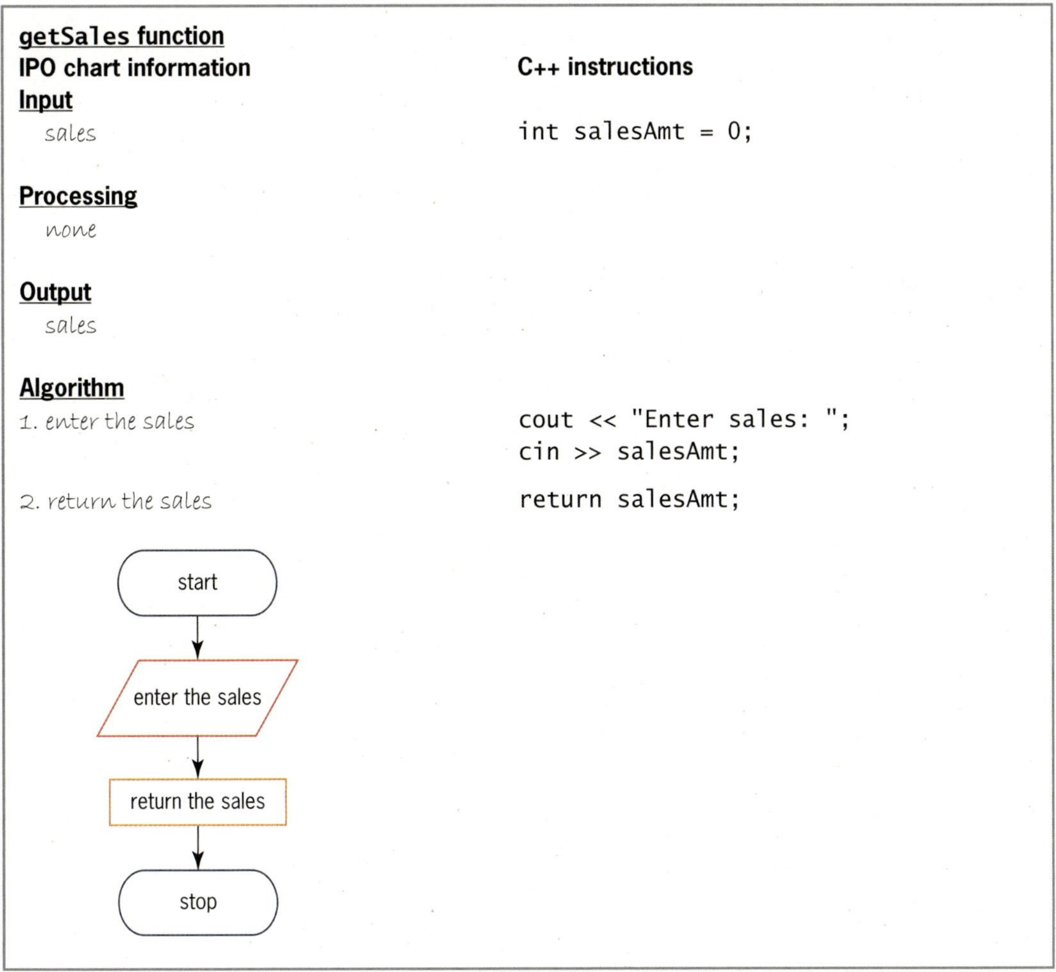

getSales function	
IPO chart information	**C++ instructions**
Input	
sales	`int salesAmt = 0;`
Processing	
none	
Output	
sales	
Algorithm	
1. enter the sales	`cout << "Enter sales: ";` `cin >> salesAmt;`
2. return the sales	`return salesAmt;`

Figure 9-32 IPO chart information and C++ code for the getSales function

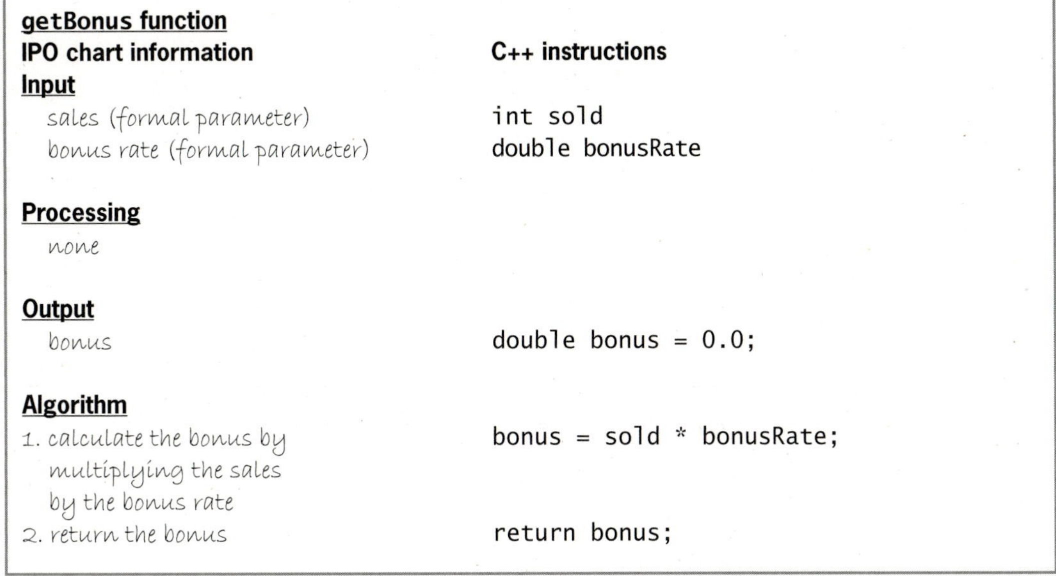

getBonus function	
IPO chart information	**C++ instructions**
Input	
sales (formal parameter)	`int sold`
bonus rate (formal parameter)	`double bonusRate`
Processing	
none	
Output	
bonus	`double bonus = 0.0;`
Algorithm	
1. calculate the bonus by multiplying the sales by the bonus rate	`bonus = sold * bonusRate;`
2. return the bonus	`return bonus;`

Figure 9-33 IPO chart information and C++ code for the getBonus function *(continues)*

(continued)

Figure 9-33 IPO chart information and C++ code for the `getBonus` function

Figure 9-34 shows a sample run of the bonus calculator program, and Figure 9-35 shows the C++ code for the entire program. The function calls appear on Lines 19 and 20 in the `main` function and are shaded in the figure. The function definitions are located below the `main` function, on Lines 31 through 44. The function prototypes are located above the `main` function, on Lines 9 and 10.

Figure 9-34 Sample run of the bonus calculator program

```
 1  //Bonus Calculator.cpp - displays the amount of a bonus
 2  //Created/revised by <your name> on <current date>
 3
 4  #include <iostream>
 5  #include <iomanip>
 6  using namespace std;
 7
 8  //function prototypes
 9  int getSales();
10  double getBonus(int sold, double bonusRate);
11
12  int main()
13  {
14      int sales    = 0;
15      double bonus = 0.0;
16
```

Figure 9-35 Bonus calculator program *(continues)*

(continued)

```
17      //call functions to get the sales and
18      //calculate the bonus
19      sales = getSales();
20      bonus = getBonus(sales, .05);
21
22      //display the bonus
23      cout << fixed << setprecision(2);
24      cout << "Bonus: $ " << bonus << endl;
25
26      //system("pause");
27      return 0;
28  } //end of main function
29
30  //*****function definitions*****
31  int getSales()
32  {
33      int salesAmt = 0;
34      cout << "Enter sales: ";
35      cin >> salesAmt;
36      return salesAmt;
37  } //end of getSales function
38
39  double getBonus(int sold, double bonusRate)
40  {
41      double bonus = 0.0;
42      bonus = sold * bonusRate;
43      return bonus;
44  } //end of getBonus function
```

your C++ development tool may require this statement

Figure 9-35 Bonus calculator program

You will desk-check the program shown in Figure 9-35 using 1575 as the sales amount. The statements on Lines 14 and 15 create and initialize an `int` variable named `sales` and a `double` variable named `bonus`. Both variables are local to the `main` function, which means they can be used only within that function. Both variables will remain in the computer's internal memory until the `main` function ends. Figure 9-36 shows the desk-check table after the variable declaration statements on Lines 14 and 15 are processed.

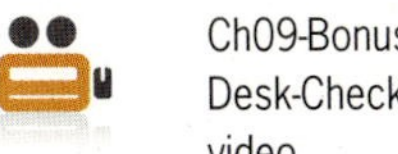

Ch09-Bonus Desk-Check video

Figure 9-36 Desk-check table after the variable declaration statements on Lines 14 and 15 are processed

When the computer encounters the `sales = getSales();` statement on Line 19, it temporarily leaves the `main` function to process the `getSales` function's code, beginning with the function header on Line 31. The function header does not contain any formal parameters, which indicates that the function does not receive any information when it is called to perform its task.

The first statement in the `getSales` function body creates and initializes an `int` variable named `salesAmt`. The variable is local to the `getSales` function, which means it can be used only within that function. The `salesAmt` variable will remain in the computer's internal memory until the `getSales` function ends. The next two statements in the `getSales` function prompt the user to enter a sales amount and then store the user's response (1575) in the `salesAmt` variable. Figure 9-37 shows the sales amount entered in the desk-check table.

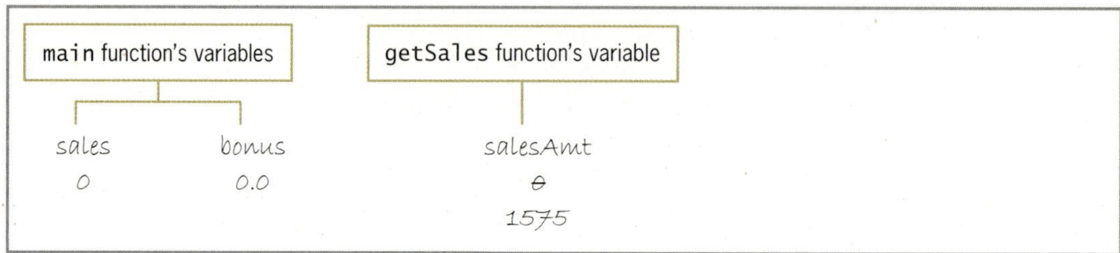

Figure 9-37 Desk-check table after the sales amount is entered

Next, the computer processes the `getSales` function's `return` statement, which returns the `salesAmt` variable's value to the statement that called the function. In this case, it returns the value to the assignment statement on Line 19 in the `main` function. The statement assigns the return value to the `sales` variable, as shown in Figure 9-38.

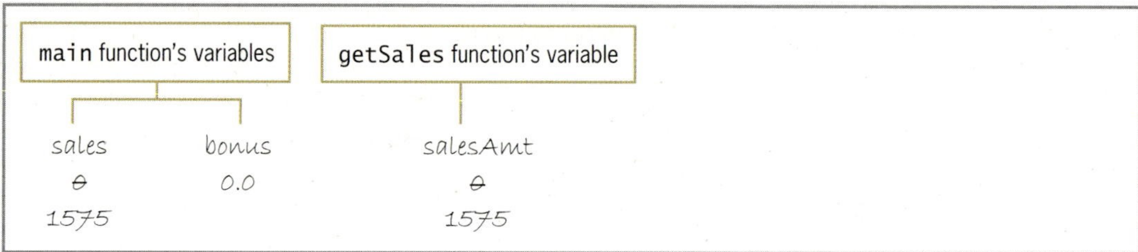

Figure 9-38 Desk-check table after the sales amount is returned to the `main` function

After its `return` statement is processed, the `getSales` function ends and the computer removes the `salesAmt` variable from memory. Figure 9-39 shows the desk-check table after the `getSales` function ends. Only the `main` function's variables are still in memory.

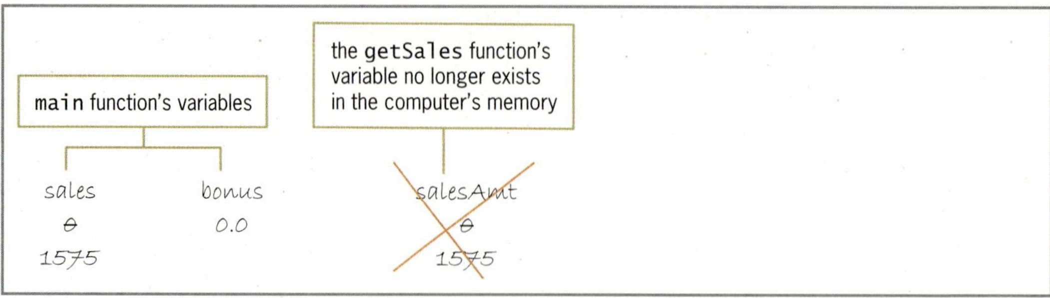

Figure 9-39 Desk-check table after the `getSales` function ends

Next, the computer processes the `bonus = getBonus(sales, .05);` statement on Line 20 in the `main` function. The statement calls the `getBonus` function, passing it two actual arguments. Here again, the computer temporarily leaves the `main` function. However, in this case, it does so to process the code in the `getBonus` function, beginning with the function header.

The two formal parameters in the `getBonus` function's *parameterList* tell the computer to create two variables: an `int` variable named `sold` and a `double` variable named `bonusRate`. The variables are local to the `getBonus` function and can be used only within that function. The computer stores the first value passed to the function in the function's first formal parameter, and it stores the second value passed to the function in the function's second formal parameter. In this case, it stores the `sales` variable's value in the `sold` variable and the numeric literal constant .05 in the `bonusRate` variable, as shown in Figure 9-40.

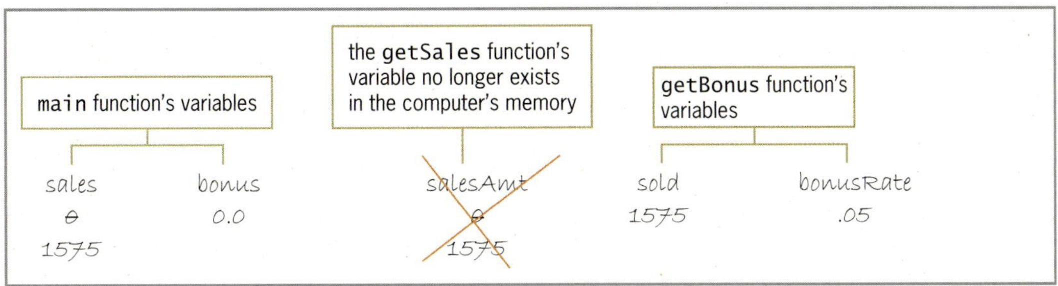

Figure 9-40 Desk-check table after the `getBonus` function header is processed

The first statement in the `getBonus` function declares an additional local variable: a `double` variable named `bonus`. The second statement multiplies the contents of the `sold` variable by the contents of the `bonusRate` variable and assigns the result (78.75) to the `bonus` variable, as shown in the desk-check table in Figure 9-41. The desk-check table indicates that two locations in the computer's memory have the same name: `bonus`. When the `bonus` name appears in a statement, the computer uses the position of the statement in the program to determine which of the two locations to use. If the program statement appears in the `main` function, the computer uses the `bonus` variable located in the `main` function's section in memory. However, if the program statement appears in the `getBonus` function, the computer uses the `bonus` variable located in the `getBonus` function's section in memory.

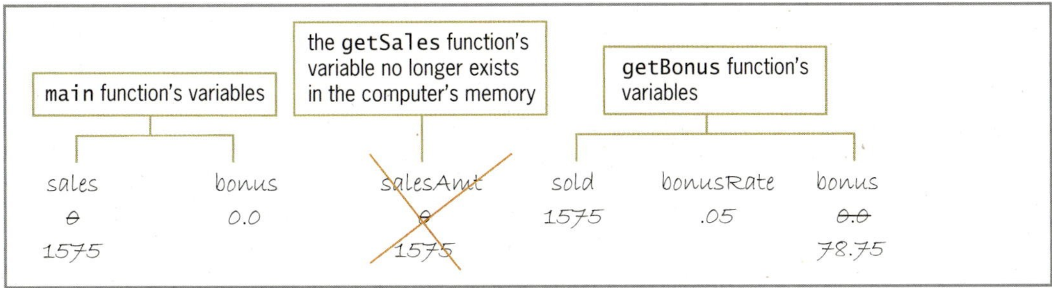

Figure 9-41 Desk-check table after the bonus is calculated

Next, the computer processes the `getBonus` function's `return` statement. The statement returns the value stored in the function's `bonus` variable to the statement that called the function. In this case, it returns the value to the assignment statement on Line 20 in the `main` function. The statement assigns the value it receives to the `main` function's `bonus` variable.

At this point, the getBonus function ends and the computer removes the function's local variables (sold, bonusRate, and bonus) from memory. Figure 9-42 shows the desk-check table after the getBonus function ends. Only the main function's variables are still in the computer's internal memory.

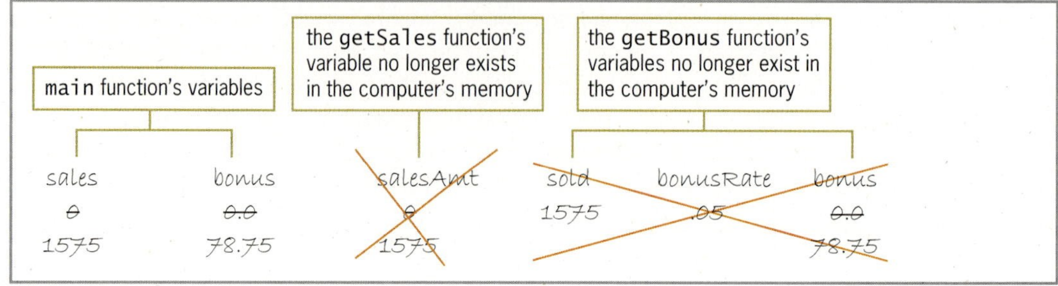

Figure 9-42 Desk-check table after the getBonus function ends

For more examples of value-returning functions, see the Value-Returning Functions section in the Ch09WantMore.pdf file.

After the getBonus function ends, the computer processes the remaining instructions in the main function. When the main function ends, the computer removes the function's variables (sales and bonus) from memory.

The answers to Mini-Quiz questions are located in Appendix A.

Mini-Quiz 9-4

1. A variable's lifetime indicates the portions of a program that can use the variable.
   a. True
   b. False
2. Unless specified otherwise, variables in C++ are passed *by contents*.
   a. True
   b. False
3. The variables in a function header have local scope.
   a. True
   b. False
4. Two functions in a program declare a variable using the same name. How does the computer know which variable to use?

LAB 9-1 Stop and Analyze

Study the program shown in Figure 9-43, and then answer the questions.

The answers to the labs are located in Appendix A.

```
1  //Lab9-1.cpp - simulates a number guessing game
2  //Created/revised by <your name> on <current date>
3
4  #include <iostream>
5  #include <ctime>
6  //#include <cstdlib>
7  using namespace std;
8
9  int main()
10 {
11     //declare variables
12     int randomNumber = 0;
13     int numberGuess  = 0;
14
15     //generate a random number from 1 through 10
16     srand(static_cast<int>(time(0)));
17     randomNumber = 1 + rand() % (10 - 1 + 1);
18
19     //get first number guess from user
20     cout << "Guess a number from 1 through 10: ";
21     cin >> numberGuess;
22
23     while (numberGuess != randomNumber)
24     {
25         cout << "Sorry, guess again: ";
26         cin >> numberGuess;
27     }   //end while
28
29     cout << endl << "Yes, the number is "
30         << randomNumber << "." << endl;
31
32     //system("pause");
33     return 0;
34 }   //end of main function
```

your C++ development tool may require this directive

your C++ development tool may require this statement

Figure 9-43 Code for Lab 9-1

QUESTIONS

1. Why is the instruction on Line 5 necessary?
2. What is the purpose of the statement on Line 16?
3. If the `rand` function on Line 17 returns the number 453, what number will be assigned to the `randomNumber` variable?
4. Follow the instructions for starting C++ and viewing the Lab9-1.cpp file, which is contained in either the Cpp7\Chap09\Lab9-1 Project folder or the Cpp7\Chap09 folder. (Depending on your C++ development tool, you may need to open Lab9-1's project/solution file first.) If necessary, delete the two forward slashes that appear

before the `system("pause");` statement and/or the `#include <cstdlib>` directive, and then save the program. Run the program. Enter a number from 1 through 10. If you entered the correct number, the program displays the "Yes, the number is *x*." message, in which *x* is the number you entered. If you did not enter the correct number, the program displays the "Sorry, guess again:" message. Continue entering numbers until you guess the correct number.

5. Modify the program so that it allows the user to make only four incorrect guesses. When the user has made the fourth incorrect guess, display the random number on the screen. Save and then run the program. Test the program appropriately.
6. Now modify the program so that it uses the `getRandomNumber` function shown in Figure 9-22 in the chapter. Save and then run the program. Test the program appropriately.
7. Finally, modify the program so that it uses the `getRandomNumber` function shown in Figure 9-23. If the `smallest` number is greater than the `largest` number, the `main` function should swap the numbers. Save and then run the program. Test the program appropriately.

LAB 9-2 Plan and Create

In this lab, you will plan and create an algorithm for Sydney Green. The problem specification along with sample calculations are shown in Figure 9-44. You can use a calculator or a spreadsheet program (such as Microsoft Excel) to verify the payments shown in the figure and also to perform your own calculations using the periodic payment formula.

Problem specification

While shopping for her dream car, Sydney Green has noticed that many auto dealers are offering buyers a choice of either a large cash rebate or an extremely low financing rate, much lower than the rate Sydney would pay by financing the car through her local credit union. Sydney is not sure whether to take the lower financing rate from the dealer or take the rebate and then finance the car through the credit union. She wants a program that will calculate and display her monthly car payment using both scenarios.

The formula for calculating a periodic payment on a loan is shown on the next page. In the formula, *principal* is the amount of the loan, *rate* is the periodic interest rate, and *term* is the number of periodic payments. Also shown on the next page are two examples that use the formula to calculate a periodic payment. Example 1 calculates the annual payment for a $9,000 loan for three years at 5% interest. The annual payment rounded to the nearest cent is $3,304.88. In other words, if you borrow $9,000 for three years at 5% interest, you would need to make three annual payments of $3,304.88 to pay off the loan. Example 2 calculates the monthly payment for a $12,000 loan for five years at 6% interest. To pay off this loan, you would need to make 60 payments of $231.99.

When you apply for a loan, the lender typically quotes you an annual interest rate and expresses the term in years. Therefore, when calculating a monthly payment, you must convert the annual interest rate to a monthly interest rate; you do this by dividing the annual rate by 12, as was done in Example 2. You also need to convert the term from years to months. As shown in Example 2, this is accomplished by multiplying the number of years by 12.

Figure 9-44 Problem specification and sample calculations for Lab 9-2 *(continues)*

(continued)

Periodic payment formula
principal * *rate* / (1 – (*rate* + 1)$^{-term}$)

Example 1	annual payment for a $9,000 loan for 3 years at 5% interest
Principal:	9,000
Annual rate:	.05
Term (years):	3
Formula:	9,000 * .05 / (1 – (.05 + 1)$^{-3}$)
Annual payment:	$3,304.88 (rounded to the nearest cent)

Example 2	monthly payment for a $12,000 loan for 5 years at 6% interest
Principal:	12,000
Monthly rate:	.005 (annual rate of .06 divided by 12)
Term (months):	60 (5 years multiplied by 12)
Formula:	12,000 * .005 / (1 – (.005 + 1)$^{-60}$)
Monthly payment:	$231.99 (rounded to the nearest cent)

Figure 9-44 Problem specification and sample calculations for Lab 9-2

First, analyze the problem, looking for the output first and then for the input. In this case, Sydney wants the program to display two monthly payments: the payment if she finances the car through her credit union and the payment if she finances it through the dealer. To calculate the monthly payments, the computer will need to know the following information: the price of the car (after any trade-in), the rebate amount, the credit union's annual interest rate, the dealer's annual interest rate, and the term (in years).

Next, plan the algorithm. Recall that most algorithms begin with an instruction to enter the input items into the computer, followed by instructions that process the input items, typically including the items in one or more calculations. Most algorithms end with one or more instructions that display, print, or store the output items.

Figure 9-45 shows the completed IPO charts for the program's `main` and `getPayment` functions. Notice that the `main` function calls the value-returning `getPayment` function twice: once to calculate and return the credit union payment, and again to calculate and return the dealer payment. The `getPayment` function uses the periodic payment formula to calculate the payments. To use the formula, the function needs to know three items of information: the principal, monthly rate, and number of months. These items will be passed to the `getPayment` function when it is invoked by a statement in the `main` function. When calling the `getPayment` function to calculate the credit union payment, the statement will pass the difference between the car price and the rebate as the principal. It also will pass the monthly credit union rate (which is the annual credit union rate divided by 12) and the number of months (which is the term times 12). Similarly, when calling the `getPayment` function to calculate the dealer payment, the `main` function will pass the car price as the principal, and also pass the monthly dealer rate and the number of months.

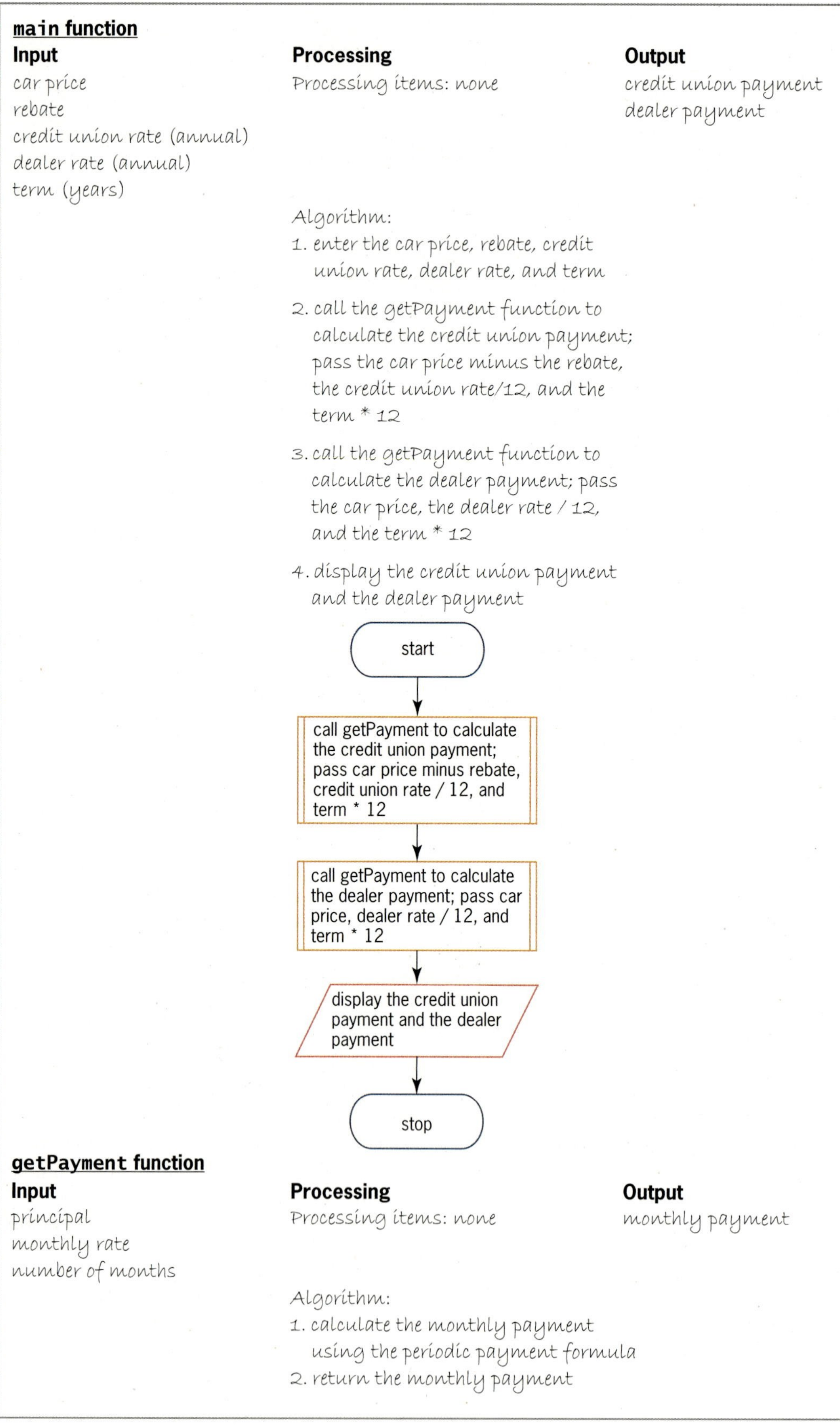

Figure 9-45 IPO charts for the `main` and `getPayment` functions *(continues)*

(continued)

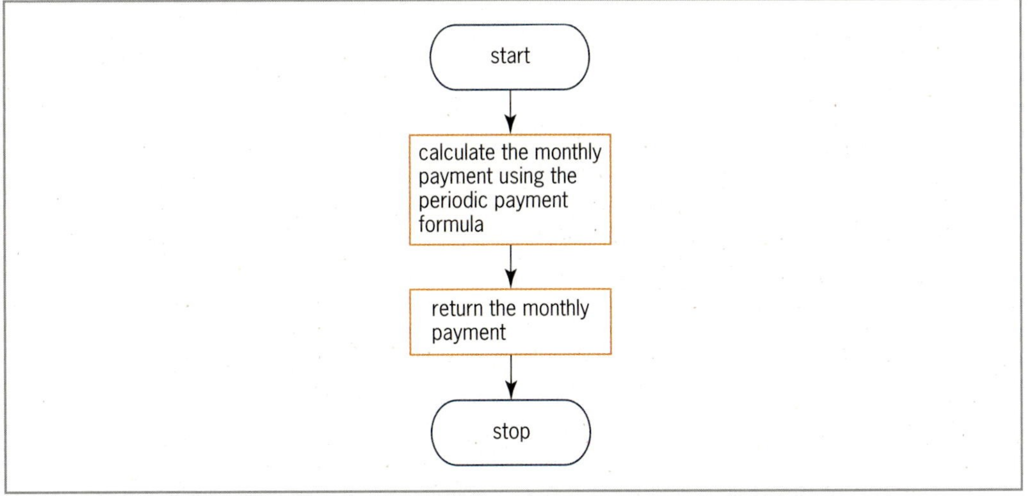

Figure 9-45 IPO charts for the `main` and `getPayment` functions

After completing the IPO chart, you then move on to the third step in the problem-solving process, which is to desk-check the algorithm. You will desk-check the algorithms in Figure 9-45 using 16000, 3000, .08, .03, and 4 as the car price (after any trade-in), rebate, credit union rate, dealer rate, and term (in years), respectively. Using these values, the monthly payments should be $317.37 (credit union) and $354.15 (dealer). Therefore, it will be cheaper for Sydney to finance the car through her credit union. Figure 9-46 shows the completed desk-check table.

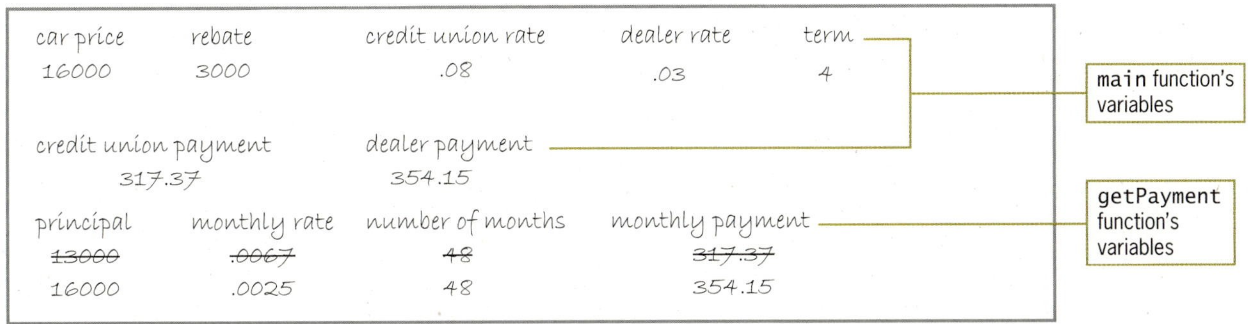

Figure 9-46 Completed desk-check table for the car payment algorithms

The fourth step in the problem-solving process is to code the algorithm into a program. The IPO chart information and C++ instructions for the `main` and `getPayment` functions are shown in Figures 9-47 and 9-48, respectively. The variables declared in Figure 9-47 are local to the `main` function and remain in memory until the `main` function ends. The variables in Figure 9-48 are local to the `getPayment` function and remain in memory until the `getPayment` function ends.

`main` function **IPO chart information**	**C++ instructions**
Input	
car price	`int carPrice = 0;`
rebate	`int rebate = 0;`
credit union rate (annual)	`double creditRate = 0.0;`
dealer rate (annual)	`double dealerRate = 0.0;`
term (years)	`int term = 0;`
Processing	
none	
Output	
credit union payment	`double creditPayment = 0.0;`
dealer payment	`double dealerPayment = 0.0;`
Algorithm	

1. enter the car price, rebate, credit union rate, dealer rate, and term	`cout << "Car price (after any trade-in): ";`
	`cin >> carPrice;`
	`cout << "Rebate: ";`
	`cin >> rebate;`
	`cout << "Credit union rate: ";`
	`cin >> creditRate;`
	`cout << "Dealer rate: ";`
	`cin >> dealerRate;`
	`cout << "Term in years: ";`
	`cin >> term;`

2. call the getPayment function to calculate the credit union payment; pass the car price minus the rebate, the credit union rate / 12, and the term * 12	`creditPayment = getPayment(carPrice - rebate, creditRate / 12, term * 12);`
3. call the getPayment function to calculate the dealer payment; pass the car price, the dealer rate / 12, and the term * 12	`dealerPayment = getPayment(carPrice, dealerRate / 12, term * 12);`
4. display the credit union payment and the dealer payment	`cout << "Credit union payment: $" << creditPayment << endl;` `cout << "Dealer payment: $" << dealerPayment << endl;`

Figure 9-47 IPO chart information and C++ code for the `main` function

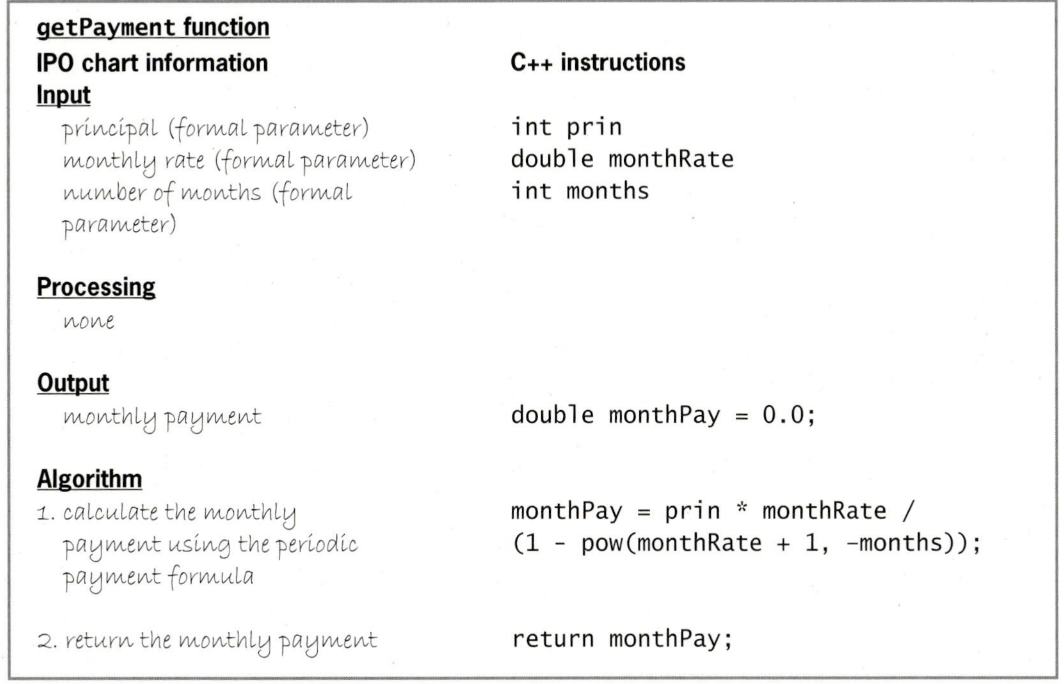

getPayment function	
IPO chart information	**C++ instructions**
Input	
principal (formal parameter)	`int prin`
monthly rate (formal parameter)	`double monthRate`
number of months (formal parameter)	`int months`
Processing	
none	
Output	
monthly payment	`double monthPay = 0.0;`
Algorithm	
1. calculate the monthly payment using the periodic payment formula	`monthPay = prin * monthRate / (1 - pow(monthRate + 1, -months));`
2. return the monthly payment	`return monthPay;`

Figure 9-48 IPO chart information and C++ code for the `getPayment` function

The fifth step in the problem-solving process is to desk-check the program. You begin by placing the names of the declared variables and named constants (if any) in a new desk-check table, along with their initial values. You then desk-check the remaining C++ instructions in order, recording in the desk-check table any changes made to the variables. Figure 9-49 shows the completed desk-check table for the car payment program. The results agree with those shown in the algorithm's desk-check table in Figure 9-46.

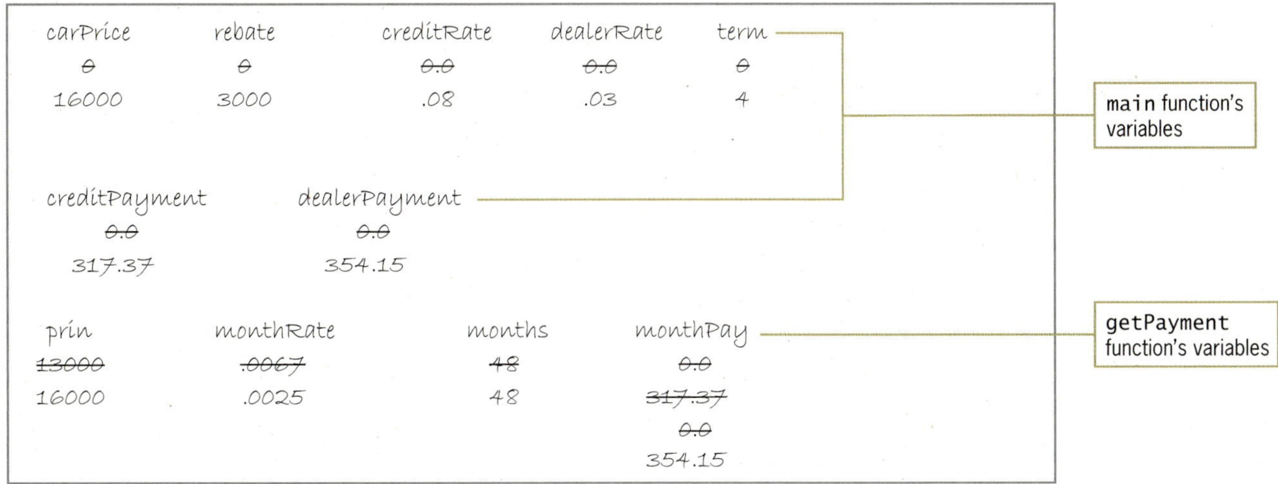

carPrice	rebate	creditRate	dealerRate	term
~~0~~	~~0~~	~~0.0~~	~~0.0~~	~~0~~
16000	3000	.08	.03	4

creditPayment	dealerPayment
~~0.0~~	~~0.0~~
317.37	354.15

main function's variables

prin	monthRate	months	monthPay
~~13000~~	~~.0067~~	~~48~~	~~0.0~~
16000	.0025	48	~~317.37~~
			~~0.0~~
			354.15

getPayment function's variables

Figure 9-49 Completed desk-check table for the car payment program

The final step in the problem-solving process is to evaluate and modify (if necessary) the program. Recall that you evaluate a program by entering its instructions into the computer and then using the computer to run (execute) it. While the program is running, you enter the same sample data used when desk-checking the program.

DIRECTIONS

Follow the instructions for starting your C++ development tool. Depending on the development tool you are using, you may need to create a new project; if so, name the project Lab9-2 Project and save it in the Cpp7\Chap09 folder. Enter the instructions shown in Figure 9-50 in a source file named Lab9-2.cpp. (Do not enter the line numbers.) Save the file in either the project folder or the Cpp7\Chap09 folder. Now follow the appropriate instructions for running the Lab9-2.cpp file. Test the program using the same data you used to desk-check the program. If necessary, correct any bugs (errors) in the program.

```
//Lab9-2.cpp - displays two monthly car payments
//Created/revised by <your name> on <current date>

#include <iostream>
#include <cmath>
#include <iomanip>
using namespace std;

//function prototype
double getPayment(int, double, int);

int main()
{
    //declare variables
    int carPrice          = 0;
    int rebate            = 0;
    double creditRate     = 0.0;
    double dealerRate     = 0.0;
    int term              = 0;
    double creditPayment = 0.0;
    double dealerPayment = 0.0;

    //get input items
    cout << "Car price (after any trade-in): ";
    cin >> carPrice;
    cout << "Rebate: ";
    cin >> rebate;
    cout << "Credit union rate: ";
    cin >> creditRate;
    cout << "Dealer rate: ";
    cin >> dealerRate;
    cout << "Term in years: ";
    cin >> term;

    //call function to calculate payments
    creditPayment = getPayment(carPrice - rebate,
        creditRate / 12, term * 12);
    dealerPayment = getPayment(carPrice,
        dealerRate / 12, term * 12);

```

the names of the formal parameters are not required

Figure 9-50 Car payment program *(continues)*

(continued)

```
    //display payments
    cout << fixed << setprecision(2) << endl;
    cout << "Credit union payment: $"
         << creditPayment << endl;
    cout << "Dealer payment: $"
         << dealerPayment << endl;

    //system("pause");
    return 0;
} //end of main function

//*****function definitions*****
double getPayment(int prin,
                  double monthRate,
                  int months)
{
    //calculates and returns a monthly payment
    double monthPay = 0.0;
    monthPay = prin * monthRate /
         (1 - pow(monthRate + 1, -months));
    return monthPay;
} //end of getPayment function
```

if your C++ development tool requires this statement, delete the two forward slashes

Figure 9-50 Car payment program

LAB 9-3 Modify

If necessary, create a new project named Lab9-3 Project and save it in the Cpp7\Chap09 folder. Enter (or copy) the Lab9-2.cpp instructions into a new source file named Lab9-3.cpp. Change Lab9-2.cpp in the first comment to Lab9-3.cpp. Make the following three modifications to the program. First, allow the user to enter the interest rates either as a whole number or as a decimal number. For example, if the interest rate is 5%, the user should be able to enter either 5 or .05. Second, the program should compare both monthly payments and then display one of the following three messages: "Take the rebate and finance through the credit union.", "Don't take the rebate. Finance through the dealer.", or "You can finance through either one." Third, the user should be able to calculate the monthly payments as many times as needed without having to run the program again. Save, run, and test the program.

LAB 9-4 Desk-Check

Desk-check the code in Figure 9-51 using the data shown in the figure. What current balance will the code display on the screen?

Test data
Beginning balance: 2000
w, 400, y
D, 1200, y
W, 45, y
w, 55, y
k, y
w, 150, y
d, 15, y
W, 1050, n

```
//Lab9-4.cpp - displays an ending balance
//Created/revised by <your name> on <current date>

#include <iostream>
#include <iomanip>
using namespace std;

//function prototype
double getBalance(double, char, double);

int main()
{
    //declare variables
    double balance    = 0.0;
    double amount     = 0.0;
    char transaction = ' ';
    char another     = 'Y';

    cout << "Beginning balance: ";
    cin >> balance;

    do
    {
        //get input items
        cout << "Withdrawal or Deposit? Enter W or D: ";
        cin >> transaction;
        transaction = toupper(transaction);

        if (transaction == 'W' || transaction == 'D')
        {
            cout << "Enter amount: ";
            cin >> amount;
            //call function to calculate balance
            balance =
                getBalance(balance, transaction, amount);
        }
        else
            cout << "Incorrect transaction type";
        //end if

```

Figure 9-51 Test data and code for Lab 9-4 *(continues)*

(continued)

```
        cout << endl << "Another transaction (Y/N)? ";
        cin >> another;
        cout << endl;
    } while (toupper(another) == 'Y');

    //display balance
    cout << fixed << setprecision(2) << endl;
    cout << "Current balance: $" << balance << endl;

    //system("pause");
    return 0;
}   //end of main function

//*****function definitions*****
double getBalance(double bal, char type, double amt)
{
    //calculates and returns the current balance
    double curBalance = 0.0;
    if (type == 'W')
        curBalance = bal - amt;
    else
        curBalance = bal + amt;
    //end if
    return curBalance;
}   //end of getBalance function
```

your C++ development tool may require this statement

Figure 9-51 Test data and code for Lab 9-4

LAB 9-5 Debug

Follow the instructions for starting C++ and viewing the Lab9-5.cpp file, which is contained in either the Cpp7\Chap09\Lab9-5 Project folder or the Cpp7\Chap09 folder. (Depending on your C++ development tool, you may need to open Lab9-5's project/solution file first.) If necessary, delete the two forward slashes that appear before the `system("pause");` statement. Test the program using 20500, 3500, and 10 as the asset cost, salvage value, and useful life, respectively. The depreciation should be $1700.00. Debug the program.

Summary

- Functions allow a programmer to avoid duplicating code in different parts of a program. They also allow large and complex programs to be broken into small and manageable tasks.
- Some of the functions used in a program are built-in functions. Others, like `main`, are program-defined functions.

- All functions are classified as either value-returning functions or void functions. A value-returning function returns precisely one value after completing its assigned task. The value is returned to the statement that called the function. Void functions, which you will learn about in Chapter 10, do not return a value.

- You can use the C++ built-in value-returning `sqrt` function to find the square root of a number. The function returns the square root as a `double` number. A program that uses the `sqrt` function must contain the `#include <cmath>` directive.
- The items within parentheses in a function call are referred to as actual arguments.
- The C++ language provides the `rand` function for generating random numbers. The `rand` function is a value-returning function. It returns an integer that is greater than or equal to 0 but less than or equal to RAND_MAX, whose value is always at least 32,767. You can use the expression *lowerBound* + `rand() %` (*upperBound* – *lowerBound* + 1) to produce random integers within a specific range.
- You can initialize the `rand` function using the C++ built-in void `srand` function. Most programmers use the built-in value-returning `time` function as the `srand` function's *seed* argument. A program that uses the `time` function must contain the `#include <ctime>` directive.
- A function definition is composed of a function header and a function body.
- The function header is the first line in the function definition. The function header for a value-returning function specifies the type of data the function returns, as well as the name of the function and an optional *parameterList* enclosed in parentheses. The items listed in the *parameterList* are called formal parameters.
- The *parameterList* in a function header contains the data type and name of each formal parameter. The quantity, data type, and sequence (order) of the formal parameters in the *parameterList* should agree with the quantity, data type, and sequence (order) of the actual arguments passed to the function. In most cases, the name of each formal parameter is different from the name of its corresponding actual argument. Functions that do not require a *parameterList* will have an empty set of parentheses after the function's name.
- The function body in a function definition contains the instructions that the function must follow to perform its assigned task. The function body begins with an opening brace and ends with a closing brace. Typically, the `return` statement, which instructs the function to return a value, is the last statement in the function body of a value-returning function.
- You call a function by including its name and actual arguments (if any) in a statement.
- Unless specified otherwise, variables in C++ are passed to a function *by value*, which means that only a copy of the value stored in the variable is passed.
- A program will have one function prototype for each function defined below the `main` function. Functions defined above the `main` function in a program do not need a function prototype.
- A variable's scope, which can be either local or global, indicates where in a program a variable can be used. A variable's lifetime indicates how long the variable remains in the computer's internal memory.
- Local variables can be used only within the function in which they are declared or in whose *parameterList* they appear, and they remain in memory until the function ends. Global variables, which you should avoid using, can be used anywhere in the program. Unlike local variables, global variables remain in memory until the program ends.
- If more than one memory location has the same name and the name appears in a statement, the computer uses the position of the statement within the program to determine which memory location to use. For clarity, you should use unique variable names within a program.

Key Terms

Actual argument—an item of information passed (sent) to a function when the function is called (invoked)

Built-in functions—blocks of code that perform a task and are included in libraries that come with the C++ language; examples include the `pow`, `sqrt`, `rand`, `srand`, and `time` functions

Formal parameters—the memory locations listed in a function header's *parameterList*; a formal parameter stores an item of information passed to a function when the function is invoked (called)

Function prototype—a statement that specifies the function's name, the data type of its return value (if any), and the data type and (optionally) name of each of its formal parameters (if any); required for every function that is defined below the `main` function in a program

Global variables—variables that are declared outside of any function in a program; global variables can be used by any statement below the variable declaration in the program, and they remain in memory until the program ends; you should avoid using global variables in a program

Lifetime—indicates how long an item, such as a variable, remains in the computer's internal memory

Local variables—variables that are either declared within a function or appear in the function header's *parameterList*; local variables can be used only by the function in which they are declared or in whose *parameterList* they appear; local variables remain in memory until the function ends

Passing *by reference*—refers to the process of passing a variable's address to a function

Passing *by value*—refers to the process of passing a copy of a variable's value to a function

Program-defined functions—blocks of code that perform a task and are written by a programmer; usually the task will avoid the duplication of code within a program or perform some common task

Pseudo-random number generator—a device that produces a sequence of numbers that meet certain statistical requirements for randomness; the `rand` function is the pseudo-random number generator in C++

`rand` function—a built-in C++ function that returns a random integer that is greater than or equal to 0 but less than or equal to the value stored in the RAND_MAX constant; the pseudo-random number generator in C++

RAND_MAX—a C++ built-in constant that represents the largest integer generated by the `rand` function; although the value of RAND_MAX varies with different computer systems, its value is always at least 32,767

`return` statement—in most cases, the last statement in a value-returning function; it returns a value to the statement that called the function and then alerts the computer that the function has completed its task

Scope—indicates where in the program an item, such as a variable, can be used

`sqrt` function—a C++ built-in function whose purpose is to return the square root of a number that has either the `double` or `float` data type; returns the square root as a `double` number; a program that uses the `sqrt` function must contain the `#include <cmath>` directive

`srand` function—a C++ built-in function used to initialize the `rand` function

time function—a built-in C++ function that returns the current time (according to your computer system's clock) as seconds elapsed since midnight on January 1, 1970; often used as the *seed* argument in the `srand` function; a program that uses the `time` function must contain the `#include <ctime>` directive

Value-returning functions—functions that return precisely one value after they complete their assigned task

Review Questions

1. Value-returning functions can return ____________.
   a. one value only
   b. one or more values
   c. the number 0 only
   d. none of the above

2. The function header specifies ____________.
   a. the data type of the function's return value (if any)
   b. the name of the function
   c. the function's formal parameters (if any)
   d. all of the above

3. Which of the following is false?
   a. The number of actual arguments should agree with the number of formal parameters.
   b. The data type of each actual argument should match the data type of its corresponding formal parameter.
   c. The name of each actual argument should be identical to the name of its corresponding formal parameter.
   d. When you pass information to a function *by value*, the function stores the value of each item it receives in a separate memory location.

4. Each memory location listed in a function header's *parameterList* is referred to as ____________.
   a. an actual argument
   b. an actual parameter
   c. a formal argument
   d. a formal parameter

5. A program contains the statement `tax = calcTax(sales);`. The `tax` and `sales` variables have the `double` data type. Which of the following is a valid function header for the `calcTax` function?
   a. `calcTax(double sales);`
   b. `double calcTax(salesAmount)`
   c. `double calcTax(double salesAmount)`
   d. `double calcTax(int sales);`

6. Which of the following is a valid function header for the `getFee` function, which receives an integer first and a number with a decimal place second? The function returns a number with a decimal place.
   a. `getFee(int base, double rate);`
   b. `double getFee(int base, double rate);`
   c. `double getFee(double base, int rate)`
   d. `double getFee(int base, double rate)`

7. Which of the following is a valid function prototype for the function described in Review Question 6?
   a. `getFee(int base, double rate);`
   b. `int getFee(int, double)`
   c. `double getFee(int base, double rate)`
   d. `double getFee(int, double);`

8. Which of the following directs a function to return the contents of the `stateTax` variable to a statement contained in the `main` function?
   a. `restore stateTax;`
   b. `return stateTax`
   c. `return to main(stateTax);`
   d. none of the above

9. If the statement `netPay = calcNet(gross, taxes);` passes a copy of the contents of the `gross` and `taxes` variables to the `calcNet` function, the variables are said to be passed ________________.
   a. *by address*
   b. *by content*
   c. *by reference*
   d. *by value*

10. A variable's ________________ indicates where in the program a variable can be used.
    a. lifetime
    b. range
    c. scope
    d. span

11. If a variable named `beginBalance` appears in a function header's *parameterList*, which of the following statements is true?
    a. The `beginBalance` variable remains in memory until the function ends.
    b. The `beginBalance` variable is called a functional variable.
    c. The `beginBalance` variable can be used anywhere in the program.
    d. both a and b

12. A program contains three functions named `main`, `calcGross`, and `displayGross`. Two of the functions—`main` and `calcGross`—declare a variable named `pay`. The `pay` variable name also appears in the `displayGross` function header. When the computer processes the statement `pay = hours * rate;` in the `calcGross` function, it multiplies the contents of the `hours` variable by the contents of the `rate` variable. It then stores the result in which function's `pay` variable?
    a. `calcGross`
    b. `displayGross`
    c. `main`
    d. none of the above because you can't have more than one memory location with the same name

13. Which of the following expressions produces a random integer from 3 to 9, inclusive?
    a. `1 + rand() % (9 - 3 + 1)`
    b. `3 + rand() % (9 - 3 + 1)`
    c. `3 + rand() % (9 + 3 - 1)`
    d. `9 + rand() % (9 + 1 - 3)`

14. Which of the following can be used to initialize the random number generator in C++?
    a. `init(static_cast<int>(time(0)));`
    b. `rand(static_cast<int>(time(0)));`
    c. `srand(static_cast<int>(time(0)));`
    d. none of the above

15. A program that uses the `sqrt` function must contain the ____________ directive.
    a. `#include <cmath>`
    b. `#include <ctime>`
    c. `#include <square>`
    d. `#include <squareRoot>`

Exercises

Pencil and Paper

TRY THIS

1. Write the C++ code for a function that receives an integer passed to it. The function should divide the integer by 2 and then return the result, which may contain a decimal place. Name the function `divideByTwo`. Name the formal parameter `wholeNumber`. (The answers to TRY THIS Exercises are located at the end of the chapter.)

TRY THIS

2. Write the function prototype for the `divideByTwo` function from Pencil and Paper Exercise 1. (The answers to TRY THIS Exercises are located at the end of the chapter.)

TRY THIS

3. Write a statement that calls the `divideByTwo` function from Pencil and Paper Exercise 1, passing the function a copy of the `total` variable's contents. The statement should assign the function's return value to a `double` variable named `quotient`. (The answers to TRY THIS Exercises are located at the end of the chapter.)

4. Rewrite the code from Pencil and Paper Exercises 1, 2, and 3 so that the `divideByTwo` function receives two integers rather than one integer. The function should add together both integers and then divide the sum by 2. Here again, the function's return value may contain a decimal place. Name the formal parameters `num1` and `num2`. Name the actual arguments `total1` and `total2`.

MODIFY THIS

5. Write a C++ statement that displays a random integer from 50 through 100 on the computer screen.

INTRODUCTORY

6. Write a C++ statement that assigns the square root of a number to a `double` variable named `sqRoot`. The number is stored in a `double` variable named `num`.

INTRODUCTORY

7. Write the C++ code for a function that prompts the user to enter a character and then stores the character in a `char` variable named `response`. The function should return the contents of the `response` variable. Name the function `getCharacter`. (The function will not have any actual arguments passed to it.) Also write an appropriate function prototype for the `getCharacter` function. In addition, write a statement that invokes the `getCharacter` function and assigns its return value to a `char` variable named `custCode`.

INTRODUCTORY

8. Write the C++ code for a function that receives four `double` numbers. The function should calculate the average of the four numbers and then return the result. Name the function `calcAverage`. Name the formal parameters `num1`, `num2`, `num3`, and `num4`. Also write an appropriate function prototype for the `calcAverage` function. In addition, write a statement that invokes the `calcAverage` function and assigns its return value to a `double` variable named `quotient`. Use the following numbers as the actual arguments: 45.67, 8.35, 125.78, and 99.56.

INTERMEDIATE

9. Write a C++ statement that adds the cube of the number stored in the `num1` variable to the square root of the number stored in the `num2` variable. The statement should assign the result to the `answer` variable. All of the variables have the `double` data type.

INTERMEDIATE

10. Write a C++ statement that assigns to the `answer` variable the square root of the following expression: $x^2 * y^3$. The `x`, `y`, and `answer` variables have the `double` data type.

INTERMEDIATE

11. Write a C++ statement that assigns to the `rate` variable the result of the following expression: $(\texttt{future} / \texttt{present})^{1 - \texttt{term}} - 1$. The three variables have the `double` data type.

ADVANCED

12. A program's `main` function declares three `double` variables named `salesTax`, `sales`, and `taxRate`. It also declares a `char` variable named `status`. The `main` function contains the following statement: `salesTax = getSalesTax(sales, status, taxRate);`. The statement calls the `getSalesTax` function, whose function header is `int getSalesTax(char code, int sold, double rate)`. Correct the function header.

SWAT THE BUGS

Computer

13. If necessary, create a new project named TryThis13 Project and save it in the Cpp7\Chap09 folder. Enter the C++ instructions shown earlier in Figure 9-6 into a source file named TryThis13.cpp. Change the filename in the first comment. Save and then run the program. Test the program using the data shown earlier in Figure 9-7. (The answers to TRY THIS Exercises are located at the end of the chapter.)

TRY THIS

14. If necessary, create a new project named TryThis14 Project and save it in the Cpp7\Chap09 folder. Code the IPO charts shown in Figure 9-52. Enter your C++ instructions into a source file named TryThis14.cpp. Also enter appropriate comments and any additional instructions required by the compiler. Display the Celsius temperature in fixed-point

TRY THIS

notation with no decimal places. Save and then run the program. Test the program using the following Fahrenheit temperatures: 32 and 212. (The answers to TRY THIS Exercises are located at the end of the chapter.)

main function

Input	Processing	Output
Fahrenheit temperature	Processing items: none Algorithm: 1. call getFahrenheit function to get the Fahrenheit temperature 2. call calcCelsius to calculate the Celsius temperature; pass the Fahrenheit temperature 3. display the Celsius temperature	Celsius temperature

getFahrenheit function

Input	Processing	Output
Fahrenheit temperature	Processing items: none Algorithm: 1. enter the Fahrenheit temperature 2. return the Fahrenheit temperature	Fahrenheit temperature

calcCelsius function

Input	Processing	Output
Fahrenheit temperature	Processing items: none Algorithm: 1. Celsius temperature = 5.0 / 9.0 * (Fahrenheit temperature - 32.0) 2. return the Celsius temperature	Celsius temperature

Figure 9-52

MODIFY THIS

15. In this exercise, you modify the code from Computer Exercise 13. If necessary, create a new project named ModifyThis15 Project and save it in the Cpp7\Chap09 folder. Enter (or copy) the TryThis13.cpp instructions into a new source file named ModifyThis15.cpp. Change TryThis13.cpp in the first comment to ModifyThis15.cpp. Remove both calculation tasks from the `main` function and assign both to a program-defined value-returning function named `getHypotenuse`. Save and then run the program. Test the program appropriately.

MODIFY THIS

16. In this exercise, you modify the code from Computer Exercise 14. If necessary, create a new project named ModifyThis16 Project and save it in the Cpp7\Chap09 folder. Enter (or copy) the TryThis14.cpp instructions into a new source file named ModifyThis16.cpp. Change TryThis14.cpp in the first comment to ModifyThis16.cpp. Modify the program so that the user can convert as many temperatures as desired without having to run the program again. Save and then run the program. Test the program appropriately.

INTRODUCTORY

17. If necessary, create a new project named Introductory17 Project and save it in the Cpp7\Chap09 folder. Enter the C++ instructions shown earlier in Figure 9-23 into a source file named Introductory17.cpp. Change the filename in the first comment.

Save and then run the program. Modify the `main` function so that it swaps the numbers if the smallest number is greater than the largest number. Also modify the program so that it performs subtraction rather than addition. However, the program should always subtract the smaller number from the larger one. Save and then run the program.

INTRODUCTORY

18. In this exercise, you modify the program from Lab 7-2 in Chapter 7. If necessary, create a new project named Introductory18 Project and save it in the Cpp7\Chap09 folder. Copy the instructions from the Lab7-2.cpp file into a source file named Introductory18.cpp. (Alternatively, you can enter the instructions from Figure 7-52 into the Introductory18.cpp file.) Change the filename in the first comment. Modify the program so that it uses a value-returning function to determine the grade. Save and then run the program. Test the program appropriately.

INTERMEDIATE

19. In this exercise, you experiment with the concepts of scope and lifetime.

    a. Follow the instructions for starting C++ and viewing the Intermediate19.cpp file, which is contained in either the Cpp7\Chap09\Intermediate19 Project folder or the Cpp7\Chap09 folder. (Depending on your C++ development tool, you may need to open this exercise's project/solution file first.) If necessary, delete the two forward slashes that appear before the `system("pause");` statement, and then save the program.

    b. Run the program. If you are asked whether you want to run the last successful build, click the No button. The C++ compiler displays an error message indicating that the `getDoubleNumber` function does not recognize the `number` variable. The error occurs because the `number` variable is local to the `main` function. To fix this error, you can either pass the `number` variable's value to the `getDoubleNumber` function or create a global variable named `number`. Passing the variable's value is the preferred way for the `main` function to communicate with the `getDoubleNumber` function. However, to give you an opportunity to see how global variables work in a program, you will fix the program's error by creating a global variable named `number`.

    c. Change the `int number = 0;` statement in the `main` function to a comment. Recall that global variables are declared outside of any function in the program. In the blank line below the `//declare global variable` comment, type `int number = 0;`. Because the `number` variable is now a global variable, both the `main` and `getDoubleNumber` functions have access to it. You will run the program to verify that fact.

    d. Save and then run the program. When prompted for a number, type 5 and press Enter. The Command Prompt window shows that doubling the number 5 results in the number 10, which is correct.

    e. Now change the statement that declares the global `number` variable to a comment. Also remove the two forward slashes from the `//int number = 0;` line in the `main` function. Fix the program's error by passing the value contained in the `number` variable to the `getDoubleNumber` function.

    f. Save and then run the program. When prompted for a number, type 5 and press Enter. The Command Prompt window shows that doubling the number 5 results in the number 10, which is correct.

INTERMEDIATE

20. In this exercise, you modify the program from Lab 6-2 in Chapter 6. If necessary, create a new project named Intermediate20 Project and save it in the Cpp7\Chap09 folder. Copy the instructions from the Lab6-2.cpp file into a source file named Intermediate20.cpp. (Alternatively, you can enter the instructions from Figure 6-37 into the Intermediate20.cpp file.) Change the filename in the first comment. Modify the program so that it uses a value-returning function to determine the commission. Save and then run the program. Test the program appropriately.

INTERMEDIATE

21. In this exercise, you modify the program from Lab 5-2 in Chapter 5. If necessary, create a new project named Intermediate21 Project and save it in the Cpp7\Chap09 folder. Copy the instructions from the Lab5-2.cpp file into a source file named Intermediate21.cpp. (Alternatively, you can enter the instructions from Figure 5-34 into the Intermediate21.cpp file.) Change the filename in the first comment. Modify the program so that it uses two value-returning functions: one to determine the fat calories and the other to determine the fat percentage. Save and then run the program. Test the program appropriately.

INTERMEDIATE

22. The payroll manager at Gerston Blankets wants a program that calculates and displays the gross pay for each of the company's employees. It also should calculate and display the total gross pay. The payroll manager will enter the number of hours the employee worked and his or her pay rate. Employees working more than 40 hours should receive time and one-half for the hours over 40. Use a value-returning function to determine an employee's gross pay. Use a different value-returning function to accumulate the total gross pay. The program should display the total gross pay only after the payroll manager has finished entering the data for all the employees. Use a sentinel value to end the program.

    a. Create IPO charts for the problem, and then desk-check the algorithm using the following four sets of hours worked and pay rates: 35, \$10.50; 43, \$15; 32, \$9.75; 20, \$6.45.

    b. List the input, processing, and output items, as well as the algorithm, in a chart similar to the one shown earlier in Figure 9-52. Then code the algorithm into a program.

    c. Desk-check the program using the same data used to desk-check the algorithm.

    d. If necessary, create a new project named Intermediate22 Project and save it in the Cpp7\Chap09 folder. Enter your C++ instructions into a source file named Intermediate22.cpp. Also enter appropriate comments and any additional instructions required by the compiler.

    e. Save and then run the program. Test the program using the same data used to desk-check the program.

ADVANCED

23. In this exercise, you create a program that calculates the average of three test scores. The program should contain three value-returning functions: `main`, `getTestScore`, and `calcAverage`. The `main` function should call the `getTestScore` function to get and return each of three test scores. The test scores may contain a decimal place. The `main` function then should call the `calcAverage` function to calculate and return the average of the three test scores. When the `calcAverage` function has completed its task, the `main` function should display the average on the screen. Display the average with one decimal place. Hint: The `main` function will need to call the `getTestScore` function three times.

    a. Create IPO charts for the problem, and then desk-check the algorithm using the following four sets of test scores: 56, 78, 90; 100, 85, 67; 74, 32, 98; 25, 99, 84.

    b. List the input, processing, and output items, as well as the algorithm, in a chart similar to the one shown earlier in Figure 9-52. Then code the algorithm into a program.

    c. Desk-check the program using the same data used to desk-check the algorithm.

    d. If necessary, create a new project named Advanced23 Project and save it in the Cpp7\Chap09 folder. Enter your C++ instructions into a source file named Advanced23.cpp. Also enter appropriate comments and any additional instructions required by the compiler.

    e. Save and then run the program. Test the program using the same data used to desk-check the program.

ADVANCED

24. In this exercise, you create a program that calculates and displays gross pay amounts. The user will enter the number of hours an employee worked and his or her pay rate. The program should contain four value-returning functions: `main`, `getHoursWorked`, `getPayRate`, and `calcGross`. The `main` function should call each of the other three functions and then display the gross pay on the screen. When coding the `calcGross` function, you do not have to worry about overtime pay. You can assume that everyone works 40 or fewer hours per week. The hours worked and rate of pay may contain a decimal place. Use a sentinel value to end the program.

    a. Create IPO charts for the problem, and then desk-check the algorithm using the following two sets of hours worked and pay rates: 25.5, $12; 40, $11.55.

    b. List the input, processing, and output items, as well as the algorithm, in a chart similar to the one shown earlier in Figure 9-52. Then code the algorithm into a program.

    c. Desk-check the program using the same data used to desk-check the algorithm.

    d. If necessary, create a new project named Advanced24 Project and save it in the Cpp7\Chap09 folder. Enter your C++ instructions into a source file named Advanced24.cpp. Also enter appropriate comments and any additional instructions required by the compiler.

    e. Save and then run the program. Test the program using the same data used to desk-check the program.

ADVANCED

25. In this exercise, you learn how to provide a default value for a formal parameter.

    a. You can provide a default value for one or more of a function's formal parameters. If a formal parameter has a default value, then you do not need to provide an actual argument for it when you call the function. Follow the instructions for starting C++ and viewing the Advanced25.cpp file, which is contained in either the Cpp7\Chap09\Advanced25 Project folder or the Cpp7\Chap09 folder. (Depending on your C++ development tool, you may need to open this exercise's project/solution file first.) If necessary, delete the two forward slashes that appear before the `system("pause");` statement, and then save the program. The program uses a value-returning function to calculate a bonus amount. The bonus rate is based on the salesperson's code: either A or B. The user enters the bonus rate only for salespeople with an "A" code. Salespeople with a "B" code always receive a 5% bonus.

    b. You provide a default value for a formal parameter in the function's prototype, using the syntax *formalParameterDataType = defaultValue*. If the prototype also contains the parameter's name, you use the syntax *formalParameterDataType formalParameterName = defaultValue*. Keep in mind that all formal parameters having a default value must be placed after those that do not have a default value in the function prototype. Change the function prototype so that it uses the number .05 as the default value for the bonus rate.

    c. Save and then run the program. Test the program appropriately.

SWAT THE BUGS

26. Follow the instructions for starting C++ and viewing the SwatTheBugs26.cpp file, which is contained in either the Cpp7\Chap09\SwatTheBugs26 Project folder or the Cpp7\Chap09 folder. (Depending on your C++ development tool, you may need to open this exercise's project/solution file first.) If necessary, delete the two forward slashes that appear before the `system("pause");` statement, and then save the program. The program should calculate and display the miles per gallon, but it is not working correctly. Debug the program.

Answers to TRY THIS Exercises

Pencil and Paper

1.
```
double divideByTwo(int wholeNumber)
{
    return wholeNumber / 2.0;
}   //end of divideByTwo function
```

2.
```
double divideByTwo(int);
```
or
```
double divideByTwo(int wholeNumber);
```

3.
```
quotient = divideByTwo(total);
```

Computer

13. No answer required.

14. See Figure 9-53.

```
//TryThis14.cpp - converts Fahrenheit to Celsius
//Created/revised by <your name> on <current date>

#include <iostream>
#include <iomanip>
using namespace std;

//function prototypes
int getFahrenheit();
double calcCelsius(int tempF);

int main()
{
    int fahrenheit = 0;
    double celsius = 0.0;

    //get input item
    fahrenheit = getFahrenheit();

    //calculate Celsius
    celsius = calcCelsius(fahrenheit);

```

Figure 9-53 *(continues)*

(continued)

```
    //display output item
    cout << fixed << setprecision(0);
    cout << "Celsius: " << celsius << endl;

    //system("pause");
    return 0;
}   //end of main function

//*****function definitions*****
int getFahrenheit()
{
    int tempF = 0;
    cout << "Enter Fahrenheit temperature: ";
    cin >> tempF;
    return tempF;
}   //end of getFahrenheit function

double calcCelsius(int tempF)
{
    double tempC = 0.0;
    tempC = 5.0 / 9.0 * (tempF - 32.0);
    return tempC;
}   //end of calcCelsius function
```

if your C++ development tool requires this statement, delete the two forward slashes

Figure 9-53

CHAPTER 10

Void Functions

After studying Chapter 10, you should be able to:

- Create a void function
- Invoke a void function
- Pass information *by reference* to a function

Functions

As discussed in Chapter 9, all built-in and program-defined functions are categorized as either value-returning functions or void functions. Recall that a value-returning function performs a task and then returns precisely one value to the statement that called it. You learned how to create and invoke value-returning functions in Chapter 9. Like value-returning functions, void functions also perform a task. However, unlike value-returning functions, **void functions** do not return a value after completing their task.

The illustration shown in Figure 10-1 may help clarify the difference between the two categories of functions. Sarah and her two siblings are planning a surprise birthday party for their mother. Being the oldest of the three children, Sarah will handle most of the party plans herself. However, she does need to delegate some tasks to her brother (Jacob) and sister (Sonja). She delegates the task of putting up the decorations (streamers, balloons, and so on) to Jacob, and delegates the task of getting the birthday present (a bottle of perfume) to Sonja. Like a void function, Jacob will perform his task but won't need to return anything to Sarah after doing so. However, like a value-returning function, Sonja will perform her task and then return a value (the bottle of perfume) to Sarah for wrapping.

Figure 10-1 Illustration of value-returning and void functions

As already mentioned, value-returning functions were covered in Chapter 9. However, the chapter also introduced you to one built-in void function: `srand`. Recall that you use the `srand` function to initialize the C++ random number generator. In this chapter, you will learn how to create and invoke program-defined void functions.

Creating Program-Defined Void Functions

A program might use a program-defined void function to display information (such as a title and column headings) at the top of each page in a report. Rather than duplicating the required code several times in the program, the code can be entered once in a void function. The program can then call the void function whenever and wherever it is needed. A void function is appropriate in this situation because the function does not need to return a value after completing its task.

Figure 10-2 shows the syntax used to create a void function in a C++ program. When you compare this syntax with the one for creating a value-returning function (shown in Figure 9-17 in Chapter 9), you will notice two differences. First, a void function's header begins with the keyword `void` rather than with a data type. The `void` keyword indicates that the function does not return a value. Second, the function body in a void function does not contain a `return` statement, which is required in the function body of a value-returning function. The `return` statement is not necessary in a void function body because a void function does not return a value. Also included in Figure 10-2 are examples of program-defined void functions.

HOW TO Create a Program-Defined Void Function

Syntax

```
void functionName([parameterList])          function header
{
     one or more statements                  function body
}    //end of functionName function
```

Example 1

```
void displayLine()                           function definition
{
     cout << "--------------------" << endl;
}    //end of displayLine function
```

The function displays a straight line composed of 20 hyphens.

Example 2

```
void displayCompanyInfo()
{
     cout << "ABC Company" << endl;
     cout << "Chicago, Illinois" << endl;
}    //end of displayCompanyInfo function
```

The function displays a company's name, city, and state.

Example 3

```
void displayTotalSales(int total)
{
     cout << "Total sales: $" << total << endl;
}    //end of displayTotalSales function
```

The function displays the total sales it receives from the statement that invoked it.

Figure 10-2 How to create a program-defined void function

Figure 10-3 shows the problem specification and IPO charts for the ABC Company program, which uses the void functions from Figure 10-2.

Problem specification
Create a program that allows the ABC Company's sales manager to enter the sales made in two stores. The program should total both sales amounts and then display the following information, in which *total* is the total sales:

```
--------------------
ABC Company
Chicago, Illinois

Total sales: $total
--------------------
```

`main` function

Input	Processing	Output
store 1's sales store 2's sales	Processing items: none	total sales straight line (2 of them) name, city, and state

Algorithm:
1. enter store 1's sales and store 2's sales
2. calculate the total sales by adding together store 1's sales and store 2's sales
3. call the displayLine function to display a straight line
4. call the displayCompanyInfo function to display the name, city, and state
5. call the displayTotalSales function to display the total sales; pass the total sales
6. call the displayLine function to display a straight line

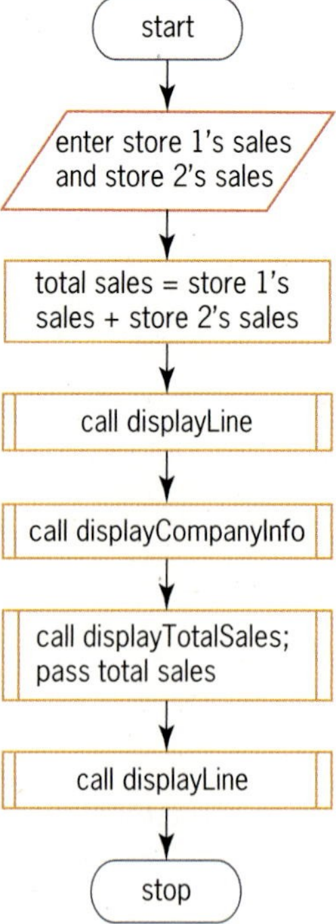

Figure 10-3 Problem specification and IPO charts for the ABC Company program *(continues)*

(continued)

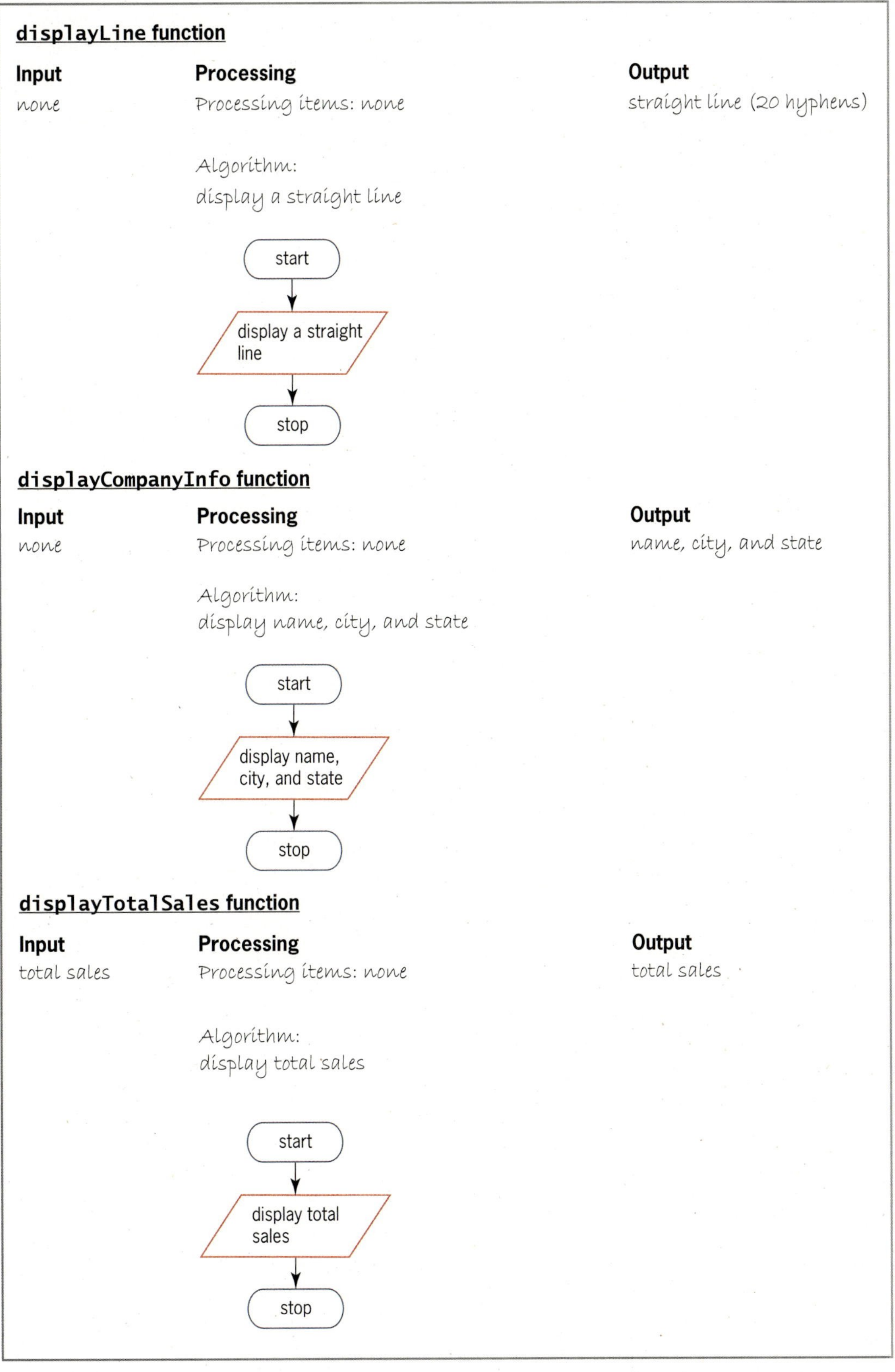

Figure 10-3 Problem specification and IPO charts for the ABC Company program

Figure 10-4 shows the IPO chart information and C++ instructions for the ABC Company program, and Figure 10-5 shows the program's code, with the function prototypes and calls shaded. As you do with a value-returning function, you call a void function by including its name and actual arguments (if any) in a statement. However, unlike a call to a value-returning function, a call to a void function appears as a statement by itself rather than as part of another statement. Each call to the void functions in Figure 10-5, for example, is a self-contained statement.

> Recall that value-returning functions typically are called from statements that do one of the following: display the function's return value, use the return value in a calculation or comparison, or assign the return value to a variable.

`main` function

IPO chart information	C++ instructions
Input	
store 1's sales	`int store1Sales = 0;`
store 2's sales	`int store2Sales = 0;`
Processing	
none	
Output	
total sales	`int totalSales = 0;` (displayed by the displayTotalSales function)
straight line (2 of them)	displayed by the displayLine function
name, city, and state	displayed by the displayCompanyInfo function
Algorithm	

1. enter store 1's sales and store 2's sales	`cout << "Store 1's sales: ";`
	`cin >> store1Sales;`
	`cout << "Store 2's sales: ";`
	`cin >> store2Sales;`

2. calculate the total sales by adding together store 1's sales and store 2's sales	`totalSales = store1Sales + store2Sales;`
3. call the displayLine function to display a straight line	`displayLine();`
4. call the displayCompanyInfo function to display the name, city, and state	`displayCompanyInfo();`
5. call the displayTotalSales function to display the total sales; pass the total sales	`displayTotalSales(totalSales);`
6. call the displayLine function to display a straight line	`displayLine();`

Figure 10-4 IPO chart information and C++ instructions for the ABC Company program *(continues)*

(continued)

`displayLine` function

IPO chart information	C++ instructions
Input	
none	
Processing	
none	
Output	
straight line (20 hyphens)	displayed using a string literal constant
Algorithm	
display a straight line	`cout << "--------------------"` `<< endl;`

`displayCompanyInfo` function

IPO chart information	C++ instructions
Input	
none	
Processing	
none	
Output	
name, city, and state	displayed using string literal constants
Algorithm	

display name, city, and state	`cout << "ABC Company" << endl;`
	`cout << "Chicago, Illinois"`
	`<< endl << endl;`

`displayTotalSales` function

IPO chart information	C++ instructions
Input	
total sales (formal parameter)	`int total`
Processing	
none	
Output	
total sales	
Algorithm	
display total sales	`cout << "Total sales: $"` `<< total << endl;`

Figure 10-4 IPO chart information and C++ instructions for the ABC Company program

```
//ABC.cpp - displays the total sales
//Created/revised by <your name> on <current date>

#include <iostream>
using namespace std;

//function prototypes
void displayLine();
void displayCompanyInfo();
void displayTotalSales(int total);

int main()
{
   int store1Sales = 0;
   int store2Sales = 0;
   int totalSales  = 0;

   //enter input items
   cout << "Store 1's sales: ";
   cin >> store1Sales;
   cout << "Store 2's sales: ";
   cin >> store2Sales;

   //calculate total sales
   totalSales = store1Sales + store2Sales;

   //display output items
   displayLine();
   displayCompanyInfo();
   displayTotalSales(totalSales);
   displayLine();

   //system("pause");
   return 0;
} //end of main function

//*****function definitions*****
void displayLine()
{
   cout << "--------------------" << endl;
} //end of displayLine function

void displayCompanyInfo()
{
   cout << "ABC Company" << endl;
   cout << "Chicago, Illinois" << endl << endl;
} //end of displayCompanyInfo function

void displayTotalSales(int total)
{
   cout << "Total sales: $" << total << endl;
} //end of displayTotalSales function
```

Figure 10-5 ABC Company program

When the computer processes a statement that calls a program-defined void function, the computer first locates the function's code in the program. If the function call contains an *argumentList*, the computer passes the values of the actual arguments (assuming the variables included in the *argumentList* are passed *by value*) to the called function. The function receives the values and stores them in the formal parameters listed in its *parameterList*. Then, the computer processes the function's code. When the function ends, the computer continues program execution with the statement immediately below the one that called the function. In the program shown in Figure 10-5, for example, the `displayLine();` statement on Line 28 calls the `displayLine` function. After processing the `displayLine` function's code, the computer returns to the `main` function to process the statement on Line 29; that statement calls the `displayCompanyInfo` function. When the computer finishes processing the code in the `displayCompanyInfo` function, it returns to the `main` function to process the statement on Line 30; that statement calls the `displayTotalSales` function. After processing the code in the `displayTotalSales` function, the computer returns to the `main` function to process the `displayLine();` statement on Line 31. After the `displayLine` function completes its task, the computer returns to the `main` function to process the `return 0;` statement on Line 34. Figure 10-6 shows a sample run of the ABC Company's program. The sample run contains output from each of the four functions in the program.

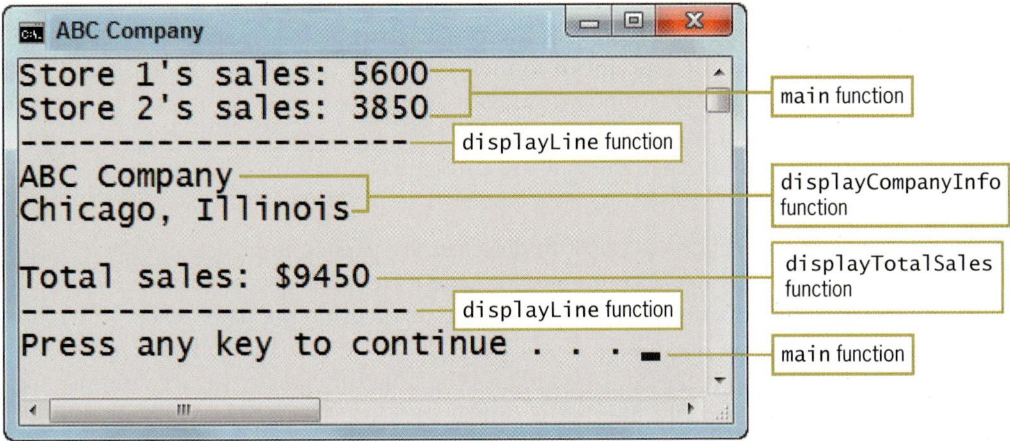

Figure 10-6 Sample run of the ABC Company program

Mini-Quiz 10-1

1. In C++, the function header for a function that does not return a value begins with the keyword ____________.
2. Write a C++ statement that calls a void function named `displayTaxes`, passing it a copy of the contents of two `double` variables named `federalTax` and `localTax`.
3. Write the function header for the `displayTaxes` function from Question 2. Use `fedTax` and `stateTax` as the names for the formal parameters.
4. The `return` statement typically is the last statement in a C++ void function.
   a. True
   b. False

The answers to Mini-Quiz questions are located in Appendix A.

Passing Variables to a Function

As you learned in Chapter 9, the items passed to a function are called actual arguments. An actual argument can be a variable, named constant, literal constant, or keyword; however, in most cases, it will be a variable. Recall that each variable declared in a program has both a value and a unique address that represents the location of the variable in the computer's internal memory. C++ allows you to pass either a copy of the variable's value or its address to a function. Passing a copy of a variable's value is referred to as passing *by value*, whereas passing its address is referred to as **passing *by reference***. The method you choose—*by value* or *by reference*—depends on whether you want the receiving function to have access to the variable in memory. In other words, it depends on whether you want to allow the receiving function to change the contents of the variable.

The internal memory of a computer is similar to a large post office. Like each post office box, each memory cell has a unique address.

Although the idea of passing information *by value* and *by reference* may sound confusing at first, it is a concept with which you are already familiar. We'll use the illustrations shown in Figure 10-7 to demonstrate this fact. Assume you have a savings account at a local bank. (Think of the savings account as a variable.) During a conversation with your friend Melissa, you mention the amount of money you have in the account, as shown in Illustration A. Sharing this information with Melissa is similar to passing a variable *by value*. Knowing the balance in your account does not give Melissa access to your bank account. It merely provides information that she can use to compare with the amount of money she has saved.

Only variables can be passed *by reference*.

Now we'll use the savings account example to demonstrate passing information *by reference*. (Here again, think of your savings account as a variable.) To either deposit money in your account or withdraw money from your account, you must provide the bank teller with your account number, as shown in Illustration B in Figure 10-7. The account number represents the location of your account at the bank and allows the teller to change the account balance. Giving the teller your bank account number is similar to passing a variable *by reference*. The account number allows the teller to change the contents of your bank account, similar to the way a variable's address allows the receiving function to change the contents of the variable.

Figure 10-7 Illustrations of passing *by value* and passing *by reference*

Before learning how to pass a variable *by reference*, you will review the concept of passing *by value*, which you learned about in Chapter 9.

Reviewing Passing Variables *by Value*

Recall that unless you specify otherwise, variables are passed *by value* in C++. This means that the computer passes only a copy of the variable's contents to the receiving function. When only a copy of the contents is passed, the receiving function is not given access to the variable in memory. Therefore, it cannot change the value stored inside of the variable.

It is appropriate to pass a variable *by value* when the receiving function needs to *know* the variable's contents, but it does not need to *change* the contents. For instance, consider the C++ program shown in Figure 10-8. The program defines and calls a void function named `displayAge`. The `displayAge` function definition is located below the `main` function (on Lines 24 through 27). Therefore, the program includes an appropriate function prototype above the `main` function (on Line 8). Because the `displayAge` function is a void function, its function call (on Line 17) appears as a statement by itself. The function call passes the `age` variable *by value* to the `displayAge` function. Notice that the data type of the actual argument in the function call—in this case, `int`—matches the data type of the formal parameter listed in both the function header and the function prototype. Also notice that the name of the actual argument (`age`) does not need to be identical to the name of the formal parameter (`years`). In fact, to avoid confusion, you should use different names for an actual argument and its corresponding formal parameter.

The receiving function can change only its copy of a variable passed *by value*. Changing the copy does not change the contents of the original variable.

```
1  //Age.cpp - displays the user's age in a message
2  //Created/revised by <your name> on <current date>
3
4  #include <iostream>
5  using namespace std;
6
7  //function prototype
8  void displayAge(int years);
9
10 int main()
11 {
12     int age = 0;
13
14     cout << "How old are you? ";
15     cin >> age;
16
17     displayAge(age);
18
19     //system("pause");
20     return 0;
21 }   //end of main function
22
23 //*****function definitions*****
24 void displayAge(int years)
25 {
26     cout << "You are " << years << " years old." << endl;
27 }   //end of displayAge function
```


Figure 10-8 Age message program

To review the concept of passing *by value*, you will desk-check the program in Figure 10-8, using the number 35 as the age. The first statement in the `main` function creates and initializes an `int` variable named `age`. The variable is local to the `main` function and will remain in memory until the `main` function ends. The next two statements prompt the user to enter an age

Ch10-Age By Value Desk-Check video

and then store the user's response (35) in the `age` variable. Figure 10-9 shows the desk-check table after the first three statements in the `main` function are processed.

Figure 10-9 Desk-check table after the first three statements in the `main` function are processed

Recall that the variables listed in a function header are local to the function and can be used only within the function. The variables will remain in memory until the function ends.

Next, the `displayAge(age);` statement on Line 17 calls the `displayAge` function, passing it a copy of the value stored in the `age` variable. In this case, the statement passes the integer 35. At this point, the computer temporarily leaves the `main` function to process the code contained in the `displayAge` function, beginning with the function header. The `displayAge` function header indicates that the computer should create one local `int` variable named `years`. The computer stores the value passed to the function in the `years` variable, as shown in Figure 10-10.

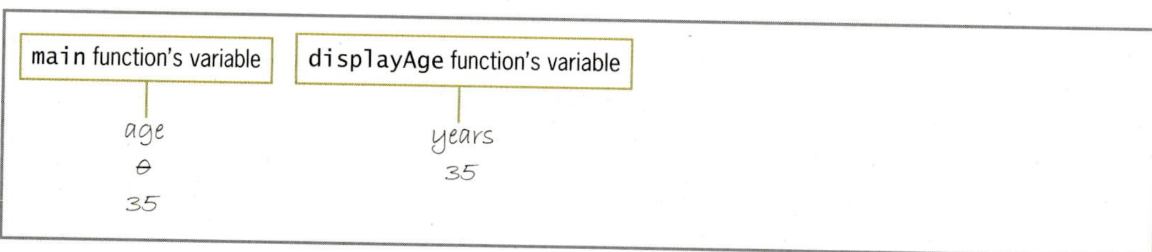

Figure 10-10 Desk-check table after the `displayAge` function header is processed

Next, the computer processes the `cout` statement contained in the `displayAge` function body. The statement displays string literal constants along with the contents of the function's local `years` variable. In this case, the statement will display the message "You are 35 years old." on the computer screen. The `displayAge` function ends when the computer encounters the function's closing brace. At that point, the computer removes the `years` variable from its internal memory. It then returns to the `main` function to process the statement immediately following the one that called the `displayAge` function; that statement is `return 0;`. Figure 10-11 shows the desk-check table after the `displayAge` function ends. Only the `main` function's local `age` variable remains in the computer's memory.

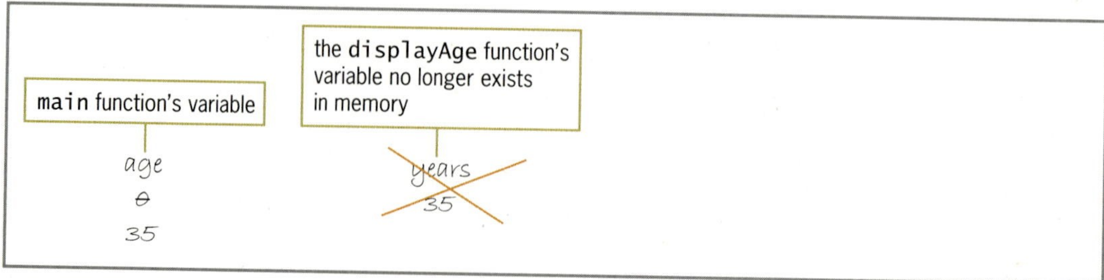

Figure 10-11 Desk-check table after the `displayAge` function ends

The `return 0;` statement returns the number 0 to the operating system to indicate that the program ended normally. When the program ends, the computer removes the `main` function's local **age** variable from its internal memory. Figure 10-12 shows a sample run of the age message program.

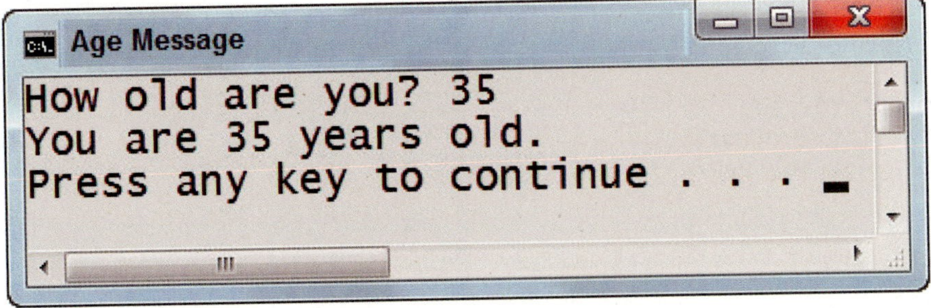

Figure 10-12 Sample run of the age message program

Passing Variables *by Reference*

Instead of passing a copy of a variable's value to a function, you can pass its address. In other words, you can pass the variable's location in the computer's internal memory. As you learned earlier, passing a variable's address is referred to as passing *by reference*, and it gives the receiving function access to the variable being passed. You pass a variable *by reference* when you want the receiving function to change the contents of the variable.

Recall that only functions defined below the `main` function require a function prototype above the `main` function.

To pass a variable *by reference* in C++, you include an ampersand (&) before the name of the corresponding formal parameter in the receiving function's header and in its prototype (if there is one). The **&** (ampersand) is called the **address-of operator**, and it tells the computer to pass the variable's address rather than a copy of its contents. If the function's prototype does not include the formal parameter's name, you enter a space followed by the address-of operator after the formal parameter's data type.

We'll use a modified version of the age message program (shown earlier in Figure 10-8) to illustrate the concept of passing *by reference*. The modified program is shown in Figure 10-13, with the modifications shaded in the figure. In addition to the `displayAge` function included in the original program, the modified program defines and calls a void function named `getAge`. The function call, which appears on Line 15, passes the `age` variable *by reference*. You can tell that the variable is passed *by reference* because the address-of operator precedes the formal parameter's name in the `getAge` function's header (on Line 24) and in its prototype (on Line 8). Notice that the statement that calls a function does not indicate whether an item is passed *by value* or *by reference*. You can determine that information only by examining the *parameterList* in either the receiving function's header or its prototype.

Like the `displayAge` function, the `getAge` function in Figure 10-13 is a void function; therefore, its function call appears as a statement by itself. Here again, notice that the data type of the actual argument in the function call matches the data type of the formal parameter listed in both the function header and the function prototype. Also notice that the name of the actual argument (`age`) is different from the name of the formal parameter (`inYears`).

```
1  //Modified Age.cpp - displays the user's age in a message
2  //Created/revised by <your name> on <current date>
3
4  #include <iostream>
5  using namespace std;
6
7  //function prototypes
8  void getAge(int &inYears);
9  void displayAge(int years);
10
11 int main()
12 {
13     int age = 0;
14
15     getAge(age);
16
17     displayAge(age);
18
19     //system("pause");
20     return 0;
21 }   //end of main function
22
23 //*****function definitions*****
24 void getAge(int &inYears)
25 {
26     cout << "How old are you? ";
27     cin >> inYears;
28 }   //end of getAge function
29
30 void displayAge(int years)
31 {
32     cout << "You are " << years << " years old." << endl;
33 }   //end of displayAge function
```

address-of operator

you also can use `void getAge(int &);`

address-of operator

Figure 10-13 Modified age message program

Ch10-Age By Reference Desk-Check video

To help you understand the concept of passing *by reference*, you will desk-check the modified program in Figure 10-13, using the number 28 as the age. The first statement in the `main` function creates and initializes an `int` variable named `age`. The variable is local to the `main` function and will remain in memory until the `main` function ends. Figure 10-14 shows the desk-check table after the declaration statement is processed.

`main` function's variable

age
0

Figure 10-14 Desk-check table after the declaration statement in the `main` function is processed

Next, the `getAge(age);` statement on Line 15 calls the `getAge` function, passing it the address of the `age` variable. At this point, the computer temporarily leaves the `main` function to process the code contained in the `getAge` function, beginning with the function header.

The formal parameter in the `getAge` function header indicates that the function receives the address of an `int` variable. When you pass a variable's address to a function, the computer uses the address to locate the variable in its internal memory. It then assigns the formal parameter's name to the memory location. In this case, the computer locates the age variable in memory and assigns the name inYears to it. As indicated in the desk-check table in Figure 10-15, the memory location now has two names: one assigned by the main function and the other assigned by the getAge function. Although both functions can access the memory location, each function uses a different name to do so. The main function uses the name age, whereas the getAge function uses the name inYears.

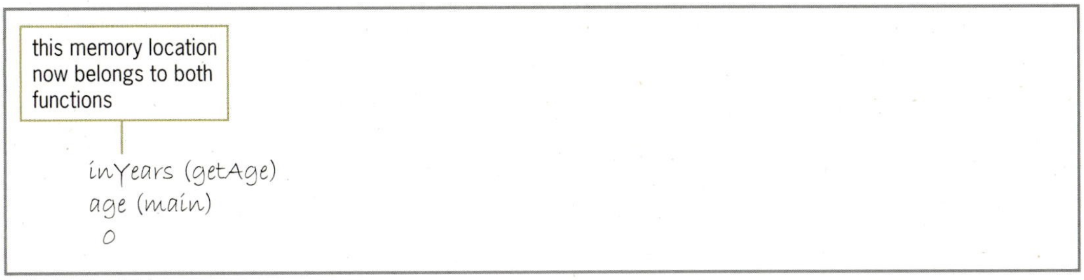

this memory location now belongs to both functions

inYears (getAge)
age (main)
0

Figure 10-15 Desk-check table after the getAge function header is processed

Next, the computer processes the two statements contained in the getAge function body. The statements prompt the user to enter an age and then store the user's response (28) in the inYears variable. Figure 10-16 shows the desk-check table after the statements in the getAge function are processed. Notice that changing the value in the inYears variable also changes the value in the age variable. This is because both variable names refer to the same location in memory.

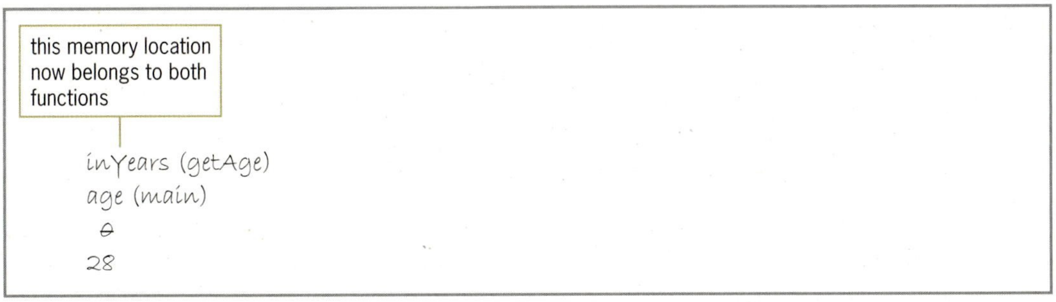

this memory location now belongs to both functions

inYears (getAge)
age (main)
~~0~~
28

Figure 10-16 Desk-check table after the statements in the getAge function are processed

The getAge function ends when the computer encounters the function's closing brace. At that point, the computer removes the name of the function's formal parameter (inYears) from the appropriate location in memory. Figure 10-17 shows the desk-check table after the getAge function ends.

this memory location now belongs only to the main function

~~inYears (getAge)~~
age (main)
~~0~~
28

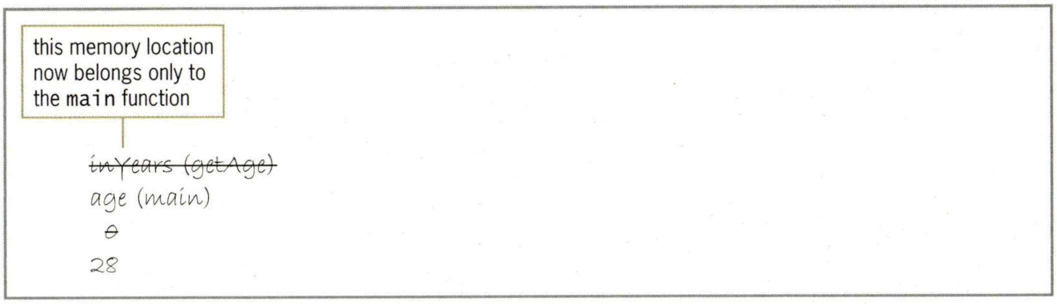

Figure 10-17 Desk-check table after the getAge function ends

After the getAge function ends, the computer returns to the main function to process the statement immediately following the one that called the getAge function. That statement is the displayAge(age); statement on Line 17. The statement calls the displayAge function, passing it a copy of the value (28) stored in the age variable. You can tell that the age variable is passed *by value* because there is no ampersand before the name of the formal parameter in the displayAge function's header and prototype. The computer temporarily leaves the main function to process the code contained in the displayAge function, beginning with the function header. The displayAge function header indicates that the computer should create one local int variable named years. The computer stores the value passed to the function in the years variable, as shown in Figure 10-18.

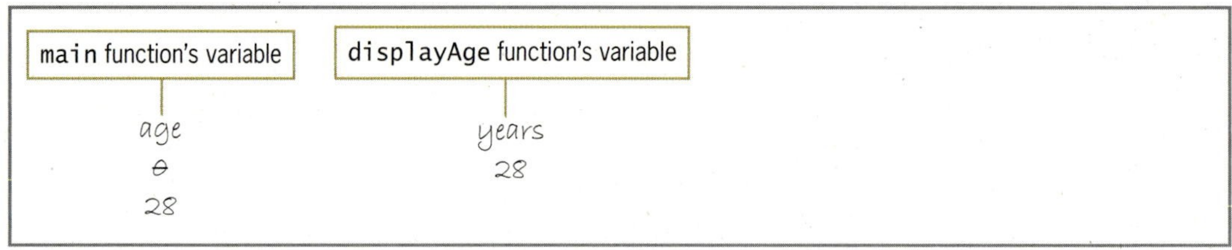

Figure 10-18 Desk-check table after the computer processes the displayAge function header

Next, the computer processes the cout statement contained in the displayAge function body. The statement will display the message "You are 28 years old." on the computer screen. When the computer encounters the displayAge function's closing brace, the function ends. The computer then removes the years variable from its internal memory. It then returns to the main function to process the return 0; statement on Line 20. Figure 10-19 shows the desk-check table after the displayAge function ends. Only the main function's local age variable remains in the computer's memory.

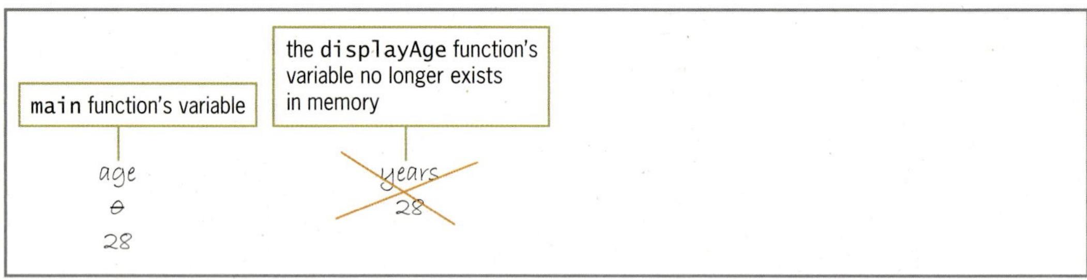

Figure 10-19 Status of the desk-check table after the displayAge function ends

The return 0; statement returns the number 0 to the operating system to indicate that the program ended normally. When the program ends, the computer removes the main function's local age variable from its internal memory. A sample run of the modified age message program is shown in Figure 10-20.

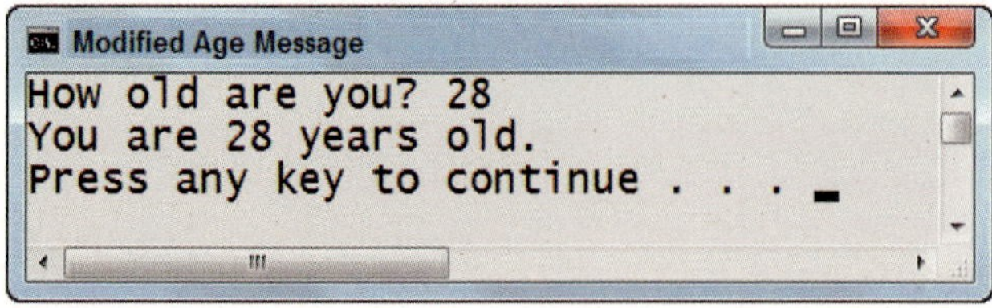

Figure 10-20 Sample run of the modified age message program

Keep in mind that when you pass a variable *by value*, the computer uses the data type and name of its corresponding formal parameter to create a separate memory location in which to store the value. When you pass a variable *by reference*, on the other hand, the computer locates the variable in memory and then assigns the name of its corresponding formal parameter to the memory location. When you pass a variable *by reference*, the variable will have two names: one assigned by the calling function and the other assigned by the receiving function. Void functions use variables that are passed *by reference* to send information back to the calling function. Value-returning functions, on the other hand, send information back to the calling function through their return value.

Mini-Quiz 10-2

The answers to Mini-Quiz questions are located in Appendix A.

1. Which of the following is a valid function header for a void function named `getInput`? The function is passed the addresses of two `double` variables.
   a. `void getInput(double &hours, double &rate)`
   b. `void getInput(&double hours, &double rate)`
   c. `void getInput(double hours, double rate)`
   d. `void getInput(double %hours, double %rate)`

2. Which of the following statements can be used to call the `getInput` function from Question 1, passing it the addresses of two `double` variables named `hoursWkd` and `payRate`?
   a. `getInput(&hoursWkd, &payRate);`
   b. `getInput(hoursWkd, payRate);`
   c. `getInput(payRate &, hoursWkd &);`
   d. `getInput(double &hoursWkd, double &payRate);`

3. Write the function prototype for the `getInput` function from Question 1.

4. When a variable is passed *by reference*, the computer assigns the name of its corresponding formal parameter to the same location in memory.
   a. True
   b. False

The Salary Program

In the modified age message program (shown earlier in Figure 10-13), each function call passed one variable to its respective function. The `getAge(age);` statement passed the `age` variable *by reference* to the `getAge` function, while the `displayAge(age);` statement passed the `age` variable *by value* to the `displayAge` function. The program discussed in this section contains a function call that passes four variables: two *by value* and two *by reference*.

Figure 10-21 shows the problem specification and IPO chart for the salary program. The program allows the user to enter an employee's current salary and raise rate. It then calculates and displays the employee's raise and new salary. Notice that the `main` function calls the `getNewPayInfo` function to calculate the raise and new salary amounts.

Problem specification
Create a program that allows the user to enter an employee's current salary and raise rate. The program should calculate and display the employee's raise and new salary.

main function

Input	Processing	Output
current salary raise rate	Processing items: none Algorithm: 1. enter the current salary and raise rate 2. call the getNewPayInfo function to calculate the raise and new salary; pass the current salary and raise rate, as well as the addresses of variables in which to store the raise and new salary 3. display the raise and new salary	raise new salary

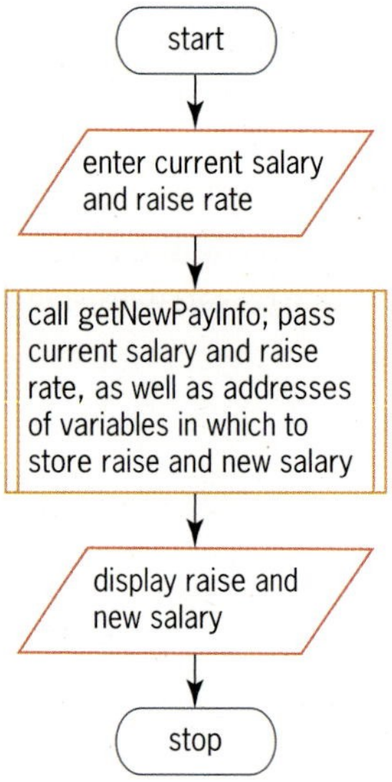

start

enter current salary and raise rate

call getNewPayInfo; pass current salary and raise rate, as well as addresses of variables in which to store raise and new salary

display raise and new salary

stop

getNewPayInfo function

Input	Processing	Output
current salary raise rate addresses of variables to store: raise new salary	Processing items: none Algorithm: 1. calculate the raise by multiplying the current salary by the raise rate 2. calculate the new salary by adding the raise to the current salary	raise new salary

Figure 10-21 Problem specification and IPO charts for the salary program *(continues)*

(continued)

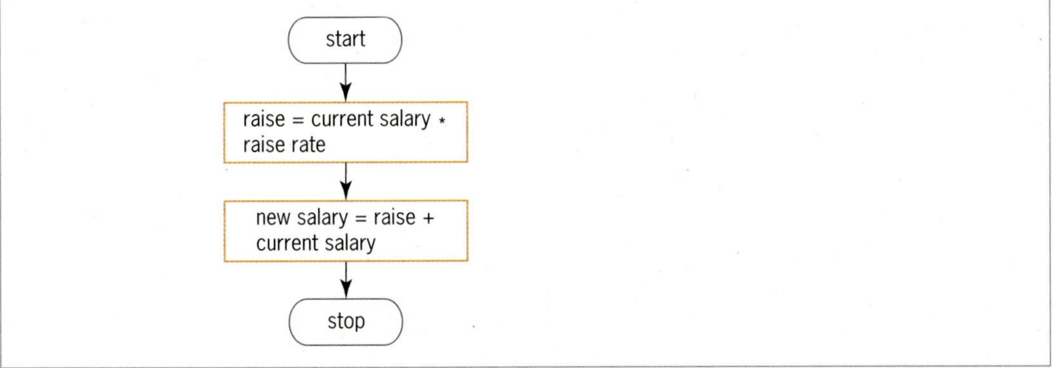

Figure 10-21 Problem specification and IPO charts for the salary program

Figure 10-22 shows the IPO chart information and C++ instructions for the program's `main` and `getNewPayInfo` functions. The `main` function passes four items of information to the `getNewPayInfo` function: the value of the current salary, the value of the raise rate, the address of the variable where the raise can be stored after it is calculated, and the address of the variable where the new salary can be stored after it is calculated. In other words, the `main` function passes its `currentSalary` and `raiseRate` variables *by value*, and it passes its `raise` and `newSalary` variables *by reference*.

`main` function

IPO chart information	**C++ instructions**
Input	
current salary	`double currentSalary = 0.0;`
raise rate	`double raiseRate = 0.0;`
Processing	
none	
Output	
raise	`double raise = 0.0;`
new salary	`double newSalary = 0.0;`
Algorithm	

1. enter the current salary and raise rate	`cout << "Current salary: ";`
	`cin >> currentSalary;`
	`cout << "Raise rate (in decimal form): ";`
	`cin >> raiseRate;`

2. call the getNewPayInfo function to calculate the raise and new salary; pass the current salary and raise rate, as well as the addresses of variables in which to store the raise and new salary	`getNewPayInfo(currentSalary,` `raiseRate, raise, newSalary);`

3. display the raise and new salary	`cout << "Raise: $" << raise << endl;`
	`cout << "New salary: $" << newSalary`
	`<< endl;`

Figure 10-22 IPO chart information and C++ instructions for the salary program *(continues)*

(continued)

getNewPayInfo function

IPO chart information	C++ instructions
Input	
current salary (formal parameter)	`double current`
raise rate (formal parameter)	`double rate`
addresses of variables to store:	
raise (formal parameter)	`double &increase`
new salary (formal parameter)	`double &pay`
Processing	
none	
Output	
raise	stored in the increase formal parameter
new salary	stored in the pay formal parameter
Algorithm	
1. calculate the raise by multiplying the current salary by the raise rate	`increase = current * rate;`
2. calculate the new salary by adding the raise to the current salary	`pay = current + increase;`

Figure 10-22 IPO chart information and C++ instructions for the salary program

Figure 10-23 shows the C++ code for the entire salary program. The `getNewPayInfo` function's prototype, call, and header are shaded in the figure. Recall that the names of the formal parameters are optional in a function prototype. Therefore, you could also write the function prototype in Figure 10-23 as follows: `void getNewPayInfo(double, double, double &, double &);`.

```
//Salary.cpp - displays the raise and new salary
//Created/revised by <your name> on <current date>

#include <iostream>
#include <iomanip>
using namespace std;

//function prototype
void getNewPayInfo(double current, double rate,
                   double &increase, double &pay);

int main()
{
    //declare variables
    double currentSalary = 0.0;
    double raiseRate     = 0.0;
    double raise         = 0.0;
    double newSalary     = 0.0;

    //get input items
    cout << "Current salary: ";
    cin >> currentSalary;
```

Figure 10-23 Salary program *(continues)*

(continued)

```
23      cout << "Raise rate (in decimal form): ";
24      cin >> raiseRate;
25
26      //get the raise and new salary
27      getNewPayInfo(currentSalary, raiseRate,
28                    raise, newSalary);
29
30      //display the raise and new salary
31      cout << fixed << setprecision(2);
32      cout << "Raise: $" << raise << endl;
33      cout << "New salary: $" << newSalary << endl;
34
35      //system("pause");
36      return 0;
37  }   //end of main function
38
39  //*****function definitions*****
40  void getNewPayInfo(double current, double rate,
41                     double &increase, double &pay)
42  {
43      increase = current * rate;
44      pay = current + increase;
45  }   //end of getNewPayInfo function
```

Figure 10-23 Salary program

You will desk-check the salary program using 32250 and .025 as the current salary and raise rate, respectively. The first four statements in the `main` function create and initialize four `double` variables. The next four statements prompt the user to enter the current salary and raise rate, storing the user's responses in the `currentSalary` and `raiseRate` variables. Figure 10-24 shows the desk-check table after the computer processes the first eight statements in the `main` function.

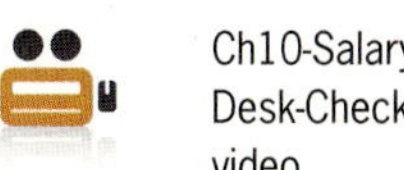

Ch10-Salary Desk-Check video

currentSalary (main)	raiseRate (main)	raise (main)	newSalary (main)
~~0.0~~	~~0.0~~	0.0	0.0
32250.0	.025		

Figure 10-24 Desk-check table after the statements on Lines 15 through 24 are processed

Next, the computer processes the `getNewPayInfo(currentSalary, raiseRate, raise, newSalary);` statement. The statement calls the `getNewPayInfo` function, passing it four variables. The `currentSalary` and `raiseRate` variables are passed *by value* because the `getNewPayInfo` function needs to *know* the values stored in the variables, but it does not need to *change* those values. You can tell that the variables are passed *by value* because their corresponding formal parameters (which are listed in the function header and function prototype) do not contain an ampersand. The `raise` and `newSalary` variables, on the other hand, are passed *by reference*, as the ampersand in their formal parameters indicates. It is necessary to pass the `raise` and `newSalary` variables *by reference* because the `getNewPayInfo` function needs to store the raise and new salary amounts in those memory locations after the amounts are calculated.

At this point, the computer temporarily leaves the `main` function to process the code contained in the `getNewPayInfo` function, beginning with the function header. When processing the `double current, double rate` portion of the function header, the computer creates two `double` memory locations named `current` and `rate`. It stores the value of the `currentSalary` variable (32250.0) in the `current` memory location and stores the value of the `raiseRate` variable (.025) in the `rate` memory location. When processing the `double &increase, double &pay` portion of the function header, the computer assigns the name `increase` to the `main` function's `raise` variable and assigns the name `pay` to the `main` function's `newSalary` variable. Figure 10-25 shows the desk-check table after the computer processes the `getNewPayInfo` function header.

currentSalary (main)	raiseRate (main)	increase (getNewPayInfo) raise (main)	pay (getNewPayInfo) newSalary (main)
~~0.0~~	~~0.0~~	0.0	0.0
32250.0	.025		

current (getNewPayInfo)	rate (getNewPayInfo)
32250.0	.025

Figure 10-25 Desk-check table after the computer processes the `getNewPayInfo` function header

The statements contained in the `getNewPayInfo` function body are processed next. The first statement multiplies the contents of the `current` variable by the contents of the `rate` variable and then assigns the result (806.25) to the `increase` variable. The second statement adds together the contents of the `current` and `increase` variables and then assigns the sum (33056.25) to the `pay` variable. Figure 10-26 shows the desk-check table after the computer processes the statements in the `getNewPayInfo` function body.

currentSalary (main)	raiseRate (main)	increase (getNewPayInfo) raise (main)	pay (getNewPayInfo) newSalary (main)
~~0.0~~	~~0.0~~	~~0.0~~	~~0.0~~
32250.0	.025	806.25	33056.25

current (getNewPayInfo)	rate (getNewPayInfo)
32250.0	.025

Figure 10-26 Desk-check table after the computer processes the statements in the `getNewPayInfo` function body

When the computer encounters the `getNewPayInfo` function's closing brace, the function ends. The computer then removes the `increase` and `pay` names from the appropriate locations in memory. It also removes the `getNewPayInfo` function's `current` and `rate` variables from memory. Figure 10-27 shows the desk-check table after the `getNewPayInfo` function ends. Notice that only the `main` function's variables remain in the computer's memory.

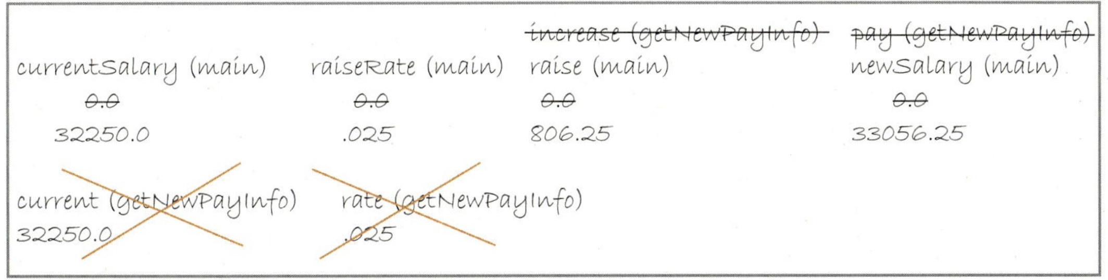

Figure 10-27 Desk-check table after the `getNewPayInfo` function ends

After the `getNewPayInfo` function ends, the computer returns to the `main` function and processes the statement immediately following the function call; that statement is the `cout << fixed << setprecision(2);` statement on Line 31. The statement tells the computer to display real numbers using fixed-point notation with two decimal places. Next, the computer processes the `cout` statements on Lines 32 and 33. Those statements display the raise and new salary amounts on the screen. The `return 0;` statement on Line 36 is processed next. When the `main` function ends, the computer removes the function's local variables (`currentSalary`, `raiseRate`, `raise`, and `newSalary`) from memory. Figure 10-28 shows a sample run of the salary program.

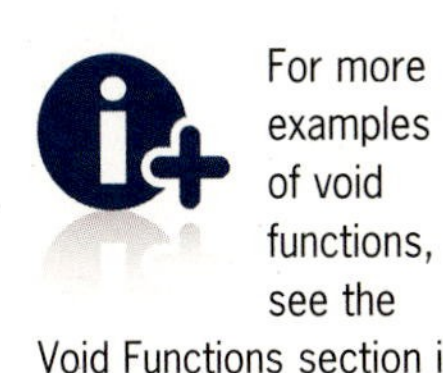

For more examples of void functions, see the Void Functions section in the Ch10WantMore.pdf file.

```
Current salary: 32250
Raise rate (in decimal form): .025
Raise: $806.25
New salary: $33056.25
Press any key to continue . . .
```

Figure 10-28 Sample run of the salary program

Mini-Quiz 10-3

The answers to Mini-Quiz questions are located in Appendix A.

1. Write the function header for a void function named `calcTaxes`. The function is passed the value of a `double` variable named `gross` and the addresses of two `double` variables named `federal` and `state`. Use `pay`, `fedTax`, and `stateTax` for the names of the formal parameters.
2. Write a C++ statement to call the `calcTaxes` function from Question 1.
3. Write the function prototype for the `calcTaxes` function from Question 1.
4. Unless specified otherwise, a variable's address is passed to a function in C++.
   a. True
   b. False

The answers to the labs are located in Appendix A.

LAB 10-1 Stop and Analyze

Figure 10-29 shows a sample run of the program for Lab 10-1. Study the program's code shown in Figure 10-30, and then answer the questions.

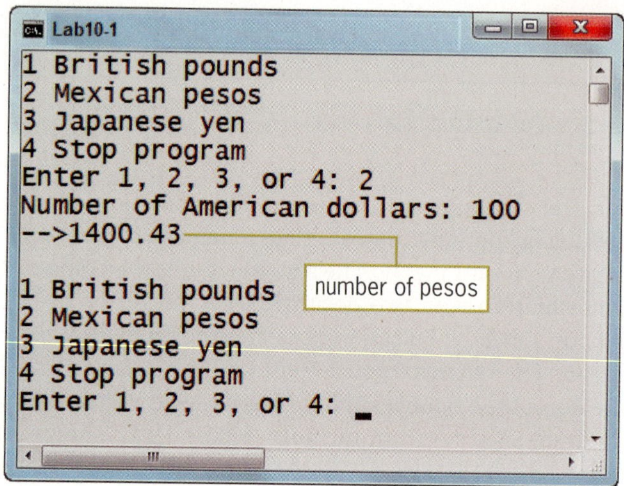

Figure 10-29 Sample run of the program for Lab 10-1

```
//Lab10-1.cpp - Converts American dollars to
//British pounds, Mexican pesos, or Japanese yen
//Created/revised by <your name> on <current date>

#include <iostream>
#include <iomanip>
using namespace std;

//function prototypes
void displayMenu();
void convertDols(double dollars,
                 double convertRate,
                 double &converted);

int main()
{
    //declare constants
    const double BRITISH_RATE  = .63071;
    const double MEXICAN_RATE  = 14.0043;
    const double JAPANESE_RATE = 79.48;

    //declare variables
    int menuChoice            = 0;
    double americanDollars    = 0.0;
    double conversionRate     = 0.0;
    double convertedCurrency = 0.0;

    //display output in fixed-point notation
    //with two decimal places
    cout << fixed << setprecision(2);

```

Figure 10-30 Code for Lab 10-1 *(continues)*

(continued)

```
    //get menu choice
    displayMenu();
    cout << "Enter 1, 2, 3, or 4: ";
    cin >> menuChoice;

    while (menuChoice > 0 && menuChoice < 4)
    {
        //get dollars to convert
        cout << "Number of American dollars: ";
        cin >> americanDollars;

        //assign rate
        if (menuChoice == 1)
            conversionRate = BRITISH_RATE;
        else if (menuChoice == 2)
            conversionRate = MEXICAN_RATE;
        else
            conversionRate = JAPANESE_RATE;
        //end if

        convertDols(americanDollars,
                    conversionRate,
                    convertedCurrency);
        cout << "-->" << convertedCurrency
             << endl << endl;

        //get menu choice
        displayMenu();
        cout << "Enter 1, 2, 3, or 4: ";
        cin >> menuChoice;
    }   //end while

    //system("pause");
    return 0;
}   //end of main function

//*****function definitions*****
void displayMenu()
{
    cout << "1 British pounds" << endl;
    cout << "2 Mexican pesos" << endl;
    cout << "3 Japanese yen" << endl;
    cout << "4 Stop program" << endl;
}   //end of displayMenu function

void convertDols(double dollars,
                 double convertRate,
                 double &converted)
{
    converted = dollars * convertRate;
}   //end of convertDols function
```

if your C++ development tool requires this statement, delete the two forward slashes

Figure 10-30 Code for Lab 10-1

QUESTIONS

1. The `main` function passes three variables to the `convertDols` function. Which lines in the program indicate whether the variables are passed *by value* or *by reference*?
2. Why are the `americanDollars` and `conversionRate` variables passed *by value*? Why is the `convertedCurrency` variable passed *by reference*?
3. Why is the `displayMenu` function a void function?
4. Which line in the program contains the priming read? Which line contains the update read?
5. The `convertDols` function in Figure 10-30 is a void function. How would you modify the function to make it a value-returning function? What other changes would you need to make to the program?
6. Follow the instructions for starting C++ and viewing the Lab10-1.cpp file, which is contained in either the Cpp7\Chap10\Lab10-1 Project folder or the Cpp7\Chap10 folder. (Depending on your C++ development tool, you may need to open Lab10-1's project/solution file first.) If necessary, delete the two forward slashes that appear before the `system("pause");` statement, and then save the program. Run the program. First, you will use the program to convert 100 American dollars to Mexican pesos. Type 2 and press Enter, and then type 100 and press Enter. The program displays the number 1400.43, as shown earlier in Figure 10-29.
7. Use the program to convert 50 American dollars to British pounds. What is the answer?
8. Use the program to convert 10 American dollars to Japanese yen. What is the answer?
9. Modify the program so that it uses a void function to assign the conversion rate. Name the function `assignRate`. Save and then run the program. Test the program using the data from Steps 6, 7, and 8.
10. Now, change the `convertDols` function to a value-returning function. (Refer to Step 5.) Save and then run the program. Test the program using the data from Steps 6, 7, and 8.

LAB 10-2 Plan and Create

In this lab, you will plan and create an algorithm for Addison Clarke. The problem specification and a sample calculation are shown in Figure 10-31.

Problem specification
Addison Clarke works for her local electric company. She wants a program that calculates a customer's electric bill. Addison will enter the current and previous meter readings. The program should calculate and display the number of units of electricity used and the total charge for the electricity. The charge for each unit of electricity is $0.11.

Example

Current reading:	32450
Previous reading:	– 30875
Units used:	1575
Charge per unit:	* .11
Total charge:	$173.25

Figure 10-31 Problem specification and a sample calculation for Lab 10-2

First, analyze the problem, looking for the output first and then for the input. In this case, Addison wants the program to display the number of units of electricity used and the total charge for the electricity. To calculate these amounts, the computer will need to know the previous meter reading, the current meter reading, and the charge per unit of electricity.

Next, plan the algorithm. Recall that most algorithms begin with an instruction to enter the input items into the computer, followed by instructions that process the input items, typically including the items in one or more calculations. Most algorithms end with one or more instructions that display, print, or store the output items.

In this program, you will use three program-defined void functions named `getInput`, `calcBill`, and `displayBill`. Each void function will be called by the program's `main` function. The `getInput` function will get the current and previous meter readings from the user. A void function is appropriate in this case because the `getInput` function needs to get two values for the `main` function, and a value-returning function can return only one value.

The `calcBill` function will be responsible for calculating both the number of units used and the total charge. Here again, a void function is appropriate because the `calcBill` function needs to calculate more than one value for the `main` function.

The `displayBill` function will perform the task of displaying both the number of units used and the total charge. The `displayBill` function should be a void function because it will not need to return a value to the `main` function after completing its task.

Figure 10-32 shows the IPO charts for the program's functions. Notice that the `getInput` function will be passed the addresses of variables that it can use to store the current and previous meter readings. The `calcBill` function will be passed five items: the current reading, the previous reading, the unit charge, the address of a variable that it can use to store the number of units used, and the address of a variable that it can use to store the total charge. The first three items are necessary to calculate both the number of units used and the total charge. The last two items provide memory locations in which to store the calculated results. The `displayBill` function will be passed two items: the number of units used and the total charge.

<u>`main` function</u>

Input	Processing	Output
current reading previous reading unit charge (.11)	Processing items: none Algorithm: 1. call the getInput function to get the current reading and previous reading; pass the addresses of variables in which to store the current reading and previous reading 2. call the calcBill function to calculate the units used and total charge; pass the current reading, previous reading, and unit charge, as well as the addresses of variables in which to store the units used and total charge 3. call the displayBill function to display the units used and total charge; pass the units used and total charge	units used total charge

Figure 10-32 IPO charts for the functions in the electric bill program *(continues)*

(continued)

start

call getInput; pass addresses of variables in which to store current reading and previous reading

call calcBill; pass current reading, previous reading, and unit charge, as well as addresses of variables in which to store units used and total charge

call displayBill; pass units used and total charge

stop

getInput function

Input	Processing	Output
addresses of variables to store: current reading previous reading	Processing items: none Algorithm: 1. enter the current reading 2. enter the previous reading	current reading previous reading

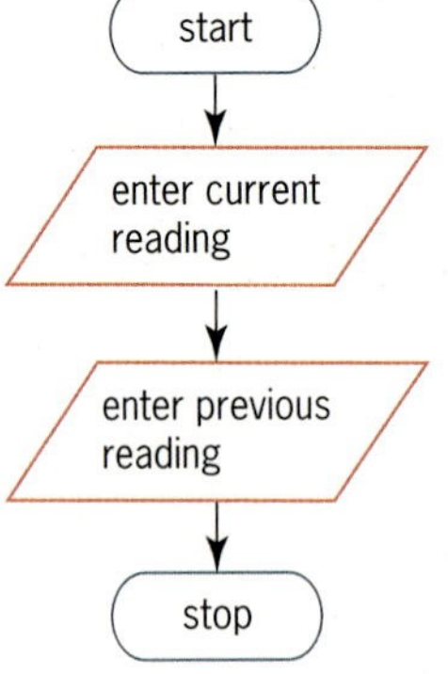

calcBill function

Input	Processing	Output
current reading previous reading unit charge addresses of variables to store: units used total charge	Processing items: none	units used total charge

Figure 10-32 IPO charts for the functions in the electric bill program *(continues)*

(continued)

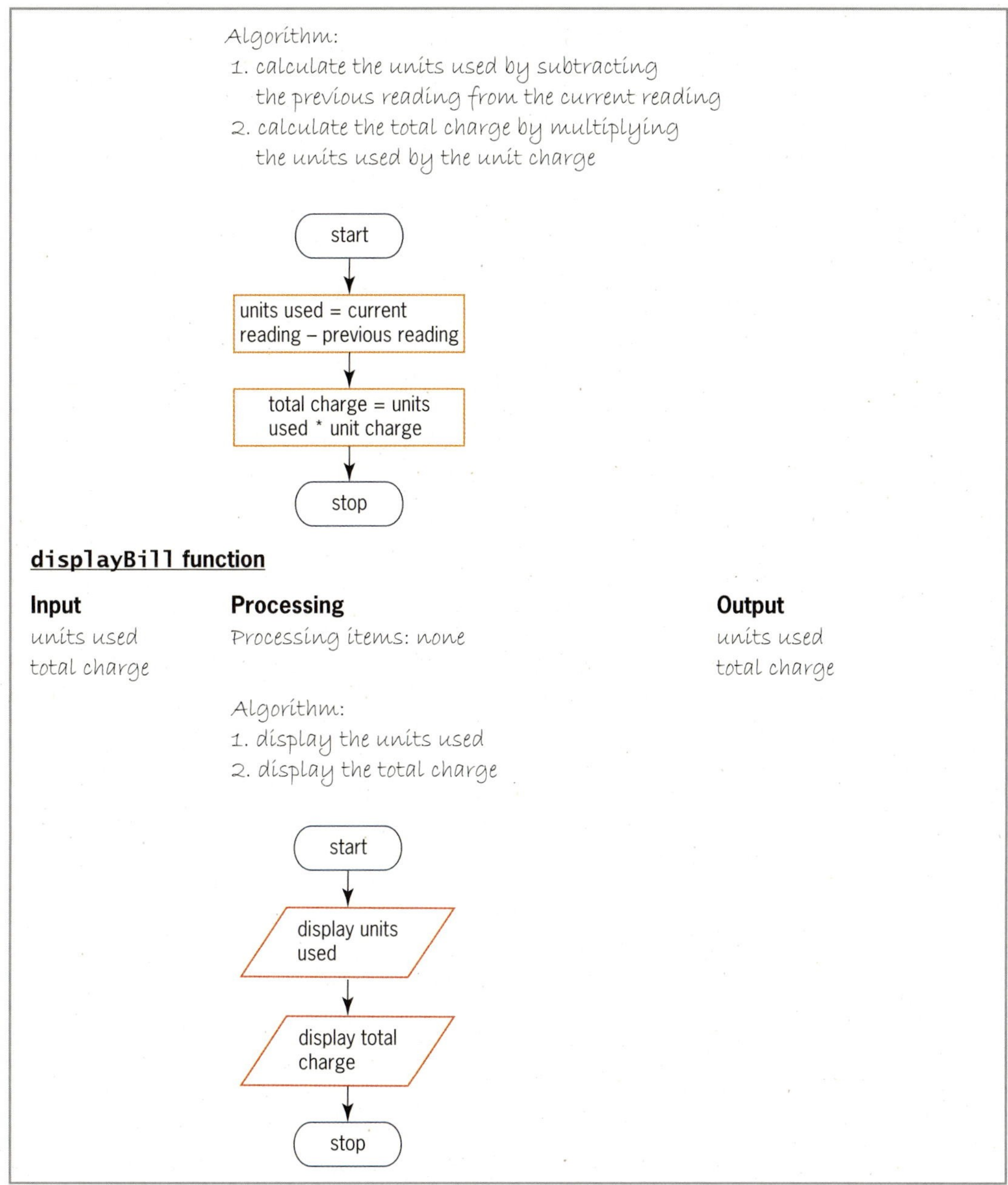

Figure 10-32 IPO charts for the functions in the electric bill program

After completing the IPO charts, you then move on to the third step in the problem-solving process, which is to desk-check the algorithm. You will desk-check the algorithms in Figure 10-32 using 32450 and 30875 as the current and previous meter readings, respectively. Using these values, the number of units used and total charge should be 1575 and $173.25, respectively. Figure 10-33 shows the completed desk-check table.

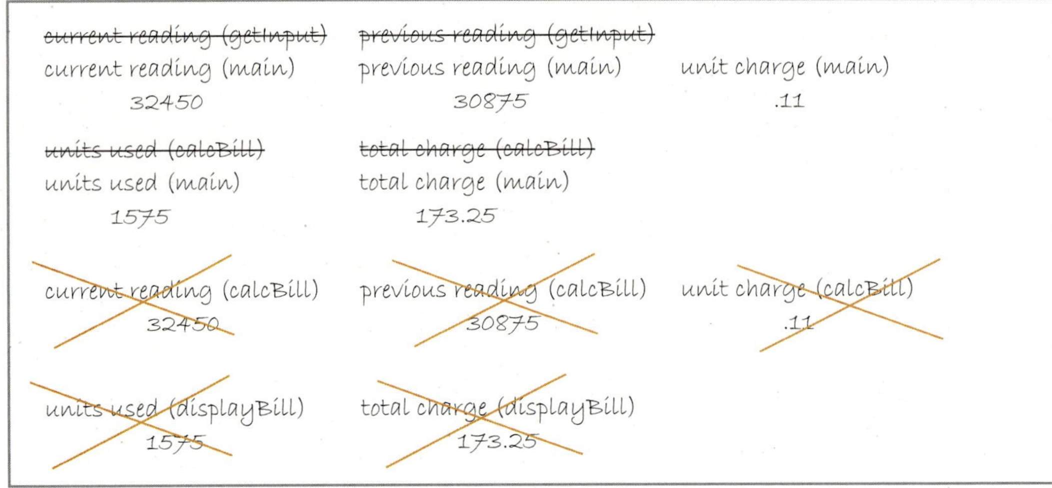

Figure 10-33 Completed desk-check table for the electric bill algorithms

The fourth step in the problem-solving process is to code the algorithm into a program. The IPO chart information and C++ instructions for the electric bill program are shown in Figure 10-34.

main function

IPO chart information	C++ instructions
Input	
current reading	`int current = 0;`
previous reading	`int previous = 0;`
unit charge (.11)	`const double UNIT_CHG = .11;`
Processing	
none	
Output	
units used	`int units = 0;`
total charge	`double total = 0.0;`
Algorithm	
1. call the getInput function to get the current reading and previous reading; pass the addresses of variables in which to store the current reading and previous reading	`getInput(current, previous);`
2. call the calcBill function to calculate the units used and total charge; pass the current reading, previous reading, and unit charge, as well as the addresses of variables in which to store the units used and total charge	`calcBill(current, previous, UNIT_CHG, units, total);`
3. call the displayBill function to display the units used and total charge; pass the units used and total charge	`displayBill(units, total);`

Figure 10-34 IPO chart information and C++ instructions for the electric bill program *(continues)*

(continued)

getInput function	
IPO chart information	**C++ instructions**
Input	
addresses of variables to store:	
current reading (formal parameter)	`int &newReading`
previous reading (formal parameter)	`int &oldReading`
Processing	
none	
Output	
current reading	stored in the newReading formal parameter
previous reading	stored in the oldReading formal parameter
Algorithm	
1. enter the current reading	`cout << "Current reading: ";` `cin >> newReading;`
2. enter the previous reading	`cout << "Previous reading: ";` `cin >> oldReading;`
calcBill function	
IPO chart information	**C++ instructions**
Input	
current reading (formal parameter)	`int curRead`
previous reading (formal parameter)	`int prevRead`
unit charge (formal parameter)	`double chgPerUnit`
addresses of variables to store:	
units used (formal parameter)	`int &numUnits`
total charge (formal parameter)	`double &totChg`
Processing	
none	
Output	
units used	stored in the numUnits formal parameter
total charge	stored in the totChg formal parameter
Algorithm	
1. calculate the units used by subtracting the previous reading from the current reading	`numUnits = curRead` `- prevRead;`
2. calculate the total charge by multiplying the units used by the unit charge	`totChg = numUnits` `* chgPerUnit;`

Figure 10-34 IPO chart information and C++ instructions for the electric bill program *(continues)*

(continued)

displayBill function	
IPO chart information	**C++ instructions**
Input	
units used (formal parameter)	`int used`
total charge (formal parameter)	`double charge`
Processing	
none	
Output	
units used	
total charge	
Algorithm	
1. display the units used	`cout << "Units used: " << used << endl;`
2. display the total charge	`cout << "Total charge: $" << charge << endl;`

Figure 10-34 IPO chart information and C++ instructions for the electric bill program

The fifth step in the problem-solving process is to desk-check the program. Figure 10-35 shows the entire electric bill program, and Figure 10-36 shows the completed desk-check table.

```
//Lab10-2.cpp - displays the number of units of
//electricity used and the total charge
//Created/revised by <your name> on <current date>

#include <iostream>
#include <iomanip>
using namespace std;

//function prototypes
void getInput(int &newReading, int &oldReading);
void calcBill(int curRead, int prevRead,
              double chgPerUnit, int &numUnits,
              double &totChg);
void displayBill(int used, double charge);

int main()
{
    //declare constant and variables
    const double UNIT_CHG = .11;
    int current  = 0;
    int previous = 0;
    int units    = 0;
    double total = 0.0;

    cout << fixed << setprecision(2);

```

Figure 10-35 Electric bill program *(continues)*

(continued)

```
    //call functions
    getInput(current, previous);
    calcBill(current, previous, UNIT_CHG, units, total);
    displayBill(units, total);

    //system("pause");
    return 0;
}   //end of main function

//*****function definitions*****
void getInput(int &newReading, int &oldReading)
{
    cout << "Current reading: ";
    cin >> newReading;
    cout << "Previous reading: ";
    cin >> oldReading;
}   //end of getInput function

void calcBill(int curRead, int prevRead,
              double chgPerUnit, int &numUnits,
              double &totChg)
{
    numUnits = curRead - prevRead;
    totChg = numUnits * chgPerUnit;
}   //end of calcBill function

void displayBill(int used, double charge)
{
    cout << "Units used: " << used << endl;
    cout << "Total charge: $" << charge << endl;
}   //end of displayBill function
```

if your C++ development tool requires this statement, delete the two forward slashes

Figure 10-35 Electric bill program

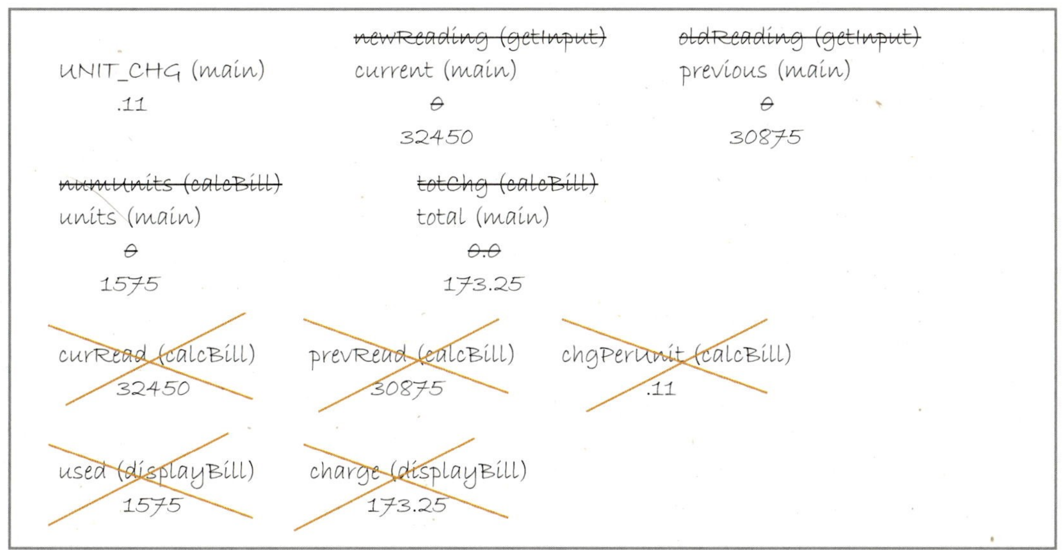

Figure 10-36 Completed desk-check table for the electric bill program

The final step in the problem-solving process is to evaluate and modify (if necessary) the program. Recall that you evaluate a program by entering its instructions into the computer and then using the computer to run (execute) it. While the program is running, you enter the same sample data used when desk-checking the program.

DIRECTIONS

Follow the instructions for starting your C++ development tool. Depending on the development tool you are using, you may need to create a new project; if so, name the project Lab10-2 Project and save it in the Cpp7\Chap10 folder. Enter the instructions shown in Figure 10-35 in a source file named Lab10-2.cpp. (Do not enter the line numbers.) Save the file in either the project folder or the Cpp7\Chap10 folder. Now, follow the appropriate instructions for running the Lab10-2.cpp file. Test the program using 32450 and 30875 as the current and previous meter readings, respectively. The number of units used and the total charge should be 1575 and $173.25, respectively. Also test the program using your own sample data. If necessary, correct any bugs (errors) in the program.

LAB 10-3 Modify

If necessary, create a new project named Lab10-3 Project and save it in the Cpp7\Chap10 folder. Enter (or copy) the Lab10-2.cpp instructions into a new source file named Lab10-3.cpp. Change Lab10-2.cpp in the first comment to Lab10-3.cpp. Currently, the electric bill program uses one void function to calculate both the number of units used and the total charge. Replace the `calcBill` function with two functions: a void function that calculates the number of units used, and a value-returning function that calculates and returns the total charge. Name the functions `getUnits` and `getTotal`, respectively. Save and then run the program. Test the program appropriately.

LAB 10-4 Desk-Check

Desk-check the code in Figure 10-37 using the following four sets of test scores: 78 and 85, 45 and 93, 87 and 98, and 54 and 32.

```
//Lab10-4.cpp - displays the average test score
//Created/revised by <your name> on <current date>

#include <iostream>
#include <iomanip>
using namespace std;

//function prototype
void calcAvg(double num1, double num2, double &avg);

```

Figure 10-37 Code for Lab 10-4 *(continues)*

(continued)

```
int main()
{
    //declare variables
    double test1   = 0.0;
    double test2   = 0.0;
    double average = 0.0;

    cout << "First test score ";
    cout << "(negative number to end): ";
    cin >> test1;
    while (test1 >= 0)
    {
        cout << "Second test score: ";
        cin >> test2;

        //call function to calculate the average
        calcAvg(test1, test2, average);

        //display the average
        cout << fixed << setprecision(1);
        cout << "Average score: " << average
             << endl << endl;

        cout << "First test score ";
        cout << "(negative number to end): ";
        cin >> test1;
    }   //end while

    //system("pause");
    return 0;
}   //end of main function

//*****function definitions*****
void calcAvg(double num1, double num2, double &avg)
{
    avg = (num1 + num2) / 2;
}   //end of calcAvg function
```

Figure 10-37 Code for Lab 10-4

LAB 10-5 Debug

Follow the instructions for starting C++ and viewing the Lab10-5.cpp file, which is contained in either the Cpp7\Chap10\Lab10-5 Project folder or the Cpp7\Chap10 folder. (Depending on your C++ development tool, you may need to open Lab10-5's project/solution file first.) If necessary, delete the two forward slashes that appear before the `system("pause");` statement and then save the program. Run the program. Enter the following scores: 93, 90, 85, and 100. The program should display 368 as the total points and A as the grade. Debug the program.

Summary

- All functions fall into one of two categories: value-returning or void. A value-returning function returns precisely one value to the statement that called the function. A void function, on the other hand, does not return a value.
- Like a value-returning function, a void function is composed of a function header and a function body. However, unlike a value-returning function, the function header for a void function begins with the keyword `void` rather than with a data type. Also unlike a value-returning function, the function body for a void function does not contain a `return` statement.
- As you do when calling a value-returning function, you call a void function by including its name and actual arguments (if any) in a statement. However, unlike a call to a value-returning function, a call to a void function appears as a statement by itself rather than as part of another statement. When the computer finishes processing a void function's code, it continues program execution with the statement immediately below the one that called the function.
- Variables can be passed to functions either *by value* (the default) or *by reference.*
- When you pass a variable *by value*, only a copy of the value stored inside of the variable is passed to the receiving function. The receiving function is not given access to a variable passed *by value*, so it cannot change the variable's contents.
- When you pass a variable *by value*, the computer uses the data type and name of the corresponding formal parameter to create a separate memory location in which to store a copy of the value.
- When you pass a variable *by reference*, the variable's address in memory is passed to the receiving function, allowing the receiving function to change the variable's contents. Only variables can be passed *by reference.*
- When you pass a variable *by reference*, the computer locates the variable in memory and then assigns the name of its corresponding formal parameter to the memory location. As a result, the variable will have two names: one assigned by the calling function and the other assigned by the receiving function.
- To pass a variable *by reference* in a C++ program, you include the address-of operator (&) before the name of the corresponding formal parameter in the function header. If the function definition appears below the `main` function in the program, you also must include the address-of operator in the function prototype. The address-of operator tells the computer to pass the variable's address rather than its contents.

Key Terms

&—the address-of operator

Address-of operator—the ampersand; tells the computer to pass a variable's address in memory rather than its contents

Passing *by reference*—refers to the process of passing a variable's address to a function

Void functions—functions that do not return a value after completing their assigned task

Review Questions

1. Which of the following is false?
   a. A void function does not return a value after completing its assigned task.
   b. A void function call typically appears as its own statement in a C++ program.
   c. A void function cannot receive any items of information when it is called.
   d. A void function header begins with the keyword `void`.

2. Which of the following C++ statements correctly calls a void function named `displayTotal`, passing it an `int` variable named `total`?
   a. `cout << displayTotal(int total);`
   b. `cout << displayTotal(total);`
   c. `displayTotal(int total);`
   d. `displayTotal(total);`

3. A void function named `calcEndingBalance` is passed the values stored in two `int` variables. Which of the following function prototypes is correct for this function?
   a. `void calcEndingBalance(int, int);`
   b. `void calcEndingBalance(int, int)`
   c. `void calcEndingBalance(int &, int &);`
   d. `int calcEndingBalance(void);`

4. A void function named `calcEndingInventory` is passed four `int` variables named `beginInventory`, `sales`, `purchases`, and `endingInventory`. The function's task is to calculate the ending inventory, using the beginning inventory, sales, and purchase amounts passed to the function. The function should store the result in the `endingInventory` variable. Which of the following function headers is correct?
   a. `void calcEndingInventory(int b, int s, int p, int &e)`
   b. `void calcEndingInventory(int b, int s, int p, int e)`
   c. `void calcEndingInventory(int &b, int &s, int &p, int e)`
   d. `void calcEndingInventory(&int b, &int s, &int p, &int e)`

5. Which of the following statements calls the `calcEndingInventory` function described in Review Question 4?
   a. `calcEndingInventory(int, int, int, int);`
   b. `calcEndingInventory(beginInventory, sales, purchases, &endingInventory);`
   c. `calcEndingInventory(beginInventory, sales, purchases, endingInventory);`
   d. `calcEndingInventory(int beginInventory, int sales, int purchases, int &endingInventory);`

6. Unless specified otherwise, variables in C++ are passed ________.
   a. *by address*
   b. *by number*
   c. *by reference*
   d. *by value*

7. If you want the receiving function to change the contents of a variable, you must pass the variable ________________.

   a. *by address*
   b. *by number*
   c. *by reference*
   d. *by value*

8. To determine whether an item is being passed *by value* or *by reference*, you must examine either the ________________ or the ________________.

   a. function call, function header
   b. function call, function prototype
   c. function header, function prototype
   d. function header, function body

9. Which of the following calls a void function named `displayName`, passing it no actual arguments?

   a. `call displayName();`
   b. `displayName;`
   c. `displayName()`
   d. `displayName();`

10. Which of the following is a correct function prototype for a void function that requires no formal parameters? The function's name is `displayName`.

    a. `displayName();`
    b. `void displayName;`
    c. `void displayName();`
    d. `void displayName(none);`

11. When a void function ends, the computer continues program execution with ________________.

    a. the statement immediately above the one that called the function
    b. the statement that called the function
    c. the statement immediately below the one that called the function

12. If the function definitions section is located below the `main` function in a program, the program will have one function prototype for each program-defined function.

    a. True
    b. False

13. Variables that can be used only by the function in which they are declared are called ________________ variables.

    a. global
    b. local
    c. separate
    d. void

14. Which of the following is false?
    a. When you pass a variable *by reference,* the receiving function can change the variable's contents.
    b. When you pass a variable *by value,* the receiving function creates a local variable that it uses to store the value.
    c. Unless specified otherwise, all variables in C++ are passed *by value.*
    d. To pass a variable *by reference* in C++, you place an ampersand (&) before the variable's name in the statement that calls the function.

15. A program contains a void function named `calcNewPrice`. The function receives two `double` variables named `oldPrice` and `newPrice`. The function multiplies the contents of the `oldPrice` variable by 1.1 and then stores the result in the `newPrice` variable. Which of the following is the appropriate function prototype for this function?
    a. `void calcNewPrice(double, double);`
    b. `void calcNewPrice(double &, double);`
    c. `void calcNewPrice(double, double &);`
    d. `void calcNewPrice(double &, double &);`

16. Which of the following can be used to call the `calcNewPrice` function described in Review Question 15?
    a. `calcNewPrice(double oldPrice, double newPrice);`
    b. `calcNewPrice(&oldPrice, newPrice);`
    c. `calcNewPrice(oldPrice, &newPrice);`
    d. `calcNewPrice(oldPrice, newPrice);`

17. Which of the following is false?
    a. The names of the formal parameters in the function header must be identical to the names of the actual arguments in the function call.
    b. When listing the formal parameters in a function header, you include each parameter's data type and name.
    c. The formal parameters should be the same data type as the actual arguments.
    d. If a function call passes an `int` variable first and a `char` variable second, the receiving function should receive an `int` variable followed by a `char` variable.

Exercises

Pencil and Paper

1. Write the C++ code for a void function that receives an integer passed to it. The function should divide the integer by 2 and then display the result, which may contain a decimal place. Name the function `divideByTwo`. Name the formal parameter `wholeNumber`. (The answers to TRY THIS Exercises are located at the end of the chapter.) TRY THIS
2. Write the function prototype for the `divideByTwo` function from Pencil and Paper Exercise 1. (The answers to TRY THIS Exercises are located at the end of the chapter.) TRY THIS
3. Write a statement that calls the `divideByTwo` function from Pencil and Paper Exercise 1, passing the function the contents of the `total` variable. (The answers to TRY THIS Exercises are located at the end of the chapter.) TRY THIS

MODIFY THIS

4. Rewrite the code from Pencil and Paper Exercises 1, 2, and 3 so that the `divideByTwo` function receives two integers rather than one integer. The function should divide the sum of both integers by 2 and then display the result. Name the formal parameters `num1` and `num2`. Name the actual arguments `total1` and `total2`.

INTRODUCTORY

5. Write the C++ code for a void function that receives three `double` variables: the first two *by value* and the last one *by reference*. Name the formal parameters `n1`, `n2`, and `answer`. The function should divide the `n1` variable by the `n2` variable and then store the result in the `answer` variable. Name the function `calcQuotient`. Also write an appropriate function prototype for the `calcQuotient` function. In addition, write a statement that invokes the `calcQuotient` function, passing it the `num1`, `num2`, and `quotient` variables.

INTERMEDIATE

6. Write the C++ code for a void function that receives four `int` variables: the first two *by value* and the last two *by reference*. Name the formal parameters `n1`, `n2`, `sum`, and `diff`. The function should calculate the sum of the two variables passed *by value* and then store the result in the first variable passed *by reference*. It also should calculate the difference between the two variables passed *by value* and then store the result in the second variable passed *by reference*. When calculating the difference, subtract the contents of the `n2` variable from the contents of the `n1` variable. Name the function `calcSumAndDiff`. Also write an appropriate function prototype for the `calcSumAndDiff` function. In addition, write a statement that invokes the `calcSumAndDiff` function, passing it the `num1`, `num2`, `numSum`, and `numDiff` variables.

INTERMEDIATE

7. Write the C++ code for a function that receives five `double` numbers: four *by value* and one *by reference*. Name the formal parameters `num1`, `num2`, `num3`, `num4`, and `avg`. The function should calculate the average of the four numbers and then assign the result to the `avg` variable. Name the function `calcAverage`. Also write an appropriate function prototype for the `calcAverage` function. In addition, write a statement that invokes the `calcAverage` function. Use the following numbers and variable as the actual arguments: 45.67, 8.35, 125.78, 99.56, and `numAvg`.

INTERMEDIATE

8. Desk-check the program shown in Figure 10-38. Show the desk-check table after the first four statements in the `main` function are processed. Also show it after the statement in the `calcEnd` function is processed. Finally, show the desk-check table after the `calcEnd` function ends.

```
//Fig10-38.cpp - displays the ending balance
//Created/revised by <your name> on <current date>

#include <iostream>
using namespace std;

void calcEnd(int beg, int pur,
             int sale, int &ending);

int main()
{
    int begVal   = 1000;
    int purchase = 500;
    int sale     = 200;
    int endVal   = 0;

```

Figure 10-38 *(continues)*

(continued)

```
    calcEnd(begVal, purchase, sale, endVal);

    cout << "Ending value: " << endVal << endl;

    //system("pause");
    return 0;
} //end of main function

//*****function definitions*****
void calcEnd(int beg, int pur,
             int sale, int &ending)
{
    ending = beg + pur - sale;
} //end of calcEnd function
```

Figure 10-38

SWAT THE BUGS

9. A program's `main` function declares three `double` variables named `sales`, `taxRate`, and `salesTax`. The `main` function contains the following statement: `calcSalesTax(sales, taxRate, salesTax);`. The `calcSalesTax` function is responsible for calculating the sales tax. Its function header looks like this: `void calcSalesTax(double sold, double rate, double tax)`. Correct the function header.

Computer

TRY THIS

10. In this exercise, you will experiment with passing variables *by value* and *by reference*. (The answers to TRY THIS Exercises are located at the end of the chapter.)
    a. Follow the instructions for starting C++ and viewing the TryThis10.cpp file, which is contained in either the Cpp7\Chap10\TryThis10 Project folder or the Cpp7\Chap10 folder. (Depending on your C++ development tool, you may need to open this exercise's project/solution file first.) If necessary, delete the two forward slashes that appear before the `system("pause");` statement, and then save the program.
    b. Notice that the `main` function passes the `age` variable *by value* to the `getAge` function. Run the program. When prompted to enter your age, type your age and press Enter. The message that appears should contain your age; however, it contains the number 0 instead. This is because the `age` variable is passed *by value* to the `getAge` function.
    c. Modify the program so that it passes the `age` variable *by reference* to the `getAge` function. Save and then run the program. When prompted to enter your age, type your age and press Enter. This time, the message contains your age.

TRY THIS

11. In this exercise, you modify the program from Lab 9-2 in Chapter 9. If necessary, create a new project named TryThis11 Project and save it in the Cpp7\Chap10 folder. Copy the instructions from the Lab9-2.cpp file into a source file named TryThis11.cpp. (The Lab9-2.cpp file is contained in either the Cpp7\Chap09\Lab9-2 Project folder or the Cpp7\Chap09 folder. Alternatively, you can enter the instructions from Figure 9-50 into the TryThis11.cpp file.) Change the filename in the first comment to TryThis11.cpp.

Modify the program to use a void function named `displayPayment`. The `displayPayment` function should accept a monthly payment and then display the monthly payment on the screen. Save and then run the program. Test the program using 16000, 3000, .08, .03, and 4 as the car price, rebate, credit union rate, dealer rate, and term, respectively. The monthly payments should be $317.37 and $354.15. (The answers to TRY THIS Exercises are located at the end of the chapter.)

TRY THIS

12. In this exercise, you modify the program from TRY THIS Exercise 14 in Chapter 9. If necessary, create a new project named TryThis12 Project and save it in the Cpp7\Chap10 folder. If you completed Chapter 9's TRY THIS Exercise 14, copy the instructions from the TryThis14.cpp file into a source file named TryThis12.cpp. (The TryThis14.cpp file is contained in either the Cpp7\Chap09\TryThis14 Project folder or the Cpp7\Chap09 folder. Alternatively, you can enter the instructions from Figure 9-53 into the TryThis12.cpp file.) Change the filename in the first comment to TryThis12.cpp. Change the `getFahrenheit` and `calcCelsius` functions to void functions. Save and then run the program. Test the program using the following Fahrenheit temperatures: 32 and 212.

MODIFY THIS

13. In this exercise, you modify the code from Computer Exercise 11. If necessary, create a new project named ModifyThis13 Project and save it in the Cpp7\Chap10 folder. Enter (or copy) the TryThis11.cpp instructions into a new source file named ModifyThis13.cpp. Change the filename in the first comment to ModifyThis13.cpp. Change the `getPayment` function to a void function named `calcPayment`. Save and then run the program. Test the program using 16000, 3000, .08, .03, and 4 as the car price, rebate, credit union rate, dealer rate, and term, respectively. The monthly payments should be $317.37 and $354.15.

MODIFY THIS

14. In this exercise, you modify the program from Lab10-1. Follow the instructions for starting C++ and viewing the ModifyThis14.cpp file, which is contained in either the Cpp7\Chap10\ModifyThis14 Project folder or the Cpp7\Chap10 folder. (Depending on your C++ development tool, you may need to open this exercise's project/solution file first.) If necessary, delete the two forward slashes that appear before the `system("pause");` statement, and then save the program. Modify the program so that it also displays the currency type (pounds, pesos, or yen). For example, Figure 10-29 in the chapter should display "-->1400.43 pesos". Save, run, and test the program.

INTRODUCTORY

15. In this exercise, you modify the program from Lab 8-2 in Chapter 8. If necessary, create a new project named Introductory15 Project and save it in the Cpp7\Chap10 folder. Copy the instructions from the Lab8-2.cpp file into a source file named Introductory15.cpp. (The Lab8-2.cpp file is contained in either the Cpp7\Chap08\Lab8-2 Project folder or the Cpp7\Chap08 folder. Alternatively, you can enter the instructions from Figure 8-42 into the Introductory15.cpp file.) Change the filename in the first comment to Introductory15.cpp. Modify the program so that it uses a void function to display the multiplication table. Save and then run the program. Test the program using multiplicands of 2 and 4, followed by a sentinel value.

INTRODUCTORY

16. In this exercise, you modify the program from Lab 7-2 in Chapter 7. If necessary, create a new project named Introductory16 Project and save it in the Cpp7\Chap10 folder. Copy the instructions from the Lab7-2.cpp file into a source file named Introductory16.cpp. (The Lab7-2.cpp file is contained in either the Cpp7\Chap07\Lab7-2 Project folder or the Cpp7\Chap07 folder. Alternatively, you can enter the instructions from Figure 7-52 into the Introductory16.cpp file.) Change the filename in the first comment to Introductory16.cpp. Modify the program so that it uses a void function to determine the grade. Save and then run the program. Test the program using the following scores and sentinel value: 45, 40, 41, 96, 89, and –1. The total points and grade should be 311 and B, respectively.

INTRODUCTORY

17. In this exercise, you modify the program from Lab 6-2 in Chapter 6. If necessary, create a new project named Introductory17 Project and save it in the Cpp7\Chap10 folder. Copy the instructions from the Lab6-2.cpp file into a source file named Introductory17.cpp. (The Lab6-2.cpp file is contained in either the Cpp7\Chap06\Lab6-2 Project folder or the Cpp7\Chap06 folder. Alternatively, you can enter the instructions from Figure 6-37 into the Introductory17.cpp file.) Change the filename in the first comment to Introductory17.cpp. Modify the program so that it uses a void function to determine the commission. Save and then run the program. Test the program using the following sales amounts: 15000 and 250125.

INTERMEDIATE

18. In this exercise, you modify the program from Lab 5-2 in Chapter 5. If necessary, create a new project named Intermediate18 Project and save it in the Cpp7\Chap10 folder. Copy the instructions from the Lab5-2.cpp file into a source file named Intermediate18.cpp. (The Lab5-2.cpp file is contained in either the Cpp7\Chap05\Lab5-2 Project folder or the Cpp7\Chap05 folder. Alternatively, you can enter the instructions from Figure 5-34 into the Intermediate18.cpp file.) Change the filename in the first comment to Intermediate18.cpp. Modify the program so that it uses two void functions: one to determine the fat calories and the other to determine the fat percentage. Save and then run the program. Test the program appropriately.

INTERMEDIATE

19. In this exercise, you create a simple payroll program using a `main` function and four void functions.

    a. Figure 10-39 shows the IPO chart information for the payroll program. Complete the C++ instructions column for the `main` function and for the three void functions (`calcFedTaxes`, `calcNetPay`, and `displayInfo`). The FWT (Federal Withholding Tax) rate is 20% of the weekly salary, and the FICA (Federal Insurance Contributions Act) rate is 8% of the weekly salary.

    b. If necessary, create a new project named Intermediate19 Project and save it in the Cpp7\Chap10 folder. Enter your C++ instructions into a source file named Intermediate19.cpp. Also enter appropriate comments and any additional instructions required by the compiler. Display the taxes and net pay with two decimal places.

    c. Save and then run the program. Test the program using 500 and 650 as the salary.

`main` function **IPO chart information**	**C++ instructions**
Input salary FWT rate (.2) FICA rate (.08) **Processing** none **Output** FWT FICA net pay	

Figure 10-39 *(continues)*

(continued)

Algorithm

1. enter the salary
2. repeat while (the salary > 0)

    call the calcFedTaxes function to calculate the FWT and FICA; pass the salary, FWT rate, FICA rate, and the addresses of variables in which to store the FWT and FICA

    call the calcNetPay function to calculate the net pay; pass the salary, FWT, FICA, and the address of the variable in which to store the net pay

    call the displayInfo function to display the FWT, FICA, and net pay; pass the FWT, FICA, and net pay

    enter the salary

   end repeat

`calcFedTaxes` function

IPO chart information | **C++ instructions**

Input

salary (formal parameter)
FWT rate (formal parameter)
FICA rate (formal parameter)
addresses of variables to store:
  FWT (formal parameter)
  FICA (formal parameter)

Processing

none

Output

FWT
FICA

Algorithm

1. calculate the FWT by multiplying the salary by the FWT rate
2. calculate the FICA by multiplying the salary by the FICA rate

`calcNetPay` function

IPO chart information | **C++ instructions**

Input

salary (formal parameter)
FWT (formal parameter)
FICA (formal parameter)
address of a variable to store:
  net pay (formal parameter)

Figure 10-39 *(continues)*

(continued)

Processing
none

Output
net pay

Algorithm
calculate the net pay by subtracting the FWT and FICA from the salary

displayInfo function

IPO chart information	C++ instructions
Input	
FWT (formal parameter)	
FICA (formal parameter)	
net pay (formal parameter)	
Processing	
none	
Output	
FWT	
FICA	
net pay	
Algorithm	
display the FWT, FICA, and net pay	

Figure 10-39

INTERMEDIATE

20. The payroll manager at Gerston Blankets wants a program that calculates and displays the gross pay for each of the company's employees. It also should calculate and display the total gross pay. The payroll manager will enter the number of hours the employee worked and his or her pay rate. Employees working more than 40 hours should receive time and one-half for the hours over 40. Use a void function to determine an employee's gross pay. Use a value-returning function to accumulate the total gross pay. The program should display the total gross pay only after the payroll manager has finished entering the data for all the employees. Use a sentinel value to end the program.

    a. Create IPO charts for the problem, and then desk-check the algorithm using the following four sets of hours worked and pay rates: 35, $10.50; 43, $15; 32, $9.75; and 20, $6.45.

    b. List the input, processing, and output items, as well as the algorithm, in a chart similar to the one shown earlier in Figure 10-39. Then, code the algorithm into a program.

    c. Desk-check the program using the same data used to desk-check the algorithm.

    d. If necessary, create a new project named Intermediate20 Project and save it in the Cpp7\Chap10 folder. Enter your C++ instructions into a source file named Intermediate20.cpp. Also enter appropriate comments and any additional instructions required by the compiler.

    e. Save and then run the program. Test the program using the same data used to desk-check the program.

INTERMEDIATE

21. The sales manager at Tompkins Company wants a program that calculates and displays each salesperson's commission, which is 10% of his or her sales. It also should display the total commission. Use a value-returning function to get the amount sold by a salesperson. The amount sold may contain a decimal place. Also use three void functions: one to calculate the 10% commission, another to display the commission, and another to calculate the total commission. The program should display the commission and total commission in fixed-point notation with two decimal places. Display the total commission only after the sales manager has finished entering the sales amounts. Use a sentinel value to end the program.

    a. Create IPO charts for the problem.

    b. List the input, processing, and output items, as well as the algorithm, in a chart similar to the one shown earlier in Figure 10-39. Then, code the algorithm into a program.

    c. If necessary, create a new project named Intermediate21 Project and save it in the Cpp7\Chap10 folder. Enter your C++ instructions into a source file named Intermediate21.cpp. Also enter appropriate comments and any additional instructions required by the compiler.

    d. Save and then run the program. Test the program using the following four sales amounts: 12000, 23000, 10000, and 25000. Then enter your sentinel value.

ADVANCED

22. In this exercise, you create a program that calculates the average of three test scores. The program should contain two value-returning functions (`main` and `calcAverage`) and two void functions (`getTestScores` and `displayAverage`). The `main` function should call the void `getTestScores` function to get three test scores. The test scores may contain a decimal place. The `main` function then should call the value-returning `calcAverage` function to calculate and return the average of the three test scores. When the `calcAverage` function has completed its task, the `main` function should call the void `displayAverage` function to display the average of the three test scores on the screen. Display the average with one decimal place. Use a sentinel value to end the program.

    a. Create IPO charts for the problem, and then desk-check the algorithm using the following four sets of test scores, followed by your sentinel value: 56, 78, 90; 100, 85, 67; 74, 32, 98; and 25, 99, 84.

    b. List the input, processing, and output items, as well as the algorithm, in a chart similar to the one shown earlier in Figure 10-39. Then, code the algorithm into a program.

    c. Desk-check the program using the same data used to desk-check the algorithm.

    d. If necessary, create a new project named Advanced22 Project and save it in the Cpp7\Chap10 folder. Enter your C++ instructions into a source file named Advanced22.cpp. Also enter appropriate comments and any additional instructions required by the compiler.

    e. Save and then run the program. Test the program using the same data used to desk-check the program.

ADVANCED

23. In this exercise, you prevent a function from changing the value of a named constant passed to it.

    a. If necessary, create a new project named Advanced23 Project and save it in the Cpp7\Chap10 folder. Copy the instructions from the Lab10-2.cpp file into a source file named Advanced23.cpp. (Alternatively, you can enter the instructions from Figure 10-35 into the Advanced23.cpp file.) Change the filename in the first comment to Advanced23.cpp.

b. The program passes the value of the `UNIT_CHG` named constant to the `calcBill` function, which stores the value it receives (.11) in the `chgPerUnit` variable. Because the function stores the value in a variable, the value can be changed by the function. First, you will verify that the `calcBill` function can change the value stored in its `chgPerUnit` variable. Insert a blank line above the `totChg = numUnits * chgPerUnit;` statement in the `calcBill` function. In the blank line, type `chgPerUnit = .25;`. Save and then run the program. Enter 3000 and 2000 as the current and previous readings, respectively. The program displays 1000 as the number of units used, which is correct. However, rather than displaying $110.00 as the total charge, the program displays $250.00.

c. To prevent the `calcBill` function from changing the charge per unit value, you must use the `const` keyword to indicate that the value being passed is a constant. Make the appropriate modification to the `calcBill` function's prototype and its header. Save and then run the program. (If you are asked whether you would like to run the last successful build, click the No button.) The compiler displays an error message indicating that you cannot assign a value to the `chgPerUnit` variable, which is defined using the `const` keyword.

d. Delete the `chgPerUnit = .25;` statement from the `calcBill` function. Save and then run the program. Enter 3000 and 2000 as the current and previous readings, respectively. The program correctly displays 1000 and $110.00 as the units used and total charge, respectively.

ADVANCED

24. In this exercise, you modify the electric bill program from Lab10-2.

a. If necessary, create a new project named Advanced24 Project and save it in the Cpp7\Chap10 folder. Copy the instructions from the Lab10-2.cpp file into a source file named Advanced24.cpp. (Alternatively, you can enter the instructions from Figure 10-35 into the Advanced24.cpp file.) Change the filename in the first comment to Advanced24.cpp.

b. Modify the program so that it allows the user to display the electric bill for more than one customer without having to run the program again. Use a sentinel value to end the program. The sentinel value should be entered as the current meter reading in the `getInput` function. When the user enters the sentinel value, the `getInput` function should not prompt the user to enter the previous reading.

c. Change the `getInput` function to a value-returning function. If the user does not enter a sentinel value as the current reading, the `getInput` function should prompt the user to enter the previous reading. It then should return a value that indicates whether the current and previous readings are valid or invalid. To be valid, the current reading must be greater than or equal to the previous reading. The `main` function should not call the `calcBill` or `displayBill` functions when the readings are not valid. Instead, it should display an error message.

d. Save and then run the program. Enter 3000 and 2000 as the current and previous readings, respectively. The program should display 1000 and $110.00 as the units used and total charge, respectively, and then prompt you to enter the current reading. Now enter 3000 and 5000 as the current and previous readings, respectively. The program should display an error message and then prompt you to enter the current reading. Enter 53512 and 51875 as the current and previous readings, respectively. The program should display 1637 and $180.07 as the units used and total charge, respectively. Enter your sentinel value to end the program.

SWAT THE BUGS

25. Follow the instructions for starting C++ and viewing the SwatTheBugs25.cpp file, which is contained in either the Cpp7\Chap10\SwatTheBugs25 Project folder or the Cpp7\Chap10 folder. (Depending on your C++ development tool, you may need to open this exercise's project/solution file first.) If necessary, delete the two forward slashes that appear before the `system("pause");` statement, and then save the program. The program should calculate and display a bonus amount, but it is not working correctly. Run the program. Enter 1000 and .1 as the sales and bonus rate, respectively. Debug the program.

SWAT THE BUGS

26. Follow the instructions for starting C++ and viewing the SwatTheBugs26.cpp file, which is contained in either the Cpp7\Chap10\SwatTheBugs26 Project folder or the Cpp7\Chap10 folder. (Depending on your C++ development tool, you may need to open this exercise's project/solution file first.) If necessary, delete the two forward slashes that appear before the `system("pause");` statement, and then save the program. The program should calculate and display the sum of two numbers, but it is not working correctly. Debug the program.

Answers to TRY THIS Exercises

Pencil and Paper

1.
```
void divideByTwo(int wholeNumber)
{
    cout << wholeNumber / 2.0;
}   //end of divideByTwo function
```

2. `void divideByTwo(int);` or `void divideByTwo(int wholeNumber);`

3. `divideByTwo(total);`

Computer

10. To modify the program, change the function prototype to `void getAge(int &years);` and change the function header to `void getAge(int &years)`.

11. See Figure 10-40. The modifications to the program are shaded in the figure.

```
//TryThis11.cpp - displays two monthly car payments
//Created/revised by <your name> on <current date>

#include <iostream>
#include <cmath>
#include <iomanip>
using namespace std;

//function prototypes
double getPayment(int, double, int);
void displayPayment(double);

```

you also can use `void displayPayment(double mthlyPay);`

Figure 10-40 *(continues)*

(continued)

```
int main()
{
    //declare variables
    int carPrice          = 0;
    int rebate            = 0;
    double creditRate     = 0.0;
    double dealerRate     = 0.0;
    int term              = 0;
    double creditPayment = 0.0;
    double dealerPayment = 0.0;

    //get input items
    cout << "Car price (after any trade-in): ";
    cin >> carPrice;
    cout << "Rebate: ";
    cin >> rebate;
    cout << "Credit union rate: ";
    cin >> creditRate;
    cout << "Dealer rate: ";
    cin >> dealerRate;
    cout << "Term in years: ";
    cin >> term;

    //call function to calculate payments
    creditPayment = getPayment(carPrice - rebate,
            creditRate / 12, term * 12);
    dealerPayment = getPayment(carPrice,
            dealerRate / 12, term * 12);

    //display payments
    cout << fixed << setprecision(2) << endl;
    cout << "Credit union payment: $";
    displayPayment(creditPayment);
    cout << endl;
    cout << "Dealer payment: $";
    displayPayment(dealerPayment);
    cout << endl;

    //system("pause");
    return 0;
}   //end of main function

//*****function definitions*****
double getPayment(int prin,
                  double monthRate,
                  int months)
{
    //calculates and returns a monthly payment
    double monthPay = 0.0;
    monthPay = prin * monthRate /
            (1 - pow(monthRate + 1, -months));
    return monthPay;
}  //end of getPayment function

void displayPayment(double mthlyPay)
{
    cout << mthlyPay;
}  //end of displayPayment function
```

if your C++ development tool requires this statement, delete the two forward slashes

Figure 10-40

12. See Figure 10-41. The modifications to the program are shaded in the figure. (Several lines of code were also removed from the two void functions.)

```
//TryThis12.cpp - converts Fahrenheit to Celsius
//Created/revised by <your name> on <current date>

#include <iostream>
#include <iomanip>
using namespace std;

//function prototypes
void getFahrenheit(int &tempF);
void calcCelsius(int tempF, double &tempC);

int main()
{
    int fahrenheit = 0;
    double celsius = 0.0;

    //get input item
    getFahrenheit(fahrenheit);

    //calculate Celsius
    calcCelsius(fahrenheit, celsius);

    //display output item
    cout << fixed << setprecision(0);
    cout << "Celsius: " << celsius << endl;

    //system("pause");
    return 0;
}   //end of main function

//*****function definitions*****
void getFahrenheit(int &tempF)
{
    cout << "Enter Fahrenheit temperature: ";
    cin >> tempF;
}   //end of getFahrenheit function

void calcCelsius(int tempF, double &tempC)
{
    tempC = 5.0 / 9.0 * (tempF - 32.0);
}   //end of calcCelsius function
```

you also can use `void getFahrenheit(int &);` and `void calcCelsius(int, double &);`

if your C++ development tool requires this statement, delete the two forward slashes

Figure 10-41

CHAPTER 11

One-Dimensional Arrays

After studying Chapter 11, you should be able to:

- Declare and initialize a one-dimensional array
- Enter data into a one-dimensional array
- Display the contents of a one-dimensional array
- Pass a one-dimensional array to a function
- Calculate the total and average of the values in a one-dimensional array
- Search a one-dimensional array
- Access an individual element in a one-dimensional array
- Find the highest value in a one-dimensional array
- Explain the bubble sort algorithm
- Use parallel one-dimensional arrays

Arrays

Ch11-Chapter Preview video

All of the variables you have used so far have been simple variables. A **simple variable**, also called a **scalar variable**, is one that is unrelated to any other variable in memory. At times, however, you will encounter situations in which some of the variables in a program *are* related to each other. In those cases, it is easier and more efficient to treat the related variables as a group.

You already are familiar with the concept of grouping. The clothes in your closet probably are separated into groups, such as coats, sweaters, shirts, and so on. Grouping your clothes in this manner allows you to easily locate your favorite sweater because you just need to look through the sweater group rather than through the entire closet. You also probably have your CD (compact disc) collection grouped by either music type or artist. If your collection is grouped by artist, it will take only a few seconds to find all of your Beatles CDs and, depending on the number of Beatles CDs you own, only a short time after that to locate a particular CD.

It takes longer for the computer to access the information stored in a disk file because the computer must wait for the disk drive to first locate the needed information and then read the information into internal memory.

When you group together related variables that have the same data type, the group is referred to as an array of variables or, more simply, an **array**. You might use an array of 50 variables to store the population of each U.S. state. Or, you might use an array of four variables to store the sales made in each of your company's four sales regions. Storing data in an array increases the efficiency of a program because data can be both stored in and retrieved from the computer's internal memory much faster than it can be written to and read from a file on a disk. In addition, after the data is entered into an array, which typically is done at the beginning of a program, the program can use the data as many times as necessary without having to enter the data again. Your company's sales program, for example, can use the sales amounts stored in an array to calculate the total company sales and the percentage that each region contributed to the total sales. It also can use the sales amounts in the array either to calculate the average sales amount or to simply display the sales made in a specific region. As you will learn in this chapter, the variables in an array can be used just like any other variables. You can assign values to them, use them in calculations, display their contents, and so on.

The most commonly used arrays in business applications are one-dimensional and two-dimensional. You will learn about one-dimensional arrays in this chapter. Two-dimensional arrays are covered in Chapter 12. Arrays having more than two dimensions are used mostly in scientific and engineering programs and are beyond the scope of this book.

As is true of functions, which you learned about in Chapters 9 and 10, arrays are one of the more challenging topics for beginning programmers. Therefore, it is important for you to read and study each section in this chapter thoroughly before moving on to the next section. For example, be sure you understand the concept of one-dimensional arrays before you continue to the sections pertaining to the bubble sort and parallel arrays. If you still feel overwhelmed by the end of the chapter, try reading the chapter again, paying particular attention to the examples and programs shown in the figures.

One-Dimensional Arrays

The variables in an array are stored in consecutive locations in the computer's internal memory. Each variable in an array has the same name and data type. You distinguish one variable in a **one-dimensional array** from another variable in the same array using a unique number. The unique number, which is always an integer, is called a subscript. The **subscript** indicates the variable's position in the array and is assigned by the computer when the array is created in internal memory. The first variable in a one-dimensional array is assigned a subscript of 0, the second a subscript of 1, and so on.

A subscript is also called an index.

You refer to each variable in an array by the array's name and the variable's subscript, which is specified in a set of square brackets immediately following the array name. Figure 11-1 illustrates a one-dimensional array named `beatles`, which contains three variables. You use `beatles[0]`—read "`beatles` sub zero"—to refer to the first variable in the array. You use `beatles[1]` to refer to the second variable in the array, and use `beatles[2]` to refer to the third (and last) variable in the array.

Notice that the last subscript in an array is always one number less than the total number of variables in the array; this is because array subscripts in C++ (and in many other programming languages) start at 0.

Figure 11-1 Illustration of the naming convention for the one-dimensional `beatles` array

Figure 11-2 uses the storage bin analogy from Chapter 3 to illustrate the variables contained in a one-dimensional array named `sales`. In this case, the array contains four variables, which are named `sales[0]`, `sales[1]`, `sales[2]`, and `sales[3]`. Here again, the last subscript in the array (3) is one number less than the total number of variables in the array (4). The `age`, `rate`, and `unitCharge` variables included in the figure are scalar (simple) variables.

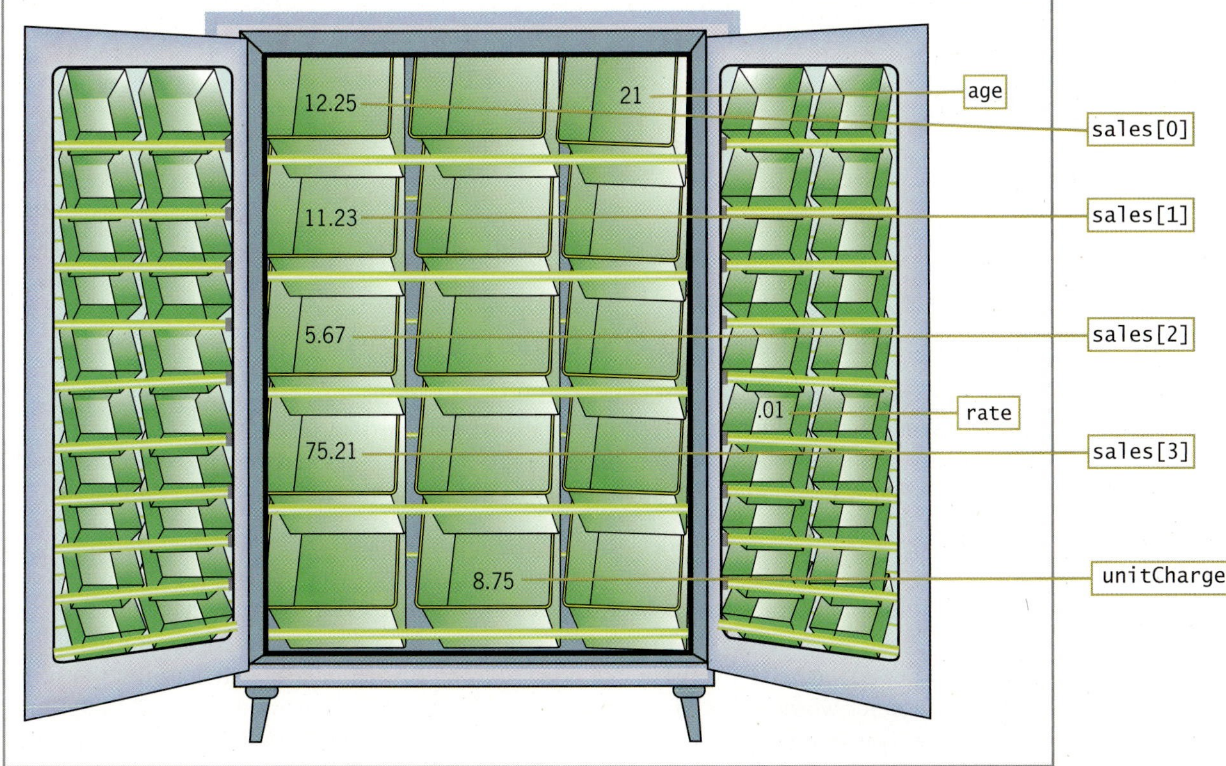

Figure 11-2 Illustration of the `sales` array

Figure 11-3 shows the problem specification and IPO chart information for the XYZ Company's sales program, which uses an array to store the sales made in each of the company's four regions. The program allows the user to enter the sales amounts and then displays the amounts on the computer screen. Before you can code the sales program, you need to learn how to declare and initialize a one-dimensional array. You also need to learn how to store data in an array and display data from an array.

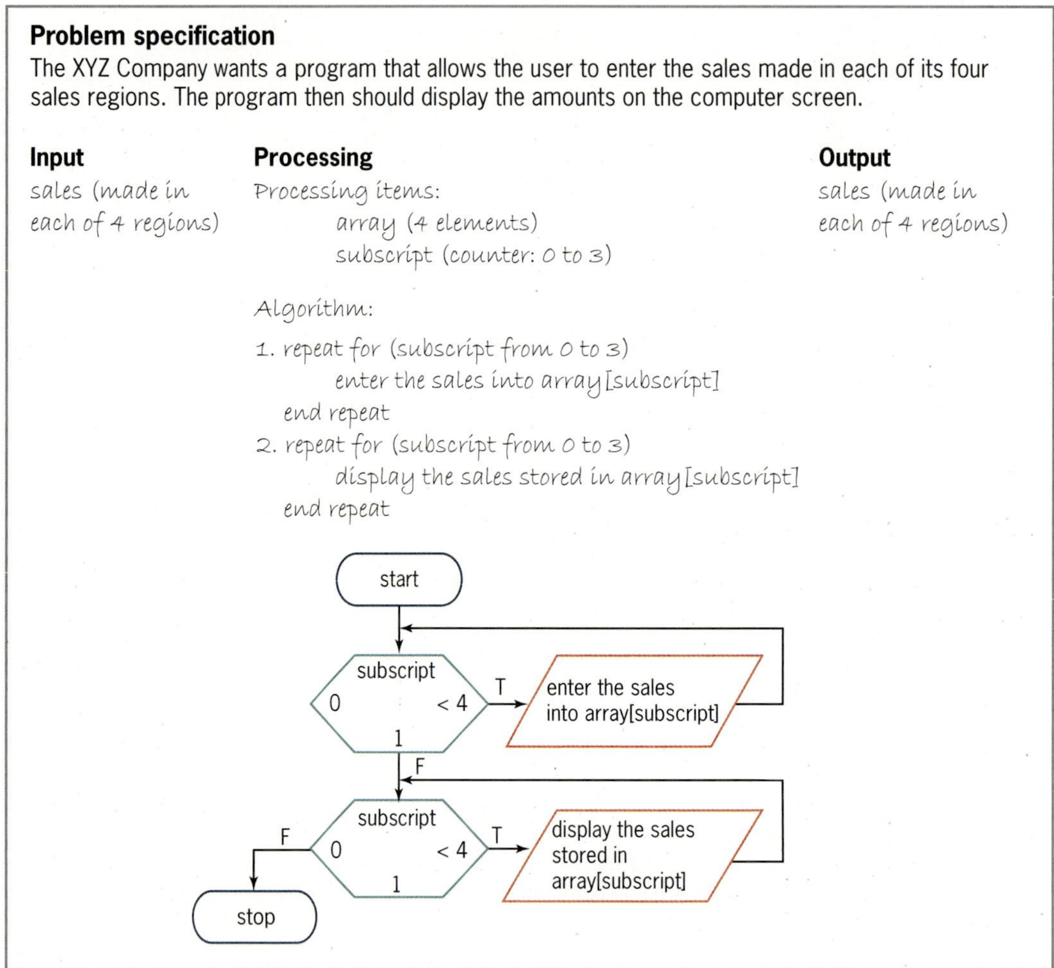

Figure 11-3 Problem specification and IPO chart for the XYZ Company's sales program

Declaring and Initializing a One-Dimensional Array

Before you can use an array in a program, you first must declare (create) it. It also is a good programming practice to initialize the array variables to ensure they will not contain garbage when the program is run. As you learned in Chapter 3, the garbage found in uninitialized variables is the remains of what was last stored at the memory location that the variable now occupies.

Figure 11-4 shows the syntax for declaring a one-dimensional array in C++ and initializing its variables. In the syntax, *dataType* is the type of data that the array variables, referred to as **elements**, will store. Recall that each of the elements (variables) in an array has the same data type. *ArrayName* in the syntax is the name of the array. You use the same rules for naming an array as you do for naming a variable. *NumberOfElements* is an integer that specifies the size of the array. In other words, it specifies the number of elements you want in the array. To declare an array that contains 10 elements, you enter the number 10 as the *numberOfElements*. Notice that you enclose the *numberOfElements* in square brackets ([]).

You can initialize the array elements at the same time you declare the array simply by entering one or more values, separated by commas, in the *initialValues* section of the syntax. You enclose the *initialValues* section in braces ({}), as shown in Figure 11-4. Assigning initial values to an array is often referred to as **populating the array**. The values used to populate an array should have the same data type as the array variables. If the data types are not the same, the computer uses implicit type conversion to either promote or demote the values to fit the array variables. However, recall from Chapter 3 that the implicit demotion of values can adversely affect a program's output. Therefore, you should always be sure to populate an array using values that have the appropriate data type.

Also included in Figure 11-4 are examples of declaring and initializing one-dimensional arrays. The declaration statement in Example 1 creates a three-element `char` array named `letters`. It initializes the `letters[0]` element to A, the `letters[1]` element to B, and the `letters[2]` element to C. Example 2 shows two statements you can use to declare a four-element `double` array, initializing each element to the `double` number 0.0. The statement `double sales[4] = {0.0, 0.0, 0.0, 0.0};` provides an initial value for each of the four array elements, whereas the statement `double sales[4] = {0.0};` provides only one value. When the array declaration statement does not provide an initial value for each of the elements in a numeric array, most C++ compilers initialize the uninitialized array elements to either 0.0 or 0 (depending on the data type of the array). However, this is done only when you provide at least one value in the *initialValues* section. If you omit the *initialValues* section from the declaration statement—for example, if you use the statement `double sales[4];` to declare the array—the compiler does not automatically initialize the elements, so the array elements may contain garbage.

Most C++ compilers initialize `char` array elements to a space, `string` array elements to the empty string, and `bool` array elements to the keyword `false`.

Example 3 in Figure 11-4 shows two statements you can use to declare a six-element `int` array named `numbers`. The statement `int numbers[6] = {12, 0, 0, 0, 0, 0};` initializes the first array element to the integer 12 and initializes the remaining elements to the integer 0. The same result can be accomplished using the `int numbers[6] = {12};` statement shown in the example.

HOW TO Declare and Initialize a One-Dimensional Array

Syntax

dataType arrayName[*numberOfElements*] = {*initialValues*};

Example 1

```
char letters[3] = {'A', 'B', 'C'};
```

declares and initializes a three-element `char` array named `letters`

Example 2

```
double sales[4] = {0.0, 0.0, 0.0, 0.0};
        or
double sales[4] = {0.0};
```

declares and initializes a four-element `double` array named `sales`; each element is initialized to 0.0

Example 3

```
int numbers[6] = {12, 0, 0, 0, 0, 0};
        or
int numbers[6] = {12};
```

declares and initializes a six-element `int` array named `numbers`; the first element is initialized to 12, whereas the others are initialized to 0

Figure 11-4 How to declare and initialize a one-dimensional array

The = {*initialValues*} portion of the syntax in Figure 11-4 is optional. Typically, optional items are enclosed in square brackets when shown in the syntax. In this case, the square brackets were omitted so as not to confuse them with the square brackets that are required by the syntax.

If you inadvertently provide more values in the *initialValues* section than the number of array elements, most C++ compilers will display the error message "too many initializers" when you attempt to compile the program. However, not all C++ compilers display a message when this error occurs. Rather, some compilers store the extra values in memory locations adjacent to, but not reserved for, the array. Therefore, you should always be careful to provide no more than the appropriate number of *initialValues*.

Entering Data into a One-Dimensional Array

As you can with a scalar (simple) variable, you can use either an assignment statement or the extraction operator to enter data into an array element. Figure 11-5 shows the syntax of such an assignment statement. In the syntax, *arrayName[subscript]* is the name and subscript of the array variable to which you want the *expression* (data) assigned. The *expression* can include any combination of constants, variables, and operators. The data type of the *expression* must match the data type of the array element to which the *expression* is assigned; otherwise, an implicit type conversion will occur, which could result in incorrect output.

Also included in Figure 11-5 are examples of assignment statements that assign data to the elements in various arrays. The arrays were declared earlier in Figure 11-4. The assignment statement in Example 1 assigns the letter Y to the second element in the `letters` array, replacing the letter B that was stored in the element when the array was declared. The code in Example 2 assigns the `double` number 0.0 to each of the four elements in the `sales` array and provides another means of initializing the array. The code in Example 3 assigns the squares of the numbers from 1 through 6 to the six-element `numbers` array, replacing the array's initial values. The square of the number 1 is assigned to the `numbers[0]` element. The square of the number 2 is assigned to the `numbers[1]` element, and so on. Notice that the `x` variable keeps track of the six numbers to be squared. Also notice that, in order to assign the square of each number to its appropriate element in the `numbers` array, the code must subtract the number 1 from the value stored in the `x` variable. This is because the `x` variable's values go from 1 through 6, whereas their corresponding array subscripts go from 0 through 5.

The code shown in Example 4 in Figure 11-5 updates the contents of each element in the `numbers` array. It does this by adding the value contained in the `increase` variable to the value contained in the current array element and then assigning the sum to the current array element.

HOW TO Use an Assignment Statement to Assign Data to a One-Dimensional Array

Syntax

arrayName[*subscript*] = *expression*;

Example 1

```
letters[1] = 'Y';
```

assigns the letter Y to the second element in the `letters` array

Example 2

```
int subscript = 0;
while (subscript < 4)
{
      sales[subscript] = 0.0;
      subscript += 1;
}     //end while
```

assigns the `double` number 0.0 to each of the four elements in the `sales` array; provides another means of initializing the array

(continues)

Figure 11-5 How to use an assignment statement to assign data to a one-dimensional array

(continued)

Example 3

```
for (int x = 1; x <= 6; x += 1)
     numbers[x - 1] = pow(x, 2);
//end for
```

assigns the squares of the numbers from 1 through 6 to the six-element `numbers` array

Example 4

```
int increase = 0;
cout << "Enter increase amount: ";
cin >> increase;
for (int x = 0; x < 6; x += 1)
     numbers[x] += increase;
//end for
```

assigns, to each element in the six-element `numbers` array, the sum of the element's current value plus the value stored in the `increase` variable

Figure 11-5 How to use an assignment statement to assign data to a one-dimensional array

The loops in Examples 2 through 4 provide a convenient way to access each element in a one-dimensional array.

As already mentioned, you also can use the extraction operator to store data in an array element; this is shown in the syntax and examples in Figure 11-6. (The arrays in Figure 11-6 were declared earlier in Figure 11-4.) The `cin` statement in Example 1 stores the user's entry in the first element in the `letters` array, replacing the element's existing data. Example 2 contains a loop that repeats its instructions four times: once for each element in the `sales` array. The loop instructions prompt the user to enter a sales amount and then store the user's response in the current element. Example 3 contains a loop that repeats its instructions for each of the six elements in the `numbers` array. The loop instructions prompt the user to enter an integer and then store the user's response in the current element.

HOW TO Use the Extraction Operator to Store Data in a One-Dimensional Array

Syntax

`cin >>` *arrayName*[*subscript*]**;**

Example 1

```
cin >> letters[0];
```

stores the user's entry in the first element in the `letters` array

(continues)

Figure 11-6 How to use the extraction operator to store data in a one-dimensional array

(continued)

Example 2

```
for (int sub = 0; sub < 4; sub += 1)
{
      cout << "Enter the sales for Region ";
      cout << sub + 1 << ": ";
      cin >> sales[sub];
}     //end for
```

stores the user's entries in the four-element `sales` array

Example 3

```
int x = 0;
while (x < 6)
{
      cout << "Enter an integer: ";
      cin >> numbers[x];
      x += 1;
}     //end while
```

stores the user's entries in the six-element `numbers` array

Figure 11-6 How to use the extraction operator to store data in a one-dimensional array

Displaying the Contents of a One-Dimensional Array

To display the contents of an array, you need to access each of its elements. You do this using a loop along with a counter variable that keeps track of each subscript in the array. Figure 11-7 shows examples of loops you can use to display the contents of the arrays declared earlier in Figure 11-4. Example 1 uses the `while` statement to display the contents of the `letters` array, which contains three elements. Example 2 uses the `for` statement to display the contents of the four-element `sales` array. Notice that the valid subscripts for the `sales` array are 0 through 3, whereas the valid region numbers are 1 through 4. Example 3 uses the `do while` statement to display the contents of the six-element `numbers` array.

HOW TO Display the Contents of a One-Dimensional Array

Example 1

```
int x = 0;
while (x < 3)
{
      cout << letters[x] << endl;
      x += 1;
}     //end while
```

displays the contents of the three-element `letters` array

(continues)

Figure 11-7 How to display the contents of a one-dimensional array

(continued)

Example 2

```
for (int sub = 0; sub < 4; sub += 1)
{
      cout << "Sales for Region " << sub + 1 << ": $";
      cout << sales[sub] << endl;
}     //end for
```

displays the contents of the four-element `sales` array

Example 3

```
int x = 0;
do    //begin loop
{
      cout << numbers[x] << endl;
      x += 1;
} while (x < 6);
```

displays the contents of the six-element `numbers` array

Figure 11-7 How to display the contents of a one-dimensional array

Now that you know how to declare and initialize a one-dimensional array, as well as how to store data in the array and display data from the array, you can code the XYZ Company's sales program.

Coding the XYZ Company's Sales Program

Earlier, in Figure 11-3, you viewed the problem specification and IPO chart for the XYZ Company's sales program. Figure 11-8 shows the IPO chart information along with the corresponding C++ instructions. Figure 11-9 shows the code for the entire program, and Figure 11-10 shows a sample run of the program.

IPO chart information	C++ instructions
Input	
sales (made in each of 4 regions)	the sales will be entered into the array
Processing	
array (4 elements)	`double sales[4] = {0.0};`
subscript (counter: 0 to 3)	declared and initialized in the for clause
Output	
sales (made in each of 4 regions)	displayed from the array by the for loop

Figure 11-8 IPO chart information and C++ instructions for the XYZ Company's sales program *(continues)*

(continued)

Algorithm

1. repeat for (subscript from 0 to 3)
   enter the sales into array[subscript]
   end repeat

```
for (int sub = 0; sub < 4; sub += 1)
{
     cout << "Enter the sales
     for Region ";
     cout << sub + 1 << ": ";
     cin >> sales[sub];
}    //end for
```

2. repeat for (subscript from 0 to 3)
   display the sales stored in array[subscript]
   end repeat

```
for (int sub = 0; sub < 4; sub += 1)
{
     cout << "Sales for Region "
     << sub + 1 << ": $";
     cout << sales[sub] << endl;
}    //end for
```

Figure 11-8 IPO chart information and C++ instructions for the XYZ Company's sales program

```
//XYZ Company.cpp
//displays the contents of an array
//Created/revised by <your name> on <current date>

#include <iostream>
#include <iomanip>
using namespace std;

int main()
{
    //declare array
    double sales[4] = {0.0};

    //store data in the array
    for (int sub = 0; sub < 4; sub += 1)
    {
         cout << "Enter the sales for Region ";
         cout << sub + 1 << ": ";
         cin >> sales[sub];
    }    //end for

    //display the contents of the array
    cout << fixed << setprecision(2) << endl << endl;
    for (int sub = 0; sub < 4; sub += 1)
    {
         cout << "Sales for Region " << sub + 1 << ": $";
         cout << sales[sub] << endl;
    }    //end for

    //system("pause");
    return 0;
}   //end of main function
```


Figure 11-9 XYZ Company's sales program

```
XYZ Company
Enter the sales for Region 1: 123.67
Enter the sales for Region 2: 350.89
Enter the sales for Region 3: 567
Enter the sales for Region 4: 224.98


Sales for Region 1: $123.67
Sales for Region 2: $350.89
Sales for Region 3: $567.00
Sales for Region 4: $224.98
Press any key to continue . . .
```

Figure 11-10 Sample run of the XYZ Company's sales program

Desk-checking the code in Figure 11-9 will help you understand how arrays operate in a program. You will desk-check the code using the following four sales amounts: 123.67, 350.89, 567, and 224.98. First, the declaration statement on Line 12 declares and initializes a four-element `double` array named `sales`. Figure 11-11 shows the desk-check table after the declaration statement is processed.

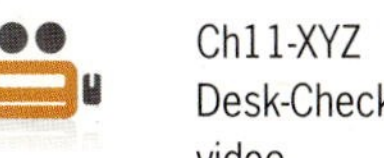

Figure 11-11 Desk-check table after the array declaration statement is processed

The `for` clause on Line 15 is processed next. The clause's *initialization* argument declares an `int` variable named `sub` and initializes it to the number 0. The `sub` variable is a counter variable that will keep track of the four array subscripts: 0, 1, 2, and 3. As you learned in Chapter 7, a variable declared in a `for` clause is local to the `for` loop and can be used only by the statements within the loop. In this case, the `sub` variable is local to the `for` loop on Lines 15 through 20. The `sub` variable will remain in memory until the `for` loop ends. Figure 11-12 shows the desk-check table after the *initialization* argument on Line 15 has been processed.

Figure 11-12 Desk-check table after the *initialization* argument on Line 15 is processed

The `for` clause's *condition* argument checks whether the value stored in the `sub` variable is less than 4. It is, so the statements in the body of the `for` loop are processed. First, the `cout` statements on Lines 17 and 18 prompt the user to enter the sales for the current region—in this case, Region 1. Notice that the current region is determined by adding the number 1 to the value stored in the `sub` variable (0). This is because, unlike the array subscripts, the region numbers go from 1 through 4 rather than from 0 through 3. The region number will always be one number more than the subscript of its corresponding element in the array. In other words,

As you learned in Chapter 7, the *condition* argument in a `for` clause is a looping condition because it specifies the requirement for processing the loop instructions.

Region 1's sales will be stored in the element whose subscript is 0. Likewise, Region 2's sales will be stored in the element whose subscript is 1, and so on. The `cin` statement on Line 19 gets Region 1's sales from the user and then stores the amount in the first array element (`sales[0]`). Figure 11-13 shows the sales for Region 1 (123.67) entered in the array.

sales[0]	sales[1]	sales[2]	sales[3]	sub
~~0.0~~	0.0	0.0	0.0	0
123.67				

Figure 11-13 Desk-check table after Region 1's sales are entered in the array

The `for` clause's *update* argument adds the number 1 to the contents of the `sub` variable; the result is 1. The *condition* argument then checks whether the `sub` variable's value is less than 4. It is, so the statements in the body of the `for` loop are processed again. The `cout` statements prompt the user to enter the sales for Region 2, and the `cin` statement stores the user's response in the second array element (`sales[1]`). Figure 11-14 shows the sales for Region 2 (350.89) entered in the array.

sales[0]	sales[1]	sales[2]	sales[3]	sub
~~0.0~~	~~0.0~~	0.0	0.0	~~0~~
123.67	350.89			1

Figure 11-14 Desk-check table after Region 2's sales are entered in the array

Next, the *update* argument adds the number 1 to the contents of the `sub` variable, giving 2. The *condition* argument then checks whether the `sub` variable's value is less than 4. It is, so the statements in the body of the `for` loop are processed again. The `cout` statements prompt the user to enter the sales for Region 3, and the `cin` statement stores the user's response in the third array element (`sales[2]`). Figure 11-15 shows the sales for Region 3 (567.0) entered in the array.

sales[0]	sales[1]	sales[2]	sales[3]	sub
~~0.0~~	~~0.0~~	~~0.0~~	0.0	~~0~~
123.67	350.89	567.0		~~1~~
				2

Figure 11-15 Desk-check table after Region 3's sales are entered in the array

Next, the *condition* argument adds the number 1 to the contents of the `sub` variable, giving 3. The *condition* argument then checks whether the `sub` variable's value is less than 4. It is, so the statements in the body of the `for` loop are processed again. The `cout` statements prompt the user to enter the sales for Region 4, and the `cin` statement stores the user's response in the fourth array element (`sales[3]`). Figure 11-16 shows the sales for Region 4 (224.98) entered in the array.

sales[0]	sales[1]	sales[2]	sales[3]	sub
~~0.0~~	~~0.0~~	~~0.0~~	~~0.0~~	~~0~~
123.67	350.89	567.0	224.98	~~1~~
				~~2~~
				3

Figure 11-16 Desk-check table after Region 4's sales are entered in the array

Once again, the *update* argument adds the number 1 to the contents of the `sub` variable; this time, the result is 4. The *condition* argument then checks whether the `sub` variable's value is less than 4. It's not, so the `for` loop on Lines 15 through 20 ends and the computer removes the loop's local `sub` variable from internal memory. Figure 11-17 shows the current status of the desk-check table.

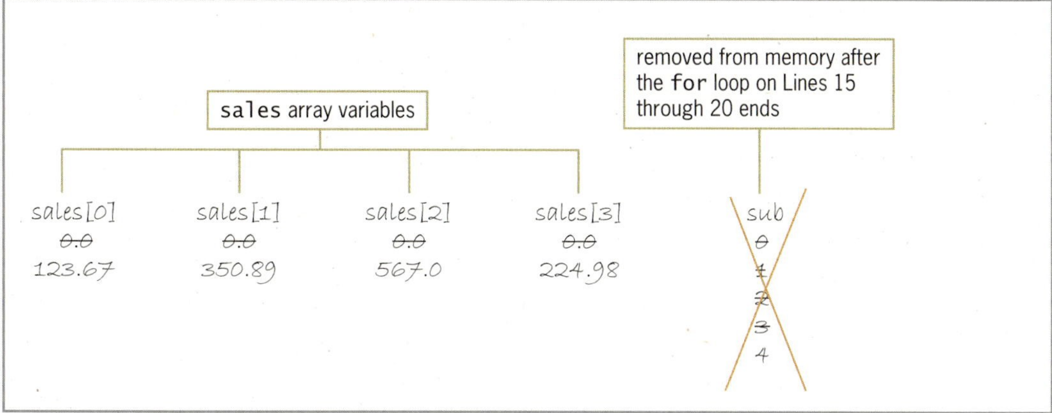

Figure 11-17 Desk-check table after the `for` loop on Lines 15 through 20 ends

The `cout` statement on Line 23 is processed next. The statement tells the computer to display real numbers in fixed-point notation with two decimal places; it also displays two blank lines. Next, the computer processes the `for` clause on Line 24. The clause's *initialization* argument declares and initializes an `int` variable named `sub`. Although the variable's name is the same as the one in the first `for` clause, which appears on Line 15, it's not the same variable. This `sub` variable is local to the `for` loop on Lines 24 through 28. The `sub` variable created by the `for` clause on Line 15 was local to the `for` loop on Lines 15 through 20 and was removed from memory when that loop ended. Figure 11-18 shows the desk-check table after the *initialization* argument on Line 24 is processed.

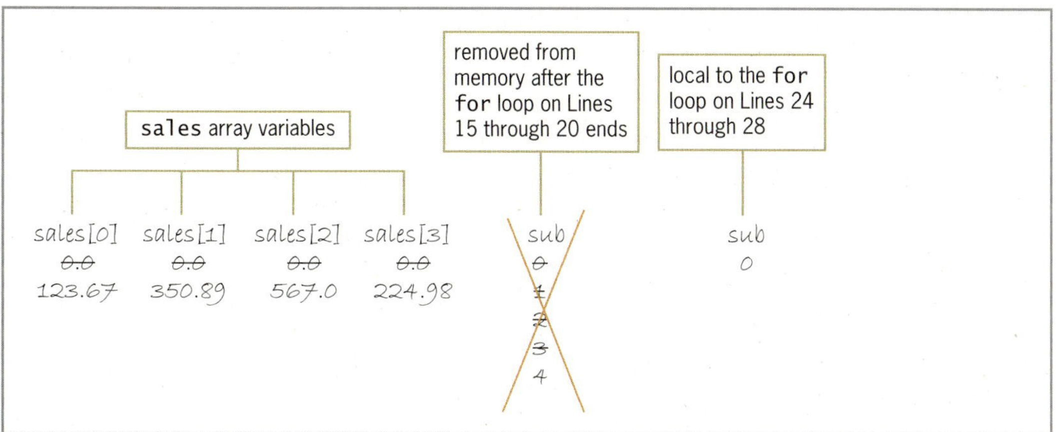

Figure 11-18 Desk-check table after the *initialization* argument on Line 24 is processed

The *condition* argument in the `for` clause on Line 24 checks whether the value in the `sub` variable is less than 4. It is, so the statements in the body of the `for` loop are processed. Those statements display Region 1's sales, which are located in the `sales[0]` element in the array, on the computer screen.

Next, the `for` clause's *update* argument adds the number 1 to the contents of the `sub` variable; the result is 1. The *condition* argument then checks whether the value in the `sub` variable is less than 4. It is, so the statements in the body of the `for` loop display Region 2's sales.

Here again, the *update* argument adds the number 1 to the contents of the `sub` variable; the result is 2. The *condition* argument then checks whether the value in the `sub` variable is less than 4. It is, so the statements in the body of the `for` loop display Region 3's sales.

The *update* argument again adds the number 1 to the contents of the `sub` variable; the result is 3. The *condition* argument then checks whether the value in the `sub` variable is less than 4. It is, so the statements in the body of the `for` loop display Region 4's sales.

Once again, the *update* argument adds the number 1 to the contents of the `sub` variable; this time, the result is 4. The *condition* argument then checks whether the value in the `sub` variable is less than 4. It's not, so the `for` loop ends and the computer removes the loop's local `sub` variable from internal memory. Figure 11-19 shows the desk-check table after the `for` loop on Lines 24 through 28 ends.

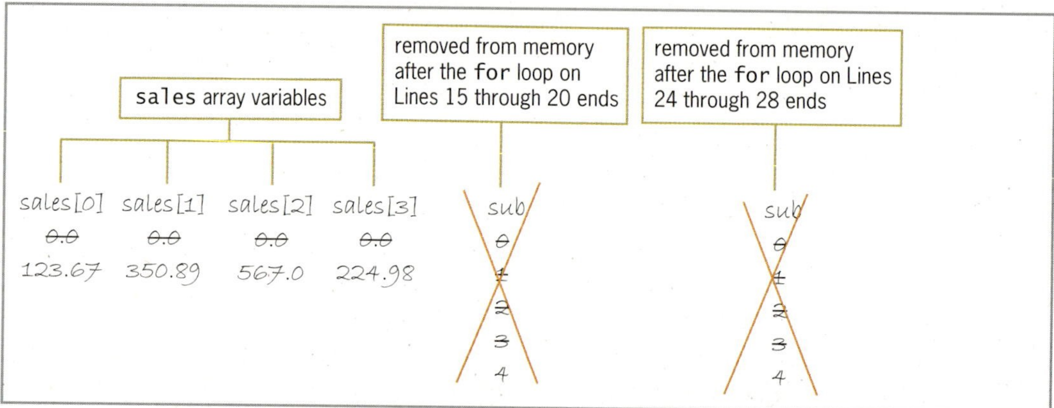

Figure 11-19 Desk-check table after the `for` loop on Lines 24 through 28 ends

Finally, the computer processes the `return 0;` statement on Line 31. When the program ends, the computer removes the `sales` array from its internal memory. (A sample run of the XYZ Company's sales program is shown earlier in Figure 11-10.)

Passing a One-Dimensional Array to a Function

Figure 11-20 shows a modified version of the XYZ Company's sales program. In the modified version, the `main` function passes the `sales` array to a program-defined void function named `displayArray`. The changes made to the original code (shown earlier in Figure 11-9) are shaded in Figure 11-20.

```
//Modified XYZ Company.cpp
//displays the contents of an array
//Created/revised by <your name> on <current date>

#include <iostream>
#include <iomanip>
using namespace std;

//function prototype
void displayArray(double dollars[], int numElements);

int main()
{
    //declare array
    double sales[4] = {0.0};

```

the name is optional (dollars)

the name is optional (numElements)

Figure 11-20 XYZ Company's modified sales program *(continues)*

(continued)

```
17     //store data in the array
18     for (int sub = 0; sub < 4; sub += 1)
19     {
20         cout << "Enter the sales for Region ";
21         cout << sub + 1 << ": ";
22         cin >> sales[sub];
23     }   //end for
24
25     //display the contents of the array
26     displayArray(sales, 4);
27
28     //system("pause");
29     return 0;
30 }   //end of main function
31
32 //*****function definitions*****
33 void displayArray(double dollars[], int numElements)
34 {
35     cout << fixed << setprecision(2) << endl << endl;
36     for (int sub = 0; sub < numElements; sub += 1)
37     {
38         cout << "Sales for Region " << sub + 1 << ": $";
39         cout << dollars[sub] << endl;
40     }   //end for
41 }   //end of displayArray function
```

if your C++ development tool requires this statement, delete the two forward slashes

Figure 11-20 XYZ Company's modified sales program

Study closely the `displayArray` function prototype, function call, and function header. The function call, which appears on Line 26, passes two items of information to the `displayArray` function: the `sales` array and the number of elements in the array. You pass an array simply by including the array's name—in this case, `sales`—as the actual argument. As you learned in Chapters 9 and 10, variables can be passed to a function either *by value* or *by reference*. Unless specified otherwise, scalar variables in C++ are passed *by value*. To pass a scalar variable *by reference*, recall that you need to include the address-of (&) operator before the formal parameter's name in the receiving function's header. You also need to include the address-of operator in the receiving function's prototype (if there is one).

Unlike scalar variables, arrays in C++ are passed automatically *by reference* rather than *by value*; this is because it is more efficient to pass arrays in that manner. Since many arrays are large, passing an array *by value* would consume a great deal of the computer's memory and time because the computer would need to duplicate the array in the receiving function's formal parameter. Passing an array *by reference* allows the computer to pass the address of only the first array element. Because array elements are stored in contiguous locations in memory, the computer can use the address to locate the remaining elements in the array.

Given that arrays are passed automatically *by reference*, you do not include the address-of (&) operator before the name of an array's formal parameter in the function header, as you do when passing scalar variables *by reference*. You also do not include the address-of operator in the function prototype. Instead, you indicate that you are passing an array to a function by entering the formal parameter's data type and name, followed by an empty set of square brackets, in the receiving function's header and in its prototype, as shown in Figure 11-20. (Recall that the formal parameter's name is optional in the prototype. Therefore, you also could write the function prototype on Line 10 in Figure 11-20 as `void displayArray(double [], int);`.)

Figure 11-21 shows the completed desk-check table for the XYZ Company's modified sales program. Recall from Chapter 10 that when you pass a variable *by reference* to a function, the computer locates the variable and then assigns the name of the corresponding formal parameter to the variable. The same process occurs with array variables and explains why each array variable in Figure 11-21 has two names: one assigned by the `main` function, and the other assigned by the `displayArray` function. Although both functions can access the memory locations where the array variables reside, each function uses a different name to do so. The `main` function uses the name `sales`, whereas the `displayArray` function uses the name `dollars`.

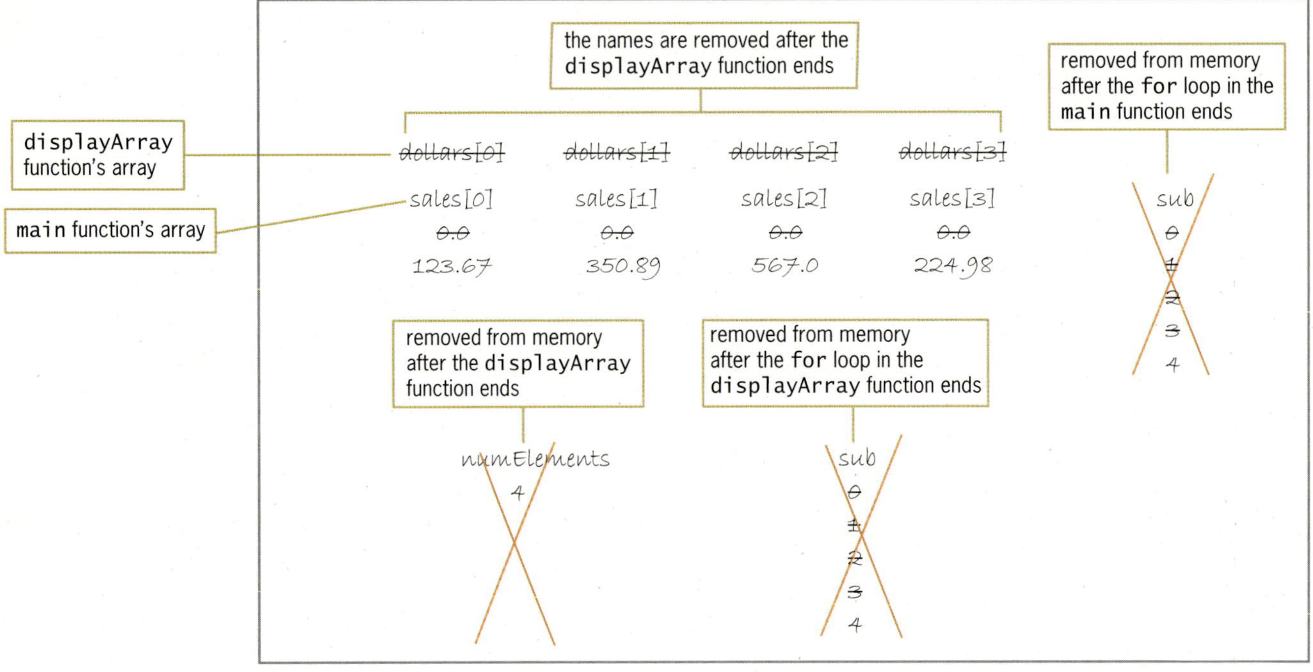

Figure 11-21 Completed desk-check table for the XYZ Company's modified sales program

The answers to Mini-Quiz questions are located in Appendix A.

Mini-Quiz 11-1

1. Which of the following declares a one-dimensional `int` array named `quantities` and initializes each of its 20 elements to the number 0?
   a. `int quantities[20] = {0};`
   b. `int quantities(20) = {0};`
   c. `int quantities{20} = 0;`
   d. none of the above
2. What is the name of the first element in the `quantities` array from Question 1?
3. What is the name of the last element in the `quantities` array from Question 1?
4. Write a C++ statement that assigns the number 7 to the fourth element in the `quantities` array from Question 1.
5. Which of the following calls the value-returning `getTotal` function, passing it the `quantities` array from Question 1 and the number of array elements?
   a. `total = getTotal(quantities[], 20);`
   b. `total = getTotal(quantities[20]);`
   c. `total = getTotal(quantities, 20);`
   d. none of the above

The Moonbucks Coffee Program—Calculating a Total and an Average

Figure 11-22 shows the problem specification, IPO chart information, and C++ instructions for the Moonbucks Coffee program. The program displays both the total and average number of pounds of coffee used in a 12-month period. The program stores the monthly usage amounts in a 12-element `double` array named `pounds`. It also uses a program-defined value-returning function named `getTotal` to calculate the total usage for the year. The `getTotal` function does this by adding together each monthly value stored in the `pounds` array, which is passed to the function when it is invoked. The `getTotal` function then returns the sum to the `main` function, where it is used to calculate the average usage.

Problem specification
The store manager at Moonbucks Coffee wants a program that displays both the total and average number of pounds of coffee used during a 12-month period. Last year, the pounds of coffee used each month were as follows: 400.5, 450, 475.5, 336.5, 457, 325, 220.5, 276, 300, 320.5, 400.5, 415. The program will use two value-returning functions: `main` and `getTotal`. The `getTotal` function will calculate the total number of pounds of coffee used.

`main` function

IPO chart information	C++ instructions
Input	
array (12 elements)	`double pounds[12] = {400.5, 450.0, 475.5, 336.5, 457.0, 325.0, 220.5, 276.0, 300.0, 320.5, 400.5, 415.0};`
Processing	
none	
Output	
total pounds	`double total = 0.0;`
average pounds	`double average = 0.0;`
Algorithm	
1. call the getTotal function to calculate the total pounds; pass the pounds array and the number of array elements	`total = getTotal(pounds, 12);`
2. calculate the average pounds by dividing the total pounds by the number of array elements	`average = total / 12;`
3. display the total pounds and average pounds	`cout << "Total pounds: " << total << endl;` `cout << "Average pounds: " << average << endl;`

Figure 11-22 Problem specification, IPO chart information, and C++ instructions for the Moonbucks Coffee program *(continues)*

(continued)

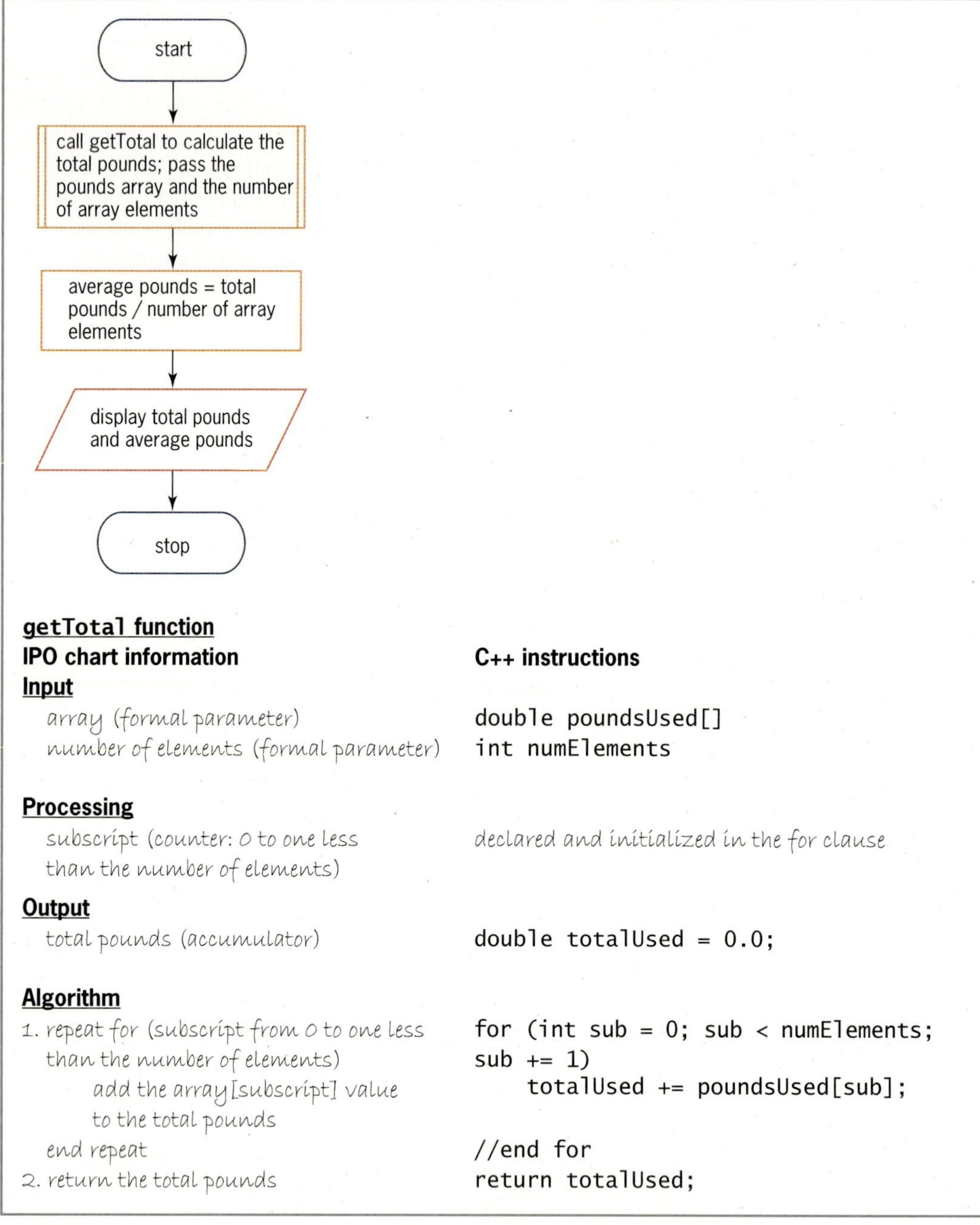

`getTotal` function

IPO chart information	**C++ instructions**
Input	
array (formal parameter)	`double poundsUsed[]`
number of elements (formal parameter)	`int numElements`
Processing	
subscript (counter: 0 to one less than the number of elements)	*declared and initialized in the for clause*
Output	
total pounds (accumulator)	`double totalUsed = 0.0;`

Algorithm

1. repeat for (subscript from 0 to one less than the number of elements)
add the array[subscript] value to the total pounds
end repeat
2. return the total pounds

```
for (int sub = 0; sub < numElements;
sub += 1)
    totalUsed += poundsUsed[sub];

//end for
return totalUsed;
```

Figure 11-22 Problem specification, IPO chart information, and C++ instructions for the Moonbucks Coffee program *(continues)*

(continued)

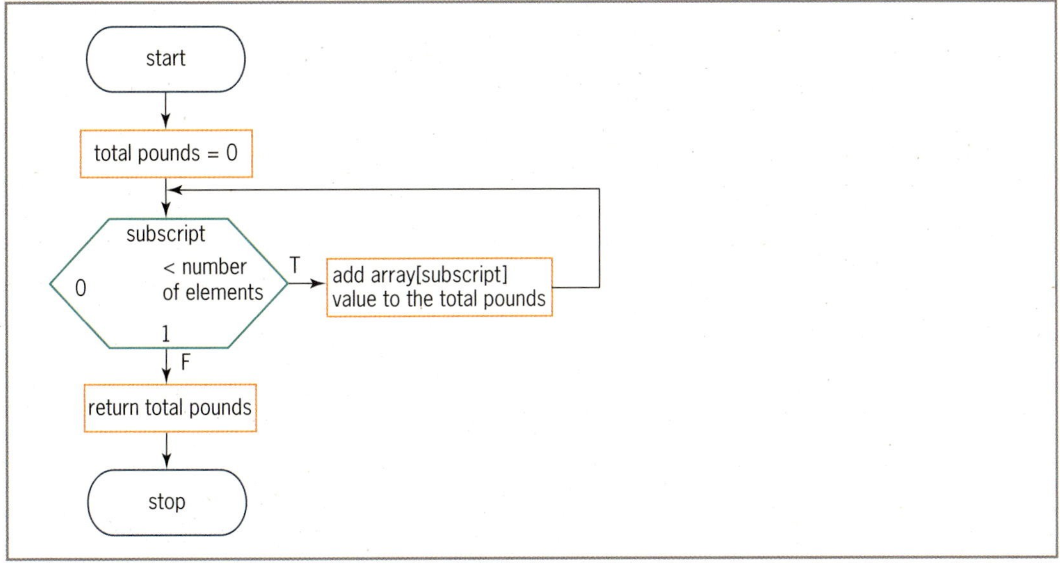

Figure 11-22 Problem specification, IPO chart information, and C++ instructions for the Moonbucks Coffee program

Figure 11-23 shows the entire Moonbucks Coffee program. The statement on Lines 15 through 17 in the `main` function declares the 12-element `double pounds` array. It uses the 12 values provided in the problem specification to initialize the array. The statements on Lines 19 and 20 declare two `double` variables named `total` and `average`. Next, the assignment statement on Line 23 calls the `getTotal` function, passing it the `pounds` array and the number of elements in the array. Recall that when an array is passed to a function, the computer passes only the address of the first array element. At this point, the computer temporarily leaves the `main` function to process the `getTotal` function's code, beginning with the function header on Line 35.

When processing the `getTotal` function's header, the computer locates the `pounds` array in memory and assigns the formal parameter's name—in this case, `poundsUsed`—to each element. As a result, each array element has two names. The first element, for example, is called `pounds[0]` in the `main` function but `poundsUsed[0]` in the `getTotal` function. After processing the `getTotal` function's header, the computer processes the statements within the function body. As Figure 11-23 indicates, those statements use a `for` loop, along with an accumulator variable named `totalUsed`, to add together each value contained in the `poundsUsed` array. The sum of those values represents the total number of pounds of coffee used. The `for` loop ends when its `sub` variable contains the integer 12 because that is the first integer that is not less than 12. When the `for` loop ends, its `sub` variable is removed from memory.

The `getTotal` function's `return` statement in Figure 11-23 is processed next. The statement returns the total number of pounds to the assignment statement on Line 23 in the `main` function. At that point, the `getTotal` function ends and the computer removes the `poundsUsed` name from the array elements. It also removes the `numElements` and `totalUsed` variables from internal memory.

The assignment statement on Line 23 in Figure 11-23 assigns the total number of pounds to the `main` function's `total` variable. Next, the assignment statement on Line 24 calculates the average number of pounds by dividing the total number of pounds by the number of array elements (12). It then assigns the result to the `average` variable. The `cout` statements on Lines 27 and 28 display the total number of pounds used and the average number of pounds used, respectively. The computer then processes the `return 0;` statement on Line 31. When the program ends, the computer removes the `pounds` array, as well as the `total` and `average` variables, from internal memory. Figure 11-24 shows the program's output.

```
//Moonbucks Coffee.cpp
//Displays the total and average number of pounds
//of coffee used during a 12-month period
//Created/revised by <your name> on <current date>

#include <iostream>
using namespace std;

//function prototype
double getTotal(double poundsUsed[], int numElements);

int main()
{
    //declare array
    double pounds[12] = {400.5, 450.0,
        475.5, 336.5, 457.0, 325.0, 220.5,
        276.0, 300.0, 320.5, 400.5, 415.0};
    //declare variables
    double total   = 0.0;
    double average = 0.0;

    //calculate the total and average pounds used
    total = getTotal(pounds, 12);
    average = total / 12;

    //display the total and average pounds used
    cout << "Total pounds: " << total << endl;
    cout << "Average pounds: " << average << endl;

    //system("pause");
    return 0;
}   //end of main function

//*****function definitions*****
double getTotal(double poundsUsed[], int numElements)
{
    double totalUsed = 0.0;    //accumulator

    //accumulate the pounds used
    for (int sub = 0; sub < numElements; sub += 1)
        totalUsed += poundsUsed[sub];
    //end for

    return totalUsed;
}   //end of getTotal function
```

if your C++ development tool requires this statement, delete the two forward slashes

Figure 11-23 Moonbucks Coffee program

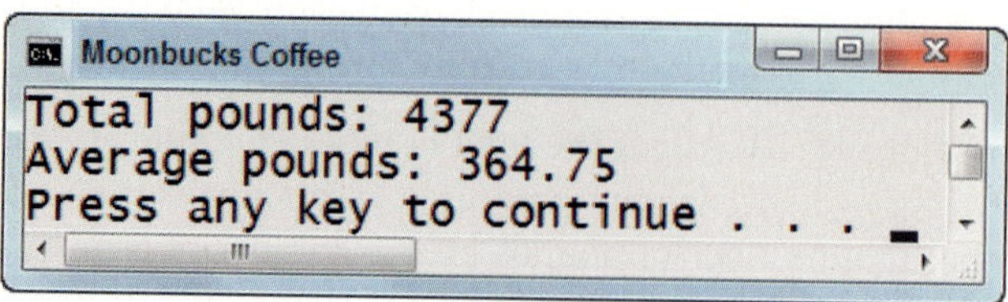

Figure 11-24 Result of running the Moonbucks Coffee program

The JK Motors Program—Searching an Array

Figure 11-25 shows the problem specification, IPO chart information, and C++ instructions for the JK Motors program. The program displays the number of employees whose salary is greater than the amount entered by the user. The program stores each employee's salary in a 10-element `int` array named `salaries`. To accomplish its task, the program uses a loop to search the `salaries` array and uses a selection structure to compare the salary in the current array element with the salary entered by the user. If the salary in the current array element is greater than the salary entered by the user, the program adds the number 1 to the `numEarnOver` counter variable. After searching each array element, the program displays the contents of the `numEarnOver` variable on the screen. It then prompts the user to enter another salary amount.

Problem specification
The payroll manager at JK Motors wants a program that displays the number of employees who earn more than a specific amount, which he will enter. The company employs 10 people. Their annual salaries are as follows: 23000, 26000, 34000, 21000, 54000, 45000, 36000, 80000, 75000, 34000. The program will use only the `main` function. It will use a sentinel value to end the program.

IPO chart information	C++ instructions
Input	
array (10 elements)	`int salaries[10] = {23000, 26000, 34000, 21000, 54000, 45000, 36000, 80000, 75000, 34000};`
salary to search for	`int searchFor = 0;`
Processing	
subscript (counter: 0 to 9)	*declared and initialized in the for clause*
Output	
number earning over the salary to search for (counter)	`int numEarnOver = 0;`
Algorithm	
1. enter the salary to search for	`cout << "Salary to search for " << "(negative number to end): "; cin >> searchFor;`
2. repeat while (the salary to search for is greater than or equal to 0)	`while (searchFor >= 0)` `{`
repeat for (subscript from 0 to 9)	`for (int sub = 0; sub < 10; sub += 1)`
if (the array[subscript] value is greater than the salary to search for)	`if (salaries[sub] > searchFor)`
add 1 to the number earning over the salary to search for	`numEarnOver += 1;`
end if	`//end if`
end repeat	`//end for`

Figure 11-25 Problem specification, IPO chart information, and C++ instructions for the JK Motors program *(continues)*

(continued)

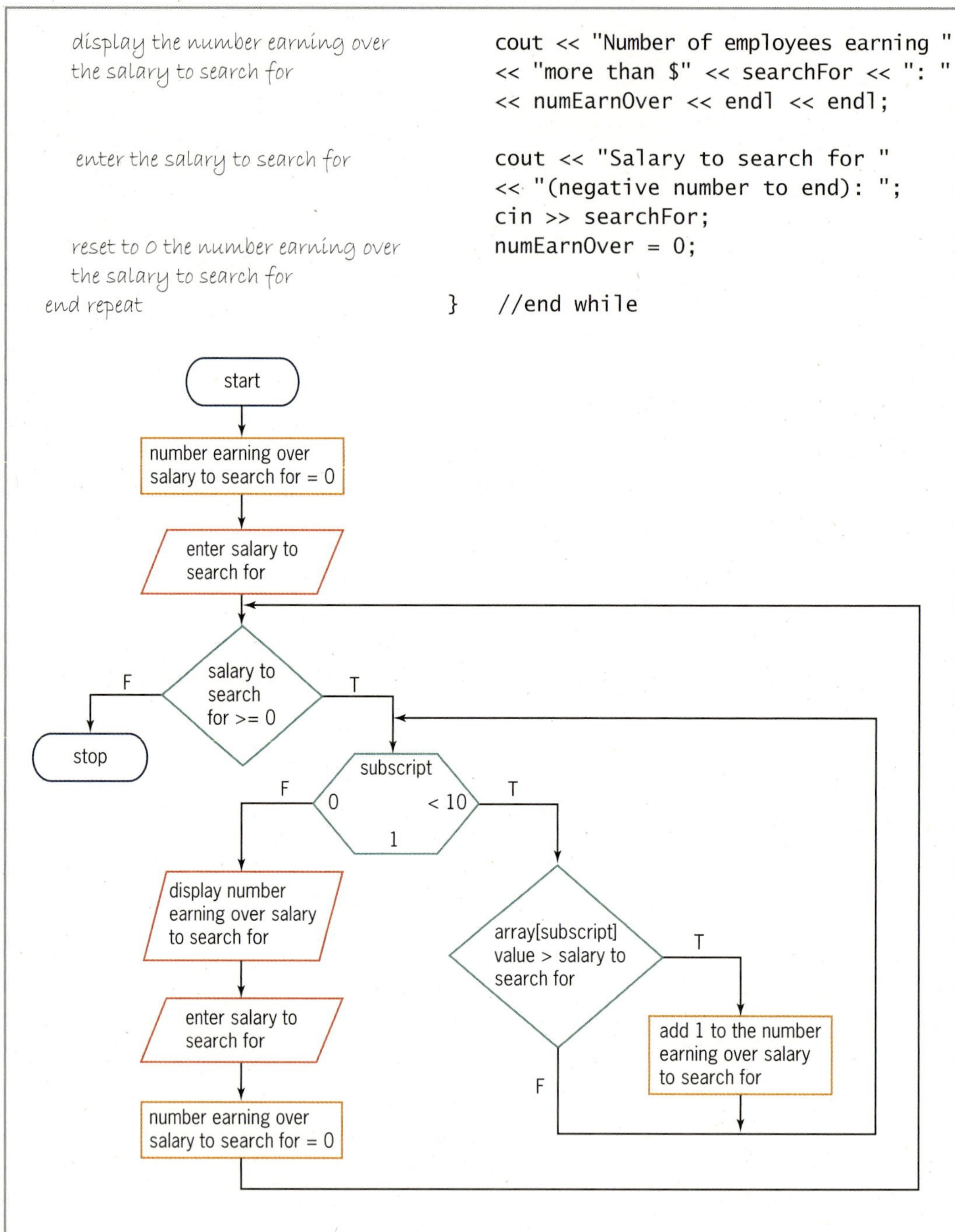

Figure 11-25 Problem specification, IPO chart information, and C++ instructions for the JK Motors program

Figure 11-26 shows the entire JK Motors program. The declaration statement on Lines 11 through 15 creates the 10-element `salaries` array and initializes it using the 10 values provided in the problem specification. The statements on Lines 16 and 17 declare two `int` variables named `searchFor` and `numEarnOver`. The `cout` statement on Lines 20 and 21 prompts the user to enter a salary amount, and the `cin` statement on Line 22 stores the user's response in the `searchFor` variable. The `while` loop in the program repeats its instructions as long as the value in the `searchFor` variable is greater than or equal to the number 0.

Within the `while` loop is a nested `for` loop, which the program uses to access each element in the `salaries` array, beginning with the element whose subscript is 0 and ending with the element whose subscript is 9. The selection structure in the nested loop compares the salary stored in the current array element with the salary stored in the `searchFor` variable. If the array element contains a salary that is greater than the salary stored in the `searchFor` variable, the selection structure's true path adds the number 1 to the contents of the `numEarnOver` variable. In the program shown in Figure 11-26, the `numEarnOver` variable is used as a counter variable to keep track of the number of employees earning more than the amount entered by the user. When the nested `for` loop ends, which is when the `sub` variable contains the number 10, the `cout` statement on Lines 34 through 36 displays an appropriate message on the screen. As shown in Figure 11-27, the `cout` statement displays the message "Number of employees earning more than $35000: 5" when the payroll manager enters 35000 as the salary to search for.

The statements on Lines 39 through 41 in Figure 11-26 then prompt the user to enter another salary amount and store the user's response in the `searchFor` variable. The statement on Line 42 resets the `numEarnOver` counter variable. Next, the condition in the `while` clause on Line 24 is evaluated again. If the `searchFor` variable's value is greater than or equal to the number 0, the instructions in the `while` loop are processed again. Otherwise, the loop ends, and the computer processes the statement on Line 45 before the program ends.

```
 1 //JK Motors.cpp - displays the number of employees
 2 //whose salary is greater than a specific amount
 3 //Created/revised by <your name> on <current date>
 4
 5 #include <iostream>
 6 using namespace std;
 7
 8 int main()
 9 {
10     //declare array and variables
11     int salaries[10] = {23000, 26000,
12                         34000, 21000,
13                         54000, 45000,
14                         36000, 80000,
15                         75000, 34000};
16     int searchFor   = 0;
17     int numEarnOver = 0;         //counter
18
19     //get salary to search for
20     cout << "Salary to search for "
21         << "(negative number to end): ";
22     cin >> searchFor;
23
24     while (searchFor >= 0)
25     {
26         //search the array
27         for (int sub = 0; sub < 10; sub += 1)
28             if (salaries[sub] > searchFor)
29                 numEarnOver += 1;
30             //end if
31         //end for
32
33         //display the search results
34         cout << "Number of employees earning "
35         << "more than $" << searchFor << ": "
36         << numEarnOver << endl << endl;
37
```

Figure 11-26 JK Motors program *(continues)*

(continued)

```
        //get another salary to search for
        cout << "Salary to search for "
             << "(negative number to end): ";
        cin >> searchFor;
        numEarnOver = 0;
    }   //end while
    //system("pause");
    return 0;
}   //end of main function
```

your C++ development tool may require this statement

Figure 11-26 JK Motors program

```
JK Motors
Salary to search for (negative number to end): 35000
Number of employees earning more than $35000: 5

Salary to search for (negative number to end): -1
Press any key to continue . . .
```

Figure 11-27 Sample run of the JK Motors program

The Hourly Rate Program—Accessing an Individual Element

Figure 11-28 shows the problem specification, IPO chart information, and C++ instructions for the hourly rate program. The program uses a six-element array to store the hourly rates, each of which is associated with a specific pay code. The program prompts the user to enter a pay code and then determines whether the pay code is valid. To be valid, the pay code must be one of the following integers: 1, 2, 3, 4, 5, or 6. If the pay code is valid, the program uses it to display the appropriate hourly rate from the array. If the pay code is not valid, the program displays the message "Invalid pay code".

Problem specification

Create a program that displays the hourly rate associated with the pay code entered by the user. The pay codes and hourly rates are as follows: 1, $11.25; 2, $10; 3, $9.85; 4, $8.65; 5, $15; 6, $25. The program should store the hourly rates in a six-element `double` array named `rates`. The array is illustrated below. The hourly rate for pay code 1 is stored in the first array element, whose subscript is 0. The hourly rate for pay code 2 is stored in the array element whose subscript is 1, and so on. Notice that the pay code is always one number more than the subscript of its corresponding hourly rate in the array.

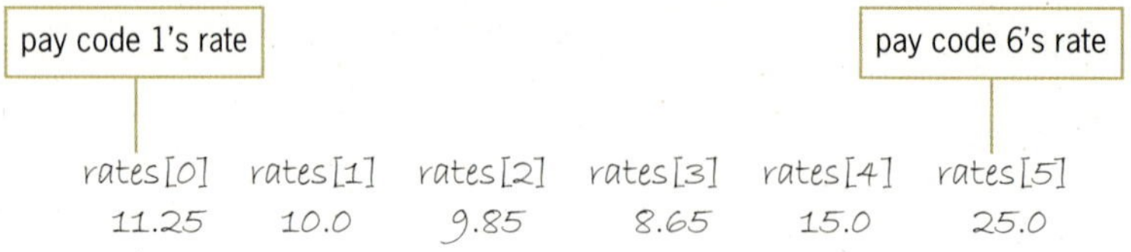

pay code 1's rate — pay code 6's rate

rates[0]	rates[1]	rates[2]	rates[3]	rates[4]	rates[5]
11.25	10.0	9.85	8.65	15.0	25.0

IPO chart information	**C++ instructions**
Input	
pay code	`int code = 0;`
Processing	
array [6 elements]	`double rates[6] = {11.25, 10.0, 9.85, 8.65, 15.0, 25.0};`
Output	
hourly rate	displayed from the array

Figure 11-28 Problem specification, IPO chart information, and C++ instructions for the hourly rate program *(continues)*

(continued)

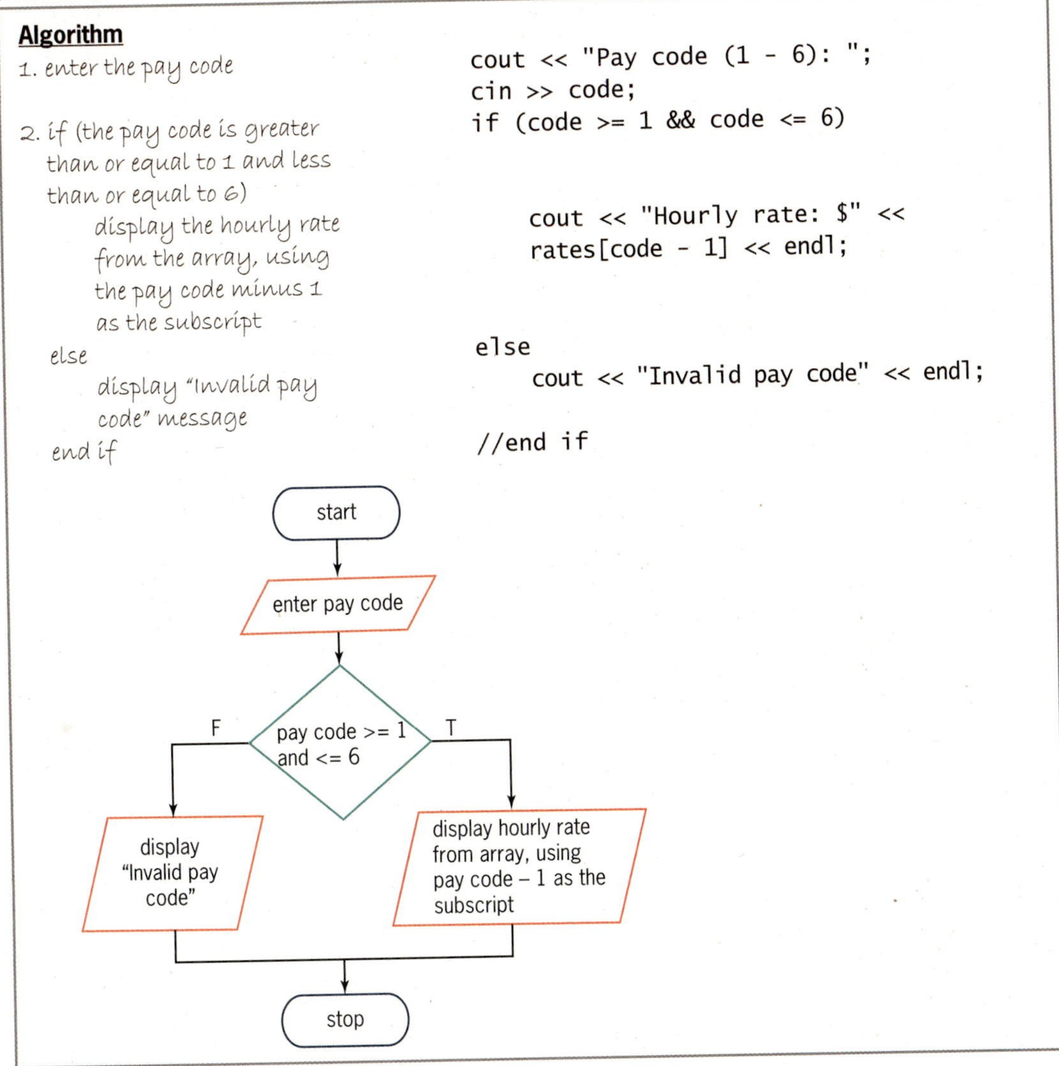

Algorithm

1. enter the pay code
2. if (the pay code is greater than or equal to 1 and less than or equal to 6)
   display the hourly rate from the array, using the pay code minus 1 as the subscript
   else
   display "Invalid pay code" message
   end if

```
cout << "Pay code (1 - 6): ";
cin >> code;
if (code >= 1 && code <= 6)


    cout << "Hourly rate: $" <<
    rates[code - 1] << endl;


else
    cout << "Invalid pay code" << endl;

//end if
```


Figure 11-28 Problem specification, IPO chart information, and C++ instructions for the hourly rate program

Figure 11-29 shows the entire hourly rate program. The declaration statement on Lines 12 and 13 creates the six-element `rates` array and initializes it using the hourly rates provided in the problem specification. The rate associated with pay code 1 is stored in the first array element (`rates[0]`). The rate associated with pay code 2 is stored in the second array element (`rates[1]`), and so on. Notice that the pay code is one number more than the subscript of its corresponding hourly rate in the array.

The statement on Line 14 in Figure 11-29 declares and initializes an `int` variable named `code`. The `code` variable will store the pay code entered by the user. It also will be used to access the corresponding hourly rate in the array. The statement on Line 17 is processed next and tells the computer to display the hourly rate in fixed-point notation with two decimal places. The `cout` statement on Line 20 prompts the user to enter the pay code, and the `cin` statement on Line 21 stores the user's response in the `code` variable.

The `if` clause on Line 22 in Figure 11-29 determines whether the pay code stored in the `code` variable is valid. If the pay code is not valid, the instruction in the `if` statement's false path displays the message "Invalid pay code"; otherwise, the instruction in its true path displays the appropriate hourly rate from the array. Notice that the true path instruction uses the `code` variable, which contains the pay code entered by the user, to access the appropriate element in the `rates` array. Also notice that to access the correct element, the number 1 must be subtracted from the contents of the `code` variable. This is because the pay code stored in the variable is one number more than the subscript of its associated hourly rate in the array. Figure 11-30 shows a sample run of the hourly rate program.

Before accessing an array element, you should always verify that the subscript is valid for the array. If the compiler encounters an invalid subscript, it will display an error message and the program will end abruptly.

```
//Hourly Rate.cpp - displays the hourly rate
//associated with the pay code entered by the user
//Created/revised by <your name> on <current date>

#include <iostream>
#include <iomanip>
using namespace std;

int main()
{
    //declare array and variable
    double rates[6] = {11.25, 10.0, 9.85,
                       8.65, 15.0, 25.0};
    int code = 0;

    //display hourly rate with two decimal places
    cout << fixed << setprecision(2);

    //get pay code
    cout << "Pay code (1 - 6): ";
    cin >> code;
    if (code >= 1 && code <= 6)
        cout << "Hourly rate: $" <<
            rates[code - 1] << endl;
    else
        cout << "Invalid pay code" << endl;
    //end if

    //system("pause");
    return 0;
}   //end of main function
```

your C++ development tool may require this statement

Figure 11-29 Hourly rate program

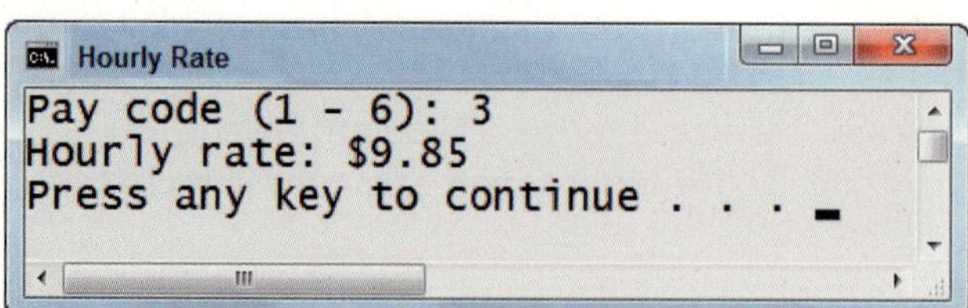

Figure 11-30 Sample run of the hourly rate program

The Random Numbers Program—Finding the Highest Value

Figure 11-31 shows the problem specification, IPO chart information, and C++ instructions for the random numbers program. The `main` function assigns five random numbers from 1 through 100 to a five-element `int` array named `randNums`. It then calls a program-defined void function to display the contents of the array. After the void function completes its task, the `main` function calls a program-defined value-returning function to determine the highest number in the array. The `main` function displays the function's return value on the screen.

Problem specification
Create a program that assigns five random integers from 1 through 100 to a five-element array. The program should display both the contents of the array and the highest number stored in the array. Use a program-defined void function to display the array's contents. Use a program-defined value-returning function to determine the highest number in the array.

`main` function IPO chart information	**C++ instructions**
Input	
random number (5 from 1 to 100)	*generated by the program and stored in the array*
Processing	
array (5 elements)	`int randNums[5] = {0};`
subscript (counter: 0 to 4)	*declared and initialized in the for clause*
Output	
random number (5 from 1 to 100)	*displayed by the displayArray function*
highest number in the array	`int highNum = 0;`
Algorithm	
1. initialize the random number generator	`srand(static_cast<int>(time(0)));`
2. repeat for (subscript from 0 to 4)	`for (int sub = 0; sub < 5; sub += 1)`
generate a random number and store it in array[subscript]	`randNums[sub] = 1 + rand() % (100 - 1 + 1);`
end repeat	`//end for`
3. call the displayArray function to display the contents of the array; pass the array and the number of elements	`displayArray(randNums, 5);`
4. call the getHighest function to determine the highest number in the array; pass the array and the number of elements	`highNum = getHighest(randNums, 5);`
5. display the highest number	`cout << endl << "Highest number: " << highNum << endl;`

Figure 11-31 Problem specification, IPO chart information, and C++ instructions for the random numbers program *(continues)*

(continued)

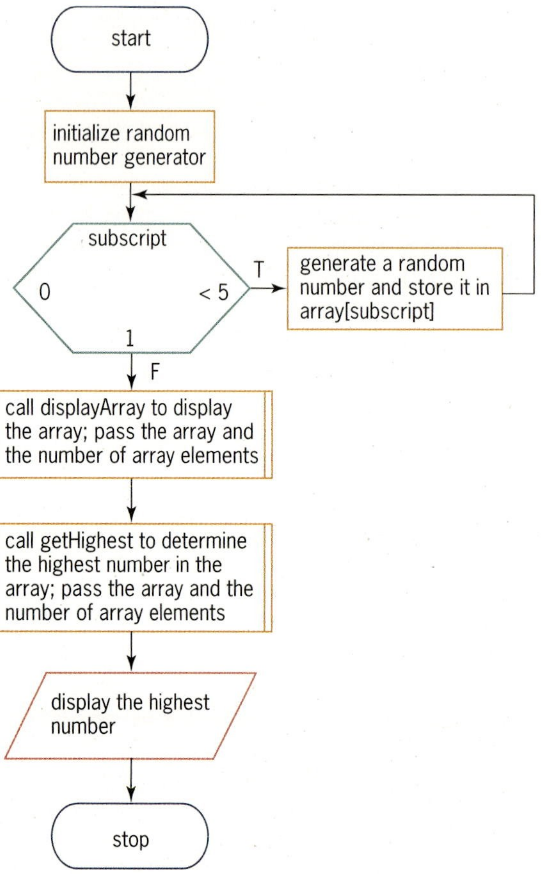

start

initialize random number generator

subscript 0 < 5 1

T: generate a random number and store it in array[subscript]

F: call displayArray to display the array; pass the array and the number of array elements

call getHighest to determine the highest number in the array; pass the array and the number of array elements

display the highest number

stop

displayArray function

IPO chart information	C++ instructions
Input	
array (5 elements) (formal parameter)	`int numbers[]`
number of elements (formal parameter)	`int numElements`
Processing	
subscript (counter: 0 to one less than the number of elements)	*declared and initialized in the for clause*
Output	
array (5 elements)	*displayed from the array by the for loop*
Algorithm	
repeat for (subscript from 0 to one less than the number of elements)	`for (int sub = 0; sub < numElements; sub += 1)`
display the contents of array[subscript]	`cout << numbers[sub] << endl;`
end repeat	`//end for`

Figure 11-31 Problem specification, IPO chart information, and C++ instructions for the random numbers program *(continues)*

(continued)

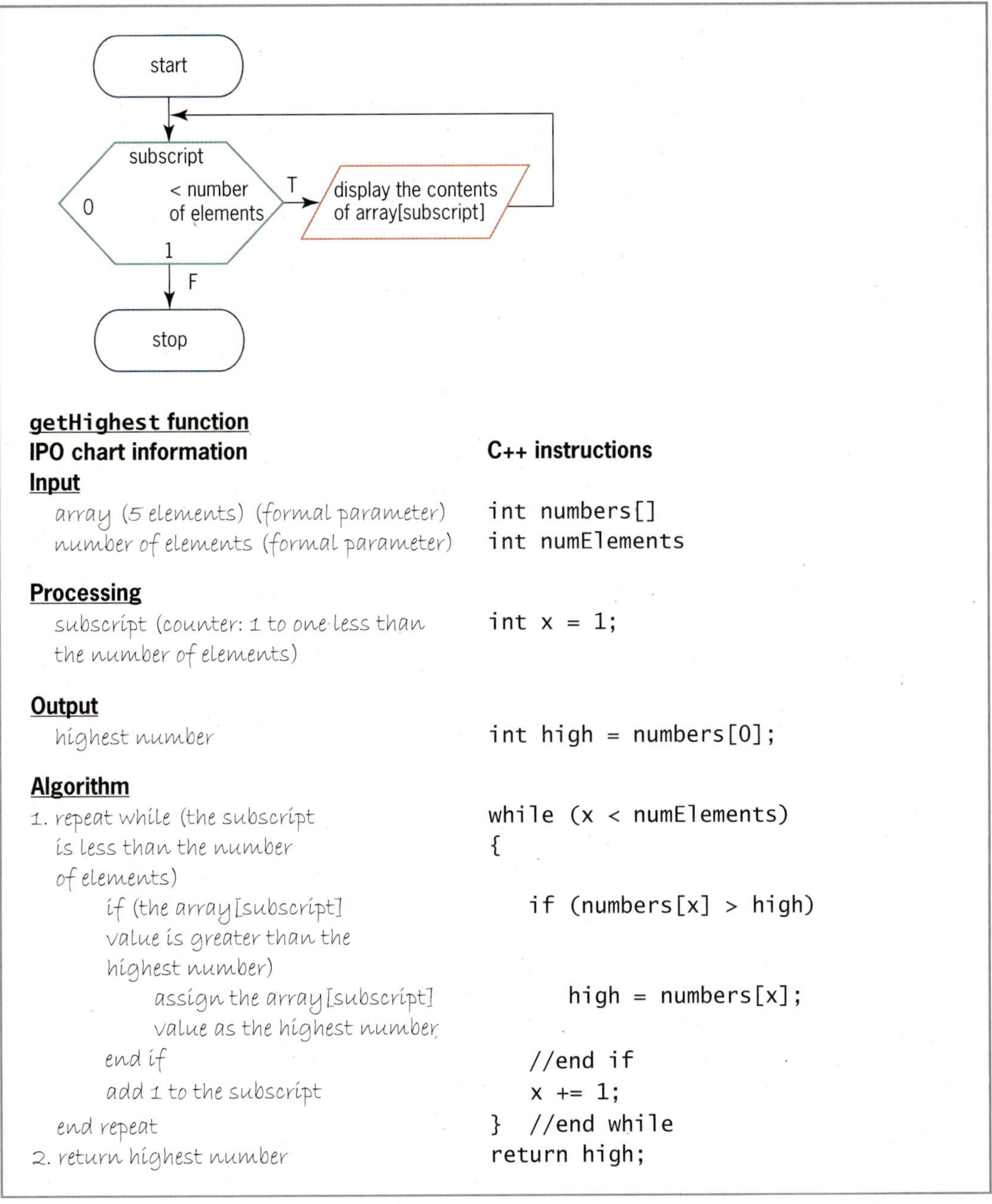

getHighest function

IPO chart information	**C++ instructions**
Input	
array (5 elements) (formal parameter)	`int numbers[]`
number of elements (formal parameter)	`int numElements`
Processing	
subscript (counter: 1 to one less than the number of elements)	`int x = 1;`
Output	
highest number	`int high = numbers[0];`
Algorithm	
1. repeat while (the subscript is less than the number of elements)	`while (x < numElements)` `{`
if (the array[subscript] value is greater than the highest number)	`if (numbers[x] > high)`
assign the array[subscript] value as the highest number	`high = numbers[x];`
end if	`//end if`
add 1 to the subscript	`x += 1;`
end repeat	`} //end while`
2. return highest number	`return high;`

Figure 11-31 Problem specification, IPO chart information, and C++ instructions for the random numbers program *(continues)*

(continued)

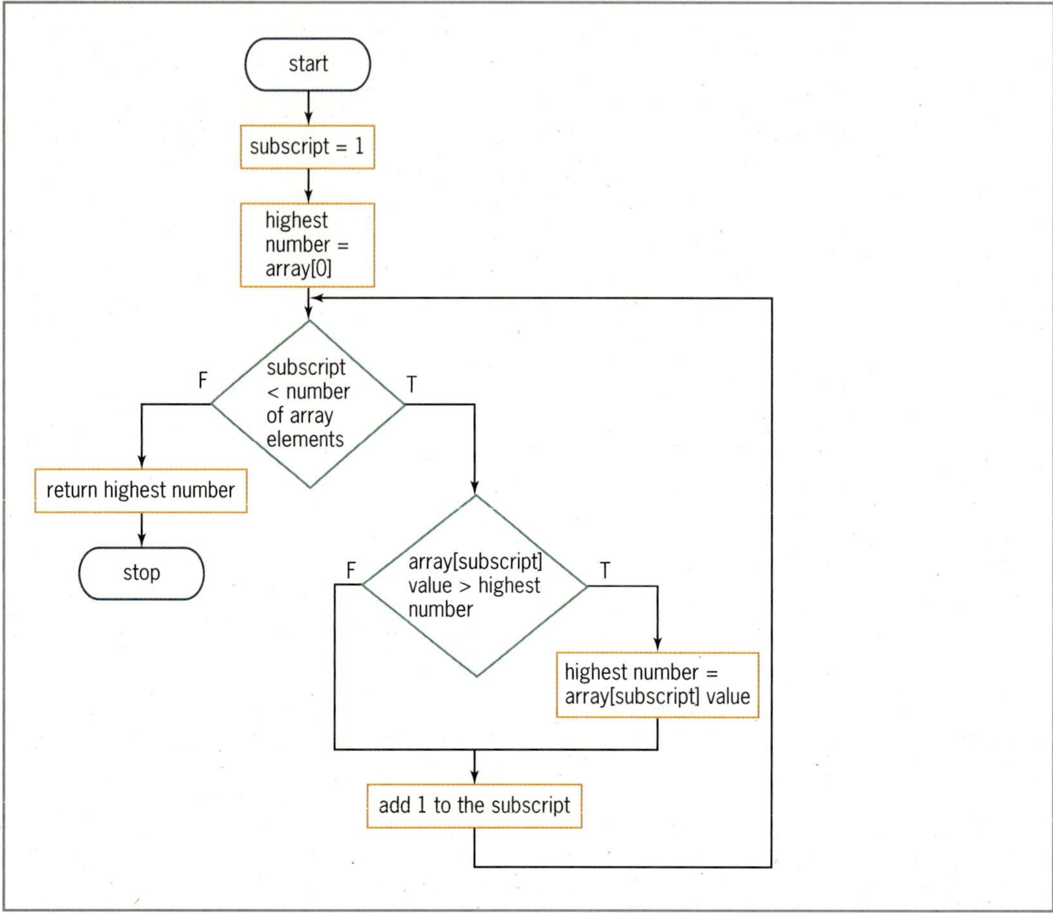

Figure 11-31 Problem specification, IPO chart information, and C++ instructions for the random numbers program

Figure 11-32 shows a sample run of the random numbers program, and Figure 11-33 shows all of the program's code. The program contains two program-defined value-returning functions: `main` and `getHighest`. It also contains a program-defined void function named `displayArray`.

Figure 11-32 Sample run of the random numbers program

```
//Random Numbers.cpp - displays the highest
//random number stored in an array
//Created/revised by <your name> on <current date>

#include <iostream>
#include <ctime>
//#include <cstdlib>
using namespace std;

//function prototypes
void displayArray(int numbers[], int numElements);
int getHighest(int numbers[], int numElements);

int main()
{
    //declare array and variable
    int randNums[5] = {0};
    int highNum = 0;

    //initialize random number generator
    srand(static_cast<int>(time(0)));
    //assign five random integers from 1
    //through 100 to the array
    for (int sub = 0; sub < 5; sub += 1)
        randNums[sub] = 1 + rand() % (100 - 1 + 1);
    //end for

    //display array
    displayArray(randNums, 5);

    //display highest number in the array
    highNum = getHighest(randNums, 5);
    cout << endl << "Highest number: "
        << highNum << endl;

    //system("pause");
    return 0;
}   //end of main function

//*****function definitions*****
void displayArray(int numbers[], int numElements)
{
    for (int sub = 0; sub < numElements; sub += 1)
        cout << numbers[sub] << endl;
    //end for
}   //end of displayArray function

int getHighest(int numbers[], int numElements)
{
    //assign first element's value
    //to the high variable
    int high = numbers[0];

    //begin the search with the second element
    int x = 1;

```

if your C++ development tool requires this directive, delete the two forward slashes

if your C++ development tool requires this statement, delete the two forward slashes

Figure 11-33 Random numbers program *(continues)*

The loop in the `getHighest` function searches the second through the last elements in the `numbers` array. It doesn't need to search the first element because that element's value is already stored in the `high` variable.

(continued)

```
57      //search for highest number
58      while (x < numElements)
59      {
60          if (numbers[x] > high)
61              high = numbers[x];
62          //end if
63          x += 1;
64      }   //end while
65
66      return high;
67 }    //end of getHighest function
```

Figure 11-33 Random numbers program

Desk-checking the random numbers program will help you understand how the highest number is determined. The statement on Line 17 in the program declares and initializes a five-element `int` array named `randNums`. The statement on Line 18 declares an `int` variable named `highNum`. The statement on Line 21 initializes the C++ random number generator, and the `for` loop on Lines 24 through 26 assigns five random integers to the `randNums` array. Figure 11-34 shows the desk-check table after the `for` loop ends, assuming the random numbers are 17, 5, 3, 96, and 77.

Ch11-Random Desk-Check video

main function's array

randNums[0]	randNums[1]	randNums[2]	randNums[3]	randNums[4]
~~0~~	~~0~~	~~0~~	~~0~~	~~0~~
17	5	3	96	77

highNum
0

removed from memory after the `for` loop in the `main` function ends

sub
~~0~~
~~1~~
~~2~~
~~3~~
~~4~~
5

Figure 11-34 Desk-check table after the `for` loop on Lines 24 through 26 ends

The statement on Line 29 calls the void `displayArray` function, passing it two actual arguments: the `randNums` array and the number of array elements (5). At this point, the computer temporarily leaves the `main` function to process the `displayArray` function's code, beginning with the function header on Line 41. When processing the function header, the computer locates the `randNums` array in memory and assigns the name of the first formal parameter (`numbers`) to each element. It also creates an `int` variable named `numElements` and stores the integer 5 in it. Figure 11-35 shows the desk-check table after the `displayArray` function header is processed.

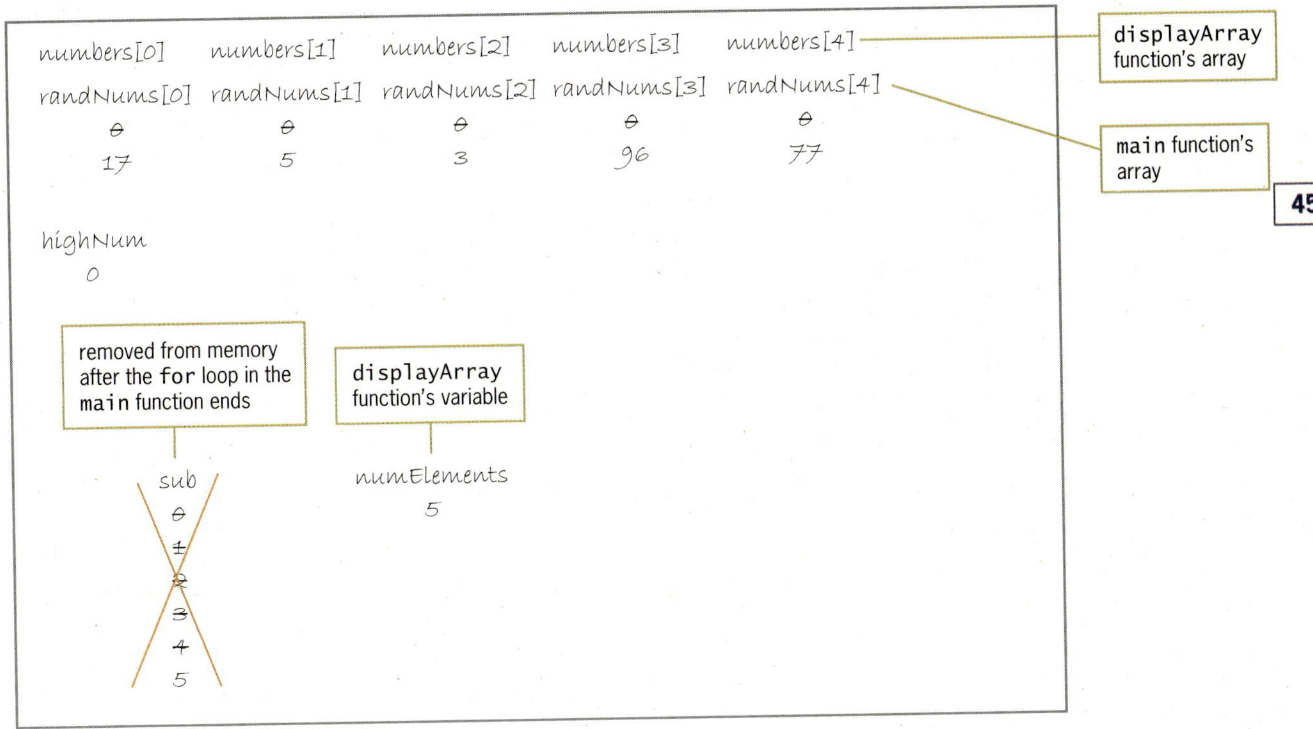

Figure 11-35 Desk-check table after the displayArray function header is processed

The `displayArray` function displays the contents of the `numbers` array (which also is the `randNums` array) on the screen. Figure 11-36 shows the desk-check table after the `displayArray` function ends.

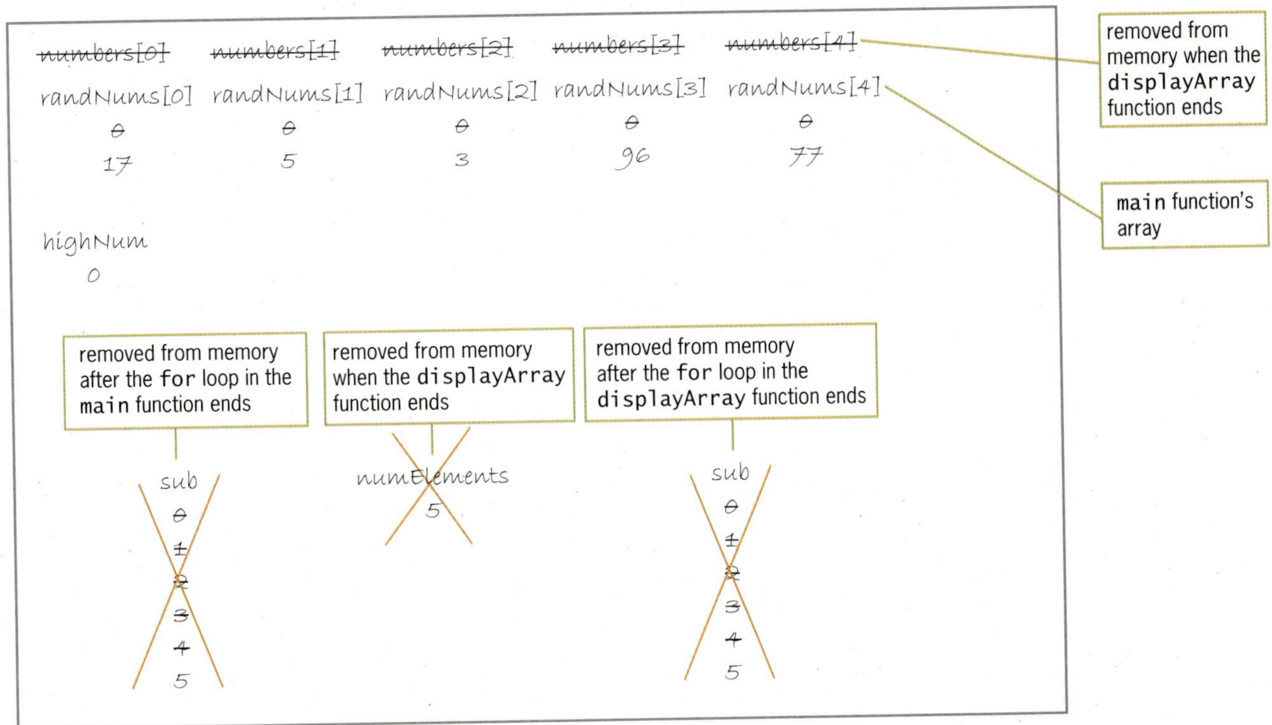

Figure 11-36 Desk-check table after the displayArray function ends

After processing the displayArray function, the computer returns to the main function to process the assignment statement that appears on Line 32. The statement calls the value-returning getHighest function, passing it two actual arguments: the randNums array and the number of array elements (5). At this point, the computer temporarily leaves the main function to process the getHighest function's code, beginning with the function header on Line 48.

When processing the getHighest function's header, the computer locates the randNums array in memory and assigns the name of the first formal parameter—numbers—to each array element. It also creates the second formal parameter—an int variable named numElements—and stores the number 5 in it. Next, the declaration statements on Lines 52 and 55 create two int variables named high and x. The high variable will keep track of the highest value stored in the array, and the x variable will keep track of the array subscripts. Notice that the high variable is initialized to the value stored in the first array element (17). The x variable is initialized to the number 1, which is the subscript of the second array element. Figure 11-37 shows the desk-check table after the declaration statements are processed.

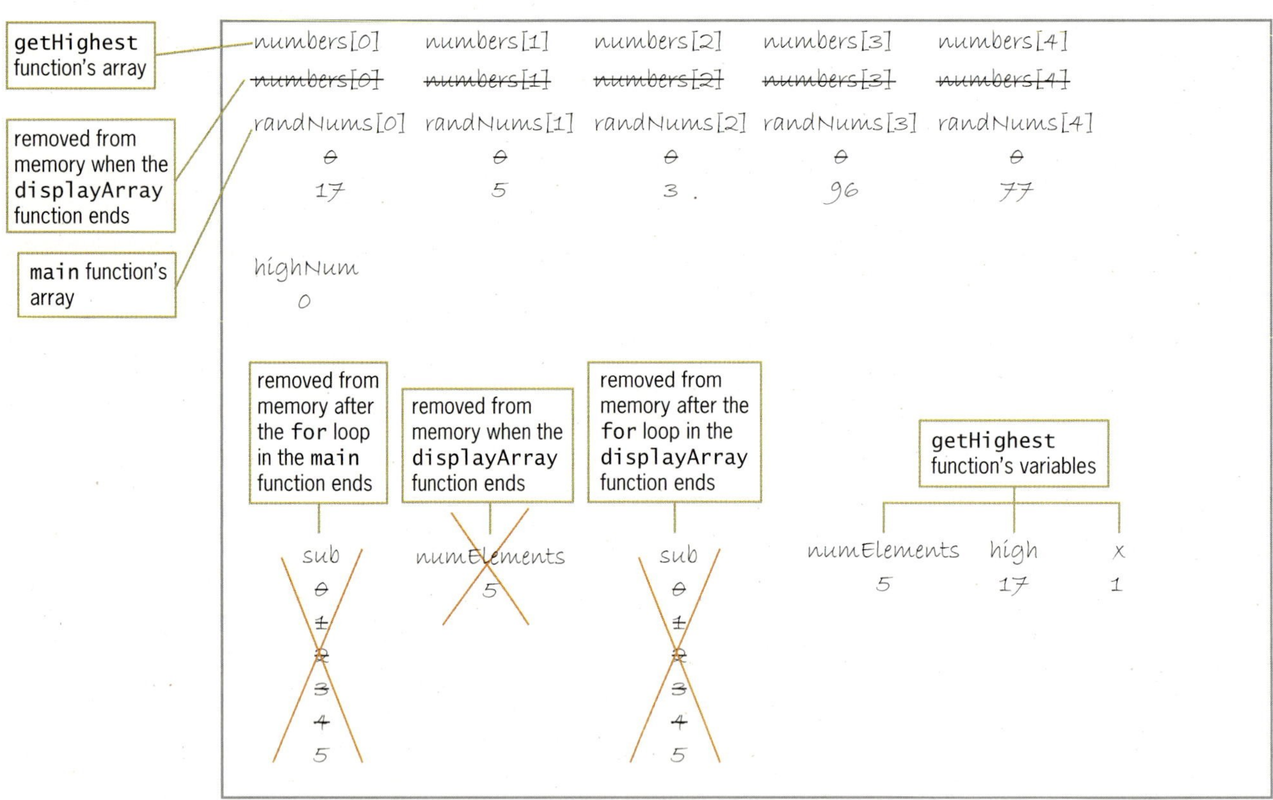

Figure 11-37 Desk-check table after the declaration statements on Lines 52 and 55 are processed

The while clause on Line 58 is processed next. The clause's condition checks whether the x variable's value is less than the number of elements stored in the numElements variable. It is, so the if statement's condition compares the value stored in the numbers[1] element, which is the second element in the array, with the value stored in the high variable. (Recall that at this point, the high variable contains the same value as the first array element.) The value in the numbers[1] element (5) is not greater than the value in the high variable (17), so the if statement ends and the computer processes the x += 1; statement on Line 63. The statement increases the value in the x variable by 1, giving 2.

Next, the condition in the while clause on Line 58 checks whether the x variable's value is less than the number of elements stored in the numElements variable. It is, so the if statement's condition compares the value stored in the numbers[2] element with the value stored in the high variable. The value in the numbers[2] element (3) is not greater than the value in the high variable (17), so the if statement ends and the computer processes the x += 1; statement on Line 63. The statement increases the value in the x variable by 1, giving 3.

The while clause on Line 58 is processed next. The clause's condition checks whether the x variable's value is less than the number of elements stored in the numElements variable. It is, so the if statement's condition compares the value stored in the numbers[3] element with the value stored in the high variable. The value in the numbers[3] element (96) is greater than the value in the high variable (17), so the instruction in the if statement's true path assigns the element's value to the high variable, as shown in Figure 11-38.

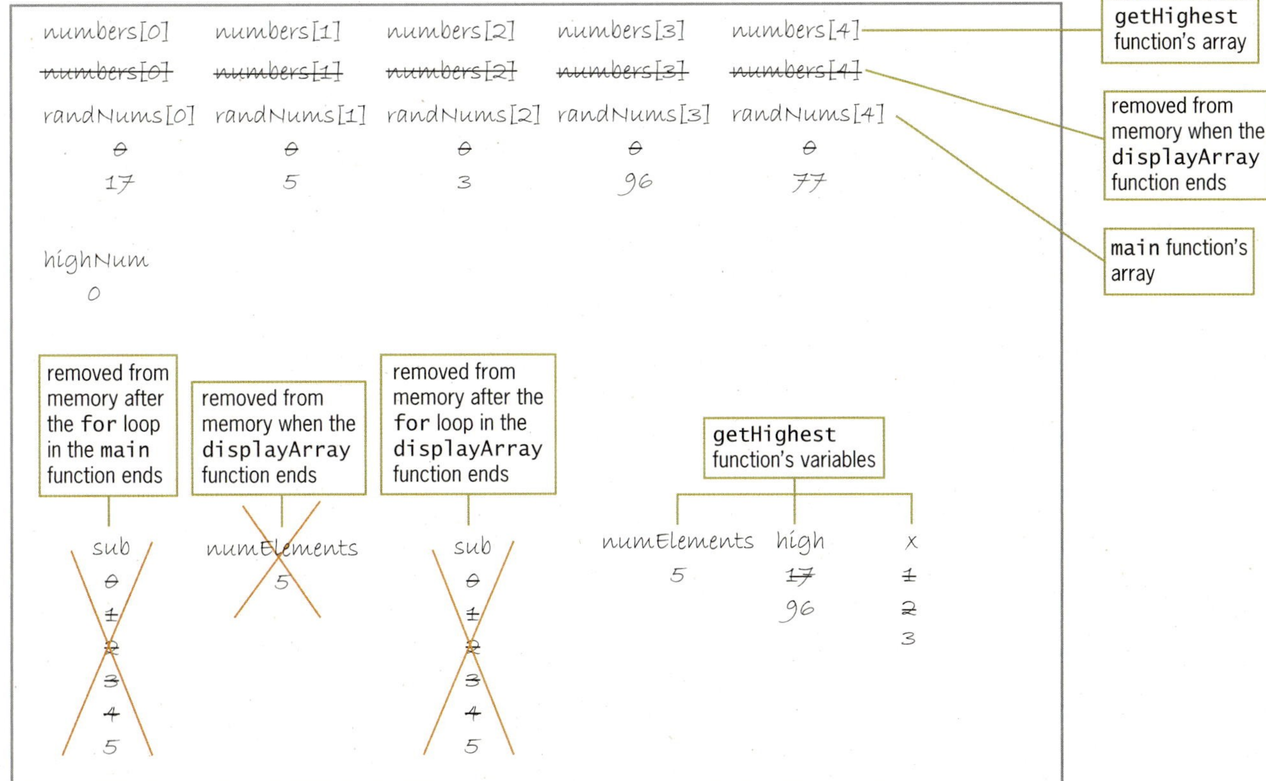

Figure 11-38 Desk-check table showing the fourth element's value entered in the high variable

Next, the computer processes the x += 1; statement on Line 63. The statement increases the value in the x variable by 1, giving 4. The while clause on Line 58 is processed next. The clause's condition checks whether the x variable's value is less than the number of elements stored in the numElements variable. It is, so the if statement's condition compares the value stored in the numbers[4] element with the value stored in the high variable. The value in the numbers[4] element (77) is not greater than the value in the high variable (96), so the if statement ends and the computer processes the x += 1; statement on Line 63. The statement increases the value in the x variable by 1, giving 5.

The condition in the while clause on Line 58 checks whether the x variable's value is less than the number of elements stored in the numElements variable. It's not, so the while loop ends and the computer processes the return statement on Line 66. The statement returns the value stored in the high variable to the statement that called the getHighest function. That statement is the assignment statement that appears on Line 32 in the main function. The assignment statement assigns the value returned by the getHighest function to the highNum variable. After the getHighest function ends, the computer removes the numbers name from each element in the array. It also removes the numElements, high, and x variables from memory. The completed desk-check table is shown in Figure 11-39.

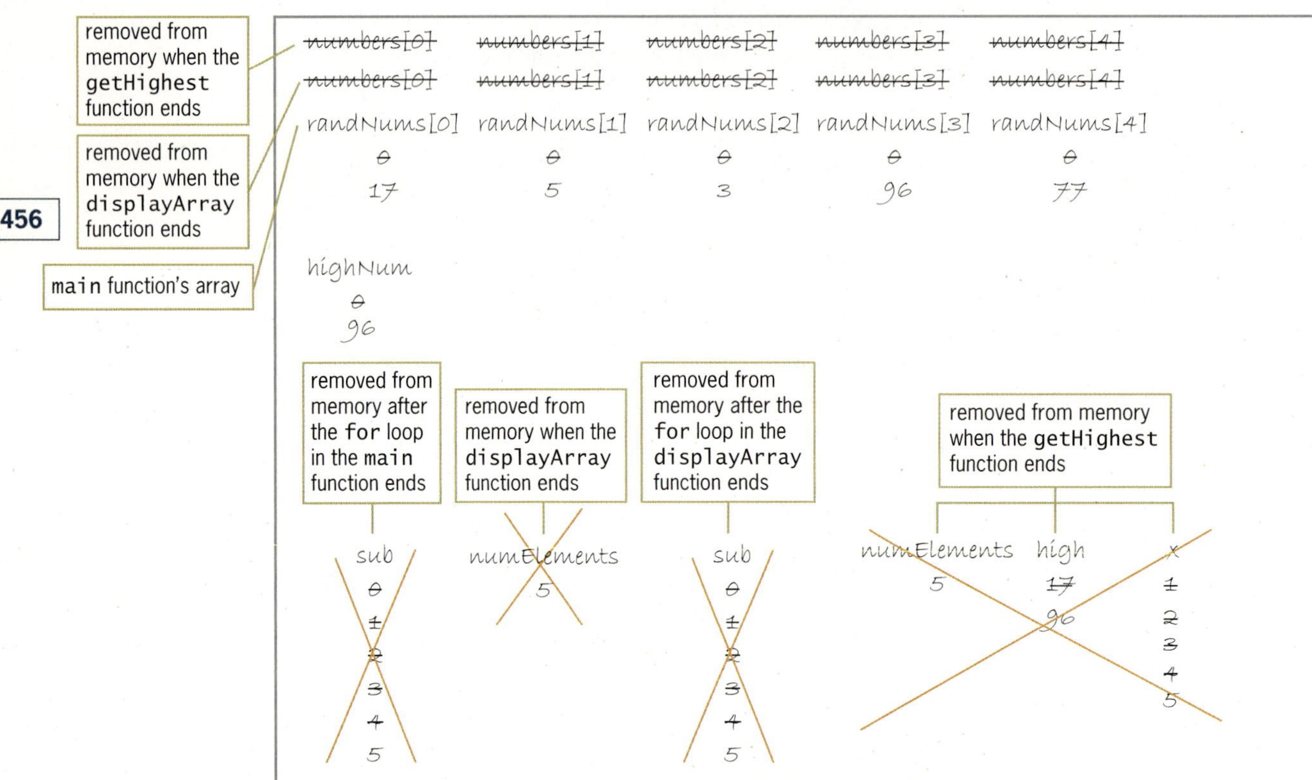

Figure 11-39 Completed desk-check table for the highest number program

The `cout` statement on Lines 33 and 34 in the `main` function displays the highest number on the computer screen. The computer then processes the `return 0;` statement on Line 37 before the program ends. When the program ends, the computer removes the `randNums` array and the `highNum` variable from memory.

Mini-Quiz 11-2

The answers to Mini-Quiz questions are located in Appendix A.

1. Which of the following adds the contents of the third element in the `orders` array to the `total` variable? Both the variable and the array have the `int` data type.
   a. `orders[2] += total;`
   b. `orders[3] += total;`
   c. `total += orders[2];`
   d. `total += orders[3];`

2. Which of the following `if` clauses determines whether the value stored in the fourth element in the `orders` array is greater than 25? The array has the `int` data type.
   a. `if (orders(3) > 25)`
   b. `if (orders{4} > 25)`
   c. `if (orders[3] > 25)`
   d. `if (orders[4] > 25)`

3. Write a C++ statement that multiplies the contents of the first element in the `sales` array by .15 and then stores the result in the `bonus` variable. Both the array and the variable have the `double` data type.

4. Which of the following `if` clauses determines whether an `int` variable named `sub` contains a valid subscript for the `scores` array? The array has 10 elements.

   a. `if (sub > 0 && sub < 10)`

   b. `if (sub >= 0 && sub <= 10)`

   c. `if (sub >= 0 && sub < 10)`

   d. `if (sub > 0 && sub <= 10)`

5. Which of the following `while` clauses tells the computer to process the loop instructions for each of the 20 elements in the `inventory` array? The program uses an `int` variable named `x` to keep track of the array subscripts. The `x` variable is initialized to 0.

   a. `while (x < 20)`

   b. `while (x <= 20)`

   c. `while (x > 0)`

   d. `while (x >= 0)`

Sorting the Data Stored in a One-Dimensional Array

In some programs, you might need to arrange the contents of a one-dimensional array in either ascending or descending order. Arranging data in a specific order is called **sorting**. When a one-dimensional array is sorted in ascending order, the first element in the array contains the smallest value and the last element contains the largest value. When a one-dimensional array is sorted in descending order, on the other hand, the first element contains the largest value and the last element contains the smallest value.

Over the years, many different sorting algorithms have been developed; one such algorithm is called the bubble sort. The **bubble sort** provides a quick and easy way to sort the items stored in an array, as long as the number of items is relatively small—for example, fewer than 50. The bubble sort algorithm works by comparing adjacent array elements and interchanging (swapping) the ones that are out of order. The algorithm continues comparing and swapping until the data in the array is sorted.

You can learn about another sorting algorithm in the Selection Sort section in the Ch11WantMore.pdf file.

To demonstrate the logic of a bubble sort, you will manually sort the contents of a three-element array in ascending order. The array, which is named `nums`, contains the following numbers: 9, 8, and 7. Figure 11-40 shows the `nums` array values before, during, and after the bubble sort.

The bubble sort algorithm begins by comparing the first value in the array with the second value. If the first value is less than or equal to the second value, then no swap is made. However, if the first value is greater than the second value, then both values are interchanged. In this case, the first value (9) is greater than the second value (8), so the values are swapped as shown in the Second Comparison column in Figure 11-40.

After comparing the first value in the array with the second value, the algorithm then compares the second value with the third value. In this case, 9 is greater than 7, so the two values are swapped as shown in the Result column in Figure 11-40. At this point, the algorithm has completed its first time through the entire array—referred to as a pass. Notice that at the end of the first pass, the largest value (9) is stored in the last element in the array. The bubble sort gets its name from the fact that as the larger values drop to the bottom of the array, the smaller values rise (like bubbles) to the top.

Now observe what the bubble sort does on its second pass through the array. The bubble sort begins the second pass by comparing the first value in the array with the second value. In this case, 8 is greater than 7, so the two values are interchanged as shown in the Second Comparison column in Figure 11-40. Notice that at this point, the data in the array is sorted.

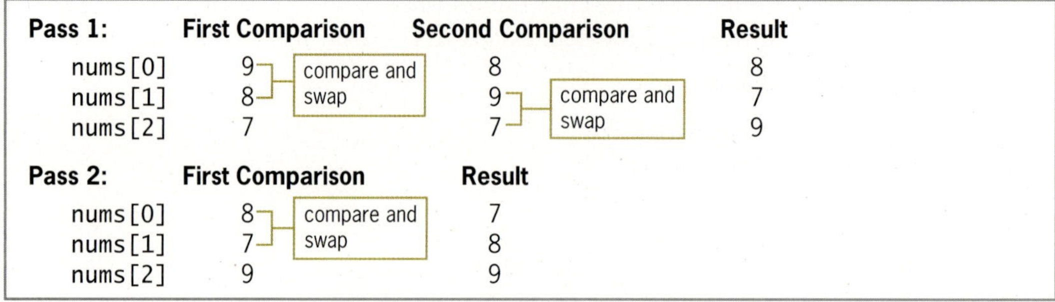

Figure 11-40 Array values before, during, and after the bubble sort

The program shown in Figure 11-41 uses the bubble sort to sort the contents of a four-element `int` array in ascending order. It then displays the contents of the sorted array on the screen.

```
//Bubble Sort.cpp - uses the bubble sort to
//sort the contents of a one-dimensional array
//in ascending order
//Created/revised by <your name> on <current date>

#include <iostream>
using namespace std;

int main()
{
    int numbers[4] = {23, 46, 12, 35};
    int sub        = 0;   //keeps track of subscripts
    int temp       = 0;   //variable used for swapping
    int maxSub     = 3;   //maximum subscript
    int lastSwap   = 0;   //position of last swap
    char swap      = 'Y'; //indicates if a swap was made

    //repeat loop instructions as long as a swap was made
    while (swap == 'Y')
    {
        swap = 'N';  //assume no swaps are necessary

        sub = 0;     //begin comparing with first
                     //array element

        //compare adjacent array elements to determine
        //whether a swap is necessary
        while (sub < maxSub)
        {
            if (numbers[sub] > numbers[sub + 1])
            {
                //a swap is necessary
                temp = numbers[sub];
                numbers[sub] = numbers[sub + 1];
                numbers[sub + 1] = temp;
                swap = 'Y';
                lastSwap = sub;
            }   //end if
            sub += 1;  //increment subscript
        }   //end while

```

Figure 11-41 Bubble sort program *(continues)*

(continued)

```
42         maxSub = lastSwap;   //reset maximum subscript
43     } //end while
44
45     //display sorted array
46     for (int x = 0; x < 4; x += 1)
47         cout << numbers[x] << endl;
48     //end for
49
50     //system("pause");
51     return 0;
52 }   //end of main function
```

your C++ development tool may require this statement

Figure 11-41 Bubble sort program

To help you understand the bubble sort, you will desk-check the program shown in Figure 11-41. (If you already understand the bubble sort program's code, you can skip the remainder of this section and continue with the section titled *Parallel One-Dimensional Arrays*.) The statements on Lines 11 through 16 create and initialize the `numbers` array and five variables. Figure 11-42 shows the desk-check table after these statements are processed.

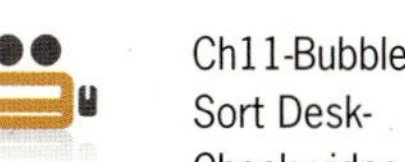

Ch11-Bubble Sort Desk-Check video

numbers[0]	numbers[1]	numbers[2]	numbers[3]	
23	46	12	35	
sub	**temp**	**maxSub**	**lastSwap**	**swap**
0	0	3	0	Y

Figure 11-42 Desk-check table after the declaration statements on Lines 11 through 16 are processed

The condition in the `while` clause on Line 19 compares the contents of the `swap` variable with the letter Y. The condition evaluates to true; therefore, the computer processes the instructions in the body of the loop. The first two instructions appear on Lines 21 and 23. The instructions assign the letter N to the `swap` variable and assign the number 0 to the `sub` variable. The `while` clause on Line 28 begins a nested loop that repeats its instructions as long as the value stored in the `sub` variable is less than the value stored in the `maxSub` variable. At this point, the `sub` variable contains the number 0, and the `maxSub` variable contains the number 3; therefore, the computer processes the instructions in the nested loop.

The first instruction in the nested loop is an `if` statement. The statement's condition, which appears on Line 30, determines whether the value stored in the `numbers[0]` variable is greater than the value stored in the `numbers[1]` variable. The condition evaluates to false because the `numbers[0]` variable contains the number 23 and the `numbers[1]` variable contains the number 46. As a result, the instructions in the `if` statement's true path are skipped over and processing continues with the `sub += 1;` statement on Line 39. The statement adds the number 1 to the contents of the `sub` variable, giving 1. Figure 11-43 shows the desk-check table after the nested loop instructions are processed the first time. The new values entered in the table are shaded in the figure.

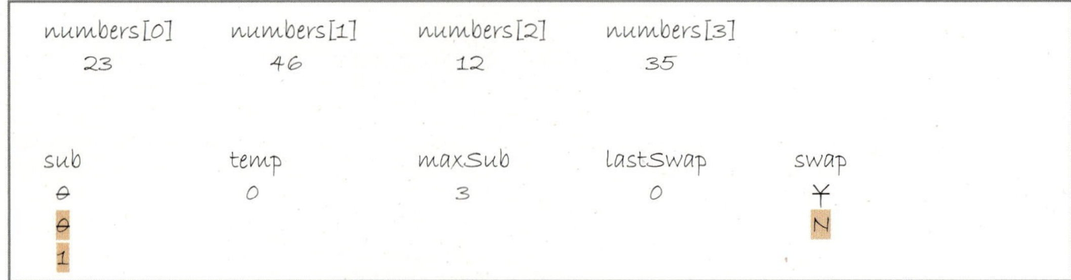

Figure 11-43 Desk-check table after the nested loop is processed the first time

Next, the computer evaluates the condition in the `while (sub < maxSub)` clause on Line 28. The condition evaluates to true because the `sub` variable's value (1) is less than the `maxSub` variable's value (3). As a result, the nested loop instructions are processed again.

The first instruction in the nested loop is an `if` statement. The statement's condition, which appears on Line 30, determines whether the value stored in the `numbers[1]` variable is greater than the value stored in the `numbers[2]` variable. In this case, the condition evaluates to true because the `numbers[1]` variable contains the number 46 and the `numbers[2]` variable contains the number 12. Because of this, the instructions in the `if` statement's true path are processed; the instructions appear on Lines 33 through 37. The first three instructions in the true path swap the values stored in the `numbers[1]` and `numbers[2]` variables. The fourth instruction assigns the letter Y to the `swap` variable to indicate that a swap was made. The last instruction in the true path assigns the value stored in the `sub` variable—in this case, the number 1—to the `lastSwap` variable, which keeps track of the position of the last swap in the array. Next, the `sub += 1;` statement on Line 39 adds the number 1 to the contents of the `sub` variable; the result is 2. Figure 11-44 shows the desk-check table after the nested loop instructions are processed the second time. The new values entered in the table are shaded in the figure.

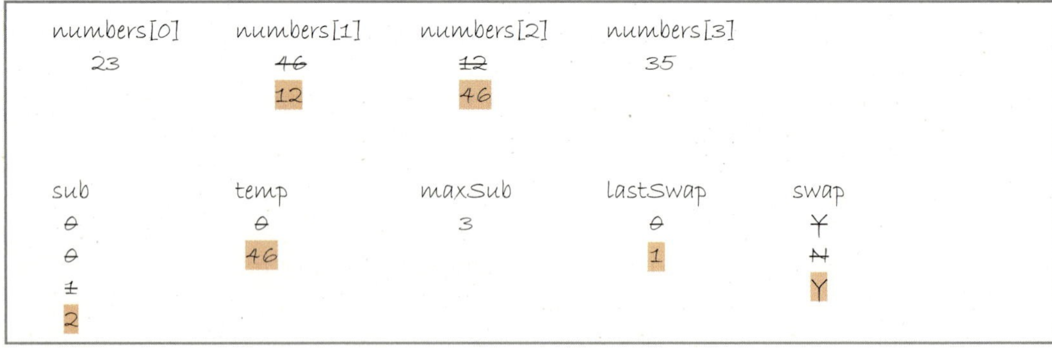

Figure 11-44 Desk-check table after the nested loop is processed the second time

Next, the computer evaluates the condition in the `while (sub < maxSub)` clause on Line 28. The condition evaluates to true because the `sub` variable's value (2) is less than the `maxSub` variable's value (3). Therefore, the computer once again processes the instructions in the nested loop.

The first instruction in the nested loop is an `if` statement. The statement's condition, which appears on Line 30, determines whether the value stored in the `numbers[2]` variable is greater than the value stored in the `numbers[3]` variable. The condition evaluates to true because the `numbers[2]` variable contains the number 46 and the `numbers[3]` variable contains the number 35. As a result, the computer processes the instructions in the `if` statement's true path. The first three instructions in the true path swap the values stored in the `numbers[2]` and `numbers[3]` variables. The fourth instruction in the true path assigns the letter Y to the `swap` variable to indicate that a swap was made. The last instruction in the true path assigns the value stored in the `sub` variable (2) to the `lastSwap` variable. Next, the `sub += 1;` statement on Line 39 adds the number 1 to the contents of the `sub` variable; the result is 3. Figure 11-45 shows the desk-check table after the nested loop instructions are processed the third time. The new values entered in the table are shaded in the figure.

numbers[0]	numbers[1]	numbers[2]	numbers[3]
23	~~46~~	~~12~~	~~35~~
	12	~~46~~	46
		35	

sub	temp	maxSub	lastSwap	swap
~~0~~	~~0~~	3	~~0~~	~~Y~~
~~0~~	~~46~~		~~1~~	~~N~~
~~1~~	46		2	~~Y~~
~~2~~				Y
3				

Figure 11-45 Desk-check table after the nested loop is processed the third time

The computer evaluates the condition in the `while (sub < maxSub)` clause on Line 28 next. The condition evaluates to false because the `sub` variable's value (3) is not less than the `maxSub` variable's value (3). As a result, the nested loop instructions are skipped over and processing continues with the `maxSub = lastSwap;` statement on Line 42. The statement assigns the number 2 to the `maxSub` variable. Figure 11-46 shows the desk-check table after the outer loop instructions are processed the first time. The new value entered in the table is shaded in the figure.

numbers[0]	numbers[1]	numbers[2]	numbers[3]
23	~~46~~	~~12~~	~~35~~
	12	~~46~~	46
		35	

sub	temp	maxSub	lastSwap	swap
~~0~~	~~0~~	~~3~~	~~0~~	~~Y~~
~~0~~	~~46~~	2	~~1~~	~~N~~
~~1~~	46		2	~~Y~~
~~2~~				Y
3				

Figure 11-46 Desk-check table after the outer loop is processed the first time

The condition in the `while (swap == 'Y')` clause on Line 19 is processed next. The condition evaluates to true, so the computer processes the outer loop's instructions again. The first two instructions in the outer loop assign the letter N to the `swap` variable and assign the number 0 to the `sub` variable, as shown in Figure 11-47. The new values entered in the table are shaded in the figure.

numbers[0]	numbers[1]	numbers[2]	numbers[3]
23	~~46~~	~~12~~	~~35~~
	12	~~46~~	46
		35	

sub	temp	maxSub	lastSwap	swap
~~0~~	~~0~~	~~3~~	~~0~~	~~Y~~
~~0~~	~~46~~	2	~~1~~	~~N~~
~~1~~	46		2	~~Y~~
~~2~~				~~Y~~
~~3~~				N
0				

Figure 11-47 Desk-check table after the instructions on Lines 21 and 23 are processed

Next, the computer evaluates the condition in the `while (sub < maxSub)` clause on Line 28. The condition evaluates to true, so the computer processes the instructions in the nested loop.

The first instruction in the nested loop is an `if` statement. The statement's condition, which appears on Line 30, determines whether the value stored in the `numbers[0]` variable is greater than the value stored in the `numbers[1]` variable. The condition evaluates to true because the `numbers[0]` variable contains the number 23 and the `numbers[1]` variable contains the number 12. As a result, the computer processes the instructions in the `if` statement's true path. The first three instructions in the true path swap the values stored in the `numbers[0]` and `numbers[1]` variables. The fourth instruction in the true path assigns the letter Y to the `swap` variable to indicate that a swap was made. The last instruction in the true path assigns the value stored in the `sub` variable (0) to the `lastSwap` variable. Next, the `sub += 1;` statement on Line 39 adds the number 1 to the contents of the `sub` variable, giving 1. Figure 11-48 shows the desk-check table after the instructions in the nested loop are processed. The new values entered in the table are shaded in the figure.

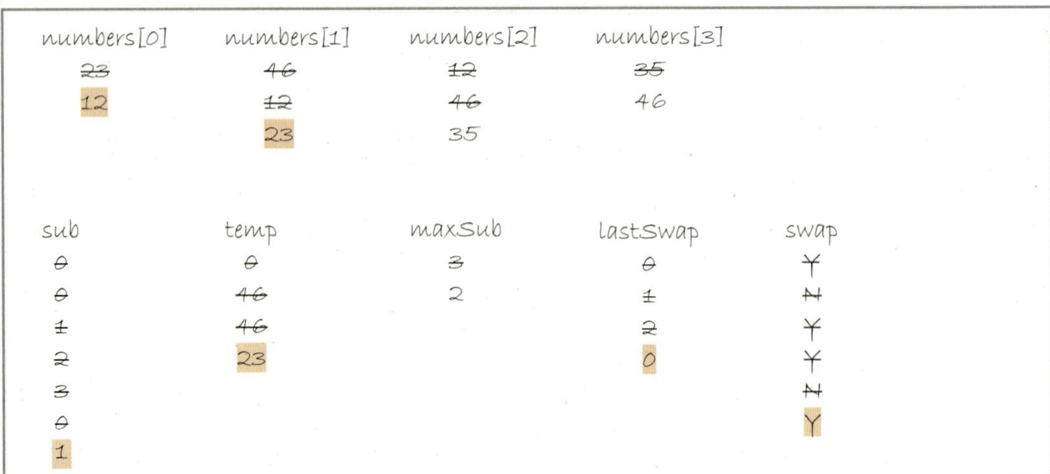

numbers[0]	numbers[1]	numbers[2]	numbers[3]
~~23~~	~~46~~	~~12~~	~~35~~
12	~~12~~	~~46~~	46
	23	35	

sub	temp	maxSub	lastSwap	swap
~~0~~	~~0~~	~~3~~	~~0~~	~~Y~~
~~0~~	~~46~~	2	~~1~~	~~N~~
~~1~~	~~46~~		~~2~~	~~Y~~
~~2~~	23		0	~~Y~~
~~3~~				~~N~~
~~0~~				Y
1				

Figure 11-48 Desk-check table after the instructions in the nested loop are processed

The computer evaluates the condition in the `while (sub < maxSub)` clause on Line 28 next. The condition evaluates to true because the `sub` variable's value (1) is less than the `maxSub` variable's value (2). Therefore, the computer processes the nested loop instructions once again.

The first instruction in the nested loop is an `if` statement. The statement's condition, which appears on Line 30, determines whether the value stored in the `numbers[1]` variable is greater than the value stored in the `numbers[2]` variable. The condition evaluates to false because the `numbers[1]` variable contains the number 23 and the `numbers[2]` variable contains the number 35. As a result, the computer skips over the instructions in the `if` statement's true path. Processing continues with the `sub += 1;` statement on Line 39. The statement increments the `sub` variable's value by 1; the result is 2.

The condition in the `while (sub < maxSub)` clause on Line 28 is processed next. The condition evaluates to false because the `sub` variable's value (2) is not less than the `maxSub` variable's value (2). Because of this, the computer skips over the instructions in the nested loop. Processing continues with the `maxSub = lastSwap;` statement on Line 42. The statement assigns the number 0 to the `maxSub` variable. Figure 11-49 shows the current status of the desk-check table. The new values entered in the table are shaded in the figure.

numbers[0]	numbers[1]	numbers[2]	numbers[3]
~~23~~	~~46~~	~~12~~	~~35~~
12	~~12~~	~~46~~	46
	23	35	

sub	temp	maxSub	lastSwap	swap
~~0~~	~~0~~	~~3~~	~~0~~	~~Y~~
~~0~~	~~46~~	~~2~~	~~1~~	~~N~~
~~1~~	~~46~~	0	~~2~~	~~Y~~
~~2~~	23		0	~~Y~~
~~3~~				~~N~~
~~0~~				Y
~~1~~				
2				

Figure 11-49 Desk-check table after the instructions in the nested loop are processed again

The computer evaluates the condition in the `while (swap == 'Y')` clause on Line 19 next. The condition evaluates to true, so the computer processes the outer loop's instructions again. The first two instructions in the outer loop assign the letter N to the `swap` variable and assign the number 0 to the `sub` variable. Next, the computer evaluates the condition in the `while (sub < maxSub)` clause on Line 28. The condition evaluates to false because the `sub` variable's value (0) is not less than the `maxSub` variable's value (0). As a result, the computer skips over the instructions in the nested loop and continues processing with the `maxSub = lastSwap;` statement on Line 42. The statement assigns the number 0 to the `maxSub` variable. Figure 11-50 shows the current status of the desk-check table. The new values entered in the table are shaded in the figure.

numbers[0]	numbers[1]	numbers[2]	numbers[3]
~~23~~	~~46~~	~~12~~	~~35~~
12	~~12~~	~~46~~	46
	23	35	

sub	temp	maxSub	lastSwap	swap
~~0~~	~~0~~	~~3~~	~~0~~	~~Y~~
~~0~~	~~46~~	~~2~~	~~1~~	~~N~~
~~1~~	~~46~~	~~0~~	~~2~~	~~Y~~
~~2~~	23	0	0	~~Y~~
~~3~~				~~N~~
~~0~~				~~Y~~
~~1~~				N
~~2~~				
0				

Figure 11-50 Current status of the desk-check table

The condition in the `while (swap == 'Y')` clause on Line 19 is processed next and evaluates to false. Because of this, the computer skips over the instructions in the outer loop. Processing continues with the `for` clause on Line 46. The clause tells the computer to repeat the `cout << numbers[x] << endl;` statement four times: once for each element in the array. Figure 11-51 shows the result of running the bubble sort program.

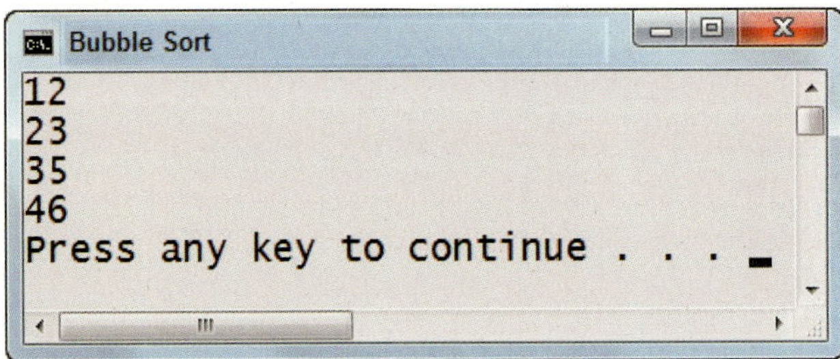

Figure 11-51 Result of running the bubble sort program

Parallel One-Dimensional Arrays

Figure 11-52 shows the problem specification and IPO chart for the motorcycle club membership program. The program displays the annual fee associated with the membership type entered by the user. Notice that the program uses two one-dimensional arrays: a `char` array named `types` and an `int` array named `fees`. The `types` array stores the five membership types, and the `fees` array stores the annual fees associated with those types. As indicated in the figure, the first element in each array pertains to membership type A; the `types` array contains the letter A, and the `fees` array contains the corresponding fee (100). The second element in each array pertains to membership type B, and so on. The two arrays are referred to as **parallel arrays** because their elements are related by their position (subscript) in the arrays. In other words, each element in the `types` array corresponds to the element located in the same position in the `fees` array. To determine the annual fee, you simply locate the membership type in the `types` array and then view its corresponding element in the `fees` array.

Problem specification

The members of a local motorcycle club are required to pay an annual fee based on their membership type. Create a program that displays a member's annual fee and membership type. The membership types and associated fees are shown here. Use a one-dimensional `char` array named `types` to store the membership types. Use a one-dimensional `int` array named `fees` to store the annual fees.

Membership type	Annual fee
A	100
B	110
C	125
D	150
E	200

types[0]	types[1]	types[2]	types[3]	types[4]
A	B	C	D	E
fees[0]	**fees[1]**	**fees[2]**	**fees[3]**	**fees[4]**
100	110	125	150	200

parallel arrays

Input

membership type
(A, B, C, D, or E)

Processing

Processing items:
types array (5 elements)
fees array (5 elements)
subscript (counter: 0 to 4)

Algorithm:
1. enter the membership type
2. repeat while (the subscript is less than 5 and the membership type has not been located in the types array)
      add 1 to the subscript
   end repeat
3. if (the subscript is less than 5)
      display types[subscript] and fees[subscript]
   else
      display "Invalid membership type"
   end if

Output

fee
membership type

Figure 11-52 Problem specification and IPO chart for the club membership program *(continues)*

(continued)

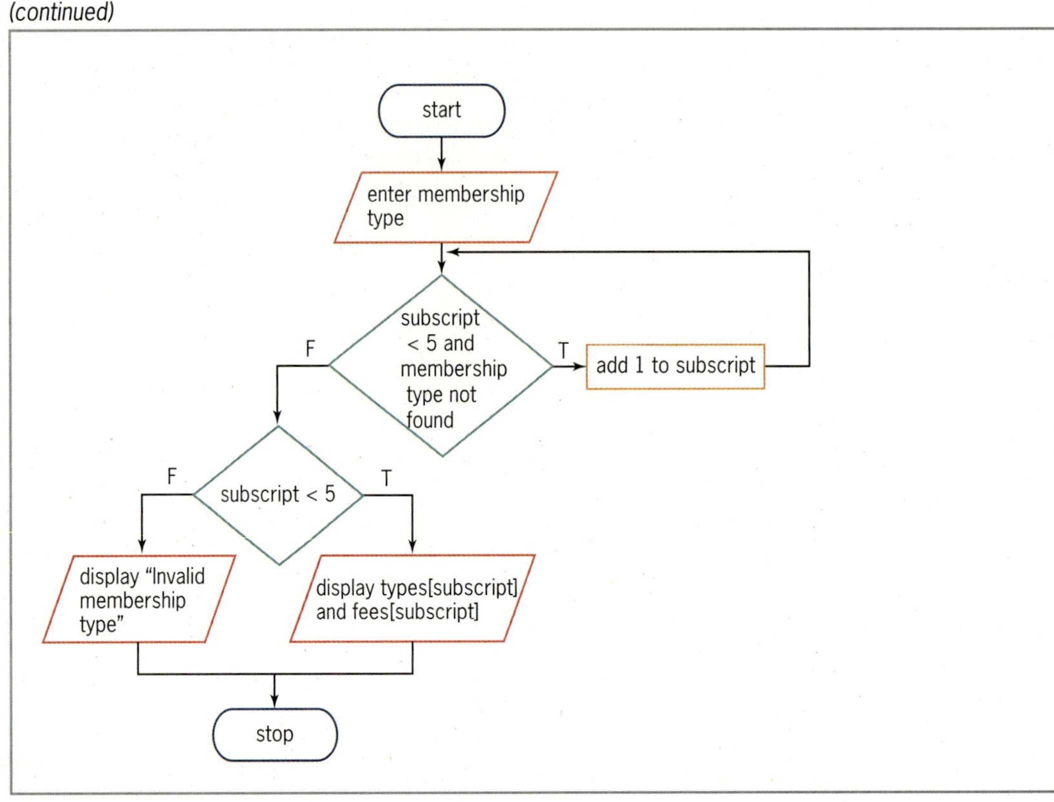

Figure 11-52 Problem specification and IPO chart for the club membership program

Figure 11-53 shows the IPO chart information and corresponding C++ instructions.

IPO chart information	C++ instructions
Input	
membership type (A, B, C, D, or E)	`char memberType = ' ';`
Processing	
types array (5 elements)	`char types[5] = {'A', 'B', 'C', 'D', 'E'};`
fees array (5 elements)	`int fees[5] = {100, 110, 125, 150, 200};`
subscript (counter: 0 to 4)	`int sub = 0;`
Output	
fee	from the fees array
membership type	from the types array

Figure 11-53 IPO chart information and C++ instructions for the club membership program *(continues)*

(continued)

Algorithm	

1. enter the membership type	`cout << "Membership type`
	`(A, B, C, D, or E): ";`
	`cin >> memberType;`
	`memberType = toupper(memberType);`

2. repeat while (the subscript is less than 5 and the membership type has not been located in the types array)	`while (sub < 5 && types[sub]` `!= memberType)`
add 1 to the subscript	`sub += 1;`
end repeat	`//end while`
3. if (the subscript is less than 5)	`if (sub < 5)`

display types[subscript] and fees[subscript]	`cout << "Annual fee for`
	`membership type " << types[sub]`
	`<< ": $" << fees[sub] << endl;`

else	`else`
display "Invalid membership type"	`cout << "Invalid membership` `type" << endl;`
end if	`//end if`

Figure 11-53 IPO chart information and C++ instructions for the club membership program

Figure 11-54 shows the code for the entire club membership program. The program declares and initializes the two parallel arrays (`types` and `fees`). It also declares and initializes two variables named `memberType` and `sub`. The `memberType` variable will store the membership type entered by the user, and the `sub` variable will keep track of the array subscripts.

The program prompts the user to enter a membership type, and it stores the user's response in the `memberType` variable. The program then converts the contents of the `memberType` variable to uppercase. The `while` loop on Lines 24 through 26 in Figure 11-54 is processed next. The loop will continue to increment the `sub` variable's value by 1 as long as the variable contains a value that is less than 5 and (at the same time) the membership type has not been located in the `types` array. The loop will stop when either of the following conditions is true: the `sub` variable contains the number 5 (which indicates that the loop reached the end of the array without finding the membership type) or the membership type is located in the array.

After the loop completes its processing, the `if` statement on Line 31 in Figure 11-54 compares the number stored in the `sub` variable with the number 5. If the `sub` variable contains a number that is less than 5, it indicates that the loop stopped processing because the membership type was located in the `types` array. In that case, the `cout` statement on Lines 32 and 33 displays both the membership type from the `types` array and the corresponding annual fee from the `fees` array. However, if the `sub` variable contains a number that is not less than 5, it indicates that the loop stopped processing because it reached the end of the `types` array without finding the membership type. In that case, the `cout` statement on Line 35 displays the message "Invalid membership type". Figure 11-55 shows a sample run of the program.

```
//Club Membership.cpp - displays the annual
//membership fee
//Created/revised by <your name> on <current date>

#include <iostream>
using namespace std;

int main()
{
    //declare arrays
    char types[5] = {'A', 'B', 'C', 'D', 'E'};
    int fees[5]   = {100, 110, 125, 150, 200};
    //declare variables
    char memberType = ' ';
    int sub         = 0;

    //get type to search for
    cout << "Membership type (A, B, C, D, or E): ";
    cin >> memberType;
    memberType = toupper(memberType);

    //locate the position of the membership
    //type in the types array
    while (sub < 5 && types[sub] != memberType)
        sub += 1;
    //end while

    //if the membership type was located in the
    //types array, display the membership type
    //and the corresponding fee
    if (sub < 5)
        cout << "Annual fee for membership type "
        << types[sub] << ": $" << fees[sub] << endl;
    else
        cout << "Invalid membership type" << endl;
    //end if

    //system("pause");
    return 0;
}   //end of main function
```

parallel one-dimensional arrays

your C++ development tool may require this statement

Figure 11-54 Club membership program

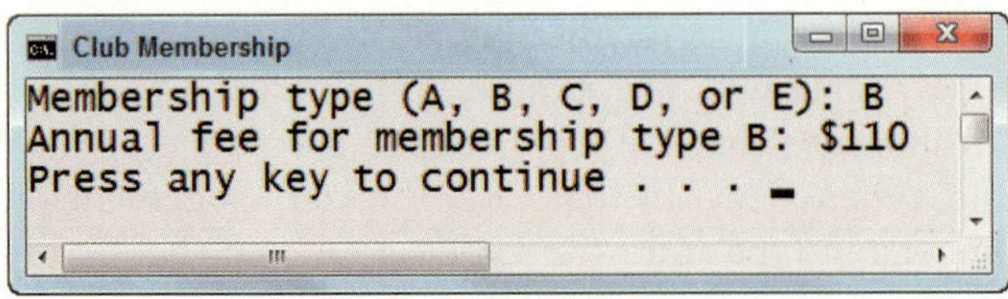

Figure 11-55 Sample run of the club membership program

Mini-Quiz 11-3

The answers to Mini-Quiz questions are located in Appendix A.

1. Write a C++ `if` clause that determines whether the value stored in the `prices[x]` variable is less than the value stored in the `lowest` variable. The array and variable have the `double` data type.
2. The process of arranging data in alphabetical or numerical order is called ________.
3. Write a `for` loop that subtracts the number 3 from each of the 10 elements in an `int` array named `orders`. Use a variable named `x` to keep track of the array subscripts. Initialize the `x` variable to 0.

LAB 11-1 Stop and Analyze

The answers to the labs are located in Appendix A.

Study the program shown in Figure 11-56, and then answer the questions. The `domestic` array contains the amounts the company sold domestically during the months of January through June. The `international` array contains the amounts the company sold internationally during the same period.

```
//Lab11-1.cpp - calculates the total sales
//Created/revised by <your name> on <current date>

#include <iostream>
using namespace std;

int main()
{
    //declare arrays and variable
    int domestic[6] = {12000, 45000, 32000,
                       67000, 24000, 55000};
    int international[6] = {10000, 56000, 42000,
                             23000, 12000, 34000};
    int totalSales = 0; //accumulator

    //accumulate sales
    for (int x = 0; x < 6; x += 1)
        totalSales += domestic[x] + international[x];
    //end for

    //display total sales
    cout << "Total sales: $" << totalSales << endl;

    //system("pause");
    return 0;
}   //end of main function
```

if your C++ development tool requires this statement, delete the two forward slashes

Figure 11-56 Code for Lab 11-1

QUESTIONS

1. What relationship exists between the `domestic` and `international` arrays?
2. What value is stored in the `domestic[1]` element?
3. How can you calculate the total company sales made in February?
4. What is the highest subscript in the `international` array?

5. If you change the `for` clause in Line 17 to `for (int x = 1; x <= 6; x += 1)`, how will the change affect the assignment statement in the `for` loop?
6. Follow the instructions for starting C++ and viewing the Lab11-1.cpp file, which is contained in either the Cpp7\Chap11\Lab11-1 Project folder or the Cpp7\Chap11 folder. (Depending on your C++ development tool, you may need to open Lab11-1's project/solution file first.) If necessary, delete the two forward slashes that appear before the `system("pause");` statement, and then save the program. Run the program. The total company sales are $412000.
7. Modify the program so that it displays the total domestic sales, total international sales, and total company sales. Save and then run the program.
8. Now modify the program so that it also displays the total sales made in each month. Use month numbers from 1 through 6. Save and then run the program.

LAB 11-2 Plan and Create

In this lab, you will plan and create an algorithm for Penelope Havert. The problem specification, IPO chart information, and C++ instructions are shown in Figure 11-57. According to the figure, the `main` function first will get the 12 rainfall amounts from the user. It then will display a menu that allows the user to select from three different options. If the user chooses to display the monthly rainfall amounts, the `main` function will call the `displayMonthly` function, passing it the `rainfall` array and the number of array elements. The `displayMonthly` function uses a `for` loop to display the 12 monthly rainfall amounts on the screen. However, if the user chooses to display the total rainfall amount, the `main` function will call the `displayTotal` function, passing it the `rainfall` array and the number of array elements. The `displayTotal` function uses a `for` loop to accumulate the 12 monthly rainfall amounts. It then displays the total rainfall amount on the screen. The program ends when the user enters any number other than 1 or 2 in response to the "Enter your choice:" prompt.

Problem specification
Penelope Havert wants a program that allows her to enter the monthly rainfall amounts for the previous year. The program then should allow her to either display the monthly rainfall amounts on the screen, or calculate and display the total annual rainfall amount. In this program, you will use two program-defined void functions named `displayMonthly` and `displayTotal`. Both functions will be passed the contents of a one-dimensional array named `rainfall`, along with the number of array elements. The `rainfall` array will contain the 12 monthly rainfall amounts entered by the user. Void functions are appropriate in this case because neither function needs to return a value to the statement that called it.

main function

IPO chart information	**C++ instructions**
Input	
menu choice	`int choice = 0;`
monthly rainfall amount (12)	`double rainfall[12] = {0.0};`
Processing	
subscript (counter: 0 to 11)	*declared and initialized in the for clause*
Output	
array (12 elements)	*displayed by the displayMonthly function*
total rainfall	*displayed by the displayTotal function*

Figure 11-57 Problem specification, IPO chart information, and C++ instructions for Lab 11-2 *(continues)*

(continued)

Algorithm

1. repeat for (subscript from 0 to 11)	`for (int x = 0; x < 12; x += 1)` `{`

enter monthly rainfall amount	`cout << "Enter rainfall`
	 `for month " << x + 1 << ": ";`
	 `cin >> rainfall[x];`

end repeat	`} //end for`
2. repeat	`do` `{`

display menu	`cout << endl;`
	 `cout << "1 Display`
	 `monthly amounts" << endl;`
	 `cout << "2 Display total`
	 `amount" << endl;`
	 `cout << "3 End program" << endl;`

enter the menu choice	`cout << "Enter your choice: ";` `cin >> choice;`
if (the menu choice is 1) call the displayMonthly function to display the array; pass the array and the number of elements	`if (choice == 1)` `displayMonthly(rainfall, 12);`

else if (the menu choice is 2) call the displayTotal function to calculate and display the total rainfall; pass the array and the number of elements	`else`
	 `if (choice == 2)`
	 `displayTotal(rainfall, 12);`

end if	`//end if`
end if	`//end if`
while (menu choice equals 1 or 2)	`} while (choice == 1 ||` `choice == 2);`

displayMonthly function

IPO chart information	C++ instructions
Input	
array (formal parameter)	`double rain[]`
number of elements (formal parameter)	`int numElements`
Processing	
subscript (counter: 0 to 11)	*declared and initialized in the for clause*
Output	
array element	*from array*

Figure 11-57 Problem specification, IPO chart information, and C++ instructions for Lab 11-2 *(continues)*

(continued)

Algorithm	
1. display heading	`cout << "Monthly rainfall amounts:" << endl;`

2. repeat for (subscript from 0 to 11)
display array[subscript]
end repeat
	`for (int x = 0; x < numElements; x += 1)`
	`cout << rain[x] << endl;`
	`//end for`

`displayTotal` function	
IPO chart information	**C++ instructions**
Input	
array (formal parameter)	`double rainAmt[]`
number of elements (formal parameter)	`int elements`
Processing	
subscript (counter: 0 to 11)	declared and initialized in the for clause
Output	
total rainfall	`double total = 0.0;`
Algorithm	

1. repeat for (subscript from 0 to 11)
add array[subscript] to the total rainfall
end repeat
	`for (int x = 0; x < elements; x += 1)`
	`total = total + rainAmt[x];`
	`//end for`

2. display the total rainfall	`cout << "Total rainfall: " << total << endl;`

Figure 11-57 Problem specification, IPO chart information, and C++ instructions for Lab 11-2

Figure 11-58 shows the code for the entire rainfall program, and Figure 11-59 shows the completed desk-check table for the program, assuming the user enters the following 12 rainfall amounts: 2.44, 2.36, 2.76, 1.2, .4, .07, .04, .23, .54, .63, 1.54, and 2.16. After entering the rainfall amounts, the user selects choice 1, followed by choice 2, followed by choice 3.

```
//Lab11-2.cpp
//Stores monthly rainfall amounts in an array
//Displays the monthly rainfall amounts or the
//total annual rainfall amount
//Created/revised by <your name> on <current date>

#include <iostream>
using namespace std;

//function prototypes
void displayMonthly(double rain[], int numElements);
void displayTotal(double rainAmt[], int elements);

```

Figure 11-58 Rainfall program *(continues)*

(continued)

```
int main()
{
    //declare array and variable
    double rainfall[12] = {0.0};
    int choice = 0;

    //get rainfall amounts
    for (int x = 0; x < 12; x += 1)
    {
        cout << "Enter rainfall for month "
            << x + 1 << ": ";
        cin >> rainfall[x];
    }   //end for

    do
    {
        //display menu and get menu choice
        cout << endl;
        cout << "1  Display monthly amounts" << endl;
        cout << "2  Display total amount" << endl;
        cout << "3  End program" << endl;
        cout << "Enter your choice: ";
        cin >> choice;

        //call appropriate function or end program
        if (choice == 1)
            displayMonthly(rainfall, 12);
        else
            if (choice == 2)
                displayTotal(rainfall, 12);
            //end if
        //end if
    }   while (choice == 1 || choice == 2);

    //system("pause");
    return 0;
}   //end of main function

//*****function definitions*****
void displayMonthly(double rain[], int numElements)
{
    cout << "Monthly rainfall amounts:" << endl;
    for (int x = 0; x < numElements; x += 1)
        cout << rain[x] << endl;
    //end for
}   //end of displayMonthly function

void displayTotal(double rainAmt[], int elements)
{
    double total = 0.0;
    for (int x = 0; x < elements; x += 1)
        total = total + rainAmt[x];
    //end for
    cout << "Total rainfall: " << total << endl;
}   //end of displayTotal function
```

if your C++ development tool requires this statement, delete the two forward slashes

Figure 11-58 Rainfall program

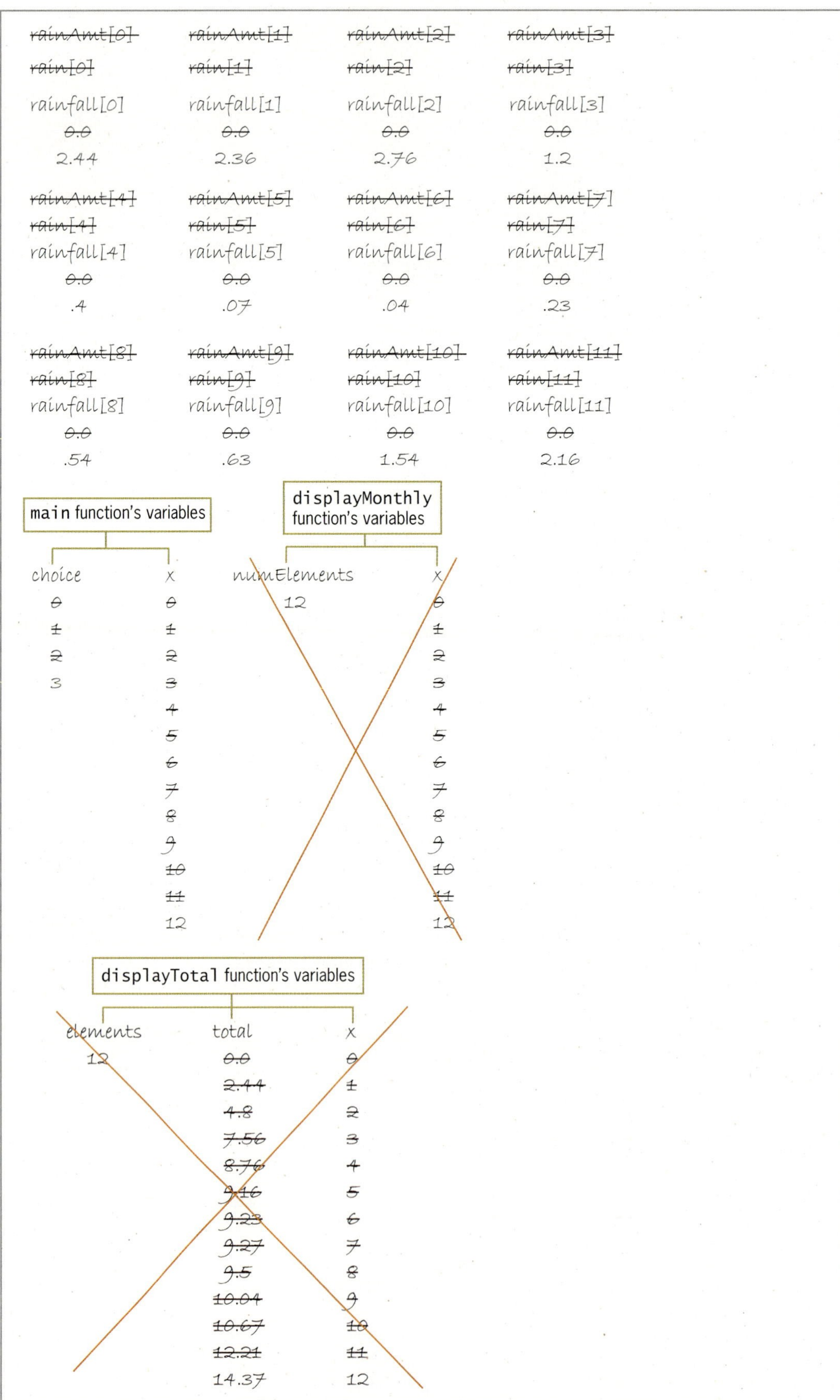

Figure 11-59 Completed desk-check table for the rainfall program

The final step in the problem-solving process is to evaluate and modify (if necessary) the program. Recall that you evaluate a program by entering its instructions into the computer and then using the computer to run (execute) it. While the program is running, you enter the same sample data used when desk-checking the program.

DIRECTIONS

Follow the instructions for starting your C++ development tool. Depending on the development tool you are using, you may need to create a new project; if so, name the project Lab11-2 Project and save it in the Cpp7\Chap11 folder. Enter the instructions shown in Figure 11-58 in a source file named Lab11-2.cpp. (Do not enter the line numbers.) Save the file in either the project folder or the Cpp7\Chap11 folder. Now follow the appropriate instructions for running the Lab11-2.cpp file. Test the program using the same data you used to desk-check the program. (The total rainfall amount should be 14.37.) If necessary, correct any bugs (errors) in the program.

LAB 11-3 Modify

If necessary, create a new project named Lab11-3 Project and save it in the Cpp7\Chap11 folder. Enter (or copy) the Lab11-2.cpp instructions into a new source file named Lab11-3.cpp. Change Lab11-2.cpp in the first comment to Lab11-3.cpp. Make the following two modifications to the program. First, change the void `displayTotal` function to a value-returning function named `getTotal`. The `getTotal` function should calculate the total rainfall and then return the result to the `main` function for displaying on the screen. Second, the `main` function should display an appropriate message when the user enters a menu choice other than 1, 2, or 3. It then should display the menu again. Save and then run the program. Test the program appropriately.

LAB 11-4 Desk-Check

Desk-check the code in Figure 11-60 using the data shown below. What will the `for` loop on Lines 31 through 34 display on the screen?

Student	Midterm	Final
1	90	100
2	88	68
3	77	75
4	85	85
5	45	32

```
//Lab11-4.cpp
//Stores averages in a one-dimensional array
//Created/revised by <your name> on <current date>

#include <iostream>
using namespace std;

int main()
{
    //declare arrays
    double midterms[5] = {0.0};
    double finals[5]   = {0.0};
    double averages[5] = {0.0};

    //get exam scores
    for (int x = 0; x < 5; x += 1)
    {
        cout << "Midterm exam score for student "
             << x + 1 << ": ";
        cin >> midterms[x];
        cout << "Final exam score for student "
             << x + 1 << ": ";
        cin >> finals[x];
        cout << endl;
        //calculate and assign average
        averages[x] = (midterms[x] + finals[x]) / 2;
    }   //end for

    //display contents of array
    cout << endl;
    for (int y = 0; y < 5; y += 1)
        cout << "Student " << y + 1 << " average: "
             << averages[y] << endl;
    //end for

    //system("pause");
    return 0;
}   //end of main function
```

your C++ development tool may require this statement

Figure 11-60 Code for Lab 11-4

LAB 11-5 Debug

Follow the instructions for starting C++ and viewing the Lab11-5.cpp file, which is contained in either the Cpp7\Chap11\Lab11-5 Project folder or the Cpp7\Chap11 folder. (Depending on your C++ development tool, you may need to open Lab11-5's project/solution file first.) If necessary, delete the two forward slashes that appear before the `system("pause");` statement and then save the program. Debug the program.

Summary

- An array is a group of variables that have the same name and data type and are related in some way. The most commonly used arrays in programs are one-dimensional arrays and two-dimensional arrays.
- Programmers use arrays to temporarily store related data in the internal memory of the computer. By doing so, a programmer can increase the efficiency of a program because data can be both stored in and retrieved from internal memory much faster than it can be written to and read from a file on a disk. In addition, after the data is entered into an array, the program can use the data as many times as it is needed.
- You must declare an array before you can use it. After declaring an array, you can use an assignment statement or the extraction operator to enter data into the array.
- Each of the array elements in a one-dimensional array is assigned a unique number, called a subscript. The first element is assigned a subscript of 0. The second element is assigned a subscript of 1, and so on. Because the first array subscript is 0, the last subscript in a one-dimensional array is always one number less than the number of elements.
- You refer to each element in a one-dimensional array by the array's name and the element's subscript, which is specified in square brackets immediately following the name.
- You can use the bubble sort algorithm to sort a small amount of data stored in an array.
- Parallel arrays are two or more arrays whose elements are related by their corresponding subscript (or position) in the arrays.

Key Terms

Array—a group of related variables that have the same name and data type

Bubble sort—one of many sorting algorithms used to sort small arrays; works by comparing adjacent array elements and swapping the ones that are out of order

Elements—the variables in an array

One-dimensional array—an array whose elements are identified by a unique subscript

Parallel arrays—two or more arrays whose elements are related by their corresponding position (subscript) in the arrays

Populating the array—refers to the process of initializing the elements in an array

Scalar variable—another term for a simple variable

Simple variable—a variable that is unrelated to any other variable in the computer's internal memory; also called a scalar variable

Sorting—the process of arranging data in a specific order

Subscript—a unique number that identifies the position of an element in an array

Review Questions

1. Which of the following is false?

   a. The elements in an array are related in some way.
   b. All of the elements in an array have the same data type.
   c. All of the elements in a one-dimensional array have the same subscript.
   d. The first element in a one-dimensional array has a subscript of 0 (zero).

2. Which of the following statements declares a five-element array named `population`?

   a. `int population[4] = {0};`
   b. `int population[5] = {0};`
   c. `int population[4] = 0`
   d. `int population[5] = {0}`

Use the `sales` array to answer Review Questions 3 through 7. The array was declared using the `int sales[5] = {10000, 12000, 900, 500, 20000};` statement.

3. The `sales[3] = sales[3] + 10;` statement will replace the number ________.

   a. 500 with 10
   b. 500 with 510
   c. 900 with 10
   d. 900 with 910

4. The `sales[4] = sales[4 - 2];` statement will replace the number ________.

   a. 20000 with 900
   b. 20000 with 19998
   c. 500 with 12000
   d. 500 with 498

5. The `cout << sales[0] + sales[1] << endl;` statement will ________.

   a. display 22000
   b. display 10000 + 12000
   c. display sales[0] + sales[1]
   d. result in an error

6. Which of the following `if` clauses verifies that the array subscript stored in the `x` variable is valid for the `sales` array?

   a. `if (sales[x] >= 0 && sales[x] < 4)`
   b. `if (sales[x] >= 0 && sales[x] <= 4)`
   c. `if (x >= 0 && x < 4)`
   d. `if (x >= 0 && x <= 4)`

7. Which of the following will correctly add the number 100 to each variable in the `sales` array? The `x` variable was declared using the `int x = 0;` statement.

   a.
   ```
   while (x <= 4)
       x += 100;
   //end while
   ```

b.
```
while (x <= 4)
{
    sales = sales + 100;
    x += 1;
} //end while
```

c.
```
while (sales < 5)
{
    sales[x] += 100;
} //end while
```

d.
```
while (x <= 4)
{
    sales[x] += 100;
    x += 1;
} //end while
```

Use the `nums` array to answer Review Questions 8 through 12. The array was declared using the `int nums[4] = {10, 5, 7, 2};` statement. The `x` and `total` variables are `int` variables and are initialized to 0. The `avg` variable is a `double` variable and is initialized to 0.0.

8. Which of the following will correctly calculate the average of the elements included in the `nums` array?

a.
```
while (x < 4)
{
    nums[x] = total + total;
    x += 1;
} //end while
avg = static_cast<double>(total) /
static_cast<double>(x);
```

b.
```
while (x < 4)
{
    total += nums[x];
    x += 1;
} //end while
avg = static_cast<double>(total) /
static_cast<double>(x);
```

c.
```
while (x < 4)
{
    total += nums[x];
    x += 1;
} //end while
avg = static_cast<double>(total) /
static_cast<double>(x) - 1;
```

d.
```
while (x < 4)
{
    total += nums[x];
    x += 1;
} //end while
avg = static_cast<double>(total) /
static_cast<double>(x - 1);
```

9. The code in Review Question 8's answer a assigns ________ to the `avg` variable.
   a. 0.0
   b. 5.0
   c. 6.0
   d. 8.0

10. The code in Review Question 8's answer b assigns ________ to the `avg` variable.
   a. 0.0
   b. 5.0
   c. 6.0
   d. 8.0

11. The code in Review Question 8's answer c assigns ________ to the `avg` variable.
   a. 0.0
   b. 5.0
   c. 6.0
   d. 8.0

12. The code in Review Question 8's answer d assigns ________ to the `avg` variable.
   a. 0.0
   b. 5.0
   c. 6.0
   d. 8.0

13. If the `cities` and `zips` arrays are parallel arrays, which of the following statements will display the city name associated with the zip code stored in the `zips[8]` variable?
   a. `cout << cities[zips[8]] << endl;`
   b. `cout << cities(zips[8]) << endl;`
   c. `cout << cities[8] << endl;`
   d. `cout << cities(8) << endl;`

Exercises

Pencil and Paper

TRY THIS

1. Write the statement to declare and initialize a one-dimensional `int` array named `scores` that has 10 elements. Then write the statement to store the number 12 in the third element in the array. (The answers to TRY THIS Exercises are located at the end of the chapter.)

TRY THIS

2. Write the code to display the contents of the `scores` array from Pencil and Paper Exercise 1. Use the `for` statement with a counter variable named `x`. (The answers to TRY THIS Exercises are located at the end of the chapter.)

MODIFY THIS

3. Rewrite the code from Pencil and Paper Exercise 2 using the `while` statement.

4. Write the statement to declare and initialize a one-dimensional `double` array named `rates` that has five elements. Use the following numbers to initialize the array: 6.5, 8.3, 4.0, 2.0, and 10.5.

INTRODUCTORY

5. Write the code to display the contents of the `rates` array from Pencil and Paper Exercise 4. Use the `for` statement.

INTRODUCTORY

INTRODUCTORY

6. Rewrite the code from Pencil and Paper Exercise 5 using the `do while` statement.

7. Write the statement to assign the C++ keyword `true` to the variable located in the third element in a one-dimensional `bool` array named `answers`.

INTERMEDIATE

8. Write the code to multiply by 2 the number stored in the first element in a one-dimensional `int` array named `nums`. Store the result in the `numDoubled` variable.

INTERMEDIATE

9. Write the code to add together the numbers stored in the first and second elements in a one-dimensional `int` array named `nums`. Display the sum on the screen.

INTERMEDIATE

10. Write the code to subtract the number 1 from each element in a one-dimensional `int` array named `quantities`. The array has 10 elements. Use the `while` statement.

INTERMEDIATE

11. Rewrite the code from Pencil and Paper Exercise 10 using the `for` statement.

INTERMEDIATE

INTERMEDIATE

12. Write the code to find the square root of the number stored in the second element in a one-dimensional `double` array named `mathNumbers`. Display the result on the screen.

13. Write the code to display the smallest number stored in a one-dimensional `int` array named `orders`. The array has five elements. Use the `while` statement.

ADVANCED

14. Rewrite the code from Pencil and Paper Exercise 13 using the `for` statement.

ADVANCED

15. Draw a flowchart for the bubble sort program shown in Figure 11-41.

ADVANCED

16. The `numbers` array is a five-element one-dimensional `int` array. The following statement should display the result of raising the first array element to the second power: `cout << pow(nums[0], 2);`. Correct the statement.

SWAT THE BUGS

Computer

17. If necessary, create a new project named TryThis17 Project and save it in the Cpp7\Chap11 folder. Enter the C++ instructions shown earlier in Figure 11-20 into a source file named TryThis17.cpp. Change the filename in the first comment to TryThis17.cpp. Save and then run the program. Test the program using the data shown in Figure 11-21 in the chapter. Change each of the `for` loops in the program to `while` loops. Save and then run the program. Test the program using the data shown in Figure 11-21 in the chapter. (The answers to TRY THIS Exercises are located at the end of the chapter.)

TRY THIS

18. If necessary, create a new project named TryThis18 Project and save it in the Cpp7\Chap11 folder. Enter the C++ instructions shown earlier in Figure 11-23 into a source file named TryThis18.cpp. Change the filename in the first comment to TryThis18.cpp. Save and then run the program. Create a void function named `getAverage`. The `getAverage` function should calculate the average number of pounds of coffee used. Hint: Pass the `average` variable *by reference*. (The answers to TRY THIS Exercises are located at the end of the chapter.)

TRY THIS

19. In this exercise, you modify the random numbers program from the chapter. If necessary, create a new project named ModifyThis19 Project and save it in the Cpp7\Chap11 folder. Enter the C++ instructions shown earlier in Figure 11-33 into a source file named ModifyThis19.cpp. Change the filename in the first comment to ModifyThis19.cpp. Add another program-defined value-returning function to the

MODIFY THIS

program. Name the function `getLowest`. The `getLowest` function should determine the lowest integer in the array. Save and then run the program. Test the program appropriately.

MODIFY THIS

20. In this exercise, you modify the hourly rate program from the chapter. If necessary, create a new project named ModifyThis20 Project and save it in the Cpp7\Chap11 folder. Enter the C++ instructions shown earlier in Figure 11-29 into a new source file named ModifyThis20.cpp. Change the filename in the first comment to ModifyThis20.cpp. Save and then run the program. Test the program appropriately. Now modify the program to use pay codes of A, B, C, D, E, and F. Store the pay codes in a parallel array, and then modify the program's code appropriately. Save and then run the program. Test the program appropriately.

INTRODUCTORY

21. Follow the instructions for starting C++ and viewing the Introductory21.cpp file, which is contained in either the Cpp7\Chap11\Introductory21 Project folder or the Cpp7\Chap11 folder. (Depending on your C++ development tool, you may need to open the project/solution file first.) If necessary, delete the two forward slashes that appear before the `system("pause");` statement, and then save the program. The program should calculate the average of the values stored in the `rates` array. It then should display the average rate on the screen. Complete the program using the `for` statement. Save and then run the program.

INTRODUCTORY

22. Follow the instructions for starting C++ and viewing the Introductory22.cpp file, which is contained in either the Cpp7\Chap11\Introductory22 Project folder or the Cpp7\Chap11 folder. (Depending on your C++ development tool, you may need to open the project/solution file first.) If necessary, delete the two forward slashes that appear before the `system("pause");` statement, and then save the program. The program should display the contents of the `orders` array. Complete the program using the `while` statement. Save and then run the program.

INTERMEDIATE

23. Follow the instructions for starting C++ and viewing the Intermediate23.cpp file, which is contained in either the Cpp7\Chap11\Intermediate23 Project folder or the Cpp7\Chap11 folder. (Depending on your C++ development tool, you may need to open the project/solution file first.) If necessary, delete the two forward slashes that appear before the `system("pause");` statement, and then save the program. The program should display the contents of the two parallel arrays. Complete the program using the `do while` statement. Save and then run the program.

INTERMEDIATE

24. In this exercise, you modify the program from Lab 11-2 in the chapter. If necessary, create a new project named Intermediate24 Project and save it in the Cpp7\Chap11 folder. Copy the instructions from the Lab11-2.cpp file into a source file named Intermediate24.cpp. (Alternatively, you can enter the instructions from Figure 11-58 into the Intermediate24.cpp file.) Change the filename in the first comment to Intermediate24.cpp. Add three additional functions to the program: `displayAverage`, `displayHigh`, and `displayLow`. The functions should display the average rainfall amount, the highest rainfall amount, and the lowest rainfall amount. Save and then run the program. Test the program appropriately.

INTERMEDIATE

25. If necessary, create a new project named Intermediate25 Project and save it in the Cpp7\Chap11 folder. Also create a new source file named Intermediate25.cpp. Declare a 12-element `int` array named `days`. Assign the number of days in each month to the array, using 28 for February. Code the program so that it displays the number of days corresponding to the month number entered by the user. For example, when the user enters the number 7, the program should display the number 31. The program also should display an appropriate message when the user enters an invalid month number. Use a sentinel value to end the program. Save and then run the program. Test the program using the valid numbers 1 through 12. Also test it using an invalid number, such as 20.

26. Follow the instructions for starting C++ and viewing the Intermediate26.cpp file, which is contained in either the Cpp7\Chap11\Intermediate26 Project folder or the Cpp7\Chap11 folder. (Depending on your C++ development tool, you may need to open the project/solution file first.) If necessary, delete the two forward slashes that appear before the `system("pause");` statement, and then save the program. Code the program so that it asks the user for a percentage amount by which each price should be increased. The program then should increase each price in the array by that amount. For example, when the user enters the number 15, the program should increase each element's value by 15%. After increasing each price, the program should display the contents of the array. Save and then run the program. Increase each price by 5%. INTERMEDIATE

27. In this exercise, you modify the program from Computer Exercise 26. If necessary, create a new project named Intermediate27 Project and save it in the Cpp7\Chap11 folder. Also create a new source file named Intermediate27.cpp. Copy the C++ instructions from the Intermediate26.cpp file into the Intermediate27.cpp file. Change the filename in the first comment to Intermediate27.cpp. Modify the program so that it also asks the user to enter a number from 1 through 10. When the user enters the number 1, the program should update only the first price in the array. When the user enters the number 2, the program should update only the second price in the array, and so on. Use a loop that stops prompting the user when he or she enters a number that is either less than or equal to 0 or greater than 10. Save and then run the program. Increase the second price by 10%. Next, increase the tenth price by 2%. Finally, decrease the first price by 10%. INTERMEDIATE

28. Follow the instructions for starting C++ and viewing the Advanced28.cpp file, which is contained in either the Cpp7\Chap11\Advanced28 Project folder or the Cpp7\Chap11 folder. (Depending on your C++ development tool, you may need to open the project/solution file first.) If necessary, delete the two forward slashes that appear before the `system("pause");` statement, and then save the program. Enter the code that prompts the user to enter a score from 0 through 100. The program should display the number of students earning that score. Use a sentinel value to end the program. Save and then run the program. Use the program to answer the following questions. ADVANCED

    How many students earned a score of 72?

    How many students earned a score of 88?

    How many students earned a score of 20?

    How many students earned a score of 99?

29. In this exercise, you modify the program from Computer Exercise 28. If necessary, create a new project named Advanced29 Project and save it in the Cpp7\Chap11 folder. Also create a new source file named Advanced29.cpp. Copy the C++ instructions from the Advanced28.cpp file into the Advanced29.cpp file. Change the filename in the first comment to Advanced29.cpp. Modify the program so that it prompts the user to enter a minimum score and a maximum score. Swap the scores if the minimum score is greater than the maximum score. The program should display the number of students who earned a score within that range. Use a sentinel value to end the program. Save and then run the program. Use the program to answer the following questions. ADVANCED

    How many students earned a score from 70 through 79?

    How many students earned a score from 65 through 85?

    How many students earned a score from 0 through 50?

30. In this exercise, you create a program that generates and displays six unique random integers for a lottery game. Each lottery number can range from 1 through 54 only. If necessary, create a new project named Advanced30 Project and save it in the Cpp7\Chap11 folder. Also create a new source file named Advanced30.cpp. Create a ADVANCED

program that generates six unique random integers from 1 through 54, and then displays the integers on the screen. Save and then run the program.

ADVANCED

31. In this exercise, you create a program that uses two parallel one-dimensional arrays. Ms. Jenkins uses the grade table shown in Figure 11-61 for her Introduction to Programming course. She wants a program that displays the grade after she enters the total points earned. If necessary, create a new project named Advanced31 Project and save it in the Cpp7\Chap11 folder. Also create a new source file named Advanced31.cpp. Store the minimum points in a one-dimensional `int` array. Store the grades in a one-dimensional `char` array. Use a sentinel value to stop the program. Save and then run the program. Test the program using the following amounts: 455, 210, 400, and 349.

Minimum points	Maximum points	Grade
0	299	F
300	349	D
350	399	C
400	449	B
450	500	A

Figure 11-61

ADVANCED

32. In this exercise, you modify the program from Computer Exercise 31. The modified program will allow the user to change the grading scale while the program is running. If necessary, create a new project named Advanced32 Project and save it in the Cpp7\Chap11 folder. Also create a new source file named Advanced32.cpp. Copy the instructions from the Advanced31.cpp file into the Advanced32.cpp file. Change the filename in the first comment. Modify the program so that it allows the user to enter the total number of possible points—in other words, the total number of points a student can earn in the course—when the program is run. Also modify the program so that it uses the grading scale shown in Figure 11-62. For example, when the user enters the number 500 as the total number of possible points, the program should use 450 (which is 90% of 500) as the minimum number of points for an A. When the user enters the number 300 as the total number of possible points, the program should use 270 (which is 90% of 300) as the minimum number of points for an A. Save and then run the program. Test the program using 300 as the total number of possible points and 185 as the number of points earned. The program should display D as the grade. Stop the program. Then test it using 500 and 363 as the total number of possible points and the total points earned, respectively. The program should display C as the grade.

Minimum points	Grade
0	F
60% of the possible points	D
70% of the possible points	C
80% of the possible points	B
90% of the possible points	A

Figure 11-62

ADVANCED

33. In this exercise, you create a program that uses two parallel one-dimensional arrays. The program displays a shipping charge that is based on the number of items ordered by a customer. The shipping charge scale is shown in Figure 11-63. If necessary, create a new project named Advanced33 Project and save it in the Cpp7\Chap11 folder. Also

create a new source file named Advanced33.cpp. Store the maximum order amounts in a one-dimensional `int` array. Store the shipping charge amounts in a parallel one-dimensional `int` array. The program should allow the user to enter the number of items a customer ordered. It then should display the appropriate shipping charge. Use a sentinel value to stop the program. Save and then run the program. Test the program appropriately.

Minimum order	Maximum order	Shipping charge
1	10	15
11	50	10
51	100	5
101	99999	0

Figure 11-63

ADVANCED

34. In this exercise, you code a program that uses three parallel numeric arrays. The program searches one of the arrays and then displays the corresponding values from the other two arrays. Follow the instructions for starting C++ and viewing the Advanced34.cpp file, which is contained in either the Cpp7\Chap11\Advanced34 Project folder or the Cpp7\Chap11 folder. (Depending on your C++ development tool, you may need to open the project/solution file first.) If necessary, delete the two forward slashes that appear before the `system("pause");` statement, and then save the program. The program should prompt the user to enter a product ID. It then should search for the product ID in the `ids` array and display the corresponding price and quantity from the `prices` and `quantities` arrays. Allow the user to display the price and quantity for as many product IDs as desired without having to execute the program again. Save and then run the program. Test the program appropriately.

SWAT THE BUGS

35. Follow the instructions for starting C++ and viewing the SwatTheBugs35.cpp file, which is contained in either the Cpp7\Chap11\SwatTheBugs35 Project folder or the Cpp7\Chap11 folder. (Depending on your C++ development tool, you may need to open the project/solution file first.) If necessary, delete the two forward slashes that appear before the `system("pause");` statement, and then save the program. Run the program. The program should display the total amount in inventory, but it is not working correctly. Debug the program.

Answers to TRY THIS Exercises

Pencil and Paper

1.
```
int scores[10] = {0};
scores[2] = 12;
```

2.
```
for (int x = 0; x < 10; x += 1)
    cout << scores[x] << endl;
//end for
```

Computer

17. See Figure 11-64. The changes are shaded in the figure.

```
//TryThis17.cpp
//displays the contents of an array
//Created/revised by <your name> on <current date>

#include <iostream>
#include <iomanip>
using namespace std;

//function prototype
void displayArray(double dollars[], int numElements);

int main()
{
     //declare array
     double sales[4] = {0.0};

     //store data in the array
     int sub = 0;
     while (sub < 4)
     {
          cout << "Enter the sales for Region ";
          cout << sub + 1 << ": ";
          cin >> sales[sub];
          sub += 1;
     }    //end while

     //display the contents of the array
     displayArray(sales, 4);

     //system("pause");
     return 0;
}    //end of main function

//*****function definitions*****
void displayArray(double dollars[], int numElements)
{
     cout << fixed << setprecision(2) << endl << endl;
     int sub = 0;
     while (sub < numElements)
     {
          cout << "Sales for Region " << sub + 1 << ": $";
          cout << dollars[sub] << endl;
          sub += 1;
     }    //end while
}    //end of displayArray function
```

if your C++ development tool requires this statement, delete the two forward slashes

Figure 11-64

18. See Figure 11-65. The changes are shaded in the figure.

```
//TryThis18.cpp
//Displays the total and average number of pounds
//of coffee used during a 12-month period
//Created/revised by <your name> on <current date>

#include <iostream>
using namespace std;

//function prototype
double getTotal(double used[], int numElements);
void getAverage(double totalLbs,
                int numElements,
                double &avg);

int main()
{
    //declare array
    double pounds[12] = {400.5, 450.0,
        475.5, 336.5, 457.0, 325.0, 220.5,
        276.0, 300.0, 320.5, 400.5, 415.0};
    //declare variables
    double total   = 0.0;
    double average = 0.0;

    //calculate the total and average pounds used
    total = getTotal(pounds, 12);
    getAverage(total, 12, average);

    //display the total and average pounds used
    cout << "Total pounds: " << total << endl;
    cout << "Average pounds: " << average << endl;

    //system("pause");
    return 0;
}   //end of main function

//*****function definitions*****
double getTotal(double poundsUsed[], int numElements)
{
    double totalUsed = 0.0;    //accumulator

    //accumulate the pounds used
    for (int sub = 0; sub < numElements; sub += 1)
        totalUsed += poundsUsed[sub];
    //end for

    return totalUsed;
}   //end of getTotal function

void getAverage(double totalLbs,
                int numElements,
                double &avg)
{
    avg = totalLbs / numElements;
}   //end of getAverage function
```

if your C++ development tool requires this statement, delete the two forward slashes

Figure 11-65

CHAPTER 12

Two-Dimensional Arrays

After studying Chapter 12, you should be able to:

- Declare and initialize a two-dimensional array
- Enter data into a two-dimensional array
- Display the contents of a two-dimensional array
- Sum the values in a two-dimensional array
- Search a two-dimensional array
- Pass a two-dimensional array to a function

Using Two-Dimensional Arrays

Ch12-Chapter Preview video

As discussed in Chapter 11, an array is a group of related variables (elements) that have the same data type. Recall that the most commonly used arrays in business applications are one-dimensional and two-dimensional. You can visualize a one-dimensional array as a column of related elements in memory, similar to the column of storage bins shown in Figure 11-2 in Chapter 11. A **two-dimensional array**, on the other hand, resembles a table in that the array elements are in rows and columns, similar to a spreadsheet or a golf scorecard. See Figure 12-1.

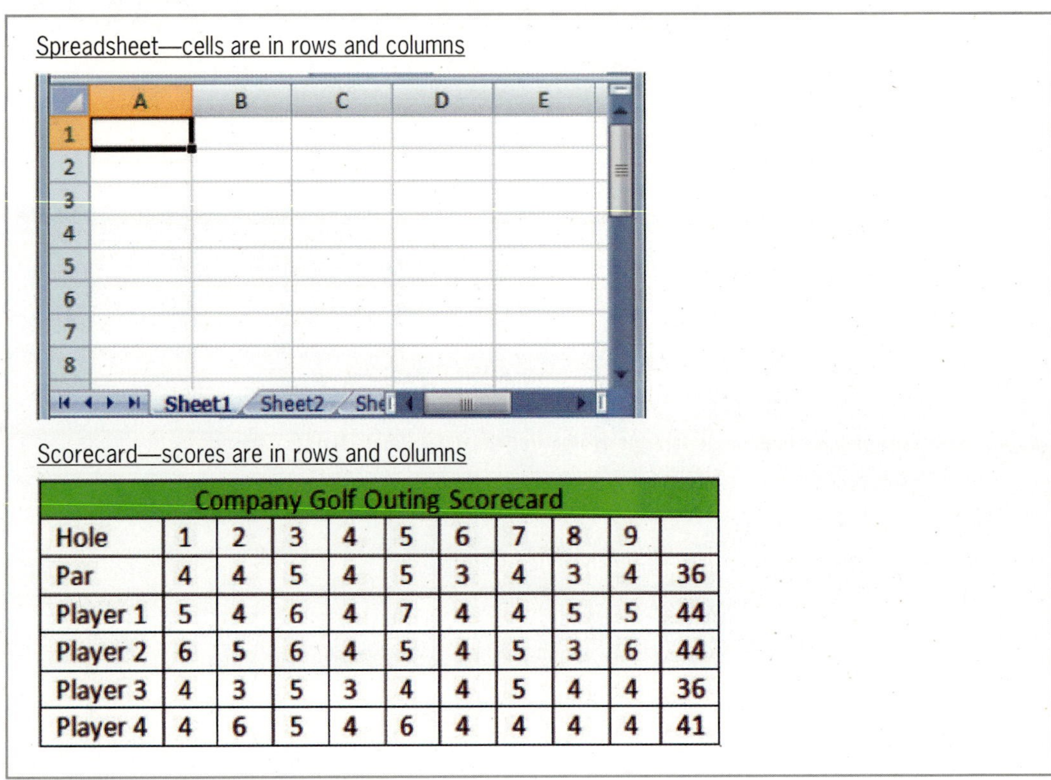

Company Golf Outing Scorecard										
Hole	1	2	3	4	5	6	7	8	9	
Par	4	4	5	4	5	3	4	3	4	36
Player 1	5	4	6	4	7	4	4	5	5	44
Player 2	6	5	6	4	5	4	5	3	6	44
Player 3	4	3	5	3	4	4	5	4	4	36
Player 4	4	6	5	4	6	4	4	4	4	41

Figure 12-1 Examples of items that use the two-dimensional array concept

Each element in a two-dimensional array is identified by a unique combination of two subscripts that the computer assigns to the element when the array is created. The subscripts specify the element's row and column positions in the array. In C++ and in many other programming languages, elements located in the first row in a two-dimensional array are assigned a row subscript of 0, elements in the second row are assigned a row subscript of 1, and so on. Similarly, elements located in the first column in a two-dimensional array are assigned a column subscript of 0, elements in the second column are assigned a column subscript of 1, and so on.

Recall that a subscript is also called an index.

You refer to each element in a two-dimensional array by the array's name and the element's row and column subscripts, with the row subscript listed first and the column subscript listed second. The row subscript is enclosed in a set of square brackets ([]) and so is the column subscript. For example, to refer to the element located in the first row, first column in a two-dimensional array named `orders`, you use `orders[0][0]`—read "`orders` sub zero zero." Similarly, to refer to the element located in the second row, third column, you use `orders[1][2]`. Notice that the subscripts are one number less than the row and column in which the element is located; this is because the row and column subscripts start at 0 rather than at 1. You will find that the last row subscript in a two-dimensional array is always one number less than the number of rows in the array. Similarly, the last column subscript is always one number less than the number of columns in the array. You can determine the number of elements in a two-dimensional array by multiplying the number of its rows by the number of its columns. An array that has four rows and three columns, for example, contains 12 variables.

Figure 12-2 illustrates the elements contained in the two-dimensional `orders` array using the storage bin analogy from Chapter 11. The `rating` and `numSold` variables included in the figure are scalar (simple) variables.

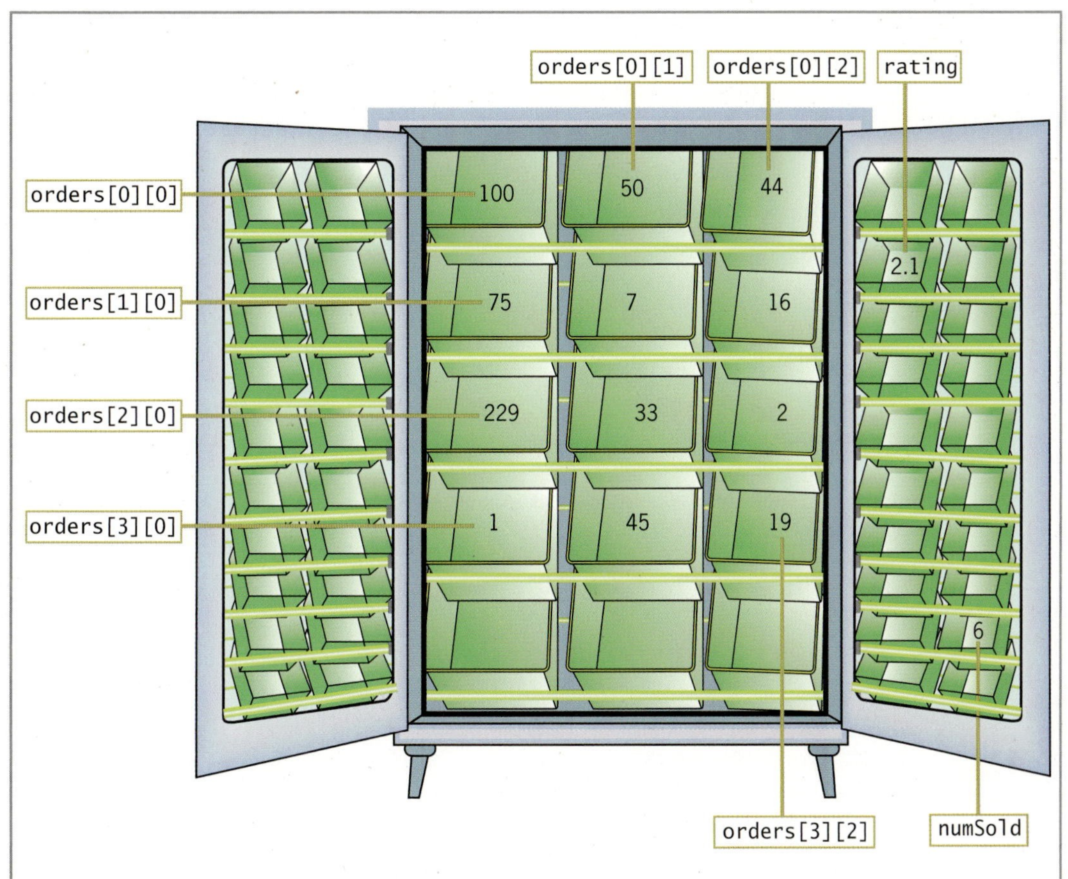

Figure 12-2 Names of some of the elements contained in the two-dimensional `orders` array

Figure 12-3 shows the problem specification and IPO chart information for the Caldwell Company program, which uses a two-dimensional array to store the number of orders received from each of the company's four sales regions during the first three months of the year. Each row in the array represents a region, and each column represents a month.

The program allows the user to enter the order amounts and then displays the amounts on the computer screen. Before you can code the program, you need to learn how to declare and initialize a two-dimensional array. You also need to learn how to store data in a two-dimensional array and display data from the array.

Problem specification
The Caldwell Company wants a program that allows the user to enter the number of orders received from each of its four sales regions during the first three months of the year. The program should store the order amounts in a two-dimensional `int` array that contains four rows and three columns. Each row in the array represents a region, and each column represents a month. The program then should display the order amounts on the computer screen. The order amounts for Region 1 should be displayed first, followed by Region 2's order amounts, and so on.

Input
number of orders (from each of 4 regions for 3 months)

Processing
Processing items:
    array (4 region rows, 3 month columns)
    region subscript (counter: 0 to 3)
    month subscript (counter: 0 to 2)

Algorithm:
```
1. repeat for (region subscript from 0 to 3)
        repeat for (month subscript from 0 to 2)
            enter the number of orders into the
            array[region subscript][month subscript]
            element
        end repeat
   end repeat
2. repeat for (region subscript from 0 to 3)
        display region subscript + 1

        repeat for (month subscript from 0 to 2)
            display month subscript + 1

            display the number of orders stored in the
            array[region subscript][month subscript]
            element
        end repeat
   end repeat
```

Output
number of orders (from each of 4 regions for 3 months)

Figure 12-3 Problem specification and IPO chart for the Caldwell Company program *(continues)*

(continued)

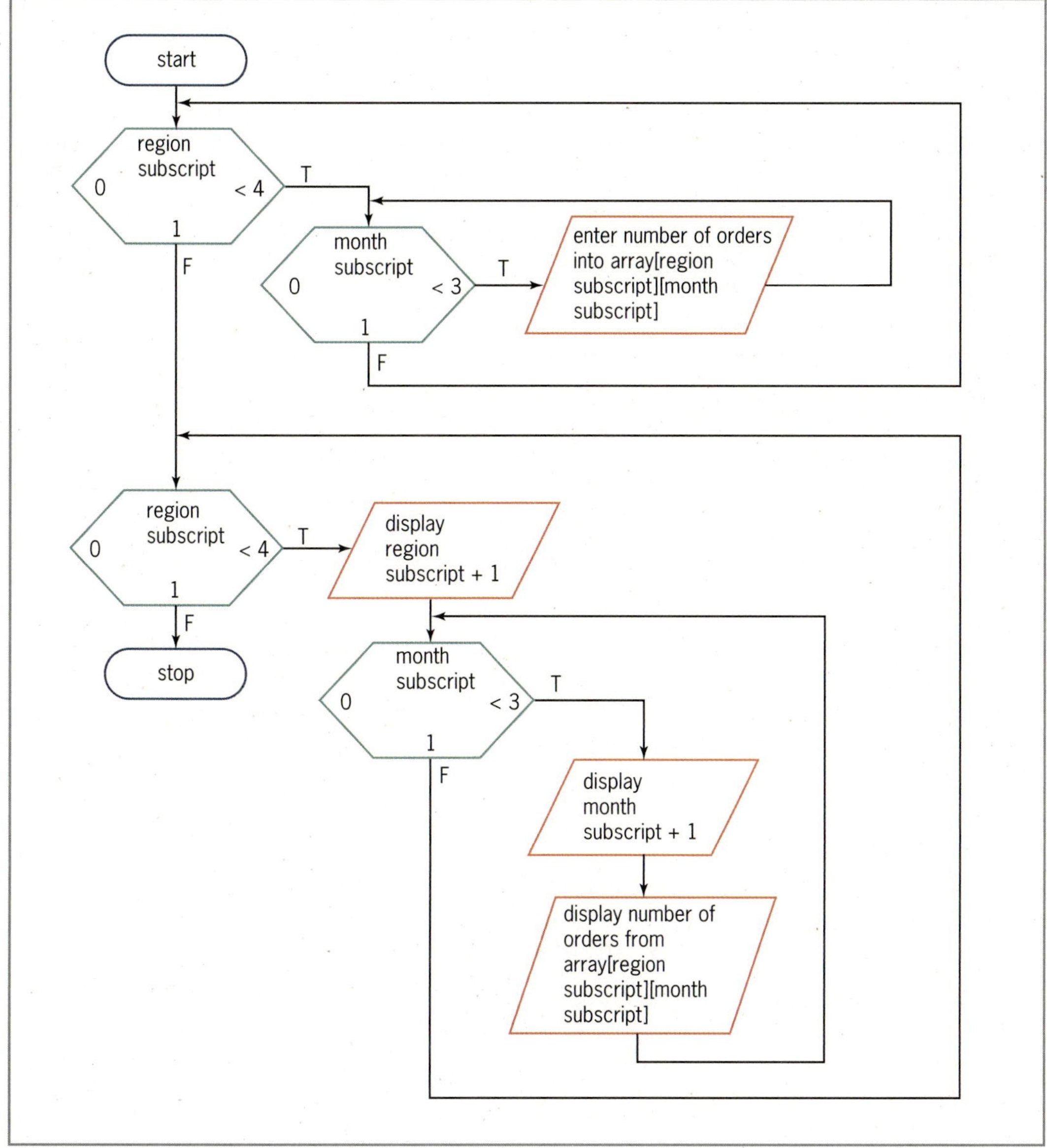

Figure 12-3 Problem specification and IPO chart for the Caldwell Company program

Declaring and Initializing a Two-Dimensional Array

Before you can use a two-dimensional array in a program, you first must declare (create) it. It also is a good programming practice to initialize the array elements to ensure they will not contain garbage when the program is run. Recall that assigning initial values to an array is often referred to as populating the array. You should populate an array using values that have the same data type as the array.

Figure 12-4 shows the syntax for declaring and initializing a two-dimensional array in C++. In the syntax, *arrayName* is the name of the array and *dataType* is the type of data the array elements will store. Recall that each of the elements in an array has the same data type. The *numberOfRows* and *numberOfColumns* items, each of which is enclosed in its own set of square brackets, are integers that specify the number of rows and columns, respectively, in the array.

You can initialize the elements in a two-dimensional array by entering a separate *initialValues* section, enclosed in braces, for each row in the array. If the array has two rows, then the statement that declares and initializes the array can have a maximum of two *initialValues* sections. If the array has five rows, then the declaration statement can have a maximum of five *initialValues* sections. Within the individual *initialValues* sections, you enter one or more values separated by commas. The maximum number of values you enter corresponds to the number of columns in the array. If the array contains 10 columns, then you can include up to 10 values in each *initialValues* section. In addition to the set of braces that surrounds each individual *initialValues* section, notice in the syntax that a set of braces also surrounds *all* of the *initialValues* sections. Also shown in Figure 12-4 are examples of declaring and initializing two-dimensional arrays.

HOW TO Declare and Initialize a Two-Dimensional Array

Syntax

dataType arrayName[*numberOfRows*][*numberOfColumns*] =
{{*initialValues*}, {*initialValues*}, ...{*initialValues*}};

Example 1

```
char grades[3][2] = {{'C', 'A'}, {'B', 'C'}, {'D', 'B'}};
```

declares and initializes a three-row, two-column `char` array named `grades`

Example 2

```
int orders[4][3] = {0};
```

or

```
int orders[4][3] = {{0}, {0}, {0}, {0}};
```

or

```
int orders[4][3] = {{0, 0, 0}, {0, 0, 0}, {0, 0, 0}, {0, 0, 0}};
```

declares and initializes a four-row, three-column `int` array named `orders`; each element is initialized to 0

Example 3

```
double prices[6][5] = {2.0};
```

declares and initializes a six-row, five-column `double` array named `prices`; the `prices[0][0]` element is initialized to 2.0; the other elements are initialized to 0.0

Figure 12-4 How to declare and initialize a two-dimensional array

The declaration statement in Example 1 in Figure 12-4 creates a two-dimensional `char` array named `grades`. The `grades` array contains three rows and two columns. The statement initializes the elements in the first row to the grades C and A, the elements in the second row to the grades B and C, and the elements in the third row to the grades D and B, as illustrated in Figure 12-5.

grades[0][0]	C	A	grades[0][1]
grades[1][0]	B	C	grades[1][1]
grades[2][0]	D	B	grades[2][1]

Figure 12-5 Illustration of the two-dimensional `grades` array

You can use any of the three statements shown in Example 2 in Figure 12-4 to declare the two-dimensional `orders` array and initialize the elements in its four rows and three columns to the number 0. When you don't provide an initial value for each of the elements in an `int` array, most C+ compilers initialize the uninitialized elements to the integer 0. The statement shown in Example 3 declares a two-dimensional `double` array named `prices`; the array contains six rows and five columns. The statement initializes the element located in the first row, first column of the array to 2.0. The remaining elements will be initialized to the `double` number 0.0 by most C++ compilers.

Keep in mind that if you inadvertently provide more *initialValues* sections than the number of rows in the array, or if you provide more values in an *initialValues* section than the number of columns in the array, most C++ compilers will display the error message "too many initializers" when you attempt to compile the program. However, not all C++ compilers display a message when this error occurs. Rather, some compilers store the extra values in memory locations adjacent to, but not reserved for, the array. Therefore, you must be careful to provide the appropriate number of *initialValues* sections and the appropriate number of values in each section.

Entering Data into a Two-Dimensional Array

As you can with one-dimensional arrays, you can use either an assignment statement or the extraction operator to enter data into the elements of a two-dimensional array. Figure 12-6 shows the syntax of an assignment statement that accomplishes the entry task. The *arrayName* [*rowSubscript*][*columnSubscript*] section of the syntax represents the name and subscripts of the element to which you want the *expression* (data) assigned. The *expression* can include any combination of constants, variables, and operators. The data type of the *expression* must match the data type of the array element to which the *expression* is assigned. If the data types do not match, an implicit type conversion will occur and may result in incorrect output.

Be sure to always use valid row and column subscripts when referring to an element in a two-dimensional array. Using an invalid subscript will result in an error message and the program ending abruptly.

Also included in Figure 12-6 are examples of assignment statements that assign data to the elements in various arrays. The arrays were declared earlier in Figure 12-4. The assignment statement in Example 1 assigns the letter F to the element located in the second row, first column in the `grades` array, replacing the letter B that was stored in the element when the array was declared. The code in Example 2 assigns the integer 0 to each of the 12 elements in the `orders` array and provides another means of initializing the array. Notice that the code uses two loops to access each element in the array. One of the loops keeps track of the row subscript, while the other loop keeps track of the column subscript. The code assigns the integer 0 to the array, row by row. In other words, it assigns 0 to each element in the first row before assigning 0 to each element in the second row, and so on.

The code in Example 3 in Figure 12-6 assigns a new price to each of the elements in the `prices` array. The new price is calculated by the assignment statement within the nested loop. The statement multiplies the old price by the contents of the `INCREASE` named constant and then assigns the result to the current array element. Like the code in Example 2, the code in Example 3 uses two loops to access each element in the array. However, unlike the code in Example 2, the code in Example 3 assigns values to the array, column by column, rather than row by row. This means that the code will assign values to each element in the first column before assigning values to each element in the second column, and so on.

HOW TO Use an Assignment Statement to Assign Data to a Two-Dimensional Array

Syntax

arrayName[*rowSubscript*][*columnSubscript*] = *expression*;

Example 1

```
grades[1][0] = 'F';
```

assigns the letter F to the element located in the second row, first column in the `grades` array

Example 2

```
for (int row = 0; row < 4; row += 1)
     for (int column = 0; column < 3; column += 1)
          orders[row][column] = 0;
     //end for
//end for
```

assigns the integer 0 to each element in the four-row, three-column `orders` array, row by row; provides another means of initializing the array

Example 3

```
int row = 0;
int column = 0;
double oldPrice = 0.0;
const double INCREASE = 1.15;
while (column < 5)
{
      while (row < 6)
      {
           cout << "Price: ";
           cin >> oldPrice;
           prices[row][column] = oldPrice * INCREASE;
           row += 1;
      }    //end while
      column += 1;
      row = 0;
}     //end while
```

assigns the new price to each element in the six-row, five-column `prices` array, column by column; the new price is calculated by multiplying the old price by the value stored in the `INCREASE` named constant

You also can use the C++ increment operator (++) to add 1 to a variable. For instance, you can use `row++` and `column++` in Example 2's `for` clauses, and use `row++;` and `column++;` in Example 3.

Figure 12-6 How to use an assignment statement to assign data to a two-dimensional array

As already mentioned, you also can use the extraction operator to store data in an element in a two-dimensional array. Figure 12-7 shows the syntax and examples of doing this using the arrays declared earlier in Figure 12-4. The `cin` statement in Example 1 stores the user's entry in the element located in the third row, second column in the `grades` array, replacing the element's existing data. The code in Example 2 contains two `for` loops. The instructions in the outer loop will be repeated once for each of the four regions, while the instructions in the nested loop will be repeated once for each of the three months within each region. The `cout` statement in the nested loop prompts the user to enter the number of orders for the current region and month. The `cin` statement stores the user's response in the current element in the `orders` array. The responses will be stored, region (row) by region (row), in the array. In other words, the three monthly sales for Region (row) 1 will be stored before the three monthly sales for Region (row) 2, and so on.

Example 3 in Figure 12-7 contains an outer `while` loop and a nested `for` loop. The `while` loop repeats its instructions for each of the five columns in the array, and the `for` loop repeats its instructions for each of the six rows in the array. The `cout` statement in the `for` loop prompts the user to enter a price, and the `cin` statement stores the user's response in the current element in the `prices` array. The responses will be stored, column by column, in the array. In other words, the six rows in the first column will be filled with prices before the six rows in the second column, and so on.

HOW TO Use the Extraction Operator to Store Data in a Two-Dimensional Array

Syntax

`cin >>` *arrayName*`[`*subscript*`][`*subscript*`];`

Example 1

```
cin >> grades[2][1];
```

stores the user's entry in the element located in the third row, second column in the `grades` array

Example 2

```
for (int region = 0; region < 4; region += 1)
     for (int month = 0; month < 3; month += 1)
     {
          cout << "Number of orders for Region "
               << region + 1 << ", Month "
               << month + 1 << ": ";
          cin >> orders[region][month];
     }    //end for
//end for
```

stores the user's entries in the four-row, three-column `orders` array, region (row) by region (row)

Example 3

```
int column = 0;
while (column < 5)
{
     for (int row = 0; row < 6; row += 1)
     {
          cout << "Price: ";
          cin >> prices[row][column];
     }    //end for
     column += 1;
}    //end while
```

stores the user's entries in the six-row, five-column `prices` array, column by column

Figure 12-7 How to use the extraction operator to store data in a two-dimensional array

In Example 2's `for` clauses, you can use `region++` and `month++`. In Example 3, you can use `row++` in the `for` clause and use `column++;` in the `while` loop.

Displaying the Contents of a Two-Dimensional Array

To display the contents of a two-dimensional array, you need to access each of its elements. You do this using two counter-controlled loops: one to keep track of the row subscript and the other to keep track of the column subscript. Figure 12-8 shows examples of loops you can use to display the contents of the arrays declared earlier in Figure 12-4. Example 1 uses two `while` loops to display the contents of the `grades` array, column by column. The `grades` array contains three rows and two columns. Example 2 uses two `for` loops to display the contents of the four-row, three-column `orders` array, region (row) by region (row). Example 3 uses both a `do while` loop and a `for` loop to display the contents of the six-row, five-column `prices` array, row by row.

You use one loop to access each element in a one-dimensional array, but two loops to access each element in a two-dimensional array.

HOW TO Display the Contents of a Two-Dimensional Array

Example 1

```
int row = 0;
int column = 0;
while (column < 2)
{
     while (row < 3)
     {
          cout << grades[row][column] << endl;
          row += 1;
     }    //end while
     column += 1;
     row = 0;
}    //end while
```

displays the contents of the three-row, two-column `grades` array, column by column

Example 2

```
for (int region = 0; region < 4; region += 1)
     for (int month = 0; month < 3; month += 1)
          cout << orders[region][month] << endl;
     //end for
//end for
```

displays the contents of the four-row, three-column `orders` array, region (row) by region (row)

Example 3

```
int row = 0;
do   //begin loop
{
     for (int column = 0; column < 5; column += 1)
          cout << prices[row][column] << endl;
     //end for
     row += 1;
} while (row < 6);
```

displays the contents of the six-row, five-column `prices` array, row by row

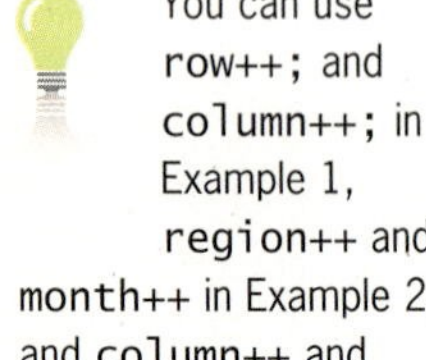

You can use `row++;` and `column++;` in Example 1, `region++` and `month++` in Example 2, and `column++` and `row++;` in Example 3.

Figure 12-8 How to display the contents of a two-dimensional array

Now that you know how to declare and initialize a two-dimensional array, and also how to store data in the array and display data from the array, you can code the Caldwell Company program.

Coding the Caldwell Company Program

Earlier, in Figure 12-3, you viewed the problem specification and IPO chart for the Caldwell Company program. Figure 12-9 shows the IPO chart information along with the corresponding C++ instructions. Figure 12-10 shows the code for the entire program, and Figure 12-11 shows a sample run of the program.

IPO chart information	C++ instructions
Input	
number of orders (from each of 4 regions for 3 months)	*the orders will be entered into the array*
Processing	
array (4 region rows, 3 month columns)	`int orders[4][3] = {0};`
region subscript (counter: 0 to 3)	*declared and initialized in the for clause*
month subscript (counter: 0 to 2)	*declared and initialized in the for clause*
Output	
number of orders (from each of 4 regions for 3 months)	*displayed from the array by the for loops*

Algorithm

1. repeat for (region subscript from 0 to 3)
repeat for (month subscript from 0 to 2)
enter the number of orders into the array[region subscript][month subscript] element
end repeat
end repeat

```
for (int region = 0; region < 4;
region += 1)
   for (int month = 0; month < 3;
   month += 1)
   {
       cout << "Number of orders
       for Region " << region + 1
       << ", Month " << month + 1
       << ": ";
       cin >> orders[region][month];
   }   //end for
//end for
```

2. repeat for (region subscript from 0 to 3)
display region subscript + 1
repeat for (month subscript from 0 to 2)
display month subscript + 1
display the number of orders stored in the array[region subscript][month subscript] element
end repeat
end repeat

```
for (int region = 0; region < 4;
region += 1)
{
   cout << "Region " << region
   + 1 << ": " << endl;

   for (int month = 0; month < 3;
   month += 1)
   {
       cout << "   Month " <<
       month + 1 << ": ";

       cout << orders[region][month]
       << endl;

   }   //end for
}  //end for
```

Figure 12-9 IPO chart information and C++ instructions for the Caldwell Company program

```
1 //Caldwell Company.cpp
2 //Displays the contents of a two-dimensional array
3 //Created/revised by <your name> on <current date>
4 
5 #include <iostream>
6 using namespace std;
7 
8 int main()
9 {
10     //declare and initialize array
11     int orders[4][3] = {0};
12 
13     //enter data into the array
14     for (int region = 0; region < 4; region += 1)
15         for (int month = 0; month < 3; month += 1)
16         {
17             cout << "Number of orders for Region "
18                  << region + 1 << ", Month "
19                  << month + 1 << ": ";
20             cin >> orders[region][month];
21         }   //end for
22     //end for
23 
24     //display the contents of the array
25     for (int region = 0; region < 4; region += 1)
26     {
27         cout << "Region " << region + 1
28             << ": " << endl;
29         for (int month = 0; month < 3; month += 1)
30         {
31             cout << "   Month " << month + 1
32                  << ": ";
33             cout << orders[region][month] << endl;
34         }   //end for
35     }   //end for
36 
37     //system("pause");
38     return 0;
39 }   //end of main function
```

array declaration (line 11)

stores data in the array (lines 14–22)

displays the contents of the array (lines 25–35)

your C++ development tool may require this statement (line 37)

You can use region++ in Lines 14 and 25, and use month++ in Lines 15 and 29.

Figure 12-10 Caldwell Company program

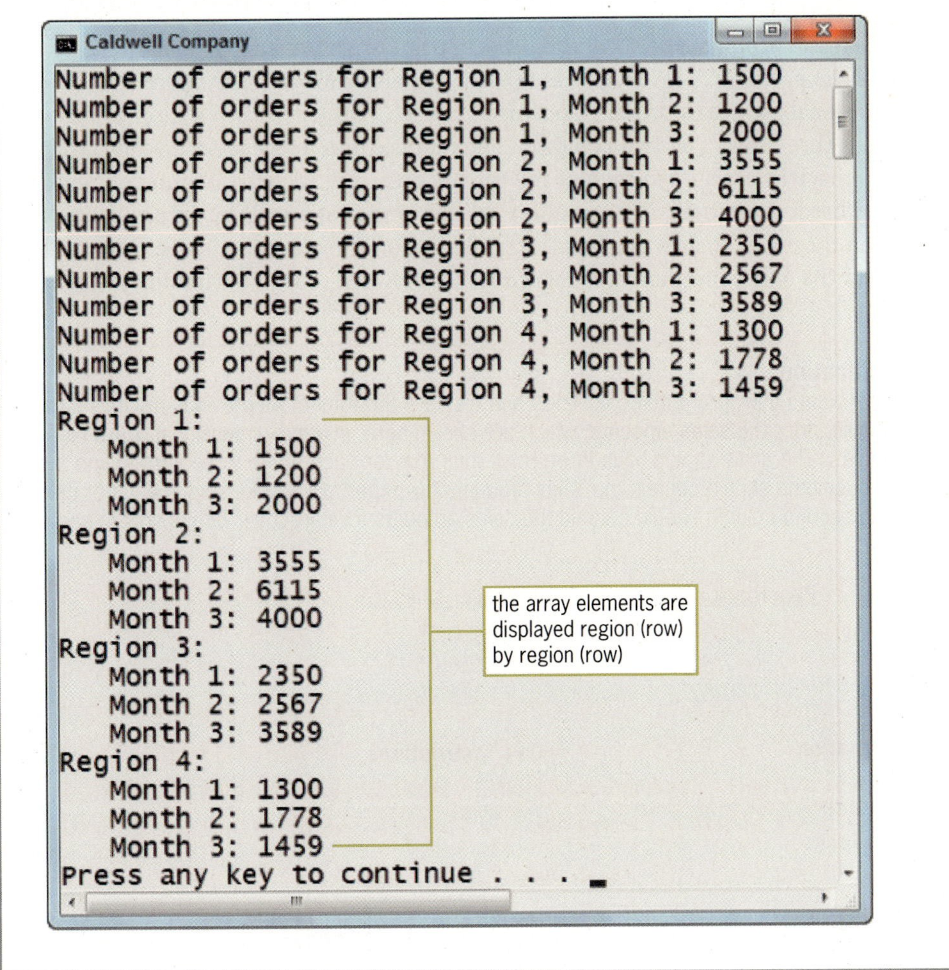

Figure 12-11 Sample run of the Caldwell Company program

Mini-Quiz 12-1

The answers to Mini-Quiz questions are located in Appendix A.

1. Which of the following declares a four-row, two-column `int` array named `quantities` and initializes each of its eight elements to the number 0?
   a. `int quantities[2][4] = {0};`
   b. `int quantities[4][2] = {0};`
   c. `int quantities{2}{4} = [0];`
   d. `int quantities{4}{2} = [0];`
2. How many elements are contained in a five-row, four-column array?
3. What is the name of the first element in the `quantities` array from Question 1?
4. What is the name of the last element in the `quantities` array from Question 1?
5. Write a C++ statement that assigns the number 5 to the element located in the second column, first row in the `quantities` array from Question 1.

Accumulating the Values Stored in a Two-Dimensional Array

Figure 12-12 shows the problem specification, IPO chart information, and C++ instructions for the Jenko Booksellers program. The program's flowchart is also shown in the figure. The program uses a two-dimensional array to store the sales made in each of the company's three bookstores. The array contains three rows and two columns. The first column in the array contains the sales amounts for paperback books sold in each of the three stores. The second column contains the sales amounts for hardcover books. The program calculates the total sales by accumulating the amounts stored in the array. It then displays the total sales on the computer screen. Figure 12-13 shows the code for the entire program, and Figure 12-14 shows the result of running the program.

Problem specification
Jenko Booksellers wants a program that calculates and displays the total of its previous month's sales. The program should store the sales amounts, which are shown here, in a two-dimensional `double` array named `sales`. The array should have three rows (one row for each of the three stores) and two columns. The first column should contain the sales amounts for paperback books sold in each of the three stores. The second column should contain the sales amounts for hardcover books sold in each of the three stores.

	Paperback sales ($)	Hardcover sales ($)
Store 1	1200.33	2350.75
Store 2	3677.80	2456.05
Store 3	750.67	1345.99

IPO chart information	**C++ instructions**
Input	
store sales (made in each of 3 stores for 2 types of books)	the sales are stored in the array
Processing	
array (3 store rows, 2 book columns)	`double sales[3][2] = {{1200.33, 2350.75}, {3677.80, 2456.05}, {750.67, 1345.99}};`
store subscript (counter: 0 to 2)	declared and initialized in the for clause
book subscript (counter: 0 to 1)	declared and initialized in the for clause
Output	
total sales (accumulator)	`double total = 0.0;`
Algorithm	
1. repeat for (store subscript from 0 to 2)	`for (int store = 0; store < 3; store += 1)`
repeat for (book subscript from 0 to 1)	`for (int book = 0; book < 2; book += 1)`
add the sales stored in array[store subscript][book subscript] to the total sales	`total += sales[store][book];`
end repeat	`//end for`
end repeat	`//end for`
2. display the total sales	`cout << "Total sales: $" << total << endl;`

Figure 12-12 Problem specification, IPO chart information (including flowchart), and C++ instructions for the Jenko Booksellers program *(continues)*

(continued)

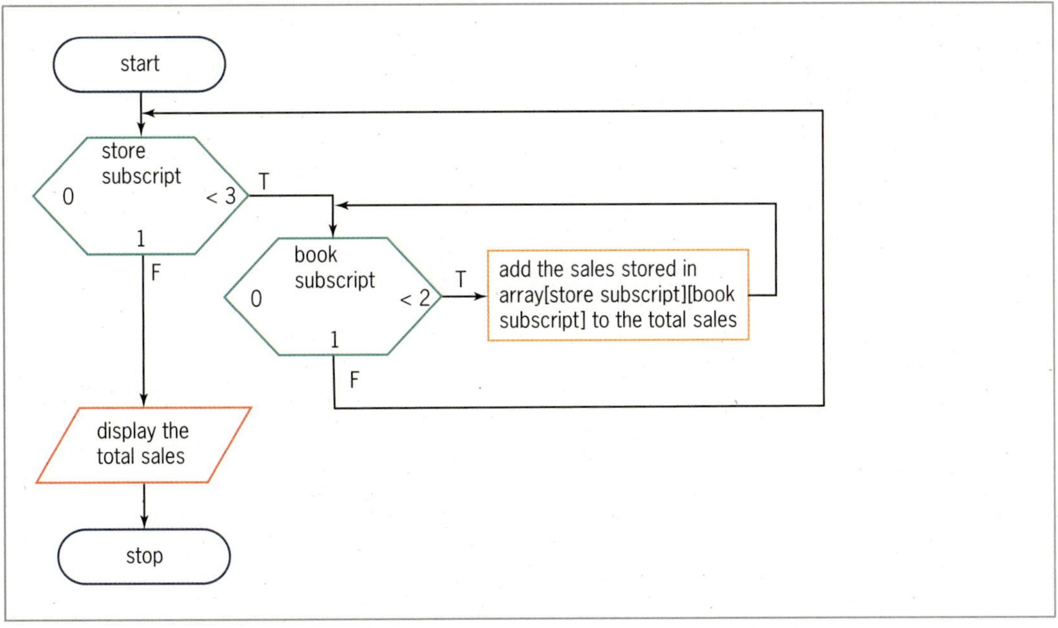

Figure 12-12 Problem specification, IPO chart information (including flowchart), and C++ instructions for the Jenko Booksellers program

```
 1 //Jenko Booksellers.cpp
 2 //Displays the total sales
 3 //Created/revised by <your name> on <current date>
 4
 5 #include <iostream>
 6 #include <iomanip>
 7 using namespace std;
 8
 9 int main()
10 {
11     //declare array and variable
12     double sales[3][2] = {{1200.33, 2350.75},
13                           {3677.80, 2456.05},
14                           {750.67, 1345.99}};
15     double total = 0.0;   //accumulator
16
17     //accumulate sales
18     for (int store = 0; store < 3; store += 1)
19         for (int book = 0; book < 2; book += 1)
20             total += sales[store][book];
21         //end for
22     //end for
23
24     //display total sales
25     cout << fixed << setprecision(2);
26     cout << "Total sales: $" << total << endl;
27
28     //system("pause");
29     return 0;
30 }   //end of main function
```

array declaration

accumulates the sales stored in the array

your C++ development tool may require this statement

Figure 12-13 Jenko Booksellers program

You can use `store++` in Line 18 and use `book++` in Line 19.

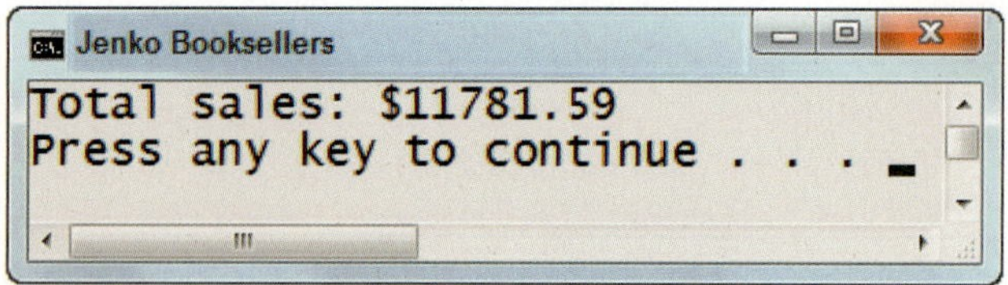

Figure 12-14 Result of running the Jenko Booksellers program

Searching a Two-Dimensional Array

Figure 12-15 shows the problem specification, IPO chart information, and C++ instructions for the Wilson Company program. The program's flowchart is also shown in the figure. The program uses a four-row, two-column array to store the company's four pay codes and their corresponding pay rates. The pay codes are stored in the first column of each row in the array. The pay rate associated with each code is stored in the same row as its pay code, but in the second column. The program gets a pay code from the user and then searches for the pay code in the array's first column. If it finds the pay code, the program displays the corresponding pay rate from the array's second column; otherwise, it displays the "Invalid pay code" message.

Problem specification

Wilson Company wants a program that displays the pay rate corresponding to the pay code entered by the user. The program should store the pay codes and pay rates, which are listed here, in a two-dimensional `int` array named `codesAndRates`. The array should have four rows (one row for each of the four pay codes) and two columns. The first column should contain the four pay codes, and the second column should contain each code's corresponding pay rate.

Pay code	Pay rate
3	8
6	14
7	18
9	20

IPO chart information	C++ instructions
Input	
4 pay codes and their pay rates	the pay codes and pay rates are stored in the array
pay code to search for	`int payCode = 0;`
Processing	
array (4 rows, 2 columns)	`int codesAndRates[4][2] = {{3, 8}, {6, 14}, {7, 18}, {9, 20}};`
row subscript (counter: 0 to 3)	`int row = 0;`
Output	
pay rate	displayed from the array

Figure 12-15 Problem specification, IPO chart information (including flowchart), and C++ instructions for the Wilson Company program *(continues)*

(continued)

Algorithm	

1. enter the pay code to search for	`cout << "Pay code (3, 6, 7, or 9). " << endl;`
	`cout << "Enter a negative number to end: ";`
	`cin >> payCode;`

2. repeat while (the pay code to search for is greater than or equal to 0)	`while (payCode >= 0)` `{`
assign 0 as the row subscript to begin searching the array with the first row	`row = 0;`
repeat while (the row subscript is less than or equal to 3 and the pay code stored in array[row subscript][0] is not the pay code to search for)	`while (row <= 3 && codesAndRates[row][0] != payCode)`
add 1 to the row subscript to continue the search with the next row	`row += 1;`
end repeat	`//end while`
if (the row subscript is less than or equal to 3)	`if (row <= 3)`
display the pay code and the pay rate stored in array[row subscript][1]	`cout << "Pay rate for pay code " << payCode << ": $" << codesAndRates[row][1] << endl << endl;`
else	`else`
display "Invalid pay code"	`cout << "Invalid pay code" << endl << endl;`
end if	`//end if`

enter the pay code to search for	`cout << "Pay code (3, 6, 7, or 9). " << endl;`
	`cout << "Enter a negative number to end: ";`
	`cin >> payCode;`

end while	`}   //end while`

Figure 12-15 Problem specification, IPO chart information (including flowchart), and C++ instructions for the Wilson Company program *(continues)*

(continued)

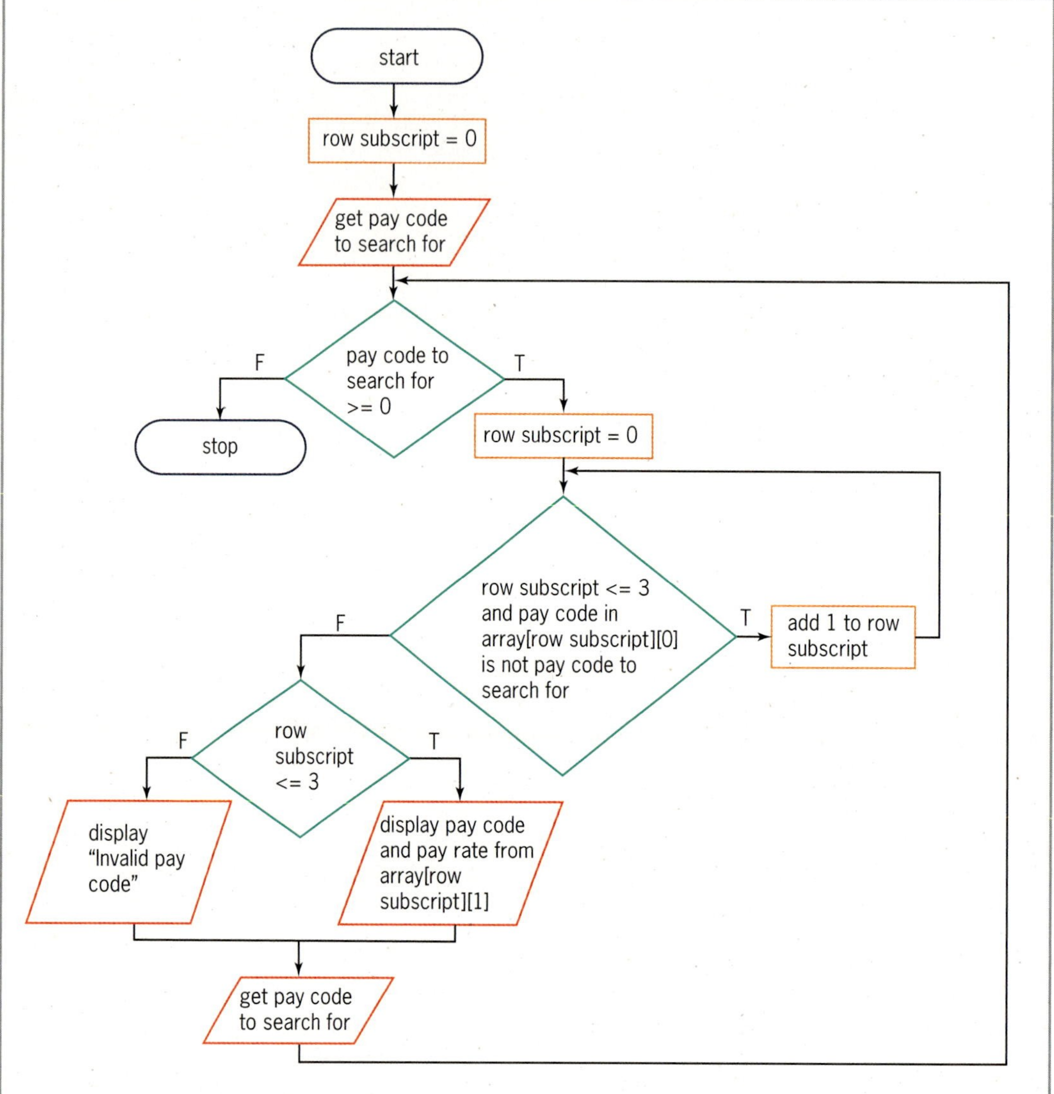

Figure 12-15 Problem specification, IPO chart information (including flowchart), and C++ instructions for the Wilson Company program

Figure 12-16 shows a sample run of the Wilson Company program. As the figure shows, the program displays $18 as the pay rate when the user enters the number 7 as the pay code. This is because the number 7 is contained in the `codesAndRates[2][0]` element, and its corresponding pay rate (18) is contained in the `codesAndRates[2][1]` element. Notice that the pay code and its associated pay rate are contained in the same row but in different columns. As the figure also shows, the program displays the "Invalid pay code" message when the user enters the number 5 as the pay code. This is because the number 5 does not appear in the first column in the array.

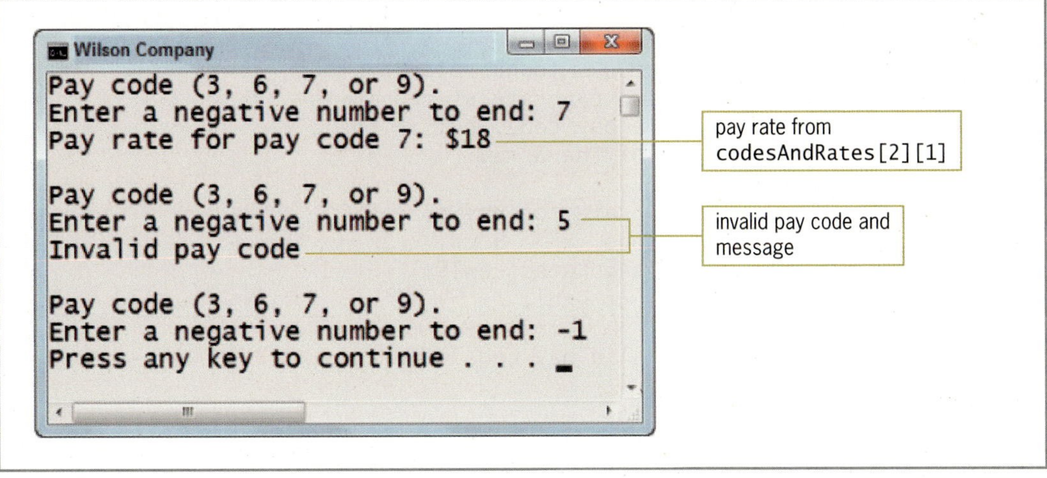

Figure 12-16 Sample run of the Wilson Company program

Figure 12-17 shows the code for the entire Wilson Company program.

```
//Wilson Company.cpp - displays the pay rate
//corresponding to the pay code entered by the user
//Created/revised by <your name> on <current date>

#include <iostream>
using namespace std;

int main()
{
    //declare array and variables
    int codesAndRates[4][2] = {{3, 8},
                               {6, 14},
                               {7, 18},
                               {9, 20}};
    int payCode = 0;
    int row     = 0;

    //get pay code
    cout << "Pay code (3, 6, 7, or 9). " << endl;
    cout << "Enter a negative number to end: ";
    cin >> payCode;

    while (payCode >= 0)
    {
        //search each row in the array, looking
        //for the pay code in the first column
        //continue the search while there are
        //array elements to search and the pay
        //code has not been found
        row = 0;
        while (row <= 3
            && codesAndRates[row][0] != payCode)
                row += 1;
        //end while

```

prevents the computer from searching beyond the memory allocated to the array

Figure 12-17 Wilson Company program *(continues)*

(continued)

```
36          //if the pay code was found, display the
37          //pay code and the pay rate stored in the
38          //same row as the pay code, but in the
39          //second column of the array
40          if (row <= 3)
41              cout << "Pay rate for pay code "
42                   << payCode << ": $"
43                   << codesAndRates[row][1]
44                   << endl << endl;
45          else
46              cout << "Invalid pay code" << endl << endl;
47          //end if
48  
49          //get pay code
50          cout << "Pay code (3, 6, 7, or 9). " << endl;
51          cout << "Enter a negative number to end: ";
52          cin >> payCode;
53      }   //end while
54  
55      //system("pause");
56      return 0;
57  }   //end of main function
```

your C++ development tool may require this statement

Figure 12-17 Wilson Company program

You will desk-check the program shown in Figure 12-17 to observe how it searches the array. The declaration statements on Lines 11 through 16 create and initialize the two-dimensional `codesAndRates` array and two variables named `payCode` and `row`. The `cout` statements on Lines 19 and 20 prompt the user to enter a pay code, and the `cin` statement on Line 21 stores the user's response in the `payCode` variable. Assume that the user enters the number 7 as the pay code. Figure 12-18 shows the desk-check table after the statements on Lines 11 through 21 are processed.

Ch12-Wilson Desk-Check video

codesAndRates[0][0] 3	codesAndRates[0][1] 8
codesAndRates[1][0] 6	codesAndRates[1][1] 14
codesAndRates[2][0] 7	codesAndRates[2][1] 18
codesAndRates[3][0] 9	codesAndRates[3][1] 20
payCode ~~0~~ 7	row 0

Figure 12-18 Desk-check table after the statements on Lines 11 through 21 are processed

The `while` clause in the program's outer loop (on Line 23) is processed next. The clause's condition evaluates to true because the value in the `payCode` variable is greater than or equal to the number 0. Therefore, the computer processes the outer loop's instructions.

The instructions on Lines 30 through 34 in the outer loop search for the pay code in the first column of the array; study these instructions closely. The instruction on Line 30 assigns the number 0 to the `row` variable to ensure that the search will begin in the first row. The `while` clause on Lines 31 and 32 marks the beginning of a nested loop. The clause's compound condition evaluates to true because both of its sub-conditions evaluate to true. The first sub-condition determines whether the value in the `row` variable is less than or equal to 3 (the highest row subscript in the array). The sub-condition evaluates to true because, at this point, the `row` variable contains the number 0. The second sub-condition compares the value in the `codesAndRates[row][0]` element with the value in the `payCode` variable. The value in the `codesAndRates[0][0]` element (3) is not equal to the value in the `payCode` variable (7), so this sub-condition also evaluates to true. As a result, the `row += 1;` statement on Line 33 in the nested loop is processed. The statement adds the number 1 to the contents of the `row` variable, giving 1. Incrementing the `row` variable by 1 allows the computer to search the next row in the array. Figure 12-19 shows the desk-check table after the nested loop is processed the first time.

codesAndRates[0][0]	codesAndRates[0][1]
3	8
codesAndRates[1][0]	**codesAndRates[1][1]**
6	14
codesAndRates[2][0]	**codesAndRates[2][1]**
7	18
codesAndRates[3][0]	**codesAndRates[3][1]**
9	20
payCode	**row**
~~0~~ 7	~~0~~ ~~0~~ 1

Figure 12-19 Desk-check table after the nested loop is processed the first time

The compound condition in the nested loop's `while` clause (on Lines 31 and 32) is evaluated again. The compound condition evaluates to true because the value in the `row` variable (1) is less than or equal to 3, and (at the same time) the value in the `codesAndRates[1][0]` element (6) is not equal to the value in the `payCode` variable (7). Therefore, the `row += 1;` statement on Line 33 increments the `row` variable by 1, giving 2. Figure 12-20 shows the desk-check table after the nested loop is processed the second time.

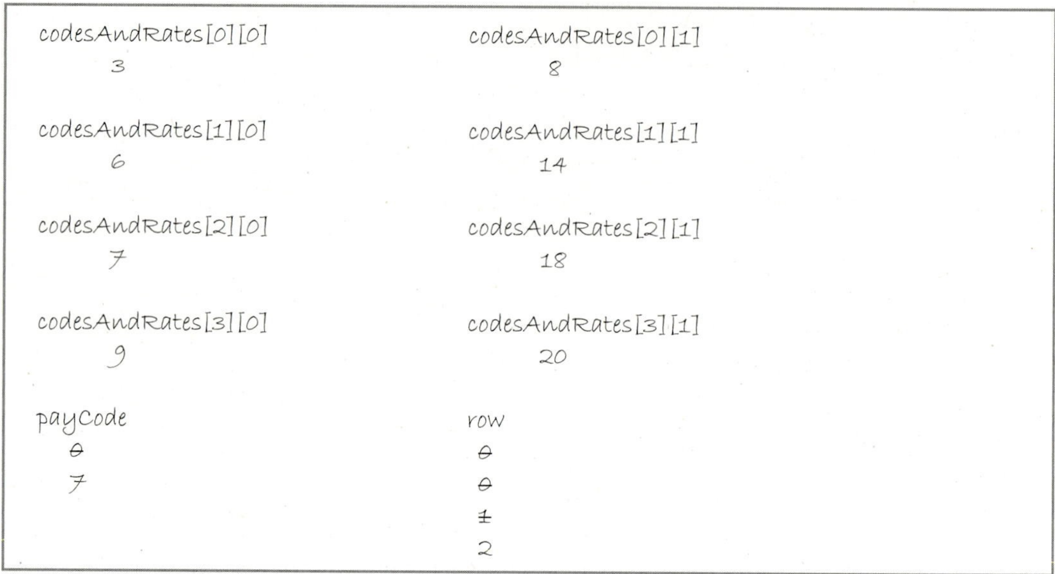

Figure 12-20 Desk-check table after the nested loop is processed the second time

The compound condition in the nested loop's `while` clause (on Lines 31 and 32) is evaluated once again. This time, the compound condition evaluates to false because the value in the `codesAndRates[2][0]` element (7) *is* equal to the value in the `payCode` variable (7). At this point, the nested loop ends and processing continues with the `if` clause on Line 40.

The `if` clause's condition determines whether the value in the `row` variable is less than or equal to 3 (the highest row subscript in the array). The condition evaluates to true because, at this point, the value in the `row` variable is 2. Therefore, the computer processes the `cout` statement that appears on Lines 41 through 44. The statement displays a message containing the pay code stored in the `payCode` variable and the pay rate stored in the `codesAndRates[2][1]` element, as shown earlier in Figure 12-16. After the message is displayed, the `if` statement ends.

The `cout` statements on Lines 50 and 51 are processed next. Those statements prompt the user to enter another pay code. The `cin` statement on Line 52 stores the user's response in the `payCode` variable. Assume that the user enters the number 5. The computer evaluates the condition in the outer loop's `while` clause (on Line 23) next. The condition evaluates to true because the value in the `payCode` variable (5) is greater than or equal to the number 0. Therefore, the computer processes the outer loop's instructions.

The instruction on Line 30 in the outer loop assigns the number 0 to the `row` variable to ensure that this new search will begin in the first row. The nested `while` clause on Lines 31 and 32 tells the computer to process the `row += 1;` statement as long as the value in the `row` variable is less than or equal to 3 (the highest row subscript in the array) and the current array element does not contain the pay code stored in the `payCode` variable. The nested loop will stop when either of the following occurs: the `row` variable contains the number 4 (which indicates that the nested loop reached the end of the array without finding the pay code) or the pay code is located in the array's first column.

Figure 12-21 shows the desk-check table after the nested loop ends. Unlike the nested loop in the previous search, which stopped when the pay code of 7 was located, the nested loop in this search stops when the `row` variable contains the number 4.

codesAndRates[0][0] 3	codesAndRates[0][1] 8
codesAndRates[1][0] 6	codesAndRates[1][1] 14
codesAndRates[2][0] 7	codesAndRates[2][1] 18
codesAndRates[3][0] 9	codesAndRates[3][1] 20
payCode ~~0~~ ~~7~~ 5	row ~~0~~ ~~0~~ ~~1~~ ~~2~~ ~~0~~ ~~1~~ ~~2~~ ~~3~~ 4

Figure 12-21 Desk-check table after the nested loop ends and the pay code is not located

When the nested loop ends, processing continues with the `if` clause on Line 40. The `if` clause's condition determines whether the value in the `row` variable is less than or equal to 3 (the highest row subscript in the array). The condition evaluates to false because the value in the `row` variable is 4. This indicates that the nested loop stopped processing because it reached the end of the array's first column without finding the pay code. Therefore, the computer processes the `cout` statement on Line 46. The statement displays the "Invalid pay code" message, as shown earlier in Figure 12-16. After the message is displayed, the `if` statement ends.

Next, the `cout` statements on Lines 50 and 51 prompt the user to enter another pay code, and the `cin` statement on Line 52 stores the user's response in the `payCode` variable. Assume that the user enters the number −1. The computer evaluates the condition in the outer loop's `while` clause (on Line 23) next. The condition evaluates to false because the value in the `payCode` variable (−1) is not greater than or equal to the number 0. As a result, the outer loop ends and the computer processes the `return 0;` statement on Line 56. After the `return` statement is processed, the program ends and the computer removes the array and the two scalar (simple) variables from internal memory.

For more examples of two-dimensional arrays, see the Two-Dimensional Arrays section in the Ch12WantMore.pdf file.

Passing a Two-Dimensional Array to a Function

Figure 12-22 shows a modified version of the Caldwell Company program, which you viewed earlier in Figure 12-10. In the modified version, the `main` function passes the `orders` array to a program-defined void function named `displayArray`. Study closely the `displayArray` function prototype, function call, and function header; each is shaded in the figure. The function call appears on Line 28 and passes one actual argument to the `displayArray` function: the `orders` array. Like one-dimensional arrays, two-dimensional arrays are passed automatically *by reference*. The `displayArray` function prototype and function header appear on Lines 9 and 35, respectively; both contain one formal parameter: `nums[4][3]`. The first set of square

When passing a two-dimensional array, the first set of square brackets in its corresponding formal parameter can be empty, like this: `[]`. This concept is covered in Computer Exercise 17 at the end of the chapter.

brackets that follows the formal parameter's name contains the number of rows in the array; the second set contains the number of columns. Recall that the formal parameter's name is optional in the prototype. Therefore, you also could write the formal parameter in the function prototype as `int [4][3]`.


```
 1 // Modified Caldwell Company.cpp
 2 // Displays the contents of a two-dimensional array
 3 // Created/revised by <your name> on <current date>
 4
 5 #include <iostream>
 6 using namespace std;
 7
 8 //function prototype
 9 void displayArray(int nums[4][3]);
10
11 int main()
12 {
13     //declare and initialize array
14     int orders[4][3] = {0};
15
16     //enter data into the array
17     for (int region = 0; region < 4; region += 1)
18         for (int month = 0; month < 3; month += 1)
19         {
20             cout << "Number of orders for Region "
21                 << region + 1 << ", Month "
22                 << month + 1 << ": ";
23             cin >> orders[region][month];
24         }   //end for
25     //end for
26
27     //display the contents of the array
28     displayArray(orders);
29
30     //system("pause");
31     return 0;
32 }   //end of main function
33
34 //*****function definitions*****
35 void displayArray(int nums[4][3])
36 {
37     for (int region = 0; region < 4; region += 1)
38     {
39         cout << "Region " << region + 1
40             << ": " << endl;
41         for (int month = 0; month < 3; month += 1)
42         {
43             cout << "   Month " << month + 1
44                 << ": ";
45             cout << nums[region][month] << endl;
46         }   //end for
47     }   //end for
48 }   //end of displayArray function
```

Figure 12-22 Modified Caldwell Company program

You can use `region++` in Lines 17 and 37, and use `month++` in Lines 18 and 41.

Mini-Quiz 12-2

The answers to Mini-Quiz questions are located in Appendix A.

1. Which of the following increases the `total` variable by the contents of the element located in the second row, first column of the `purchases` array? The variable and array have the `int` data type.
   a. `purchases[2][1] += total;`
   b. `purchases[1][2] += total;`
   c. `total += purchases[2][1];`
   d. `total += purchases[1][0];`

2. Which of the following `if` clauses determines whether the value stored in the fourth column, third row in the `scores` array is greater than 25? The array has the `int` data type.
   a. `if (scores[3, 4] > 25)`
   b. `if (scores[4, 3] > 25)`
   c. `if (scores[2][3] > 25)`
   d. `if (scores[3][4] > 25)`

3. Write a C++ statement that multiplies the contents of the element located in the first row, second column in the `sales` array by .15 and then stores the result in the `bonus` variable. The `sales` array and `bonus` variable have the `double` data type.

4. Which of the following `if` clauses determines whether an `int` variable named `row` contains a valid subscript for the `scores` array? The array has 10 rows and 20 columns.
   a. `if (row >= 0 && row < 10)`
   b. `if (row >= 0 && row <= 10)`
   c. `if (row >= 0 && row < 9)`
   d. `if (row > 0 && row <= 10)`

LAB 12-1 Stop and Analyze

The answers to the labs are located in Appendix A.

Study the program shown in Figure 12-23, and then answer the questions. The `company` array contains the amounts the company sold both domestically and internationally during the months of January through June. The first row contains the domestic sales for the three months. The second row contains the international sales during the same period.

```
//Lab12-1.cpp - calculates the total sales
//Created/revised by <your name> on <current date>

#include <iostream>
using namespace std;

```

Figure 12-23 Code for Lab 12-1 *(continues)*

(continued)

```
 7 int main()
 8 {
 9     //declare arrays and variable
10     int company[2][6] = {{12000, 45000, 32000,
11                           67000, 24000, 55000},
12                          {10000, 56000, 42000,
13                           23000, 12000, 34000}};
14     int companySales = 0;   //accumulator
15 
16     //accumulate sales
17     for (int location = 0; location < 2; location += 1)
18         for (int month = 0; month < 6; month += 1)
19             companySales += company[location][month];
20         //end for
21     //end for
22 
23     //display total sales
24     cout << "Company sales: $" << companySales << endl;
25 
26     //system("pause");
27     return 0;
28 }   //end of main function
```

Figure 12-23 Code for Lab 12-1

QUESTIONS

1. What value is stored in the `company[1][5]` element?
2. How can you calculate the total company sales made in February?
3. What is the highest row subscript in the `company` array? What is the highest column subscript in the array?
4. If the January domestic sales are stored in the `company[0][0]` element, where are the January international sales stored?
5. If you change the `for` clause in Line 18 to `for (int month = 1; month <= 6; month += 1)`, how will the change affect the assignment statement in the `for` loop?
6. Follow the instructions for starting C++ and viewing the Lab12-1.cpp file, which is contained in either the Cpp7\Chap12\Lab12-1 Project folder or the Cpp7\Chap12 folder. (Depending on your C++ development tool, you may need to open Lab12-1's project/solution file first.) If necessary, delete the two forward slashes that appear before the `system("pause");` statement, and then save the program. Run the program. The total company sales are $412000.
7. Modify the program so that it displays the total domestic sales, total international sales, and total company sales. Save and then run the program. (The total domestic sales are $235000.)
8. Next, modify the program so that it also displays the total sales made in each month. Save and then run the program. (The total January sales are $22000.)
9. Now, modify the program to use the `while` statement rather than the `for` statement. Save and then run the program.

LAB 12-2 Plan and Create

In this lab, you will plan and create an algorithm for Falcon Incorporated. The problem specification, IPO chart information, and C++ instructions are shown in Figure 12-24. The program displays a shipping charge based on the number of items ordered, which is entered by the user. The problem specification shows the three shipping charges along with their associated minimum and maximum orders. Notice that the maximum order amounts are stored in the first column of the two-dimensional `shipCharges` array, while their corresponding shipping charges are stored in the second column. To find the appropriate shipping charge, you search the first column for the number of items ordered, beginning with the first row. You continue searching the first column in each row as long as there are rows left to search and the number of items ordered is greater than the value in the first column. You stop searching either when there are no more rows to search or when the number of items ordered is less than or equal to the value in the first column. For example, if the number of items ordered is 75, the first value you would look at in the array is 50. The number of items ordered (75) is greater than 50, so you continue searching with the value in the second row (100). The number 100 is greater than the number of items ordered (75), so you stop searching. The appropriate shipping charge is located in the same row—in this case, the second row—but in the second column. The appropriate shipping charge is $10.

Problem specification
Falcon Incorporated wants a program that displays a shipping charge based on the number of items ordered by the customer. The shipping charge information is shown here.

Minimum order	Maximum order	Shipping charge ($)
1	50	20
51	100	10
101	999999	0

IPO chart information	**C++ instructions**
Input	
number ordered	`int numOrdered = 0;`
maximum orders and shipping charges	*stored in the array*
Processing	
array (3 rows, 2 columns)	`int shipCharges[3][2] = {{50, 20}, {100, 10}, {999999, 0}};`
row subscript (counter: 0 to 2)	`int rowSub = 0;`
Output	
shipping charge	*displayed from the array*
Algorithm	
1. enter the number ordered	`cout << "Number ordered "; cout << "(negative number or 0 to end): "; cin >> numOrdered;`
2. repeat while (the number ordered is greater than 0 and less than or equal to 999999)	`while (numOrdered > 0 && numOrdered <= 999999) {`
assign 0 to the row subscript to ensure the search begins in the first row	`rowSub = 0;`

Figure 12-24 Problem specification, IPO chart information, and C++ instructions for Lab 12-2 *(continues)*

(continued)

repeat while (the row subscript is less than 3 and the number ordered is greater than the value stored in the array[row subscript][0]) element	`while (rowSub < 3 && numOrdered > shipCharges[rowSub][0])`
add 1 to the row subscript to continue the search in the next row	`rowSub += 1;`
end repeat	`//end while`
display the shipping charge	`cout << "Shipping charge for a quantity of " << numOrdered << " is $" << shipCharges[rowSub][1] << endl << endl;`
enter the number ordered	`cout << "Number ordered "; cout << "(negative number or 0 to end): "; cin >> numOrdered;`
end repeat	`} //end while`

Figure 12-24 Problem specification, IPO chart information, and C++ instructions for Lab 12-2

Figure 12-25 shows the code for the entire Falcon Incorporated program, and Figure 12-26 shows the completed desk-check table for the program, assuming the user enters the numbers 75, 200, and –1 as the number of items ordered.

```
//Lab12-2.cpp - displays the shipping charge
//Created/revised by <your name> on <current date>

#include <iostream>
using namespace std;

int main()
{
    //declare array and variables
    int shipCharges[3][2] = {{50, 20},
                             {100, 10},
                             {999999, 0}};
    int numOrdered = 0;
    int rowSub     = 0;

    //enter the number ordered
    cout << "Number ordered ";
    cout << "(negative number or 0 to end): ";
    cin >> numOrdered;

```

Figure 12-25 Falcon Incorporated program *(continues)*

(continued)

```
21      while (numOrdered > 0 && numOrdered <= 999999)
22      {
23          //search array
24          rowSub = 0;
25          while (rowSub < 3 &&
26              numOrdered > shipCharges[rowSub][0])
27                  rowSub += 1;
28          //end while
29
30          //display shipping charge
31          cout << "Shipping charge for a quantity of "
32               << numOrdered << " is $"
33               << shipCharges[rowSub][1] << endl << endl;
34
35          //enter the number ordered
36          cout << "Number ordered ";
37          cout << "(negative number or 0 to end): ";
38          cin >> numOrdered;
39      }   //end while
40
41      //system("pause");
42      return 0;
43  }   //end of main function
```

if your C++ development tool requires this statement, delete the two forward slashes

Figure 12-25 Falcon Incorporated program

You can use `rowSub++;` in Line 27.

shipCharges[0][0] 50	shipCharges[0][1] 20
shipCharges[1][0] 100	shipCharges[1][1] 10
shipCharges[2][0] 999999	shipCharges[2][1] 0
numOrdered ~~0~~ ~~75~~ ~~200~~ -1	rowSub ~~0~~ ~~0~~ ~~1~~ ~~0~~ ~~1~~ 2

Figure 12-26 Completed desk-check table for the Falcon Incorporated program

The final step in the problem-solving process is to evaluate and modify (if necessary) the program. Recall that you evaluate a program by entering its instructions into the computer and then using the computer to run (execute) it. While the program is running, you enter the same sample data used when desk-checking the program.

DIRECTIONS

Follow the instructions for starting your C++ development tool. Depending on the development tool you are using, you may need to create a new project; if so, name the project Lab12-2 Project and save it in the Cpp7\Chap12 folder. Enter the instructions shown in Figure 12-25 in a source file named Lab12-2.cpp. (Do not enter the line numbers.) Save the file in either the project folder or the Cpp7\Chap12 folder. Now, follow the appropriate instructions for running the Lab12-2.cpp file. Test the program using the same data you used to desk-check the program. If necessary, correct any bugs (errors) in the program.

LAB 12-3 Modify

If necessary, create a new project named Lab12-3 Project and save it in the Cpp7\Chap12 folder. Enter (or copy) the Lab12-2.cpp instructions into a new source file named Lab12-3.cpp. Change Lab12-2.cpp in the first comment to Lab12-3.cpp. Replace the maximum amounts in the `shipCharges` array with the minimum amounts. Then, make the appropriate modifications to the program. Save and then run the program. Test the program appropriately.

LAB 12-4 Desk-Check

Desk-check the Jenko Booksellers program, which is shown in Figure 12-13 in the chapter.

LAB 12-5 Debug

Follow the instructions for starting C++ and viewing the Lab12-5.cpp file, which is contained in either the Cpp7\Chap12\Lab12-5 Project folder or the Cpp7\Chap12 folder. (Depending on your C++ development tool, you may need to open Lab12-5's project/solution file first.) If necessary, delete the two forward slashes that appear before the `system("pause");` statement and then save the program. Read the program's comments and then run the program. Notice that the program is not working correctly. Debug the program.

Summary

- A two-dimensional array resembles a table in that the elements are in rows and columns. Each element has the same data type.
- You can determine the number of elements in a two-dimensional array by multiplying the number of its rows by the number of its columns.
- Each element in a two-dimensional array is identified by a unique combination of two subscripts. The first subscript represents the element's row location in the array, and the second subscript represents its column location. You refer to each element in a two-dimensional array by the array's name and the element's subscripts, which are specified in two sets of square brackets immediately following the name.
- The first row subscript in a two-dimensional array is 0; the first column subscript also is 0. The last row subscript is always one number less than the number of rows in the array. The last column subscript is always one number less than the number of columns in the array.
- You must declare a two-dimensional array before you can use it. When declaring a two-dimensional array, you must provide the number of rows and the number of columns.
- After declaring a two-dimensional array, you can use an assignment statement or the extraction operator to enter data into the array.
- You need to use two loops to access every element in a two-dimensional array. One of the loops keeps track of the row subscript. The other loop keeps track of the column subscript.
- To pass a two-dimensional array to a function, you include the array's name in the statement that calls the function. The array's corresponding formal parameter in the function header must specify the formal parameter's data type and name, followed by two sets of square brackets. The first bracket contains the number of rows, and the second bracket contains the number of columns.

Key Term

Two-dimensional array—an array made up of rows and columns; each element has the same data type and is identified by a unique combination of two subscripts: a row subscript and a column subscript

Review Questions

1. The first element in a two-dimensional array has a row subscript of ________ and a column subscript of ________.
   a. 0, 0
   b. 0, 1
   c. 1, 0
   d. 1, 1

2. Which of the following statements creates a two-dimensional `int` array named `rates` that contains three rows and four columns?

   a. `int rates[3, 4] = {0};`

   b. `int rates[4, 3] = {0};`

   c. `int rates[3][4] = {0};`

   d. `int rates[4][3] = {0};`

Use the `sales` array to answer Review Questions 3 through 6. The array was declared using the `int sales[2][5] = {{10000, 12000, 900, 500, 20000}, {350, 600, 700, 800, 100}};` statement.

3. The statement `sales[1][3] = sales[1][3] + 10;` will replace the number ____________.

   a. 900 with 910

   b. 500 with 510

   c. 700 with 710

   d. 800 with 810

4. The statement `sales[0][4] = sales[0][4 - 2];` will replace the number ____________.

   a. 20000 with 900

   b. 20000 with 19998

   c. 20000 with 19100

   d. 500 with 12000

5. The statement `cout << sales[0][3] + sales[1][3] << endl;` will ____________.

   a. display 1300

   b. display 1600

   c. display `sales[0][3] + sales[1][3]`

   d. result in an error

6. Which of the following `if` clauses verifies that the array subscripts stored in the `row` and `col` variables are valid for the `sales` array?

   a. `if (sales[row][col] >= 0 && sales[row][col] < 5)`

   b. `if (sales[row][col] >= 0 && sales[row][col] <= 5)`

   c. `if (row >= 0 && row < 3 && col >= 0 && col < 6)`

   d. `if (row >= 0 && row <= 1 && col >= 0 && col <= 4)`

Exercises

Pencil and Paper

TRY THIS

1. Write the code to declare and initialize a two-dimensional `double` array named `balances` that has four rows and six columns. (The answers to TRY THIS Exercises are located at the end of the chapter.)

2. Write the code to display the contents of the `balances` array from Pencil and Paper Exercise 1. Use two `for` statements to display the array, row by row. (The answers to TRY THIS Exercises are located at the end of the chapter.) TRY THIS
3. Rewrite the code from Pencil and Paper Exercise 2 to display the array, column by column. MODIFY THIS
4. Write the code to store the number 100 in each element in the `balances` array from Pencil and Paper Exercise 1. Use two `for` statements. INTRODUCTORY

5. Rewrite the code from Pencil and Paper Exercise 4 using two `while` statements. INTRODUCTORY
6. Rewrite the code from Pencil and Paper Exercise 4 using the `do while` statement in the outer loop and the `while` statement in the nested loop. INTRODUCTORY
7. Write the statement to assign the C++ keyword `true` to the variable located in the third row, first column of a `bool` array named `answers`. INTERMEDIATE
8. Write the code to display the sum of the numbers stored in the following three elements contained in a two-dimensional `double` array named `sales`: the first row, first column; the second row, third column; and the third row, fourth column. INTERMEDIATE
9. Write the code to subtract the number 1 from each element in a two-dimensional `int` array named `quantities`. The array has 10 rows and 25 columns. Use two `for` statements. INTERMEDIATE
10. Rewrite the code from Pencil and Paper Exercise 9 using two `while` statements. INTERMEDIATE
11. Write the code to find the square root of the number stored in the first row, third column in a two-dimensional `double` array named `mathNumbers`. Display the result on the screen. INTERMEDIATE
12. Rewrite the code shown in Example 3 in Figure 12-8 so it displays the contents of the `prices` array, column by column. Use an outer `for` loop and a nested `while` loop. INTERMEDIATE
13. Write the code to display the largest number stored in the first column of a two-dimensional `int` array named `orders`. The array has five rows and two columns. Use the `for` statement. ADVANCED
14. Rewrite the code from Pencil and Paper Exercise 13 using the `while` statement. ADVANCED
15. The `numbers` array is a two-dimensional `int` array that contains three rows and five columns. The following statement should call the void `calcTotal` function, passing it the `numbers` array: `calcTotal(numbers[3][5]);`. Correct the statement. SWAT THE BUGS

Computer

16. If necessary, create a new project named TryThis16 Project and save it in the Cpp7\Chap12 folder. Enter the C++ instructions shown earlier in Figure 12-10 into a source file named TryThis16.cpp. Change the filename in the first comment. Save and then run the program. Test the program using the data shown in Figure 12-11 in the chapter. Change the `for` loops that enter data into the array to `while` loops. Change the `for` loops that display the array's contents to `do while` loops. Save and then run the program. Test the program using the data shown in Figure 12-11 in the chapter. (The answers to TRY THIS Exercises are located at the end of the chapter.) TRY THIS
17. If necessary, create a new project named TryThis17 Project and save it in the Cpp7\Chap12 folder. Enter the C++ instructions shown earlier in Figure 12-22 into a source file named TryThis17.cpp. Change the filename in the first comment. Save and TRY THIS

then run the program. As mentioned in the chapter, when you pass a two-dimensional array to a function, the first set of square brackets in its corresponding formal parameter can be empty. Remove the number 4 from the first formal parameter in the function prototype and function header. The `main` function will now need to pass two actual arguments to the `displayArray` function: the array and the number of rows (regions) in the array. Make the appropriate modifications to the `displayArray` function prototype, function header, and function call. Also modify the outer loop's `for` clause in the `displayArray` function so it uses the number of rows passed to the function rather than the literal constant 4. (The answers to TRY THIS Exercises are located at the end of the chapter.)

MODIFY THIS

18. If necessary, create a new project named ModifyThis18 Project and save it in the Cpp7\Chap12 folder. Enter the C++ instructions shown earlier in Figure 12-13 into a source file named ModifyThis18.cpp. Change the filename in the first comment. Save and then run the program. Jenko Booksellers has opened another store. The store's sales of paperback and hardcover books are $650.85 and $246.85, respectively. Add the new sales information to the array, and then modify the program appropriately. Save and then run the program.

MODIFY THIS

19. If necessary, create a new project named ModifyThis19 Project and save it in the Cpp7\Chap12 folder. Enter the C++ instructions shown earlier in Figure 12-17 into a new source file named ModifyThis19.cpp. Change the filename in the first comment. Save and then run the program. Test the program using the following two pay codes: 6 and 5. Enter –1 to stop the program. Add a new pay code and pay rate to the array. The new pay code is 11, and its corresponding pay rate is $23. Make the appropriate modifications to the code. Save and then run the program. Test the program using the following three pay codes: 6, 5, and 11. Enter –1 to stop the program.

INTRODUCTORY

20. Follow the instructions for starting C++ and viewing the Introductory20.cpp file, which is contained in either the Cpp7\Chap12\Introductory20 Project folder or the Cpp7\Chap12 folder. (Depending on your C++ development tool, you may need to open the project/solution file first.) If necessary, delete the two forward slashes that appear before the `system("pause");` statement, and then save the program. The program should calculate the average of the values stored in the `rates` array. It then should display the average rate on the screen. Display the average with two decimal places. Complete the program using the `for` statement. Save and then run the program.

INTRODUCTORY

21. Follow the instructions for starting C++ and viewing the Introductory21.cpp file, which is contained in either the Cpp7\Chap12\Introductory21 Project folder or the Cpp7\Chap12 folder. (Depending on your C++ development tool, you may need to open the project/solution file first.) If necessary, delete the two forward slashes that appear before the `system("pause");` statement, and then save the program. The program should display the contents of the two-dimensional array, column by column and also row by row. Complete the program using a `while` statement in the outer loops and a `for` statement in the nested loops. Save and then run the program.

INTERMEDIATE

22. If necessary, create a new project named Intermediate22 Project and save it in the Cpp7\Chap12 folder. Also create a new source file named Intermediate22.cpp. Declare a seven-row, two-column `int` array named `temperatures`. The program should prompt the user to enter the highest and lowest temperatures for seven days. Store the highest temperatures in the first column in the array. Store the lowest temperatures in the second column. The program should display the average high

temperature and the average low temperature. Display the average temperatures with one decimal place. Save and then run the program. Test the program using the data shown in Figure 12-27.

Day	Highest	Lowest
1	95	67
2	98	54
3	86	70
4	99	56
5	83	34
6	75	68
7	80	45

Figure 12-27

INTERMEDIATE

23. In this exercise, you modify the program from Computer Exercise 22. If necessary, create a new project named Intermediate23 Project and save it in the Cpp7\Chap12 folder. Copy the instructions from the Intermediate22.cpp file into a source file named Intermediate23.cpp. Change the filename in the first comment. In addition to displaying the average high temperature and average low temperature, the program also should display the highest temperature stored in the first column in the array and the lowest temperature stored in the second column. Save and then run the program. Test the program using the data shown in Figure 12-27.

ADVANCED

24. Follow the instructions for starting C++ and viewing the Advanced24.cpp file, which is contained in either the Cpp7\Chap12\Advanced24 Project folder or the Cpp7\Chap12 folder. (Depending on your C++ development tool, you may need to open the project/solution file first.) If necessary, delete the two forward slashes that appear before the `system("pause");` statement, and then save the program. Code the program so that it asks the user for a dollar amount by which each price should be increased. The program then should increase each price in the array's first column by that amount. For example, when the user enters the number 10, the program should increase each price in the array's first column by $10. Store the updated prices in the second column of the array. After increasing each price, the program should display the contents of the array, row by row. Display the array contents in two columns. Save and then run the program. Increase each price by $10.

ADVANCED

25. In this exercise, you code an application that displays the number of times a value appears in a two-dimensional array. Follow the instructions for starting C++ and viewing the Advanced25.cpp file, which is contained in either the Cpp7\Chap12\Advanced25 Project folder or the Cpp7\Chap12 folder. (Depending on your C++ development tool, you may need to open the project/solution file first.) If necessary, delete the two forward slashes that appear before the `system("pause");` statement, and then save the program. Code the program so that it displays the number of times each of the numbers from 1 through 9 appears in the `numbers` array. Save and then run the program. Hint: Use a one-dimensional array of counter variables.

ADVANCED

26. If necessary, create a new project named Advanced26 Project and save it in the Cpp7\Chap12 folder. Also create a new source file named Advanced26.cpp. JM Sales employs 10 salespeople. The sales made by the salespeople during the months of January, February, and March are listed in Figure 12-28. Store the sales amounts in a two-dimensional array. The sales manager wants an application that allows him to enter the current bonus rate. The program should display each salesperson's number (1 through 10), total sales amount, and total bonus amount. It also should display the total bonus paid to all salespeople. Display the bonus amounts with two decimal places. Save and then run the program. Test the program using 10% as the bonus rate.

Salesperson	January	February	March
1	2400	3500	2000
2	1500	7000	1000
3	600	450	2100
4	790	240	500
5	1000	1000	1000
6	6300	7000	8000
7	1300	450	700
8	2700	5500	6000
9	4700	4800	4900
10	1200	1300	400

Figure 12-28

ADVANCED

27. Follow the instructions for starting C++ and viewing the Advanced27.cpp file, which is contained in either the Cpp7\Chap12\Advanced27 Project folder or the Cpp7\Chap12 folder. (Depending on your C++ development tool, you may need to open the project/solution file first.) If necessary, delete the two forward slashes that appear before the `system("pause");` statement, and then save the program. Notice that the pay codes in the array are in ascending numerical order. The user will enter the pay code to search for in the array. The program should search for the pay code in the first column of the array, but the search should begin in the middle row, which is row 4. If the pay code the user is searching for is located in the first column of row 4, the program should display the corresponding pay rate from the second column in row 4. If the pay code the user is searching for is *greater* than the pay code in row 4's first column, the search should continue in rows 5, 6, and 7. However, if the pay code the user is searching for is *less* than the pay code in row 4's first column, the search should continue in rows 3, 2, and 1. Save and then run the program. Hint: To verify that the search works appropriately, use counters to keep track of the number of greater than comparisons made and the number of less than comparisons made.

SWAT THE BUGS

28. Follow the instructions for starting C++ and viewing the SwatTheBugs28.cpp file, which is contained in either the Cpp7\Chap12\SwatTheBugs28 Project folder or the Cpp7\Chap12 folder. (Depending on your C++ development tool, you may need to open the project/solution file first.) If necessary, delete the two forward slashes that appear before the `system("pause");` statement, and then save the program. Read the program's comments and then run the program. Notice that the program is not working correctly. Debug the program.

Answers to TRY THIS Exercises

Pencil and Paper

1.
```
double balances[4][6] = {0.0};
```

2.
```
for (int row = 0; row < 4; row += 1)
    for (int col = 0; col < 6; col += 1)
        cout << balances[row][col] << endl;
    //end for
//end for
```

You also can use `row++` and `col++` in Pencil and Paper Answer 2.

Computer

16. See Figure 12-29.

```
 1 //TryThis16.cpp
 2 //Displays the contents of a two-dimensional array
 3 //Created/revised by <your name> on <current date>
 4 
 5 #include <iostream>
 6 using namespace std;
 7 
 8 int main()
 9 {
10     //declare and initialize array
11     int orders[4][3] = {0};
12 
13     //enter data into the array
14     int region = 0;
15     int month = 0;
16     while (region < 4)
17     {
18         while (month < 3)
19         {
20             cout << "Number of orders for Region "
21                  << region + 1 << ", Month "
22                  << month + 1 << ": ";
23             cin >> orders[region][month];
24             month += 1;
25         }   //end while
26         region += 1;
27         month = 0;
28     }   //end while
29 
30     //display the contents of the array
31     region = 0;
32     month = 0;
33     do  //begin outer loop
34     {
35         cout << "Region " << region + 1
36              << ": " << endl;
37         do  //begin nested loop
38         {
39             cout << "   Month " << month + 1
40                  << ": ";
41             cout << orders[region][month] << endl;
42             month += 1;
43         } while (month < 3);
44         region += 1;
45         month = 0;
46     }   while (region < 4);
47 
48     //system("pause");
49     return 0;
50 }   //end of main function
```

your C++ development tool may require this statement

Figure 12-29

You can use `month++;` in Lines 24 and 42, and `region++;` in Lines 26 and 44.

17. See Figure 12-30. The changes are shaded in the figure.

```
1 //TryThis17.cpp
2 //Displays the contents of a two-dimensional array
3 //Created/revised by <your name> on <current date>
4
5 #include <iostream>
6 using namespace std;
7
8 //function prototype
9 void displayArray(int nums[][3], int numRegions);
10
11 int main()
12 {
13     //declare and initialize array
14     int orders[4][3] = {0};
15
16     //enter data into the array
17     for (int region = 0; region < 4; region += 1)
18         for (int month = 0; month < 3; month += 1)
19         {
20             cout << "Number of orders for Region "
21                  << region + 1 << ", Month "
22                  << month + 1 << ": ";
23             cin >> orders[region][month];
24         }   //end for
25     //end for
26
27     //display the contents of the array
28     displayArray(orders, 4);
29
30     //system("pause");
31     return 0;
32 }   //end of main function
33
34 //*****function definitions*****
35 void displayArray(int nums[][3], int numRegions)
36 {
37     for (int region = 0; region < numRegions; region += 1)
38     {
39         cout << "Region " << region + 1
40              << ": " << endl;
41         for (int month = 0; month < 3; month += 1)
42         {
43             cout << "    Month " << month + 1
44                  << ": ";
45             cout << nums[region][month] << endl;
46         }   //end for
47     }   //end for
48 }   //end of displayArray function
```

your C++ development tool may require this statement

Figure 12-30

You can use region++ in Lines 17 and 37, and use month++ in Lines 18 and 41.

CHAPTER 13

Strings

After studying Chapter 13, you should be able to:

- Utilize `string` memory locations in a program
- Get string input using the `getline` function
- Ignore characters using the `ignore` function
- Determine the number of characters in a string
- Access the characters in a string
- Search a string
- Remove characters from a string
- Replace characters in a string
- Insert characters within a string
- Duplicate characters within a string
- Concatenate strings

The string Data Type

In the programs created in the previous chapters, you used memory locations (variables and named constants) having the int and double data types. In this chapter, you will use string memory locations. As you learned in Chapter 3, the string data type is not one of the fundamental data types in C++. Rather, it was added to the C++ language through the use of a class, called the string class. Recall that a class is simply a group of instructions that the computer uses to create an object. The instructions for creating a string object, which can be either a string variable or a string named constant, are contained in the string file. Therefore, for a program to use the string class, it must contain the #include <string> directive. Also included in the string file are functions that you can use to manipulate strings. The functions are called member functions because they are members of a class—in this case, the string class. You will explore some of the more commonly used string class member functions in this chapter. First, however, you need to learn how to declare a string memory location.

You will learn how to create your own classes and objects in Chapter 15.

Figure 13-1 shows examples of using the string class to create and initialize string variables and string named constants. Memory locations having the string data type are initialized using string literal constants. Recall from Chapter 3 that a string literal constant is zero or more characters enclosed in double quotation marks. The declaration statement in Example 1 creates a string variable named zipCode and initializes it to the empty string (""), which is two double quotation marks with no space between. Most string variables are initialized to the empty string. The declaration statement in Example 2 creates a string variable named playAgain and initializes it to the string "Y". Examples 3 and 4 create and initialize string named constants called VALID_LENGTH and COMPANY_NAME, respectively.

Ch13-Chapter Preview video

HOW TO Declare and Initialize string Variables and Named Constants

Example 1
```
string zipCode = "";
```
declares and initializes a string variable named zipCode

Example 2
```
string playAgain = "Y";
```
declares and initializes a string variable named playAgain

Example 3
```
const string VALID_LENGTH = "Valid length";
```
declares and initializes a string named constant called VALID_LENGTH

Example 4
```
const string COMPANY_NAME = "ABC Company";
```
declares and initializes a string named constant called COMPANY_NAME

Figure 13-1 How to declare and initialize string variables and named constants

The Creative Sales Program

Figure 13-2 shows the problem specification and IPO chart for the Creative Sales program, which gets a salesperson's name and sales amount from the user. It then calculates the salesperson's bonus and displays the salesperson's name and bonus amount on the screen.

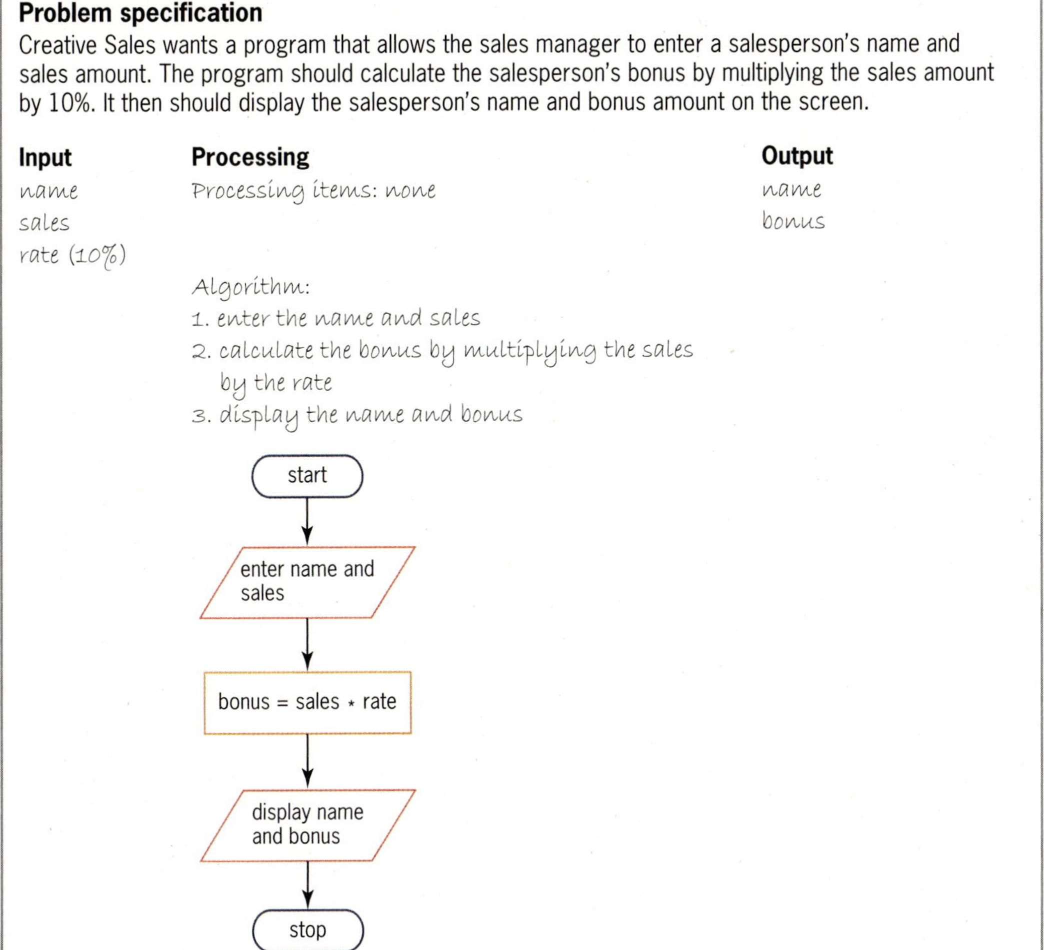

Figure 13-2 Problem specification and IPO chart for the Creative Sales program

So far, you have used the extraction operator (>>) to get numbers and characters from the user at the keyboard. The extraction operator also can be used to get string input from the keyboard, as shown in the examples in Figure 13-3. (For clarity, the variable declaration statements are included in the examples.) However, keep in mind that the extraction operator stops reading characters when it encounters a white-space character in the input. A white-space character is a blank, tab, or newline. You enter a blank character when you press the Spacebar on your keyboard. You enter a tab character when you press the Tab key, and you enter a newline character when you press the Enter key. As a result, if the user inadvertently enters the string "45 602" (rather than "45602") as the ZIP code in Example 1, the extraction operator in the `cin >> zipCode;` statement will store only the string "45" in the `zipCode` variable.

HOW TO Use the Extraction Operator (>>) to Get String Input

Example 1

```
string zipCode = "";
cout << "Enter your zip code: ";
cin >> zipCode;
```

gets a string from the keyboard and stores it in the `zipCode` variable

Example 2

```
string playAgain = "Y";
cout << "Play the game again? (Y/N): ";
cin >> playAgain;
```

gets a string from the keyboard and stores it in the `playAgain` variable

Figure 13-3 How to use the extraction operator (>>) to get string input

Because many strings entered at the keyboard contain one or more blank characters (such as "Bowling Green, Kentucky" and "Gerald R. Jones"), the `string` class provides a member function for accepting that type of input. The function is called `getline`. You will need to use the `getline` function to get the salesperson's name in the Creative Sales program.

The `getline` Function

Figure 13-4 shows the syntax for using the `getline` function to get string input from the keyboard; it also includes examples of using the function. The semicolon that appears as the last character in the syntax indicates that the `getline` function is a self-contained statement. The function has three actual arguments, two of which are required. The required `cin` argument refers to the computer keyboard, and the required *stringVariableName* argument is the name of a `string` variable in which to store the input. You can use the optional *delimiterCharacter* argument to indicate the end of the string. The argument represents the character that immediately follows the last character in the string. The **`getline` function** will continue to read the characters entered at the keyboard until it encounters the delimiter character. If you omit the *delimiterCharacter* argument, the default delimiter character is the newline character. For example, if the user types the words "Good night" and then presses the Enter key, the string will end with the letter t, which is the last character the user typed before pressing the Enter key. When the `getline` function encounters the delimiter character in the input, it discards the character—a process C++ programmers refer to as **consuming the character**.

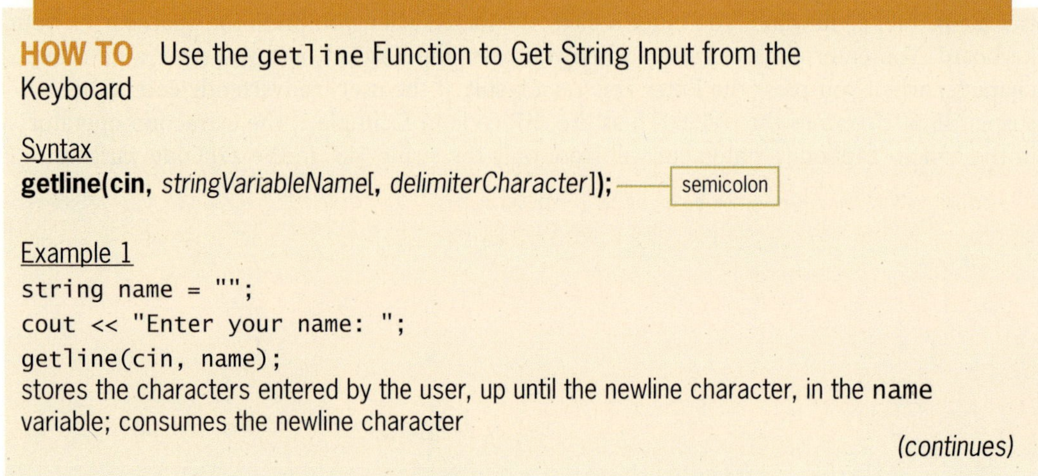

HOW TO Use the `getline` Function to Get String Input from the Keyboard

Syntax

getline(cin, *stringVariableName*[**,** *delimiterCharacter*]**);** — semicolon

Example 1

```
string name = "";
cout << "Enter your name: ";
getline(cin, name);
```

stores the characters entered by the user, up until the newline character, in the `name` variable; consumes the newline character

(continues)

Figure 13-4 How to use the `getline` function to get string input from the keyboard

Example 2 *(continued)*

```
string name = "";
cout << "Enter your name: ";
getline(cin, name, '\n');
```

same as Example 1, but specifies the newline delimiter character

Example 3

```
string city = "";
cout << "City: ";
getline(cin, city, '#');
```

stores the characters entered by the user, up until the # character, in the `city` variable; consumes the # character

Figure 13-4 How to use the `getline` function to get string input from the keyboard

The `getline` function in Example 1 in Figure 13-4 reads the characters entered at the keyboard and then stores the characters in the `name` variable. The function will stop reading and storing characters when it encounters the newline character, which is when the user presses the Enter key. As mentioned earlier, the newline character is the default delimiter character in the `getline` function. At that point, the function will consume (discard) the newline character.

Like the `getline` function in Example 1, the `getline` function in Example 2 also reads the characters entered at the keyboard and stores them in the `name` variable. Here too, the function will stop reading and storing characters when it encounters the newline character, which it will consume (discard). The newline character is designated in C++ by a backslash and the letter n, both enclosed in single quotation marks, like this: `'\n'`. Although the newline character consists of two characters, it is treated as one character by the computer. The backslash in the newline character is called an escape character, and it indicates that the character that follows it—in this case, the letter n—has a special meaning. The combination of the backslash and the character that follows it is called an **escape sequence**. An example of another escape sequence is `'\t'`, which represents the Tab key.

The `getline` function in Example 3 in Figure 13-4 reads the characters entered at the keyboard and stores them in the `city` variable. In this case, the function will stop reading and storing characters when it encounters the # character, which it will consume (discard).

Figure 13-5 shows the Creative Sales program, with the code pertaining to `string` data shaded. The `#include <string>` directive, which is necessary when using `string` memory locations, appears on Line 7. The declaration statement on Line 13 declares a `string` variable called `name` and initializes it to the empty string. The `getline` function on Line 19 waits for the user to respond to the "Salesperson's name: " prompt. When the user presses the Enter key, the function stores the characters typed by the user, up until the newline character, in the `name` variable; it then consumes the newline character. Figure 13-6 shows a sample run of the program.

```
//Creative Sales.cpp
//displays a salesperson's name and bonus
//Created/revised by <your name> on <current date>

#include <iostream>
#include <iomanip>
#include <string>
using namespace std;

int main()
{
    const double RATE = .1;
    string name   = "";
    int sales     = 0;
    double bonus = 0.0;

    //get input
    cout << "Salesperson's name: ";
    getline(cin, name);
    cout << "Sales: ";
    cin >> sales;

    //calculate bonus
    bonus = sales * RATE;

    //display output
    cout << fixed << setprecision(2);
    cout << "Bonus for " << name
         << ": $" << bonus << endl;

    //system("pause");
    return 0;
}   //end of main function
```

your C++ development tool may require this statement

Figure 13-5 Creative Sales program

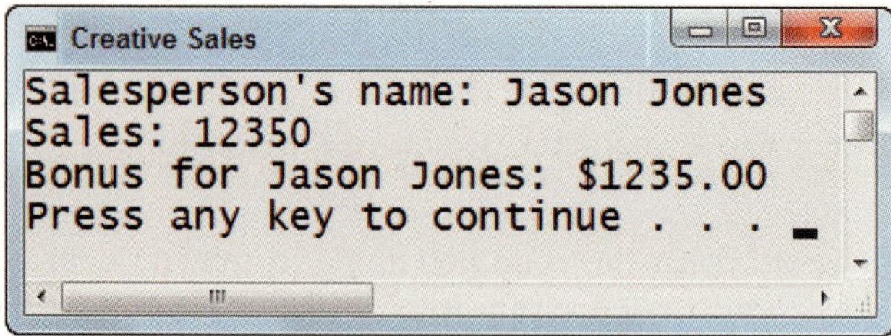

Figure 13-6 Sample run of the Creative Sales program

Now let's make a slight change to the problem specification for Creative Sales. In addition to entering the salesperson's name and sales amount, the sales manager also should enter the state in which the sales were made. The program should now display the state name along with the salesperson's name and bonus amount. Consider how these changes will affect the original program shown earlier in Figure 13-5. The modified program will need to declare and initialize a `string` variable to store the state name entered by the user. It also will need both a `cout` statement that prompts the user to enter the state name and a `getline` function to get the user's input. A `getline` function is appropriate because some state names—for example, North Carolina—contain a blank character. In addition, the program will need to include the state name in the `cout` statement that displays the salesperson's name and bonus amount. The modifications made to the original program are shaded in Figure 13-7. Figure 13-8 shows a sample run of the modified program. Notice that the program does not pause to allow the user to enter the state name.

```
//Modified Creative Sales.cpp
//displays a salesperson's name, bonus, and state
//Created/revised by <your name> on <current date>

#include <iostream>
#include <iomanip>
#include <string>
using namespace std;

int main()
{
    const double RATE = .1;
    string name    = "";
    int sales      = 0;
    double bonus = 0.0;
    string state = "";

    //get input
    cout << "Salesperson's name: ";
    getline(cin, name);
    cout << "Sales: ";
    cin >> sales;
    cout << "State name: ";
    getline(cin, state);

    //calculate bonus
    bonus = sales * RATE;

    //display output
    cout << fixed << setprecision(2);
    cout << "Bonus for " << name << " in "
         << state << ": $" << bonus << endl;

    //system("pause");
    return 0;
}   //end of main function
```

your C++ development tool may require this statement

Figure 13-7 Creative Sales program showing the modifications

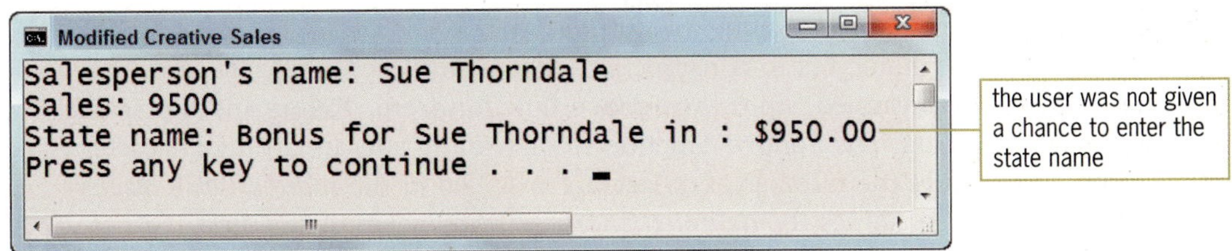

the user was not given a chance to enter the state name

Figure 13-8 Result of running the modified Creative Sales program

To understand why the modified program is not working correctly, you need to understand how the extraction operator and `getline` function get keyboard input. Toward this end, you will desk-check Lines 19 through 24 in the program shown in Figure 13-7. You will use Sue Thorndale, 9500, and Tennessee as the salesperson's name, sales amount, and state, respectively.

The `cout` statement on Line 19 prompts the user to enter the salesperson's name. Before allowing the user to enter the name, the `getline` function on Line 20 checks the `cin` object to determine whether it contains any characters. As you learned in Chapter 4, the `cin` object stores the characters entered at the keyboard. Because the `cin` object is empty at this point in the program, the `getline` function waits for the user to enter a name. In this case, the user types the string "Sue Thorndale" and then presses the Enter key to indicate that he or she is finished entering the name. The computer stores the string and the newline character (`'\n'`) in the `cin` object. It then alerts the `getline` function that the object now contains data. The `getline` function removes both the string and the newline character from the `cin` object. It stores the string in the `name` variable and then consumes the newline character.

Next, the `cout` statement on Line 21 prompts the user to enter the sales. Before allowing the user to enter the sales, the extraction operator in the `cin >> sales;` statement on Line 22 checks the `cin` object to determine whether it contains any characters. The object is empty at this point, so the extraction operator waits for the user to enter a sales amount. In this case, the user types the four numbers 9, 5, 0, and 0 and then presses the Enter key to indicate that he or she is finished entering the sales amount. The computer stores the four numbers and the newline character (`'\n'`) in the `cin` object. It then alerts the extraction operator that the object now contains data. The extraction operator removes the four numbers from the `cin` object and stores them in the `sales` variable. However, it leaves the newline character in the object.

Next, the `cout` statement on Line 23 prompts the user to enter the state name. Before allowing the user to respond to the prompt, the `getline` function on Line 24 checks the `cin` object to determine whether it contains any characters. At this point, the object contains the newline character, which the `getline` function interprets as the end of the state name entry. As a result, the `getline` function stores the empty string in the `state` variable and then consumes the newline character. Processing continues with the bonus calculation statement on Line 27. Obviously, the program is not working correctly because of the newline character that the extraction operator on Line 22 leaves in the `cin` object. You can fix the program by telling the computer to ignore that character.

The `ignore` Function

You can use the C++ **`ignore` function** to first read and then ignore characters stored in the `cin` object. The function ignores the characters by consuming (discarding) them. Figure 13-9 shows the function's syntax and examples of using the function. Like the `getline` function, the `ignore` function is a self-contained statement, as the semicolon at the end of the syntax indicates. The function has two actual arguments, both of which are optional. The *numberOfCharacters* argument is an integer that represents the maximum number of characters the function should consume. If you omit the *numberOfCharacters* argument, the default number of characters to consume is 1. The *delimiterCharacter* argument is a character that, when consumed, stops the `ignore` function from reading and discarding any additional characters. The `ignore` function stops reading and discarding characters either when it consumes the number of characters specified in the *numberOfCharacters* argument or when it consumes the *delimiterCharacter*, whichever occurs first.

HOW TO Use the `ignore` Function

Syntax

cin.ignore([*numberOfCharacters*] [, *delimiterCharacter*]**);** — semicolon

Example 1
```
cin.ignore();
```
reads and consumes one character; also can be written as `cin.ignore(1);`

Example 2
```
cin.ignore(5);
```
reads and consumes five characters

Example 3
```
cin.ignore(100, '\n');
```
reads and consumes characters until either 100 characters are consumed or the newline character is consumed, whichever occurs first

Example 4
```
cin.ignore(25, '#');
```
reads and consumes characters until either 25 characters are consumed or the # character is consumed, whichever occurs first

Figure 13-9 How to use the `ignore` function

As indicated in Example 1 in Figure 13-9, you can use either the statement `cin.ignore();` or the statement `cin.ignore(1);` to read and then discard (consume) one character. The `ignore` function in Example 2 reads and consumes five characters. Example 3's `ignore` function reads and consumes characters until either 100 characters are consumed or the newline character is consumed, whichever occurs first. The `ignore` function in Example 4 reads and discards characters until either 25 characters are consumed or the # character is consumed, whichever occurs first.

Lab 13-5 provides another example of a program that requires the `ignore` function.

In the modified Creative Sales program, you will use the `ignore` function to consume the newline character that is left in the `cin` object after the sales amount is entered. You do this by entering the `ignore` function immediately after the `cin` statement that gets the sales amount, as shown in the partial program in Figure 13-10. The `ignore` function appears on Line 23. Figure 13-11 shows a sample run of the modified program.

Note: Lines 1 through 17 are the same as in Figure 13-7.
```
18      //get input
19      cout << "Salesperson's name: ";
20      getline(cin, name);
21      cout << "Sales: ";
22      cin >> sales;
23      cin.ignore(100, '\n');    ignore function
24      cout << "State name: ";
25      getline(cin, state);
```
Note: The remainder of the program is the same as Lines 25 through 36 in Figure 13-7.

Figure 13-10 Partial modified Creative Sales program showing the `ignore` function

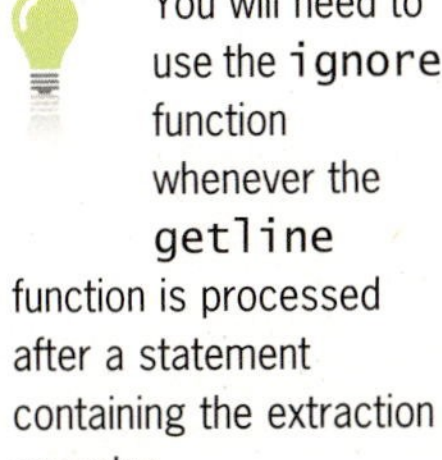

You will need to use the `ignore` function whenever the `getline` function is processed after a statement containing the extraction operator.

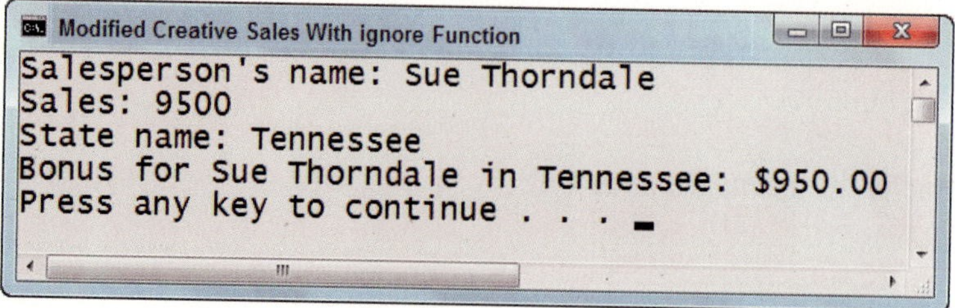

Figure 13-11 Sample run of the modified Creative Sales program with the `ignore` function

You may be wondering why the modified program in Figure 13-10 uses the `cin.ignore(100, '\n');` statement rather than the simpler `cin.ignore();` statement. Although both statements will consume the newline character left in the `cin` object after the sales amount is entered, there is an advantage to using the `cin.ignore(100, '\n');` statement in the program. To illustrate, assume that when entering the sales amount, the user types the four numbers 9, 5, 0, and 0, followed inadvertently by the letter L, and then presses the Enter key. The computer stores the four numbers, along with the letter L and the newline character, in the `cin` object. It then alerts the extraction operator in the `cin >> sales;` statement that the object now contains data. The extraction operator removes the four numbers from the `cin` object and stores them in the `sales` variable. However, it leaves both the letter L (which cannot be stored in an `int` variable) and the newline character in the object; at this point, the `cin` object contains two characters. If the program used the `cin.ignore();` statement, the `ignore` function would consume only the letter L. The newline character would still be in the `cin` object when the `getline(cin, state);` statement is processed. As you learned earlier, the `getline` function will interpret the newline character as the end of the state name entry. The `cin.ignore(100, '\n');` statement, on the other hand, will consume both the letter L and the newline character. This is because the statement tells the computer to read and discard characters until either 100 characters are consumed or the newline character is consumed, whichever occurs first. As a result, the `getline` function will not find any characters in the `cin` object and will wait for the user to enter the state name.

The answers to Mini-Quiz questions are located in Appendix A.

Mini-Quiz 13-1

1. Which of the following declares a named constant and initializes it to the name of the first U.S. president?

   a. `const String FIRST_PRES = "George Washington";`
   b. `const string FIRST_PRES = 'George Washington';`
   c. `const string FIRST_PRES = "George Washington";`
   d. `constant string FIRST_PRES = "George Washington";`

2. Which of the following declares a `string` variable named `country` and initializes it to the empty string?

   a. `String country = "";`
   b. `string country = "";`
   c. `string country = ' ';`
   d. `String country = '';`

3. Which of the following gets a string of characters from the `cin` object and stores them in a `string` variable named `streetAddress`?

   a. `getline(cin, streetAddress, '\n');`

   b. `getline(streetAddress, cin);`

   c. `cin.getline(streetAddress);`

   d. `getline.cin(streetAddress);`

4. Which of the following will stop reading and discarding characters either when 10 characters are consumed or when the user presses the Enter key, whichever occurs first?

   a. `cin.ignore('\n', 10);`

   b. `cin.ignore(10);`

   c. `cin.ignore(10, '\n');`

   d. both b and c

The ZIP Code Program

Many times, a program will need to manipulate (process) string data in some way. For example, it may need to look at the first character in an inventory part number to determine the part's location in the warehouse. Or, it may need to search an address to determine the street name. Or, as in the ZIP code program created in this section, it may need to determine the number of characters in a ZIP code.

The problem specification and IPO chart for the ZIP code program are shown in Figure 13-12. As the problem specification states, the program should get a ZIP code from the user and then verify that the user's entry contains exactly five characters. If the ZIP code contains the required five characters, the program should display the message "Valid length"; otherwise, it should display the message "Invalid length". The program will store the ZIP code in a `string` variable and store the messages in two `string` named constants.

Problem specification

Create a program that allows the user to enter a ZIP code. The program should verify that the user entered exactly five characters and then display either the "Valid length" message or the "Invalid length" message. The ZIP code will not be used in a calculation, so the program should store its value in a `string` variable. The program should store the two messages in two `string` named constants.

Input	Processing	Output
ZIP code	Processing items: none	"Valid length" message or "Invalid length" message

```
Algorithm:
1. enter the ZIP code
2. repeat while (the ZIP code is not "-1")
     if (the ZIP code has exactly 5 characters)
          display the "Valid length" message
     else
          display the "Invalid length" message
     end if
     enter the ZIP code
   end repeat
```

Figure 13-12 Problem specification and IPO chart for the ZIP code program *(continues)*

(continued)

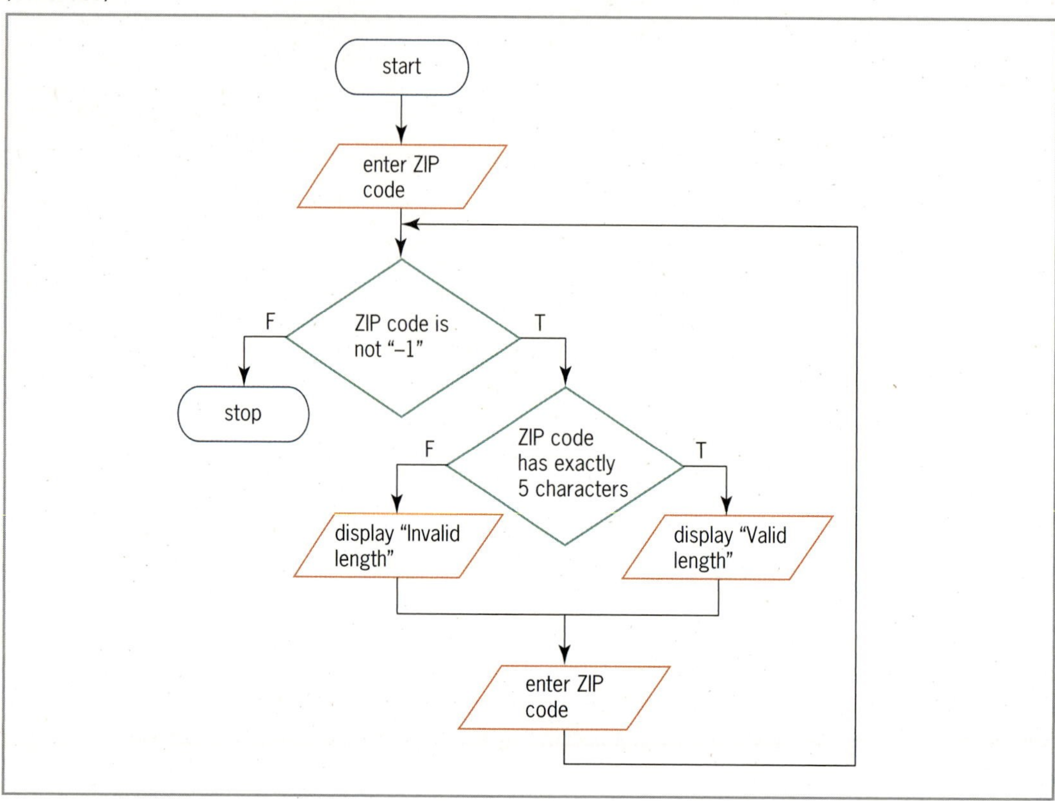

Figure 13-12 Problem specification and IPO chart for the ZIP code program

Determining the Number of Characters Contained in a `string` Variable

You can use the `string` class's **`length` function** to determine the number of characters contained in a `string` variable. The function's syntax is shown in Figure 13-13 along with examples of using the function. In the syntax, *string* is the name of the `string` variable whose length you want to determine. The `length` function returns the number of characters contained in the variable. The `cout` statement in Example 1 uses the `length` function to display the number of characters (15) contained in the `name` variable. The `if` clause in Example 2 uses the `length` function to compare the number of characters stored in the `zipCode` variable with the number 5. The `while` clause in Example 3 uses the `length` function to repeat the loop instructions as long as the `partNum` variable does not contain exactly six characters.

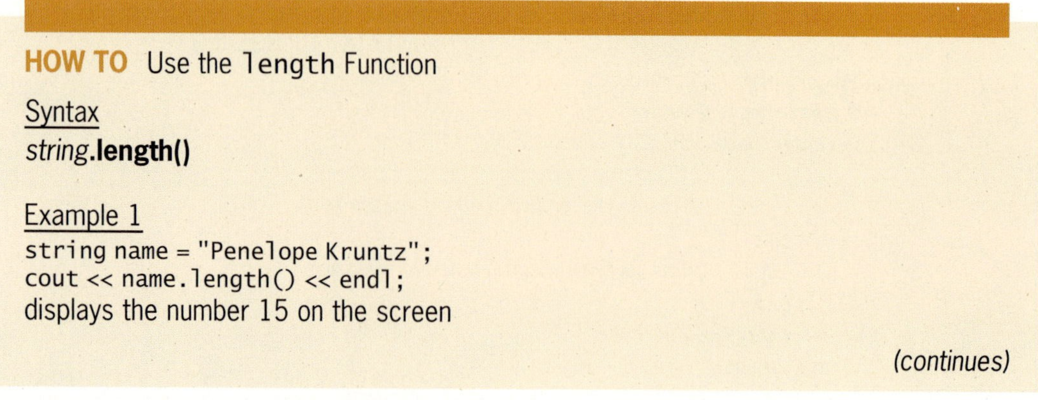

HOW TO Use the `length` Function

Syntax
string.**length()**

Example 1
```
string name = "Penelope Kruntz";
cout << name.length() << endl;
```
displays the number 15 on the screen

(continues)

Figure 13-13 How to use the `length` Function

(continued)

Example 2

```
const string VALID_MSG = "Valid length";
const string INVALID_MSG = "Invalid length";
string zipCode = "";
cout << "Five-character ZIP code: ";
cin >> zipCode;
if (zipCode.length() == 5)
        cout << VALID_MSG << endl;
else
        cout << INVALID_MSG << endl;
//end if
```

compares the number of characters stored in the `zipCode` variable with the number 5 and then displays an appropriate message

Example 3

```
string partNum = "";
cout << "Six-character part number: ";
getline(cin, partNum);
while (partNum.length() != 6)
{
        cout << "Six-character part number: ";
        getline(cin, partNum);
}       //end while
```

continues getting a part number until the user enters exactly six characters

Figure 13-13 How to use the `length` function

Figure 13-14 shows the ZIP code program. The `length` function appears in the `if` clause on Line 21 and is shaded in the figure. Figure 13-15 shows a sample run of the program.

```
 1 //ZIP Code.cpp
 2 //displays a message indicating whether a ZIP
 3 //code's length is valid or invalid
 4 //Created/revised by <your name> on <current date>
 5
 6 #include <iostream>
 7 #include <string>
 8 using namespace std;
 9
10 int main()
11 {
12     const string VALID_MSG   = "Valid length";
13     const string INVALID_MSG = "Invalid length";
14     string zipCode = "";
15
16     cout << "Five-character ZIP code (-1 to end): ";
17     cin >> zipCode;
18
```

Figure 13-14 ZIP code program *(continues)*

(continued)

```
    while (zipCode != "-1")
    {
        if (zipCode.length() == 5)
            cout << VALID_MSG << endl << endl;
        else
            cout << INVALID_MSG << endl << endl;
        //end if

        cout << "Five-character ZIP code (-1 to end): ";
        cin >> zipCode;
    }   //end while

    //system("pause");
    return 0;
}   //end of main function
```

your C++ development tool may require this statement

Figure 13-14 ZIP code program

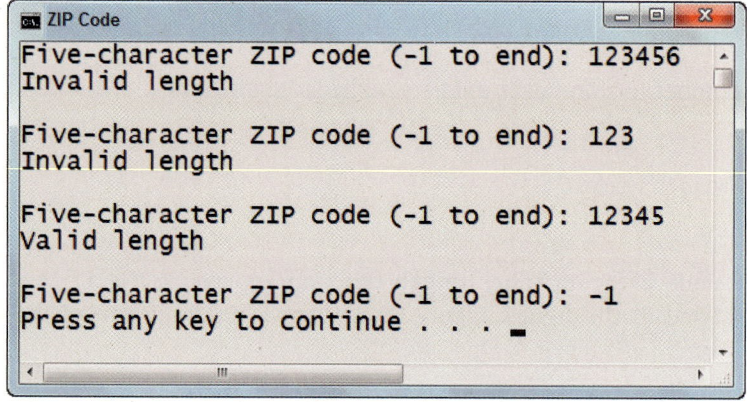

Figure 13-15 Sample run of the ZIP code program

Modifying the ZIP Code Program

Now, you will modify the ZIP code program from Figure 13-14. The modified program will verify that each character entered by the user is a number. Figure 13-16 shows the modified problem specification and IPO charts for the `main` and `verifyNumeric` functions. The `main` function passes the ZIP code to the `verifyNumeric` function, whose task is to determine whether the ZIP code contains only numbers.

Problem specification
Create a program that allows the user to enter a ZIP code. The program should verify that the user entered exactly five characters. If the user entered the required number of characters, the program should display the message "Valid length" and then verify that each of the five characters is a number. If all five characters are numbers, the program should display the message "All numbers"; otherwise, it should display the message "Not all numbers". However, if the user did not enter exactly five characters, the program should display the message "Invalid length". The ZIP code will not be used in a calculation, so the program should store its value in a `string` variable. The program should store the four messages in four `string` named constants.

`main` function

Input	Processing	Output
ZIP code	Processing items: isAllNumbers variable (a char variable to store the value returned by the verifyNumeric function)	"Valid length" message or "Invalid length" message "All numbers" message or "Not all numbers" message

Algorithm:
1. enter the ZIP code
2. repeat while (the ZIP code is not "-1")
    - if (the ZIP code has exactly 5 characters)
        - display the "Valid length" message
        - call the verifyNumeric function to determine whether the ZIP code contains only numbers; pass the ZIP code; store the function's return value in the isAllNumbers variable
        - if (the isAllNumbers variable contains 'Y', it means that the ZIP code contains only numbers)
            - display the "All numbers" message
        - else
            - display the "Not all numbers" message
        - end if
    - else
        - display the "Invalid length" message
    - end if
    - enter the ZIP code

   end repeat

Figure 13-16 Problem specification and IPO chart for the modified ZIP code program *(continues)*

(continued)

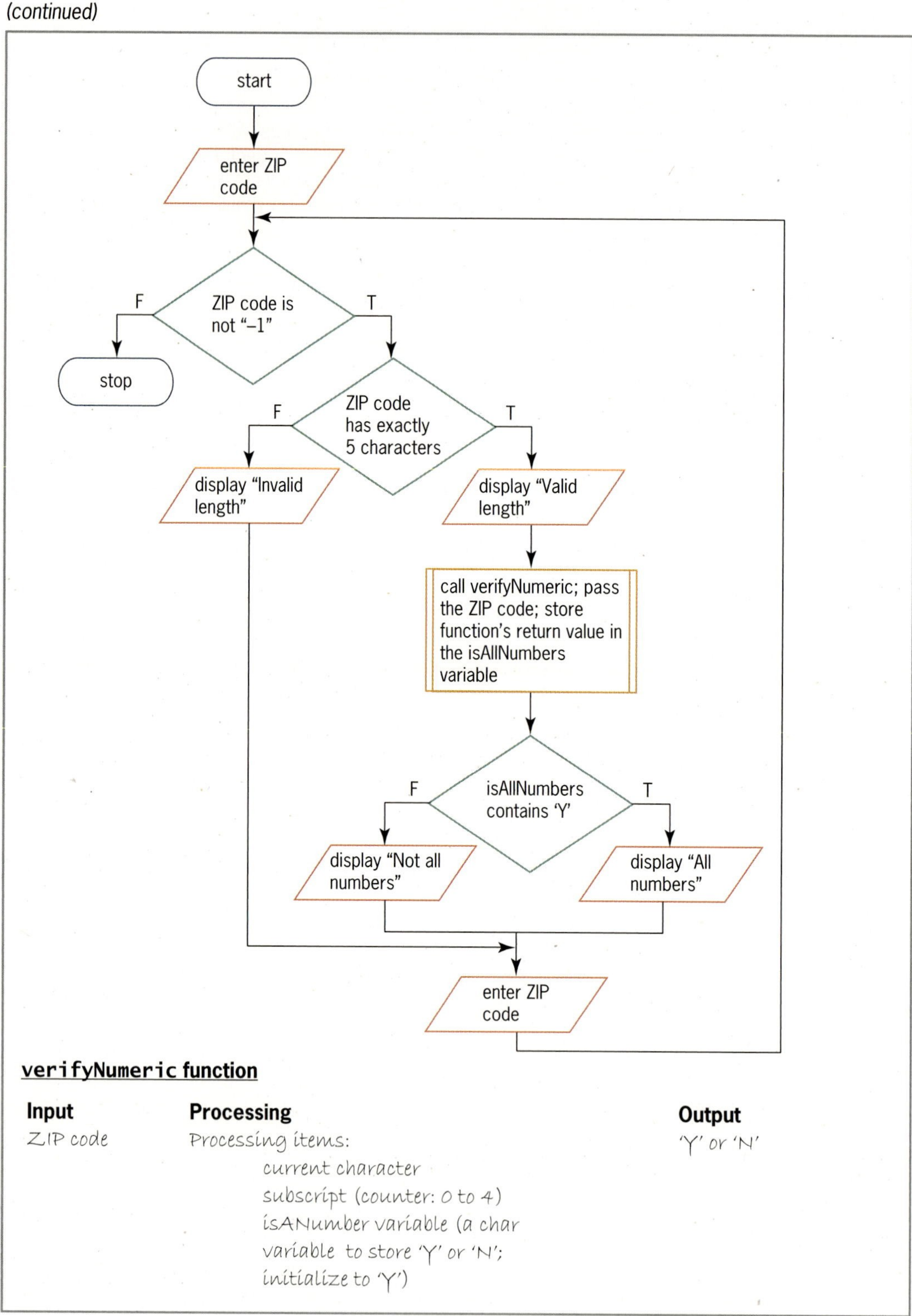

`verifyNumeric` function

Input	**Processing**	**Output**
ZIP code	Processing items: current character subscript (counter: 0 to 4) isANumber variable (a char variable to store 'Y' or 'N'; initialize to 'Y')	'Y' or 'N'

Figure 13-16 Problem specification and IPO chart for the modified ZIP code program *(continues)*

(continued)

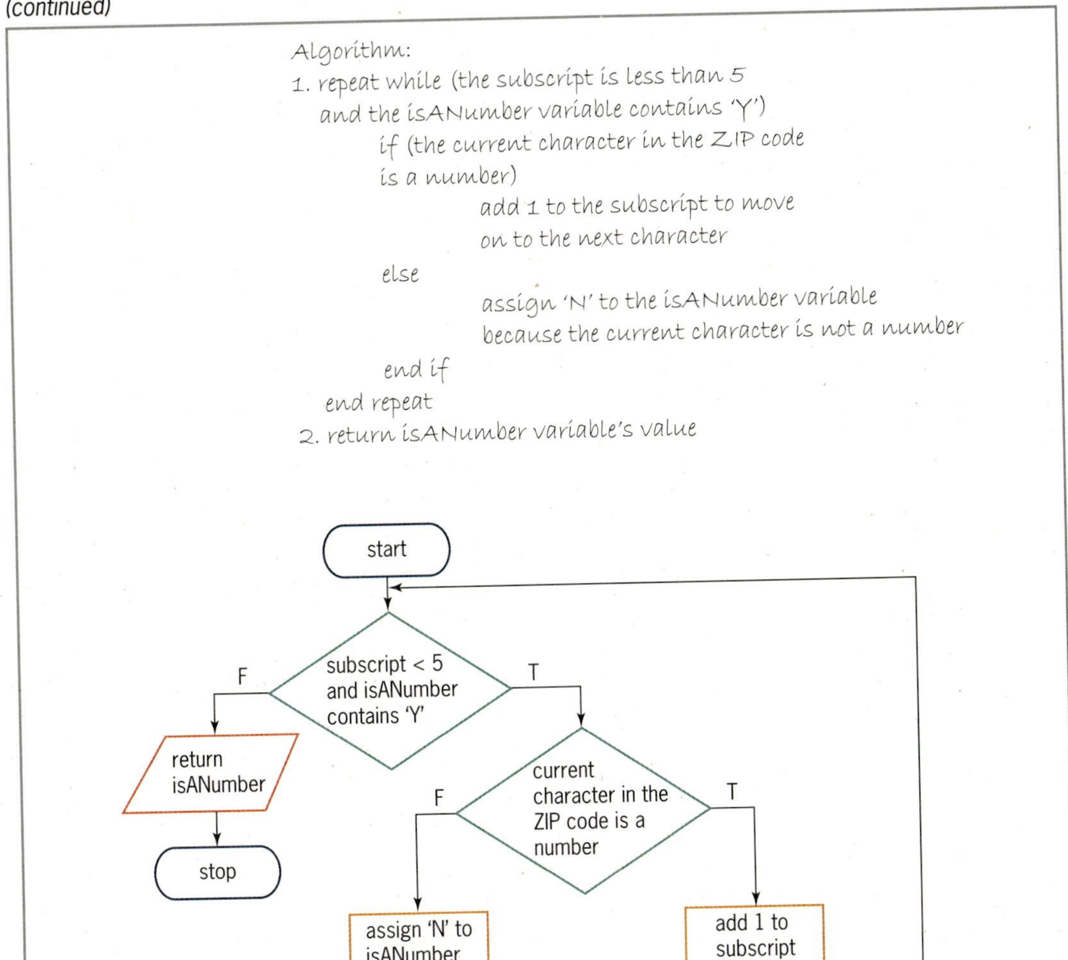

Figure 13-16 Problem specification and IPO chart for the modified ZIP code program

Before you can code the modified ZIP code program, you need to learn how to access the characters contained in a `string` variable.

Accessing the Characters Contained in a `string` Variable

You can access each character stored in a `string` variable using a loop along with the `string` class's `length` and `substr` (substring) functions. In the `substr` function's syntax, which is shown in Figure 13-17, *string* is the name of the `string` variable that contains the characters you want to access. The **`substr` function** allows you to access any number of characters contained in the `string` variable; it then returns those characters. As its syntax indicates, the `substr` function has two actual arguments: *subscript* and *count*. The arguments can be numeric literal constants or the names of numeric variables.

The required *subscript* argument in the `substr` function's syntax represents the subscript of the first character you want to access in the *string*. You learned about subscripts in Chapter 11, which covered one-dimensional arrays. A string is equivalent to a one-dimensional array of characters, with each character having a unique subscript that indicates its position in the string. The first character in a string has a subscript of 0, the second has a subscript of 1, and so on.

The optional *count* argument in the `substr` function's syntax indicates the number of characters you want to access. To have the `substr` function access the first four characters in a string, you use 0 as the *subscript* argument and 4 as the *count* argument. Similarly, to have the function access the tenth through the twelfth characters, you use 9 as the *subscript* argument and 3 as the *count* argument. The `substr` function returns a string that contains *count* number of characters, beginning with the character whose subscript is specified in the *subscript* argument. If you omit the *count* argument, the `substr` function returns all of the characters from the *subscript* position through the end of the *string*.

HOW TO Use the `substr` Function

Syntax

string.**substr(***subscript*[, *count*]**)**

Example 1

```
string name = "Jack Blackfeather";
string first = "";
string last = "";
first = name.substr(0, 4);
last = name.substr(5);
```

assigns "Jack" to the `first` variable and "Blackfeather" to the `last` variable

Example 2

```
string sales = "";
cout << "Enter the sales: ";
getline(cin, sales);
if (sales.substr(0, 1) == "$")
    sales = sales.substr(1);
//end if
```

if the string stored in the `sales` variable begins with the dollar sign, the code assigns the variable's contents, excluding the dollar sign, to the variable

Example 3

```
string rate = "";
cout << "Enter the rate: ";
getline(cin, rate);
if (rate.substr(rate.length() - 1, 1) == "%")
    rate = rate.substr(0, rate.length() - 1);
//end if
```

if the string stored in the `rate` variable ends with the percent sign, the code assigns the variable's contents, excluding the percent sign, to the variable

Figure 13-17 How to use the `substr` function

Study the examples shown in Figure 13-17. The `first = name.substr(0, 4);` statement in Example 1 assigns the first four characters stored in the `name` variable ("Jack") to the `first` variable. The `last = name.substr(5);` statement assigns all of the characters contained in the `name` variable, beginning with the character whose subscript is 5, to the `last` variable. The character whose subscript is 5 is the letter B; therefore, the statement assigns "Blackfeather" to the `last` variable.

The condition in the `if` clause in Example 2 uses the `substr` function to compare the first character contained in the `sales` variable with the dollar sign. If the first character is the dollar sign, the `sales = sales.substr(1);` statement assigns all of the characters from the `sales` variable, beginning with the character whose subscript is 1, to the `sales` variable. In other words, the statement assigns all of the characters *except* the dollar sign to the variable.

The condition in the `if` clause in Example 3 uses the `substr` and `length` functions to determine whether the string stored in the `rate` variable ends with the percent sign. If it does, the `rate = rate.substr(0, rate.length() - 1);` statement assigns the `rate` variable's contents, excluding the last character (which is the percent sign), to the `rate` variable.

Figure 13-18 shows the IPO chart information and C++ code for the modified ZIP code program. The `verifyNumeric` function contains a loop that determines whether each character in the ZIP code received from the `main` function is a number. The loop's `while` clause tells the computer to repeat the loop instructions as long as both of the following sub-conditions evaluate to true. First, the contents of the `x` variable, which keeps track of the subscripts in the `zips` variable, must be less than 5 (the number of characters in the ZIP code). Second, the `isANumber` variable, which keeps track of whether a non-numeric character appears in the `zips` variable, must contain the character 'Y'. If both sub-conditions evaluate to true, the first statement in the loop uses the `substr` function and `x` variable to access the current character in the `zips` variable. Next, the condition in the `if` statement determines whether the current character is greater than or equal to "0" and less than or equal to "9". If the condition evaluates to true, it means that the character is a number. In that case, the statement in the `if` statement's true path adds the number 1 to the subscript, which is stored in the `x` variable; doing this allows the loop to look at the next character in the `zips` variable. Otherwise, the statement in its false path assigns the character 'N' to the `isANumber` variable.

Recall that a string is equivalent to a one-dimensional array of characters.

When the `while` loop in the `verifyNumeric` function ends, the `return isANumber;` statement returns (to the `main` function) a character that indicates whether the ZIP code either contains only numbers ('Y') or contains at least one non-numeric character ('N'). As Figure 13-18 shows, the returned character is assigned to the `isAllNumbers` variable. The `if` statement in the `main` function is processed next. The statement compares the value stored in the `isAllNumbers` variable with the character 'Y'. If the variable contains the character 'Y', the `if` statement's true path displays the "All numbers" message; otherwise, its false path displays the "Not all numbers" message.

`main` function

IPO chart information	**C++ instructions**
Input	
ZIP code	`string zipCode = "";`
Processing	
isAllNumbers variable (a char variable to store the value returned by the verifyNumeric function)	`char isAllNumbers = ' ';`
Output	
"Valid length" message or	`const string VALID_MSG = "Valid length";`
"Invalid length" message	`const string INVALID_MSG = "Invalid length";`
"All numbers" message or	`const string ALL_NUMBERS = "All numbers";`
"Not all numbers" message	`const string NOT_ALL_NUMBERS = "Not all numbers";`
Algorithm	
1. enter the ZIP code	`cout << "Five-character ZIP code (-1 to end): ";` `cin >> zipCode;`

Figure 13-18 IPO chart information and C++ instructions for the modified ZIP code problem *(continues)*

(continued)

IPO chart information	C++ instructions
2. repeat while (the ZIP code is not "-1")	`while (zipCode != "-1")` `{`
if (the ZIP code has exactly 5 characters)	`if (zipCode.length() == 5)` `{`
display the "Valid length" message	`cout << VALID_MSG << endl;`
call the verifyNumeric function to determine whether the ZIP code contains only numbers; pass the ZIP code; store the function's return value in the isAllNumbers variable	`isAllNumbers =` `verifyNumeric(zipCode);`
if (the isAllNumbers variable contains 'Y', it means that the ZIP code contains only numbers)	`if (isAllNumbers == 'Y')`
display the "All numbers" message	`cout << ALL_NUMBERS` `<< endl << endl;`
else	`else`
display the "Not all numbers" message	`cout << NOT_ALL_NUMBERS` `<< endl << endl;`
end if	`//end if` `}`
else	`else`
display the "Invalid length" message	`cout << INVALID_MSG` `<< endl << endl;`
end if	`//end if`

enter the ZIP code	`cout << "Five-character ZIP`
	`code (-1 to end): ";`
	`cin >> zipCode;`

end repeat	`} //end while`

verifyNumeric function

Input	
ZIP code (formal parameter)	`string zips`
Processing	

current character
subscript (counter: 0 to 4)
isANumber variable (a char variable to store 'Y' or 'N'; initialize to 'Y')
	`string currentChar = "";`
	`int x = 0;`
	`char isANumber = 'Y';`

Output	
'Y' or 'N'	
Algorithm	

1. repeat while (the subscript is less than 5 and the isANumber variable contains 'Y')	`while (x < 5 &&`
	`isANumber == 'Y')`
	`{`

Figure 13-18 IPO chart information and C++ instructions for the modified ZIP code problem *(continues)*

(continued)

if (the current character in the ZIP code is a number)	`currentChar =`
	`zips.substr(x, 1);`
	`if (currentChar >= "0"`
	`&& currentChar <= "9")`

add 1 to the subscript to move on to the next character	`x += 1;`
else	`else`
assign 'N' to the isANumber variable because the current character is not a number	`isANumber = 'N';`
end if	`//end if`
end repeat	`} //end while`
2. return isANumber variable's value	`return isANumber;`

Figure 13-18 IPO chart information and C++ instructions for the modified ZIP code problem

The modified ZIP code program is shown in Figure 13-19, with the modifications made to the original program (shown earlier in Figure 13-14) shaded. Figure 13-20 shows a sample run of the modified program.

```
//Modified ZIP Code.cpp
//displays a message indicating whether a ZIP
//code's length is valid or invalid
//also displays a message indicating whether
//each character in the ZIP code is a number
//Created/revised by <your name> on <current date>

#include <iostream>
#include <string>
using namespace std;

//function prototype
char verifyNumeric(string);

int main()
{
    const string VALID_MSG        = "Valid length";
    const string INVALID_MSG      = "Invalid length";
    const string ALL_NUMBERS      = "All numbers";
    const string NOT_ALL_NUMBERS = "Not all numbers";

    string zipCode = "";
    char isAllNumbers = ' ';

    cout << "Five-character ZIP code (-1 to end): ";
    cin >> zipCode;

    while (zipCode != "-1")
    {
        if (zipCode.length() == 5)
        {
            cout << VALID_MSG << endl;
            isAllNumbers = verifyNumeric(zipCode);

```

Figure 13-19 Modified ZIP code program *(continues)*

(continued)

```
35              if (isAllNumbers == 'Y')
36                  cout << ALL_NUMBERS << endl << endl;
37              else
38                  cout << NOT_ALL_NUMBERS << endl << endl;
39              //end if
40
41          }
42          else
43              cout << INVALID_MSG << endl << endl;
44          //end if
45
46          cout << "Five-character ZIP code (-1 to end): ";
47          cin >> zipCode;
48      }   //end while
49
50      //system("pause");
51      return 0;
52  }   //end of main function
53
54  //*****function definitions*****
55  char verifyNumeric(string zips)
56  {
57      //determine whether each character
58      //is a number
59      string currentChar = "";
60      int x              = 0;     //character subscript
61      char isANumber     = 'Y';   //assume all numbers
62
63      while (x < 5 && isANumber == 'Y')
64      {
65          currentChar = zips.substr(x, 1);
66          if (currentChar >= "0"
67            && currentChar <= "9")
68              //the character is a number, so
69              //move on to the next character
70              x += 1;
71          else
72              //the character is not a number
73              isANumber = 'N';
74          //end if
75      }   //end while
76      return isANumber;
77  }   //end of verifyNumeric function
```

your C++ development tool may require this statement

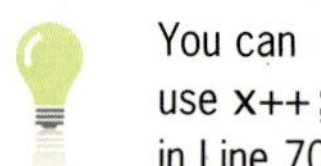

You can use x++; in Line 70.

Figure 13-19 Modified ZIP code program

```
Modified ZIP Code
Five-character ZIP code (-1 to end): 123
Invalid length

Five-character ZIP code (-1 to end): 12345
Valid length
All numbers

Five-character ZIP code (-1 to end): 123x5
Valid length
Not all numbers

Five-character ZIP code (-1 to end): -1
Press any key to continue . . .
```

Figure 13-20 Sample run of the modified ZIP code program

Mini-Quiz 13-2

The answers to Mini-Quiz questions are located in Appendix A.

1. Which of the following `while` clauses will process the loop instructions as long as the `employee` variable contains more than 20 characters?
   a. `while (employee.length() > 20)`
   b. `while (employee.length() > "20");`
   c. `while (employee.length() > '20');`
   d. `while (employee.length() > 20);`
2. Write a C++ `if` clause that determines whether a `string` variable named `code` contains seven characters.
3. The `cityState` variable contains the string "Los Angeles, CA". Which of the following assigns the state ID ("CA") to a `string` variable named `state`?
   a. `state = cityState.substr(13);`
   b. `state = cityState.substr(13, 2);`
   c. `state = cityState.substr(14, 2);`
   d. both a and b
4. Write a `cout` statement that displays the last character contained in a `string` variable named `college`.

The Rearranged Name Program

Figure 13-21 shows the problem specification and IPO chart for the rearranged name program. The program should allow the user to enter a person's first and last names, separated by a space. The program should display the person's last name followed by a comma, a space, and the person's first name. For example, if the user enters "Henry Smith", the program should display "Smith, Henry". As the algorithm indicates, you can accomplish this task by searching for the space character that separates the first name from the last name. The characters to the left of the space character represent the first name. The characters to the right of the space character represent the last name. You will learn how to search the contents of a `string` variable in the next section.

Problem specification
Create a program that allows the user to enter a person's first and last names, separated by a space. The program should display the person's last name followed by a comma, a space, and the person's first name. For example, if the user enters "Henry Smith", the program should display "Smith, Henry".

Input
name (first name followed by a space and the last name)

Processing
Processing items:
space's location

Algorithm:
1. enter the name
2. search the name, looking for the space's location
3. assign the characters to the left of the space's location as the first name
4. assign the characters to the right of the space's location as the last name
5. display the rearranged name

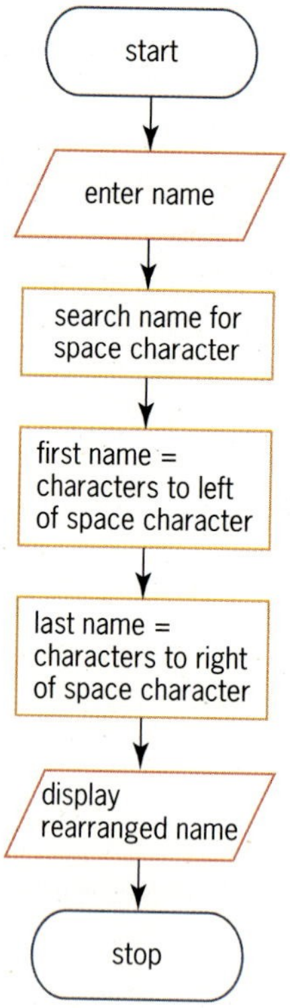

start
enter name
search name for space character
first name = characters to left of space character
last name = characters to right of space character
display rearranged name
stop

Output
rearranged name (last name followed by a comma, a space, and the first name)

Figure 13-21 Problem specification and IPO chart for the rearranged name program

Searching the Contents of a `string` Variable

You can use the `string` class's **`find` function** to search the contents of a `string` variable to determine whether it contains a specific sequence of characters. For example, you can use the function to determine whether a phone number contains a certain area code. Or, you can use the function to determine whether a specific street name appears in an address. You also can use it to determine the location of the space character that separates a first name from a last name.

Figure 13-22 shows the `find` function's syntax. In the syntax, *string* is the name of the `string` variable whose contents you want to search, and *searchString* is the string for which you are searching. The *searchString* argument can be a `string` literal constant or the name of either a `string` variable or a `string` named constant. The *subscript* argument specifies the starting position for the search. In other words, it specifies the subscript of the character at which the search should begin. The `find` function searches for the *searchString* in the *string*, starting with the character whose subscript is specified in the *subscript* argument. The function performs a case-sensitive search, which means that uppercase letters are not equivalent to their lowercase counterparts. When the *searchString* is contained within the *string*, the `find` function returns an integer that indicates the beginning position (subscript) of the *searchString* within the *string*. The function returns the number –1 when the *searchString* is not contained within the *string*.

HOW TO Use the `find` Function

Syntax

string.**find(***searchString*, *subscript***)**

Example 1

```
int location = 0;
string phone = "(312) 999-9999";
location = phone.find("(312)", 0);
```

searches the `phone` variable, starting with the first character (subscript 0), to determine the location of the string "(312)"; stores the result (0) in the `location` variable

Example 2

```
int spaceLocation = 0;
string name = "Carol Cho";
spaceLocation = name.find(" ", 1);
```

searches the `name` variable, starting with the second character (subscript 1), to determine the location of the space character; stores the result (5) in the `spaceLocation` variable

Example 3

```
int location = 0;
string address = "210 Elm Street, Elmwood, NJ";
location = address.find("Elm ", 2);
```

searches the `address` variable, starting with the third character (subscript 2), to determine the location of the string "Elm "; stores the result (4) in the `location` variable

(continues)

Figure 13-22 How to use the `find` Function

Notice the space after the letter m in the `find` function in Examples 3, 4, and 5.

(continued)

Example 4

```
int location = 0;
string address = "210 Elm Street, Elmwood, NJ";
location = address.find("elm ", 0);
```

searches the `address` variable, starting with the first character (subscript 0), to determine the location of the string "elm "; stores the result (–1) in the `location` variable

Example 5

```
int location = 0;
string address = "210 Elm Street, Elmwood, NJ";
location = address.find("Elm ", 9);
```

searches the `address` variable, starting with the tenth character (subscript 9), to determine the location of the string "Elm "; stores the result (–1) in the `location` variable

Figure 13-22 How to use the `find` function

Study the examples shown in Figure 13-22. The `location = phone.find("(312)", 0);` statement in Example 1 searches for the *searchString* "(312)" in the `phone` variable, beginning with the first character (whose subscript is 0) in the variable. It then assigns the result—in this case, the number 0—to the `location` variable. The number 0 is assigned because the *searchString* "(312)" begins with the character whose subscript is 0 in the `phone` variable.

The `spaceLocation = name.find(" ", 1);` statement in Example 2 searches for the space character in the `name` variable, starting with the second character (whose subscript is 1). It then assigns the number 5 to the `spaceLocation` variable; this is because the space character in the `name` variable has a subscript of 5.

The `location = address.find("Elm ", 2);` statement in Example 3 searches the third through the last characters in the `address` variable, looking for the string "Elm " (notice the space after the letter m). The statement assigns the number 4 to the `location` variable because the string "Elm " begins with the character whose subscript is 4 in the `address` variable.

The `location = address.find("elm ", 0);` statement in Example 4 searches for the string "elm " (notice the space after the letter m) in the `address` variable, starting with the first character. The statement assigns the number –1 to the `location` variable because the `address` variable does not contain the string "elm ".

The `location = address.find("Elm ", 9);` statement in Example 5 searches for the string "Elm " (notice the space after the letter m) in the tenth through the last characters in the `address` variable. The statement assigns the number –1 to the `location` variable because the string "Elm " does not appear in the tenth through the last characters in the `address` variable. In other words, it doesn't appear in the characters "treet, Elmwood, NJ".

Figure 13-23 shows the code for the rearranged name program. The `find` function appears on Line 24 and is shaded in the figure. After the `find` function determines the location of the space, the program uses the location in the two `substr` functions to separate the first name from the last name. The `substr` functions appear on Lines 25 and 26 and are shaded in the figure. Figure 13-24 shows a sample run of the program.

```
//Rearranged Name.cpp
//displays the last name followed by a comma,
//a space, and the first name
//Created/revised by <your name> on <current date>

#include <iostream>
#include <string>
using namespace std;

int main()
{
    //declare variables
    string firstLast   = "";
    string first       = "";
    string last        = "";
    int spaceLocation = 0;

    //get first and last name
    cout << "Name (first and last, ";
    cout << "separated by a space): ";
    getline(cin, firstLast);
    //locate space, then pull out first and
    //last names
    spaceLocation = firstLast.find(" ", 0);
    first = firstLast.substr(0, spaceLocation);
    last = firstLast.substr(spaceLocation + 1);

    //display rearranged name
    cout << last << ", " << first << endl;

    //system("pause");
    return 0;
}   //end of main function
```

your C++ development tool may require this statement

Figure 13-23 Rearranged name program

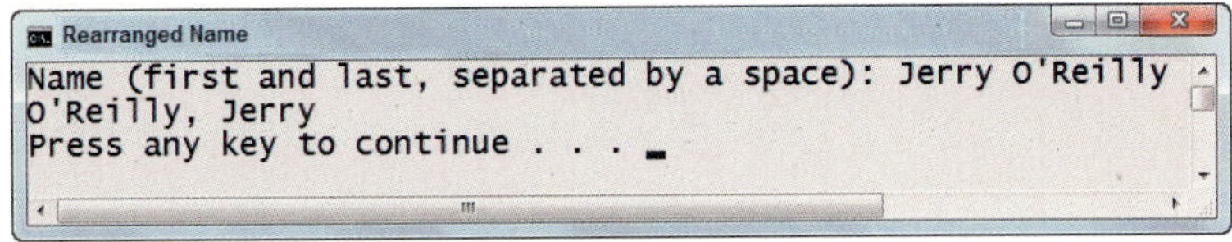

Figure 13-24 Sample run of the rearranged name program

The Annual Income Program

Figure 13-25 shows the problem specification and IPO chart for the annual income program. The program should allow the user to enter a company's annual income. It then should remove any dollar signs, commas, and spaces from the user's entry before displaying the annual income on the screen. You will learn how to remove characters from a `string` variable in the next section.

Problem specification
Create a program that allows the user to enter a company's annual income. The program should remove any dollar signs, commas, and spaces from the annual income before displaying it on the screen.

Input	Processing	Output
annual income	Processing items: subscript (counter: 0 to one less than the number of characters in the annual income)	annual income with no commas or spaces

Algorithm:

```
1. enter the annual income
2. repeat while (the annual income is not "-1")
       repeat while (the subscript is less than
       the number of characters in the annual
       income)
             if (the current character is a
             dollar sign, a comma, or a space)
                   remove the current character
                   from the annual income
             else
                   add 1 to the subscript to move
                   on to the next character in
                   the annual income
             end if

       end repeat
       display the annual income with no
       dollar signs, commas, or spaces

       enter the annual income
       reset the subscript to 0
   end repeat
```

Figure 13-25 Problem specification and IPO chart for the annual income program *(continues)*

(continued)

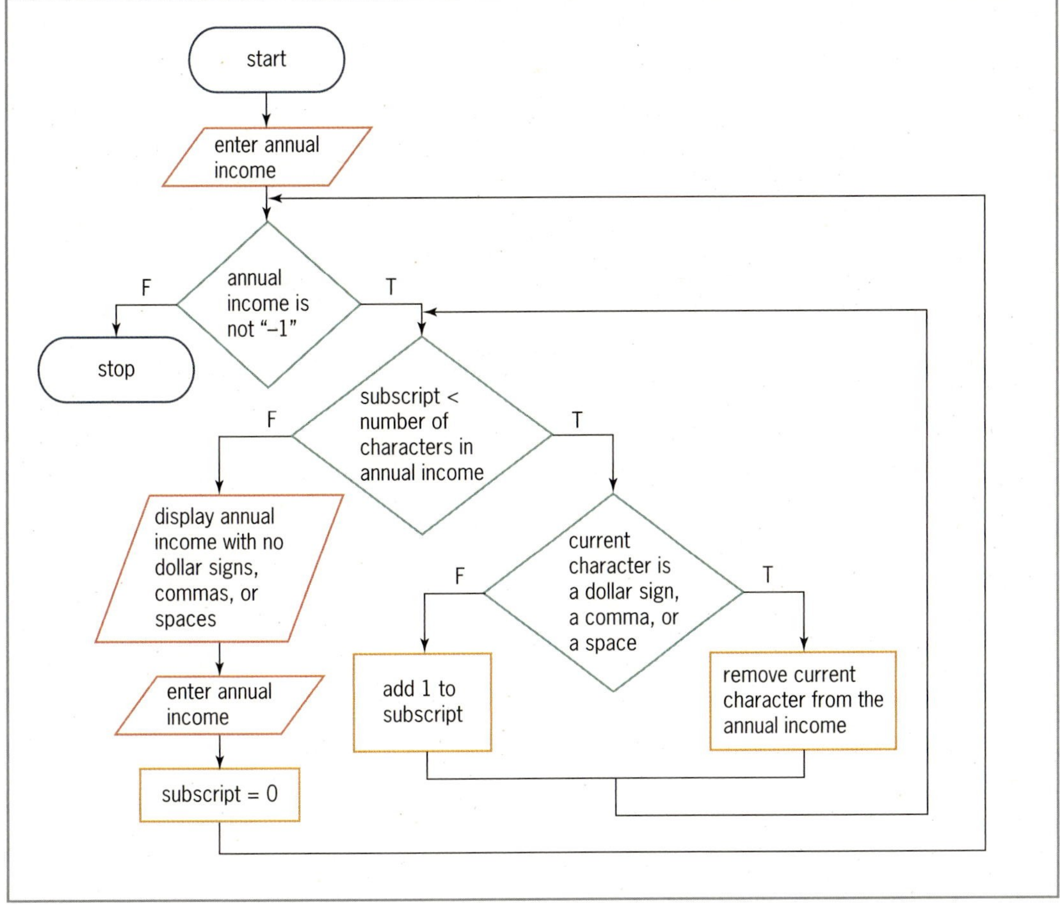

Figure 13-25 Problem specification and IPO chart for the annual income program

Removing Characters from a `string` Variable

At times, you may need to remove one or more characters from an item of data entered by the user, such as a dollar sign from the beginning of a sales amount or a percent sign from the end of a tax rate. In C++, you can use the `string` class's **erase function** to remove one or more characters located anywhere in a `string` variable. Figure 13-26 shows the function's syntax. In the syntax, *string* is the name of a `string` variable, and the *subscript* argument is the subscript of the first character you want to remove (erase) from the variable's contents. Recall that the first character in a string has a subscript of 0. The optional *count* argument is an integer that specifies the number of characters you want removed. If you omit the *count* argument, the `erase` function removes all characters from the *subscript* position through the end of the string.

HOW TO Use the `erase` Function

Syntax

string.**erase(***subscript* [, *count*]**);**

Example 1
```
string place = "Salem, Oregon";
place.erase(0, 7);
```
removes the first seven characters from the `place` variable, changing the variable's contents to "Oregon"

Example 2
```
string place = "Salem, Oregon";
place.erase(5);
```
removes all of the characters from the `place` variable, beginning with the character whose subscript is 5, changing the variable's contents to "Salem"

Example 3
```
string name = "John";
name.erase(2, 1);
```
removes the third character from the `name` variable, changing the variable's contents to "Jon"

Example 4
```
int x = 0;
string sales = "";
cout << "Sales: ";
getline(cin, sales);
while (x < sales.length())
    if (sales.substr(x, 1) == "$"
       || sales.substr(x, 1) == ",")
           sales.erase(x, 1);
    else
           x += 1;
    //end if
//end while
```
removes (erases) any dollar signs and commas from the `sales` variable

Figure 13-26 How to use the `erase` function

Study the examples shown in Figure 13-26. The `erase` function in Example 1 removes the first seven characters from the string stored in the `place` variable. The first seven characters are the letters S, a, l, e, and m and the comma and space characters. After the function is processed, the `place` variable contains the string "Oregon".

The `erase` function in Example 2 removes all of the characters from the `place` variable, beginning with the character whose subscript is 5. In this case, the function removes the ", Oregon" portion of the string from the variable. After the function is processed, the `place` variable contains the string "Salem".

The `erase` function in Example 3 removes one character from the string stored in the `name` variable, beginning with the character whose subscript is 2. In other words, it removes the letter h. After the function is processed, the `name` variable contains the string "Jon".

The code in Example 4 contains a loop that looks at each character in the `sales` variable, one at a time. The condition in the `if` statement within the loop compares the current character to both a dollar sign and a comma. If the current character is either of those characters, the `erase` function in the `if` statement's true path removes the character from the variable. Otherwise, the statement in its false path increments the `x` variable by 1; doing this allows the loop to look at the next character in the `sales` variable.

Figure 13-27 shows the annual income program. The `erase` function appears on Line 28 and is shaded in the figure. Figure 13-28 shows a sample run of the program.

```
1 //Annual Income.cpp - displays the annual
2 //income without any dollar signs, commas,
3 //or spaces
4 //Created/revised by <your name> on <current date>
5
6 #include <iostream>
7 #include <string>
8 using namespace std;
9
10 int main()
11 {
12      string income      = "";
13      string currentChar = "";
14      int x = 0;  //keeps track of subscripts
15
16      cout << "Annual income (-1 to end): ";
17      getline(cin, income);
18
19      while (income != "-1")
20      {
21          //remove dollar signs, commas, and spaces
22          while (x < income.length())
23          {
24              currentChar = income.substr(x, 1);
25              if (currentChar == "$"
26                 || currentChar == ","
27                 || currentChar == " ")
28                  income.erase(x, 1);
29              else
30                  x += 1;
31              //end if
32          }   //end while
33
34          //display annual income
35          cout << "Annual income with no dollar "
36               << "signs, commas, or spaces: "
37               << income << endl << endl;
38
39          cout << "Annual income (-1 to end): ";
40          getline(cin, income);
41          x = 0;
42      }   //end while
43
44      //system("pause");
45      return 0;
46 }   //end of main function
```

your C++ development tool may require this statement

Figure 13-27 Annual income program

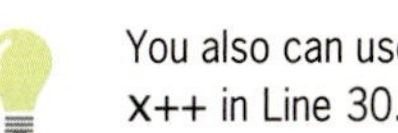

You also can use x++ in Line 30.

```
Annual Income With erase Function
Annual income (-1 to end): 1234
Annual income with no dollar signs, commas, or spaces: 1234

Annual income (-1 to end): 1,234,567
Annual income with no dollar signs, commas, or spaces: 1234567

Annual income (-1 to end): $ 1,234
Annual income with no dollar signs, commas, or spaces: 1234

Annual income (-1 to end): 1 2, 3 4
Annual income with no dollar signs, commas, or spaces: 1234

Annual income (-1 to end): -1
Press any key to continue . . .
```

Figure 13-28 Sample run of the annual income program with the `erase` function

Replacing Characters in a `string` Variable

Rather than using the `erase` function to code the annual income program from the previous section, you also can use the `string` class's `replace` function. The **`replace` function** replaces a sequence of characters in a `string` variable with another sequence of characters. For example, you can use the `replace` function to replace area code "800" with area code "877" in a phone number. Or, you can use it to replace the dashes in a Social Security number with the empty string. You also can use it to replace a character, such as a dollar sign or a comma, with the empty string.

Figure 13-29 shows the `replace` function's syntax and includes examples of using the function. In the syntax, *string* is the name of a `string` variable, and the *subscript* argument specifies where to begin replacing characters in the *string*. The *count* argument indicates the number of characters to replace, and the *replacementString* argument contains the replacement characters. The `replace` function in Example 1 replaces the "800" in the `phone` variable with "877". After the function is processed, the `phone` variable contains 1-877-111-0000. The `replace` function in Example 2 replaces the letter X, whose subscript is 3 in the `item` variable, with the letter "D". After the function is processed, the `item` variable will contain "ABCD34" rather than "ABCX34". The `replace` function in Example 3 replaces the string "Wilson" in the `name` variable with the string "Farley"; doing this changes the variable's contents to "Karena Farley". The code in Example 4 removes the dollar signs and commas from the `sales` variable. It does this by replacing the dollar signs and commas with the empty string.

HOW TO Use the `replace` Function

Syntax
string.**replace(***subscript*, *count*, *replacementString***);**

Example 1
```
string phone = "1-800-111-0000";
phone.replace(2, 3, "877");
```
beginning with the character whose subscript is 2, replaces three characters in the `phone` variable with "877"; changes the contents of the `phone` variable to "1-877-111-0000"

(continues)

Figure 13-29 How to use the `replace` function

(continued)

Example 2

```
string item = "ABCX34";
item.replace(3, 1, "D");
```

beginning with the character whose subscript is 3, replaces one character in the `item` variable with "D"; changes the contents of the `item` variable to "ABCD34"

Example 3

```
string name = "Karena Wilson";
name.replace(7, 6, "Farley");
```

beginning with the character whose subscript is 7, replaces six characters in the `name` variable with "Farley"; changes the contents of the `name` variable to "Karena Farley"

Example 4

```
int x = 0;
string sales = "";
cout << "Sales: ";
getline(cin, sales);
while (x < sales.length())
    if (sales.substr(x, 1) == "$"
       || sales.substr(x, 1) == ",")
          sales.replace(x, 1, "");
    else
          x += 1;
    //end if
//end while
```

replaces any dollar signs and commas in the `sales` variable with the empty string

Figure 13-29 How to use the `replace` function

Figure 13-30 shows how you can use the `replace` function, instead of the `erase` function, in the annual income program. The modification made to the original code (shown earlier in Figure 13-27) is shaded in Figure 13-30. Figure 13-31 shows a sample run of the program containing the `replace` function.

Note: Lines 1 through 20 are the same as in Figure 13-27.

```
21          //remove dollar signs, commas, and spaces
22          while (x < income.length())
23          {
24              currentChar = income.substr(x, 1);
25              if (currentChar == "$"
26                 || currentChar == ","
27                 || currentChar == " ")
28                  income.replace(x, 1, "");
29              else
30                  x += 1;
31              //end if
32          }   //end while
```

Note: The remainder of the program is the same as Lines 33 through 46 in Figure 13-27.

Figure 13-30 Partial annual income program showing the `replace` function

```
Annual Income With replace Function
Annual income (-1 to end): 78000
Annual income with no dollar signs, commas, or spaces: 78000

Annual income (-1 to end): $78,0 00
Annual income with no dollar signs, commas, or spaces: 78000

Annual income (-1 to end): -1
Press any key to continue . . .
```

Figure 13-31 Sample run of the annual income program with the `replace` function

The answers to Mini-Quiz questions are located in Appendix A.

Mini-Quiz 13-3

1. Which of the following searches for a comma in a `string` variable named `cityState` and then assigns the result to an `int` variable named `location`?
   a. `location = cityState.find(",", 0);`
   b. `location = cityState.find(0, ",");`
   c. `location = cityState.search(",", 0);`
   d. `location = cityState.searchFor(",");`
2. If the `cityState` variable contains the string “Bowling Green, KY”, what will the statement from Question 1 assign to the `location` variable?
3. If the `cityState` variable contains the string “Bowling Green, KY”, which of the following changes the variable’s contents to “Bowling Green”?
   a. `cityState.erase(13);`
   b. `cityState.erase(13, 4);`
   c. `cityState.replace(13, 4, "");`
   d. all of the above

The Social Security Number Program

Figure 13-32 shows the problem specification and IPO chart for the Social Security number program. The program should allow the user to enter a Social Security number without the hyphens. If the user’s entry contains nine characters, the program should insert hyphens in the appropriate places in the Social Security number and then display the result on the screen. If the user did not enter nine characters, the program should display an appropriate message. You will learn how to insert characters within a `string` variable in the next section.

Problem specification

Create a program that allows the user to enter a Social Security number without the two hyphens. The user's entry should contain nine characters. If the user did not enter the required number of characters, the program should display the message "The number must contain 9 characters". Otherwise, the program should insert the two missing hyphens and then display the result on the screen.

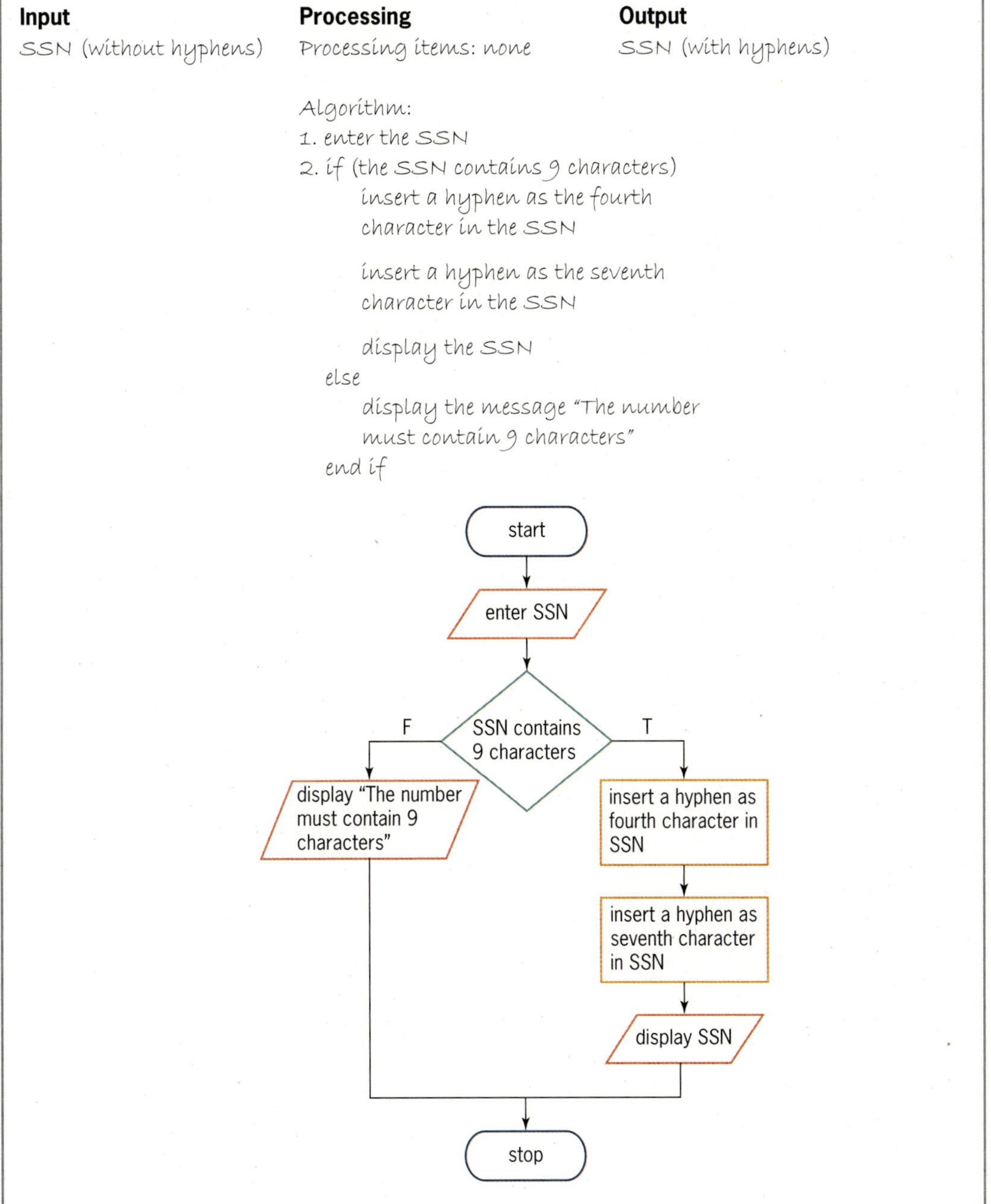

Figure 13-32 Problem specification and IPO chart for the Social Security number program

Inserting Characters Within a `string` Variable

In addition to removing and replacing characters in a `string` variable, you also can insert characters within a `string` variable. For example, you can insert an employee's middle initial between his or her first and last names. Or, you can insert parentheses around the area code in a phone number. You also can insert hyphens in a Social Security number.

The `string` class provides the **`insert` function** for inserting characters within a `string` variable. The function's syntax and examples of using the function are shown in Figure 13-33. In the syntax, *string* is the name of a `string` variable, and *subscript* specifies where in the *string* you want the *insertString* inserted. To insert the *insertString* at the beginning of the *string*, you use the number 0 as the *subscript*. To insert the *insertString* starting with the second character in the *string*, you use the number 1 as the *subscript*, and so on.

HOW TO Use the `insert` Function

Syntax

string.**insert(***subscript*, *insertString***);**

Example 1

```
string name = "Harold Cruthers";
name.insert(7, "G. ");
```

inserts the letter G, followed by a period and a space, between the first and last names stored in the `name` variable; changes the contents of the `name` variable to "Harold G. Cruthers"

Example 2

```
string phone = "312 050-1111";
phone.insert(0, "(");
phone.insert(4, ")");
```

inserts the opening and closing parentheses at the beginning and end, respectively, of the area code; changes the contents of the `phone` variable to "(312) 050-1111"

Example 3

```
string ssn = "111220000";
ssn.insert(3, "-");
ssn.insert(6, "-");
```

inserts two hyphens in the Social Security number, one after the third number and the other after the fifth number; changes the contents of the `ssn` variable to "111-22-0000"

Figure 13-33 How to use the `insert` function

Study the examples shown in Figure 13-33. The `insert` function in Example 1 inserts the *insertString*—in this case, "G. " (the letter G, a period, and a space)—in the `name` variable. The letter G is inserted in subscript 7, which makes it the eighth character in the `name` variable. The period and space are inserted in subscripts 8 and 9, respectively, making them the ninth and tenth characters in the variable. After the function is processed, the `name` variable contains the string "Harold G. Cruthers".

In Example 2, the first `insert` function changes the contents of the `phone` variable from "312 050-1111" to "(312 050-1111". The second `insert` function in the example then changes the variable's contents to "(312) 050-1111". In Example 3, the first `insert` function changes the contents of the `ssn` variable from "111220000" to 111-220000", and the second `insert` function then changes the variable's contents to "111-22-0000".

Figure 13-34 shows the Social Security number program. The `insert` function appears on Lines 18 and 19; both lines are shaded in the figure. Figures 13-35 and 13-36 show sample runs of the program.

```
1 //Social Security Number.cpp
2 //displays the Social Security number with hyphens
3 //Created/revised by <your name> on <current date>
4
5 #include <iostream>
6 #include <string>
7 using namespace std;
8
9 int main()
10 {
11     string ssn = "";
12     cout << "Social Security number without hyphens: ";
13     getline(cin, ssn);
14
15     if (ssn.length() == 9)
16     {
17         //insert hyphens
18         ssn.insert(3, "-");  //xxx-xxxxxx
19         ssn.insert(6, "-");  //xxx-xx-xxxx
20         cout << "Social Security number: " << ssn << endl;
21     }
22     else
23         cout << "The number must contain "
24              << "9 characters" << endl;
25     //end if
26
27     system("pause");
28     return 0;
29 }   //end of main function
```

your C++ development tool may require this statement

Figure 13-34 Social Security number program

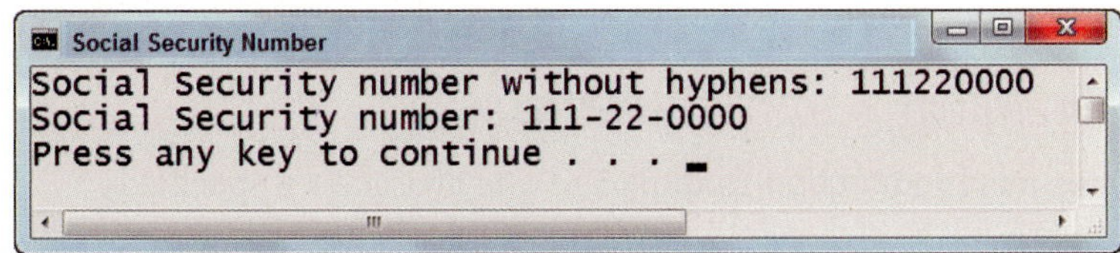

Figure 13-35 Sample run of the Social Security number program

```
Social Security Number
Social Security number without hyphens: 11122000
The number must contain 9 characters
Press any key to continue . . .
```

Figure 13-36 Another sample run of the Social Security number program

The Company Name Program

Figure 13-37 shows the problem specification and IPO chart for the company name program. The program should allow the user to enter the name of a company. It then should display the name with a row of hyphens below it. You will learn how to display the appropriate number of hyphens in the next section.

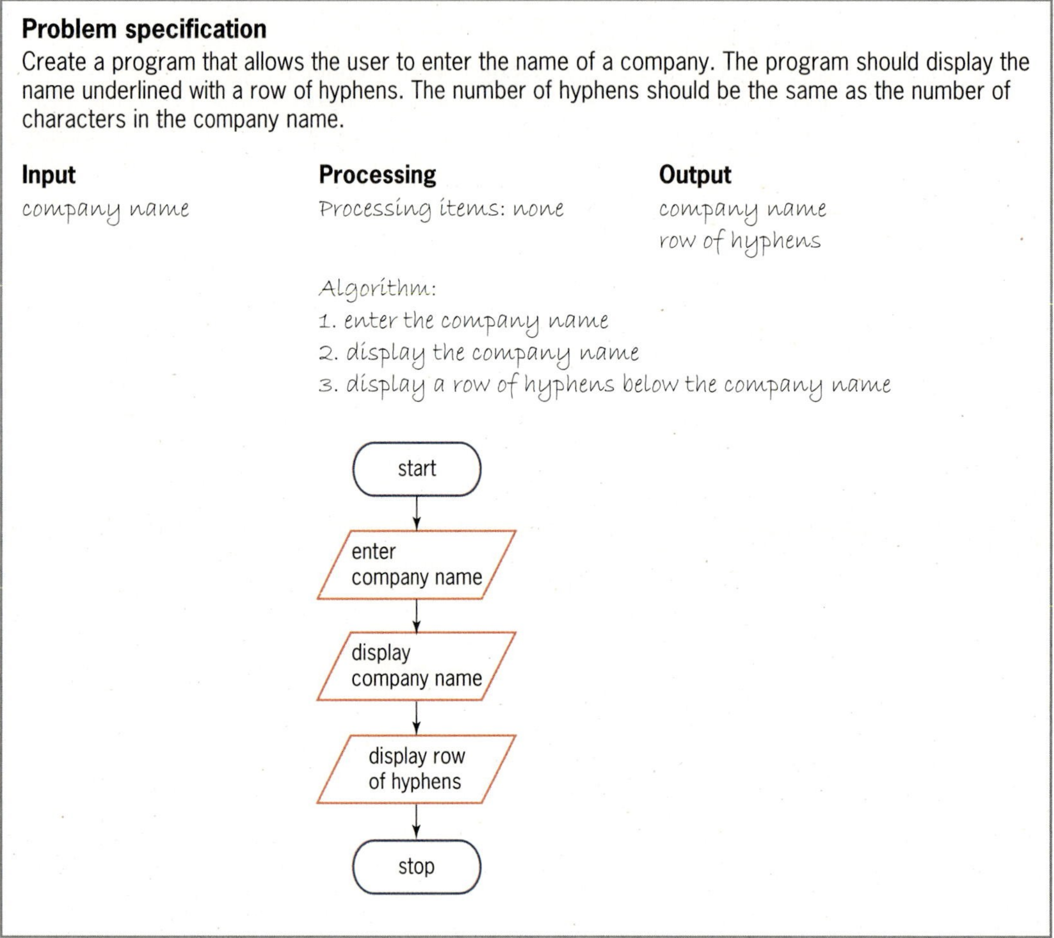

Figure 13-37 Problem specification and IPO chart for the company name program

Duplicating a Character Within a `string` Variable

You can use the `string` class's **`assign` function** to duplicate one character a specified number of times, assigning the resulting string to a `string` variable. Figure 13-38 shows the function's syntax and includes examples of using the function. In the syntax, *string* is the name of a `string` variable that will store the duplicated characters. The *count* argument is an integer that indicates the number of times you want to duplicate the character specified in the function's *character* argument. The *character* argument can be either a character literal constant enclosed in single quotation marks or the name of a `char` memory location. The `assign` function in Example 1 duplicates the asterisk character 10 times and then assigns the resulting string to the `asterisks` variable. The `assign` function in Example 2 duplicates the hyphen character zero or more times, depending on the number of characters in the `companyName` variable. It then assigns the resulting string to the `underline` variable.

HOW TO Use the `assign` Function

Syntax

string.**assign(***count*, *character***);**

Example 1

```
string asterisks = "";
asterisks.assign(10, '*');
```

assigns 10 asterisks to the `asterisks` variable

Example 2

```
string companyName = "";
string underline = "";
cout << "Company name: ";
getline(cin, companyName);
underline.assign(companyName.length(), '-');
```

assigns zero or more hyphens to the `underline` variable; the number of hyphens depends on the number of characters in the `companyName` variable

Figure 13-38 How to use the `assign` function

Figure 13-39 shows the company name program. The `assign` function appears on Line 19 and is shaded in the figure. Figure 13-40 shows a sample run of the program.

```
 1 //Company Name.cpp - displays the company name
 2 //underlined with a row of hyphens
 3 //Created/revised by <your name> on <current date>
 4
 5 #include <iostream>
 6 #include <string>
 7 using namespace std;
 8
 9 int main()
10 {
11     string companyName = "";
12     string underline   = "";
13
14     //get the company name
15     cout << "Company name: ";
16     getline(cin, companyName);
17
18     //assign the appropriate number of hyphens
19     underline.assign(companyName.length(), '-');
20
21     //display the company name and row of hyphens
22     cout << endl << companyName << endl;
23     cout << underline << endl;
24
25     //system("pause");
26     return 0;
27 }   //end of main function
```

your C++ development tool may require this statement

Figure 13-39 Company name program

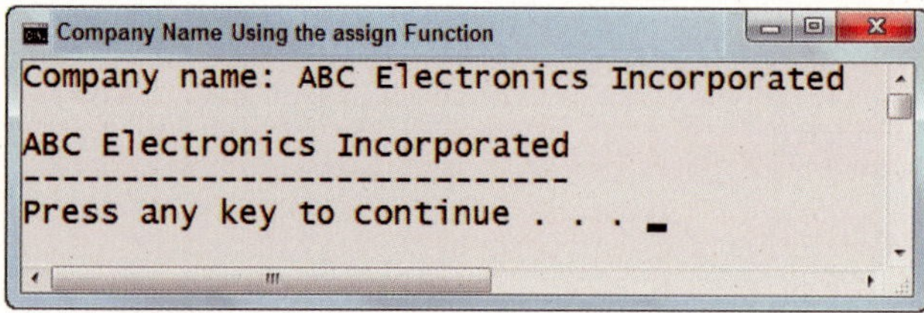

Figure 13-40 Sample run of the company name program using the `assign` function

Concatenating Strings

The company name program, which you viewed in the previous section, used the `assign` function to assign zero or more hyphens to a `string` variable named `underline`. You can accomplish the same result using string concatenation (rather than the `assign` function). **String concatenation** refers to the process of connecting (or linking) strings together. You concatenate strings using the **concatenation operator**, which is the + sign in C++.

Figure 13-41 shows examples of using the concatenation operator in a C++ statement. The `full = first + " " + last;` statement in Example 1 concatenates the contents of the `first` variable, a space, and the contents of the `last` variable. It then assigns the concatenated string ("Sydney Holmes") to the `full` variable. The `sentence = sentence + "?";` statement in Example 2 concatenates the contents of the `sentence` variable and a question mark (?) and then assigns the concatenated string ("How are you?") to the `sentence` variable. The `underline = underline + "-";` statement in Example 3 appears within a loop that will repeat the statement for each character in the `companyName` variable. The statement concatenates a hyphen (–) and the current contents of the `underline` variable and then assigns the result to the `underline` variable.

HOW TO Use the Concatenation Operator

Example 1

```
string first = "Sydney";
string last = "Holmes";
string full = "";
full = first + " " + last;
```

concatenates the contents of the `first` variable, a space, and the contents of the `last` variable and then assigns the result ("Sydney Holmes") to the `full` variable

Example 2

```
string sentence = "How are you";
sentence = sentence + "?";
```

concatenates the contents of the `sentence` variable and a question mark and then assigns the result ("How are you?") to the `sentence` variable

Example 3

```
string companyName = "";
string underline = "";
cout << "Company name: ";
getline(cin, companyName);
for (int x = 1; x <= companyName.length(); x += 1)
     underline = underline + "-";
//end for
```

concatenates zero or more hyphens within the `underline` variable; the number of hyphens depends on the number of characters in the `companyName` variable

Figure 13-41 How to use the concatenation operator

Figure 13-42 shows how you can use string concatenation, instead of the `assign` function, in the company name program. The modifications made to the original code (shown earlier in Figure 13-39) are shaded in Figure 13-42. Although you could use the loop shown in Figure 13-42 to assign the appropriate number of hyphens to the `underline` variable, it is much easier to use the `underline.assign(companyName.length(), '-');` statement. Figure 13-43 shows a sample run of the program using string concatenation.

You also can use `x++` in Line 19 and `underline += "-";` in Line 20.

Note: Lines 1 through 17 are the same as in Figure 13-39.

```
18      //assign the appropriate number of hyphens
19      for (int x = 1; x <= companyName.length(); x += 1)
20          underline = underline + "-";
21      //end for
22
23      //display the company name and row of hyphens
24      cout << endl << companyName << endl;
25      cout << underline << endl;
```

Note: The remainder of the program is the same as Lines 24 through 27 in Figure 13-39.

Figure 13-42 Partial company name program showing string concatenation

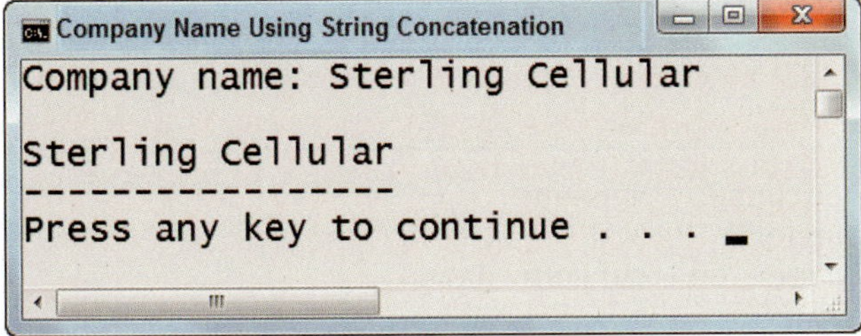

Figure 13-43 Sample run of the company name program using string concatenation

Mini-Quiz 13-4

The answers to Mini-Quiz questions are located in Appendix A.

1. Which of the following changes the contents of the `cityState` variable from "Las Vegas Nevada" to "Las Vegas, Nevada"?

   a. `cityState.insert(10, ",");`

   b. `cityState.replace("s N", "s, N");`

   c. `cityState.assign(9, ",");`

   d. none of the above

2. The `temp` and `sentence` variables are `string` variables. Which of the following assigns four exclamation points to the `temp` variable and then concatenates the variable and the `sentence` variable?
   a. `sentence = sentence + temp.assign(4, '!');`
   b. `sentence = sentence + temp.assign(4, "!");`
   c. `sentence = sentence + temp.assign('!', 4);`
   d. none of the above

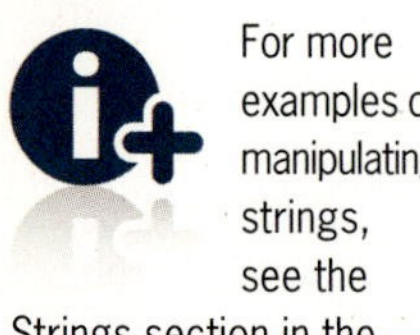

For more examples of manipulating strings, see the Strings section in the Ch13WantMore.pdf file.

3. Which of the following concatenates the opening parentheses, the contents of the `areaCode` variable, and the closing parentheses and then assigns the result to the `areaCode` variable?
   a. `areaCode = "(" + "areaCode" + ")";`
   b. `areaCode = "(" + areaCode + ")";`
   c. `areaCode = '(' & areaCode & ')';`
   d. none of the above

LAB 13-1 Stop and Analyze

The answers to the labs are located in Appendix A.

Study the program shown in Figure 13-44 and then answer the questions.

```
//Lab13-1.cpp - removes parentheses, hyphens,
//and spaces from a phone number
//Created/revised by <your name> on <current date>

#include <iostream>
#include <string>
using namespace std;

int main()
{
    string phone        = "";
    string currentChar = "";
    int numChars        = 0;
    int subscript       = 0;

    //get phone number
    cout << "Enter a phone number "
         << "in this format (xxx) xxx-xxxx: ";
    getline(cin, phone);

```

Figure 13-44 Code for Lab 13-1 *(continues)*

(continued)

```
21    //determine number of characters
22    numChars = phone.length();
23
24    //remove parentheses, hyphens, and spaces
25    while (subscript < numChars)
26    {
27        currentChar = phone.substr(subscript, 1);
28        if (currentChar == "("
29          || currentChar == ")"
30          || currentChar == "-"
31          || currentChar == " ")
32        {
33            phone.erase(subscript, 1);
34            numChars -= 1;
35        }
36        else
37            subscript += 1;
38        //end if
39    }   //end while
40
41    //display phone number
42    cout << "Phone number without "
43         << "parentheses, hyphens, or spaces: "
44         << phone << endl;
45
46    //system("pause");
47    return 0;
48 }  //end of main function
```

if your C++ development tool requires this statement, delete the two forward slashes

Figure 13-44 Code for Lab 13-1

QUESTIONS

1. What is the purpose of the loop in Lines 25 through 39?
2. What is the purpose of the statement in Line 27?
3. What is the purpose of the selection structure in Lines 28 through 38?
4. Why is the statement in Line 34 necessary?
5. Why is the statement in Line 37 processed only when the current character is not an opening parentheses, a closing parentheses, a hyphen, or a space? In other words, why isn't it necessary to update the `subscript` variable when the character is an opening parentheses, a closing parentheses, a hyphen, or a space?
6. Follow the instructions for starting C++ and viewing the Lab13-1.cpp file, which is contained in either the Cpp7\Chap13\Lab13-1 Project folder or the Cpp7\Chap13 folder. (Depending on your C++ development tool, you may need to open Lab13-1's project/solution file first.) If necessary, delete the two forward slashes that appear before the `system("pause");` statement, and then save the program. Run the program. When you are prompted to enter a phone number, type (312) 050-1234 and press Enter. The program removes the parentheses, hyphen, and space from the phone number and then displays 3120501234 on the screen.
7. Modify the program to use the `replace` function rather than the `erase` function. Save and then run the program.

LAB 13-2 Plan and Create

In this lab, you will plan and create an algorithm for Mr. Coleman. The problem specification, IPO chart information, and C++ instructions are shown in Figure 13-45.

Problem specification

Mr. Coleman teaches second grade at Hinsbrook School. On days when the weather is bad and the students cannot go outside to play, he spends recess time playing a simplified version of the Hangman game with his class. The game requires two people to play. Currently, Mr. Coleman thinks of a word that has five letters. He then draws five dashes on the chalkboard—one for each letter in the word. One student then is chosen to guess the word, letter by letter. When the student guesses a correct letter, Mr. Coleman replaces the appropriate dash or dashes with the letter. For example, if the original word is *moose* and the student guesses the letter *o*, Mr. Coleman changes the five dashes on the chalkboard to *-oo--*. The game is over when the student either guesses all of the letters in the word or makes 10 incorrect guesses, whichever occurs first. Mr. Coleman wants a program that allows two students to play the game on the computer.

IPO chart information	**C++ instructions**
Input	
original word (from player 1) letter (from player 2)	`string origWord = "";` `string letter = "";`
Processing	
variable that keeps track of whether a dash was replaced ('N')	`char dashReplaced = 'N';`
variable that keeps track of whether the game is over ('N')	`char gameOver = 'N';`
number of incorrect guesses	`int numIncorrect = 0;`
Output	
display word (5 dashes when the program begins)	`string displayWord = "-----";`
Algorithm	
1. repeat	`do //begin loop` `{`
get original word	`cout << "Enter a 5-letter word in uppercase: ";` `getline(cin, origWord);`
while (the original word does not contain exactly five characters)	`} while (origWord.length() != 5);`
2. clear the screen	`system("cls");`
3. display the five dashes contained in the display word	`cout << "Guess this word: " << displayWord << endl;`
4. repeat while (the game is not over)	`while (gameOver == 'N')` `{`
get an uppercase letter	`cout << "Enter an uppercase letter: ";` `cin >> letter;`
repeat for (each letter in the original word)	`for (int x = 0; x < 5; x += 1)` `{`
if (the current character in the original word matches the letter)	`if (origWord.substr(x, 1) == letter)`

Figure 13-45 Problem specification, IPO chart information, and C++ instructions for Lab 13-2 *(continues)*

(continued)

IPO chart information	C++ instructions
	{
replace the dash in the display word with the letter	displayWord.replace(x, 1, letter);
assign 'Y' to the variable that keeps track of whether a dash was replaced	dashReplaced = 'Y';
end if	} //end if
end repeat	} //end for
if (a dash was replaced)	if (dashReplaced == 'Y') {
if (the display word does not contain any dashes)	if (displayWord.find("-", 0) == -1) {
assign 'Y' to the variable that keeps track of whether the game is over	gameOver = 'Y';
display the original word	cout << endl << "Yes, the word is " << origWord << endl;
display "Great guessing" message	cout << "Great guessing!" << endl; }
else	else {
display the status of the display word	cout << endl << "Guess this word: " << displayWord << endl;
reset to 'N' the variable that keeps track of whether a dash was replaced	dashReplaced = 'N';
end if	} //end if }
else	else {
add 1 to the number of incorrect guesses	numIncorrect += 1;
if (the number of incorrect guesses is 10)	if (numIncorrect == 10) {
assign 'Y' to the variable that keeps track of whether the game is over	gameOver = 'Y';
display "Sorry, the word is" and the original word	cout << endl << "Sorry, the word is " << origWord << endl;
end if	} //end if
end if	} //end if
end repeat	} //end while

Figure 13-45 Problem specification, IPO chart information, and C++ instructions for Lab 13-2

Figure 13-46 shows the code for the entire Hangman game program, and Figures 13-47 and 13-48 show sample runs of the program using APPLE and HOUSE as the original words.

```
 1 //Lab13-2.cpp - simulates the Hangman game
 2 //Created/revised by <your name> on <current date>
 3
 4 #include <iostream>
 5 #include <string>
 6 //#include <cstdlib>
 7 using namespace std;
 8
 9 int main()
10 {
11     //declare variables
12     string origWord    = "";
13     string letter      = "";
14     char dashReplaced  = 'N';
15     char gameOver      = 'N';
16     int numIncorrect   = 0;
17     string displayWord = "-----";
18
19     //get original word
20     do   //begin loop
21     {
22         cout << "Enter a 5-letter word in uppercase: ";
23         getline(cin, origWord);
24     } while (origWord.length() != 5);
25
26     //clear the screen
27     system("cls");
28
29     //start guessing
30     cout << "Guess this word: " <<
31     displayWord << endl;
32     while (gameOver == 'N')
33     {
34         cout << "Enter an uppercase letter: ";
35         cin >> letter;
36
37         //search for the letter in the original word
38         for (int x = 0; x < 5; x += 1)
39         {
40             //if the current character matches
41             //the letter, replace the corresponding
42             //dash in the displayWord variable and then
43             //set the dashReplaced variable to 'Y'
44             if (origWord.substr(x, 1) == letter)
45             {
46                 displayWord.replace(x, 1, letter);
47                 dashReplaced = 'Y';
48             } //end if
49         }   //end for
50
51         //if a dash was replaced, check whether the
52         //displayWord variable contains another dash
53         if (dashReplaced == 'Y')
54         {
55             //if the displayWord variable does not
```

your C++ development tool may require this directive to use the statement on Line 27

Figure 13-46 Hangman game program *(continues)*

(continued)

```
            //contain any dashes, the game is over
            if (displayWord.find("-", 0) == -1)
            {
                gameOver = 'Y';
                cout << endl << "Yes, the word is "
                     << origWord << endl;
                cout << "Great guessing!" << endl;
            }
            else  //otherwise, continue guessing
            {
                cout << endl << "Guess this word: "
                     << displayWord << endl;
                dashReplaced = 'N';
            } //end if
        }
        else  //processed when dashReplaced contains 'N'
        {
            //add 1 to the number of incorrect guesses
            numIncorrect += 1;
            //if the number of incorrect guesses is 10,
            //the game is over
            if (numIncorrect == 10)
            {
                gameOver = 'Y';
                cout << endl << "Sorry, the word is "
                     << origWord << endl;
            } //end if
        } //end if
    }  //end while

    //system("pause");
    return 0;
}   //end of main function
```

if your C++ development tool requires this statement, delete the two forward slashes

Figure 13-46 Hangman game program

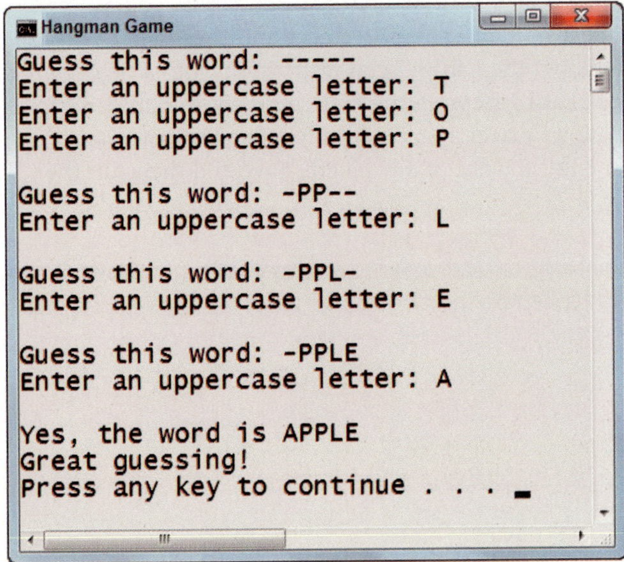

Figure 13-47 Sample run of the Hangman game program

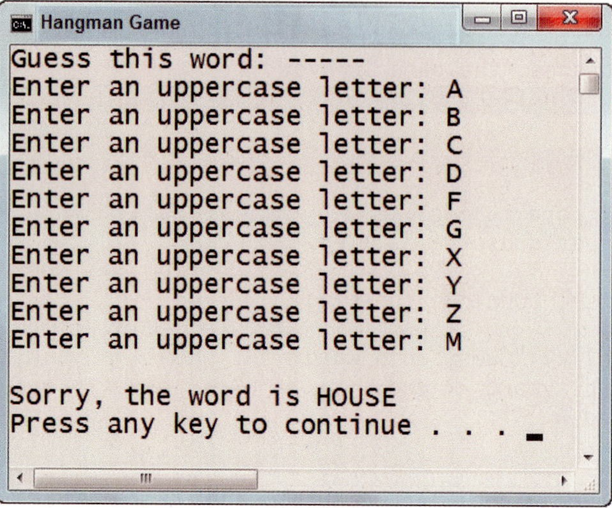

Figure 13-48 Another sample run of the Hangman game program

DIRECTIONS

Follow the instructions for starting your C++ development tool. Depending on the development tool you are using, you may need to create a new project; if so, name the project Lab13-2 Project and save it in the Cpp7\Chap13 folder. Enter the instructions shown in Figure 13-46 in a source file named Lab13-2.cpp. (Do not enter the line numbers.) Save the file in either the project folder or the Cpp7\Chap13 folder. Now follow the appropriate instructions for running the Lab13-2.cpp file. Test the program using an original word that does not contain exactly five characters. Also test the program using the words and letters shown in Figures 13-47 and 13-48. If necessary, correct any bugs (errors) in the program.

LAB 13-3 Modify

If necessary, create a new project named Lab13-3 Project and save it in the Cpp7\Chap13 folder. Enter (or copy) the Lab13-2.cpp instructions into a new source file named Lab13-3.cpp. Change Lab13-2.cpp in the first comment to Lab13-3.cpp. Currently, the Hangman game program allows player 1 to enter only a five-character word. Modify the program so that player 1 can enter a word of any length. Save and then run the program. Test the program appropriately.

LAB 13-4 Desk-Check

Desk-check the code shown in Figure 13-49. What will the code display on the screen?

```
//Lab13-4.cpp - displays a message
//Created/revised by <your name> on <current date>

#include <iostream>
#include <string>
using namespace std;

int main()
{
    string message      = "praogxwrazingmun";
    string subMessage1 = "";
    string subMessage2 = "";

    message.erase(5, 2);
    message.insert(11, "is");
    message.replace(13, 1, "f");

    subMessage1 = message.substr(0, 11);
    subMessage1.replace(7, 1, "mm");
    subMessage1.erase(2, 2);
    subMessage1.replace(0, 1, "P");
    subMessage1.insert(2, "o");

    subMessage2 = subMessage2.assign(5, '!');
    subMessage2 = message.substr(11) + subMessage2;
    subMessage2.insert(0, " ");
    subMessage2.insert(3, " ");

    message = subMessage1 + subMessage2;

    //display message
    cout << "Message: " << message << endl;

    //system("pause");
    return 0;
}   //end of main function
```

your C++ development tool may require this statement

Figure 13-49 Code for Lab 13-4

LAB 13-5 Debug

Follow the instructions for starting C++ and viewing the Lab13-5.cpp file, which is contained in either the Cpp7\Chap13\Lab13-5 Project folder or the Cpp7\Chap13 folder. (Depending on your C++ development tool, you may need to open Lab13-5's project/solution file first.) If necessary, delete the two forward slashes that appear before the `system("pause");` statement and then save the program. Run the program. Type Joe and press Enter. Rather than displaying the letters J, o, and e on three separate lines, the program displays Joe, oe, and e. Stop and then debug the program.

Summary

- The `string` data type was added to the C++ language using the `string` class.
- Memory locations (variables and named constants) whose data type is `string` are initialized using string literal constants, which are zero or more characters enclosed in double quotation marks. Most `string` variables are initialized to the empty string.
- You can use the extraction operator to get a string from the user at the keyboard, but only if the string does not contain a white-space character (blank, tab, or newline).
- The `getline` function gets a string of characters entered at the keyboard and stores them in a `string` variable. The string can contain any characters, including white-space characters (blanks, tabs, and newlines). The `getline` function stops reading and storing characters when it encounters the delimiter character in the input. The function's default delimiter character is the newline character. The function reads and then consumes (discards) the delimiter character.
- The computer stores the characters entered at the keyboard in the `cin` object. Both the extraction operator and the `getline` function remove characters from the object. However, unlike the extraction operator, which leaves the newline character in the `cin` object, the `getline` function consumes the newline character.
- The `ignore` function reads and then consumes characters entered at the keyboard. The function stops reading and consuming characters when it consumes either a specified number of characters or the delimiter character, whichever occurs first. The default number of characters to consume is 1.
- Figure 13-50 shows the syntax and purpose of each function covered in the chapter. It also includes the string concatenation operator. The `assign`, `erase`, `insert`, and `replace` functions are self-contained statements that change the value of the *string* variable.

Function/Operator	Syntax	Purpose
+		concatenate strings
`assign` function	*string*.**assign(***count*, *character***);**	duplicate a character within a `string` variable
`erase` function	*string*.**erase(***subscript* [, *count*]**);**	remove one or more characters located anywhere in a `string` variable
`find` function	*string*.**find(***searchString*, *subscript***)**	search a `string` variable to determine whether it contains a specific sequence of characters
`getline` function	**getline(cin,** *stringVariableName* [, *delimiterCharacter*]**);**	get string input from the keyboard
`ignore` function	**cin.ignore(**[*numberOfCharacters*][, *delimiterCharacter*]**);**	read and consume characters entered at the keyboard

Figure 13-50 Summary of `string` functions and the concatenation operator *(continues)*

(continued)

Function/Operator	Syntax	Purpose
`insert` function	*string*.**insert(***subscript*, *insertString***);**	insert characters within a `string` variable
`length` function	*string*.**length()**	determine the number of characters contained in a `string` variable
`replace` function	*string*.**replace(***subscript*, *count*, *replacementString***);**	replace a sequence of characters in a `string` variable with another sequence of characters
`substr` function	*string*.**substr(***subscript* [, *count*]**)**	access any number of characters contained in a `string` variable

Figure 13-50 Summary of `string` functions and the concatenation operator

Key Terms

`assign` function—used to duplicate one character a specified number of times within a string

Concatenation operator—used to concatenate (connect) strings; the + sign in C++

Consuming the character—another term for discarding the character

`erase` function—used to remove (erase) characters from a string

Escape sequence—the combination of the backslash and the character that follows; for example, the escape sequences `'\n'` and `'\t'` represent the Enter key and Tab key, respectively

`find` function—returns an integer that indicates the beginning position of a string within a `string` variable

`getline` function—reads characters entered at the keyboard until it encounters the delimiter character, which it consumes

`ignore` function—tells the computer to first read and then consume (discard) one or more characters

`insert` function—used to insert characters within a string

`length` function—returns the number of characters contained in a `string` variable

`replace` function—used to replace characters within a string

String concatenation—the process of connecting (or linking) strings together; accomplished with the concatenation operator

`substr` function—returns the characters you want to access from a `string` variable

Review Questions

1. Which of the following statements displays the number of characters contained in a `string` variable named `address`?

   a. `cout << address.length() << endl;`

   b. `cout << numChars(address) << endl;`

   c. `cout << length(address) << endl;`

   d. `cout << size.address << endl;`

2. Which of the following statements should a program use to get the name of any city and store it in a `string` variable named `cityName`?

   a. `cin >> cityName;`

   b. `cin(cityName);`

   c. `getline(cityName, cin);`

   d. `getline(cin, cityName);`

3. If the `amount` variable contains the string "$56.55", which of the following statements will remove the dollar sign from the variable's contents?

   a. `amount.erase("$");`

   b. `amount.erase(0, 1);`

   c. `amount = amount.substr(1);`

   d. both b and c

4. If the `state` variable contains the string "MI   " (the letters M and I followed by three spaces), which of the following statements will remove the three spaces from the variable's contents?

   a. `state.erase("   ");`

   b. `state.erase(3, "");`

   c. `state.remove(2, 3);`

   d. none of the above

5. The subscript of the first character contained in a `string` variable is ________.

   a. 0 (zero)

   b. 1 (one)

6. Which of the following `if` clauses determines whether the string stored in the `part` variable begins with the letter A?

   a. `if (part.begins("A"))`

   b. `if (part.beginswith("A"))`

   c. `if (part.substr(0, 1) == "A")`

   d. `if (part.substr(1) == "A")`

7. Which of the following `if` clauses determines whether the string stored in the `part` variable ends with the letter B?

   a. `if (part.ends("B"))`

   b. `if (part.endswith("B")`

   c. `if (part.substr(part.length() - 1, 1) == "B")`

   d. none of the above

8. Which of the following statements assigns the first three characters in the `part` variable to the `code` variable?

    a. `code = part.assign(0, 3);`
    b. `code = part.substr(0, 3);`
    c. `code = part.substr(1, 3);`
    d. `code = part.substring(0, 3);`

9. If the `word` variable contains the string "Bells", which of the following statements will change the contents of the variable to "Bell"?

    a. `word.erase(word.length() - 1, 1);`
    b. `word.replace(word.length() - 1, 1, "");`
    c. `word = word.substr(0, word.length() - 1);`
    d. all of the above

10. Which of the following statements changes the contents of the `word` variable from "men" to "mean"?

    a. `word.addTo(2, "a");`
    b. `word.insert(2, "a");`
    c. `word.insert(3, "a");`
    d. none of the above

11. If the `msg` variable contains the string "Happy holidays", what will the `cout << msg.find("day", 0);` statement display on the screen?

    a. –1
    b. 0
    c. 10
    d. 11

12. If the `msg` variable contains the string "Happy holidays", what will the `location = msg.find("Day", 0);` statement assign to the `location` variable?

    a. –1
    b. 0
    c. 10
    d. 11

13. Which of the following assigns the location of the comma in the `amount` variable to an `int` variable named `loc`?

    a. `loc = amount.contains(",");`
    b. `loc = amount.substr(",");`
    c. `loc = amount.find(",", 0);`
    d. none of the above

14. Which of the following statements searches for the string "CA" in a `string` variable named `state` and then assigns the result to an `int` variable named `result`? The search should begin with the character located in subscript 5 in the `state` variable. The `state` variable's contents are uppercase.

    a. `result = find(state, 5, "CA");`

    b. `result = state.find(5, "CA");`

    c. `result = state.find("CA", 5);`

    d. `result = state.find("CA", 5, 2);`

15. If the `state` variable contains the string "San Francisco, CA", what will the correct statement in Question 14 assign to the `result` variable?

    a. –1

    b. 0

    c. 11

    d. 15

16. Which of the following statements replaces the two characters located in subscripts 4 and 5 in a `string` variable named `code` with the string "AB"?

    a. `code.replace(2, 4, "AB");`

    b. `code.replace(4, 2, "AB");`

    c. `code.replace(4, 5, "AB");`

    d. `replace(code, 4, "AB");`

17. Which of the following statements assigns five asterisks (*) to a `string` variable named `divider`?

    a. `divider.assign(5, '*');`

    b. `divider.assign(5, "*");`

    c. `divider.assign('*', 5);`

    d. `assign(divider, '*', 5);`

18. Which of the following statements concatenates the contents of a `string` variable named `city`, a comma, a space, and the contents of a `string` variable named `state` and then assigns the result to a `string` variable named `cityState`?

    a. `cityState = "city" + ", " + "state";`

    b. `cityState = city + ", " + state;`

    c. `cityState = city & ", " & state;`

    d. `cityState = "city, + state";`

19. Which of the following statements assigns the fifth character in the `word` variable to the `letter` variable?

    a. `letter = word.substr(4);`

    b. `letter = word.substr(4, 1);`

    c. `letter = word(5).substring;`

    d. `letter = substring(word, 5);`

20. Which of the following tells the computer to consume the next 100 characters?
    a. `cin.ignore(100);`
    b. `cin.ignore('100');`
    c. `ignore(cin, 100);`
    d. none of the above

21. When processed, the ______ can consume the newline character.
    a. >> operator
    b. << operator
    c. `getline` function
    d. both a and c

Exercises

Pencil and Paper

1. Write a C++ statement that assigns the number of characters contained in the `message` variable to an `int` variable named `numChars`. (The answers to TRY THIS Exercises are located at the end of the chapter.) TRY THIS
2. Write a C++ statement that uses the `erase` function to remove the first two characters from the `message` variable. (The answers to TRY THIS Exercises are located at the end of the chapter.) TRY THIS
3. Rewrite the code from Pencil and Paper Exercise 2 using the `replace` function. MODIFY THIS
4. Write a C++ statement that replaces the first character in a `string` variable named `code` with the letter B. INTRODUCTORY
5. Write a C++ statement that assigns the first four characters in a `string` variable named `address` to a `string` variable named `streetNum`. INTRODUCTORY
6. The `part` variable contains the string "ABCD34G". Write a C++ statement that assigns the 34 in the `part` variable to a `string` variable named `code`. INTRODUCTORY
7. Write a C++ statement to change the contents of the `word` variable from "mend" to "amend". INTRODUCTORY
8. Write a C++ statement to change the contents of the `word` variable from "mouse" to "mouth". INTRODUCTORY
9. The `amount` variable contains the string "3,123,560". Write the C++ code to remove the commas from the contents of the variable. INTERMEDIATE
10. Write the C++ code that uses the `substr` function to determine whether the string stored in the `rate` variable ends with the percent sign. If it does, the code should use the `replace` function to remove the percent sign from the variable's contents. INTERMEDIATE
11. Write the C++ code to determine whether the `address` variable contains the street name "Grove Street". Begin the search with the fifth character in the `address` variable and assign the result to an `int` variable named `subNum` variable. INTERMEDIATE
12. Write a C++ statement that searches for the period in a `string` variable named `amount` and then assigns the location of the period to an `int` variable named `location`. Begin the search with the first character in the `amount` variable. INTERMEDIATE

ADVANCED

13. The `total` and `dollars` variables are `string` variables. Write the C++ code that uses the `assign` function to assign 10 asterisks to the `total` variable. The code then should concatenate the contents of the `total` variable and the contents of the `dollars` variable and then assign the resulting string to the `total` variable.

ADVANCED

14. A `string` variable named `amount` contains a string that has zero or more commas. Write the C++ code to count the number of commas in the string. Assign the result to an `int` variable named `numCommas`.

SWAT THE BUGS

15. Correct the following statement, which should change the contents of the `day` variable from "731" to "7/31": `day = day.insert(2, "/");`.

Computer

TRY THIS

16. If necessary, create a new project named TryThis16 Project and save it in the Cpp7\Chap13 folder. Enter the C++ instructions from Figure 13-23 into a source file named TryThis16.cpp. Change the filename in the first comment to TryThis16.cpp. Save and then run the program. Test the program using the data shown in Figure 13-24 in the chapter. Now, modify the program so the user enters the last name followed by a comma, a space, and the first name. The program should display the first name followed by a space and the last name. Be sure to modify the comments that document the program's purpose. Save and then run the program. Test the program appropriately. (The answers to TRY THIS Exercises are located at the end of the chapter.)

TRY THIS

17. If necessary, create a new project named TryThis17 Project and save it in the Cpp7\Chap13 folder. Also create a new source file named TryThis17.cpp. Write a program that allows the user to enter a string that represents a date. The date should be entered in the following format: mm/yy. Verify that the user entered exactly five characters and that the third character is the slash character (/). If the user did not enter the required number of characters, or if the third character is not a slash, display a message that indicates the type of entry error made by the user. Otherwise, the program should display the date in the following format: mm/20yy. Use a sentinel value to end the program. Save and then run the program. Test the program by entering the following dates: 6/08, 12/09, 05/10, and 123/4. (The answers to TRY THIS Exercises are located at the end of the chapter.)

MODIFY THIS

18. In this exercise, you modify the program from TRY THIS Exercise 17. If necessary, create a new project named ModifyThis18 Project and save it in the Cpp7\Chap13 folder. Copy the instructions from the TryThis17.cpp file into a source file named ModifyThis18.cpp. Change the filename in the first comment to ModifyThis18.cpp. Modify the program so that it allows the user to enter the date in the following format: mm/dd/yy. Verify that the user entered exactly eight characters and that the third and sixth characters are slashes (/). If the user did not enter the required number of characters, or if the third and sixth characters are not slashes, display a message that indicates the type of entry error made by the user. Otherwise, the program should display the date in the following format: mm/dd/20yy together. Save and then run the program. Test the program appropriately.

MODIFY THIS

19. In this exercise, you modify the annual income program from the chapter. If necessary, create a new project named ModifyThis19 Project and save it in the Cpp7\Chap13 folder. Enter the C++ instructions from Figure 13-27 into a new source file named ModifyThis19.cpp. Change the filename in the first comment. Save and then run the program. Test the program using the data shown in Figure 13-28 in the chapter. Now, modify the program so that it verifies that the other characters in the annual income are numbers. Display an appropriate message if a non-numeric character is found; otherwise, display the annual income. Save and then run the program. Test the program appropriately.

MODIFY THIS

20. In this exercise, you modify the ZIP code program from the chapter. If necessary, create a new project named ModifyThis20 Project and save it in the Cpp7\Chap13 folder. Enter the C++ instructions from Figure 13-19 into a new source file named ModifyThis20.cpp. Change the filename in the first comment. Save and then run the program. Test the program using the data shown in Figure 13-20 in the chapter. Now, modify the program so that it also passes to the `verifyNumeric` function the number of characters contained in the `zipCode` variable. Save and then run the program. Test the program appropriately.

INTRODUCTORY

21. If necessary, create a new project named Introductory21 Project and save it in the Cpp7\Chap13 folder. Also create a new source file named Introductory21.cpp. Write a program that displays the appropriate shipping charge based on the ZIP code entered by the user. To be valid, the ZIP code must contain exactly five digits and the first three digits must be either "605" or "606". The shipping charge for "605" ZIP codes is $25. The shipping charge for "606" ZIP codes is $30. Display an appropriate message if the ZIP code is invalid. Use a sentinel value to end the program. Save and then run the program. Test the program using the following ZIP codes: 60677, 60511, 60344, and 7130.

INTRODUCTORY

22. If necessary, create a new project named Introductory22 Project and save it in the Cpp7\Chap13 folder. Also create a new source file named Introductory22.cpp. Write a program that allows the user to enter three separate strings: a city name, state name, and ZIP code. The program should use string concatenation to display the city name followed by a comma, a space, the state name, two spaces, and the ZIP code. Use a sentinel value to end the program. Save and then run the program. Test the program.

INTERMEDIATE

23. If necessary, create a new project named Intermediate23 Project and save it in the Cpp7\Chap13 folder. Also create a new source file named Intermediate23.cpp. Write a program that displays the color of the item whose item number is entered by the user. All item numbers contain exactly seven characters. All items are available in four colors: blue, green, red, and white. The fourth character in the item number indicates the item's color, as follows: a B or b indicates Blue, a G or g indicates Green, an R or r indicates Red, and a W or w indicates White. If the item number does not contain exactly seven characters, or if the fourth character is not one of the valid color characters, the program should display an appropriate message. Use a sentinel value to end the program. Save and then run the program. Test the program using the following item numbers: 123B567, 34AG123, 111r222, 111w222, 123, 1234567, and 111k456.

INTERMEDIATE

24. In this exercise, you modify the Social Security number program from the chapter. If necessary, create a new project named Intermediate24 Project and save it in the Cpp7\Chap13 folder. Enter the instructions from Figure 13-34 into a source file named Intermediate24.cpp. Change the filename in the first comment. Before inserting the missing hyphens, verify that the nine characters entered by the user are numeric. Save and then run and test the program.

INTERMEDIATE

25. If necessary, create a new project named Intermediate25 Project and save it in the Cpp7\Chap13 folder. Also create a new source file named Intermediate25.cpp. Write a program that accepts a string of characters from the user. The program should display the characters in reverse order. In other words, if the user enters the string "Programming", the program should display "gnimmargorP". Save and then run and test the program.

INTERMEDIATE

26. If necessary, create a new project named Intermediate26 Project and save it in the Cpp7\Chap13 folder. Also create a new source file named Intermediate26.cpp. Write a program that allows the user to enter a part number that consists of four or five characters. The second and third characters represent the delivery method, as follows: "MS" represents "Mail – Standard", "MP" represents "Mail – Priority", "FS" represents

"FedEx – Standard", "FO" represents "FedEx – Overnight", and "UP" represents "UPS". Display an appropriate message when the part number does not contain either four or five characters. Also display an appropriate message when the second and third characters are not one of the delivery methods. If the part number is valid, the program should display the delivery method. Use a sentinel value to end the program. Save and then run the program. Test the program using the following part numbers: 7MP6, 3fs5, 2UP7, 7mS89, 9FO8, 9fo89, 8ko89, and 1234MS.

INTERMEDIATE

27. In this exercise, you modify the program from Lab 13-2. If necessary, create a new project named Intermediate27 Project and save it in the Cpp7\Chap13 folder. Also create a new source file named Intermediate27.cpp. Copy the C++ instructions from the Lab13-2.cpp file into the Intermediate27.cpp file. Change the filename in the first comment. Modify the program so that it displays a message indicating the number of incorrect guesses remaining. Display the message each time the user enters an incorrect guess.

ADVANCED

28. If necessary, create a new project named Advanced28 Project and save it in the Cpp7\Chap13 folder. Also create a new source file named Advanced28.cpp. Write a program that determines whether the user entered an item number in the required format: three digits, a hyphen, and two digits. Display an appropriate message indicating whether the format is correct. Use a sentinel value to end the program. Save and then run the program.

ADVANCED

29. Follow the instructions for starting C++ and viewing the Advanced29.cpp file, which is contained in either the Cpp7\Chap13\Advanced29 Project folder or the Cpp7\Chap13 folder. (Depending on your C++ development tool, you may need to open the project/solution file first.) If necessary, delete the two forward slashes that appear before the `system("pause");` statement and/or the `#include <cstdlib>` directive, and then save the program. The program assigns the letters of the alphabet to a `string` variable named `letters`. It also prompts the user to enter a letter. Complete the program by entering instructions to perform the tasks listed in Figure 13-51. Save and then run the program. Test the program appropriately.

1. Generate a random number that can be used to select one of the letters from the `letters` variable. Assign the letter to the `randomLetter` variable.
2. Verify that the user entered exactly one lowercase letter. If the user did not enter exactly one lowercase letter, display an appropriate error message.
3. If the user entered exactly one lowercase letter, compare the letter to the random letter. If the letter entered by the user is the same as the random letter, display the message "You guessed the correct letter." and then end the program. Otherwise, display messages indicating whether the correct letter comes alphabetically before or after the letter entered by the user.
4. Allow the user to enter a letter until he or she guesses the random letter.

Figure 13-51

ADVANCED

30. In this exercise, you modify the program from ADVANCED Exercise 29. If necessary, create a new project named Advanced30 Project and save it in the Cpp7\Chap13 folder. Also create a new source file named Advanced30.cpp. Copy the C++ instructions from the Advanced29.cpp file into the Advanced30.cpp file. Research the C++ `compare` function. Modify the program to use the `compare` function. Save and then run the program. Test the program appropriately.

ADVANCED

31. In this exercise, you modify the program from Lab 13-2. If necessary, create a new project named Advanced31 Project and save it in the Cpp7\Chap13 folder. Also create a new source file named Advanced31.cpp. Copy the C++ instructions from the Lab13-2.cpp file into the Advanced31.cpp file. Change the filename in the first comment. Modify the program so that it keeps track of the letters guessed by the user. If the user enters a

letter that he or she has already entered, display an appropriate message and do not include the letter in the number of incorrect guesses. Save and then run the program. Test the program appropriately.

ADVANCED

32. In this exercise, you modify the program from ADVANCED Exercise 31. If necessary, create a new project named Advanced32 Project and save it in the Cpp7\Chap13 folder. Also create a new source file named Advanced32.cpp. Copy the instructions from the Advanced31.cpp file into the Advanced32.cpp file. Change the filename in the first comment. Modify the program so that it displays the letters already entered by the user. Display the letters immediately before prompting the user to enter a letter. Save and then run the program. Test the program appropriately.

ADVANCED

33. If necessary, create a new project named Advanced33 Project and save it in the Cpp7\Chap13 folder. Also create a new source file named Advanced33.cpp. Create a program that allows the user to enter a word. The program should display the word in pig latin form. The rules for converting a word into pig latin form are listed in Figure 13-52. Use a sentinel value to end the program.

1. When the word begins with a vowel (A, E, I, O, or U), add the string "-way" (a dash followed by the letters w, a, and y) to the end of the word. For example, the pig latin form of the word "ant" is "ant-way".
2. When the word does not begin with a vowel, first add a dash to the end of the word. Then continue moving the first character in the word to the end of the word until the first character is the letter A, E, I, O, U, or Y. Then add the string "ay" to the end of the word. For example, the pig latin form of the word "Chair" is "air-Chay".
3. When the word does not contain the letter A, E, I, O, U, or Y, add the string "-way" to the end of the word. For example, the pig latin form of "56" is "56-way".

Figure 13-52

ADVANCED

34. Some credit card companies assign a special digit, called a check digit, to the end of each customer's credit card number. Many methods for creating the check digit have been developed. One very simple method is to append the second digit in the credit card number to the end of the number. For example, if the first four characters in the credit card number are 1357, you would append the number 3 to the end of the number, making the credit card number 13573. If necessary, create a new project named Advanced34 Project and save it in the Cpp7\Chap13 folder. Also create a new source file named Advanced34.cpp. Write a program that prompts the user to enter a five-digit credit card number, with the fifth digit being the check digit. Verify that the user entered exactly five numbers. If the user entered the required number of numbers, verify that the last number is the check digit. Display appropriate messages indicating whether the credit card number is valid or invalid. Use a sentinel value to end the program. Save and then run the program. Test the program appropriately.

ADVANCED

35. If necessary, create a new project named Advanced35 Project and save it in the Cpp7\Chap13 folder. Also create a new source file named Advanced35.cpp. Create a program that allows the user to enter a password. The program then should create and display a new password using the rules listed in Figure 13-53. Use a sentinel value to end the program.

1. All vowels (A, E, I, O, and U) in the original password should be replaced with the letter X.
2. All numbers in the original password should be replaced with the letter Z.
3. All of the characters in the original password should be reversed.

Figure 13-53

ADVANCED

36. In this exercise, you modify the program from Lab 13-2. If necessary, create a new project named Advanced36 Project and save it in the Cpp7\Chap13 folder. Also create a new source file named Advanced36.cpp. Copy the C++ instructions from the Lab13-2.cpp file into the Advanced36.cpp file. Change the prompt on Line 21 to "Enter a 5-letter word: ". Also change the prompt on Line 33 to "Enter a letter: ". Modify the program so that it converts both the 5-letter word and the letter to uppercase. Save and then run the program. Test the program appropriately. Hint: Recall that a string is equivalent to a one-dimensional array of characters.

SWAT THE BUGS

37. Follow the instructions for starting C++ and viewing the SwatTheBugs37.cpp file, which is contained in either the Cpp7\Chap13\SwatTheBugs37 Project folder or the Cpp7\Chap13 folder. (Depending on your C++ development tool, you may need to open the project/solution file first.) If necessary, delete the two forward slashes that appear before the `system("pause");` statement, and then save the program. The program should calculate and display the total of the prices entered by the user. Run the program. Use your own data to test the program. Notice that the program is not working correctly. Debug the program.

Answers to TRY THIS Exercises

Pencil and Paper

1. `numChars = message.length();`
2. `message.erase(0, 2);`

Computer

16. See Figure 13-54.

```
//TryThis16.cpp
//displays the first name followed by a space
//and the last name
//Created/revised by <your name> on <current date>

#include <iostream>
#include <string>
using namespace std;

int main()
{
    //declare variables
    string firstLast  = "";
    string first      = "";
    string last       = "";
    int commaLocation = 0;

    //get first and last name
    cout << "Name (last, comma, space, first): ";
    getline(cin, firstLast);
    //locate comma, then pull out first and
    //last names
    commaLocation = firstLast.find(",", 0);
    last = firstLast.substr(0, commaLocation);
    first = firstLast.substr(commaLocation + 2);

    //display rearranged name
    cout << first << " " << last << endl;

    //system("pause");
    return 0;
}   //end of main function
```

your C++ development tool may require this statement

Figure 13-54

17. See Figure 13-55.

```
//TryThis17.cpp
//displays a date using the format mm/20yy
//Created/revised by <your name> on <current date>

#include <iostream>
#include <string>
using namespace std;

int main()
{
    string date = "";

    cout << "Enter date (mm/yy). Enter -1 to end. ";
    getline(cin, date);

    while (date != "-1")
    {
        if (date.length() != 5)
            cout << "Invalid length" << endl << endl;
        else
            if (date.substr(2, 1) != "/")
                cout << "Invalid third character"
                    << endl << endl;
            else
            {
                date.insert(3, "20");
                cout << date << endl << endl;
            }   //end if
        //end if

        cout << "Enter date (mm/yy). Enter -1 to end. ";
        getline(cin, date);
    }   //end while

    //system("pause");
    return 0;
}   //end of main function
```

your C++ development tool may require this statement

Figure 13-55

CHAPTER 14

Sequential Access Files

After studying Chapter 14, you should be able to:

- Create file objects
- Open a sequential access file
- Determine whether a sequential access file was opened successfully
- Write data to a sequential access file
- Read data from a sequential access file
- Test for the end of a sequential access file
- Close a sequential access file

File Types

In addition to getting data from the keyboard and sending data to the computer screen, a program also can get data from and send data to a file on a permanent or secondary storage device (such as a flash drive). Getting data from a file is referred to as "reading the file," and sending data to a file is referred to as "writing to the file." Files to which data is written are called **output files** because the files store the output produced by a program. Files that are read by the computer are called **input files** because a program uses the data in the files as input.

Ch14-Chapter Preview video

Most input and output files are composed of lines of text that are both read and written sequentially. In other words, they are read and written in consecutive order, one line at a time, beginning with the first line in the file and ending with the last line in the file. Such files are referred to as **sequential access files** because of the manner in which the lines of text are accessed. They also are referred to as **text files** because they store text. Figure 14-1 shows examples of text you might find stored in sequential access files. The examples include an employee list, a quarterly sales report, and a company memo.

Employee list
Bratomello, Irene
Dobanski, Charles
Hetting, Susan
Myers, Jacob
Sanders, Jerry

Quarterly sales report

January sales	75,000	83,000	85,000
February sales	64,000	63,000	75,000
March sales	78,000	80,000	76,000
Total sales	217,000	226,000	236,000

Company memo
To: All Employees

From: Sharon Jones

The company picnic will be held on July 25th at Rosewood Park. All employees and their families are invited. Please join us for some food, beverages, and fun!

Figure 14-1 Examples of text stored in sequential access files

You also can create random access and binary access files in C++. The data stored in a random access file can be accessed in either consecutive or random order. The data in a binary access file can be accessed by its byte location in the file. Random access and binary access files are used less often in programs and, therefore, are not covered in this book.

The CD Collection Program

The CD (compact disc) collection program, which you code in this chapter, will use a sequential access file to store the names of CDs along with the names of the artists. Figure 14-2 shows the program's problem specification and IPO charts. In addition to the `main` function, the CD collection program will use two void functions named `saveCd` and `displayCds`. The `saveCd` function will get both the CD's name and the artist's name from the user at the keyboard. It then will save the user's entries in a sequential access file. The `displayCds` function will display the contents of the sequential access file on the computer screen. You will learn how to code this program in the remainder of the chapter.

Problem specification

Create a program that keeps track of a CD (compact disc) collection. The program should display a menu containing the following three options:

1 Enter CD information
2 Display CD information
3 End the program

If the user selects option 1, the program should call a function that first prompts the user to enter the CD's name and the artist's name, and then saves the user's entries in a sequential access file named cds.txt. If the user selects option 2, the program should call a function that displays the contents of the cds.txt file on the screen. The program should end only when the user selects option 3. If the cds.txt file cannot be opened, the program should display a message indicating that fact.

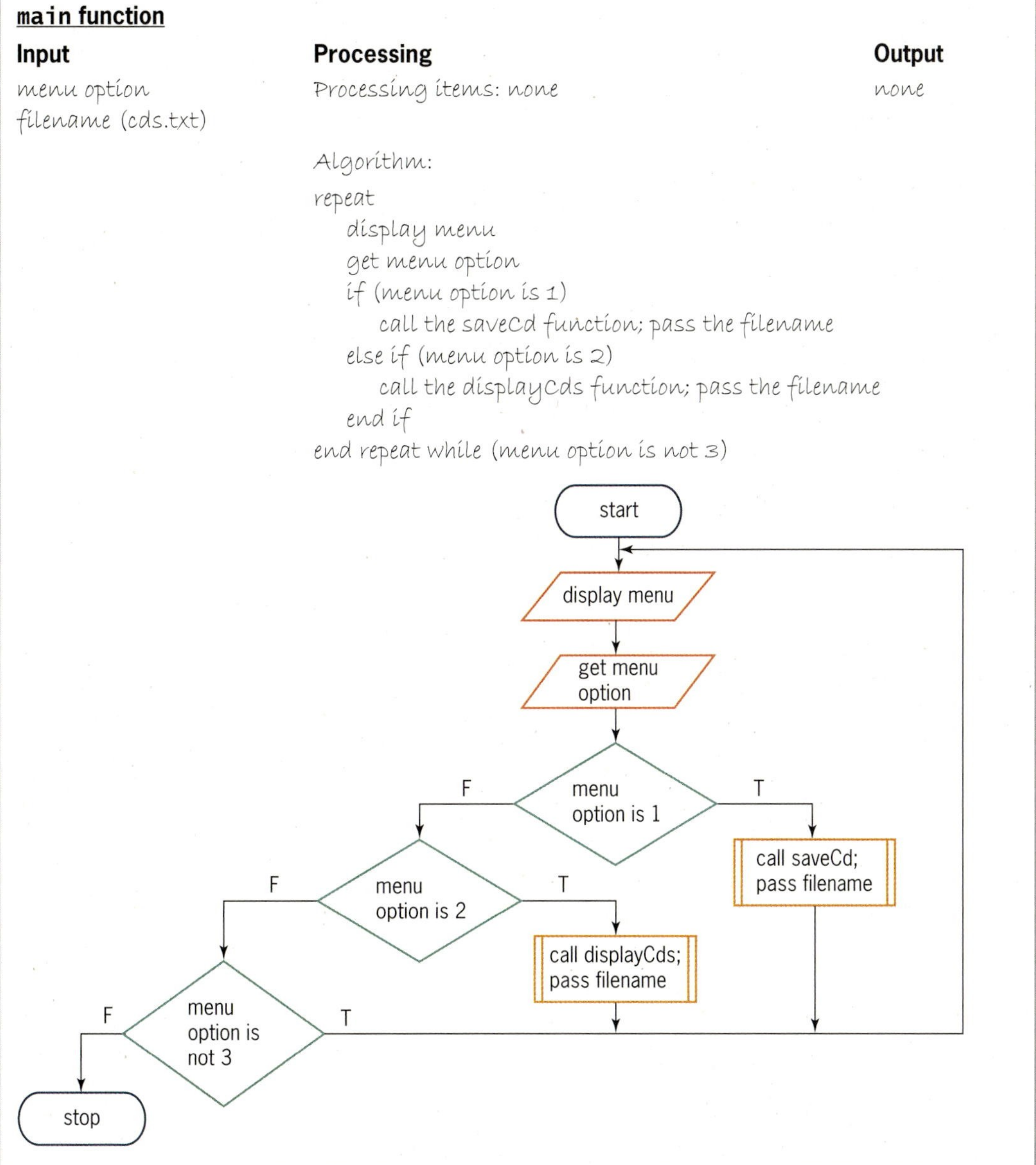

`main` function

Input	**Processing**	**Output**
menu option *filename (cds.txt)*	*Processing items: none*	*none*

Algorithm:

```
repeat
   display menu
   get menu option
   if (menu option is 1)
      call the saveCd function; pass the filename
   else if (menu option is 2)
      call the displayCds function; pass the filename
   end if
end repeat while (menu option is not 3)
```


Figure 14-2 Problem specification and IPO charts for the CD collection program *(continues)*

(continued)

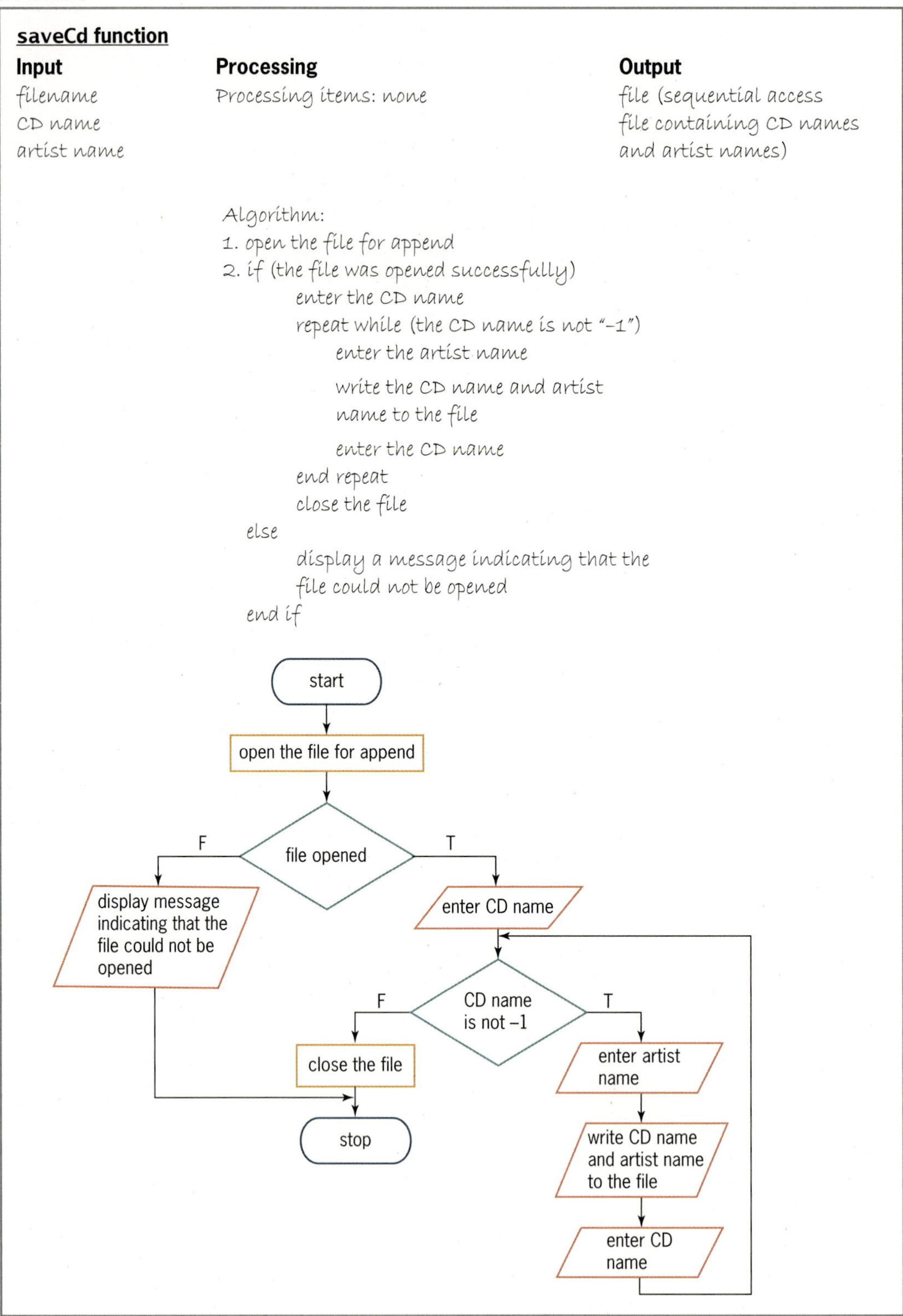

Figure 14-2 Problem specification and IPO charts for the CD collection program *(continues)*

(continued)

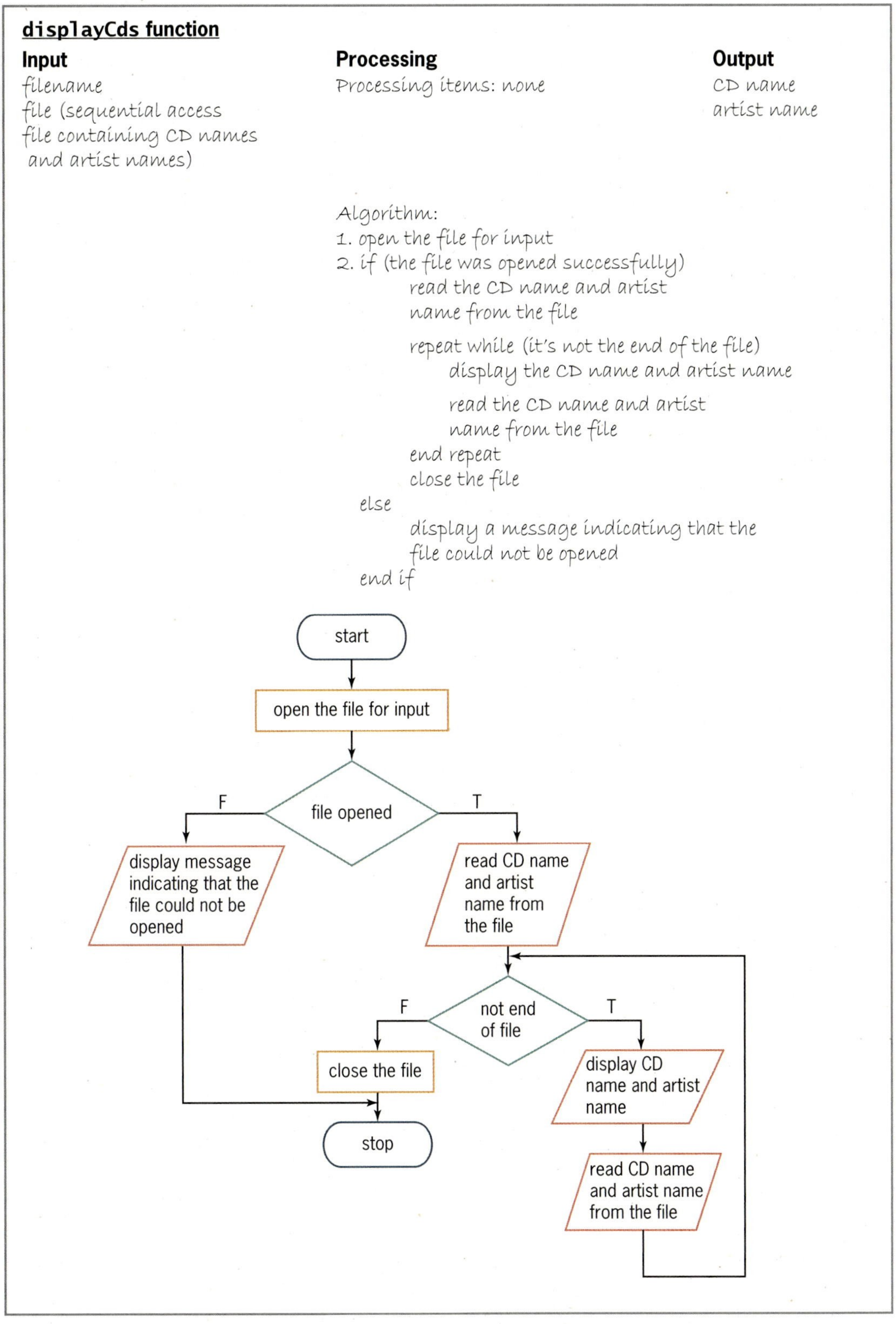

Figure 14-2 Problem specification and IPO charts for the CD collection program

Creating File Objects

In previous chapters, you used stream objects to perform standard input and output operations in a program. The standard input stream object (`cin`) refers to the computer keyboard, and the standard output stream object (`cout`) refers to the computer screen. As you already know, a program that uses the `cin` and `cout` objects must contain the `#include <iostream>` directive, which tells the compiler to include the contents of the iostream file in the program. The iostream file contains the definitions of the `istream` and `ostream` classes from which the `cin` and `cout` objects, respectively, are created. You do not have to create the `cin` and `cout` objects in a program because C++ creates those objects for you.

All objects in C++ are created from a class and are referred to as an instance of the class. For example, a `cin` object is an instance of the `istream` class, whereas an input file object is an instance of the `ifstream` class.

Objects are also used to perform file input and output operations in C++. However, unlike the standard `cin` and `cout` objects, the input and output file objects must be created by the programmer. To create a file object in a program, the program must contain the `#include <fstream>` directive, which tells the compiler to include the contents of the fstream file in the program. The fstream file contains the definitions of the `ifstream` (input file stream) and `ofstream` (output file stream) classes, which allow you to create input and output file objects, respectively.

Figure 14-3 shows the syntax for creating input file objects and the syntax for creating output file objects. In the first syntax, `ifstream` is the name of the class from which all input file objects are created. Similarly, `ofstream` in the second syntax is the name of the class from which all output file objects are created. In each syntax, *fileObject* is the name of the file object you want to create. Notice that a semicolon appears at the end of each syntax.

Also included in Figure 14-3 are examples of creating file objects. The statements in Examples 1 and 2 create input file objects named `inFile` and `inEmploy`, respectively. The statements in Examples 3 and 4 create output file objects named `outFile` and `outSales`, respectively. Notice that the names of the input file objects in the examples begin with the two letters `in`, whereas the names of the output file objects begin with the three letters `out`. Although the C++ syntax does not require you to begin file object names with either `in` or `out`, using this naming convention helps to distinguish a program's input file objects from its output file objects.

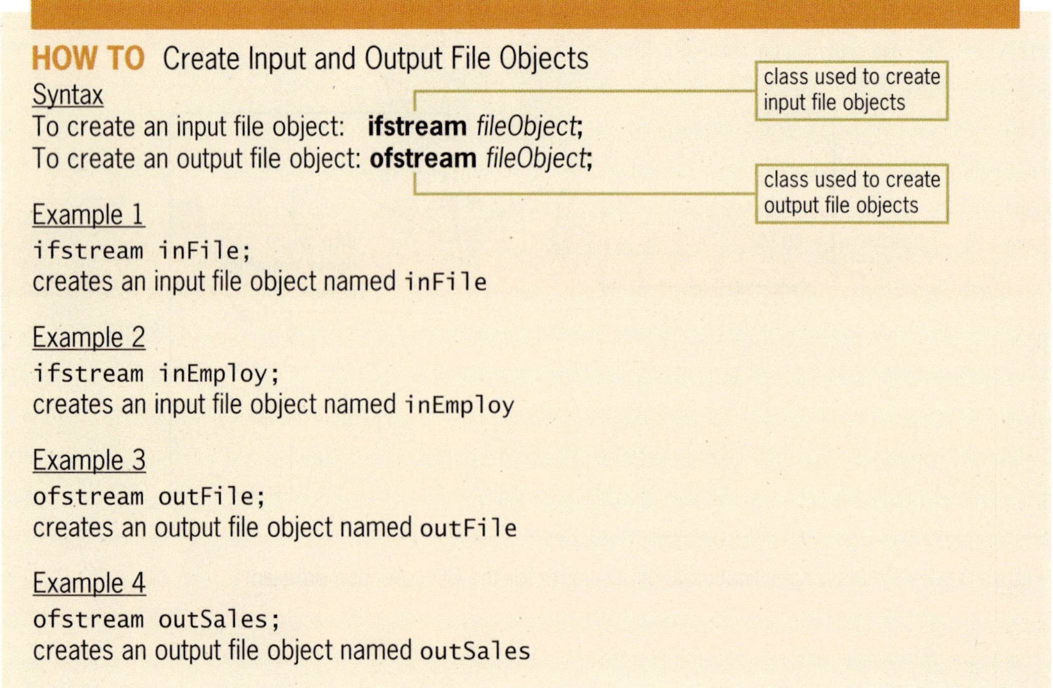
HOW TO Create Input and Output File Objects

Syntax

To create an input file object: **ifstream** *fileObject*;

To create an output file object: **ofstream** *fileObject*;

Example 1

```
ifstream inFile;
```

creates an input file object named `inFile`

Example 2

```
ifstream inEmploy;
```

creates an input file object named `inEmploy`

Example 3

```
ofstream outFile;
```

creates an output file object named `outFile`

Example 4

```
ofstream outSales;
```

creates an output file object named `outSales`

Figure 14-3 How to create input and output file objects

Opening a Sequential Access File

You use a program's input and output file objects, along with the C++ `open` function, to open actual files on your computer's disk. Figure 14-4 shows the `open` function's syntax and describes the modes most commonly used to open a sequential access file. In the syntax, *fileObject* is the name of either an existing `ifstream` file object or an existing `ofstream` file object, and *fileName* is the name of the file (including an optional path) you want to open. The *fileName* argument can be either a string literal constant or a `string` variable. If the *fileName* argument does not contain a path, the computer assumes that the file is located in the same folder as the program file. (See the second TIP on this page.) The **open function** opens the file whose name is specified in the *fileName* argument and associates the file with the *fileObject*. When a subsequent statement in the program needs to refer to the file, it does so using the name of the *fileObject* rather than the *fileName* itself.

The `open` function is defined in the `ifstream` and `ofstream` classes and is referred to as a class member function.

The optional *mode* argument in the syntax indicates how the file is to be opened. As Figure 14-4 indicates, you use the `ios::in` mode to open a file for input, which allows the computer to read the data stored in the file. The `ios::out` and `ios::app` modes are used to open output files. Both of these modes allow the computer to write data to the file. You use the `ios::app` (`app` stands for *append*) mode when you want to add data to the end of an existing file. If the file does not exist, the computer creates the file for you. You use the `ios::out` mode to open a new, empty file for output. If the file already exists, the computer erases the contents of the file before writing any data to it. The two colons (`::`) in each mode are called the **scope resolution operator** and indicate that the keywords `in`, `out`, and `app` are defined in the `ios` class.

In most cases, the program file refers to the .exe file. However, when running a program from the Microsoft Visual C++ IDE, the program file refers to the .cpp file.

HOW TO Open a Sequential Access File

Syntax

fileObject.**open(***fileName*[**,** *mode*]**);**

mode	Description
`ios::in`	Used with an `ifstream` object. Opens the file for input, which allows the computer to read the file's contents. This is the default mode for input files.
`ios::out`	Used with an `ofstream` object. Opens the file for output, which creates a new, empty file to which data can be written. If the file already exists, the computer erases the file's contents before the new data is written to it. This is the default mode for output files.
`ios::app`	Used with an `ofstream` object. Opens the file for append, which allows the computer to write new data to the end of the existing data in the file. If the file does not exist, the computer creates the file before writing any data to it.

Example 1

```
inFile.open("payroll.txt", ios::in);
```

or

```
inFile.open("payroll.txt");
```

opens the payroll.txt file for input

(continues)

Figure 14-4 How to open a sequential access file

(continued)

Example 2

```
outFile.open("employ.txt", ios::out);
```

or

```
outFile.open("employ.txt");
```

opens the employ.txt file for output

Example 3

```
outSales.open("F:/FirstQtr/sales.txt", ios::app);
```

opens the sales.txt file for append

Figure 14-4 How to open a sequential access file

Also included in Figure 14-4 are examples of statements that open sequential access files. Although it is not a requirement, many programmers use "txt" (short for "text") as the filename extension when naming sequential access files. You can use either of the statements in Example 1 to open the payroll.txt file for input. Because the *fileName* argument in both statements does not contain a path, the computer will look for the payroll.txt file in the same location as the program file. Notice that the *mode* argument is omitted in the second statement in Example 1. Because all files associated with an `ifstream` file object are opened automatically for input, it is not necessary to specify `ios::in` when opening an input file.

Unlike files associated with an `ifstream` object, files associated with an `ofstream` object are opened automatically for output. In other words, `ios::out` is the default mode when opening output files. This explains why you can use either of the statements in Example 2 to open the employ.txt file for output. Here too, because the *fileName* argument in both statements does not contain a path, the computer will look for the employ.txt file in the same location as the program file.

In cases for which the program needs to add data to the end of the existing data stored in an output file, you need to specify the `ios::app` mode in the `open` function, as shown in Example 3. In this case, the `outSales.open("F:/FirstQtr/sales.txt", ios::app);` statement tells the computer to open the sales.txt file, which is located in the FirstQtr folder on the F drive, for append.

The computer uses a file pointer to keep track of the next character either to read from or to write to a file. When you open a file for input, the computer positions the file pointer at the beginning of the file, immediately before the first character. When you open a file for output, the computer also positions the file pointer at the beginning of the file, but recall that the file is empty. (As you learned earlier, when you open a file for output, the computer either creates a new, empty file or erases the contents of an existing file.) However, when you open a file for append, the computer positions the file pointer immediately after the last character in the file. Figure 14-5 illustrates the position of the file pointer when files are opened for input, output, and append.

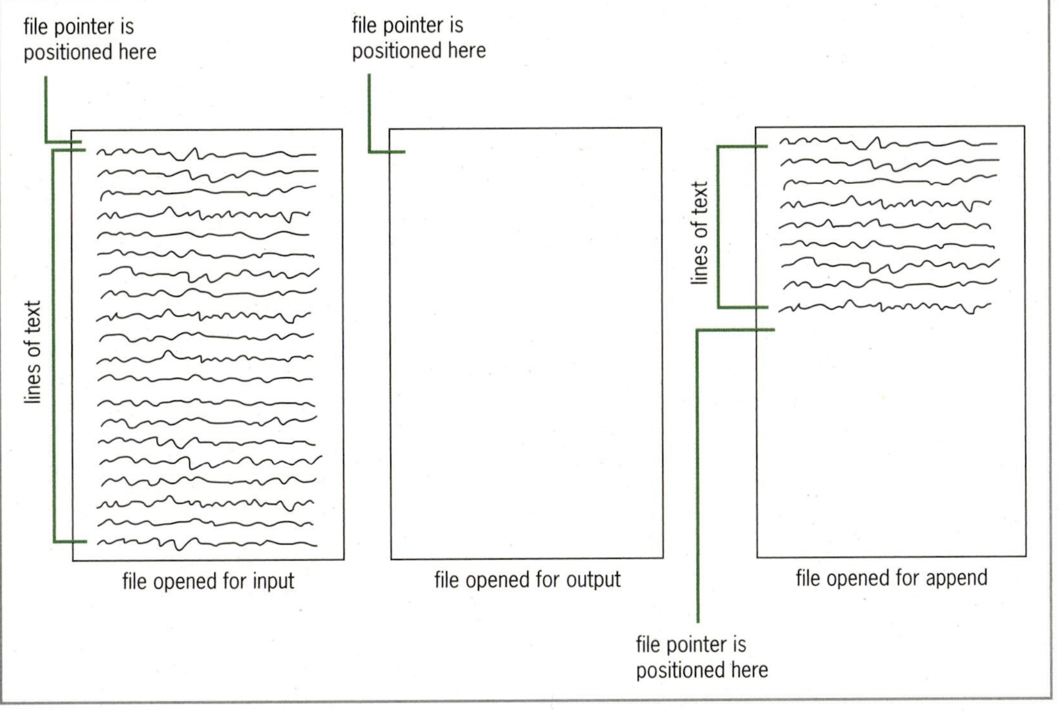

Figure 14-5 Position of the file pointer when files are opened for input, output, and append

Mini-Quiz 14-1

The answers to Mini-Quiz questions are located in Appendix A.

1. To create an input file in a program, the program must contain the ________ directive.
   a. `#include <filestream>`
   b. `#include <fstream>`
   c. `#include <instream>`
   d. `#include <iofilestream>`

2. Which mode tells the computer to open a file for input?
   a. `add::ios`
   b. `in::file`
   c. `ios::app`
   d. `ios::in`

3. Write the C++ statement to create an output file object named `outAlbums`.

4. Which of the following statements uses the `outAlbums` file object from Question 3 to open an output file named mine.txt? New information should be written following the existing information in the file.
   a. `outAlbums.open("mine.txt", ios::in);`
   b. `outAlbums.open("mine.txt", ios::out);`
   c. `outAlbums.open("mine.txt", ios::app);`
   d. `outAlbums.open("mine.txt", ios::add);`

Determining Whether a File Was Opened Successfully

The `is_open` function is a class member function in the `ifstream` and `ofstream` classes.

Keep in mind that it is possible for the `open` function to fail when attempting to open a file. For example, the `open` function will not be able to create an output file when either the path specified in the *fileName* argument does not exist or the disk is full. It also will not be able to open an input file that does not exist or one that you don't have permission to open. Immediately after using the `open` function in a program, you should use the `is_open` function to determine whether the file was opened successfully. The **`is_open` function** returns the Boolean value true if the `open` function was able to open the file; otherwise, it returns the Boolean value false.

Figure 14-6 shows the `is_open` function's syntax and includes examples of using the function. In the syntax, *fileObject* is the name of an existing file object in the program. Most times, you will use the `is_open` function in an `if` statement's condition, as shown in the examples. (For clarity, an appropriate `open` function is included in each example.)

HOW TO Determine the Success of the `open` Function

Syntax

fileObject.**is_open()**

Example 1

```
inFile.open("payroll.txt");

if (inFile.is_open() == true)
  or
if (inFile.is_open())
```

determines whether the `open` function succeeded in opening the file associated with the `inFile` object

Example 2

```
outFile.open("employ.txt");

if (outFile.is_open() == false)
  or
if (!outFile.is_open())
```

determines whether the `open` function failed to open the file associated with the `outFile` object

Figure 14-6 How to determine the success of the `open` function

You can use either of the conditions shown in Example 1 to determine whether the `open` function was able to open the file associated with the `inFile` object. The first condition in Example 1, `inFile.is_open() == true`, compares the `is_open` function's return value to the Boolean value true. If the condition evaluates to true, it means that the `open` function was successful in opening the file. If the condition evaluates to false, it means that the `open` function was not able to open the file. As the second condition in Example 1 shows, you can omit the `== true` text from the condition and use `inFile.is_open()` instead.

Unlike the conditions in Example 1, the conditions in Example 2 determine whether the `open` function failed to open the file associated with the `outFile` object. The `outFile.is_open() == false` condition compares the `is_open` function's return value to the Boolean value false. In this case, you can omit the `== false` text by preceding the condition with an exclamation point (!), as shown in the second condition in Example 2. The **!** is the **Not logical operator** in C++, and its purpose is to reverse the truth-value of the condition. In other words, if the value of `outFile.is_open()` is true, then the value of `!outFile.is_open()` is false. Likewise, if the value of `outFile.is_open()` is false, then the value of `!outFile.is_open()` is true.

Writing Data to a Sequential Access File

Figure 14-7 shows the syntax for writing data to a sequential access file in C++. In the syntax, *fileObject* is the name of an existing `ofstream` object in the program, and *data* is the information you want written to the file. The figure also includes examples of using the syntax.

HOW TO Write Data to a Sequential Access File

Syntax
fileObject << *data*;

Example 1
```
outFile << "XYZ Corporation" << endl;
```
writes the string "XYZ Corporation" to the file associated with the `outFile` object and then advances the file pointer to the next line in the file

Example 2
```
outFile << "Gross pay: ";
outFile << gross << endl;
```
writes the string "Gross pay: " and the contents of the `gross` variable to the file associated with the `outFile` object and then advances the file pointer to the next line in the file

Example 3
```
outSales << custName << endl;
```
writes the contents of the `custName` variable to the file associated with the `outSales` object and then advances the file pointer to the next line in the file

Example 4
```
outEmploy << name << '#' << salary << endl;
```
writes the contents of the `name` variable, the number sign (#), and the contents of the `salary` variable to the file associated with the `outEmploy` object and then advances the file pointer to the next line in the file

Figure 14-7 How to write data to a sequential access file

The statement in Example 1 writes the string "XYZ Corporation" followed by a newline character to the file associated with the `outFile` object. The newline character, which represents the Enter key, advances the file pointer to the next line in the file. The first statement in Example 2 writes the string "Gross pay: " to the file associated with the `outFile` object, but it leaves the file pointer after the last character written—in this case, after the space character. The second statement in Example 2 writes the contents of the `gross` variable followed by a newline character to the file. If the `gross` variable contains the number 450, the statements in Example 2 write "Gross pay: 450" (without the quotes) to the file before advancing the file pointer.

Fields and records are like columns and rows, respectively, in a table.

In many programs, a sequential access file is used to store fields and records. A **field** is a single item of information about a person, place, or thing—such as a name, a salary, a Social Security number, or a price. A **record** is a collection of one or more related fields that contain all of the necessary data about a specific person, place, or thing. The college you are attending keeps a student record on you. Examples of fields contained in your student record include your Social Security number, name, address, phone number, credits earned, and grades earned. The place where you are employed also keeps a record on you. Your employee record contains your Social Security number, name, address, phone number, starting date, salary or hourly wage, and so on.

To distinguish one record from another in a sequential access file, programmers typically write each record on a separate line in the file. You do this by including the `endl` stream manipulator at the end of the statement that writes the record. The `outSales << custName << endl;` statement in Example 3 in Figure 14-7, for instance, writes a record that contains one field (the name stored in the `custName` variable) to the file associated with the `outSales` object. The `endl` stream manipulator writes a newline character at the end of the record, which advances the file pointer to the next line in the file.

You also can use a string literal constant, such as "#", to separate each field.

When writing a record that contains more than one field, programmers typically separate each field with a character literal constant. The character literal constant `'#'`, which is the number sign (or hash mark) enclosed in single quotation marks, is commonly used as the separator character. The `'#'` character appears in the `outEmploy << name << '#' << salary << endl;` statement in Example 4 in Figure 14-7. The statement writes a record that contains two fields: the name stored in the `name` variable and the salary amount stored in the `salary` variable. The statement writes the record on a separate line in the file, with the number sign separating the data in the `name` field from the data in the `salary` field.

You can use Notepad to create a text file. However, when saving the file, be sure to enclose the filename in quotation marks, like this: "employees.txt". You also can use Notepad to create a .cpp file, as long as you enclose the filename in quotation marks.

You can verify that the information was written correctly to a sequential access file by opening the file in a text editor, such as the text editor in Visual C++, Dev-C++, Code::Blocks, or Notepad. The instructions for opening a sequential access file depend on the text editor you are using. However, in most cases, you click File on the text editor's menu bar. If you are using either Microsoft Visual C++ or Dev-C++, you then display the Open File dialog box by pointing to Open and then clicking File (Visual C++) or by clicking Open Project or File (Dev-C++). If you are using Code::Blocks, you display the Open file dialog box by clicking Open and then (if necessary) clicking Open it inside the Code::Blocks editor. If you are using Notepad, you display the Open dialog box by clicking Open on the File menu. Next, you click the name of the appropriate file in the Open File (Open file or Open) dialog box and then click the Open button. Figure 14-8 shows a sequential access file named yearsAndSalaries.txt opened in a text editor. The file contains four records: one for each of the company's four employees. Each record has two fields separated by a number sign (#). The first field in each record represents the number of years the employee has worked for the company; the second field represents the employee's salary. A newline character separates one record from the next. Because the newline character is invisible, you will not see it when you open a sequential access file.

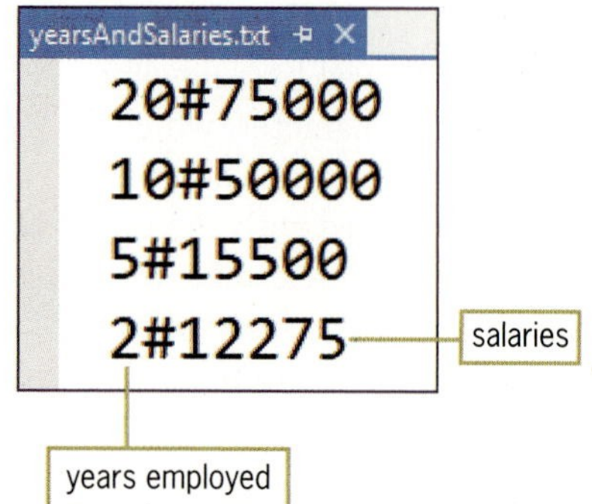

Figure 14-8 The yearsAndSalaries.txt sequential access file opened in a text editor

Reading Information from a Sequential Access File

Figure 14-9 shows the syntax for reading numeric and `char` data from a sequential access file in C++, as well as the syntax for reading `string` data. The figure also includes examples of using each syntax. In each syntax, *fileObject* is the name of an existing `ifstream` object in the program. The *variableName* and *stringVariableName* arguments represent the name of the variable that will store the information read from the file.

HOW TO Read Data from a Sequential Access File

Syntax

To read numeric and `char` data: *fileObject* **>>** *variableName*;
To read `string` data: **getline(***fileObject*, *stringVariableName*[, *delimiterCharacter*]**);**

Example 1

```
int years = 0;
double salary = 0.0;
inFile >> years;
inFile.ignore(1);
inFile >> salary;
inFile.ignore(1);
```

reads a number from the file associated with the `inFile` object and stores the number in the `years` variable, then ignores (consumes) one character, then reads the next number and stores it in the `salary` variable, and then ignores (consumes) one character; when used to read a record from the yearsAndSalaries.txt file shown earlier in Figure 14-8, the first `ignore` function will consume the # character, and the second `ignore` function will consume the newline character

Example 2

```
char letter = ' ';
inAlphabet >> letter;
```

reads a character from the file associated with the `inAlphabet` object and stores the character in the `letter` variable

Example 3

```
string name = "";
getline(inEmploy, name);
```

reads a string from the file associated with the `inEmploy` object and stores the string in the `name` variable, and then ignores (consumes) the newline character

Example 4

```
string name = "";
double salary = 0.0;
getline(inEmploy, name, '#');
inEmploy >> salary;
inEmploy.ignore(1);
```

reads a string from the file associated with the `inEmploy` object and stores the string in the `name` variable, then ignores (consumes) the # character, then reads a number from the file and stores the number in the `salary` variable, and then ignores (consumes) one character

Figure 14-9 How to read data from a sequential access file

As Figure 14-9 indicates, you use the extraction operator (>>) to read `char` and numeric data from a file. Study each of the examples shown in the figure. If the `inFile` object in Example 1 is associated with the yearsAndSalaries.txt file (shown earlier in Figure 14-8), you can use Example 1's code to read the first record from the file. The `inFile >> years;` statement in the example reads the first number from the file (20) and stores the number in the `years` variable. The first `inFile.ignore(1);` statement then consumes (ignores) the number sign (#) that separates the years field from the salary field. Next, the `inFile >> salary;` statement reads the employee's salary (75000) from the file and stores it in the `salary` variable. Finally, the second `inFile.ignore(1);` statement consumes the newline character that separates the first record from the second record.

In Example 2 in Figure 14-9, the `inAlphabet >> letter;` statement reads a character from the file associated with the `inAlphabet` object and stores the character in the `letter` variable.

To read `string` data from a sequential access file, you use the `getline` function, which you learned about in Chapter 13. The `getline` function will continue to read characters from the file associated with the *fileObject* until it encounters the *delimiterCharacter*, which it consumes. Recall that when a function consumes a character, it means that the function reads and discards the character. If you omit the *delimiterCharacter* argument in the `getline` function, the default delimiter character is the newline character. The `getline(inEmploy, name);` statement in Example 3 in Figure 14-9 uses the `getline` function to read a string from the file associated with the `inEmploy` object. Because the `getline` function does not specify a *delimiterCharacter*, the function stops reading when it encounters the newline character. The function stores the string in the `name` variable and then consumes the newline character.

The `getline(inEmploy, name, '#');` statement in Example 4 in Figure 14-9 also reads a string from the file associated with the `inEmploy` object. In this case, however, the `getline` function's *delimiterCharacter* argument indicates that the string ends with the character immediately preceding the # character. After storing the string in the `name` variable, the `getline` function consumes the # character. The next statement in the example, `inEmploy >> salary;`, reads a number from the file and stores the number in the `salary` variable. The `inEmploy.ignore(1);` statement then consumes the next character in the file.

The answers to Mini-Quiz questions are located in Appendix A.

Mini-Quiz 14-2

1. What value does the `is_open` function return when the `open` function fails?
2. Which of the following statements writes the contents of the `quantity` variable to the inventory.txt file, which is associated with a file object named `outInv`?
   a. `inventory.txt << quantity << endl;`
   b. `ofstream << quantity << endl;`
   c. `outInv << quantity << endl;`
   d. `outInv >> quantity >> endl;`
3. Which of the following statements writes a record to the test.txt file? The file is associated with a file object named `outFile`. The record contains two scores, which are stored in the `score1` and `score2` variables.
   a. `test.txt << score1 << score2 << endl;`
   b. `ofstream << score1 << '#' << score2 << endl;`
   c. `outFile << score1 << score2 << endl;`
   d. `outFile << score1 << '#' << score2 << endl;`

4. Which of the following statements reads a record written by the statement from Question 2 and stores the record in the `number` variable? The inventory.txt file is associated with a file object named `inInv`.

   a. `ifstream >> number;`

   b. `inventory.txt >> number;`

   c. `inInv << number;`

   d. `inInv >> number;`

Testing for the End of a Sequential Access File

As you learned earlier, the computer uses a file pointer to keep track of the next character either to read from a file or to write to a file. When a sequential access file is opened for input, the computer positions the file pointer before the first character in the file. Each time a character is read from the file, the file pointer is moved to the next character. When an entire line from the file is read, the computer moves the file pointer to the beginning of the next line in the file.

Most times, a program will need to read each line contained in a sequential access file, one line at a time, beginning with the first line and ending with the last line. You can accomplish this task using a loop along with the `eof` (end of file) function. The **`eof` function** determines whether the last character in a file has been read. In other words, it determines whether the file pointer is located after the last character in the file. If the file pointer is located at the end of the file, the `eof` function returns the Boolean value true; otherwise, it returns the Boolean value false. Figure 14-10 shows the function's syntax and includes examples of using the function. In the syntax, *fileObject* is the name of an existing `ifstream` object in the program. The condition in the `while` clause in Example 1 tells the computer to repeat the loop instructions as long as the end of the file has not been reached. You also can write the condition using the Not logical operator (`!`), as shown in Example 2. As the examples indicate, you should enter the priming read above the `while` clause that contains the `eof` function.

The `eof` function is a class member function in the `ifstream` class.

HOW TO Test for the End of a Sequential Access File

Syntax
fileObject.**eof()**

Example 1
priming read instruction
`while (inFile.eof() == false)`
tells the computer to repeat the loop instructions as long as (or while) the end of the file associated with the `inFile` object has not been reached

Example 2
priming read instruction
`while (!inFile.eof())`
same as Example 1

Figure 14-10 How to test for the end of a sequential access file

Closing a Sequential Access File

To prevent the loss of data, you should use the **`close` function** to close a sequential access file as soon as the program is finished using it. The function's syntax is shown in Figure 14-11 along with examples of using the function. In the syntax, *fileObject* is the name of either an existing `ifstream` object or an existing `ofstream` object in the program. Notice that the `close` function does not require the name of the file you want to close. This is because the computer automatically closes the file whose name is associated with the *fileObject*. (Recall that the `open` function associates the file's name with the *fileObject* when the file is opened.) The `close` function in Example 1 closes the input file associated with the `inFile` object. The `close` function in Example 2 closes the output file associated with the `outFile` object. Because it is so easy to forget to close the files used in a program, you should enter the statement to close the file as soon as possible after entering the one that opens it.

The `close` function is a class member function in the `ifstream` and `ofstream` classes.

HOW TO Close a Sequential Access File

Syntax

fileObject.**close()**

Example 1

```
inFile.close()
```

closes the file associated with the `inFile` object

Example 2

```
outFile.close()
```

closes the file associated with the `outFile` object

Figure 14-11 How to close a sequential access file

Keep in mind that after a file has been read, the only way to access the first record again is to close the file and then reopen it.

Coding the CD Collection Program

Figure 14-12 shows the IPO chart information and C++ instructions for the CD collection program, which keeps track of a CD (compact disc) collection. The problem specification and IPO charts are shown earlier in Figure 14-2. Recall that the program displays a menu containing three options: Enter CD information, Display CD information, and End the program. If the user selects the first option, the program calls a function that prompts the user to enter the CD's name and the artist's name. The function then saves the user's entries in a sequential access file named cds.txt. If the user selects the second option, the program calls a function that displays the contents of the cds.txt file on the screen. The program will end only when the user selects the third option. If the cds.txt file cannot be opened, the program displays an appropriate message.

main function	
IPO chart information	**C++ instructions**
Input	
menu option	`int menuOption = 0;`
filename (cds.txt)	`const string FILE_NAME = "cds.txt";`
Processing	
none	
Output	
none	
Algorithm	
repeat	`do        //begin loop` `{`

display menu	`cout << "1  Enter CD information"`
	`<< endl;`
	`cout << "2  Display CD information"`
	`<< endl;`
	`cout << "3  End the program"`
	`<< endl;`

get menu option	`cout << "Enter menu option: ";`
	`cin >> menuOption;`
	`cin.ignore(100, '\n');`
	`cout << endl;`

if (menu option is 1) call the saveCd function; pass the filename	`if (menuOption == 1)` `saveCd(FILE_NAME);`
else if (menu option is 2) call the displayCds function; pass the filename	`else if (menuOption == 2)` `displayCds(FILE_NAME);`
end if	`//end if` `cout << endl;`
end repeat while (menu option is not 3)	`} while (menuOption != 3);`
saveCd function	
IPO chart information	**C++ instructions**
Input	
filename (formal parameter)	`string nameOfFile`
CD name	`string cdName     = "";`
artist name	`string artistName = "";`
Processing	
none	
Output	
file (sequential access file containing CD names and artist names)	`ofstream outFile;`

Figure 14-12 IPO chart information and C++ instructions for the CD collection program *(continues)*

(continued)

you may need to use nameOfFile.c_str()

Algorithm

Algorithm	C++ instructions
1. open the file for append	`outFile.open(nameOfFile, ios::app);`
2. if (the file was opened successfully)	`if (outFile.is_open())` `{`
enter the CD name	`cout << "CD name (-1 to stop): ";` `getline(cin, cdName);`
repeat while (the CD name is not "-1")	`while (cdName != "-1")` `{`
enter the artist name	`cout << "Artist's name: ";` `getline(cin, artistName);`
write the CD name and artist name to the file	`outFile << cdName << '#'` `<< artistName << endl;`
enter the CD name	`cout << "CD name (-1 to stop): ";` `getline(cin, cdName);`
end repeat	`}  //end while`
close the file	`outFile.close();` `}`
else	`else`
display a message indicating that the file could not be opened	`cout << nameOfFile << " file could not be opened" << endl;`
end if	`//  end if`

displayCds function

IPO chart information	C++ instructions
Input	
filename (formal parameter)	`string nameOfFile`
file (sequential access file containing CD names and artist names)	`ifstream inFile;`
Processing	
none	
Output	
CD name	`string cdName = "";`
artist name	`string artistName = "";`
Algorithm	
1. open the file for input	`inFile.open(nameOfFile, ios::in);`
2. if (the file was opened successfully)	`if (inFile.is_open())` `{`
read the CD name and artist name from the file	`getline(inFile, cdName, '#');` `getline(inFile, artistName);`
repeat while (it's not the end of the file)	`while (!inFile.eof())` `{`
display the CD name and artist name	`cout << cdName << ", " << artistName << endl;`

you may need to use nameOfFile.c_str()

Figure 14-12 IPO chart information and C++ instructions for the CD collection program *(continues)*

(continued)

IPO chart information	C++ instructions
read the CD name and artist name from the file	`getline(inFile, cdName, '#');` `getline(inFile, artistName);`
end repeat	`} //end while`
close the file	`inFile.close();` `}`
else	`else`
display a message indicating that the file could not be opened	`cout << nameOfFile << " file could not be opened" << endl;`
end if	`//end if`

Figure 14-12 IPO chart information and C++ instructions for the CD collection program

Figure 14-13 shows the entire CD collection program, with the instructions pertaining to sequential access files shaded. Figure 14-14 shows a sample run of the program, and Figure 14-15 shows the cds.txt file opened in a text editor.

```
//CD Collection.cpp - keeps track of a CD collection
//Created/revised by <your name> on <current date>

#include <iostream>
#include <string>
#include <fstream>
using namespace std;

//function prototypes
void saveCd(string nameOfFile);
void displayCds(string nameOfFile);

int main()
{
     const string FILE_NAME = "cds.txt";
     int menuOption = 0;

     do //begin loop
     {
        //display menu and get option
        cout << "1  Enter CD information" << endl;
        cout << "2  Display CD information" << endl;
        cout << "3  End the program" << endl;
        cout << "Enter menu option: ";
        cin >> menuOption;
        cin.ignore(100, '\n');
        cout << endl;

        //call appropriate function
        //or display error message
        if (menuOption == 1)
            saveCd(FILE_NAME);
        else if (menuOption == 2)
            displayCds(FILE_NAME);
        //end if
        cout << endl;
     } while (menuOption != 3);

```

Figure 14-13 CD collection program *(continues)*

(continued)

```
    //system("pause");
    return 0;
}   //end of main function

//*****function definitions*****
void saveCd(string nameOfFile)
{
    //writes records to a sequential access file
    string cdName     = "";
    string artistName = "";

    //create file object and open the file
    ofstream outFile;
    outFile.open(nameOfFile, ios::app);

    //determine whether the file was opened
    if (outFile.is_open())
    {
       //get the CD name
       cout << "CD name (-1 to stop): ";
       getline(cin, cdName);
       while (cdName != "-1")
       {
           //get the artist's name
           cout << "Artist's name: ";
           getline(cin, artistName);
           //write the record
           outFile << cdName << '#'
                << artistName << endl;
           //get another CD name
           cout << "CD name (-1 to stop): ";
           getline(cin, cdName);
       }   //end while

       //close the file
       outFile.close();
    }
    else
       cout << nameOfFile
            << " file could not be opened" << endl;
    //end if
}   //end of saveCd function

void displayCds(string nameOfFile)
{
    //displays the records stored in the cds.txt file
    string cdName     = "";
    string artistName = "";

    //create file object and open the file
    ifstream inFile;
    inFile.open(nameOfFile, ios::in);

    //determine whether the file was opened
    if (inFile.is_open())
```

your C++ development tool may require this statement

you may need to use nameOfFile.c_str()

you may need to use nameOfFile.c_str()

Figure 14-13 CD collection program *(continues)*

(continued)

```
    {
        //read a record
        getline(inFile, cdName, '#');
        getline(inFile, artistName);

        while (!inFile.eof())
        {
            //display the record
            cout << cdName << ", " <<
                artistName << endl;
            //read another record
            getline(inFile, cdName, '#');
            getline(inFile, artistName);
        }   //end while

        //close the file
        inFile.close();
    }
    else
        cout << nameOfFile <<
            " file could not be opened" << endl;
    //end if
}   //end of displayCds function
```

Figure 14-13 CD collection program

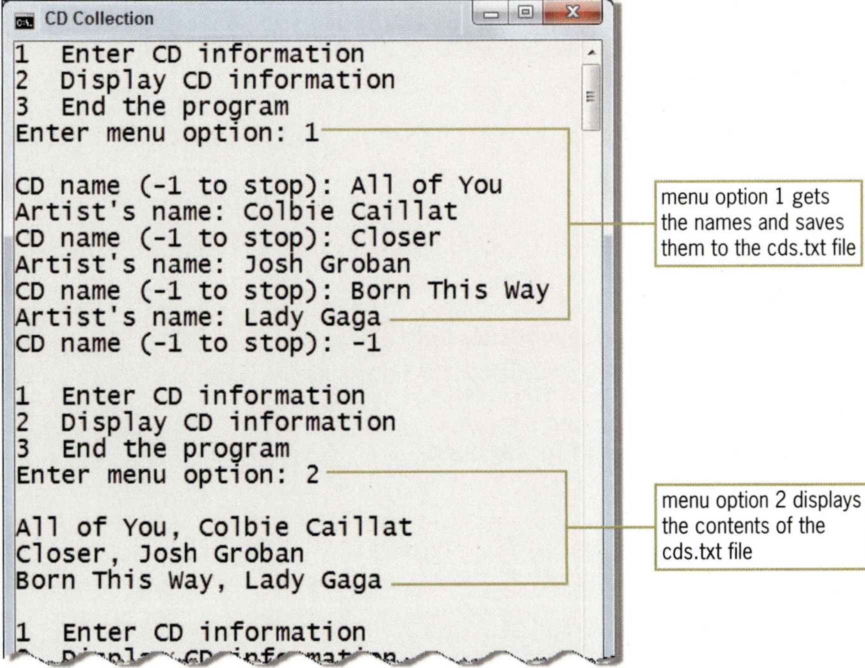

Figure 14-14 Sample run of the CD collection program

Figure 15-15 The cds.txt sequential access file opened in a text editor

The answers to Mini-Quiz questions are located in Appendix A.

Mini-Quiz 14-3

1. Which of the following `while` clauses tells the computer to continue reading the inventory.txt file until the end of the file is reached? The file object is named `inInv`.
   a. `while (inventory.txt.end())`
   b. `while (inInv.end())`
   c. `while (!inInv.eof())`
   d. `while (!inventory.txt.eof())`
2. What value does the `eof` function return when the file pointer is not at the end of the file?
3. Write the statement to close the inventory.txt file, which is associated with a file object named `outInv`.

LAB 14-1 Stop and Analyze

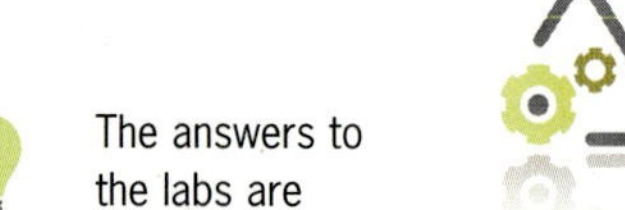

The answers to the labs are located in Appendix A.

Study the program shown in Figure 14-16 and then answer the questions.

```
//Lab14-1.cpp - saves movie titles and release
//years in a sequential access file
//Created/revised by <your name> on <current date>

#include <iostream>
#include <string>
#include <fstream>

using namespace std;

int main()
{
    string title = "";
    string year  = "";

    //create file object and open the file
    ofstream outFile;
    outFile.open("movies.txt", ios::out);

    //determine whether the file is open
    if (outFile.is_open())
    {
        //get movie title
        cout << "Movie title (-1 to stop): ";
        getline(cin, title);

        while (title != "-1")
        {
            //get the release year
            cout << "Year released: ";
            getline(cin, year);

            //write the record to the file
            outFile << title << '#' << year << endl;

```

Figure 14-16 Code for Lab 14-1 *(continues)*

(continued)

```
36              //get another movie title
37              cout << "Movie title (-1 to stop): ";
38              getline(cin, title);
39          }   //end while
40
41          //close the file
42          outFile.close();
43      }
44      else
45          cout << "The movies.txt file could not be opened."
46               << endl;
47      //end if
48
49      //system("pause");
50      return 0;
51 }    //end of main function
```

if your C++ development tool requires this statement, delete the two forward slashes

Figure 14-16 Code for Lab 14-1

QUESTIONS

1. Why are the instructions in Lines 5, 6, and 7 necessary?
2. The program writes records to a sequential access file. How many fields are in each record and what are they?
3. Suppose you run the program twice, entering three records the first time and two records the second time. If you open the movies.txt file in a text editor, how many records will the file contain and why?
4. How can you modify the program so that the existing records in the movies.txt file are not erased when the program is run?
5. What is another way of writing the `if` clause in Line 21?
6. What is the purpose of the # character in Line 34?
7. Why is the statement in Line 42 necessary?
8. Follow the instructions for starting C++ and viewing the Lab14-1.cpp file, which is contained in either the Cpp7\Chap14\Lab14-1 Project folder or the Cpp7\Chap14 folder. (Depending on your C++ development tool, you may need to open Lab14-1's project/solution file first.) If necessary, delete the two forward slashes that appear before the `system("pause");` statement, and then save the program. Run the program. When you are prompted to enter a movie title, type Titanic and press Enter. When you are prompted to enter the release year, type 1997 and press Enter. Next, enter The Dark Knight as the movie title and 2008 as the release year. Finally, enter –1 as the movie title.
9. Use a text editor to open the movies.txt file. The file contains two records. Close the movies.txt file.
10. Run the program again. Enter Shrek 2 as the movie title and 2004 as the release year, and then enter –1 as the movie title. Use a text editor to open the movies.txt file. The file contains one record. Close the movies.txt file.
11. Modify the program so that the existing records in the movies.txt file are not erased when the program is run.

12. Save and then run the program. Enter the following movie titles and release years, followed by the sentinel value, which is −1:

Titanic	1997
The Dark Knight	2008
Star Wars: Episode IV – A New Hope	1977
E.T.: The Extra-Terrestrial	1982

13. Use a text editor to open the movies.txt file. The file contains five records. Close the movies.txt file.

LAB 14-2 Plan and Create

In this lab, you will plan and create an algorithm for Cheryl Liu, the owner of a candy shop named Sweets-4-You. The problem specification is shown in Figure 14-17.

Problem specification
Cheryl Liu is the owner of a candy shop named Sweets-4-You. She wants a program that displays the following menu:

Menu Options
1 Add Records
2 Display Total Sales
3 Exit

If Cheryl selects option 1, the program should call a function that prompts her to enter each salesperson's name and sales amount. The function should save Cheryl's entries in a sequential access file named sales.txt. If Cheryl selects option 2, the program should call a function that calculates and displays the total of the sales amounts stored in the sales.txt file. The program should end only when Cheryl selects option 3.

Figure 14-17 Problem specification for Lab 14-2

The Sweets-4-You program will use four functions: `main`, `getChoice`, `addRecords`, and `displayTotal`. Figure 14-18 shows the IPO chart information and C++ instructions for the `main` and `getChoice` functions; it also includes each function's flowchart. The `main` function begins by declaring and initializing an `int` variable named `choice`. It then calls the `getChoice` function to display the menu, which contains three options. After displaying the menu, the `getChoice` function prompts Cheryl to enter her choice of menu options: 1 to add records, 2 to display the total sales, or 3 to exit the program. The `getChoice` function returns Cheryl's response to the `main` function, which assigns the value to the `choice` variable.

The next instruction in the `main` function in Figure 14-18 is a selection structure that compares the contents of the `choice` variable with the number 1. If the `choice` variable contains the number 1, the `main` function calls the `addRecords` function to add one or more records to the sequential access file. When the `addRecords` function ends, the `main` function calls the `getChoice` function to display the menu again and get another choice from the user. If the `choice` variable does not contain the number 1, the nested selection structure in the `main` function compares the contents of the `choice` variable with the number 2. If the `choice` variable contains the number 2, the `main` function calls the `displayTotal` function to total the sales amounts stored in the sequential access file and then display the total on the screen. When the `displayTotal` function ends, the `main` function calls the `getChoice` function once again. If the `choice` variable contains the number 3, the program ends. If the `choice` variable contains a value other than 1, 2, or 3, the `main` function calls the `getChoice` function to get another selection from the user.

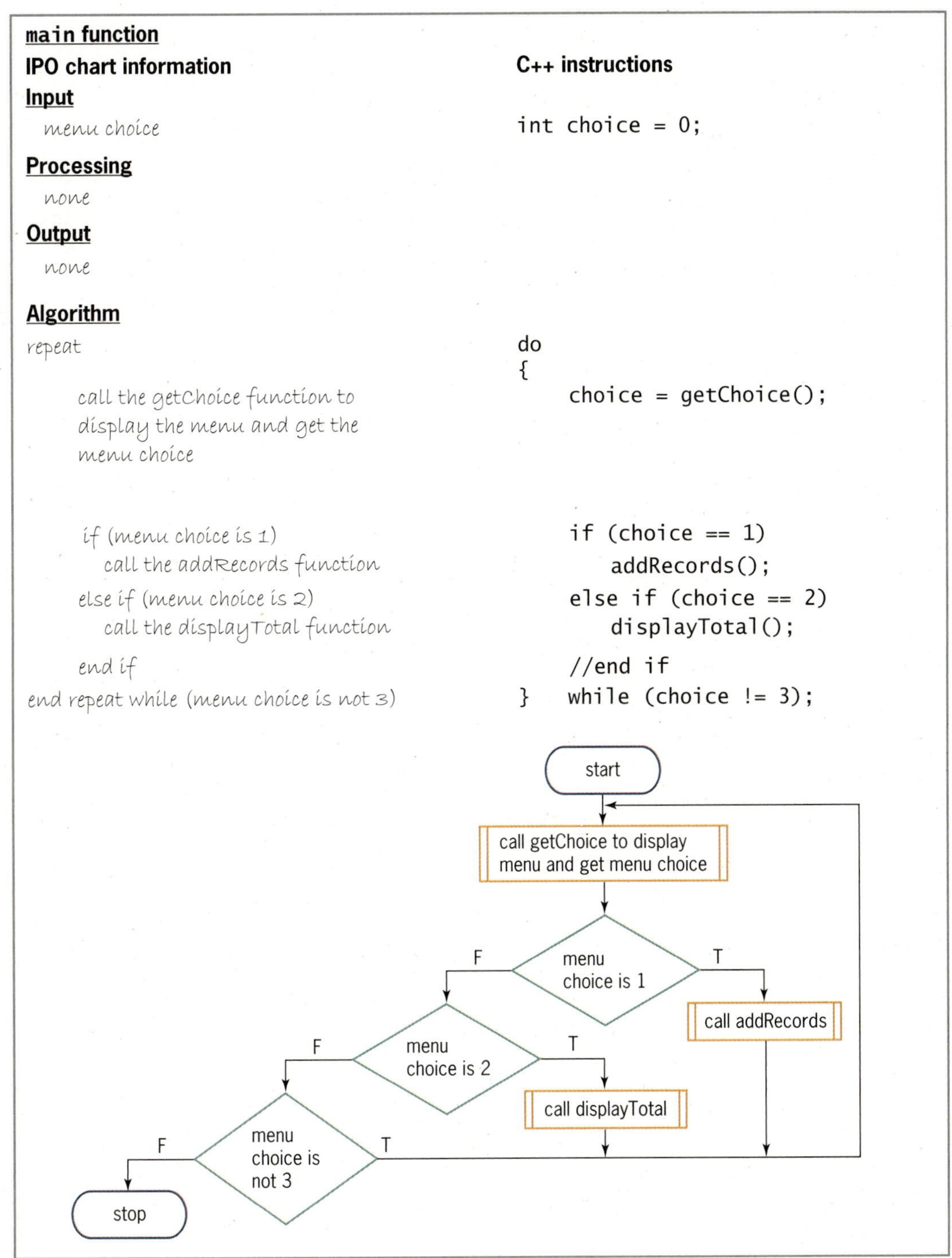

`main` function

IPO chart information	C++ instructions
Input	
menu choice	`int choice = 0;`
Processing	
none	
Output	
none	
Algorithm	
repeat	`do` `{`
call the getChoice function to display the menu and get the menu choice	`choice = getChoice();`
if (menu choice is 1)	`if (choice == 1)`
call the addRecords function	`addRecords();`
else if (menu choice is 2)	`else if (choice == 2)`
call the displayTotal function	`displayTotal();`
end if	`//end if`
end repeat while (menu choice is not 3)	`} while (choice != 3);`

Figure 14-18 IPO chart information (including flowcharts) and C++ instructions for the `main` and `getChoice` functions *(continues)*

(continued)

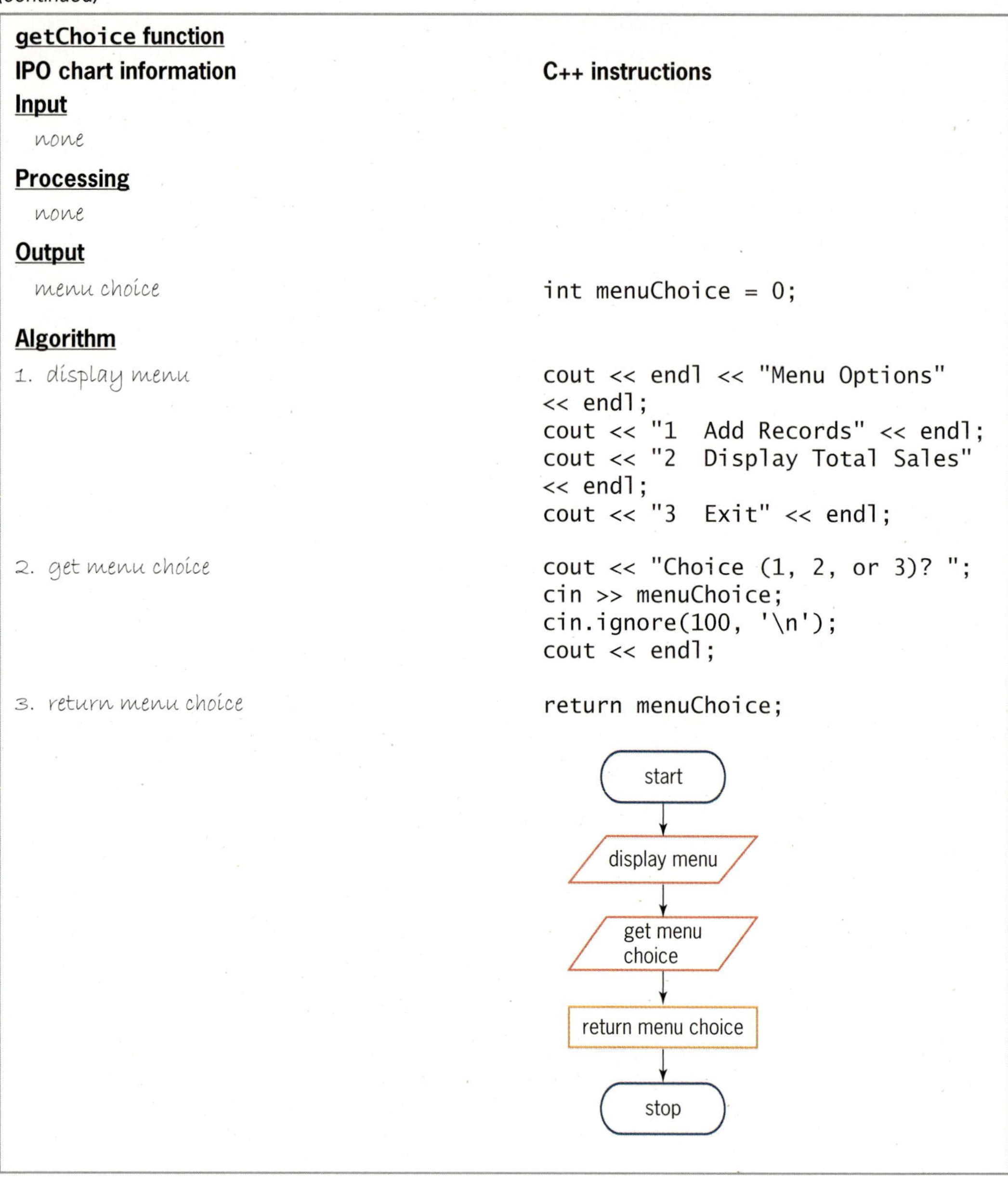

getChoice function

IPO chart information	C++ instructions
Input	
none	
Processing	
none	
Output	
menu choice	`int menuChoice = 0;`
Algorithm	

1. display menu	`cout << endl << "Menu Options"`
	`<< endl;`
	`cout << "1  Add Records" << endl;`
	`cout << "2  Display Total Sales"`
	`<< endl;`
	`cout << "3  Exit" << endl;`

2. get menu choice	`cout << "Choice (1, 2, or 3)? ";`
	`cin >> menuChoice;`
	`cin.ignore(100, '\n');`
	`cout << endl;`

3. return menu choice	`return menuChoice;`

Figure 14-18 IPO chart information (including flowcharts) and C++ instructions for the `main` and `getChoice` functions

Figure 14-19 shows the IPO chart information and C++ instructions for the `addRecords` function; it also includes the function's flowchart. The function creates an output file object named `outFile` and then uses the object, along with the `open` function, to open the sales.txt file for append. The condition in the `if` clause determines whether the sales.txt file was opened successfully. If the condition evaluates to false, it means that the `open` function failed to open the file. In that case, the `addRecords` function displays an appropriate error message and then the function ends. If the condition evaluates to true, on the other hand, it means that the `open` function was successful in opening the sales.txt file. As a result, the instructions in the `if` statement's true path are processed.

The first two statements in the `if` statement's true path in Figure 14-19 prompt the user to enter the salesperson's name and then store the user's response in the `name` variable. The `while` clause in the true path is processed next. The `while` clause indicates that the loop body instructions should be repeated as long as the `name` variable does not contain either the letter X or the letter x. The first two statements in the loop body prompt the user to enter the sales amount and then store the user's response in the `sales` variable. The `cin.ignore(100, '\n');` statement instructs the computer to consume the newline character that remains in the `cin` object after the sales amount is entered. The `outFile << name << '#' << sales << endl;` statement then writes a record, followed by a newline character, to the file. The record contains the contents of the `name` variable, the # character, and the contents of the `sales` variable. The last two statements in the loop body prompt the user to enter another salesperson's name and then store the user's response in the `name` variable. The loop will end when the `name` variable contains either the string "X" or the string "x". When the loop ends, the `outFile.close();` statement closes the sales.txt file before the `addRecords` function ends.

addRecords function

IPO chart information	C++ instructions
Input	
salesperson's name	`string name = "";`
sales amount	`int sales = 0;`
Processing	
none	
Output	
sales.txt file (sequential access)	`ofstream outFile;`
Algorithm	
1. open the sales.txt file for append	`outFile.open("sales.txt", ios::app);`
2. if (the sales.txt file was opened successfully)	`if (outFile.is_open())` `{`
enter the salesperson's name	`cout << "Salesperson's name (X to stop): ";` `getline(cin, name);`
repeat while (the salesperson's name is not "X" or "x")	`while (name != "X" && name != "x")` `{`

enter the sales amount	`cout << "Sales: ";`
	`cin >> sales;`
	`cin.ignore(100, '\n');`

write the salesperson's name and sales amount to the sales.txt file	`outFile << name << '#' << sales << endl;`
enter the salesperson's name	`cout << "Salesperson's name (X to stop): ";` `getline(cin, name);`
end repeat	`} //end while`
close the sales.txt file	`outFile.close();` `}`
else	`else`
display the "sales.txt file could not be opened" message	`cout << "sales.txt file could not be opened" << endl;`
end if	`// end if`

Figure 14-19 IPO chart information (including flowchart) and C++ instructions for the addRecords function *(continues)*

(continued)

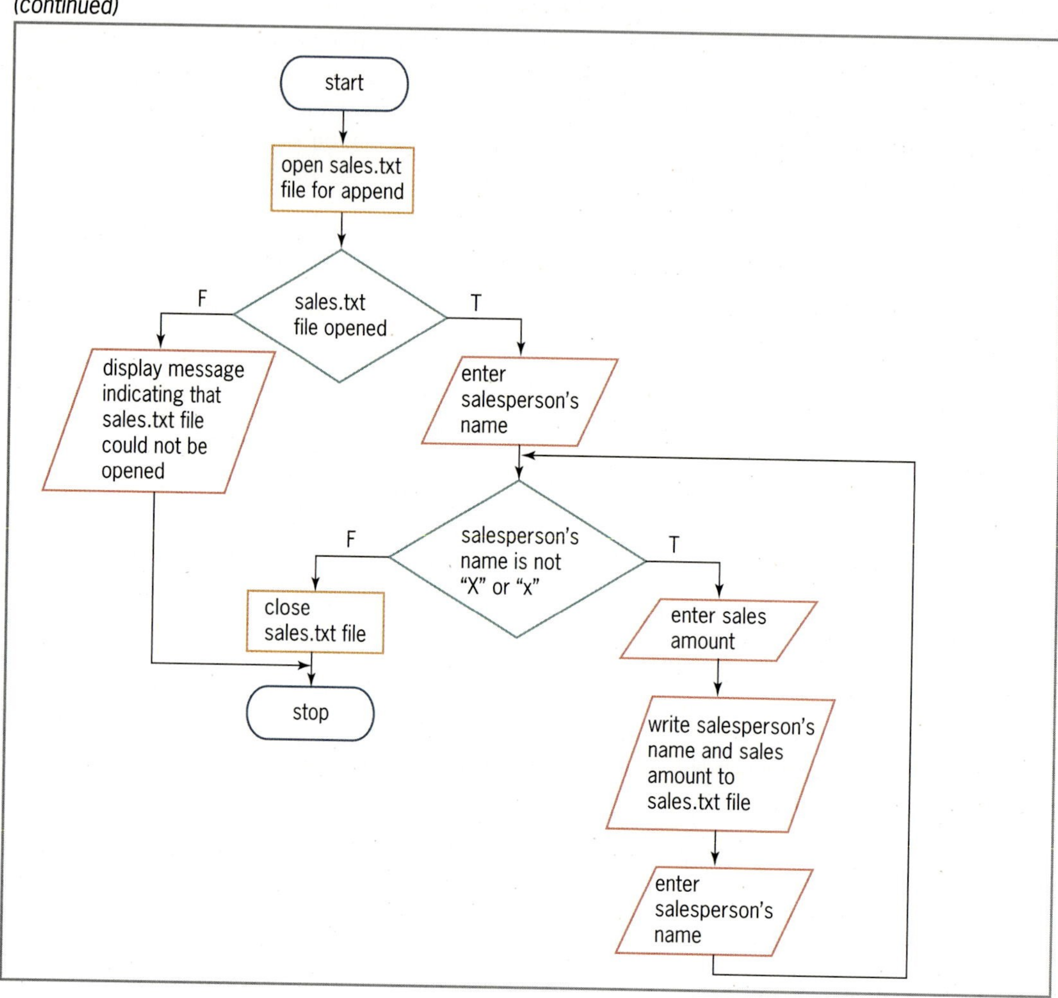

Figure 14-19 IPO chart information (including flowchart) and C++ instructions for the `addRecords` function

Finally, Figure 14-20 shows the IPO chart information and C++ instructions for the `displayTotal` function; it also contains the function's flowchart. The function creates an input file object named `inFile` and then uses the object, along with the `open` function, to open the sales.txt file for input. The condition in the `if` clause determines whether the sales.txt file was opened successfully. If the condition evaluates to false, the `displayTotal` function displays an appropriate error message and then the function ends. If the condition evaluates to true, on the other hand, the instructions in the `if` statement's true path are processed.

The instructions in the `if` statement's true path in Figure 14-20 read a record from the sales.txt file, assigning the name to the `name` variable and assigning the sales to the `sales` variable. The `while` clause in the true path tells the computer to repeat the loop body instructions as long as the file pointer is not at the end of the file. The first statement in the loop body adds the sales amount to the accumulator variable, which is named `total`. The remaining instructions in the loop body read another record from the file. When the loop ends, which occurs when the file pointer is at the end of the sales.txt file, the last two statements in the `if` statement's true path close the sales.txt file and then display the total sales amount on the screen. After displaying the total sales amount, the `displayTotal` function ends.

displayTotal function	
IPO chart information	**C++ instructions**
Input	
sales.txt file (sequential access)	`ifstream inFile;`
Processing	
salesperson's name *sales amount*	`string name = "";` `int sales = 0;`
Output	
total sales amount (accumulator)	`int total = 0;`
Algorithm	

1. open the sales.txt file for input
2. if (the sales.txt file was opened successfully)
	`inFile.open("sales.txt");`
	`if (inFile.is_open())`
	`{`

read the salesperson's name and sales amount from the sales.txt file	`getline(inFile, name, '#');`
	`inFile >> sales;`
	`inFile.ignore();`

repeat while (it's not the end of the sales.txt file)	`while (!inFile.eof())` `{`
add the sales amount to the total sales amount	`total += sales;`

read the salesperson's name and sales amount from the sales.txt file
end repeat
	`getline(inFile, name, '#');`
	`inFile >> sales;`
	`inFile.ignore();`
	`} //end while`

close the sales.txt file
display the total sales amount
	`inFile.close();`
	`cout << "Total sales $"`
	`<< total << endl << endl;`
	`}`

else
display the "sales.txt file could not be opened" message
end if
	`else`
	`cout << "sales.txt file could`
	`not be opened" << endl;`
	`//end if`

Figure 14-20 IPO chart information (including flowchart) and C++ instructions for the `displayTotal` function *(continues)*

(continued)

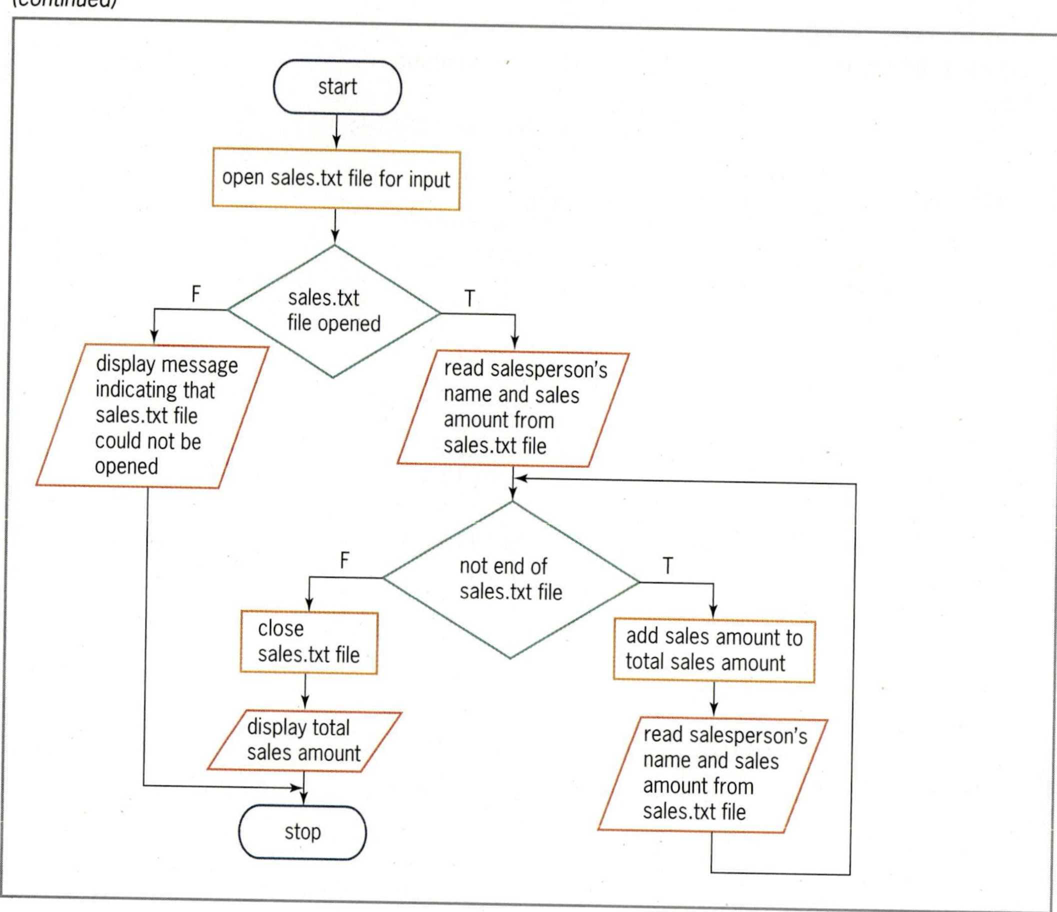

Figure 14-20 IPO chart information (including flowchart) and C++ instructions for the `displayTotal` function

Figure 14-21 shows the code for the entire CD collection program, and Figure 14-22 shows a sample run of the program.

```
//Lab14-2.cpp - saves records to a sequential access
//file and also calculates and displays the total
//of the sales amounts stored in the file
//Created/revised by <your name> on <current date>

#include <iostream>
#include <string>
#include <fstream>
using namespace std;

//function prototypes
int getChoice();
void addRecords();
void displayTotal();

```

Figure 14-21 CD collection program *(continues)*

(continued)

```
int main()
{
    int choice = 0;
    do
    {
        //get user's menu choice
        choice = getChoice();
        if (choice == 1)
            addRecords();
        else if (choice == 2)
            displayTotal();
        //end if
    }   while (choice != 3);

    //system("pause");
    return 0;
}   //end of main function

//*****function definitions*****
int getChoice()
{
    //displays menu and returns choice
    int menuChoice = 0;
    cout << endl << "Menu Options" << endl;
    cout << "1  Add Records" << endl;
    cout << "2  Display Total Sales" << endl;
    cout << "3  Exit" << endl;
    cout << "Choice (1, 2, or 3)? ";
    cin >> menuChoice;
    cin.ignore(100, '\n');
    cout << endl;
    return menuChoice;
}   //end of getChoice function

void addRecords()
{
    //saves records to a sequential access file
    string name = "";
    int sales   = 0;
    ofstream outFile;

    //open file for append
    outFile.open("sales.txt", ios::app);

    //if the open was successful, get the
    //salesperson's name and sales amount and
    //then write the information to the file;
    //otherwise, display an error message
    if (outFile.is_open())
    {
        cout << "Salesperson's name (X to stop): ";
        getline(cin, name);

        while (name != "X" && name != "x")
        {
            cout << "Sales: ";
            cin >> sales;
            cin.ignore(100, '\n');

            outFile << name << '#' << sales << endl;
```

if your C++ development tool requires this statement, delete the two forward slashes

Figure 14-21 CD collection program *(continues)*

(continued)

```

            cout << "Salesperson's name "
                 << "(X to stop): ";
            getline(cin, name);
        }   //end while

        outFile.close();
    }
    else
        cout << "sales.txt file could not be opened"
             << endl;
    //end if
}   //end of addRecords function

void displayTotal()
{
    //calculates and displays the total sales
    string name = "";
    int sales   = 0;
    int total   = 0;
    ifstream inFile;

    //open file for input
    inFile.open("sales.txt");

    //if the open was successful, read the
    //salesperson's name and sales amount, then add
    //the sales amount to the accumulator, and then
    //display the accumulator; otherwise, display
    //an error message
    if (inFile.is_open())
    {
        getline(inFile, name, '#');
        inFile >> sales;
        inFile.ignore();

        while (!inFile.eof())
        {
            total += sales;
            getline(inFile, name, '#');
            inFile >> sales;
            inFile.ignore();
        }   //end while
        inFile.close();
        cout << "Total sales $" << total
             << endl << endl;
    }
    else
        cout << "sales.txt file could not be opened"
             << endl;
    //end if
}   //end of displayTotal function
```

Figure 14-21 CD collection program

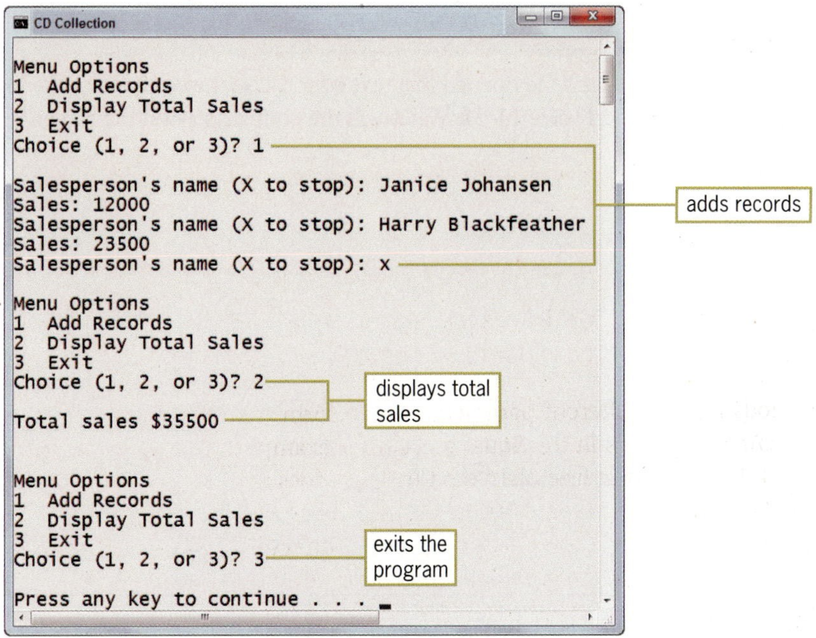

Figure 14-22 Sample run of the CD collection program

DIRECTIONS

Follow the instructions for starting your C++ development tool. Depending on the development tool you are using, you may need to create a new project; if so, name the project Lab14-2 Project and save it in the Cpp7\Chap14 folder. Enter the instructions shown in Figure 14-21 in a source file named Lab14-2.cpp. (Do not enter the line numbers.) Save the file in either the project folder or the Cpp7\Chap14 folder. Now, follow the appropriate instructions for running the Lab14-2.cpp file. Test the program using the data shown in Figure 14-22. If necessary, correct any bugs (errors) in the program.

LAB 14-3 Modify

If necessary, create a new project named Lab14-3 Project and save it in the Cpp7\Chap14 folder. Enter (or copy) the Lab14-2.cpp instructions into a new source file named Lab14-3.cpp. Change Lab14-2.cpp in the first comment to Lab14-3.cpp. Modify the menu so that it contains five options: Add Records, Display Records, Display Total Sales, Display Average Sales, and Exit. When the user selects the Display Records option, the program should call a function to display the contents of the sales.txt file on the screen. When the user selects the Display Average Sales option, the program should call a function to calculate and display the average sales amount stored in the file. Save and then run the program. Test the program appropriately.

LAB 14-4 Desk-Check

Figure 14-23 shows the Lab14-4.txt file opened in a text editor. Use the contents of the file to desk-check the code shown in Figure 14-24. What will the code display on the screen?

```
Lab14-4.txt
7500#6000
4750#3675
8000#9500
4200#5400
```

Figure 14-23 Contents of the Lab14-4.txt sequential access file

```
//Lab14-4.cpp - displays each region's total sales
//Created/revised by <your name> on <current date>

#include <iostream>
#include <fstream>
using namespace std;

int main()
{
    int store1Sales = 0;
    int store2Sales = 0;
    int store1Total = 0;
    int store2Total = 0;

    //create file object and open the file
    ifstream inFile;
    inFile.open("Lab14-4.txt");

    //determine whether the file was opened
    if (inFile.is_open())
    {
        //read store 1's sales amount
        inFile >> store1Sales;
        inFile.ignore();

        while (!inFile.eof())
        {
            //read store 2's sales amount
            inFile >> store2Sales;
            inFile.ignore();

            //accumulate each store's sales amount
            store1Total += store1Sales;
            store2Total += store2Sales;

            //read store 1's sales amount
            inFile >> store1Sales;
            inFile.ignore();
        }   //end while

```

Figure 14-24 Code for Lab 14-4 *(continues)*

(continued)

```
        //close the file
        inFile.close();

        //display the total sales amount for each store
        cout << "Store 1's total sales: $"
             << store1Total << endl;
        cout << "Store 2's total sales: $"
             << store2Total << endl;
    }
    else
        cout << "Can't open Lab14-4.txt file." << endl;
    //end if

    //system("pause");
    return 0;
}   //end of main function
```

your C++ development tool may require this statement

Figure 14-24 Code for Lab 14-4

LAB 14-5 Debug

Follow the instructions for starting C++ and viewing the Lab14-5.cpp file, which is contained in either the Cpp7\Chap14\Lab14-5 Project folder or the Cpp7\Chap14 folder. (Depending on your C++ development tool, you may need to open Lab14-5's project/solution file first.) If necessary, delete the two forward slashes that appear before the `system("pause");` statement and then save the program. The program should write records consisting of a name and two numbers to a sequential access file named records.txt. Run the program. Type your name and press Enter. Type 5000 and press Enter, and then type 2000 and press Enter. Notice that the program is not working correctly. Debug the program. After debugging the program, be sure to open the records.txt file to verify that it contains the information you entered.

Summary

- Sequential access files can be either input files or output files. Input files are files whose contents are read by a program. Output files are files to which a program writes data.
- To create a file object in a program, the program must contain the `#include <fstream>` directive.
- You use the `ifstream` and `ofstream` classes, which are defined in the fstream file, to create input and output file objects, respectively. The file objects are used to represent the actual files stored on your computer's disk.
- After creating a file object, you then use the `open` function (which is a member function in the `ifstream` and `ofstream` classes) to open the file for input, output, or append.
- You can use the `is_open` function (which is a member function in the `ifstream` and `ofstream` classes) to determine whether the `open` function either succeeded or failed to open a sequential access file. The `is_open` function returns the Boolean value true if the `open` function was able to open the file. It returns the Boolean value false if the `open` function could not open the file.
- To distinguish one record from another in a sequential access file, programmers usually write each record on a separate line in the file. You do this by including the `endl` stream

manipulator at the end of the statement that writes the record to the file. If the record contains more than one field, programmers use a character (such as `'#'`) to separate the data in one field from the data in another field.

- When reading data from a file, you use the `eof` function (which is a member function in the `ifstream` class) to determine whether the file pointer is at the end of the file. If the file pointer is located after the last character in the file, the `eof` function returns the Boolean value true; otherwise, it returns the Boolean value false.
- When a program is finished with a file, you should use the `close` function (which is a member function in the `ifstream` and `ofstream` classes) to close it. Failing to close an open file can result in the loss of data.

Key Terms

`!`—the Not logical operator

`close` function—closes a sequential access file in a program

`eof` function—determines whether an entire sequential access file has been read; it returns true when the file pointer is located after the last character in a sequential access file; otherwise, it returns false

Field—a single item of information about a person, place, or thing

Input files—files that contain information used as input by a program

`is_open` function—used in a program to determine whether a sequential access file was opened successfully; returns true when the open operation succeeded; otherwise, returns false

Not logical operator—an exclamation point (`!`); reverses the truth-value of a condition

open function—used to open input and output files in a program

Output files—files that store the output produced by a program

Record—a collection of one or more related fields that contain all of the necessary data about a person, place, or thing

Scope resolution operator—two colons (`::`); indicates that the keyword to the right of the operator is a member of the class whose name appears to the left of the operator

Sequential access files—files composed of lines of text; also referred to as text files

Text files—another name for sequential access files

Review Questions

1. A ________ is a single item of information about a person, place, or thing.
   a. field
   b. file
   c. record
   d. none of the above

2. A group of related fields that contain all of the data about a specific person, place, or thing is called a ________.
   a. field
   b. file
   c. record
   d. none of the above

3. For a program to create a file object, it must include the ______ file.

   a. fileStream
   b. fstream
   c. outFile
   d. sequential

4. You use the ______ class to instantiate an output file object.

   a. `cout`
   b. `fstream`
   c. `ofstream`
   d. `outstream`

5. Which of the following statements creates an object named `outPayroll` that represents an output file in the program?

   a. `fstream outPayroll;`
   b. `ofstream outPayroll;`
   c. `outPayroll as ofstream;`
   d. `outPayroll as outstream;`

6. Which of the following statements opens the payroll.txt file for output? The file is associated with the `outPayroll` object.

   a. `outPayroll.open("payroll.txt");`
   b. `outPayroll.open("payroll.txt", ios::out);`
   c. `outPayroll.open("payroll.txt", ios::output);`
   d. both a and b

7. To add records to the end of an existing output file, you use the ______ *mode* in the `open` function.

   a. `add`
   b. `ios::add`
   c. `ios::app`
   d. `ios::out`

8. You use the ______ function to close a sequential access file.

   a. `close`
   b. `end`
   c. `exit`
   d. `finish`

9. You can use the ______ function to determine whether the `open` function was successful.

   a. `is_open`
   b. `isopen`
   c. `isFileOpen`
   d. `is_FileOpen`

10. Which of the following statements writes the contents of the `city` variable to an output file named address.txt? The file is associated with the `outFile` object.
    a. `address.txt << city << endl;`
    b. `ofstream << city << endl;`
    c. `outFile << city << endl;`
    d. `outFile >> city >> endl;`

11. Which of the following statements reads a number from an input file named managers.txt and stores the number in the `salary` variable? The file is associated with the `inFile` object.
    a. `managers.dat << salary;`
    b. `ifstream << salary;`
    c. `inFile << salary;`
    d. none of the above

12. Which of the following statements writes the contents of the `city` and `state` variables to an output file named address.txt? The file is associated with the `outFile` object.
    a. `address.txt << city << state << endl;`
    b. `ofstream << city << state << endl;`
    c. `outFile >> city >> state >> endl;`
    d. `outFile << city << '#' << state << endl;`

13. Which of the following `while` clauses tells the computer to repeat the loop instructions until the end of the file is reached? The file is associated with the `inFile` object.
    a. `while (inFile.eof())`
    b. `while (!ifstream.eof())`
    c. `while (!inFile.eof())`
    d. `while (!ifstream.fail())`

14. Which of the following statements creates an object named `inPayroll` that represents an input file in the program?
    a. `instream inPayroll;`
    b. `ifstream inPayroll;`
    c. `inPayroll ifstream;`
    d. `inPayroll as ifstream;`

15. Which of the following statements opens the payroll.txt file for input? The file is associated with the `inFile` object.
    a. `inFile.open("payroll.txt", ios::app);`
    b. `inFile.open("payroll.txt");`
    c. `inFile.open("payroll.txt", ios::in);`
    d. both b and c

Exercises

Pencil and Paper

1. Write the statement to declare an input file object named `inSales`. (The answers to TRY THIS Exercises are located at the end of the chapter.) TRY THIS
2. Write the statement to open a sequential access file named jansales.txt for output. The file is associated with the `outJan` object. (The answers to TRY THIS Exercises are located at the end of the chapter.) TRY THIS
3. Rewrite the statement from Pencil and Paper Exercise 2 so it opens the jansales.txt file for append. MODIFY THIS
4. Write the statement to open a sequential access file named inventory.txt for input. The file is associated with the `inInventory` object. INTRODUCTORY
5. Write the statement to open a sequential access file named firstQtr.txt for append. The file is associated with the `outSales` object. INTRODUCTORY
6. Write the statement to open a sequential access file named febsales.txt for output. The file is associated with the `outFeb` object. INTRODUCTORY
7. Write an `if` clause that determines whether an output file was opened successfully. The file is associated with the `outSales` object. INTRODUCTORY
8. Write the statement to read a string from the sequential access file associated with the `inFile` object. Assign the string to the `textLine` variable. INTRODUCTORY
9. Write the statement to read a number from the sequential access file associated with the `inFile` object. Assign the number to the `number` variable. INTRODUCTORY
10. Write the statement to close the jansales.txt file, which is associated with the `outFile` object. INTRODUCTORY
11. A program needs to write the string "Employee" and the string "Name" to the sequential access file associated with the `outFile` object. Each string should appear on a separate line in the file. Write the code to accomplish this task. INTRODUCTORY
12. A program needs to write the contents of a `string` variable named `capital` and the newline character to the sequential access file associated with the `outFile` object. Write the code to accomplish this task. INTERMEDIATE
13. Write a `while` clause that tells the computer to stop processing the loop instructions when the end of the file has been reached. The file is associated with the `inFile` object. INTERMEDIATE
14. A program needs to read a sequential access file, line by line, and display each line on the computer screen. The file, which was opened successfully, is associated with the `inFile` object. Write the code to read and then close the file. ADVANCED
15. Correct the condition in the following `if` clause, which should determine whether the `open` function was able to open the file associated with the `outFile` object: `if (outFile.open())`. SWAT THE BUGS

Computer

TRY THIS

16. If necessary, create a new project named TryThis16 Project and save it in the Cpp7\Chap14 folder. Also create a new source file named TryThis16.cpp. Write a program that allows the user to enter the 26 letters of the alphabet. The program should save each letter on a separate line in a sequential access file named TryThis16.txt. Save and then run the program. Test the program by entering the 26 lowercase letters of the alphabet, one at a time. Verify that the program worked correctly by opening the TryThis16.txt file in a text editor. Close the TryThis16.txt file. (The answers to TRY THIS Exercises are located at the end of the chapter.)

TRY THIS

17. If necessary, create a new project named TryThis17 Project and save it in the Cpp7\Chap14 folder. Also create a new source file named TryThis17.cpp. Write a program that saves records to a sequential access file named TryThis17.txt. Each record should appear on a separate line and contain two fields separated by the number sign (#). The first field should contain numbers from 10 through 25. The second field should contain the square of the number in the first field. For example, the first record will contain 10#100 followed by the newline character. Display the message "Numbers saved in file." if the program was able to save the numbers. Save and then run the program. Verify that the program worked correctly by opening the TryThis17.txt file in a text editor. Close the TryThis17.txt file. (The answers to TRY THIS Exercises are located at the end of the chapter.)

MODIFY THIS

18. In this exercise, you modify the program from TRY THIS Exercise 17. If necessary, create a new project named ModifyThis18 Project and save it in the Cpp7\Chap14 folder. Copy the instructions from the TryThis17.cpp file into a source file named ModifyThis18.cpp. Change the filename in the first comment to ModifyThis18.cpp. Also change the name of the sequential access file in both the `open` function and the `cout` statement to ModifyThis18.txt. Modify the program so that each record contains an additional field: the cube of the number in the first field. For example, the first record will contain 10#100#1000 followed by the newline character. Save and then run the program. Verify that the program worked correctly by opening the ModifyThis18.txt file in a text editor. Close the ModifyThis18.txt file.

INTRODUCTORY

19. If necessary, create a new project named Introductory19 Project and save it in the Cpp7\Chap14 folder. Also create a new source file named Introductory19.cpp. Create a program that saves a company's payroll amounts in a sequential access file. Save the amounts in fixed-point notation with two decimal places. Name the sequential access file Introductory19.txt and open the file for append. Use a negative number as the sentinel value. Save and then run the program. Enter the following payroll amounts and sentinel value: 45678.99, 67000.56, and –1. Now, run the program again. This time, enter the following payroll amounts and sentinel value: 25000.89, 35600.55, and –1. Open the Introductory19.txt file in a text editor. The file should contain four payroll amounts, with each amount appearing on a separate line in the file. Close the Introductory19.txt file.

INTRODUCTORY

20. If necessary, create a new project named Introductory20 Project and save it in the Cpp7\Chap14 folder. Also create a new source file named Introductory20.cpp. Create a program that saves prices in a sequential access file. Save the prices in fixed-point notation with two decimal places. Name the sequential access file Introductory20.txt and open the file for append. Use a negative number as the sentinel value. Save and then run the program. Enter the following prices and sentinel value: 10.50, 15.99, and –1. Now, run the program again. This time, enter the following prices and sentinel value: 20, 76.54, 17.34, and –1. Open the Introductory20.txt file in a text editor. The file should contain five prices, with each price appearing on a separate line in the file. Close the Introductory20.txt file.

INTRODUCTORY

21. If necessary, create a new project named Introductory21 Project and save it in the Cpp7\Chap14 folder. Also create a new source file named Introductory21.cpp. If you are using Microsoft Visual C++, copy the Introductory21.txt file from the Cpp7\Chap14 folder to the Cpp7\Chap14\Introductory21 Project folder. Use a text editor to open the Introductory21.txt file, which contains the 26 uppercase letters of the alphabet. Close the Introductory21.txt file. Create a program that counts the number of letters stored in the file. The program should display the number of letters on the computer screen. Save and then run the program.

INTERMEDIATE

22. If necessary, create a new project named Intermediate22 Project and save it in the Cpp7\Chap14 folder. Also create a new source file named Intermediate22.cpp. If you are using Microsoft Visual C++, copy the Intermediate22.txt file from the Cpp7\Chap14 folder to the Cpp7\Chap14\Intermediate22 Project folder. Use a text editor to open the Intermediate22.txt file, which contains payroll amounts. Close the Intermediate22.txt file. Create a program that calculates and displays the total of the payroll amounts stored in the file. Display the total with a dollar sign and two decimal places. Save and then run the program.

INTERMEDIATE

23. If necessary, create a new project named Intermediate23 Project and save it in the Cpp7\Chap14 folder. Also create a new source file named Intermediate23.cpp. If you are using Microsoft Visual C++, copy the Intermediate23.txt file from the Cpp7\Chap14 folder to the Cpp7\Chap14\Intermediate23 Project folder. Use a text editor to open the Intermediate23.txt file, which contains prices. Close the Intermediate23.txt file. Create a program that calculates and displays the average price stored in the file. Display the average with a dollar sign and two decimal places. Save and then run the program.

INTERMEDIATE

24. If necessary, create a new project named Intermediate24 Project and save it in the Cpp7\Chap14 folder. Also create a new source file named Intermediate24.cpp. If you are using Microsoft Visual C++, copy the Intermediate24.txt file from the Cpp7\Chap14 folder to the Cpp7\Chap14\Intermediate24 Project folder. Use a text editor to open the Intermediate24.txt file, which contains payroll codes and salaries. Close the Intermediate24.txt file. Create a program that allows the user to enter a payroll code. The program should search for the payroll code in the file and then display the appropriate salary. If the payroll code is not in the file, the program should display an appropriate message. The program should allow the user to display as many salaries as needed without having to run the program again. Save and then run the program. Test the program by entering the following payroll codes: 10, 24, 55, 32, and 6. Stop the program.

ADVANCED

25. If necessary, create a new project named Advanced25 Project and save it in the Cpp7\Chap14 folder. Also create a new source file named Advanced25.cpp. If you are using Microsoft Visual C++, copy the Advanced25.txt file from the Cpp7\Chap14 folder to the Cpp7\Chap14\Advanced25 Project folder. Use a text editor to open the Advanced25.txt file, which contains the names of the items in inventory, as well as each item's quantity and price. Close the Advanced25.txt file. Write a program that displays the contents of the file in three columns titled "Name", "Quantity", and "Price". The program should also display a fourth column that contains the result of multiplying each item's quantity by its price. Use "Value" as the column's title. (You can align the columns using `'\t'`, which is the escape sequence for the Tab key.) In addition, the program should calculate and display the total value of the items in inventory. Display the price, value, and total value with two decimal places. Save and then run the program.

ADVANCED

26. If necessary, create a new project named Advanced26 Project and save it in the Cpp7\Chap14 folder. Also create a new source file named Advanced26.cpp. Write a program that allows the user to record the names of cities and their corresponding ZIP codes in a sequential access file named Advanced26.txt. The program should also allow the user to look up a ZIP code in the file and display the name of its corresponding city. If the ZIP code is not in the file, the program should display an appropriate message.

Save and then run the program. Enter the ZIP codes and city names listed in Figure 14-25. Next, display the name of the city corresponding to the following ZIP codes: 60135, 60544, and 55555.

ZIP code	City
60561	Darien
60544	Hinsdale
60137	Glen Ellyn
60135	Downers Grove
60136	Burr Ridge

Figure 14-25

ADVANCED

27. If necessary, create a new project named Advanced27 Project and save it in the Cpp7\Chap14 folder. Also create a new source file named Advanced27.cpp. If you are using Microsoft Visual C++, copy the Advanced27.txt file from the Cpp7\Chap14 folder to the Cpp7\Chap14\Advanced27 Project folder. Each salesperson at BobCat Motors is assigned a code that consists of two characters. The first character is either the letter F (which indicates a full-time employee) or the letter P (which indicates a part-time employee). The second character is either a 1 (indicating the salesperson sells new cars) or a 2 (indicating the salesperson sells used cars). Use a text editor to open the Advanced27.txt file, which contains the names of BobCat's salespeople along with each salesperson's code, and then close the file. Write a program that prompts the user to enter the code (F1, F2, P1, or P2). The program should search the Advanced27.txt file for the code and then display only the names of the salespeople assigned that code. Display an appropriate message if the user enters an invalid code. Save and then run the program. Test the program by entering F2 as the code. The program should display three records: Mary Jones, Joel Adkari, and Janice Paulo. Now, test the program using codes of F1, P1, P2, and S3.

ADVANCED

28. If necessary, create a new project named Advanced28 Project and save it in the Cpp7\Chap14 folder. Also create a new source file named Advanced28.cpp. If you are using Microsoft Visual C++, copy the Advanced28.txt file from the Cpp7\Chap14 folder to the Cpp7\Chap14\Advanced28 Project folder. Use a text editor to open the Advanced28.txt file, which contains 20 numbers. Close the Advanced28.txt file. Write a program that performs the following for each number in the Advanced28.txt file: read the number, add 1 to the number, and write the new number to another sequential access file named UpdatedAdvanced28.txt. Save and then run the program. Use a text editor to open the UpdatedAdvanced28.txt file. Each number in the file should be one greater than its corresponding number in the Advanced28.txt file. Close the UpdatedAdvanced28.txt file.

ADVANCED

29. If necessary, create a new project named Advanced29 Project and save it in the Cpp7\Chap14 folder. Also create a new source file named Advanced29.cpp. If you are using Microsoft Visual C++, copy the Advanced29.txt file from the Cpp7\Chap14 folder to the Cpp7\Chap14\Advanced29 Project folder. Use a text editor to open the Advanced29.txt file, which contains 12 numbers. Close the Advanced29.txt file. Write a program that reads the numbers contained in the Advanced29.txt file and writes only the even numbers to a new sequential access file named EvenAdvanced29.txt. Save and then run the program. Use a text editor to open the EvenAdvanced29.txt file, which should contain only the even numbers. Close the EvenAdvanced29.txt file.

SWAT THE BUGS

30. Follow the instructions for starting C++ and viewing the SwatTheBugs30.cpp file, which is contained in either the Cpp7\Chap14\SwatTheBugs30 Project folder or the Cpp7\Chap14 folder. Depending on your C++ development tool, you may need to open the project/solution file first.) If necessary, delete the two forward slashes that appear

before the `system("pause");` statement, and then save the program. The program should display the contents of the SwatTheBugs30.txt file. Run the program. Notice that the program is not working correctly. Debug the program.

Answers to TRY THIS Exercises

Pencil and Paper

1. `ifstream inSales;`
2. `outJan.open("jansales.txt");` or `outJan.open("jansales.txt", ios::out);`

Computer

16. See Figures 14-26 and 14-27.

```
1 //TryThis16.cpp
2 //writes 26 letters to a sequential access file
3 //Created/revised by <your name> on <current date>
4
5 #include <iostream>
6 #include <fstream>
7 using namespace std;
8
9 int main()
10 {
11     char letter = ' ';
12
13     //create file object and open the file
14     ofstream outFile;
15     outFile.open("TryThis16.txt");
16
17     //determine whether the file was opened
18     if (outFile.is_open())
19     {
20         //get the 26 letters of the alphabet and
21         //write each to the file
22         for (int x = 1; x <= 26; x += 1)
23         {
24             cout << "Enter letter " << x << ": ";
25             cin >> letter;
26             outFile << letter << endl;
27         }   //end for
28
```

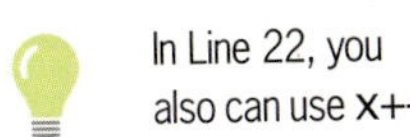

In Line 22, you also can use x++.

Figure 14-26 *(continues)*

(continued)

```
        //close the file
        outFile.close();
    }
    else
        cout << "Can't open the TryThis16.txt file."
             << endl;
    //end if

    //system("pause");
    return 0;
}   //end of main function
```

your C++ development tool may require this statement

Figure 14-26

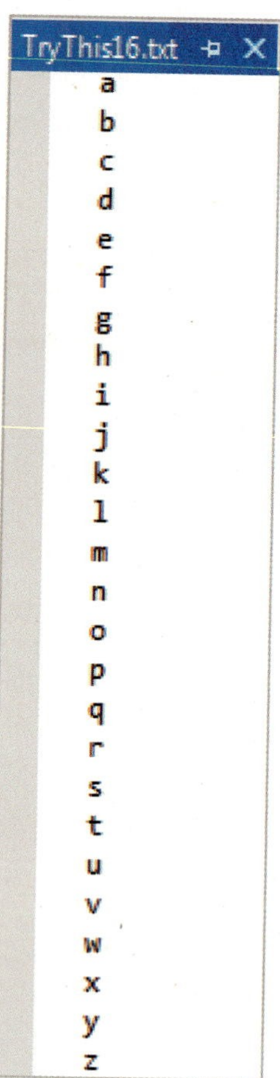

Figure 14-27

17. See Figures 14-28 and 14-29.

```
1 //TryThis17.cpp - saves numbers from 10 through
2 //25, along with the square of each number,
3 //in a sequential access file
4 //Created/revised by <your name> on <current date>
5
6 #include <iostream>
7 #include <cmath>
8 #include <fstream>
9 using namespace std;
10
11 int main()
12 {
13     ofstream outNumbers;
14     outNumbers.open("TryThis17.txt");
15
16     if (outNumbers.is_open())
17     {
18         for (int x = 10; x < 26; x += 1)
19             outNumbers << x << '#'
20                 << pow(x, 2.0) << endl;
21         //end for
22         outNumbers.close();
23         cout << "Numbers saved in file." << endl;
24     }
25     else
26         cout << "Can't open the TryThis17.txt file."
27              << endl;
28     //end if
29
30     //system("pause");
31     return 0;
32 }   //end of main function
```

your C++ development tool may require this statement

Figure 14-28

In Line 18, you also can use x++.

```
TryThis17.txt
10#100
11#121
12#144
13#169
14#196
15#225
16#256
17#289
18#324
19#361
20#400
21#441
22#484
23#529
24#576
25#625
```

Figure 14-29

CHAPTER 15

Classes and Objects

After studying Chapter 15, you should be able to:

- Differentiate between procedure-oriented and object-oriented programming
- Define the terms used in object-oriented programming
- Create a class definition
- Instantiate an object from a class that you define
- Create a default constructor
- Create a parameterized constructor
- Include methods other than constructors in a class
- Overload the methods in a class

Object-Oriented Terminology

Ch15-Chapter Preview video

In Chapter 1, you learned that some programs are procedure oriented and some are object oriented. All of the programs you created in the previous chapters were procedure oriented. Recall that when writing a procedure-oriented program, the programmer concentrates on the major tasks that the program must perform to accomplish its goal. A payroll program, for example, typically performs several major tasks, such as inputting the employee data, calculating the gross pay, calculating the taxes, calculating the net pay, and outputting a paycheck. The programmer usually assigns each major task to a function, which is the primary component in a procedure-oriented program.

The primary component in an object-oriented program, on the other hand, is an object. An **object** is anything that can be seen, touched, or used. In other words, an object is nearly any *thing.* When writing an object-oriented program, the programmer focuses on the objects (rather than the tasks) that the program can use to accomplish its goal. The objects can take on many different forms. Programs written for the Windows environment typically use objects such as check boxes, list boxes, and buttons. A payroll program, on the other hand, might utilize objects found in real life, such as a time card object, an employee object, or a paycheck object. Because each object is viewed as an independent unit, an object can be used in more than one program, usually with little or no modification. A check object used in a payroll program, for example, also can be used in a sales revenue program (which receives checks from customers) and an accounts payable program (which issues checks to creditors). The ability to use an object for more than one purpose enables code-reuse, which saves programming time and money—advantages that contribute to the popularity of object-oriented programming.

Every object in an object-oriented program is created from a **class**, which is a pattern or blueprint that the computer uses to create the object. Using object-oriented programming (**OOP**) terminology, objects are **instantiated** (created) from a class, and each object is referred to as an **instance** of the class. A `string` object (variable or named constant), for example, is an instance of the `string` class and is instantiated when its declaration statement is processed in a program. Similarly, the input and output file objects discussed in Chapter 14 are instances of the `ifstream` and `ofstream` classes, respectively. Keep in mind that the class itself is not an object. Only an instance of a class is an object.

Every object has **attributes**, which are the characteristics that describe the object. When you tell someone that your wristwatch is a Valenti Model VI, you are describing the watch (an object) in terms of some of its attributes—in this case, its maker and model number. A watch also has many other attributes, such as a crown, a dial, an hour hand, a minute hand, and movement. In addition to attributes, most objects also have behaviors. An object's **behaviors** fall into two categories: actions that the object is capable of performing and actions to which the object can respond. A watch, for example, can keep track of the time and date. Some watches also can illuminate their dials when a button on the watch is pushed. A class contains—or, in OOP terms, **encapsulates**—all of the attributes and behaviors of the object it instantiates. The term "encapsulate" means "to enclose in a capsule." In the context of OOP, the "capsule" is a class.

"Abstraction" is another term used in OOP discussions. **Abstraction** refers to the hiding of the internal details of an object from the user. Hiding the internal details helps prevent the user from making inadvertent changes to the object. The internal mechanism of a watch, for example, is enclosed (**hidden**) in a case to protect the mechanism from damage. Attributes and behaviors that are not hidden are said to be **exposed** to the user. Exposed on a Valenti Model VI watch are the crown used to set the hour and minute hands, and the button used to illuminate the dial. The idea behind abstraction is to expose to the user only those attributes and behaviors that are necessary to use the object, and to hide everything else.

Another OOP term, **inheritance**, refers to the fact that you can create one class from another class. The new class, called the **derived class**, inherits the attributes and behaviors of the original class, called the **base class**. For example, the Valenti company might create a blueprint of the Model VII watch from the blueprint of the Model VI watch. The Model VII blueprint (the derived class) will inherit all of the attributes and behaviors of the Model VI blueprint (the base class), but it then can be modified to include an additional feature, such as an alarm.

Finally, you also will hear the term "polymorphism" in OOP discussions. **Polymorphism** is the object-oriented feature that allows the same instruction to be carried out differently depending on the object. For example, you open a door, but you also open an envelope, a jar, and your eyes. Similarly, you can set the time, date, and alarm on a Valenti watch. Although the meaning of the verbs "open" and "set" are different in each case, you can understand each instruction because the combination of the verb and the object makes the instruction clear.

You can use the acronym APIE (Abstraction, Polymorphism, Inheritance, and Encapsulation) to help you remember some of the OOP terms.

Mini-Quiz 15-1

The answers to Mini-Quiz questions are located in Appendix A.

1. OOP is an acronym for ________.
2. A class is an object.
   a. True
   b. False
3. An object created from a class is called ________.
   a. an attribute
   b. an instance of the class
   c. the base class
   d. the derived class
4. The actions that an object can perform or to which an object can respond are called the object's ________.
   a. attributes
   b. behaviors
   c. qualities
   d. traits

Defining a Class in C++

In previous chapters, you instantiated objects using existing classes, such as the `string` and `ofstream` classes. You used the instantiated objects in a variety of ways in many different programs. In some programs, you used a `string` object (variable or named constant) to store a name, whereas in others you used it to store a phone number. Similarly, one of the programs in Chapter 14 used an output file object to save CD (compact disc) information. Another program in the same chapter used an output file object to save a store's sales information.

The creation of a good class, which is one whose objects can be used in a variety of ways by many different programs, requires a lot of planning.

You also can define your own classes in C++ and then create instances (objects) from those classes. As do the `string` and `ofstream` classes, your classes must specify the attributes and behaviors of the objects they create. You specify the attributes and behaviors using a **class definition**. Figure 15-1 shows the syntax used in this book to define a class. The figure also includes an example of defining a class named `FormattedDate`.

HOW TO Define a Class

Syntax

//declaration section
class *className*
{
public: — colon
public attributes (data members)
public behaviors (member methods)
private: — colon
private attributes (data members)
private behaviors (member methods)
}; — semicolon

[//implementation section
member method definitions]

Example

```
//declaration section
class FormattedDate
{
public:
     FormattedDate();
     void setDate(string, string, string);
     string getFormattedDate();
private:
     string month;
     string day;
     string year;
};

//implementation section
FormattedDate::FormattedDate()
{
     //initializes the private variables
     month = "0";
     day   = "0";
     year  = "0";
}    //end of default constructor

void FormattedDate::setDate(string m, string d, string y)
{
     //assigns program values to the private variables
     month = m;
     day   = d;
     year  = y;
}    //end of setDate method

string FormattedDate::getFormattedDate()
{
     //formats and returns values stored
     //in the private variables
     return month + "/" + day + "/" + year;
}    //end of getFormattedDate method
```

(Annotations: the three public lines are labeled "method prototypes"; the three private string lines are labeled "variable declarations".)

Figure 15-1 How to define a class

Notice that the class definition syntax contains two sections: a declaration section and an optional implementation section. The **declaration section** contains the C++ **`class` statement**, which begins with the keyword `class` followed by the name of the class; the statement ends with a semicolon. Although it is not a requirement, the convention is to enter the class name using **Pascal case**, which means you capitalize the first letter in the name and the first letter in any subsequent words in the name. Examples of class names that follow this naming convention include `Check`, `FormattedDate`, and `TimeCard`.

The `class` statement groups related items into one unit.

Within the `class` statement, you list the attributes and behaviors of the objects that the class will create; you enclose the attributes and behaviors in a set of braces. In most cases, the attributes (called data members) are represented by variable declarations, and the behaviors (called member methods) are represented by method prototypes. A **method** is simply a function that is defined in a class definition. You enter the method definitions in the **implementation section** of a class definition. The implementation section will contain one definition for each prototype listed in the declaration section. If no method prototypes appear in the declaration section, the implementation section is not needed.

Some C++ programmers refer to the methods in a class as member functions.

As Figure 15-1 indicates, a class can contain both public members and private members. You record the public members below the keyword `public` in the `class` statement. The private members are recorded below the keyword `private`. When you use a class to instantiate (create) an object in a program, only the public members of the class are exposed (made available) to the program; the private members are hidden. In most cases, you will want to expose the member methods and hide the data members. Therefore, in most class definitions, you will list the method prototypes below the keyword `public` in the `class` statement and list the variable declarations below the keyword `private`, as shown in the `FormattedDate` class definition in Figure 15-1. You expose the member methods to allow the program to use the service each method provides. You hide the variables (data members) to protect their contents from being changed inadvertently by the program.

When a program needs to assign data to a private variable, it must use a public member method to do so. For example, a program would need to use the `setDate` method in Figure 15-1 to assign data to a FormattedDate object's `month`, `day`, and `year` variables. It is the public member method's responsibility to validate the data, if necessary, and then either assign the data to the private data member (if the data is valid) or reject the data (if the data is not valid). Keep in mind that a program does not have direct access to the private members of a class. Rather, it must access the private members indirectly, through a public member method.

Instantiating an Object and Referring to a Public Member

Figure 15-2 shows the syntax for instantiating an object in a C++ program. In the syntax, *className* and *objectName* are the names of the class and object, respectively. The figure also includes an example of instantiating a `FormattedDate` object named `reportDate`.

HOW TO Instantiate an Object

Syntax

className objectName; — semicolon

Example

```
FormattedDate reportDate;
```

uses the `FormattedDate` class from Figure 15-1 to instantiate an object named `reportDate`

Figure 15-2 How to instantiate an object

After an object has been instantiated in a program, the program can refer to a public member of the class using the syntax shown in Figure 15-3. In the syntax, *objectName* and *publicMember* are the names of the object and public member, respectively. The figure also includes examples of referring to the `reportDate` object's `getFormattedDate` and `setDate` methods. Both methods are public members of the `FormattedDate` class used to instantiate a `reportDate` object.

HOW TO Refer to a Public Member of an Object's Class

Syntax

objectName.publicMember

Example 1

```
cout << reportDate.getFormattedDate();
```

refers to the `reportDate` object's `getFormattedDate` method, which is a public method of the `FormattedDate` class (shown earlier in Figure 15-1)

Example 2

```
reportDate.setDate(monthNum, dayNum, yearNum);
```

refers to the `reportDate` object's `setDate` method, which is a public method of the `FormattedDate` class (shown earlier in Figure 15-1)

Figure 15-3 How to refer to a public member of an object's class

The answers to Mini-Quiz questions are located in Appendix A.

Mini-Quiz 15-2

1. A program cannot access a class's public member method directly.
   a. True
   b. False
2. In C++, you enter the `class` statement in the ________ section of a class definition, and you enter the method definitions in the ________ section.

3. Typically, the data members (attributes) of a class are represented by ______ in a class definition.

   a. constant declarations
   b. method prototypes
   c. method definitions
   d. variable declarations

4. A class's private data member can be accessed directly by a public member method within the class.

   a. True
   b. False

5. Write the C++ statement to instantiate a `Check` object named `payCheck`.

6. Which of the following refers to the `payCheck` object's `getCheck` method?

   a. `payCheck.getCheck()`
   b. `payCheck::getCheck()`
   c. `getCheck()`
   d. `getCheck().payCheck`

In this chapter, you will view examples of defining and using classes. The first example is a class that contains a private data member and public member methods.

Example 1—A Class that Contains a Private Data Member and Public Member Methods

Figure 15-4 shows the class definition for the `Square` class, which a program can use to instantiate a `Square` object. A `Square` object has one attribute: the length of one of its sides. The attribute is represented within the `class` statement by a private data member: a `double` variable named `side`. When a variable is declared below the `private` keyword in a `class` statement, it can be used only by the code entered in the class definition. In this case, the code uses the `side` variable to both store and retrieve the side measurement of a `Square` object.

A `Square` object also has four behaviors: It can initialize its side measurement when it is created; it can assign a value to its side measurement after it has been created; it can retrieve its side measurement value; and it can calculate and return its area. In the class definition shown in Figure 15-4, these behaviors are represented by four public member methods named `Square`, `setSide`, `getSide`, and `calcArea`. The method prototypes for these methods appear below the `public` keyword in the `class` statement. The definitions of the methods appear in the implementation section of the class definition.

```
//declaration section
class Square
{
public:
     Square();
     void setSide(double);
     double getSide();
     double calcArea();
```

Figure 15-4 `Square` class definition *(continues)*

(continued)

```
private:
      double side;
};

//implementation section
Square::Square()
{
      side = 0.0;
} //end of default constructor

void Square::setSide(double sideValue)
{
      if (sideValue > 0.0)
            side = sideValue;
      else
            side = 0.0;
      //end if
} //end of setSide method

double Square::getSide()
{
      return side;
} //end of getSide method

double Square::calcArea()
{
      return side * side;
} //end of calcArea method
```

Figure 15-4 Square class definition

In the Square class definition in Figure 15-4, the first method prototype (in the declaration section) and the first method definition (in the implementation section) pertain to the default constructor. A **constructor** is a class method whose instructions the computer automatically processes each time an object is instantiated from the class. The sole purpose of a constructor is to initialize the class's private variables. Every class should have at least one constructor. Each of a class's constructors must have the same name as the class, but its formal parameters (if any) must be different from any other constructor in the class. A constructor that has no formal parameters is called the **default constructor**. A class can have only one default constructor.

Because a constructor does not return a value, its prototype and definition do not begin with a data type. However, notice that its definition begins with the name of the class followed by the scope resolution operator (`::`), the name of the constructor, and a set of empty parentheses—in this case, `Square::Square()`. The scope resolution operator indicates that the Square method is a member of (or is contained in) the Square class. The Square method's definition in Figure 15-4 contains the code to initialize the Square class's private side variable to the number 0.0.

As you learned earlier, a program does not have direct access to a private variable in a class. Rather, it must access the private variable indirectly, through a public method. A program that instantiates a Square object, for instance, can use the public setSide method in Figure 15-4 to assign a value to the private side variable. In this case, the setSide method receives the value from the program that invokes it and then stores the value in its formal parameter: a double variable named sideValue. The code contained in the setSide method's definition verifies that the value received from the program is greater than the number 0.0. If it is, the code assigns the value to the private side variable; otherwise, it assigns the number 0.0 to the variable. Notice that the setSide method's prototype and definition begin with the keyword void, which indicates that the method does not return a value.

A program that instantiates a `Square` object can use the public `getSide` method in Figure 15-4 to retrieve the value stored in the private `side` variable. Unlike the void `setSide` method, the `getSide` method is a value-returning method; it returns the `double` number stored in the object's `side` variable.

The last method in the `Square` class, `calcArea`, is also a value-returning method. The method first calculates the area of the `Square` object by multiplying the value stored in its private `side` variable by itself. It then returns the area as a `double` number.

Figure 15-5 shows the patio area program, which uses the `Square` class to instantiate a `Square` object that represents a square patio. The program uses the `Square` object to calculate and display the area of the patio. The `Square` class definition appears on Lines 8 through 43. The code pertaining to the `Square` object is shaded in the figure.

```
1  //Patio Area.cpp
2  //Displays the area of a square patio
3  //Created/revised by <your name> on <current date>
4
5  #include <iostream>
6  using namespace std;
7
8  //declaration section
9  class Square
10 {
11 public:
12     Square();
13     void setSide(double);
14     double getSide();
15     double calcArea();
16 private:
17     double side;
18 };
19
20 //implementation section
21 Square::Square()
22 {
23     side = 0.0;
24 } //end of default constructor
25
26 void Square::setSide(double sideValue)
27 {
28     if (sideValue > 0.0)
29         side = sideValue;
30     else
31         side = 0.0;
32     //end if
33 } //end of setSide method
34
35 double Square::getSide()
36 {
37     return side;
38 } //end of getSide method
39
40 double Square::calcArea()
41 {
42     return side * side;
43 } //end of calcArea method
44
```

Figure 15-5 Patio area program *(continues)*

(continued)

```
45  int main()
46  {
47      //instantiate Square object
48      Square patio;
49      //declare variables
50      double sideMeasurement = 0.0;
51      double area            = 0.0;
52
53      //get side measurement
54      cout << "Side measurement (feet): ";
55      cin >> sideMeasurement;
56      //assign side measurement to Square object
57      patio.setSide(sideMeasurement);
58
59      //calculate and display area
60      area = patio.calcArea();
61      cout <<
62          "The area of a square patio "
63          << "with a side measurement of " << endl
64          << patio.getSide() << " feet is "
65          << area << "  square feet." << endl;
66      //system("pause");
67      return 0;
68  } //end of main function
```

your C++ development tool may require this statement

Figure 15-5 Patio area program

The `Square patio;` statement on Line 48 instantiates a `Square` object named `patio`. When the object is created, the default constructor is called, automatically, to initialize the private data member (the `side` variable) to the number 0.0. The `patio.setSide(sideMeasurement);` statement on Line 57 calls the `Square` object's `setSide` method, passing it the side measurement value entered by the user. Recall that the `setSide` method is a public member of the `Square` class. The `setSide` method verifies that the value passed to it is greater than the number 0.0. If it is, the method assigns the value to the `Square` object's private `side` variable; otherwise, it assigns the number 0.0 to the variable.

The `area = patio.calcArea();` statement on Line 60 is processed next. The statement calls the `Square` object's `calcArea` method to calculate and return the `Square` object's area. The statement assigns the method's return value to the program's `area` variable. The `cout` statement on Lines 61 through 65 displays a message on the computer screen. The message contains the `Square` object's side measurement and area. When processing the `cout` statement, the `patio.getSide()` code on Line 64 calls the `Square` object's `getSide` method, which simply retrieves the value stored in the private `side` variable. A sample run of the patio area program is shown in Figure 15-6.

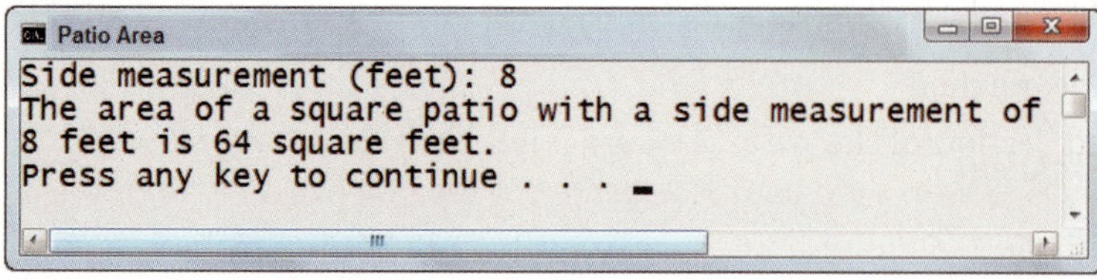

Figure 15-6 Sample run of the patio area program

Header Files

Although you can enter a class definition in the program that uses the class, as shown earlier in Figure 15-5, most programmers enter a class definition in a separate text file called a **header file**. Figure 15-7 shows the definition of the `Square` class entered in a header file named Square.h. Unlike program filenames, which end with .cpp, header filenames end with .h. You will learn how to add a header file to a solution in Lab 15-2.

```
//Square.h
//Created/revised by <your name> on <current date>

//declaration section
class Square
{
public:
   Square();
   void setSide(double);
   double getSide();
   double calcArea();
private:
   double side;
};

//implementation section
Square::Square()
{
   side = 0.0;
} //end of default constructor

void Square::setSide(double sideValue)
{
   if (sideValue > 0.0)
      side = sideValue;
   else
      side = 0.0;
   //end if
} //end of setSide method

double Square::getSide()
{
   return side;
} //end of getSide method

double Square::calcArea()
{
   return side * side;
} //end of calcArea method
```

Figure 15-7 `Square` class definition entered in the Square.h header file

Figure 15-8 shows a modified version of the patio area program. Unlike the original program, the modified program does not contain the `Square` class definition. Instead, the modified program uses the class definition contained in the Square.h header file from Figure 15-7. Typically, a header file is stored in the same location as the program file that employs the class. In this case, for example, the Square.h file would be stored in the same location as the Modified Patio Area.cpp file. The programmer uses a `#include` directive to tell the compiler to include the contents of the header file in the program. In the modified patio area program, the

`#include "Square.h"` directive (which is shaded in Figure 15-8) tells the compiler to merge the contents of the Square.h file with the contents of the current program. In other words, it tells the compiler to include the `Square` class definition in the current program. The quotation marks before and after the header filename indicate that the header file is located in the same folder as the program file.

```
//Modified Patio Area.cpp
//Displays the area of a square patio
//Created/revised by <your name> on <current date>

#include <iostream>
#include "Square.h"
using namespace std;

int main()
{
    //instantiate Square object
    Square patio;
    //declare variables
    double sideMeasurement = 0.0;
    double area            = 0.0;

    //get side measurement
    cout << "Side measurement (feet): ";
    cin >> sideMeasurement;
    //assign side measurement to Square object
    patio.setSide(sideMeasurement);

    //calculate and display area
    area = patio.calcArea();
    cout <<
        "The area of a square patio "
        << "with a side measurement of " << endl
        << patio.getSide() << " feet is "
        << area << " square feet." << endl;
    //system("pause");
    return 0;
}   //end of main function
```

your C++ development tool may require this statement

The angle brackets (<>) in a directive indicate that the file is located in the folder that contains the C++ Standard Library header files.

Figure 15-8 Modified patio area program

The answers to Mini-Quiz questions are located in Appendix A.

Mini-Quiz 15-3

1. The `::` operator is called the ________.
2. Write the default constructor's prototype for a class named `Item`.
3. The `Item` class in Question 2 contains two private data members: a `char` variable named `code` and an `int` variable named `price`. Write the definition for the default constructor.

Example 2—A Class that Contains a Parameterized Constructor

Figure 15-9 shows a modified version of the `Square` class from Example 1. The modifications made to the original class (shown earlier in Figure 15-7) are shaded in the figure. Notice that this version of the `Square` class contains an additional constructor. The additional constructor has one parameter: a `double` variable named `num`. Constructors that contain at least one parameter are called **parameterized constructors**. In this case, the parameterized constructor allows you to specify the `side` variable's initial value in the statement that instantiates a `Square` object. You specify the value by enclosing it in a set of parentheses after the object's name. For example, either of the following program statements will invoke the parameterized constructor shown in Figure 15-9: `Square picture(9.5);` or `Square picture(sideLength);`. When the parameterized constructor is invoked, it calls the `setSide` method, passing it the value it receives from the program. The `setSide` method determines whether the value is greater than 0.0 and then assigns either the value or the number 0.0 to the private `side` variable.

```
//Modified Square.h
//Created/revised by <your name> on <current date>

//declaration section
class Square
{
public:
    Square();
    Square(double);
    void setSide(double);
    double getSide();
    double calcArea();
private:
    double side;
};

//implementation section
Square::Square()
{
    side = 0.0;
} //end of default constructor

Square::Square(double num)
{
    setSide(num);
} //end of constructor

void Square::setSide(double sideValue)
{
    if (sideValue > 0.0)
        side = sideValue;
    else
        side = 0.0;
    //end if
} //end of setSide method

```

default constructor

parameterized constructor

Figure 15-9 Modified `Square` class definition entered in the Modified Square.h header file *(continues)*

If the `setSide` method did not contain validation code, you could replace the statement in the parameterized constructor with `side = num;`.

(continued)

```
double Square::getSide()
{
    return side;
} //end of getSide method

double Square::calcArea()
{
    return side * side;
} //end of calcArea method
```

Figure 15-9 Modified `Square` class definition entered in the Modified Square.h header file

A method's name combined with its optional *parameterList* is called the method's **signature**. When a program statement instantiates an object, the computer compares the statement with the signature of each of the class constructors; it stops comparing when it finds a match. Put another way, the computer determines the appropriate class constructor by matching the quantity, data type, and position (or order) of the arguments in the statement that instantiates the object with the quantity, data type, and position (order) of the parameters listed in each constructor's *parameterList*. For example, the computer will invoke the default constructor when you use the `Square picture;` statement to instantiate a `Square` object. However, as mentioned earlier, it will use the parameterized constructor when you instantiate a `Square` object using statements such as `Square picture(9.5);` or `Square picture(sideLength);`. Figure 15-10 shows how you could use the parameterized constructor, which is defined in the Modified Square.h header file from Figure 15-9, in the modified patio area program.

```
//Modified Patio Area.cpp
//Displays the area of a square patio
//Created/revised by <your name> on <current date>

#include <iostream>
#include "Modified Square.h"
using namespace std;

int main()
{
    //declare variables
    double sideMeasurement = 0.0;
    double area            = 0.0;

    //get side measurement
    cout << "Side measurement (feet): ";
    cin >> sideMeasurement;

    //instantiate Square object
    Square patio(sideMeasurement);

    //calculate and display area
    area = patio.calcArea();
```

instantiates a `Square` object

Figure 15-10 Modified patio area program using the parameterized constructor *(continues)*

(continued)

```
    cout <<
        "The area of a square patio "
        << "with a side measurement of " << endl
        << patio.getSide() << " feet is "
        << area << " square feet." << endl;
    //system("pause");
    return 0;
}   //end of main function
```

your C++ development tool may require this statement

Figure 15-10 Modified patio area program using the parameterized constructor

Compare the code shown in Figure 15-10 with the code shown earlier in Figure 15-8. Notice that the statement to instantiate a `Square` object now appears after the `cin` statement that gets the side measurement, and it now contains an argument (the `sideMeasurement` variable). In Figure 15-8, the instantiation code appears before the variable declaration statements, on Line 12, and it doesn't contain any arguments. Also notice that the code in Figure 15-10 does not call the `setSide` method, as the code on Line 21 in Figure 15-8 does. The `setSide` method is not necessary in Figure 15-10's code because the parameterized constructor will set the private `side` variable's value when the `Square` object is instantiated.

Example 3—Reusing a Class

In Examples 1 and 2, you used the `Square` class to create an object that represented a square patio. In this example, you will use the `Square` class to create objects that represent a square pizza and a square pizza slice. As mentioned earlier, the ability to use an object for more than one purpose saves programming time and money, which contributes to the popularity of object-oriented programming.

Figure 15-11 shows the pizza slices program, which calculates and displays the number of square pizza slices that can be cut from a square pizza. The program instantiates two `Square` objects named `wholePizza` and `pizzaSlice` to represent the whole pizza and a pizza slice, respectively. The program then declares five `double` variables to store the side measurement of the whole pizza, the side measurement of a pizza slice, the area of the whole pizza, the area of a pizza slice, and the number of slices. The `cout` and `cin` statements on Lines 23 through 26 prompt the user for the side measurements of the whole pizza and a pizza slice, and store the user's responses in the `wholeSide` and `sliceSide` variables, respectively. The statement on Line 29 calls the `wholePizza` object's `setSide` method, passing it the side measurement of the whole pizza. The statement on Line 30 calls the `pizzaSlice` object's `setSide` method, passing it the side measurement of a pizza slice. Each time the `setSide` method is invoked, it validates the value passed to it and then assigns either the value or the number 0.0 to the appropriate object's `side` variable.

The assignment statement on Line 34 in Figure 15-11 is processed next. The statement calls the `wholePizza` object's `calcArea` method to calculate and return the area of the whole pizza. Similarly, the assignment statement on Line 35 calls the `pizzaSlice` object's `calcArea` method to calculate and return the area of a pizza slice. Next, the condition in the `if` clause on Line 38 checks whether the pizza slice area is greater than 0.0. This determination is necessary because the pizza slice area is used as the divisor in the statement on Line 39. That statement calculates the number of slices by dividing the area of the whole pizza by the area of a pizza slice. The `cout` statement on Line 41 displays a message that contains the number of slices. A sample run of the pizza slices program is shown in Figure 15-12.

```
//Pizza Slices.cpp
//Displays the number of square slices
//that can be cut from a square pizza
//Created/revised by <your name> on <current date>

#include <iostream>
#include "Modified Square.h"
using namespace std;

int main()
{
   //instantiate Square objects
   Square wholePizza;
   Square pizzaSlice;
   //declare variables
   double wholeSide = 0.0;
   double sliceSide = 0.0;
   double wholeArea = 0.0;
   double sliceArea = 0.0;
   double numSlices = 0.0;

   //get side measurements
   cout << "Whole pizza side measurement (inches): ";
   cin >> wholeSide;
   cout << "Pizza slice side measurement (inches): ";
   cin >> sliceSide;

   //assign side measurements to Square objects
   wholePizza.setSide(wholeSide);
   pizzaSlice.setSide(sliceSide);

   //calculate area of whole pizza and
   //area of a pizza slice
   wholeArea = wholePizza.calcArea();
   sliceArea = pizzaSlice.calcArea();

   //calculate number of slices
   if (sliceArea > 0.0)
       numSlices = wholeArea / sliceArea;
   //end if
   cout << "Number of slices: " << numSlices << endl;
   //system("pause");
   return 0;
} //end of main function
```

your C++ development tool may require this statement

Figure 15-11 Pizza slices program

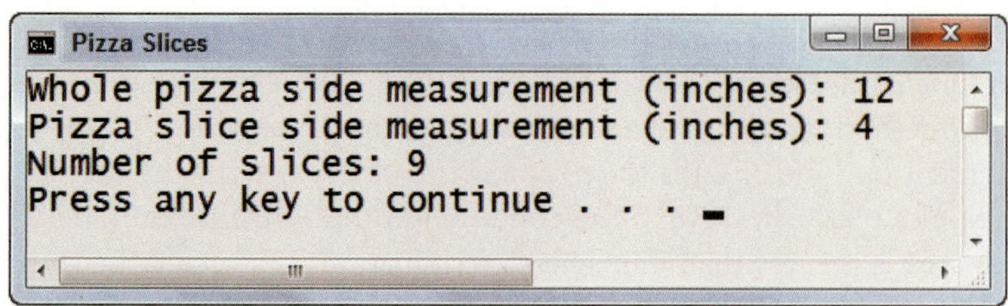

Figure 15-12 Sample run of the pizza slices program

Example 4—A Class that Contains Overloaded Methods

Figure 15-13 shows a different version of the `Square` class used in the previous examples. This version contains two (rather than one) `calcArea` methods. Although both methods have the same name, notice that their *parameterLists* differ. The *parameterList* in the first `calcArea` method is empty, as it was in the previous examples. The *parameterList* in the second `calcArea` method, however, contains one formal parameter: a `double` variable named `sideValueFromProgram`. (The second method's prototype and definition are shaded in the figure.) When two or more methods have the same name but different *parameterLists*, the methods are referred to as **overloaded methods**.

```
//Overloaded Square.h
//Created/revised by <your name> on <current date>

//declaration section
class Square
{
public:
   Square();
   Square(double);
   void setSide(double);
   double getSide();
   double calcArea();
   double calcArea(double);
private:
   double side;
};

//implementation section
Square::Square()
{
   side = 0.0;
} //end of default constructor

Square::Square(double num)
{
   setSide(num);
} //end of constructor

void Square::setSide(double sideValue)
{
   if (sideValue > 0.0)
       side = sideValue;
   else
       side = 0.0;
   //end if
} //end of setSide method

double Square::getSide()
{
   return side;
} //end of getSide method

double Square::calcArea()
{
   return side * side;
} //end of calcArea method
```

Figure 15-13 `Square` class definition entered in the Overloaded Square.h file *(continues)*

The two constructors in Figure 15-13 are overloaded methods because both have the same name but a different *parameterList*.

(continued)

```

double Square::calcArea(double sideValueFromProgram)
{
   setSide(sideValueFromProgram);
   return side * side;
} //end of calcArea method
```

Figure 15-13 Square class definition entered in the Overloaded Square.h file

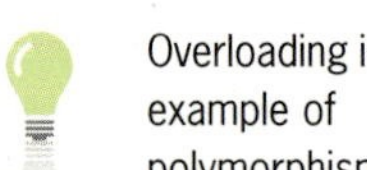
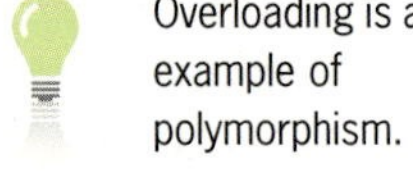

Overloading is an example of polymorphism.

Overloading is useful when two or more methods require different parameters to perform essentially the same task. Both overloaded `calcArea` methods in the `Square` class, for example, calculate and return the area of a `Square` object. However, the first `calcArea` method does not require a program to pass it any information. The second `calcArea` method, on the other hand, requires a program to pass it one item of information: the side measurement of the `Square` object. Like the parameterized constructor, the parameterized `calcArea` method calls the `setSide` method to validate the side measurement provided by the program. After the `setSide` method assigns the appropriate value to the object's private `side` variable, the `calcArea` method calculates and returns the `Square` object's area.

Figure 15-14 shows a modified version of the pizza slices program from Example 3, with the modifications shaded in the figure. The modified version uses the parameterized `calcArea` method.

```
//Modified Pizza Slices.cpp
//Displays the number of square slices
//that can be cut from a square pizza
//Created/revised by <your name> on <current date>

#include <iostream>
#include "Overloaded Square.h"
using namespace std;

int main()
{
   //instantiate Square objects
   Square wholePizza;
   Square pizzaSlice;
   //declare variables
   double wholeSide = 0.0;
   double sliceSide = 0.0;
   double wholeArea = 0.0;
   double sliceArea = 0.0;
   double numSlices = 0.0;

   //get side measurements
   cout << "Whole pizza side measurement (inches): ";
   cin >> wholeSide;
   cout << "Pizza slice side measurement (inches): ";
   cin >> sliceSide;

   //calculate area of whole pizza and
   //area of a pizza slice
   wholeArea = wholePizza.calcArea(wholeSide);
   sliceArea = pizzaSlice.calcArea(sliceSide);
```

Figure 15-14 Modified pizza slices program *(continues)*

(continued)

```

    //calculate number of slices
    if (sliceArea > 0.0)
        numSlices = wholeArea / sliceArea;
    //end if
    cout << "Number of slices: " << numSlices << endl;
    //system("pause");
    return 0;
} //end of main function
```

your C++ development tool may require this statement

Figure 15-14 Modified pizza slices program

Compare the code shown in Figure 15-14 with the code shown earlier in Figure 15-11. Unlike the code in Figure 15-11 (on Lines 29 and 30), the code in Figure 15-14 does not call the `setSide` method to assign a value to each `Square` object's `side` variable. The `setSide` method is not necessary in Figure 15-14's code because each object's parameterized `calcArea` method calls the `setSide` method before it calculates and returns the area. Figure 15-15 shows another sample run of the pizza slices program.

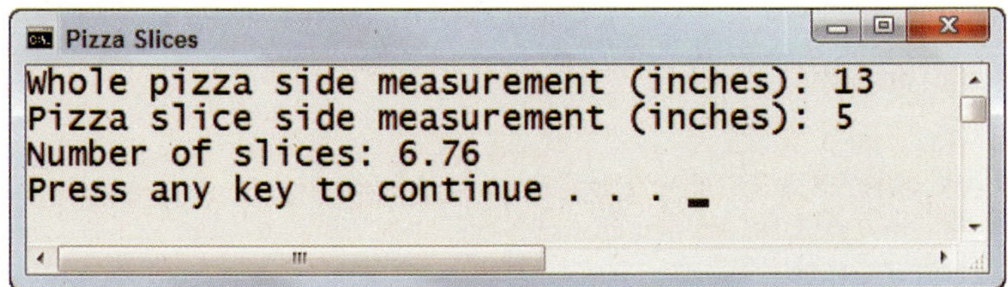

Figure 15-15 Another sample run of the pizza slices program

Mini-Quiz 15-4

The answers to Mini-Quiz questions are located in Appendix A.

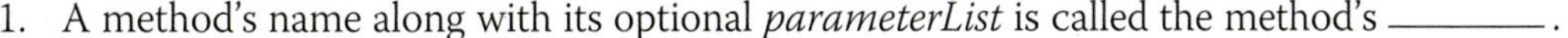

1. A method's name along with its optional *parameterList* is called the method's ________.

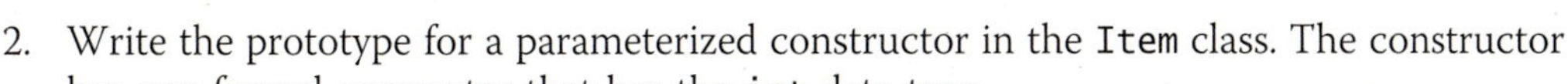

2. Write the prototype for a parameterized constructor in the `Item` class. The constructor has one formal parameter that has the `int` data type.

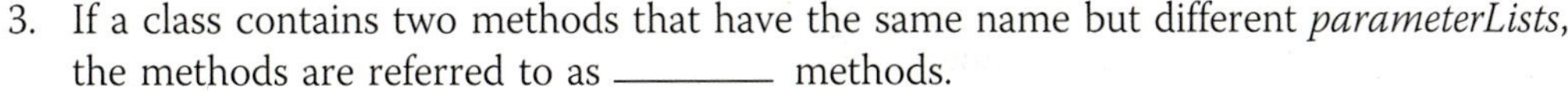

3. If a class contains two methods that have the same name but different *parameterLists*, the methods are referred to as ________ methods.

The answers to the labs are located in Appendix A.

LAB 15-1 Stop and Analyze

Study the program shown in Figure 15-16 and then answer the questions.

```
//Lab15-1.cpp - increases and then displays a price
//Created/revised by <your name> on <current date>

#include <iostream>
#include <string>
#include <iomanip>
using namespace std;

//declaration section
class Item
{
public:
    Item();
    void setData(string, double);
    double getIncreasedPrice(double);
private:
    string id;
    double price;
};

//implementation section
Item::Item()
{
    id    = "";
    price = 0.0;
} //end of default constructor

void Item::setData(string idNum, double p)
{
    id = idNum;
    price = p;
}  //end of setData method

double Item::getIncreasedPrice(double rate)
{
    if (rate > 1.0)
        rate = rate / 100;
    //end if
    return price + price * rate;
}  //end of getIncreasedPrice method


int main()
{
    //instantiate Item object
    Item computer;

    //declare variables
    string computerId    = "";
    double computerPrice = 0.0;
```

Figure 15-16 Code for Lab 15-1 *(continues)*

(continued)

```
51      double incRate         = 0.0;
52
53      cout << fixed << setprecision(2);
54
55      //get computer ID
56      cout << "Computer ID (X to end): ";
57      getline(cin, computerId);
58      while (computerId != "X" && computerId != "x")
59      {
60          //get price and increase
61          cout << "Enter the price: ";
62          cin >> computerPrice;
63          cin.ignore(100, '\n');
64          cout << "Increase rate in decimal form: ";
65          cin >> incRate;
66          cin.ignore(100, '\n');
67
68          //assign the ID and price
69
70
71          //display the increased price
72          cout << "The new price of computer "
73               << computerId << " is $"
74
75               << endl;
76
77          //get computer ID
78          cout << endl
79               << "Computer ID (X to end): ";
80          getline(cin, computerId);
81      }   //end while
82
83      //system("pause");
84      return 0;
85 }    //end of main function
```

if your C++ development tool requires this statement, delete the two forward slashes

Figure 15-16 Code for Lab 15-1

QUESTIONS

1. What are the names of the private data members in the `Item` class?
2. What are the name and purpose of the default constructor?
3. What is the purpose of the `setData` method?
4. What is the purpose of the `getIncreasedPrice` method?
5. What is the purpose of the code on Lines 36 and 37?
6. What statement is missing from Line 69?
7. Line 74 should display the increased price. What code is missing from that line?
8. Follow the instructions for starting C++ and viewing the Lab15-1.cpp file, which is contained in either the Cpp7\Chap15\Lab15-1 Project folder or the Cpp7\Chap15 folder. (Depending on your C++ development tool, you may need to open Lab15-1's project/solution file first.) If necessary, delete the two forward slashes that appear before the `system("pause");` statement, and then save the program.

9. Enter the missing statement and code from Steps 6 and 7. Save and then run the program. Enter ABX-12 as the computer ID, 2500 as the price, and .1 as the increase rate. The program displays the message "The new price of computer ABX-12 is $2750.00."

10. Test the program using different computer IDs, prices, and rates. When you are finished testing the program, enter the letter x as the computer ID.

LAB 15-2 Plan and Create

Figure 15-17 shows the problem specification for Lab 15-2.

Problem specification
Sharon Terney of Terney Landscaping wants a program that estimates the cost of laying sod on a rectangular piece of land. Jack Sysmanski, the owner of All-Around Fence Company, wants a program that calculates the cost of installing a fence around a rectangular yard. You will create the Terney Landscaping program in this lab and then create the All-Around Fence Company program in Computer Exercise 13 at the end of the chapter.

While analyzing both problems, you notice that each involves a rectangular shape. In the Terney Landscaping program, you need to find the area of the rectangle on which the sod is to be laid. In the All-Around Fence Company program, on the other hand, you need to find the perimeter of the rectangle around which a fence is to be constructed. To save time, you can create a `Rectangle` class that contains the attributes and behaviors of a rectangle and then use the class to instantiate a `Rectangle` object in both programs.

Figure 15-17 Problem specification for Lab 15-2

Recall that a class defines an object's attributes and behaviors. When determining the attributes, it is helpful to consider how you would describe the object. Rectangles typically are described in terms of two dimensions: length and width. Therefore, the length and width dimensions are the attributes of a `Rectangle` object. You will include both attributes as private data members in the `Rectangle` class, using the `double` variables `length` and `width`.

Next, you determine the object's behaviors. To be useful in both the Terney Landscaping and All-Around Fence Company programs, a `Rectangle` object must be capable of performing the four tasks shown in Figure 15-18.

A `Rectangle` object should be able to:

1. initialize its private data members (default constructor)
2. assign values to its private data members
3. calculate and return its area
4. calculate and return its perimeter

Figure 15-18 Tasks a `Rectangle` object should be capable of performing

As Figure 15-18 indicates, a `Rectangle` object will need to initialize its private data members. You will provide a default constructor for this purpose. A `Rectangle` object also will need to provide a means for the program to assign values to the private data members. This task will be handled by a void member method named `setDimensions`. You will use two value-returning member methods named `calcArea` and `calcPerimeter` to perform the third and fourth tasks listed in Figure 15-18. Figure 15-19 shows the completed class definition for the `Rectangle` class.

```
//Lab15-2 Rectangle.h
//Created/revised by <your name> on <current date>

//declaration section
class Rectangle
{
public:
    Rectangle();
    void setDimensions(double, double);
    double calcArea();
    double calcPerimeter();
private:
    double length;
    double width;
};

//implementation section
Rectangle::Rectangle()
{
    length = 0.0;
    width  = 0.0;
} //end of default constructor

void Rectangle::setDimensions(double len, double wid)
{
    //assigns length and width to private data members
    if (len > 0.0 && wid > 0.0)
    {
        length = len;
        width  = wid;
    }   //end if
} //end of setDimensions method

double Rectangle::calcArea()
{
    return length * width;
} //end of calcArea method

double Rectangle::calcPerimeter()
{
    return (length + width) * 2;
} //end of calcPerimeter method
```

Figure 15-19 `Rectangle` class definition

Now that you have defined the `Rectangle` class, you can begin creating the Terney Landscaping program, which will use the class to create a `Rectangle` object. Figure 15-20 shows the IPO chart information and C++ instructions for the program. According to the IPO chart, the output is the area (in square yards) and the total price. The input is the length and width of the rectangle (both in feet) and the price of a square yard of sod. Notice that a `Rectangle` object is used as a processing item in the program.

IPO chart information	C++ instructions
Input	
length (in feet)	`double lawnLength = 0.0;`
width (in feet)	`double lawnWidth = 0.0;`
sod price (per square yard)	`double priceSqYd = 0.0;`
Processing	
Rectangle object	`Rectangle lawn;`
Output	
area (in square yards)	`double lawnArea = 0.0;`
total price	`double totalPrice = 0.0;`
Algorithm	

1. enter length, width, and sod price	`cout << "Length (in feet): ";`
	`cin >> lawnLength;`
	`cout << "Width (in feet): ";`
	`cin >> lawnWidth;`
	`cout << "Sod price (per square yard): ";`
	`cin >> priceSqYd;`

2. use the Rectangle object's setDimensions method to assign the length and width to the Rectangle object	`lawn.setDimensions(lawnLength,` `lawnWidth);`
3. use the Rectangle object's calcArea method to calculate the area in square feet, then divide the result by 9 to get the area in square yards	`lawnArea = lawn.calcArea() / 9;`
4. calculate the total price by multiplying the area by the sod price	`totalPrice = lawnArea * priceSqYd;`

5. display the area and the total price	`cout << "Square yards: " <<`
	`lawnArea << endl;`
	`cout << "Total price: $" <<`
	`totalPrice << endl;`

Figure 15-20 IPO chart information and C++ instructions for the Terney Landscaping program

As the algorithm in Figure 15-20 indicates, the program first gets the length, width, and sod price information from the user. The program passes the length and width information to the `Rectangle` object's `setDimensions` method, which assigns the values (assuming that both are greater than 0.0) to the `Rectangle` object's private data members. The third instruction in the algorithm is to calculate the area of the `Rectangle` object in square yards. To do this, the program first calls the `Rectangle` object's `calcArea` method to calculate the area in square feet. It then converts the value returned by the `calcArea` method from square feet to square yards by dividing the return value by the number 9, which is the number of square feet in a square yard. The fourth instruction in the algorithm is to calculate the total price by multiplying the number of square yards by the price per square yard of sod. The last instruction in the algorithm is to display the area (in square yards) and the total price on the screen. Notice that, although the `Rectangle` object also is capable of calculating its perimeter, the current program does not require the object to perform that task.

Figure 15-21 shows the code for the entire Terney Landscaping program, and Figure 15-22 shows a sample run of the program.

```
//Lab15-2.cpp
//Calculates and displays the cost of laying sod
//Created/revised by <your name> on <current date>

#include <iostream>
#include <iomanip>
#include "Lab15-2 Rectangle.h"
using namespace std;

int main()
{
    //instantiate Rectangle object
    Rectangle lawn;

    //declare variables
    double lawnLength = 0.0;
    double lawnWidth  = 0.0;
    double priceSqYd  = 0.0;
    double lawnArea   = 0.0;
    double totalPrice = 0.0;

    //get length, width, and sod price
    cout << "Length (in feet): ";
    cin >> lawnLength;
    cout << "Width (in feet): ";
    cin >> lawnWidth;
    cout << "Sod price (per square yard): ";
    cin >> priceSqYd;

    //assign input to Rectangle object
    lawn.setDimensions(lawnLength, lawnWidth);

    //calculate area and total price
    lawnArea = lawn.calcArea() / 9;
    totalPrice = lawnArea * priceSqYd;

    //display area and total price
    cout << fixed << setprecision(2) << endl;
    cout << "Square yards: " << lawnArea << endl;
    cout << "Total price: $" << totalPrice << endl;

    //system("pause");
    return 0;
}   //end of main function
```

if your C++ development tool requires this statement, delete the two forward slashes

Figure 15-21 Terney Landscaping program

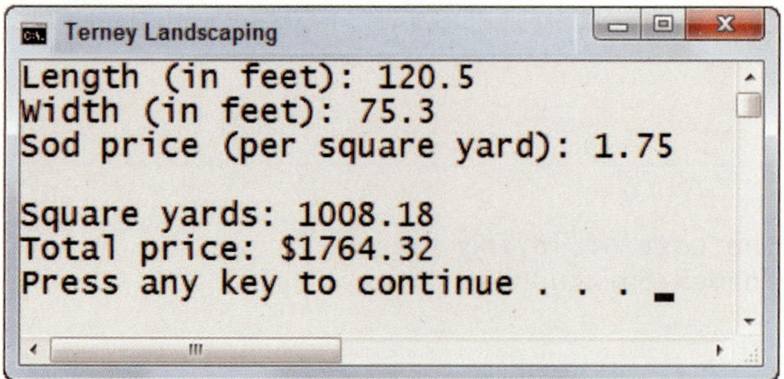

Figure 15-22 Sample run of the Terney Landscaping program

DIRECTIONS

Follow the instructions for starting your C++ development tool. Depending on the development tool you are using, you may need to create a new project; if so, name the project Lab15-2 Project and save it in the Cpp7\Chap15 folder. Enter the instructions shown in Figure 15-21 in a source file named Lab15-2.cpp. (Do not enter the line numbers.) Save the file in either the project folder or the Cpp7\Chap15 folder.

Next, you will add a header file to either the project folder (if you are using Microsoft Visual C++) or the Cpp7\Chap15 folder (if you are using Dev-C++ or Code::Blocks). The instructions for doing this are shown in Figure 15-23. (If you are using a different C++ development tool, you will need to ask your instructor how and where to add a header file.)

If you are using Microsoft Visual C++, click PROJECT on the menu bar and then click Add New Item. If necessary, click Visual C++. Click Header File (.h) in the Add New Item dialog box and then type Lab15-2 Rectangle in the Name box. Finally, click the Add button.

If you are using Dev-C++, click File on the menu bar, point to New, and then click Source File. Click File, then click Save As. Type Lab15-2 Rectangle.h in the File name box and then click the Save button.

If you are using CODE::BLOCKS, click File on the menu bar, point to New, and then click File. In the New from template dialog box, click C/C++ header, and then click Go to start the C/C++ header file wizard. Click Next. Click the Browse button that appears next to the Filename with full path box. In the Select filename dialog box, type Lab15-2 Rectangle.h and then click Save. Finally, click Finish.

Figure 15-23 Instructions for adding a header file

In the header file, enter the `Rectangle` class definition shown in Figure 15-19. Save the program. Now, follow the appropriate instructions for running the Lab15-2.cpp file. Test the program using the data shown in Figure 15-22. If necessary, correct any bugs (errors) in the program.

LAB 15-3 Modify

If necessary, create a new project named Lab15-3 Project and save it in the Cpp7\Chap15 folder. Enter (or copy) the Lab15-2.cpp instructions into a new source file named Lab15-3.cpp. Change Lab15-2.cpp in the first comment to Lab15-3.cpp. Also change "Lab15-2 Rectangle.h" in the #include directive to "Lab15-3 Rectangle.h".

Next, enter (or copy) the Lab15-2 Rectangle.h instructions into a new header file named Lab15-3 Rectangle.h. Change Lab15-2 Rectangle.h in the first comment to Lab15-3 Rectangle.h. Add a second `setDimensions` method to the `Rectangle` class. The method should accept two integers rather than two `double` numbers. It should convert the integers to `double` numbers before assigning them to the class's private variables. Now, modify the program so that it uses integers (rather than `double` numbers) for the length and width measurements. Save and then run the program. Test the program using 10 as the length, 15 as the width, and 1.95 as the sod price. The number of square yards and total price are 16.67 and $32.50, respectively.

LAB 15-4 Desk-Check

Desk-check the code shown in Figure 15-24 using Thomas Johans and 2500.75 as the salesperson's name and sales amount, respectively. Then use X to stop the program. What will the code display on the computer screen?

```
//Lab15-4.cpp - displays a bonus amount
//Created/revised by <your name> on <current date>

#include <iostream>
#include <string>
#include <iomanip>
using namespace std;

//declaration section
class Bonus
{
public:
    Bonus();
    void setSales(double);
    double getBonus(double);
private:
    double sales;
};

//implementation section
Bonus::Bonus()
{
    sales = 0.0;
} //end of default constructor

void Bonus::setSales(double s)
{
    if (s > 0.0)
        sales = s;
    else
        sales = 0.0;
    //end if
} //end of setSales method

```

Figure 15-24 Code for Lab 15-4 *(continues)*

(continued)

```
double Bonus::getBonus(double r)
{
   return sales * r;
} //end of getBonus method

int main()
{
   //declare constant and variables
   const double BONUS_RATE = .05;
   string name    = "";
   double dollars = 0.0;
   double bonus   = 0.0;

   //instantiate Bonus object
   Bonus dollarAmt;

   cout << fixed << setprecision(2);

   cout << "Salesperson's name (X to exit): ";
   getline(cin, name);
   while (name != "X" && name != "x")
   {
       cout << "Sales amount: ";
       cin >> dollars;
       cin.ignore(100, '\n');
       dollarAmt.setSales(dollars);

       //calculate the bonus
       bonus = dollarAmt.getBonus(BONUS_RATE);

       //display the name and bonus
       cout << name << " bonus:  $"  << bonus << endl;

       cout << endl << "Salesperson's name (X to exit): ";
       getline(cin, name);
    } //end while

    //system("pause");
    return 0;
}   //end of main function
```

Figure 15-24 Code for Lab 15-4

LAB 15-5 Debug

Follow the instructions for starting C++ and viewing the Lab15-5.cpp file, which is contained in either the Cpp7\Chap15\Lab15-5 Project folder or the Cpp7\Chap15 folder. (Depending on your C++ development tool, you may need to open Lab15-5's project/solution file first.) If necessary, delete the two forward slashes that appear before the `system("pause");` statement and then save the program. The program should display the item number and inventory quantity entered by the user. Run the program. Notice that the program is not working correctly. Debug the program.

Summary

- A class is a pattern for creating one or more instances of the class. Each instance is considered an object.
- A class encapsulates all of an object's attributes and behaviors. An object's attributes are the characteristics that describe the object. Its behaviors are the actions that the object can perform or to which the object can respond.
- The OOP term "abstraction" refers to the hiding of an object's internal details from the user. Hiding the internal details prevents the user from making inadvertent changes to the object.
- The idea behind abstraction is to expose to the user only the attributes and behaviors that are necessary to use the object and to hide everything else. In most classes, you expose an object's behaviors (member methods) and you hide its attributes (data members).
- Polymorphism is the object-oriented feature that allows the same instruction to be carried out differently depending on the object.
- You use a class definition to create a class. The class definition contains two sections: declaration and implementation. The declaration section contains the `class` statement. The implementation section contains the method definitions.
- You instantiate (create) an object using the syntax *className objectName*`;`, in which *className* is the name of the class and *objectName* is the name of the object.
- You refer to a public member of a class using the syntax *objectName*`.`*publicMember*.
- Most C++ programmers enter class definitions in header files. Header filenames end with .h.
- You can use a constructor to initialize the data members in a class when an object is instantiated. A class can have more than one constructor, but only one can be the default constructor. The default constructor has no formal parameters.
- Each constructor in a class has the same name, but its formal parameters (if any) must be different from any other constructor in the class. A constructor that has one or more formal parameters is called a parameterized constructor.
- A constructor does not have a data type because it cannot return a value.
- You can overload the methods in a class. Doing this allows you to use the same name for methods that require different information to perform the same task. The computer uses the method's signature to determine which overloaded method to process.

Key Terms

Abstraction—the OOP term that refers to the hiding of the internal details of an object from the user

Attributes—the characteristics that describe an object

Base class—the class from which a derived class is created

Behaviors—the actions that an object is capable of performing or to which the object can respond

Class—a pattern or blueprint used to instantiate an object in a program

Class definition—used to specify the attributes and behaviors of an object

`class` statement—the statement used to create a class in C++

Constructor—a class method whose instructions the computer automatically processes each time an object is instantiated from the class

Declaration section—the section that contains the `class` statement in a class definition

Default constructor—a constructor that has no formal parameters

Derived class—the class that inherits the attributes and behaviors of a base class

Encapsulates—the OOP term that refers to the grouping together of the attributes and behaviors of an object within a class

Exposed—the OOP term that refers to the attributes and behaviors that the user can access

Header file—a file that contains a class definition; header filenames end with .h

Hidden—the OOP term that refers to the attributes and behaviors that the user cannot access

Implementation section—the section that contains the method definitions in a class definition

Inheritance—the OOP term that refers to the fact that you can create one class (the derived class) from another class (the base class); the derived class inherits the attributes and behaviors of the base class

Instance—in OOP terminology, an object instantiated (created) from a class

Instantiated—the OOP term that refers to objects being created from a class

Method—a function that is defined in a class definition

Object—anything that can be seen, touched, or used

OOP—an acronym for object-oriented programming

Overloaded methods—two or more class methods that share the same name but have different *parameterLists*

Parameterized constructors—constructors that have one or more formal parameters

Pascal case—the practice of capitalizing the first letter in a name and the first letter in any subsequent words in the name

Polymorphism—the object-oriented feature that allows the same instruction to be carried out differently depending on the object

Signature—the combination of a method's name with its optional *parameterList*

Review Questions

1. A blueprint for creating an object in C++ is called a(n) ________.
   a. class
   b. instance
   c. map
   d. pattern

2. Which of the following statements is false?
   a. An example of an attribute is the `minutes` variable in a `Time` class.
   b. An example of a behavior is the `setTime` method in a `Time` class.
   c. An object created from a class is referred to as an instance of the class.
   d. A class is considered an object.

3. You hide a member of a class by recording the member below the keyword ________ in the `class` statement.

   a. `confidential`
   b. `hidden`
   c. `private`
   d. `restricted`

4. You expose a member of a class by recording the member below the ________ keyword in the `class` statement.

   a. `common`
   b. `exposed`
   c. `public`
   d. `unrestricted`

5. A program can access the private members of a class ________.

   a. directly
   b. only through the public members of the class
   c. only through other private members of the class
   d. none of the above because the program cannot access the private members of a class in any way

6. In most classes, you expose the ________ and hide the ________.

   a. attributes, data members
   b. data members, member methods
   c. member methods, data members
   d. variables, member methods

7. The method definitions for a class are entered in the ________ section in the class definition.

   a. declaration
   b. implementation
   c. method
   d. program-defined

8. Which of the following is the scope resolution operator?

   a. `::` (two colons)
   b. `*` (asterisk)
   c. `.` (period)
   d. `->` (hyphen and greater than symbol)

9. The name of the constructor for a class named `Animal` is ________.

   a. `Animal`
   b. `AnimalConstructor`
   c. `ConstAnimal`
   d. Any of the above could be used as the name of the constructor.

10. Which of the following statements is false?
    a. You typically use a public member method to change the value stored in a private data member.
    b. Because a constructor does not return a value, you place the keyword `void` before the constructor's name.
    c. The public member methods in a class can be accessed by any program that uses an object created from the class.
    d. An instance of a class is considered an object.

11. Which of the following creates an `Animal` object named `dog`?
    a. `Animal dog;`
    b. `Animal "dog";`
    c. `dog = "Animal";`
    d. `dog Animal();`

12. A program creates an `Animal` object named `dog`. Which of the following calls the `displayBreed` method, which is a public member method contained in the `Animal` class?
    a. `Animal::displayBreed();`
    b. `displayBreed();`
    c. `dog::displayBreed();`
    d. `dog.displayBreed();`

Exercises

Pencil and Paper

TRY THIS

1. Write the class definition for a class named `Employee`. The class should include private data members for an `Employee` object's name and salary. The salary may contain a decimal place. The class should contain two constructors: the default constructor and a constructor that allows a program to assign initial values to the data members. (The answers to TRY THIS Exercises are located at the end of the chapter.)

TRY THIS

2. Include an additional public method in the `Employee` class from Pencil and Paper Exercise 1. The method should allow a program to assign values to the data members after an `Employee` object has been instantiated. (The answers to TRY THIS Exercises are located at the end of the chapter.)

MODIFY THIS

3. Include two additional public methods in the `Employee` class from Pencil and Paper Exercise 2. One method should allow a program to view the contents of the salary data member. The other method should allow a program to view the contents of the employee name data member.

MODIFY THIS

4. Include another public method in the `Employee` class from Pencil and Paper Exercise 3. The method should calculate an `Employee` object's new salary, which is based on the raise percentage provided by the program using the object. Before making the calculation, the method should verify that the raise percentage is greater than or equal to 0.0. If the raise percentage is less than 0.0, the method should assign the number 0.0 as the new salary.

INTRODUCTORY

5. Write the code for two overloaded methods named `getArea`. The methods belong to the `Square` class. The first `getArea` method should accept two integers. The second

getArea method should accept two double numbers. Both methods should calculate the area by multiplying the first number by the second number. Each should then return the calculated value.

6. Correct the errors in the Item class shown in Figure 15-25. SWAT THE BUGS


```
//declaration section
class Item
{
private:
    item();
    void assignItem(string, double);
public:
    string name;
    double price;
}

//implementation section
Item()
{
    name = "";
    price = 0.0;
}  //end of default constructor

void assignItem(string n, double p)
{
    name = n;
    price = p;
}  //end of assignItem method
```

Figure 15-25

Computer

7. In this exercise, you use the Employee class from Pencil and Paper Exercise 4 to create an Employee object. Follow the instructions for starting C++ and viewing the TryThis7.cpp file, which is contained in either the Cpp7\Chap15\TryThis7 Project folder or the Cpp7\Chap15 folder. (Depending on your C++ development tool, you may need to open this exercise's project/solution file first.) If necessary, delete the two forward slashes that appear before the system("pause"); statement and then save the file. Add a header file named TryThis7 Employee.h. In the header file, enter the #include <string> and using namespace std; directives. Then enter the class definition you created in Pencil and Paper Exercise 4. Next, complete the TryThis7.cpp file by entering the appropriate instructions. Use the comments as a guide. Save and then run the program. Test the program by entering your name, a current salary amount of 54000, and a raise rate of .1. The program should display your name, current salary ($54000), and new salary ($59400). (The answers to TRY THIS Exercises are located at the end of the chapter.) TRY THIS

8. In this exercise, you complete a program that uses the FormattedDate class shown in Figure 15-1 in the chapter. Follow the instructions for starting C++ and viewing the TryThis8.cpp file, which is contained in either the Cpp7\Chap15\TryThis8 TRY THIS

Project folder or the Cpp7\Chap15 folder. (Depending on your C++ development tool, you may need to open this exercise's project/solution file first.) If necessary, delete the two forward slashes that appear before the `system("pause");` statement and then save the file. Add a header file named TryThis8 FormattedDate.h. In the header file, enter the `#include <string>` and `using namespace std;` directives. Then enter the class definition from Figure 15-1. Next, complete the TryThis8.cpp file by entering the appropriate instructions. Use the comments as a guide. Save and then run the program. Test the program appropriately. (The answers to TRY THIS Exercises are located at the end of the chapter.)

MODIFY THIS

9. In this exercise, you modify the program from TRY THIS Exercise 8. If necessary, create a new project named ModifyThis9 Project and save it in the Cpp7\Chap15 folder. Copy the instructions from the TryThis8.cpp file into a source file named ModifyThis9.cpp. Change the filename in the first comment. Also copy the instructions from the TryThis8 FormattedDate.h file into a header file named ModifyThis9 FormattedDate.h file. If necessary, change the filename in the first comment. Modify the program so that it asks the user whether he or she wants to display the formatted date using either slashes (/) or hyphens (-). Save and then run the program. Test the program by entering 12 as the month, 5 as the day, 2013 as the year, and a - (hyphen) as the separator. The program displays 12-5-2013 on the computer screen. Run the program again. Enter 9 as the month, 30 as the day, 2014 as the year, and a / (slash) as the separator. The program displays 9/30/2014 on the computer screen. Hint: The `getFormattedDate` method should receive a string that indicates whether the user wants slashes or hyphens in the date.

MODIFY THIS

10. In this exercise, you modify the pizza slices program shown in Figure 15-11 in the chapter. If necessary, create a new project named ModifyThis10 Project and save it in the Cpp7\Chap15 folder. Enter the C++ instructions from the figure into a source file named ModifyThis10.cpp. Change the filename in the first comment. Enter the instructions shown in Figure 15-9 in the chapter in a header file named ModifyThis10 Square.h. Change the filename in the first comment. Modify the pizza slices program so it uses the parameterized constructor in the ModifyThis10 Square.h file. Save, run, and test the program.

MODIFY THIS

11. In this exercise, you modify the patio area program shown in Figure 15-8 in the chapter. If necessary, create a new project named ModifyThis11 Project and save it in the Cpp7\Chap15 folder. Enter the C++ instructions from the figure into a source file named ModifyThis11.cpp. Change the filename in the first comment. Enter the instructions shown in Figure 15-13 in the chapter in a header file named ModifyThis11 Square.h. Change the filename in the first comment. Modify the patio area program so it uses the parameterized `calcArea` method. Save, run, and test the program.

INTRODUCTORY

12. In this exercise, you complete a program that uses the `Square` class shown in Figure 15-7 in the chapter. Follow the instructions for starting C++ and viewing the Introductory12.cpp file, which is contained in either the Cpp7\Chap15\Introductory12 Project folder or the Cpp7\Chap15 folder. (Depending on your C++ development tool, you may need to open this exercise's project/solution file first.) If necessary, delete the two forward slashes that appear before the `system("pause");` statement and then save the file. Enter the `Square` class definition from Figure 15-7 in a header file named Introductory12 Square.h. Change the filename in the first comment. Next, complete the Introductory12.cpp file by entering the appropriate instructions. Use the comments as a guide. Save, run, and test the program.

INTERMEDIATE

13. In this exercise, you use the `Rectangle` class from Lab 15-2 to instantiate a `Rectangle` object in the All-Around Fence Company program. If necessary, create a new project named Intermediate13 Project. Copy the instructions from the Lab15-2 Rectangle.h file (which is located in either the Cpp7\Chap15\Lab15-2 Project folder or the Cpp7\Chap15 folder) into a header file named Intermediate13 Rectangle.h. Change the filename in the first comment. The owner of All-Around Fence Company wants a program that calculates the cost of installing a fence. Use the IPO chart shown in Figure 15-26 to code the program. Enter your C++ instructions into a source file named Intermediate13.cpp. Display the perimeter as an integer. Display the total price with a dollar sign and two decimal places. Also enter appropriate comments and any additional instructions required by the compiler. Save and then run the program. Test the program using 120 as the length, 75 as the width, and 10 as the cost per linear foot. The program should display 390 linear feet as the perimeter and $3900.00 as the total price.

Input	**Processing**	**Output**
length (in feet) width (in feet) fence cost (per linear foot)	Processing items: Rectangle object Algorithm: 1. enter length, width, and fence cost 2. use the Rectangle object's setDimensions method to assign the length and width to the Rectangle object 3. use the Rectangle object's calcPerimeter method to calculate and return the perimeter 4. calculate the total price by multiplying the perimeter by the fence cost 5. display the perimeter and total price	perimeter total price

Figure 15-26

INTERMEDIATE

14. In this exercise, you modify the `Rectangle` class from Lab 15-2 so that it allows a program to view the contents of the `length` and `width` data members. You also modify the Terney Landscaping program so that it displays the length and width measurements.

    a. If necessary, create a new project named Intermediate14 Project and save it in the Cpp7\Chap15 folder. Copy the instructions from the Lab15-2.cpp file into a source file named Intermediate14.cpp. Change the filename in the first comment.

    b. Copy the instructions from the Lab15-2 Rectangle.h file (which is located in either the Cpp7\Chap15\Lab15-2 Project folder or the Cpp7\Chap15 folder) into a header file named Intermediate14 Rectangle.h file. Change the filename in the first comment.

    c. Add two value-returning methods to the `Rectangle` class. Each method should return the value of one of the private variables.

    d. Modify the Terney Landscaping program so that it uses the methods to display the length and width of the `Rectangle` object. (The program also should display the area and total price.) Save and then run the program. Test the program appropriately.

INTERMEDIATE

15. In this exercise, you modify the `Rectangle` class from Lab 15-2 so that its `setDimensions` method returns a value. You also modify the Terney Landscaping program.

  a. If necessary, create a new project named Intermediate15 Project and save it in the Cpp7\Chap15 folder. Copy the instructions from the Lab15-2.cpp file into a source file named Intermediate15.cpp. Change the filename in the first comment.

  b. Copy the instructions from the Lab15-2 Rectangle.h file (which is located in either the Cpp7\Chap15\Lab15-2 Project folder or the Cpp7\Chap15 folder) into a header file named Intermediate15 Rectangle.h file. Change the filename in the first comment.

  c. Modify the `setDimensions` method so that it returns a value that indicates whether the length and width dimensions passed to the method are valid. To be valid, each dimension must be greater than 0.0. If the `setDimensions` method indicates that the length and width dimensions are valid, the program should calculate and display both the area and the total price; otherwise, it should display an error message. Modify the program appropriately.

  d. Save and then run the program. Test the program using 120 feet as the length, 75 feet as the width, and 1.55 as the price. The program should display 1000.00 as the area in square yards and $1550.00 as the total price. Now, run the program again. Enter –5 as the length, 6 as the width, and 3 as the price. The program should display an error message because the length dimension is less than 0.0.

INTERMEDIATE

16. In this exercise, you create a `Triangle` class and a program that uses the `Triangle` class to instantiate a `Triangle` object.

  a. If necessary, create a new project named Intermediate16 Project and save it in the Cpp7\Chap15 folder. Create a `Triangle` class. Enter the class definition in a header file named Intermediate16 Triangle.h. The class should include a void method that allows the program to set the triangle's dimensions. The method should verify that all of the dimensions are greater than 0.0 before assigning the values to the private data members. The class also should include two value-returning methods. One value-returning method should calculate the area of a triangle, and the other should calculate the perimeter of a triangle. The formula for calculating the area of a triangle is $1/2 * b * h$, where b is the base and h is the height. The formula for calculating the perimeter of a triangle is $a + b + c$, where a, b, and c are the lengths of the sides. Determine the appropriate variables to include in the class. Be sure to include a default constructor that initializes the variables.

  b. Create a program that prompts the user for the triangle's dimensions and then displays the triangle's area and perimeter amounts. Enter your C++ instructions in a source file named Intermediate16.cpp. Display the amounts with zero decimal places. Also enter appropriate comments and any additional instructions required by the compiler. Save and then run the program. Test the program appropriately.

ADVANCED

17. In this exercise, you modify an existing header file.

  a. Follow the instructions for starting C++ and viewing the Advanced17.cpp and Advanced17 MyDate.h files, which are contained in either the Cpp7\Chap15\Advanced17 Project folder or the Cpp7\Chap15 folder. The program uses the `MyDate` class to create an object named `today`. Notice that the program prompts the user to enter the month, day, and year. It then uses the `MyDate` class's public methods (`setDate` and `displayDate`) to set and display the date entered by the user. The program also uses a public method named `updateDate` to increase the day number by 1. It then displays the new date on the screen.

b. Run the program. Enter 3 as the month, 15 as the day, and 2014 as the year. The computer screen shows that today is 3/15/2014 and tomorrow is 3/16/2014, which is correct.

c. Run the program again. This time, enter 3 as the month, 31 as the day, and 2015 as the year. The computer screen shows that today is 3/31/2015 and tomorrow is 3/32/2015, which is incorrect.

d. Modify the `updateDate` method so that it updates the date correctly. For example, if today is 3/31/2015, then tomorrow is 4/1/2015. If today is 12/31/2013, then tomorrow is 1/1/2014. You do not have to worry about leap years; treat February as though it always has 28 days. Save and then run the program. Test the program four times, using the following dates: 3/15/2014, 4/30/2015, 2/28/2011, and 12/31/2013.

ADVANCED

18. In this exercise, you modify the Terney Landscaping program from Lab 15-2 so that it passes an object to a function.

    a. If necessary, create a new project named Advanced18 Project and save it in the Cpp7\Chap15 folder. Copy the instructions from the Lab15-2.cpp file into a source file named Advanced18.cpp. Change the filename in the first comment. Copy the instructions from the Lab15-2 Rectangle.h file (which is located in either the Cpp7\Chap15\Lab15-2 Project folder or the Cpp7\Chap15 folder) into a header file named Advanced18 Rectangle.h file. Change the filename in the first comment.

    b. Modify the program so that it uses a function named `calcAndDisplay` to calculate and display the area and the total price. Pass the `Rectangle` object and the price per square yard to the function. Save and then run the program. Test the program using 120 feet as the length, 75 feet as the width, and 1.55 as the price. The program should display 1000.00 as the area in square yards and $1550.00 as the total price.

ADVANCED

19. In this exercise, you modify the `Rectangle` class from Lab 15-2 so that it includes an overloaded method.

    a. If necessary, create a new project named Advanced19 Project and save it in the Cpp7\Chap15 folder. Copy the instructions from the Lab15-2 Rectangle.h file (which is located in either the Cpp7\Chap15\Lab15-2 Project folder or the Cpp7\Chap15 folder) into a header file named Advanced19 Rectangle.h. Change the filename in the first comment.

    b. Pool-Time, a company that sells in-ground pools, wants a program that its salespeople can use to determine the number of gallons of water required to fill an in-ground pool. To calculate the number of gallons, you need to find the volume of the pool. The volume formula is *length * width * depth*. Modify the `Rectangle` class so that it can be used to represent a pool. You will need to include an additional private variable to store the depth value, as well as an additional public method to calculate and return the volume. You also will need to modify the default constructor and also overload the `setDimensions` method. Be sure to verify that the depth value is greater than 0.0 before assigning the value to the private variable.

    c. Use the IPO chart shown in Figure 15-27 to code the program. Enter your C++ instructions in a source file named Advanced19.cpp. Also enter appropriate comments and any additional instructions required by the compiler. Display the volume and number of gallons with two decimal places.

    d. Save and then run the program. Use 25 feet as the length, 15 feet as the width, and 6.5 feet as the depth. The program should display 2437.50 as the volume and 18233.84 as the number of gallons of water.

Input	**Processing**	**Output**
length (in feet) width (in feet) depth (in feet)	Processing items: Rectangle object Algorithm: 1. enter length, width, and depth 2. use the Rectangle object's setDimensions method to assign the length, width, and depth to the Rectangle object 3. use the Rectangle object's calcVolume method to calculate and return the volume 4. calculate the gallons of water by dividing the volume by .13368 5. display the volume and gallons of water	volume (in cubic feet) gallons of water

Figure 15-27

Answers to TRY THIS Exercises

Pencil and Paper

1. See Figure 15-28.

```
//declaration section
class Employee
{
public:
    Employee();
    Employee(string, double);
private:
    string name;
    double salary;
};

//implementation section
Employee::Employee()
{
    name = "";
    salary = 0.0;
} //end of default constructor

Employee::Employee(string n, double s)
{
    name = n;
    salary = s;
} //end of constructor
```

Figure 15-28

2. See Figure 15-29.

```
//declaration section
class Employee
{
public:
    Employee();
    Employee(string, double);
    void setEmployee(string, double);
private:
    string name;
    double salary;
};

//implementation section
Employee::Employee()
{
    name = "";
    salary = 0.0;
}  //end of default constructor

Employee::Employee(string n, double s)
{
    name = n;
    salary = s;
} //end of constructor

void Employee::setEmployee(string n, double s)
{
    name = n;
    salary = s;
} //end of setEmployee method
```

Figure 15-29

Computer

7. See Figures 15-30 and 15-31.

```
//TryThis7.cpp
//calculates and displays a new salary
//Created/revised by <your name> on <current date>

#include <iostream>
#include <string>
#include "TryThis7 Employee.h"
using namespace std;

int main()
{
    //instantiate Employee object
    Employee myEmployee;

    //declare variables
    string name = "";
    double pay  = 0;
    double rate = 0.0;

    //get name, salary, and raise percentage
    cout << "Employee's name: ";
    getline(cin, name);
    cout << "Employee's current salary: ";
    cin >> pay;
    cin.ignore(100, '\n');
    cout << "Raise rate (in decimal form): ";
    cin >> rate;
    cin.ignore(100, '\n');

    //assign name and salary to the Employee object
    myEmployee.setEmployee(name, pay);

    //use the Employee object to display the
    //name and current salary
    cout << "Name: " << myEmployee.getName() << endl;
    cout << "Current salary: $" << myEmployee.getSalary()
         << endl;

    //use the Employee object to calculate the new salary
    myEmployee.calcNewSalary(rate);

    //use the Employee object to display the new salary
    cout << "New salary: $" << myEmployee.getSalary()
         << endl;

    //system("pause");
    return 0;
}   //end of main function
```

your C++ development tool may require this statement

Figure 15-30

```
//TryThis7 Employee.h
//Created/revised by <your name> on <current date>

#include <string>
using namespace std;

//declaration section
class Employee
{
public:
   Employee();
   Employee(string, double);
   void setEmployee(string, double);
   double getSalary();
   string getName();
   void calcNewSalary(double);
private:
   string name;
   double salary;
};

//implementation section
Employee::Employee()
{
   name   = "";
   salary = 0.0;
} //end of default constructor

Employee::Employee(string n, double s)
{
   name   = n;
   salary = s;
} //end of constructor

void Employee::setEmployee(string n, double s)
{
   name   = n;
   salary = s;
} //end of setEmployee method

double Employee::getSalary()
{
   return salary;
} //end of getSalary method

string Employee::getName()
{
   return name;
} //end of getName method

```

Figure 15-31 *(continues)*

(continued)

```
void Employee::calcNewSalary(double r)
{
    if (r >= 0.0)
         salary = salary * r + salary;
    else
         salary = 0.0;
    //end if
} //end of calcNewSalary method
```

Figure 15-31

8. See Figures 15-32 and 15-33.

```
//TryThis8.cpp - displays a formatted date
//Created/revised by <your name> on <current date>

#include <iostream>
#include <string>
#include "TryThis8 FormattedDate.h"
using namespace std;

int main()
{
    //create a FormattedDate object
    FormattedDate hireDate;

    //declare variables
    string hireMonth = "";
    string hireDay   = "";
    string hireYear  = "";

    //get month, day, and year
    cout << "Enter the month number: ";
    cin >> hireMonth;
    cout << "Enter the day number: ";
    cin >> hireDay;
    cout << "Enter the year number: ";
    cin >> hireYear;

    //use the FormattedDate object to set the date
    hireDate.setDate(hireMonth, hireDay, hireYear);

    //display the formatted date
    cout << "Employee hire date: "
         << hireDate.getFormattedDate() << endl;

    //system("pause");
    return 0;
}   //end of main function
```

your C++ development tool may require this statement

Figure 15-32

```
//TryThis8 FormattedDate.h
//Created/revised by <your name> on <current date>

#include <string>
using namespace std;

//declaration section
class FormattedDate
{
public:
    FormattedDate();
    void setDate(string, string, string);
    string getFormattedDate();
private:
    string month;
    string day;
    string year;
};

//implementation section
FormattedDate::FormattedDate()
{
    //initializes the private variables
    month  =  "0";
    day    =  "0";
    year   =  "0";
} //end of default constructor

void FormattedDate::setDate(string m, string d, string y)
{
    //assigns program values to the private variables
    month = m;
    day = d;
    year = y;
} //end of setDate method

string FormattedDate::getFormattedDate()
{
    //formats and returns values stored
    //in the private variables
    return month + "/" + day + "/" + year;
} //end of getFormattedDate method
```

Figure 15-33

APPENDIX A

Answers to Mini-Quizzes and Labs

Answers to Chapter 1 Mini-Quizzes

Mini-Quiz 1-1

1. machine
2. a. a procedure-oriented
3. b. an object-oriented
4. compiler

Mini-Quiz 1-2

1. sequence, selection, repetition
2. sequence
3. algorithm
4. repetition
5. repetition
6. selection

Answers to Chapter 1 Labs

LAB 1-1 Stop and Analyze

1. sequence and repetition
2. Mary Smith and 60
3. change the last instruction to *display the salesperson's name, sales amount, and bonus amount*
4. The modifications are shaded in the algorithm.

```
repeat for (each salesperson)
      enter the salesperson's name and sales amount
      calculate the bonus amount by multiplying the sales amount by 3%
      display the salesperson's name and bonus amount
end repeat
```

5. The modifications are shaded in the algorithm.

```
enter the bonus rate
repeat (5 times)
      enter the salesperson's name and sales amount
      calculate the bonus amount by multiplying the sales amount by the bonus rate
      display the salesperson's name and bonus amount
end repeat
```

LAB 1-2 Plan and Create

```
repeat (25 times)
      read the student's answer and the correct answer
      if (the student's answer is not the same as the correct answer)
            mark the student's answer incorrect
      end if
end repeat
```

LAB 1-3 Modify

You can use either of the following algorithms. The modifications are shaded in each.

Algorithm 1

```
repeat (5 times)
      enter the salesperson's name and sales amount
      if (the sales amount is greater than 2000)
            calculate the bonus amount by multiplying the sales amount by 3.5%
      else
            calculate the bonus amount by multiplying the sales amount by 3%
      end if
      display the salesperson's name and bonus amount
end repeat
```

Algorithm 2

```
repeat (5 times)
    enter the salesperson's name and sales amount
    if (the sales amount is less than or equal to 2000)
        calculate the bonus amount by multiplying the sales amount by 3%
    else
        calculate the bonus amount by multiplying the sales amount by 3.5%
    end if
    display the salesperson's name and bonus amount
end repeat
```

Answers to Chapter 2 Mini-Quizzes

Mini-Quiz 2-1

1. Output: sales tax
   Input: purchase amount
   sales tax rate
   Missing information: none

2. Output savings
   Input: number of CDs purchased
   club CD price
   store CD price
   Missing information: store CD price

3. Output: total amount saved in January
   Input: amount saved per day
   number of days in January
   Missing information: none (Although the number of days in January is not specified in the problem specification, that information can be found in any calendar.)

4. Output: yearly savings
   Input: amount saved per day
   number of days in the year
   Missing information: number of days in the year (Because some years are leap years, you would need to know the number of days in the year.)

Mini-Quiz 2-2

1. input/output
2. rectangular
3.

Input	Processing	Output
purchase amount sales tax rate	Processing items: none Algorithm: 1. enter the purchase amount and sales tax rate 2. calculate the sales tax by multiplying the purchase amount by the sales tax rate 3. display the sales tax	sales tax

4.

Input	Processing	Output
number of CDs purchased club CD price store CD price	Processing items: total club cost total store cost	savings

Algorithm:

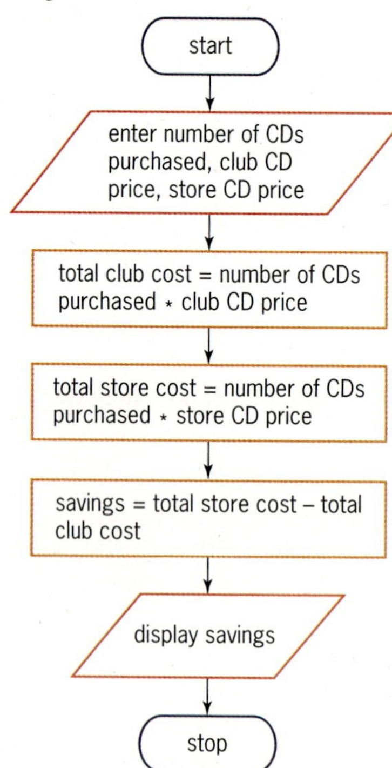

Mini-Quiz 2-3

1.

purchase amount	sales tax rate	sales tax
~~67~~	~~.05~~	~~3.35~~
100	.02	2.00

2.

first number	second number	sum	average
~~5~~	~~11~~	~~16~~	~~8~~
6	12	18	9

Answers to Chapter 2 Labs

LAB 2-1 Stop and Analyze

1. The algorithm will display 306 when the user enters 300 and .02 as the current weekly pay and raise percentage, respectively. The algorithm will display 512.50 when the user enters 500 and .025 as the current weekly pay and raise percentage, respectively.

2.

Input	Processing	Output
current weekly pay raise percentage	Processing items: raise	new weekly pay

Algorithm:
1. enter the current weekly pay and raise percentage
2. calculate the raise by multiplying the current weekly pay by the raise percentage
3. calculate the new weekly pay by adding the raise to the current weekly pay
4. display the new weekly pay

current weekly pay	raise percentage	raise	new weekly pay
~~300~~	~~.02~~	~~6~~	~~306~~
500	.025	12.50	512.50

3.

Input	Processing	Output
current weekly pay raise percentage	Processing items: none	raise new weekly pay

Algorithm:
1. enter the current weekly pay and raise percentage
2. calculate the raise by multiplying the current weekly pay by the raise percentage
3. calculate the new weekly pay by adding the raise to the current weekly pay
4. display the raise and new weekly pay

current weekly pay	raise percentage	raise	new weekly pay
~~300~~	~~.02~~	~~6~~	~~306~~
500	.025	12.50	512.50

LAB 2-2 Plan and Create

No answer required.

LAB 2-3 Modify

Input	**Processing**	**Output**
number of nights per-night rate room service charge telephone charge entertainment tax rate	Processing items: room charge entertainment tax	total bill

Algorithm:
1. enter the number of nights, per-night rate, room service charge, telephone charge, and entertainment tax rate
2. calculate the room charge by multiplying the number of nights by the per-night rate
3. calculate the entertainment tax by multiplying the room charge by the entertainment tax rate
4. calculate the total bill by adding together the room charge, entertainment tax, room service charge, and telephone charge
5. display the total bill

number of nights	per-night rate	room service charge	telephone charge	entertainment tax rate
~~3~~	~~70~~	~~0~~	~~10~~	~~.05~~
7	100	25	6	.03

room charge	entertainment tax	total bill
~~210~~	~~10.50~~	~~230.50~~
700	21	752

LAB 2-4 Desk-Check

assessed value	tax rate	annual property tax
~~104000~~	~~1.50~~	~~1560~~
~~239000~~	~~1.15~~	~~2748.50~~
86000	.98	842.80

LAB 2-5 Debug

first number	second number	third number	sum	average
~~25~~	~~63~~	~~14~~	~~102~~	~~34~~
33	56	70	159	53

Answers to Chapter 3 Mini-Quizzes

Mini-Quiz 3-1

1. one
2. a. `quantity`
3. c. `COMMISSION_RATE`
4. variables and named constants

Mini-Quiz 3-2

1. b. False
2. c. 100000
3. 98, 01100010
4. d. both a and c

Mini-Quiz 3-3

1. b. '%'
2. d. all of the above
3. 10
4. `int population = 0;`
5. `const double MAX_PAY = 25.55;`
6. $5

Answers to Chapter 3 Labs

LAB 3-1 Stop and Analyze

1. The problem requires three memory locations.
2. The problem requires three variables, but no named constants. Variables were chosen so that the values of the input and output items can vary during runtime.
3. The input and output items could be stored in either `float` or `double` memory locations.
4. ```
   double currentPay = 0.0;
   double raiseRate = 0.0;
   double newPay = 0.0;
   ```
5. `const double RAISE_RATE = .02;`

LAB 3-2 Plan and Create

No answer required.
   ```

LAB 3-3 Modify

The modifications made to Figure 3-17 are shaded in the IPO chart.

Input	Processing	Output
radius pi (3.14)	Processing items: radius squared Algorithm: 1. enter the radius 2. calculate the radius squared by multiplying the radius by itself 3. calculate the area by multiplying the radius squared by pi 4. display the area	area

The modifications made to Figure 3-20 are shaded in the IPO chart information and C++ instructions.

IPO chart information	C++ instructions
Input	
radius	`double radius = 0.0;`
pi (3.14)	`const double PI = 3.14;`
Processing	
radius squared	`double radiusSquared = 0.0;`
Output	
area	`double area = 0.0;`

LAB 3-4 Desk-Check

The modifications made to Figure 3-18 are shaded in the manual calculations.

First desk-check

```
   4     (radius)
*  4     (radius)
----------------------
  16     (radius squared)
*  3.14  (pi)
----------------------
  50.24  (area)
```

Second desk-check

```
   5.5   (radius)
*  5.5   (radius)
----------------------
  30.25  (radius squared)
*  3.14  (pi)
----------------------
  94.985 (area)
```

The modifications made to Figure 3-19 are shaded in the desk-check table.

radius	pi	radius squared	area
~~4~~	~~3.14~~	~~16~~	~~50.24~~
5.5	3.14	30.25	94.985

LAB 3-5 Debug

The modifications made to Figure 3-21 are shaded in the C++ instructions column.

IPO chart information	C++ instructions
Input	
first number	`double first = 0.0;`
second number	`double second = 0.0;`
third number	`double third = 0.0;`
Processing	
sum	`double sum = 0.0;`
Output	
average	`double average = 0.0;`

Answers to Chapter 4 Mini-Quizzes

Mini-Quiz 4-1

1. b. `cin >> grossPay;`
2. c. `cout << grossPay;`
3. d. all of the above
4. `<<`

Mini-Quiz 4-2

1. `grossPay = 9.55 * hours;`
2. `grossPay = 9.55 * static_cast<double>(hours);`
3. The expression will evaluate to 13.5. It should evaluate to 15.75. The expression evaluates incorrectly because dividing the integer 7 by the integer 2 results in the integer 3 rather than in the `double` number 3.5. Multiplying the integer 3 by the `double` number 4.5 results in the incorrect answer of 13.5.
4. You can use any of the following expressions. You also can use the `static_cast` operator to type cast at least one of the integers in the expression.

```
7.0 / 2.0 * 4.5
7.0 / 2 * 4.5
7 / 2.0 * 4.5
```

5. `age += 1;`

Mini-Quiz 4-3

1. syntax
2. c. source
3. a. braces

Answers to Chapter 4 Labs

LAB 4-1 Stop and Analyze

1. When evaluating the `totalCost = numberOfPeople * costPerPerson;` statement, the computer converts the integer stored in the `numberOfPeople` variable to the `double` number 10.0 before multiplying it by the value stored in the `costPerPerson` variable (the `double` number 7.45). The result is the `double` number 74.5, which the computer assigns to the `double` variable `totalCost`. The value assigned to the `totalCost` variable is correct.

2. When evaluating the `numberOfPeople = numberOfPeople / 2;` statement, the computer divides the integer 10 by the integer 2. The result is the integer 5, which the computer assigns to the `numberOfPeople` variable. The value assigned to the `numberOfPeople` variable is correct.

3. When evaluating the `costPerPerson = costPerPerson + 3;` statement, the computer converts the integer 3 to the `double` number 3.0 before adding it to the value stored in the `costPerPerson` variable (the `double` number 7.45). The result is the `double` number 10.45, which the computer assigns to the `costPerPerson` variable. The value assigned to the `costPerPerson` variable is correct.

4. When evaluating the `average = score1 + score2 / 2;` statement, the computer converts the integer 2 to the `double` number 2.0 before dividing it into the value stored in the `score2` variable (the `double` number 90.0). The result is the `double` number 45.0, which the computer adds to the value stored in the `score1` variable (the `double` number 100.0). The result is the `double` number 145.0, which the computer assigns to the `double` variable `average`. The value assigned to the `average` variable is incorrect. You can fix the statement as follows: `average = (score1 + score2) / 2;`

5. When evaluating the `avgSales = (juneSales + julySales) / 2;` statement, the computer adds the integer stored in the `juneSales` variable (933) to the integer stored in the `julySales` variable (1216). The result is the integer 2149, which the computer divides by the integer 2. The quotient is the integer 1074, which the computer converts to the `double` number 1074.0 before assigning it to the `double` variable `avgSales`. The value assigned to the `avgSales` variable is incorrect. Two ways you can fix the statement are shown here:

```
avgSales = (juneSales + julySales) / 2.0;
avgSales = static_cast<double>(juneSales + julySales) / 2;
```

LAB 4-2 Plan and Create

No answer required.

LAB 4-3 Modify

The modifications made to the Lab4-2.cpp file are shaded.

```
//Lab4-3.cpp - displays the total owed
//Created/revised by <your name> on <current date>

#include <iostream>
using namespace std;

int main()
{
    //declare variables and named constants
    double hours              = 0.0;
    double totalOwed          = 0.0;
    const int FEE_PER_HOUR = 105;
    const int ROOM_BOARD    = 2000;

    //enter hours enrolled
    cout << "Hours enrolled? ";
    cin >> hours;

    //calculate total owed
    totalOwed = hours * FEE_PER_HOUR + ROOM_BOARD;

    //display total owed
    cout << "Total owed: $" << totalOwed << endl;

    //system("pause");
    return 0;
} //end of main function
```

LAB 4-4 Desk-Check

num	answer
~~75~~	~~0~~
	1

LAB 4-5 Debug

To debug the program, you need to convert at least one of the items on the right side of the assignment operator in the `raise = salary * 3 / 100;` statement to the `double` data type. For example, you can use any of the following:

```
raise = salary * 3 / 100.0;
raise = salary * 3.0 / 100;
static_cast<double>(salary) * 3 / 100;
static_cast<double>(salary) * 3.0 / 100.0;
```

Answers to Chapter 5 Mini-Quizzes

Mini-Quiz 5-1

1. end if
2. b. False
3. a. diamond
4. b. single-alternative
5. a. dual-alternative

Mini-Quiz 5-2

1. d. none of the above
2. c. `if (quantity == 100)`
3. a. `if (sales >= 300.99)`
4. c. `!=`
5. b. `>=`

Mini-Quiz 5-3

1. true
2. false
3. true
4. b. `if (age >= 30 && age <= 40)`
5. a. `if (code == 'R' || code == 'r')`

Mini-Quiz 5-4

1. d. `cout << fixed << setprecision(2);`
2. c. `letter = tolower(letter);`
3. d. 34.650000

Answers to Chapter 5 Labs

LAB 5-1 Stop and Analyze

1. The number .03 will be assigned to the `rate` variable when the user enters a pay grade of 1. The number .02 will be assigned to the `rate` variable when the user enters either 3 or 5 as the pay grade.

2. The directive on Line 5 is necessary because the program uses the `setprecision` stream manipulator.

3. The 1 in the `if` statement is enclosed in single quotation marks because the `payGrade` variable's data type is `char`.

4.
```
if (payGrade != '1')
   rate = .02;
else
   rate = .03;
//end if
```

5. You also can write the `salary = salary + salary * rate;` statement as follows:

   `salary = salary * (1 + rate);`

   or `salary *= (1 + rate);`

   or `salary += (salary * rate);`

6. You would need to remove the `double rate = 0.0;` and `salary = salary + salary * rate;` statements. You also would need to change the `rate = .03;` statement to `salary = salary + salary * .03;`, and change the `rate = .02;` statement to `salary = salary + salary * .02;`.

LAB 5-2 Plan and Create

No answer required.

LAB 5-3 Modify

```
if (totalCals < 0 || fatGrams < 0)
     cout << "Input error" << endl;
else
{
    //calculate and display the output
    fatCals = fatGrams * 9;
    fatPercent = static_cast<double>(fatCals)
         / static_cast<double>(totalCals) * 100;

    cout << "Fat calories: " << fatCals << endl;
    cout << fixed << setprecision(0);
    cout << "Fat percentage: " << fatPercent << "%" << endl;
}   //end if
```

LAB 5-4 Desk-Check

letter
P

When the user enters the letter P, the compound condition in the first `if` statement evaluates to true and the statement's true path displays the "Pass" message on the computer screen. Although the correct message already appears on the screen, the computer still evaluates the second `if` statement's compound condition, which determines whether to display the "Fail" message. The second evaluation is unnecessary and makes the code inefficient. You can fix the code by deleting the first `//end if` comment and replacing the `if (letter != 'P' || letter != 'p')` clause with `else`.

LAB 5-5 Debug

To debug the program, change `if (code = '2')` to `if (code == '2')`.

Answers to Chapter 6 Mini-Quizzes

Mini-Quiz 6-1

1. c. in either an outer selection structure's false path or its true path

2.
```
if (the bag contains trash)
    if (the lid is on the Trash container)
        lift the Trash container's lid using your left hand
    end if
    drop the bag of trash in the Trash container
    put the lid back on the Trash container using your left hand
else
    if (the lid is on the Recycle container)
        lift the Recycle container's lid using your left hand
    end if
    drop the bag of recyclables in the Recycle container
    put the lid back on the Recycle container using your left hand
end if
```

3.
```
ask the store clerk whether the store accepts the Discovery card
if (the store accepts the Discovery card)
    pay for your items using your Discovery card
else
    ask the store clerk whether the store accepts the Vita card
    if (the store accepts the Vita card)
        pay for your items using your Vita card
    else
        pay for your items using cash
    end if
end if
```

Mini-Quiz 6-2

1.
```
if (the test score is at least 90)
    display "Great score!"
else
    if (the test score is at least 70)
        display "Good score"
    else
        display "Retake the test"
    end if
end if
```

2.

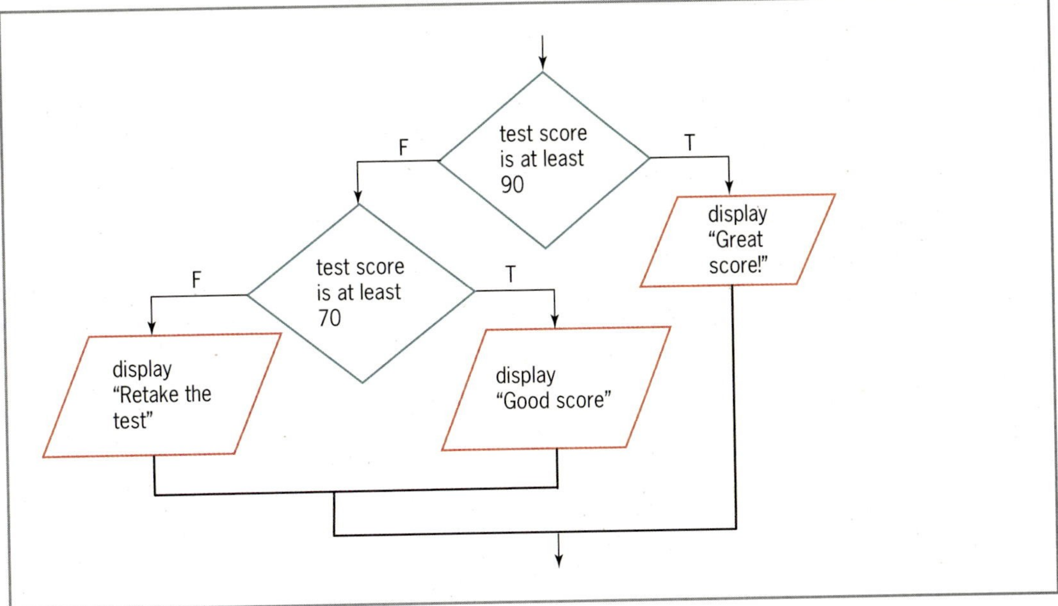

3.
```
if (score >= 90)
     cout << "Great score!" << endl;
else
     if (score >= 70)
          cout << "Good score" << endl;
     else
          cout << "Retake the test" << endl;
     //end if
//end if
```

4. a. membership status, day of the week

Mini-Quiz 6-3

1. Using a compound condition rather than a nested selection structure
   Reversing the decisions in the outer and nested selection structures
   Using an unnecessary nested selection structure
2. Using an unnecessary nested selection structure
3. It is inefficient because the nested selection structure is unnecessary. If the first selection structure's condition evaluates to false, it means that the basketball did *not* go through the hoop. Therefore, there is no need for a nested selection structure that determines whether the basketball did not go through the hoop.
4. Algorithm A in Figure 6-24 will not give you the same results as the solution shown in Figure 6-2. Algorithm A has Maleek saying "I did it!" and "3 points for me" even when the basketball does not go through the hoop.
5. Algorithm B in Figure 6-24 will give you the same results as the solution shown in Figure 6-2.

Mini-Quiz 6-4

1.
```
if (score >= 90)
   cout << "Great score!" << endl;
else if (score >= 70)
   cout << "Good score" << endl;
else if (score >= 0)
   cout << "Retake the test" << endl;
else
   cout << "Invalid test score" << endl;
//end if
```

2. b. `case 2:`

3. `break`

Answers to Chapter 6 Labs

LAB 6-1 Stop and Analyze

1. The program will display the number 35 when the code is C.

2.
```
if (code == 'S')
    fee = 40;
else
    if (code == 'F')
        fee = 50;
    else
        if (code == 'A')
            fee = 30;
        else
            if (code == 'C')
                fee = 35;
            else
                fee = 0;
            //end if
        //end if
    //end if
//end if
```

3.
```
if (code == 'S')
    fee = 40;
else if (code == 'F')
    fee = 50;
else if (code == 'A')
    fee = 30;
else if (code == 'C')
    fee = 35;
else
    fee = 0;
//end if
```

4.
```
switch (code)
{
case 'S':
    fee = 40;
```

```
        break;
    case 'F':
        fee = 50;
        break;
    case 'A':
        fee = 30;
        break;
    case 'C':
        fee = 35;
        break;
    default:
        fee = 0;
    }    //end switch
```

5.
```
switch (code)
{
case 'S':
    cout << 40 << endl;
    break;
case 'F':
    cout << 50 << endl;
    break;
case 'A':
    cout << 30 << endl;
    break;
case 'C':
    cout << 35 << endl;
    break;
default:
   cout << "Invalid code";
} //end switch
```

LAB 6-2 Plan and Create

No answer required.

LAB 6-3 Modify

```
//Lab6-3.cpp - displays a salesperson's commission
//Created/revised by <your name> on <current date>

#include <iostream>
#include <iomanip>
using namespace std;

int main()
{
    //declare variables
    int sales          = 0;
    double commission = 0.0;
    char code          = ' ';
```

```

    //enter the code
    cout << "Code (1, 2, or 3): ";
    cin >> code;

    //determine whether the code is valid
    if (code != '1' && code != '2' && code != '3')
        cout << "Invalid code" << endl;
    else
    {
        //enter the sales
        cout << "Sales: ";
        cin >> sales;

        //determine whether the sales are valid
        if (sales < 0)
            cout << "The sales cannot be less than 0." << endl;
        else
        {
            //calculate and display the commission
            switch (code)
            {
            case '1':
                commission = sales * .02;
                break;
            case '2':
                commission = (sales - 100000)  * .05 + 2000;
                break;
            case '3':
                commission = (sales - 400000) * .1 + 17000;
                break;
            }  //end switch

            cout << fixed << setprecision(2);
            cout << "Commission: $" << commission << endl;
        }    //end if
    }  //end if

    //system("pause");
    return 0;
} //end of main function
```

LAB 6-4 Desk-Check

number

~~0~~
~~2~~
~~4~~
~~0~~
~~5~~
~~10~~
~~0~~
~~100~~
50

LAB 6-5 Debug

The modifications are shaded in the code.

```
//Lab6-5.cpp
//displays the salary associated with a code
//Valid codes      Salary
//1                $45,000
//2, 5             $33,000
//3, 4             $25,000
//Created/revised by <your name> on <current date>

#include <iostream>
using namespace std;

int main()
{
    //declare variable
    int code = 0;

    //get code
    cout << "Enter the code (1 through 5): ";
    cin >> code;

    //display salary
    if (code == 1)
        cout << "$45,000" << endl;
    else if (code == 2 || code == 5)
        cout << "$33,000" << endl;
    else if (code == 3 || code == 4)
        cout << "$25,000" << endl;
    else
        cout << "Entry error" << endl;
    //end if

    //system("pause");
    return 0;
} //end of main function
```

Answers to Chapter 7 Mini-Quizzes

Mini-Quiz 7-1

1.
```
1. print the first page
2. repeat while (there is another page to print)
        print the next page
   end repeat
   say "Done printing"
```

2.
```
1. print the first page
2. repeat while (there is another page to print)
       if (the next page is not page 3)
           print the next page
       end if
   end repeat
   say "Done printing"
```

3.
```
1. try to pick a rose
2. repeat while (a rose was picked)
       if (the rose is pink)
           put the rose in the pink basket
       else
           put the rose in the brown basket
       end if
       try to pick a rose
   end repeat
```

Mini-Quiz 7-2

1. `while (quantity > 0)`
2. `while (quantity >= 0)`
3. `while (inStock > reorder)`
4. `while (toupper(letter) == 'Y')` [You also can use `while (tolower(letter) == 'y')` or `while (letter == 'Y' || letter == 'y')`.]
5. a. –9

Mini-Quiz 7-3

1. a. accumulator
2. `quantity += 2;` (or `quantity = quantity + 2;`)
3. `total -= 3;` (or `total = total - 3;` or `total += -3;` or `total = total + -3;`)
4. `totalPurchases += purchases;` (or `totalPurchases = totalPurchases + purchases;`)

Mini-Quiz 7-4

1.
```
while (evenNum < 9)
 {
     cout << evenNum << endl;
     evenNum += 2;  (or evenNum = evenNum + 2;)
 } //end while
```
2. a. `for (int x = 10; x <= 100; x = x + 10)`
3. d. 110
4. `for (int x = 25; x > 0; x = x - 5)` (You also can use `x -= 5`, `x += -5`, or `x = x + -5` as the *update* argument.)
5. 0
6. `for (int num = 2; num < 9; num += 2)` (You also can use `num = num + 2` as the *update* argument.)

Answers to Chapter 7 Labs

LAB 7-1 Stop and Analyze

1. The program inputs a temperature. It uses two processing items: a counter that keeps track of the number of temperatures and an accumulator that totals the temperatures. The program displays the average temperature.
2. The number 999 was chosen as a sentinel value because it's not a valid outside temperature. A negative number was not chosen as a sentinel value because the temperature outside can be below zero.
3. The selection structure on Lines 32 through 43 is necessary to prevent the program from calculating the average temperature when the counter variable (`numberOfTemps`) contains the number 0. Dividing by zero will cause the program to end abruptly with an error.
4. Although the statement on Lines 35 and 36 doesn't need both type casts, it does need at least one of them. Without at least one type cast, the quotient obtained when dividing the contents of the `totalTemp` variable by the contents of the `numberOfTemps` variable would be an integer (rather than a `double` number). This is because both of those variables have the `int` data type; when you divide two integers, the result is an integer. At least one type cast is needed to force the computer to perform the division using `double` numbers, which will result in a quotient that also is a `double` number.
5. The `cout << fixed << setprecision(1);` statement on Line 37 tells the computer to display the output in fixed-point notation with one decimal place.
6. The `numberOfTemps` counter variable keeps track of the number of temperatures entered. Therefore, it should be initialized to 0 at the beginning of the program and then updated only when a temperature has been entered.

7. The average temperature is 76.666... (with the 6 repeating).

numberOfTemps	totalTemp	temp	average
~~0~~	~~0~~	~~0~~	~~0.0~~
~~1~~	~~78~~	~~78~~	
~~2~~	~~163~~	~~85~~	
3	230	~~67~~	
		999	76.666...

8. The program displays 76.7.
9. The program displays the "No temperatures were entered." message.
10. The program (shown below) displays the "No temperatures were entered." message.

```
//Lab7-1.cpp - calculates and displays the average temperature
//Created/revised by <your name> on <current date>

#include <iostream>
#include <iomanip>
using namespace std;

int main()
{
    //declare variables
    int numberOfTemps = 0;  //counter
    int totalTemp     = 0;  //accumulator
    int temp          = 0;
    double average    = 0.0;

    //get first temperature
    cout << "First temperature (999 to stop): ";
    cin >> temp;

    for (; temp != 999;)
    {
        //update counter and accumulator
        numberOfTemps += 1;
        totalTemp += temp;

        //get remaining temperatures
        cout << "Next temperature (999 to stop): ";
        cin >> temp;
    }  //end for

    //verify that at least one temperature was entered
    if (numberOfTemps > 0)
    {
        //calculate and display average temperature
        average = static_cast<double>(totalTemp) /
            static_cast<double>(numberOfTemps);
        cout << fixed << setprecision(1);
        cout << endl << "Average temperature: "
            << average << endl;
    }
    else
        cout << "No temperatures were entered." << endl;
    //end if

    //system("pause");
    return 0;
}  //end of main function
```

11. The average temperature is 14.8.

LAB 7-2 Plan and Create

No answer required.

LAB 7-3 Modify

The program (shown below) displays the correct total points (255) and grade (C). The program shows that the professor entered 7 scores.

```
//Lab7-3.cpp - displays the total points earned and grade
//Created/revised by <your name> on <current date>

#include <iostream>

using namespace std;

int main()
{
   //declare variables
   int score       = 0;
   int totalPoints = 0;  //accumulator
   char grade      = ' ';
   int numScores   = 0;  //counter

   //get first score
   cout << "First score (-1 to stop): ";
   cin >> score;

   while (score != -1)
   {
       //update accumulator and counter, then get another score
       totalPoints += score;
       numScores += 1;
       cout << "Next score (-1 to stop): ";
       cin >> score;
   }  //end while

   //determine grade
   if (totalPoints >= 315)
       grade = 'A';
   else if (totalPoints >= 280)
       grade = 'B';
   else if (totalPoints >= 245)
       grade = 'C';
   else if (totalPoints >= 210)
       grade = 'D';
   else
       grade = 'F';
   //end if

   //display the total points, grade, and number of scores
   cout << "Total points earned: " << totalPoints << endl;
```

```
    cout << "Grade: " << grade << endl;
    cout << "Number of scores: " << numScores << endl;

    //system("pause");
    return 0;
}   //end of main function
```

LAB 7-4 Desk-Check

First desk-check:

squaredNumber	number
~~0~~	~~1~~
~~1~~	~~2~~
~~4~~	~~3~~
~~9~~	~~4~~
16	5

The original code contains an error because it will not display the square of the number 5.

Corrected code:

```
//declare variables
int squaredNumber = 0;

for (int number = 1; number <= 5; number = number + 1)
{
    squaredNumber = number * number;
    cout << squaredNumber << endl;
}   //end for
```

Second desk-check:

squaredNumber	number
~~0~~	~~1~~
~~1~~	~~2~~
~~4~~	~~3~~
~~9~~	~~4~~
~~16~~	~~5~~
25	6

LAB 7-5 Debug

To debug the program, enter a `cin >> price;` statement below the `cout << "Next price: ";` statement.

Answers to Chapter 8 Mini-Quizzes

Mini-Quiz 8-1

1. 4
2. 1
3. 3
4. 1
5.
```
1. repeat while (you are not directly in front of your bedroom door)
       walk forward
   end repeat
2. if (the bedroom door is closed)
       open the bedroom door
   end if
3. walk forward

1. if (you are not directly in front of your bedroom door)
       repeat
           walk forward
       end repeat while (you are not directly in front of your bedroom door)
   end if
2. if (the bedroom door is closed)
       open the bedroom door
   end if
3. walk forward
```

Mini-Quiz 8-2

1. b. False
2. d. semicolon
3. `} while (inStock > reorder);`
4. `} while (toupper(letter) == 'Y');`

Mini-Quiz 8-3

1. b. False
2. a. True

3. a. outer, nested
4. d. all of the above
5.
```
repeat while (there are customers in line)
   repeat while (the customer has a book that needs signing)
      accept the book from the customer
      place the book on the table
      open the front cover of the book
      sign your name on the first page
      close the book
      return the book to the customer
   end repeat
   thank the customer
end repeat
```

Answers to Chapter 8 Labs

LAB 8-1 Stop and Analyze

1. The program contains two pretest loops. It does not contain any posttest loops.
2. The loop that keeps track of the region number is controlled by a counter. The loop's condition will evaluate to true for the following counter values: 1 and 2. A counter value of 3 will make the loop's condition evaluate to false.
3. The loop that keeps track of the sales amounts is controlled by a sentinel value. The valid sentinel values for the loop are any numbers that are less than zero.
4. Desk-check:

sales	region	totalRegionSales
~~0~~	~~1~~	~~0~~
~~1000~~		~~1000~~
~~2000~~		~~3000~~
~~-1~~	~~2~~	
~~400~~		~~3400~~
~~500~~		3900
-3	3	

The missing statement on Line 39 is `totalRegionSales = 0;`. Without this statement, the program is adding both regions' sales to the accumulator. As a result, it's displaying $3000 as the total sales for Region 1 (which is correct) and $3900 as the total sales for Region 2 (which is not correct). The program should be accumulating each region's sales separately and then displaying $3000 as the total sales for Region 1 and $900 as the total sales for Region 2. The `totalRegionSales = 0;` statement is needed to reset the accumulator to 0 before adding the next region's sales to it. You can modify the comment on Line 37 as follows: `//update counter and reset accumulator`.

5. Desk-check:

sales	region	totalRegionSales
~~0~~	~~1~~	~~0~~
~~1000~~		~~1000~~
~~2000~~		~~3000~~
~~-1~~	~~2~~	
		~~0~~
~~400~~		~~400~~
~~500~~		900
-3	3	

The total sales for Region 1 are $3000. The total sales for Region 2 are $900.

6. The program displays $3000 as Region 1's total sales and $900 as Region 2's total sales.

7. The program displays $3000 as Region 1's total sales and $900 as Region 2's total sales. You should remove the "(negative number to end)" text from the `cout` statement on Lines 16 and 17. That statement prompts the user to enter the first sales amount for the current region. However, because the loop that controls the sales amount entries is a posttest loop, the condition will not be evaluated until the second sales amount is entered for the current region. Therefore, a negative number will not end the loop if it is entered as the first sales amount for the region.

```
1 //Lab8-1.cpp - displays each region's total sales
2 //Created/revised by <your name> on <current date>
3
4 #include <iostream>
5 using namespace std;
6
7 int main()
8 {
9      //declare variables
10     int sales            = 0;
11     int totalRegionSales = 0;    //accumulator
12
13     for (int region = 1; region < 3; region += 1)
14     {
15         //get current region's first sales amount
16         cout << "First sales amount for Region "
17              << region << ": ";
18         cin >> sales;
19
20         do      //begin loop
21         {
22             //add sales amount to region total
23             totalRegionSales += sales;
24             //get next sales amount for
25             //current region
26             cout << "Next sales amount for Region "
27                  << region << " (negative number to end): ";
28             cin >> sales;
29         }   while (sales >= 0);
30
31         //display current region's total sales
32         cout << "****************Region " << region
33              << " sales: $" << totalRegionSales
34              << endl << endl;
35
36         //reset accumulator
37         totalRegionSales = 0;
38     }   //end for
```

```

    //system("pause");
    return 0;
} //end of main function
```

LAB 8-2 Plan and Create

No answer required.

LAB 8-3 Modify

```
//Lab8-3.cpp - displays a multiplication table
//Created/revised by <your name> on <current date>

#include <iostream>
using namespace std;

int main()
{
    //declare variables
    int multiplicand = 0;
    int product      = 0;

    cout << "Multiplicand (negative number to end): ";
    cin >> multiplicand;

    do   //begin loop
    {
        int multiplier = 1;
        do   //begin loop
        {
            product = multiplicand * multiplier;
            cout << multiplicand << " * "
                 << multiplier << " = "
                 << product << endl;
            multiplier += 1;
        }   while (multiplier < 10);

        cout << endl;
        cout << "Multiplicand (negative number to end): ";
        cin >> multiplicand;
    }   while (multiplicand >= 0);

    //system("pause");
    return 0;
} //end of main function
```

LAB 8-4 Desk-Check

Desk-check:

number	x
~~1~~	~~1~~
	~~2~~
	~~3~~
	~~4~~
	~~5~~
~~2~~	~~1~~
	~~2~~
	~~3~~
	~~4~~
	5
3	

The code will display the following:

1 2 3 4 5

2 3 4 5 6

LAB 8-5 Debug

To debug the program, cut the `//update the month counter` comment and `month += 1;` statement from the nested loop and paste them below the `cout << endl;` statement in the outer loop. Also, change the `totalSales += totalSales + sales;` statement to either `totalSales = totalSales + sales;` or `totalSales += sales;`.

Answers to Chapter 9 Mini-Quizzes

Mini-Quiz 9-1

1. b. `sqrt(16.0)`
2. c. `25 + rand() % (50 - 25 + 1)`
3. d. none of the above
4. a. `#include <ctime>`

Mini-Quiz 9-2

1. d. all of the above
2. a. `double getArea()`
3. `double getGrossPay (int hours, double rate)`
4. `return gross;`

Mini-Quiz 9-3

1. b. `area = getArea();`
2. c. `double getArea();`
3. `cout << getArea();`
4. `double getGrossPay(int hours, double rate);` or `double getGrossPay(int, double);`
5. `weekGross = getGrossPay(40, payRate);`

Mini-Quiz 9-4

1. b. False
2. b. False
3. a. True
4. When the variable appears in a statement in the program, the computer uses the location of the statement to determine which variable to use.

Answers to Chapter 9 Labs

LAB 9-1 Stop and Analyze

1. The `#include <ctime>` instruction on Line 5 is necessary because the program uses the `time` function.
2. The `srand(static_cast<int>(time(0)));` statement on Line 16 uses the `srand` and `time` functions to initialize the random number generator.
3. The number 4 will be assigned to the `randomNumber` variable.
4. No answer required.

5.

```
//Lab9-1.cpp - simulates a number guessing game
//Created/revised by <your name> on <current date>

#include <iostream>
#include <ctime>
//#include <cstdlib>
using namespace std;

int main()
{
     //declare variables
     int randomNumber     = 0;
     int numberGuess      = 0;
     int incorrectGuesses = 0;
     char moreGuesses     = 'Y';

     //generate a random number from 1 through 10
     srand(static_cast<int>(time(0)));
     randomNumber = 1 + rand() % (10 - 1 + 1);

     //get first number guess from user
     cout << "Guess a number from 1 through 10: ";
     cin >> numberGuess;

     while (moreGuesses == 'Y')
     {
          if (numberGuess != randomNumber)
          {
               incorrectGuesses += 1;
               if (incorrectGuesses < 4)
               {
                    cout << "Sorry, guess again: ";
                    cin >> numberGuess;
               }
               else
               {
                    cout << endl << "Sorry, the number is "
                    << randomNumber << "." << endl;
                    moreGuesses = 'N';
               }   //end if
          }
          else
          {
               moreGuesses = 'N';
               cout << endl << "Yes, the number is "
               << randomNumber << "." << endl;
          }  //end if

     }  //end while

     //system("pause");
     return 0;
}  //end of main function
```

6.

```
//Lab9-1.cpp - simulates a number guessing game
//Created/revised by <your name> on <current date>

#include <iostream>
#include <ctime>
//#include <cstdlib>
using namespace std;
```

```

//function prototype
int getRandomNumber();

int main()
{
    //declare variables
    int randomNumber     = 0;
    int numberGuess      = 0;
    int incorrectGuesses = 0;
    char moreGuesses     = 'Y';

    //generate a random number from 1 through 10
    srand(static_cast<int>(time(0)));
    randomNumber = getRandomNumber();

    //get first number guess from user
    cout << "Guess a number from 1 through 10: ";
    cin >> numberGuess;

    while (moreGuesses == 'Y')
    {
        if (numberGuess != randomNumber)
        {
            incorrectGuesses += 1;
            if (incorrectGuesses < 4)
            {
                cout << "Sorry, guess again: ";
                cin >> numberGuess;
            }
            else
            {
                cout << endl << "Sorry, the number is "
                << randomNumber << "." << endl;
                moreGuesses = 'N';
            }  //end if
        }
        else
        {
            moreGuesses = 'N';
            cout << endl << "Yes, the number is "
            << randomNumber << "." << endl;
        }     //end if

    }  //end while

    //system("pause");
    return 0;
}  //end of main function

//*****function definitions*****
int getRandomNumber()
{
    int randInteger = 0;
    //generate random integer from 1 through 10
    randInteger = 1 + rand() % (10 - 1 + 1);
    return randInteger;
}   //end of getRandomNumber function
```

7.

```
//Lab9-1.cpp - simulates a number guessing game
//Created/revised by <your name> on <current date>

#include <iostream>
#include <ctime>
//#include <cstdlib>
using namespace std;

//function prototype
int getRandomNumber(int lower, int upper);

int main()
{
    //declare variables
    int randomNumber     = 0;
    int numberGuess      = 0;
    int incorrectGuesses = 0;
    char moreGuesses     = 'Y';
    int smallest         = 0;
    int largest          = 0;

    cout << "Smallest integer: ";
    cin >> smallest;
    cout << "Largest integer: ";
    cin >> largest;
    cout << endl;

    //if necessary, swap the numbers
    if (smallest > largest)
    {
        int temp = largest;
        largest = smallest;
        smallest = temp;
    }   //end if

    //generate a random number from smallest through largest
    srand(static_cast<int>(time(0)));
    randomNumber = getRandomNumber(smallest, largest);

    //get first number guess from user
    cout << "Guess a number from " << smallest << " through "
    << largest << ": ";
    cin >> numberGuess;

    while (moreGuesses == 'Y')
    {
        if (numberGuess != randomNumber)
        {
            incorrectGuesses += 1;
            if (incorrectGuesses < 4)
            {
                cout << "Sorry, guess again: ";
                cin >> numberGuess;
            }
            else
            {
                cout << endl << "Sorry, the number is "
                << randomNumber << "." << endl;
                moreGuesses = 'N';
            }   //end if
        }
        else
```

```
            {
                 moreGuesses = 'N';
                 cout << endl << "Yes, the number is "
                 << randomNumber << "." << endl;
            }  //end if

        }  //end while

        //system("pause");
        return 0;
} //end of main function

//*****function definitions*****
int getRandomNumber(int lower, int upper)
{
    int randInteger = 0;
    //generate random integer from lower through upper
    randInteger = lower + rand() % (upper - lower + 1);
    return randInteger;
} //end of getRandomNumber function
```

LAB 9-2 Plan and Create

No answer required.

LAB 9-3 Modify

```
//Lab9-3.cpp - displays two monthly car payments
//Created/revised by <your name> on <current date>

#include <iostream>
#include <cmath>
#include <iomanip>
using namespace std;

//function prototype
double getPayment(int, double, int);

int main()
{
   //declare variables
   int carPrice            = 0;
   int rebate              = 0;
   double creditRate       = 0.0;
   double dealerRate       = 0.0;
   int term                = 0;
   double creditPayment = 0.0;
   double dealerPayment = 0.0;
   char again              = 'Y';

   do
   {
       //get input items
       cout << "Car price (after any trade-in): ";
       cin >> carPrice;
```

```
        cout << "Rebate: ";
        cin >> rebate;
        cout << "Credit union rate: ";
        cin >> creditRate;
        cout << "Dealer rate: ";
        cin >> dealerRate;
        cout << "Term in years: ";
        cin >> term;

        //convert rates to decimal format, if necessary
        if (creditRate >= 1.0)
            creditRate /= 100;
        //end if
        if (dealerRate >= 1.0)
            dealerRate /= 100;
        //end if

        //call function to calculate payments
        creditPayment = getPayment(carPrice - rebate,
            creditRate / 12, term * 12);
        dealerPayment = getPayment(carPrice,
            dealerRate / 12, term * 12);

        //display payments
        cout << fixed << setprecision(2) << endl;
        cout << "Credit union payment: $"
            << creditPayment << endl;
        cout << "Dealer payment: $"
            << dealerPayment << endl;

        if (creditPayment < dealerPayment)
            cout << "Take the rebate and finance
            through the credit union." << endl;
        else
            if (creditPayment > dealerPayment)
                cout << "Don't take the rebate.
                Finance through the dealer." << endl;
            else
                cout << "You can finance through either one."
                << endl;
            //end if
        //end if

        cout << endl << "Make another calculation? (Y/N): ";
        cin >> again;
        cout << endl;
    } while (toupper(again) == 'Y');

    //system("pause");
    return 0;
} //end of main function

//*****function definitions*****
double getPayment(int prin,
                  double monthRate,
                  int months)
{
    //calculates and returns a monthly payment
    double monthPay = 0.0;
    monthPay = prin * monthRate /
        (1 - pow(monthRate + 1, -months));
    return monthPay;
} //end of getPayment function
```

LAB 9-4 Desk-Check

Desk-check:

balance	amount	transaction	another
~~0.0~~	~~0.0~~	–	~~Y~~
~~2000.0~~	~~400.0~~	~~w~~	~~y~~
~~1600.0~~	~~1200.0~~	~~W~~	~~y~~
~~2800.0~~	~~45.0~~	~~D~~	~~y~~
~~2755.0~~	~~55.0~~	~~D~~	~~y~~
~~2700.0~~	~~150.0~~	~~W~~	~~y~~
~~2550.0~~	~~15.0~~	~~W~~	~~y~~
~~2565.0~~	1050.0	~~w~~	~~y~~
1515.0		~~W~~	n
		~~k~~	
		~~K~~	
		~~w~~	
		~~W~~	
		~~d~~	
		~~D~~	
		~~W~~	
		W	

bal	type	amt	curBalance
~~2000.0~~	~~W~~	~~400.0~~	~~0.0~~
			~~1600.0~~
~~1600.0~~	~~D~~	~~1200.0~~	~~0.0~~
			~~2800.0~~
~~2800.0~~	~~W~~	~~45.0~~	~~0.0~~
			~~2755.0~~
~~2755.0~~	~~W~~	~~55.0~~	~~0.0~~
			~~2700.0~~
~~2700.0~~	~~W~~	~~150.0~~	~~0.0~~
			~~2550.0~~
~~2550.0~~	~~D~~	~~15.0~~	~~0.0~~
			~~2565.0~~
~~2565.0~~	~~W~~	~~1050.0~~	~~0.0~~
			~~1515.0~~

The code will display a current balance of $1515.00.

LAB 9-5 Debug

To debug the program, change the statement that calls the `getDepreciation` function to `depreciation = getDepreciation(cost, salvage, lifeYears);`.

Answers to Chapter 10 Mini-Quizzes

Mini-Quiz 10-1

1. `void`
2. `displayTaxes(federalTax, localTax);`
3. `void displayTaxes(double fedTax, double stateTax)`
4. b. False

Mini-Quiz 10-2

1. a. `void getInput(double &hours, double &rate)`
2. b. `getInput(hoursWkd, payRate);`
3. `void getInput(double &hours, double &rate);` or `void getInput(double &, double &);`
4. a. True

Mini-Quiz 10-3

1. `void calcTaxes(double pay, double &fedTax, double &stateTax)`
2. `calcTaxes(gross, federal, state);`
3. `void calcTaxes(double pay, double &fedTax, double &stateTax);` or `void calcTaxes(double, double &, double &);`
4. b. False

Answers to Chapter 10 Labs

LAB 10-1 Stop and Analyze

1. The function prototype on Lines 11 through 13, and the function header on Lines 77 through 79.
2. The `americanDollars` and `conversionRate` variables are passed *by value* because the `convertDols` function needs to know their values but does not need to change their contents. The `convertedCurrency` variable is passed *by reference* because the `convertDols` function needs to store a value (the converted dollars) inside the variable.

3. The `displayMenu` function is a void function because it does not return a value after completing its task.
4. Line 35 contains the priming read. Line 61 contains the update read.
5. You would need to modify the function as shown here:

```
double convertDols(double dollars, double convertRate)
{
      double converted = 0.0;
      converted = dollars * convertRate;
      return converted;
}   //end of convertDols function
```

   You also need to change the function prototype on Lines 11 through 13 to `double convertDols(double dollars, double convertRate);`, and change the function call on Lines 52 through 54 to `convertedCurrency = convertDols(americanDollars, conversionRate);`.
6. No answer required.
7. 31.54
8. 794.80
9.

```
1 //Lab10-1.cpp - Converts American dollars to
2 //British pounds, Mexican pesos, or Japanese yen
3 //Created/revised by <your name> on <current date>
4
5 #include <iostream>
6 #include <iomanip>
7 using namespace std;
8
9 //function prototypes
10 void displayMenu();
11 void convertDols(double dollars,
12                  double convertRate,
13                  double &converted);
14 void assignRate(int choice, double &convertRate);
15
16 int main()
17 {
18      //declare variables
19      int menuChoice               = 0;
20      double americanDollars       = 0.0;
21      double conversionRate        = 0.0;
22      double convertedCurrency     = 0.0;
23
24      //display output in fixed-point notation
25      //with two decimal places
26      cout << fixed << setprecision(2);
27
28      //get menu choice
29      displayMenu();
30      cout << "Enter 1, 2, 3, or 4: ";
31      cin >> menuChoice;
32
33      while (menuChoice > 0 && menuChoice < 4)
34      {
35            //get dollars to convert
36            cout << "Number of American dollars: ";
37            cin >> americanDollars;
38
39            //assign rate
40            assignRate(menuChoice, conversionRate);
```

```

            convertDols(americanDollars,
                    conversionRate,
                    convertedCurrency);
            cout << "-->" << convertedCurrency
                 << endl << endl;

            //get menu choice
            displayMenu();
            cout << "Enter 1, 2, 3, or 4: ";
            cin >> menuChoice;
    }    //end while

    //system("pause");
    return 0;
} //end of main function

//*****function definitions*****
void displayMenu()
{
    cout << "1 British pounds" << endl;
    cout << "2 Mexican pesos" << endl;
    cout << "3 Japanese yen" << endl;
    cout << "4 Stop program" << endl;
} //end of displayMenu function

void convertDols(double dollars,
                 double convertRate,
                 double &converted)
{
    converted = dollars * convertRate;
} //end of convertDols function

void assignRate(int choice, double &convertRate)
{
    //declare constants
    const double BRITISH_RATE  = .63071;
    const double MEXICAN_RATE  = 14.0043;
    const double JAPANESE_RATE = 70.4800;

    if (choice == 1)
        convertRate = BRITISH_RATE;
    else if (choice == 2)
        convertRate = MEXICAN_RATE;
    else
        convertRate = JAPANESE_RATE;
    //end if
} //end of assignRate function
```

10.

```
//Lab10-1.cpp - Converts American dollars to
//British pounds, Mexican pesos, or Japanese yen
//Created/revised by <your name> on <current date>

#include <iostream>
#include <iomanip>
using namespace std;

//function prototypes
void displayMenu();
double convertDols(double dollars,
                   double convertRate);
void assignRate(int choice, double &convertRate);
```

```

int main()
{
	//declare variables
	int menuChoice            = 0;
	double americanDollars    = 0.0;
	double conversionRate     = 0.0;
	double convertedCurrency = 0.0;

	//display output in fixed-point notation
	//with two decimal places
	cout << fixed << setprecision(2);

	//get menu choice
	displayMenu();
	cout << "Enter 1, 2, 3, or 4: ";
	cin >> menuChoice;

	while (menuChoice > 0 && menuChoice < 4)
	{
		//get dollars to convert
		cout << "Number of American dollars: ";
		cin >> americanDollars;

		//assign rate
		assignRate(menuChoice, conversionRate);

		convertedCurrency =
		   convertDols(americanDollars, conversionRate);
		cout << "-->" << convertedCurrency
		     << endl << endl;

		//get menu choice
		displayMenu();
		cout << "Enter 1, 2, 3, or 4: ";
		cin >> menuChoice;
	  }  //end while

  //system("pause");
  return 0;
} //end of main function

//*****function definitions*****
void displayMenu()
{
	cout << "1 British pounds" << endl;
	cout << "2 Mexican pesos" << endl;
	cout << "3 Japanese yen" << endl;
	cout << "4 Stop program" << endl;
}  //end of displayMenu function

double convertDols(double dollars,
                   double convertRate)
{
	double converted = 0.0;
	converted = dollars * convertRate;
	return converted;
}  //end of convertDols function

void assignRate(int choice, double &convertRate)
{
	//declare constants
	const double BRITISH_RATE = .63071;
	const double MEXICAN_RATE = 14.0043;
```

```
    const double JAPANESE_RATE = 79.48;

    if (choice == 1)
        convertRate = BRITISH_RATE;
    else if (choice == 2)
        convertRate = MEXICAN_RATE;
    else
        convertRate = JAPANESE_RATE;
    //end if
} //end of assignRate function
```

LAB 10-2 Plan and Create

No answer required.

LAB 10-3 Modify

```
//Lab10-3.cpp - displays the number of units of
//electricity used and the total charge
//Created/revised by <your name> on <current date>

#include <iostream>
#include <iomanip>
using namespace std;

//function prototypes
void getInput(int &newReading, int &oldReading);
void getUnits(int curRead, int prevRead, int &numUnits);
double getTotal(int numUnits, double chgPerUnit, double &totChg);
void displayBill(int used, double charge);

int main()
{
    //declare constant and variables
    const double UNIT_CHG = .11;
    int current  = 0;
    int previous = 0;
    int units    = 0;
    double total = 0.0;

    cout << fixed << setprecision(2);

    //call functions
    getInput(current, previous);
    getUnits(current, previous, units);
    total = getTotal(units, UNIT_CHG, total);
    displayBill(units, total);

    //system("pause");
    return 0;
}   //end of main function

//*****function definitions*****
void getInput(int &newReading, int &oldReading)
```

```
{
    cout << "Current reading: ";
    cin >> newReading;
    cout << "Previous reading: ";
    cin >> oldReading;
} //end of getInput function

void getUnits(int curRead, int prevRead, int &numUnits)
{
    numUnits = curRead - prevRead;
} //end of getUnits function

double getTotal(int numUnits, double chgPerUnit, double &totChg)
{
    totChg = numUnits * chgPerUnit;
    return totChg;
} //end of getTotal function

void displayBill(int used, double charge)
{
    cout << "Units used: " << used << endl;
    cout << "Total charge: $" << charge << endl;
} //end of displayBill function
```

LAB 10-4 Desk-Check

test1 (main)	test2 (main)	~~avg (calcAvg)~~ average (main)	~~num1 (calcAvg)~~	~~num2 (calcAvg)~~
~~0.0~~	~~0.0~~	~~0.0~~	~~78.0~~	~~85.0~~
~~78.0~~	~~85.0~~	~~81.5~~	~~45.0~~	~~93.0~~
~~45.0~~	~~93.0~~	~~69.0~~	~~87.0~~	~~98.0~~
~~87.0~~	~~98.0~~	~~92.5~~	~~54.0~~	~~32.0~~
54.0	32.0	43.0		

LAB 10-5 Debug

To debug the program, change the function prototype to either `void assignGrade(int pointsEarned, char &letter);` or `void assignGrade(int, char &);` and change the function header to `void assignGrade(int pointsEarned, char &letter)`.

Answers to Chapter 11 Mini-Quizzes

Mini-Quiz 11-1

1. a. `int quantities[20] = {0};`
2. `quantities[0]`
3. `quantities[19]`
4. `quantities[3] = 7;`
5. c. `total = getTotal(quantities, 20);`

Mini-Quiz 11-2

1. c. `total += orders[2];`
2. c. `if (orders[3] > 25)`
3. `bonus = sales[0] * .15;`
4. c. `if (sub >= 0 && sub < 10)`
5. a. `while (x < 20)`

Mini-Quiz 11-3

1. `if (prices[x] < lowest)`
2. sorting
3.
```
for (int x = 0; x < 10; x += 1)
     orders[x] -= 3;
//end for
```

Answers to Chapter 11 Labs

LAB 11-1 Stop and Analyze

1. The `domestic` and `international` arrays are parallel arrays because the elements in one array are related by their subscripts to the elements in the other array. For example, the first element in both arrays contains the sales made in January, the second element contains the February sales, and so on.

2. The `domestic[1]` element contains 45000.
3. The total company sales made in February can be calculated by adding the contents of the `domestic[1]` element to the contents of the `international[1]` element.
4. The highest subscript in the `international` array is 5.
5. The assignment statement would need to be changed to `totalSales += domestic[x - 1] + international[x - 1];`.
6. No answer required.
7.

```
//Lab11-1.cpp - calculates the total domestic sales,
//total international sales, and total sales
//Created/revised by <your name> on <current date>

#include <iostream>
using namespace std;

int main()
{
    //declare arrays and variable
    int domestic[6] = {12000, 45000, 32000,
                       67000, 24000, 55000};
    int international[6] = {10000, 56000, 42000,
                            23000, 12000, 34000};
    int totalSales          = 0;  //accumulator
    int totalDomestic       = 0;  //accumulator
    int totalInternational  = 0;  //accumulator

    //accumulate sales
    for (int x = 0; x < 6; x += 1)
    {
        totalDomestic += domestic[x];
        totalInternational += international[x];
        totalSales += domestic[x] + international[x];
    } //end for

    //display total domestic sales, total
    //international sales, and total sales
    cout << "Total domestic sales: $"
         << totalDomestic << endl;
    cout << "Total international sales: $"
         << totalInternational << endl;
    cout << "Total sales: $" << totalSales << endl;

    //system("pause");
    return 0;
} //end of main function
```

8.

```
//Lab11-1.cpp - calculates the total domestic sales,
//total international sales, total sales, and
//total sales made in each month
//Created/revised by <your name> on <current date>

#include <iostream>
using namespace std;

```

```
int main()
{
    //declare arrays and variable
    int domestic[6] = {12000, 45000, 32000,
                      67000, 24000, 55000};
    int international[6] = {10000, 56000, 42000,
                           23000, 12000, 34000};
    int totalSales         = 0;  //accumulator
    int totalDomestic      = 0;  //accumulator
    int totalInternational = 0;  //accumulator
    int monthSales[6]      = {0};

    //accumulate sales
    for (int x = 0; x < 6; x += 1)
    {
        totalDomestic += domestic[x];
        totalInternational += international[x];
        totalSales += domestic[x] + international[x];
        monthSales[x] = domestic[x] + international[x];
    } //end for

    //display total domestic sales, total
    //international sales, and total sales
    cout << "Total domestic sales: $"
         << totalDomestic << endl;
    cout << "Total international sales: $"
         << totalInternational << endl;
    cout << "Total sales: $" << totalSales
         << endl << endl;

    //display total sales made in each month
    for (int x = 0; x < 6; x += 1)
        cout << "Month " << x + 1 << " sales: $"
             << monthSales[x] << endl;
    //end for

    //system("pause");
    return 0;
} //end of main function
```

LAB 11-2 Plan and Create

No answer required.

LAB 11-3 Modify

```
//Lab11-3.cpp
//Stores monthly rainfall amounts in an array
//Displays the monthly rainfall amounts or the
//total annual rainfall amount
//Created/revised by <your name> on <current date>

#include <iostream>
using namespace std;

```

```
//function prototypes
void displayMonthly(double rain[], int numElements);
double getTotal(double rainAmt[], int elements);

int main()
{
   //declare array and variable
   double rainfall[12] = {0.0};
   int choice = 0;
   double totalRainfall = 0.0;

   //get rainfall amounts
   for (int x = 0; x < 12; x += 1)
   {
       cout << "Enter rainfall for month "
            << x + 1 << ": ";
       cin >> rainfall[x];
   } //end for

   do
   {
       //display menu and get menu choice
       cout << endl;
       cout << "1  Display monthly amounts" << endl;
       cout << "2  Display total amount" << endl;
       cout << "3  End program" << endl;
       cout << "Enter your choice: ";
       cin >> choice;

       if (choice != 1 && choice != 2 && choice != 3)
           cout << "Invalid choice" << endl << endl;
       else
       {
           //call appropriate function or end program
           if (choice == 1)
               displayMonthly(rainfall, 12);
           else
               if (choice == 2)
               {
                   totalRainfall = getTotal(rainfall, 12);
                   cout << "Total rainfall: " <<
                   totalRainfall << endl;
               }   //end if
           //end if
       } //end if
   } while (choice != 3);

   //system("pause");
   return 0;
} //end of main function

//*****function definitions*****
void displayMonthly(double rain[], int numElements)
{
   cout << "Monthly rainfall amounts:" << endl;
   for (int x = 0; x < numElements; x += 1)
       cout << rain[x] << endl;
   //end for
} //end of displayMonthly function

double getTotal(double rainAmt[], int elements)
```

```
{
    double total = 0.0;
    for (int x = 0; x < elements; x += 1)
        total = total + rainAmt[x];
    //end for
    return total;
} //end of getTotal function
```

LAB 11-4 Desk-Check

Desk-check:

midterms[0]	midterms[1]	midterms[2]	midterms[3]	midterms[4]
~~0.0~~	~~0.0~~	~~0.0~~	~~0.0~~	~~0.0~~
90.0	88.0	77.0	85.0	45.0

finals[0]	finals[1]	finals[2]	finals[3]	finals[4]
~~0.0~~	~~0.0~~	~~0.0~~	~~0.0~~	~~0.0~~
100.0	68.0	75.0	85.0	32.0

averages[0]	averages[1]	averages[2]	averages[3]	averages[4]
~~0.0~~	~~0.0~~	~~0.0~~	~~0.0~~	~~0.0~~
95.0	78.0	76.0	85.0	38.5

x
~~0~~
~~1~~
~~2~~
~~3~~
~~4~~
5

The `for` loop will display the following:
Student 1 average: 95
Student 2 average: 78
Student 3 average: 76
Student 4 average: 85
Student 5 average: 38.5

LAB 11-5 Debug

To debug the program, change the `increase += quantities[x];` statement in the `for` loop to `quantities[x] += increase;`.

Answers to Chapter 12 Mini-Quizzes

Mini-Quiz 12-1

1. b. `int quantities[4][2] = {0};`
2. 20
3. `quantities[0][0]`
4. `quantities[3][1]`
5. `quantities[0][1] = 5;`

Mini-Quiz 12-2

1. d. `total += purchases[1][0];`
2. c. `if (scores[2][3] > 25)`
3. `bonus = sales[0][1] * .15;`
4. a. `if (row >= 0 && row < 10)`

Answers to Chapter 12 Labs

LAB 12-1 Stop and Analyze

1. 34000
2. The total company sales made in February can be calculated by adding the contents of the `company[0][1]` element to the contents of the `company[1][1]` element.
3. The highest row subscript in the `company` array is 1. The highest column subscript is 5.
4. The January international sales are stored in the `company[1][0]` element.
5. The assignment statement would need to be changed to `companySales += company[location][month - 1];`.
6. No answer required.
7.

```
//Lab12-1.cpp - calculates the total domestic sales,
//total international sales, and total company sales
//Created/revised by <your name> on <current date>

#include <iostream>
using namespace std;

```

```
int main()
{
   //declare arrays and variable
   int company[2][6] = {{12000, 45000, 32000,
                         67000, 24000, 55000},
                        {10000, 56000, 42000,
                         23000, 12000, 34000}};
   int companySales       = 0;
   int domesticSales      = 0;    //accumulator
   int internationalSales = 0;    //accumulator

   //accumulate sales
   for (int month = 0; month < 6; month += 1)
   {
       domesticSales += company[0][month];
       internationalSales += company[1][month];
   } //end for
   companySales = domesticSales + internationalSales;

   //display total sales
   cout << "Domestic sales: $" << domesticSales << endl;
   cout << "International sales: $" << internationalSales << endl;
   cout << "Company sales: $" << companySales << endl;

   //system("pause");
   return 0;
} //end of main function
```

8.

```
//Lab12-1.cpp - calculates the total domestic sales,
//total international sales, and total company sales
//also calculates the total sales made in each month
//Created/revised by <your name> on <current date>

#include <iostream>
using namespace std;

int main()
{
   //declare arrays and variable
   int company[2][6] = {{12000, 45000, 32000,
                         67000, 24000, 55000},
                        {10000, 56000, 42000,
                         23000, 12000, 34000}};

   int monthSales[6]      = {0};
   int companySales       = 0;
   int domesticSales      = 0;
   int internationalSales = 0;

   //accumulate sales
   for (int month = 0; month < 6; month += 1)
   {
       domesticSales += company[0][month];
       internationalSales += company[1][month];
       monthSales[month] = company[0][month] + company[1][month];
   } //end for
   companySales = domesticSales + internationalSales;

   //display total sales
   cout << "Domestic sales: $" << domesticSales << endl;
   cout << "International sales: $" << internationalSales << endl;
   cout << "Company sales: $" << companySales << endl << endl;
```

```
    //display monthly sales
    for (int x = 0; x < 6; x += 1)
        cout << "Month " << x + 1 << " sales: $"
             << monthSales[x] << endl;
    //end for

    //system("pause");
    return 0;
}   //end of main function
```

9.

```
//Lab12-1.cpp - calculates the total domestic sales,
//total international sales, and total company sales
//also calculates the total sales made in each month
//Created/revised by <your name> on <current date>

#include <iostream>
using namespace std;

int main()
{
    //declare arrays and variable
    int company[2][6] = {{12000, 45000, 32000,
                          67000, 24000, 55000},
                         {10000, 56000, 42000,
                          23000, 12000, 34000}};

    int monthSales[6]      = {0};
    int companySales       = 0;
    int domesticSales      = 0;
    int internationalSales = 0;
    int month              = 0;

    //accumulate sales
    while (month < 6)
    {
        domesticSales += company[0][month];
        internationalSales += company[1][month];
        monthSales[month] = company[0][month] + company[1][month];
        month += 1;
    }  //end while
    companySales = domesticSales + internationalSales;

    //display total sales
    cout << "Domestic sales: $" << domesticSales << endl;
    cout << "International sales: $" << internationalSales << endl;
    cout << "Company sales: $" << companySales << endl << endl;

    //display monthly sales
    for (int x = 0; x < 6; x += 1)
        cout << "Month " << x + 1 << " sales: $"
             << monthSales[x] << endl;
    //end for

    //system("pause");
    return 0;
}   //end of main function
```

LAB 12-2 Plan and Create

No answer required.

LAB 12-3 Modify

```
//Lab12-3.cpp - displays the shipping charge
//Created/revised by <your name> on <current date>

#include <iostream>
using namespace std;

int main()
{
    //declare array and variables
    int shipCharges[3][2] = {{101, 0},
                             {51, 10},
                             {1, 20}};
    int numOrdered = 0;
    int rowSub     = 0;
    char found     = 'N';

    //enter the number ordered
    cout << "Number ordered ";
    cout << "(negative number or 0 to end): ";
    cin >> numOrdered;

    while (numOrdered > 0 && numOrdered <= 999999)
    {
        //search array
        rowSub = 0;
        while (rowSub < 3 && found == 'N')
            if (numOrdered >= shipCharges[rowSub][0])
                found = 'Y';
            else
                rowSub += 1;
            //end if
        //end while

        //display shipping charge
        cout << "Shipping charge for a quantity of "
             << numOrdered << " is $"
             << shipCharges[rowSub][1] << endl << endl;

        //enter the number ordered
        cout << "Number ordered ";
        cout << "(negative number or 0 to end): ";
        cin >> numOrdered;
        found = 'N';
    } //end while

    //system("pause");
    return 0;
} //end of main function
```

LAB 12-4 Desk-Check

sales[0][0]	sales[0][1]
1200.33	2350.75

sales[1][0]	sales[1][1]
3677.8	2456.05

sales[2][0]	sales[2][1]
750.67	1345.99

total	store	book
~~0.0~~	~~0~~	~~0~~
~~1200.33~~	~~1~~	~~1~~
~~3551.08~~	~~2~~	~~2~~
~~7228.88~~	3	~~0~~
~~9684.93~~		~~1~~
~~10435.6~~		~~2~~
11781.59		~~0~~
		~~1~~
		2

LAB 12-5 Debug

To debug the program, change the `numbers[row][0] = counter * counter;` statement in the first `for` loop to `numbers[row][1] = counter * counter;`, and then enter the `counter += 1;` (or `counter = counter + 1;`) statement below the `numbers[row][1] = counter * counter;` statement.

Answers to Chapter 13 Mini-Quizzes

Mini-Quiz 13-1

1. c. `const string FIRST_PRES = "George Washington";`
2. b. `string country = "";`
3. a. `getline(cin, streetAddress, '\n');`
4. c. `cin.ignore(10, '\n');`

Mini-Quiz 13-2

1. a. `while (employee.length() > 20)`
2. `if(code.length() == 7)`
3. d. both a and b
4. `cout << college.substr(college.length() - 1);`

Mini-Quiz 13-3

1. a. `location = cityState.find(",", 0);`
2. 13
3. d. all of the above

Mini-Quiz 13-4

1. d. none of the above
2. a. `sentence = sentence + temp.assign(4, '!');`
3. b. `areaCode = "(" + areaCode + ")";`

Answers to Chapter 13 Labs

LAB 13-1 Stop and Analyze

1. The purpose of the loop in Lines 25 through 39 is to access each character in the `phone` variable, one character at a time, in order to remove any parentheses, hyphens, or space characters.
2. The statement in Line 27 assigns the current character from the `phone` variable to the `currentChar` variable.
3. The selection structure in Lines 28 through 38 compares the current character in the `phone` variable with the opening and closing parentheses, the hyphen, and a space character. If the current character is one of those characters, the statement in Line 33 removes the current character from the `phone` variable. The statement in Line 34 then subtracts the number 1 from the `numChars` variable, which keeps track of the number of characters in the `phone` variable. If the current character is not one of those characters, the statement in Line 37 adds 1 to the contents of the `subscript` variable, which allows the loop to access the next character in the `phone` variable.

4. Before the loop in the program is processed, the statement in Line 22 assigns the number of characters stored in the `phone` variable to the `numChars` variable. If the `phone` variable contains the eight characters 111-2222, the statement assigns the number 8 to the `numChars` variable. When the statement in Line 33 removes a character from the `phone` variable, the variable contains one fewer character. For example, if the statement in Line 33 removes the hyphen from the 111-2222 stored in the `phone` variable, the variable contains seven characters rather than eight characters. If the statement in Line 34 did not subtract the number 1 from the `numChars` variable, the loop would attempt to access the eighth character in the `phone` variable, even though the variable now contains only seven characters.
5. Assume that the `phone` variable contains (500)333-4444. The statement in Line 27 assigns the opening parentheses, whose subscript is 0, to the `currentChar` variable. When the statement in Line 33 removes the opening parentheses from the `phone` variable, the number 5 becomes the first character in the variable and, therefore, it has a subscript of 0. In other words, when you remove a character from a variable, the next character in the variable assumes the same subscript. However, when a character is not removed from the variable, you need to update the subscript to access the next character in the variable. The statement in Line 37 performs the update task.
6. No answer required.
7. Change the `phone.erase(subscript, 1);` statement in Line 33 to `phone.replace(subscript, 1, "");`.

LAB 13-2 Plan and Create

No answer required.

LAB 13-3 Modify

```
//Lab13-3.cpp - simulates the Hangman game
//Created/revised by <your name> on <current date>

#include <iostream>
#include <string>
using namespace std;

int main()
{
    //declare variables
    string origWord    = "";
    string letter      = "";
    char dashReplaced  = 'N';
    char gameOver      = 'N';
    int numIncorrect   = 0;
    string displayWord = "";
    int numChars       = 0;

    //get original word
```

```
    cout << "Enter a word in uppercase: ";
    getline(cin, origWord);
    numChars = origWord.length();
    displayWord.assign(numChars, '-');

    //clear the screen
    system("cls");

    //start guessing
    cout << "Guess this word: " <<
    displayWord << endl;
    while (gameOver == 'N')
    {
        cout << "Enter an uppercase letter: ";
        cin >> letter;

        //search for the letter in the original word
        for (int x = 0; x < numChars; x += 1)
        {
            //if the current character matches
            //the letter, replace the corresponding
            //dash in the displayWord variable and then
            //set the dashReplaced variable to 'Y'
            if (origWord.substr(x, 1) == letter)
            {
                displayWord.replace(x, 1, letter);
                dashReplaced = 'Y';
            } //end if
        } //end for

        //if a dash was replaced, check whether the
        //displayWord variable contains another dash
        if (dashReplaced == 'Y')
        {
            //if the displayWord variable does not
            //contain any dashes, the game is over
            if (displayWord.find("-", 0) == -1)
            {
                gameOver = 'Y';
                cout << endl << "Yes, the word is "
                    << origWord << endl;
                cout << "Great guessing!" << endl;
            }
            else //otherwise, continue guessing
            {
                cout << endl << "Guess this word: "
                    << displayWord << endl;
                dashReplaced = 'N';
            } //end if
        }
        else //processed when dashReplaced contains 'N'
        {
            //add 1 to the number of incorrect guesses
            numIncorrect += 1;
            //if the number of incorrect guesses is 10,
            //the game is over
            if (numIncorrect == 10)
            {
                gameOver = 'Y';
                cout << endl << "Sorry, the word is "
                    << origWord << endl;
            } //end if
        } //end if
    } //end while
```

```
    //system("pause");
    return 0;
} //end of main function
```

LAB 13-4 Desk-Check

Desk-check:

message	subMessage1	subMessage2
~~praogxwrazingmun~~	————	————
~~praograzingmun~~	~~praograzing~~	~~!!!!!~~
~~praograzingismun~~	~~praogramming~~	~~isfun!!!!!~~
~~praograzingisfun~~	~~prgramming~~	~~isfun!!!!!~~
Programming is fun!!!!!	~~Prgramming~~	is fun!!!!!
	Programming	

The code will display the following: Message: Programming is fun!!!!!

LAB 13-5 Debug

To debug the program, change the `cout << message.substr(x) << endl;` statement in the `for` loop to `cout << message.substr(x, 1) << endl;`.

Answers to Chapter 14 Mini-Quizzes

Mini-Quiz 14-1

1. b. `#include <fstream>`
2. d. `ios::in`
3. `ofstream outAlbums;`
4. c. `outAlbums.open("mine.txt", ios::app);`

Mini-Quiz 14-2

1. the Boolean value `false`
2. c. `outInv << quantity << endl;`
3. d. `outFile << score1 << '#' << score2 << endl;`
4. d. `inInv >> number;`

Mini-Quiz 14-3

1. c. `while (!inInv.eof())`
2. the Boolean value `false`
3. `outInv.close();`

Answers to Chapter 14 Labs

LAB 14-1 Stop and Analyze

1. The instruction on Line 5 is necessary because the program uses the `cin` and `cout` objects. The instruction on Line 6 is necessary because the program uses the `string` class. The instruction on Line 7 is necessary because the program uses the `ofstream` class.
2. Each record contains two fields: the movie title and the year the movie was released.
3. The movies.txt file will contain only the two records written during the second run of the program. This is because the program opens the movies.txt file for output, which means the file's contents will be erased each time the program is run.
4. To save the previous records, you need to open the file for append. You do this by changing the *mode* in the `open` function in Line 18 to `ios::app`.
5. `if (outFile.is_open() == true)`
6. The purpose of the # character is to separate the movie title field from the year released field in each record.
7. The statement in Line 42 closes the output file. Neglecting to close a file can result in a loss of data.
8. No answer required.
9. No answer required.
10. No answer required.

11. Change the `outFile.open("movies.txt", ios::out);` statement in Line 18 to `outFile.open("movies.txt", ios::app);`.

12. No answer required.

LAB 14-2 Plan and Create

No answer required.

LAB 14-3 Modify

```
//Lab14-3.cpp - saves records to a sequential access
//file, displays the records, calculates and displays
//the total of the sales amounts stored in the file,
//and displays the average sales amount
//Created/revised by <your name> on <current date>

#include <iostream>
#include <string>
#include <fstream>
using namespace std;

//function prototypes
int getChoice();
void addRecords();
void displayRecords();
void displayTotal();
void displayAvg();

int main()
{
    int choice = 0;
    do
    {
        //get user's menu choice
        choice = getChoice();
        if (choice == 1)
            addRecords();
        else if (choice == 2)
            displayRecords();
        else if (choice == 3)
            displayTotal();
        else if (choice == 4)
            displayAvg();
        //end if
    } while (choice != 5);

    //system("pause");
    return 0;
} //end of main function

//*****function definitions*****
int getChoice()
```

```
{
   //displays menu and returns choice
   int menuChoice = 0;
   cout << endl << "Menu Options" << endl;
   cout << "1  Add Records" << endl;
   cout << "2  Display Records" << endl;
   cout << "3  Display Total Sales" << endl;
   cout << "4  Display Average Sales" << endl;
   cout << "5  Exit" << endl;
   cout << "Choice (1, 2, 3, 4, or 5)? ";
   cin >> menuChoice;
   cin.ignore(100, '\n');
   cout << endl;
   return menuChoice;
}  //end of getChoice function

void addRecords()
{
   //saves records to a sequential access file
   string name = "";
   int sales   = 0;
   ofstream outFile;

   //open file for append
   outFile.open("sales.txt", ios::app);

   //if the open was successful, get the
   //salesperson's name and sales amount and
   //then write the information to the file;
   //otherwise, display an error message
   if (outFile.is_open())
   {
       cout << "Salesperson's name (X to stop): ";
       getline(cin, name);

       while (name != "X" && name != "x")
       {
           cout << "Sales: ";
           cin >> sales;
           cin.ignore(100, '\n');

           outFile << name << '#' << sales << endl;

           cout << "Salesperson's name "
               << "(X to stop): ";
           getline(cin, name);
       }  //end while

       outFile.close();
   }
   else
       cout << "sales.txt file could not be opened"
           << endl;
   //end if
}  //end of addRecords function

void displayRecords()
{
   //displays the contents of the sales.txt file

   string name = "";
```

```
    int sales    = 0;
    ifstream inFile;

    //open file for input
    inFile.open("sales.txt");

    //if the open was successful, read a
    //record and then display the record
    //otherwise, display an error message
    if (inFile.is_open())
    {
        getline(inFile, name, '#');
        inFile >> sales;
        inFile.ignore();

        while (!inFile.eof())
        {
            cout << name << "      $" << sales << endl;
            getline(inFile, name, '#');
            inFile >> sales;
            inFile.ignore();
        }   //end while
        inFile.close();
    }
    else
        cout << "sales.txt file could not be opened." << endl;
    //end if
}   //end of displayRecords function

void displayTotal()
{
    //calculates and displays the total sales
    string name = "";
    int sales    = 0;
    int total    = 0;
    ifstream inFile;

    //open file for input
    inFile.open("sales.txt");

    //if the open was successful, read the
    //salesperson's name and sales amount, then add
    //the sales amount to the accumulator, and then
    //display the accumulator; otherwise, display
    //an error message
    if (inFile.is_open())
    {
        getline(inFile, name, '#');
        inFile >> sales;
        inFile.ignore();

        while (!inFile.eof())
        {
            total += sales;
            getline(inFile, name, '#');
            inFile >> sales;
            inFile.ignore();
        }   //end while
```

```
        inFile.close();
        cout << "Total sales $" << total
            << endl << endl;
    }
    else
        cout << "sales.txt file could not be opened"
            << endl;
    //end if
} //end of displayTotal function

void displayAvg()
{
    //calculates and displays the average sales

    string name      = "";
    int sales        = 0;
    int totalSales   = 0;
    int numSales     = 0;
    double avgSales = 0.0;

    ifstream inFile;

    //open file for input
    inFile.open("sales.txt");

    //if the open was successful, read the
    //salesperson's name and sales amount, then add
    //the sales amount to the accumulator and add 1
    //to the counter; otherwise, display an error message
    if (inFile.is_open())
    {
        getline(inFile, name, '#');
        inFile >> sales;
        inFile.ignore();

        while (!inFile.eof())
        {
            totalSales += sales;
            numSales += 1;
            getline(inFile, name, '#');
            inFile >> sales;
            inFile.ignore();
        } //end while
        inFile.close();

        //calculate and display the average sales
        avgSales =
            static_cast<double>(totalSales) / numSales;
        cout << "Average sales $" << avgSales
            << endl << endl;
    }
    else
        cout << "sales.txt file could not be opened." << endl;
    //end if
} //end of displayAvg function
```

LAB 14-4 Desk-Check

Desk-check:

store1Sales	store2Sales	store1Total	store2Total
~~0~~	~~0~~	~~0~~	~~0~~
~~7500~~	~~6000~~	~~7500~~	~~6000~~
~~4750~~	~~3675~~	~~12250~~	~~9675~~
~~8000~~	~~9500~~	~~20250~~	~~19175~~
4200	5400	24450	24575

The code will display the following:

Store 1's total sales: $24450
Store 2's total sales: $24575

LAB 14-5 Debug

To debug the program, add the `cin.ignore(100, '\n');` statement below the `cin >> num2;` statement.

Answers to Chapter 15 Mini-Quizzes

Mini-Quiz 15-1

1. object-oriented programming
2. b. False
3. b. an instance of the class
4. b. behaviors

Mini-Quiz 15-2

1. b. False
2. declaration, implementation
3. d. variable declarations
4. a. True

5. Check payCheck;
6. a. paycheck.getCheck()

Mini-Quiz 15-3

1. scope resolution operator
2. Item();
3.
```
Item::Item()
{
      code = ' ';
      price = 0;
} //end of default constructor
```

Mini-Quiz 15-4

1. signature
2. Item(int);
3. overloaded

Answers to Chapter 15 Labs

LAB 15-1 Stop and Analyze

1. The names of the private data members are id and price.
2. The name of the default constructor is Item. The constructor's purpose is to initialize the private variables in the class.
3. The setData method's purpose is to assign the program values to the private variables in the class.
4. The getIncreasedPrice method's purpose is to calculate and return the new price of the item, given the item's current price and the increase rate.
5. The code on Line 36 determines whether the value stored in the rate variable is greater than 1.0, which indicates that the rate was entered as an integer rather than as a decimal number. (For example, the user entered 15 rather than .15 as the rate.) The code on Line 37 converts the integer to its decimal equivalent by dividing the integer by 100.

6. The `computer.setData(computerId, computerPrice);` statement is missing from Line 69.

7. The `<< computer.getIncreasedPrice(incRate)` code is missing from Line 74.

LAB 15-2 Plan and Create

No answer required.

LAB 15-3 Modify

The modifications are shaded in the code.

```
//Lab15-3 Rectangle.h
//Created/revised by <your name> on <current date>

//declaration section
class Rectangle
{
public:
    Rectangle();
    void setDimensions(double, double);
    void setDimensions(int, int);
    double calcArea();
    double calcPerimeter();
private:
    double length;
    double width;
};

//implementation section
Rectangle::Rectangle()
{
    length = 0.0;
    width  = 0.0;
} //end of default constructor

void Rectangle::setDimensions(double len, double wid)
{
    //assigns length and width to private data members
    if (len > 0.0 && wid > 0.0)
    {
        length = len;
        width  = wid;
    } //end if
} //end of setDimensions method

void Rectangle::setDimensions(int len, int wid)
{
    //assigns length and width to private data members
    if (len > 0 && wid > 0)
    {
        length = static_cast<double>(len);
        width  = static_cast<double>(wid);
```

```
    } //end if
} //end of setDimensions method

double Rectangle::calcArea()
{
   return length * width;
} //end of calcArea method

double Rectangle::calcPerimeter()
{
   return (length + width) * 2;
} //end of calcPerimeter method
```

```
//Lab15-3.cpp
//Calculates and displays the cost of laying sod
//Created/revised by <your name> on <current date>

#include <iostream>
#include <iomanip>
#include "Lab15-3 Rectangle.h"
using namespace std;

int main()
{
   //instantiate Rectangle object
   Rectangle lawn;

   //declare variables
   int lawnLength    = 0;
   int lawnWidth     = 0;
   double priceSqYd  = 0.0;
   double lawnArea   = 0.0;
   double totalPrice = 0.0;

   //get length, width, and sod price
   cout << "Length (in feet): ";
   cin >> lawnLength;
   cout << "Width (in feet): ";
   cin >> lawnWidth;
   cout << "Sod price (per square yard): ";
   cin >> priceSqYd;

   //assign input to Rectangle object
   lawn.setDimensions(lawnLength, lawnWidth);

   //calculate area and total price
   lawnArea = lawn.calcArea() / 9;
   totalPrice = lawnArea * priceSqYd;

   //display area and total price
   cout << fixed << setprecision(2) << endl;
   cout << "Square yards: " << lawnArea << endl;
   cout << "Total price: $" << totalPrice << endl;

   //system("pause");
   return 0;
} //end of main function
```

LAB 15-4 Desk-Check

Desk-check:

BONUS_RATE	name	dollars	bonus
.05	———	~~0.0~~	~~0.0~~
	~~Thomas Johans~~	2500.75	125.04
	X		

dollarAmt.sales
~~0.0~~
2500.75

The code will display the following: Thomas Johans bonus: $125.04

LAB 15-5 Debug

To debug the program, enter the `#include "Lab15-5 Inventory.h"` directive in the Lab15-5.cpp file. Also change the `if` clause in the `setItem` method in the Lab15-5 Inventory.h file to `if (num > 0)`.

APPENDIX B

C++ Keywords

abstract	dynamic_cast	mutable	struct
and	else	namespace	switch
and_eq	enum	new	template
array	event	not	this
asm	explicit	not_eq	throw
auto	export	nullptr	true
bitand	extern	operator	try
bitor	false	or	typedef
bool	finally	or_eq	typeid
break	float	private	typename
case	for	property	union
catch	friend	protected	unsigned
char	gcnew	public	using
class	generic	register	virtual
compl	goto	reinterpret_cast	void
const	if	return	volatile
const_cast	initonly	safe_cast	wchar_t
continue	inline	sealed	while
default	int	short	xor
delegate	interface	signed	xor_eq
delete	interior_ptr	sizeof	
do	literal	static	
double	long	static_cast	

APPENDIX C

ASCII Codes

Character	ASCII	Binary
SPACE	32	00100000
!	33	00100001
“	34	00100010
#	35	00100011
$	36	00100100
%	37	00100101
&	38	00100110
'	39	00100111
(	40	00101000
)	41	00101001
*	42	00101010
+	43	00101011
‘	44	00101100
–	45	00101101
.	46	00101110
/	47	00101111
0	48	00110000
1	49	00110001
2	50	00110010
3	51	00110011
4	52	00110100
5	53	00110101
6	54	00110110
7	55	00110111
8	56	00111000
9	57	00111001
:	58	00111010
;	59	00111011
<	60	00111100
=	61	00111101
>	62	00111110
?	63	00111111
@	64	01000000
A	65	01000001
B	66	01000010
C	67	01000011
D	68	01000100
E	69	01000101
F	70	01000110
G	71	01000111
H	72	01001000
I	73	01001001
J	74	01001010
K	75	01001011
L	76	01001100
M	77	01001101
N	78	01001110
O	79	01001111
P	80	01010000
Q	81	01010001
R	82	01010010
S	83	01010011
T	84	01010100
U	85	01010101
V	86	01010110
W	87	01010111
X	88	01011000
Y	89	01011001
Z	90	01011010
[	91	01011011
\	92	01011100
]	93	01011101
^	94	01011110
_	95	01011111
`	96	01100000
a	97	01100001
b	98	01100010
c	99	01100011
d	100	01100100
e	101	01100101
f	102	01100110
g	103	01100111
h	104	01101000
i	105	01101001
j	106	01101010
k	107	01101011
l	108	01101100
m	109	01101101

(continues)

(continued)

Character	ASCII	Binary	Character	ASCII	Binary	Character	ASCII	Binary
n	110	01101110	t	116	01110100	z	122	0111101
o	111	01101111	u	117	01110101	{	123	0111101
p	112	01110000	v	118	01110110	|	124	0111110
q	113	01110001	w	119	01110111	}	125	0111110
r	114	01110010	x	120	01111000	~	126	0111111
s	115	01110011	y	121	01111001	DELETE	127	0111111

APPENDIX D

Common Syntax Errors

1. A statement that does not end with a semicolon
2. A missing #include directive (such as #include <iostream>, #include <string>, #include <fstream>, #include <cmath>, #include <ctime>, #include <iomanip>, or #include <cstdlib>)
3. No using namespace std; statement
4. Unmatched braces in a function, selection structure, or loop (for example, an opening brace that does not have a corresponding closing brace or vice versa)
5. A statement block (function, multi-statement selection structure, multi-statement loop) not enclosed in a set of braces
6. Braces facing the wrong way (for example, using } as the opening brace or { as the closing brace)
7. A reserved word used as the name of a variable or named constant
8. cin used with the insertion operator (<<) rather than with the extraction operator (>>)
9. cout used with the extraction operator (>>) rather than with the insertion operator (<<)
10. The extraction operator entered as > rather than as >>
11. The insertion operator entered as < rather than as <<
12. A variable, named constant, class, object, keyword, function, or method whose name is either misspelled or entered in the wrong case
13. A space entered between two characters in an arithmetic assignment operator (for example, using + = rather than +=)
14. An arithmetic assignment operator whose characters are reversed (for example, using =* rather than *=)
15. A space entered between two characters in a comparison operator (for example, using > = rather than >=)
16. A comparison operator whose characters are reversed (for example, using => rather than >=)
17. A comparison made using one equal sign (=) rather than two equal signs (==)
18. In an if statement, an else clause that does not have a matching if clause
19. A do while statement that does not end with a semicolon

20. A `string` enclosed in single quotation marks rather than in double quotation marks (for example, using `'Mary'` rather than `"Mary"`)
21. A `char` character enclosed in double quotation marks rather than in single quotation marks (for example, using `"A"` rather than `'A'`)
22. A `char` memory location initialized using two single quotation marks (`''`) rather than two single quotation marks separated by a space character (`' '`)
23. An array declared using parentheses rather than square brackets
24. Accessing an element that is beyond the memory allocated to an array
25. A `for` clause that contains commas rather than semicolons, or one that does not contain two semicolons
26. In a `switch` statement, a missing colon (`:`) in a `case` clause
27. In a `switch` statement, using semicolons in a `case` clause
28. A missing `break;` statement in a `switch` statement
29. A value-returning function that does not contain a `return` statement
30. A missing function prototype for a function that is defined below the `main` function
31. A missing `#include` directive for a header file that contains a class definition

APPENDIX E

How To Boxes

How To	Figure	Page(s)
Create a Computer Solution to a Problem	2-3	23
Name a Memory Location in C++	3-2	52
Use the Decimal (*Base 10*) Number System	3-7	55
Use the Binary (*Base 2*) Number System	3-8	56
Declare a Variable in C++	3-11	60
Declare a Named Constant in C++	3-13	61
Use `cin` and >> to Get Numeric or Character Data	4-3	76
Use the `cout` Object	4-5	77
Use the `static_cast` Operator	4-10	82
Write an Assignment Statement	4-11	83-84
Use an Arithmetic Assignment Operator	4-13	86
Use the `if` Statement	5-6	121-122
Use Comparison Operators in an `if` Statement's Condition	5-7	123
Use Logical Operators in an `if` Statement's Condition	5-16	129-130
Use the `toupper` and `tolower` Functions	5-25	137
Use the `fixed` and `scientific` Stream Manipulators	5-26	138
Use the `setprecision` Stream Manipulator	5-27	139
Use the `switch` Statement	6-28	182
Use the `while` Statement	7-13	220
Use the `for` Statement	7-32	232
Use the `do while` Statement	8-9	268-269
Use the `pow` Function	8-27	281
Use the `sqrt` Function	9-4	310
Use the `rand` Function	9-10	314

(continues)

(continued)

Index

D

N

O

P

W

X

Z